SCHLACHTFLIEGER!

GERMANY AND THE ORIGINS OF AIR/GROUND SUPPORT 1916-1918

SCHLACHTFLIEGER!

GERMANY AND THE ORIGINS OF AIR/GROUND SUPPORT 1916-1918

Rick Duiven & Dan-San Abbott

Schiffer Military History
Atglen, PA

Acknowledgements

A great number of World War I aviation historians have been helpful in compiling this effort on the *Schutzstaffeln/Schlachtstaffeln*. These include but are not limited to: Bill Bailey, Mark Berger, Augie Blume, Bernard Deneckere, Helge Dittmann, Jim DuBois, the late Harry van Dorrsen, Marco Fernández-Sommerau, Immo Frese, Dr. Achim Fuchs of the Bavarian Military Archives, Peter Grosz, Jan Hayzlett, Glenn Jewison, Ingrid Johanson, Reinhard Kastner, Ron Kintner, Steve Lawson, Frederic Liefferinckx, Rick Lundström, Grzegorz Mazurowski, the late Neal O'Connor, Frank Olynyk, Douglass Pardee, Thorsten Pietsch, Terry Phillips, Markus Pleyer, Johan Ryheul, Jeffery Sands, The Aviation Historical Collection at the University of Texas at Dallas and its Director Dr. Larry Sall, Marton Szigeti, Hannes Täger, Manfred Thiemeyer, Alan D. Toelle, Jan Vancoillie, Alain Van Geeteruyen, Lothair Vanoverbeke, Greg VanWyngarden, David Watts, Aaron Weaver, Tobias Weber, Ralph Whitehead, Charles Woolley, and to all our friends at the Aerodrome Forum: www.theaerodrome.com.

A special thanks is due to Jörg Mückler and Gunnar Söderbaum who painstakingly reviewed the rosters, combat logs, airfields, victory lists, and losses for each of the thirty-eight units. Without their eye for detail this work would be so much the poorer. Also a special thanks to Adam Wait who was solely responsible for the translation of many of the German articles found herein. And an especial thanks must go to Dr. Dieter H.M. Gröschel who was instrumental in obtaining and then helping to translate the *Bavarian Kriegsstammrollen* which, by the way, are all handwritten in the old German Schrift. And, of course, to Lin and Patti for their encouragement and understanding while this project was being undertaken.

Despite all this wonderful help however, we, the authors, are solely responsible for the final text. Any errors, either of commission or omission, are ours alone. In our defense we quickly point out that there are many errors of omission with respect to the individual *Schusta/Schlasta* unit histories. The relevant material is just not available. Additions and/or corrections to supplement this effort would be most welcome.

Book design by Robert Biondi.

Library of Congress Catalog Number: 2006930609.

Printed in China.
ISBN: 0-7643-2441-1

Published by Schiffer Publishing Ltd.
4880 Lower Valley Road
Atglen, PA 19310
Phone: (610) 593-1777
FAX: (610) 593-2002
E-mail: Info@schifferbooks.com.
Visit our web site at: www.schifferbooks.com
Please write for a free catalog.
This book may be purchased from the publisher.
Please include $3.95 postage.
Try your bookstore first.

In Europe, Schiffer books are distributed by:
Bushwood Books
6 Marksbury Ave.
Kew Gardens, Surrey TW9 4JF
England
Phone: 44 (0)20 8392-8585
FAX: 44 (0)20 8392-9876
E-mail: info@bushwoodbooks.co.uk
www.bushwoodbooks.co.uk
Free postage in the UK. Europe: air mail at cost.
Try your bookstore first.

FOREWORD

The greater part of literature concerning the history of aviation during the First World War has been devoted to the fighter pilot and fighter squadrons. There is a natural fascination for the relatively individualistic nature of combat between opposing airmen, and the accomplishments of fighter pilots are readily measurable in the tally of aerial victories. Their recorded exploits have captured the imagination of readers for generations and during the Great War served as useful propaganda for the war-weary population at home. The aerial duels fought with the greatest intensity over the fields of northeastern France and Belgium – the Western Front – provided a welcome contrast to the massed infantry attacks on the ground, which took such a tremendous toll in human lives for little gain in territory.

Students of military aviation history are familiar, however, with the important role played by other branches of the air service, such as the reconnaissance and bomber squadrons. Photographic reconnaissance was the initial – and strategically most important – function of aviation in the First World War. No major or minor offensive could be planned without the tireless efforts of reconnaissance squadrons which throughout the war produced hundreds of thousands of photographic plates illuminating details of the enemy's positions and movements, both on the immediate front and in the rear areas which fed men and supplies to the combat zone.

Although restricted in numbers and payload capacity, the achievements of both tactical and strategic bomber squadrons made an indelible impression on future planners of aerial warfare. Certainly the nature of aerial bombing campaigns of the Second World War was influenced by lessons gained from the preceding world conflict.

Beginning in the 1960s, the accomplishments of bomber and reconnaissance aviation in the First World War began to receive greater attention, allowing a more balanced view of this pioneer era of military aviation. The creation of fighter, reconnaissance, and bombing squadrons during World War I was a natural consequence of the evolution of aviation technology and the development of task-specific aircraft designs. The fighter squadron, reconnaissance squadron, and bomber squadron of the Allied air services on the Western Front found a rough counterpart in the *Jagdstaffel, Flieger Abteilung,* and *Bombenstaffel* of the opposing German air service.

This present volume, however, involves a unique development in aviation during the First World War: the formation of aerial units devoted specifically to the material support of the infantry in ground combat operations. These squadrons were developed solely by the German air service. The Allied air services deployed fighter squadrons on occasion for ground attack missions and late in the war were developing for this purpose specially modified fighter aircraft, with localized armor plating and fixed downward-firing armament. However, it was the German air service, the *Luftstreitkräfte*, which placed enough value on direct, low-level air-ground support to create specialized ground-attack squadrons. Once beyond the initial stage of formation, these units were equipped with specially designed, light and maneuverable two-seater aircraft. The name given to such a unit was *Schlachtstaffel*, literally "battle squadron," which was developed from the earlier *Schutzstaffel*, or "protection squadron."

The *Schlachtstaffeln* (to use the plural term) gained no wide public recognition by means of aerial conquests, although they did boast a few 'aces' (in Allied parlance, flyers with five or more victories) among their ranks. As a tactical weapon, their operations lacked the strategic scope of the short- and long-range reconnaissance units which functioned as the "eyes" of the army. They also launched no assaults which stirred debate in the governments of the warring nations, as did the bombing squadrons which ranged over targets such as Paris, London, and centers of industry in the German Ruhr and Saar regions.

However, the services they rendered do merit special distinction. In the First World War the *raison d'être* of the army air services was to support the ground campaign in cooperation with the infantry. Reconnaissance squadrons supplied information about the disposition of the opposing army. They also ranged their artillery onto enemy targets through wireless telegraphy using Morse code. Bomber squadrons attacked railway junctions and other points of strategic interest involving the line of supply and movement of enemy troops to the front. It was the task of the fighter squadrons to interfere with all such activity and leave the sky clear for the operation of their own squadrons supporting strategic and tactical operations on the front. These were the types of squadrons which operated in the service of all nations involved in the conflict – but in the German air service, the *Schlachtstaffeln* performed a somewhat special function.

These units were, in the most immediate sense, an offensive weapon working in close cooperation with the infantry. They flew low-level missions, directly over the heads of their own troops, attacking enemy infantry with machine guns, hand grenades, and small bombs. Unlike the reconnaissance, bomber, and fighter squadrons, which generally operated at altitudes measured in thousands of feet, these flyers regularly flew through the gauntlet of enemy fire at a low height that could be measured in hundreds of feet – and often considerably less.

The autobiographical novel *Winged Victory* by Victor M. Yeates, who piloted Sopwith Camel fighters with 46 Squadron RFC/RAF, gives one a fair impression of the stresses involved in such ground attack missions. Describing the effect such activity had on the character Tom Cundall, Yeates wrote how "(t)he thought of ground-strafing made him feel like a jelly that would not set." He was plagued by a "feeling of terror that gripped his vitals when he went near the gun-bristling earth ... it was as though fear had gathered there like an invisible gas, and every time he dived into it he was inevitably overcome." No doubt many, if not most, fighter pilots would have shared Yeates' sentiments regarding such extra hazardous duty and felt some relief in returning to normal offensive patrols far above the front, where he could at least deal with a more visible enemy on more equal terms. For the *Schlachtstaffeln*, though, these perilous ground attack sorties constituted their "daily bread."

Aviators often expressed sympathy for their earth-bound brethren. British flyers referred to the soldiers in the trenches as the "P.B.I," i.e, "Poor Bloody Infantry." These feelings were sometimes based on personal experiences amidst the shell holes, barbed wire, and mud on the Western Front before transferring to the air service. However, the aircrews who signed up for service in the *Schlachtstaffeln* often voiced a sense of solidarity with the ground troops which was translated into direct action. They accompanied the infantry in striking at enemy positions. They flew low enough to be raked by machine guns manned by enemy infantry and to encounter clouds of poisonous gas crawling over the shell-pocked terrain. A glance at the casualty lists will reveal the cost of their devotion.

It is interesting to speculate whether the *Schlachtstaffeln* could have had a decisive material effect on the outcome of the spring offensives of 1918, had they been available in greater numbers. However, military planners of the time felt that the greatest asset of the ground-attack units was their positive effect on the morale of the German infantry, who were able to visibly acknowledge the protective presence of these low-flying airmen with the wave of a hand, rifle, or helmet. It is worthy of note that considerations regarding the psychological effects of attacks from the air also guided the policies of strategic bombing raids during the First World War. This was of course also true of the subsequent cataclysm of 1939-1945, which saw in addition the effective implementation of the *Blitzkrieg,* itself an outgrowth of the cooperative tactics developed by the earth-bound *Sturmtruppen* and aerial *Schlachtstaffeln* of World War I.

The name developed for these units can be rendered literally, and somewhat awkwardly, into English as "battle squadron," but is perhaps best translated as "ground-attack squadron." The aviators who flew with the ground-attack squadrons also had a special designation, which might likewise be translated only roughly into English as "ground-attack flyers." All linguistic difficulties aside, it is hoped that the following pages will convey to the reader a better understanding and appreciation of the term: *Schlachtflieger!*

Adam Wait
Sacramento, California
February 1, 2005

CONTENTS

PREFACE

Much has been written about the fighter units, *Jagdstaffeln*, and other units of the German Air Force during the Great War of 1914-1918, however little has been told of the *Schutzstaffeln*, the Protection Flights, and the *Schlachtstaffeln*, the Battle Flights, which evolved from the *Schutzstaffeln* in 1918.

The story of the *Schutzstaffeln* begins in 1916 as a consequence of the failure in the tactics of the German *Fliegertruppe* (Aviation Troops) during the Verdun and Somme battles of 1916, which resulted in the loss of aerial superiority over the German front and rear areas. The tactics the *Fliegertruppe* employed were the institution of blockade flights by the *Kampfstaffeln* (Combat Flights) of the *Kampfgeschwader der Obersten Heersleitung* (Combat Squadrons of the Army High Command). Barrage patrols of two-seat reconnaissance/bomber aircraft flying over the front lines in an attempt to prevent French or British aircraft from entering German airspace were a costly waste of all resources including fuel, oil, men and machines. The outcome of these flawed tactics was that the French and British were able to gain control of the air over the German front as well as the rear areas.

After a review of the situation in the air war by the German High Command, they decided to reorganize the *Fliegertruppe* and from it form a new Air Force, the *Luftstreitkräfte*, under the command of *Generalleutnant* Ernst von Hoeppner.

In *Generalleutnant* von Hoeppner's study of the situation, he determined that four of the Combat Squadrons (*Kampfgeschwader*) would be dissolved; from the twenty-four *Kampfstaffeln* twenty-four *Schutzstaffeln* (Protection Flights) would be formed. An additional three more were created from other front units, making a total of twenty-seven Protection Flights.

Each *Schutzstaffel* was commanded by an officer, the *Schustaführer*, and, in general, consisted of enlisted aircrews. Each unit was equipped with six single-engine, armed, two-seater biplanes. The mission of the *Schusta* was escorting reconnaissance and artillery-spotting aircraft and protecting them from attack by Allied aircraft. The *Schusta* were usually based on the same airfield as the *Flieger Abteilung*, (*Fl.Abt.*) Flying Detachment, or *Artillerie Flieger Abteilung*, (*Fl.Abt. A*) Flying Detachment Artillery for which they would fly escort.

Some of the *Schustaführer* had the insight to consider the possibility of employing the *Schusta* in an offensive role. This change of mission from defense to offense led to the creation of the *Schlachtstaffeln* in 1918. This book will tell the story, in words and pictures, of the birth and organization of the *Schusta* and the *Schlasta* – the men and machines that invented Air Ground Support.

• • •

1917-1918 German *vs*. Allied Time

A one-hour discrepancy usually occurred between Allied time and German time in their respective records, but occasionally the times corresponded. Although a comparison of German time versus Allied time has been previously presented in a variety of sources, it will be repeated here for the sake of completeness:

- Until 24Mar17 German time was one hour ahead of Allied time e.g. 13.00 hours German = 12.00 hours Allied

- 25Mar17 – 15Apr17 times were the same

• 16Apr17 – 17Sep17 German time was one hour ahead of Allied time

• 18Sep17 – 5Oct17 times were the same

• 6Oct17 – 9Mar18 German time was one hour ahead of Allied time

• 10Mar18 – 15Apr18 times were the same

• 16Apr18 – 15Sep18 German time was one hour ahead of Allied time

• 16Sep18 – 5Oct18 times were the same

• 6Oct18 – EOW German time was one hour ahead of Allied time

• • •

A Timeline of 1917/1918 Events as They Pertain to the *Schutzstaffeln/Schlachtstaffeln*

1Jan17: *Schutzstaffeln 1* through *21* are formed by order KM Nr. 1425.16.g.A.7.L. *Schutzstaffeln 22b* through *27b* are formed by order BKM Nr. 148032.

15Mar17: *Schutzstaffeln 28b* through *30b* are established by order BKM Nr. 21943A.

9Apr17: The Arras-Vimy Ridge British Offensive.

16Apr17: The German *1. Armee* is pulled from the northern Somme area and relocated to the Champagne front between the *7.* and *3. Armeen.*

16Apr17: The Nivelle Offensive between Reims and Soissons on the Chemin des Dames.

24Apr17: The first recorded use of *Schutzstaffeln* aircraft as ground attack units.

7Jun17: The First Battle of Messines Ridge.

31Jul17: The First Battle of Passchendaele.

20Aug17: The Third Battle of Verdun.

20Nov17: The British Offensive against Cambrai.

30Nov17: The German Counter-Offensive at Cambrai.

27Dec17: German *18. Armee* formed, inserted between the *2.* and *7. Armeen.*

1Feb18: German *17. Armee* formed, inserted between the *6.* and *2. Armeen.*

4Feb18: German *19. Armee* formed, inserted between *Armee Abteilung C.* and *Armee Abteilung A.*

21Mar18: 'Der Tag' – The German Offensive in Picardy (Operation Michael).

27Mar18: The *Schutzstaffeln* are renamed *Schlachtstaffeln* by order KM Nr. 5126.18.A.7.L.IV.C.

1Apr18: The RAF is formed by combining the RFC and RNAS.

9Apr18: The Battle of the Lys (Operation Georgette).

25Apr18: The Battle for the Kemmel Ridge.

27May18: The German Offensive of the Chemin des Dames (Operation Blücher).

9Jun18: The Battle of the Matz (Operation Gneisenau-Yorck).

4Jul18: The Battle for Hamel.

5Jul18: German *9. Armee* (in West) formed and inserted between the *18.* and *7. Armeen.*

15Jul18: The Final German Offensive on the Marne, the Battle of Reims (Operation Friedensturm – Peace Offensive).

8Aug18: The Battle of Amiens.

23Aug18: The Battle of Bapaume.

26Aug18: The Battle of the Scarpe.

2Sep18: The Battle of the Drocourt-Quéant Line.

12Sep18: The St. Mihiel Offensive.

18Sep18: The Battle of Havrincourt and Epéhy.

18Sep18: German *9. Armee* withdrawn from the Western Front.

26Sep18: The Battle of the Meuse-Argonne.

27Sep18: The Battle of the Canal du Nord.

28Sep18: The Battles in Flanders.

29Sep18: The Battle for the Hindenburg Line.

8Oct18: The Second Battle of Le Cateau.

14Oct18: The Belgium Attack in Flanders.

11Nov18: Waffenstillstand.

PART I
THE SCHUTZSTAFFELN

(JANUARY 1917 TO FEBRUARY 1918)

CHAPTER I

INTRODUCTION

The history of the *Schlachtstaffeln* starts with the Battle of Verdun, which began on February 21, 1916. At this time the philosophy of the German *Fliegertruppe* (Air Troops) was to establish *Sperre* (blockade) patrols in an effort to create a barrier to the French aircraft. In essence they wanted to build an aerial trench system, similar to that of the ground forces that the enemy airmen could not cross. The units assigned to undertake this task were the existing *Kampfgeschwader 1-7*, flying two-seaters with a pilot, unarmed, and an observer armed with a single Parabellum machine gun.

The reason that these tactics were obviously doomed to fail is that the sky is three-dimensional. The opposing French aircraft could easily elude the barrage patrol aircraft by flying around, under, or over them and thus avoid the German 'trench in the sky.' However, the Germans continued this defensive policy in the British sector to the north with the advent of the Battle of the Somme, which commenced on 2 July 1916, with the same results. The British flyers were easily able to skirt the 'trench' and could penetrate far beyond the German lines to reconnointer, bomb, strafe, and in general wrest control of the sky from the Germans.

Meanwhile the Germans discovered that their blockade patrols were extremely costly in terms of crew and aircraft losses, let alone a waste of petrol, oil, and material supplies. Furthermore, they had completely lost control of the air. These tactics by the *Fliegertruppe* gave rise to the German Infantry expression, "*Gott strafe England, unser Artillerie und unser Fliegertruppe*" (May God punish England, our artillery and our aviation troops). The *Fliegertruppen* got pushed so far away from the trenches that the Infantry began to scrawl such remarks as "has anyone around here ever seen a German aviator?" on the walls of their dugouts. [Cuneo, 1947, 251].

This deplorable situation, comprising a complete loss of aerial supremacy during 1916, led the German High Command to order a reorganization of the *Fliegertruppe*. On October 8, 1916 the Air Force became known as the *Luftstreitkräfte* and was placed under the command of *Generalleutnant* Ernst von Hoeppner. As his Chief of Staff, von Hoeppner chose *Oberstleutnant* Hermann von der Lieth-Thomsen, the former *Feldflugchef*. They immediately began a complete overhaul of the German Flying Corps.

CHAPTER II

FORMATION OF THE SCHUTZSTAFFELN

Von Hoeppner's and von der Lieth-Thomsen's first step was to eliminate the 78 existing *Feldfliegerabteilungen* (*F.Fl.Abt.*, field flying sections) and to renumber and redesignate 48 of the old units as long-range reconnaissance *Flieger Abteilungen* (*Fl.Abt.*). The other 30 units were redesignated and joined the existing *Artillerie-Flieger-Abteilungen* (*Fl.Abt.(A)*) in performing artillery ranging and infantry support missions. This renumbering and reorganization took place from December 1916 through January 1917. A further development of great significance was the formation of the first *Jagdstaffeln*, beginning in late August of 1916.

However, the most important event pertaining to the formation of ground attack squadrons occurred on 1 January 1917 by order KM Nr. 1425.16.g.A.7.L. when three *Kampfgeschwader* were dissolved and their respective *Kampfstaffeln* were redesignated *Schutzstaffeln (Schusta)*. By this same order the three existing *Sondern Staffeln* (Special Squadrons) *Ks S.1, Ks S.2,* and *Ks S.3* were also redesignated as *Schutzstaffeln*. The Bavarians followed suit by order BKM Nr. 148032 of 31 December 1916, and renamed the *Kampfstaffeln* assigned to *Kampfgeschwader 6* as *Schusta* on 1 January 1917. Thus *KG 3 (Ks 13-18)* became *Schusta 1-6; KG 5 (Ks 25-30)* became *Schusta 7-12; KG 7 (Ks 37-42)* became *Schusta 13-18*; *Ks S.1*, *Ks S.2*, and *Ks S.3*, became *Schusta 20, 19,* and *21*; and *KG 6 (Ks 31-36)* became *Schusta 22b-27b*, respectively.

Order KM 1425.16.g.A.7.L. also spelled out the numerical establishment of a *Schusta*, both in terms of personnel and equipment. The unit would be commanded by an officer. Under him would be 79 men of enlisted rank. These were designated as: 6 pilots; 6 machine gunners; 1 foreman *(Werkmeister)*; 1 Top Sergeant *(Feldwebel)*; 1 Sergeant *(Vizefeldwebel)*; 1 medical officer; 7 non-commissioned officers including 3 tent maintenance personnel and 1 for book-keeping; 6 primary aircraft maintenance personnel; 10 Privates First Class *(Gefreite)* consisting of 4 aircraft maintenance personnel, 4 engine mechanics, 1 electrician, and 1 carpenter; 31 lower ranks including 2 aircraft maintenance men, 14 engine mechanics, 2 electricians, 2 carpenters, 2 saddlers, 1 shoemaker, 1 tailor, 1 clerk, 2 telephone operators, and 4 optional professions; 1 armament officer; 2 armament assistants; 1 service unit soldier; 1 motorcyclist; and 5 motor vehicle drivers. The equipment was to consist of 2 personnel transports; 2 trucks; 1 maintenance truck; 2 additional vehicles as lighting truck and water-heating truck; and 6 C-type aircraft.

This same order also specified the *Train* or *Parkzug* that would be held at the *Armee Flug Park* as the support detachment for each *Schusta*. These 13 personnel would consist of 1 pilot; 1 machine gunner; 1 non-commissioned officer; 2 Privates First Class (*Gefreite)* and 7 lower ranks consisting of 2 aircraft maintenance personnel, 2 engine mechanics, 1 electrician, 1 carpenter, 3 various professions; and 1 truck driver.

Order KM 1425.16.g.A.7.L. also provided instructions for the commander of a *Schutzstaffel* as follows:

1. When battle conditions require it, a *Schutzstaffel* will be assigned to a *Flieger Abteilung (A)* or *Flieger Abteilung* to protect the artillery aircraft and will be placed under its command with respect to finances and disciplinary measures.

2. The *Staffel* and its component parts will be at the disposal of the commander of the *Flieger Abteilung* with respect to its tactical deployment and its utilization.

3. The *Staffel* commander has the disciplinary authority and leave-granting powers of a company commander.

4. The replacement of personnel and material will be regulated by the *Kommandeur der Flieger* to whom the *Staffel* is assigned.

Additionally, by order BKM Nr. 21943A. of 15 March 1917, Bavaria formed *Schusta 28b-30b* during February and March. Thus, as the year 1917 began, the *Luftstreitkräfte* were equipped with 30 *Schutzstaffeln* to escort, support, and defend the aircraft of the *Fl.Abt.* and *Fl.Abt.(A)*.

Above: Since *KG 3/Ks 16* was renamed *Schusta 4*, and since this photo is undated, it is not possible to determine exactly with which unit it was taken. As it comes from the album of Anton Schmitz, it had to be one of these units. Note the black stripe on the white wheel cover of this Albatros C.VII, possibly an early unit marking of *Schusta 4*. Photo credit: Terry Phillips.

Left: An Albatros C.VII of either *KG 3/Ks 16* or its successor unit *Schusta 4*. Note the black stripe on the white wheel cover, probably an early unit marking of *Schusta 4*. Photo credit: Terry Phillips.

Two unknown crews of *KG 3/16*, the predecessor of *Schusta 4*, winter 1916. Photo credit: Terry Phillips.

Above: A Roland C.II *Walfisch* of *Schusta 28b*. This unit was formed at *FEA 1b* in February 1917. Photo credit: Terry Phillips.

Below: Probably the same Roland C.II of *Schusta 28b* with *Oblt.d.R.* Eduard Schleich in the pilot's cockpit. The gunner is not identified. Photo credit: Terry Phillips.

KG 7/Ks 39 the forerunner of *Schutzstaffel 15*. Left to right: *Ltn.* Gerhard Bassenge (P), the C.O. *Oblt.* Heinz Pflugk-Harttung (O), *Ltn.* Rossteuscher (O) and *Gefr.* Beese (P). All four men became original members of *Schusta 15*.

The *KG 7/Ks 39* crew of *Ltn.* Gerhard Bassenge, pilot, and *Vzfw.* Ernst Flöel, gunner, standing 2nd and 3rd from left. Their aircraft is an Albatros C.III. This unit became *Schusta 15* on 1Jan17 and both men became members.

KG 7/Ks 39 with *Vzfw.* Ernst Flöel and *Ltn.* Gerhard Bassenge, in their Albatros C.III, before being converted to *Schusta 15*. Bassenge went on to become a Jasta pilot, serving with *Jasta 6, 5*, and 2 and was credited with 7 victories.

CHAPTER III

ROLE OF THE SCHUTZSTAFFELN

By late December 1916, the German *Fl.Abt.* and *Fl.Abt.(A)* were manned by observers who were essentially young Lieutenants. These men had little or no experience with regard to air combat. Their role with the *Fl.Abt.* was to photograph the enemy lines – trenches, build-up of troops, train activity, etc. Alternatively, the observers of the *Fl.Abt.(A)* were expected to range their artillery, correct and rerange the fire, to keep track of where their batteries shells fell and to make the appropriate corrections.

Observers occupied with such tasks, especially when inexperienced, were hard-pressed to keep a simultaineous look out for enemy aircraft every ten or fifteen seconds. The German High Command therefore decided that this valuable resource, the observer, needed protection from enemy attack, so that they could safely carry out their missions.

The role assigned to the *Schutzstaffeln* was to escort the *Fl.Abt.* and *Fl.Abt.(A)* aircraft and protect them from aerial attack. Thus during 1917 the reconnaisance aircraft, either *Fl.Abt.* or *Fl.Abt.(A),* would be accompanied by a 'protective' aircraft, the *Schusta* often being stationed at the same airfield as the unit they were designated to escort. British combat reports are filled with instances of their fighter aircraft attacking a pair of two-seaters, with the result that one immediately 'flew East,' while the other 'stayed to fight.' The most well-documented accounts of this typical occurrence are recorded by Capt. James McCudden, where one two-seater fled East (the *Fl.Abt.* or *Fl.Abt.(A)* aircraft containing the important information the high command would want) and the other aircraft stayed to engage in combat and allow the *Fl.Abt.* aircraft to escape. That McCudden had good results against these 'protective' aircraft is reflected in the 'G' lists appearing in a later section. Despite McCudden's success however, it must be pointed out that he allowed the more important aircraft to escape.

To present a few of these protection flights one may refer to existing *Kofl* (*Kommandeur der Flieger*) reports. For example, on 22 April 1917, the *1. Armee* had at its disposal *Gruppe Aisne* with *Schusta 5* and *16* escorting *Fl.Abt. 226(A)* and *228(A); Gruppe Brimont* with *Schusta 23b, 1,* and *29b* supporting *Fl.Abt. 278(A), Fl.Abt. 286(A)b*, and *Fl.Abt. 248(A)*, respectively; *Gruppe Reims* having *Schusta 9* and *12* with *Fl.Abt. 245(A)* and *Fl.Abt. 203(A)*; and *Gruppe Prosnes* with *Schusta 15, 18*, and *28b* escorting *Fl.Abt. 296(A)b, 272(A)*, and *Fl.Abt. 252(A)w*, respectively. By 30 June 17, *1. Armee* only reported *Gruppe Prosnes* containing *Schusta 15* and *18* still with *Fl.Abt. 296(A)b* and *Fl.Abt. 272(A)*.

During August 1917, *5. Armee* consisted of *Grufl 14* having *Schusta 20, 14,* and *8* escorting *Fl.Abt. 278(A), Fl.Abt. 296(A)b*, and *Fl.Abt. 249(A); Grufl 1* with *Schusta 6, 18,* and *15* supporting *Fl.Abt. 36, Fl.Abt. 44,* and *Fl.Abt. 228(A); Grufl 10* having *Schusta 22b* escorting *Fl.Abt. 291(A)b*; and *Grufl 16* with *Schusta 2* protecting *Fl.Abt. 207(A)*.

As a final example, the *7. Armee* during November-December 1917 consisted of *Gruppe Vaille* with *Schusta 14, 2, 20, 8*, and *18* escorting *Fl.Abt. 10, 209(A), 212(A), 216(A)*, and *265(A)*, respectively; *Gruppe Liese* with *Schusta 6* supporting *Fl.Abt. 234(A)*; and *Gruppe Crépy* with *Schusta 3* escorting *Fl.Abt. 277(A)*. As can be seen, the *Schutzstaffeln* were as mobile as the *Jagdstaffeln* with respect to supporting active portions of the front, or those locations where offensive and/or defensive battles were occurring. A more detailed accounting of these protection flights can be found in Part V, where the airfield locations and escort duties of the individual *Schutzstaffel* are presented.

A Roland C.II *Walfisch* of *Schutzstaffel 2* that came to grief in early 1917, probably at the airfield at Cerny les Bucy in the *7. Armee*, while they were escorting *Fl.Abt. 222(A)*. The crew is unknown but it is not thought that either occupant was killed. Photo credit: Helge Dittmann.

Opposite
Top: The *Schutzstaffel 8* DFW C.V (Av) 9030/17 marked '2.' The gunner, *Uffz.* Otto Kutter, is on the left in his cockpit. Photo credit: Marcus Pleyer.

Bottom: Albatros C.VII (OAW) 3540/16 of *Schusta 27b* photographed on 23May17 at Bellincamps in the *6. Armee* while they were escorting *Fl.Abt. 224(A)w*. At this time the unit marking was a black chevron and a black number, in this case '3.'

Right: The *Schusta 13* crew of *Vzfw.* Wilhelm Littig (P) and *Uffz.* Karl Kubitza (G) and their Rumpler C.I at Ham airfield on January 26, 1917. Littig served with *Schusta/Schlasta 13* from 1 January 1917 to 8 May 1918.

Below: *Vzfw.* Otto Gawron and *Vzfw.* Reisberg making one of their first front flights with *Schusta 2* in April 1917. The aircraft is a Rumpler C.I marked 4.

2

C.VII.3540

CHAPTER IV

INFANTRY SUPPORT

Schusta 2 under the command of *Oblt.* Oskar Kuppinger moved from *Armee Abteilung A* to the *7. Armee* in early March 1917, and settled in at their new base at Cerny les Bucy, near Laon. In early April the *7. Armee* learned of an impending attack by the French on the Chemin des Dames, which was to commence on 16 April 1917. Prior to this attack, French aircraft were bombing German rear positions every night to hinder their activities and shield the preparations for the offensive. Kuppinger pled with *Kofl 7* to allow some sort of German response to these nightly flights. Finally he was given permission and with his long-time pilot *Vzfw.* Julius Tillmann they selected the French airfield at Cramoiselle, northwest of Fère en Tardenois, as their target.

They took off during the night of April 13th and proceeded to circle over the airfield, shooting at French bomber aircraft which were attempting to land following their bombing sorties, and generally raising as much commotion as they could. Kuppinger's mission report of this night's activity so impressed *Kofl 7* that it was quoted verbatim in the *Nachrichtenblatt der Luftstreitkräfte*, No. 9, dated 26 April 1917. It is presented below as published in the *Over The Front Journal*, Vol. 14, No. 3, Fall 1999, pp. 276-277, courtesy of and by permission of Jan Hayzlett, who provided the translation:

> "The airplane flew south from Laon towards a row of bright lights. Shortly after crossing the Aisne [River], it was determined that the lights were arranged in the same manner as the French airfield illumination during the fighting on the Somme. Six to eight kilometers northeast of the row of lights, roughly eight to ten small, dim lights were observed in a right angle. The communication lines from the suspected, brightly-lighted airfield over the point of this angle of lights pointed directly towards Laon.

"The airplane approached the hangars in a glide, amid constant '*Schurpsen*' [turning the engine off and on]. Down below on the airfield, a searchlight then shined, clearly showing the landing direction with its beam and at the same time indicating that the runway was clear. Opposite the bright row of lights, the hangars stood out in darkness; it was Cramoiselle airfield.

"The bright lamps were shaded against the landing airplane and against the field. The shades had the shape of a right angle. They didn't reach all the way to the ground, giving the field an even, bright light shimmer, which was quite favorable for landing.

"I now strafed the airfield with 200 cartridges from my Parabellum [machine] gun. The searchlight, on the western edge of the field, went out. Two other searchlights, located three kilometers northeast of the field, now shined, searching for my airplane, but failed to find it in the hour and a quarter that I was circling over the airfield. The airplane was at an average altitude of 1,000 meters.

"Some time later, an enemy flier returned. Judging from the distance between his red and green position lanterns, it must have been a 'G-type' [multi-engine] airplane. I positioned my airplane directly behind the enemy [airplane] and fired at it with my fixed machine gun. The airplane had extinguished its lights after 15 – 20 rounds. By doing so, the enemy airman avoided any further pursuit; he disappeared into the darkness in a steep glide.

"Ten minutes later, another enemy airplane approached. It signaled its intention to land using a bright, white spotlight. The spotlight was situated in the front, between the red and green lanterns. The searchlight down below on the field did not answer. The airplane was attacked. It disappeared into the darkness in a glide after a few rounds.

"With dawn approaching, I flew for home. My airplane was fired on by neither anti-aircraft fire nor machine guns the entire flight."

The famous, or perhaps infamous, Nivelle Offensive on the Chemin des Dames launched on April 16, 1917, ended in complete failure due to the timely advance warning for the Germans and, in fact, was the direct contributor to the mutiny of the French Army in 1917. From this date until the Fall of 1918, the French never again launched offensive operations. The ordinary *Poilu* refused to attack again. They vowed to defend French soil, but would no longer go like lambs to the slaughter. This debacle cost the French over 120,000 casualties and can be laid squarely at the feet of General Robert Nivelle.

The first use of *Schutzstaffeln* aircraft in direct support of the infantry occurred during an attack on April 24, 1917, when *Hptm*. Eduard Wolfgang Zorer, the C.O. of *Schusta 7*, and his pilot, *Vzfw*. Josef Schleiffer, supported their ground comrades during a local attack. The infantry was slated to attack the English trenches along the Gavrelle-Roeux Road before Arras. But let Zorer tell of this attack in his own words:

"On the evening of April 23rd I had my best pilot, *Vizefeldwebel* Schleiffer, come to my room. 'Tomorrow morning an infantry support flight, my dear Schleiffer. Take-off at the break of dawn. Attack on our side in sector Gavrelle-Roeux. Important mission!' 'Very well, Herr *Hauptmann*. Aircraft ready for take-off at 5:45 a.m.,' Schleiffer answers and departs. Once more I closely inspect the territory on the map over which I was to fly on the next morning during the attack by our troops. Then I lay down on my bed with some misgivings, in order to go through the flight alone.

"Shortly before 5 o'clock my orderly Küchler reported to me. I got ready for the flight and at 6 a.m. was sitting in the aircraft. Streamers on the wings, flare cartridges for giving various signals in the air, electric lamp, machine gun – everything in perfect order. The take-off had to be postponed for five minutes, as it was too dark. From the direction of the front one hears the booming of the most terrible barrage. 6:05 a.m. We both extend our hands to one another. 'Happy landings!' The engine clatters. The mechanics await the order to take off. 'Ready. Let's go!' My men still stood there smartly for a moment in the manner of a salute and then waved to us, for everyone knew that we had a dark, difficult flight before us.

"The aircraft rolls away dully across the still dark field and heads up to the sky in the fresh, vigorous morning air. It was still fairly dark. The land lay before us in the mist. Only over Douai did the day begin to break. The heavy guns to the west of the canal spat their destructive fire of the heaviest caliber into the enemy lines. A rare and beautiful sight! First here, then there appear the incessant flashes and then arrives the rosy-fingered dawn. It was a wonderful feeling to steer toward the enemy in calm, secure flight so utterly alone in the fresh morning air. As I came toward the front the sounds of battle reached my ear in spite of the roar of the engine. We were 600 meters high. We flew along the front once in order to orient ourselves precisely concerning the course of the difficult battle. In all my life I have never seen such murderous fire of all calibers with and without gas shells. It was intolerable at 500 to 600 meters height. The turbulence from the passing shells was terrible. Like a ship without sail in a storm the aircraft danced back and forth, hanging first on one and then the other wing.

"Up here death threatened us every second with the shells flying thickly around us, which brought the air into a wild uproar and desired to draw the aircraft after them into the precipitous abyss, first on one side and then the other according to position. Sometimes I felt as though I were seeing a black monster roar past me to create beneath me in the next moment a horrible crater in the earth, thundering and spewing poisonous gas.

"I gave the signal to descend. At the edge of the barrage fire Schleiffer goes down in a sharp turn to 100 meters in the dead space between the fire on both sides. I clearly perceived from above and from the side that at a low altitude between the lines a narrow space had formed which could be flown through at a minimal height. And it was in fact more calm here. Upon my firing of green and red signal flares, the infantry had lain out their white cloths. Thus with their aid I could determine the general course of our forwardmost line at 6:40 a.m. At this time two English fighter aircraft appeared beyond their lines. They probably had their eyes on us, but we were on our guard. There was no surprise. At the same time two German airplanes also showed up – an artillery spotter with his bodyguard. They soon disappeared.

"Around 6:50 a wonderful sight presented itself to me: the barrage fire on both sides of the road from Gavrelle to Roeux. The fire directed toward Gavrelle itself ceased. And now I could hardly believe my eyes. Down below, where hell was yet raging, life was stirring again in the shell holes and dug-out trenches. We head down again and again to about 20 meters above the earth. There were really people, soldiers, beneath us. Jump up. Jump. Individual infantrymen. Each time Schleiffer dropped down closely above them, I bent far over out of the aircraft and yelled as loud as I could 'Go get 'em!' and shouted 'Hurrah!' At 6:55 there was also movement in the English trenches. Now I saw first here, then there the Tommies with their dish-like helmets. Already Schleiffer and I began to fire on the fellows alternately, he with his fixed and I with my flexible machine gun. He from the front through the propeller-disc and I from the side. The English head backward, our troops forward.

"We both fired off about 500 rounds at the enemy. But gradually the business became more and more unpleasant, more dangerous for us. Round after round from rifles and machine guns whistled about our ears. Then a machine gun bullet even smashed through the fuselage closely behind my seat and ricocheted off the ammunition drum of my machine gun with a loud clank. Our infantry had advanced up to the road from Gavrelle to Roeux. Now I wanted to also observe the battle around Gavrelle. I was still looking at the fight in the ruins of houses in the northeast part of Gavrelle when a machine gun bullet smacks into my engine. Schleiffer calls out amidst the predicament: 'Where should I land?' I direct him with a wave of the hand in order to lead him back out of the fight. Again and again it appeared as though the motor was about to stop. It was spewing out an awful lot of oil. It was a difficult bit of work for Schleiffer to get back to the field at Douai with a defective motor, but he made it. The last drop of oil had been used up when he brought the airplane to a smooth landing. I turned around. 'Schleiffer, you did great! Many thanks!' '*Herr Hauptmann*, that was a nice flight,' was his answer.

"Immediately I submitted my report by telephone to headquarters. The general staff officers thanked me. 'Come by yourself immediately.' said *Hauptmann* Rutz, *Gruppenführer der Flieger* in Douai. I appeared and he shook my hand. 'Go directly to corps headquarters.' I gave the report to *Hauptmann* Kr. I C. of the 1st Bavarian Reserve Corps. A report about everything that had happened at the front was probably seldom submitted to him so quickly. On the next day an officer from the staff of the *Kommandierender General der Luftstreitkräfte* at main headquarters spoke with me on the telephone and had me relate all the details of the flight.

"When I had returned from duty to my quarters at four in the afternoon, I found there on my table the army report of April 25th. Therein was the following:

"'During one of our counterthrusts at Gavrelle *Hauptmann* Zorer the commander of a *Schutzstaffel*, flew at the head of the storming infantry at 150 meters height and fired upon the English lines from his aircraft with his machine gun.'"

Although only a 'minor' line-straightening operation, Zorer noted that this attack was 'the birth of the *Sturmflieger*'. Be that as it may, the next ground attack isn't noted until two months later. On June 6, 1917, the British attacked Messines Ridge, beginning the battle by blowing up 19 mines filled with over a million pounds of explosive that had been tunneled under the German trenches. The *Schusta* in the immediate area were called on to support their infantry and to help stem the British advance that followed in the wake of the tremendous explosions. The supporting *Schusta* had little success in halting this attack, and it was not until mid-July 1917 that the initial attack petered out, only to be renewed with vigor by the British on 31 July 1917 (the first battle of Passchendaele), against the German *4. Armee.*

The attack immediately became bogged down in the muck and mire that comprised both front lines as well as no man's land and was soon discontinued with little gain. However, this attack may also have been seriously hampered by the defensive actions of the opposing *Schutzstaffeln*. It is known that at least 18 of these units were stationed in *4. Armee* opposing this British attack. An example of their work is provided by *Uffz.* Josef Gerl, a gunner with *Schusta 26b*, who had only recently joined the unit. His story, '*Schlachtflieger*,' which was published in Max Zeidelhack's *Bayerische Flieger im Weltkrieg,* is presented below. It was a dramatic beginning for the new arrival, as can be seen in his report on the *Staffel's* activities that day, which demonstrates the multiple roles of a typical *Schusta:*

"The day of a big battle in Flanders! The uninterrupted rumble of thousands and thousands of exploding shells reached our airfield, which lay close to the front. The force of the pounding shells caused the ground to tremble as though it were an earthquake. For the flyers in Flanders there was no concept of 'weather unfit for flying.' We had to take off in spite of pouring rain and low-lying mist. We had to bring aid to the infantry which was involved in very heavy fighting against a force several times its own strength.

"The airfield of our *Schlachtstaffel* (sic) was bristling with activity. We had received orders to maintain a high state of alert for take-off. The machines stood before the tents; the mechanics checked the engines at the test stands; the machine guns were being installed and loaded. Bombs were unpacked from their crates, equipped with fuses, and placed in the racks. Dozens of hand grenades and thousands of rounds for the machine guns loaded onto drums were stowed in the observer's compartments. The aircraft crews, protected from the cold by their special flight clothing, supervised the readying of their machines.

"The *Staffel* commander rushed to the airfield, had the aircrews assembled, and with the aid of a map explained the latest tactical situation to them, which he had just learned from the division staff officers. 'There is an impending attack by the enemy infantry.' The raging artillery and mortar fire of our opponent had reached its climax. It was as though Hell wanted to give birth to an all new Hell. 'Neighboring divisions have observed the advance of masses of enemy infantry. The attack is expected between ... Farm and the village of ... Both names were to be found on the map. In reality they were just heaps of rubble and ruins, not a single stone rested upon another. Everything had been swept away by the devastating, pulverizing fire. But the *Schlachtflieger* couldn't have any difficulties finding these points. Figuratively speaking, he had to recognize every single stone in the area.

"The *Staffel* commander read off the scanty reports which came back amidst the bombardment and told of enemy reserves in the vicinity of ... He ordered individual crews to bomb these enemy nests in particular and to range artillery batteries upon them. The flight path and position of every individual machine in the air during a formation flight and in the battle were determined.

"Then everyone proceeded to the aircraft standing ready for take-off. A brief command was issued and then they lifted off the ground one after the other, circling over the field. The *Staffel* commander took off last. Upon his firing a signal flare, the others assembled around him and flew in a wedge formation toward the front. During the flight every machine had to maintain precisely the position assigned to it in the formation.

"We arrived in the proximity of the battle zone. A beautiful and yet horrible drama presented itself to the crews. The entire front between Dixmuide and Passchendaele was enveloped in a sea of fire and smoke. A thousand fiery fingers flashed through the dense fumes. These were the muzzle flashes of the amassed enemy artillery around Boesinghe. The shells exploding in the flooded region sent towering fountains of water into the air and in Houthulst tree trunks were uprooted. They covered the graves of many of our brave soldiers.

"Dozens of observation balloons hung here and there. They presented an enticing target for the fighter pilots who were flying in formation along the front and who were to protect our own airplanes while constantly on the look-out for prey. The leader of our formation first headed in the direction of the nests of enemy artillery. We bombed them and they in turn responded with furious shrapnel fire. After dropping their bombs, all the aircraft turned around and assembled behind our lines. Then, spread out in an extended line, they flew toward the enemy infantry positions. In a dive these were shot up with the fixed machine guns. In the meantime, the gunners in the rear cockpit searched the area for enemy reserves in various hiding places and for pieces of artillery.

"When the pilot had exhausted his supply of ammunition, he went into a turn and the machine gunner rattled away at the enemy infantry with his gun. Many occupants of the trenches were readily visible because we were flying at a very low altitude over the positions, about 70 to 100 meters. Hand grenades were thrown at especially worthwhile targets, such as machine gun nests in shell craters, mortars, and tanks. But soon our ammunition was used up. The formation assembled at a previously agreed upon point behind our lines and followed a path to our home airfield.

"Important targets, the assembling of storm troops, reserves on the march, and heavy battery positions were reported to the division and the *Gruppenführer der Flieger* on the flight back by way of message drops. The course of the front line – which was indicated to the *Schlachtflieger* by laying out cloths, igniting smoke signals, and often just by waving helmets and rifles – was relayed to the command posts.

"The machines landed in perfect order. But the pause was often very short. When the tactical situation required it, we took off a second time with more ammunition for the same task. The work of the *Schlachtflieger* was difficult and dangerous. But they had become faithful comrades of the infantry and the enemy learned to fear them."

In his account, Gerl describes the *Staffel*'s organized tactics in first dropping their explosive ordnance, turning around, reassembling at an agreed-upon point, and then approaching in an 'extended line' formation for a second wave of attacks using machine guns. Once their attacks were completed, they once again assembled at the designated area prior to the return flight to the airfield.

Major a.D. Hans Arndt described such tactics in the aviation section of Friedrich Sesselberg's book *Der Stellungskrieg, 1914-1918.* He explained:

"While the first attack flights encountered little ground opposition, later the losses increased. Gradually a

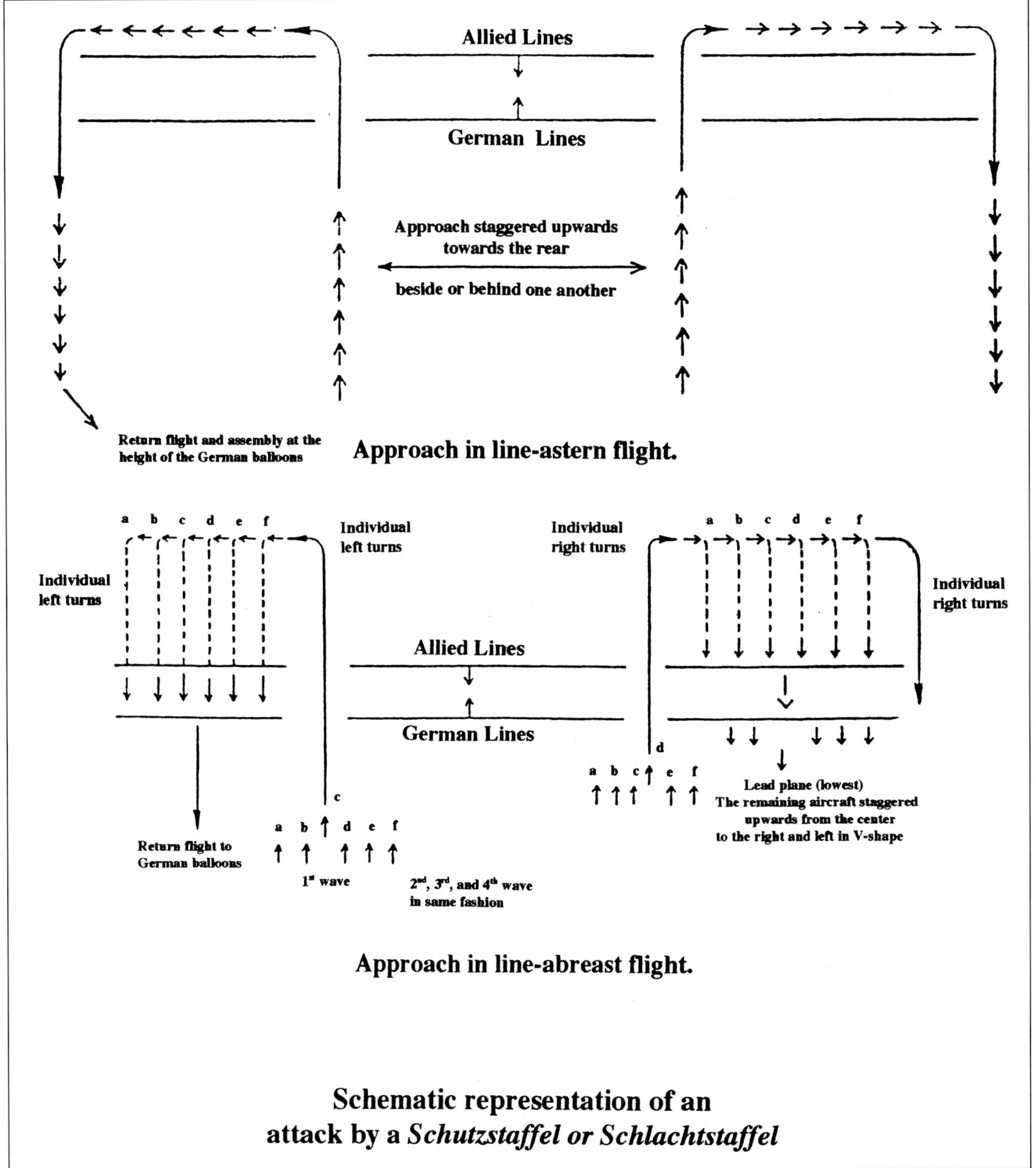

Schematic representation of an attack by a *Schutzstaffel or Schlachtstaffel*

formal attack tactic developed which is to be characterized as 'formation flight line-astern' or with an approach in 'line-abreast.'

"In 'line-astern' flight the target could be maintained under fire longer. It offered ground defenses only a narrow and therefore difficult target. In a 'line-abreast attack' a broader section lay under unified concentrated fire. It had a greater moral effect on friend and foe because of the closed approach in waves, however, it was more intensely subject to ground fire. But it was increasingly chosen because in this closed form one could more easily fend off enemy fighters which now also sought aerial combat at the lowest altitudes".

Sesselberg also included a schematic diagram of such attack formations, which is reproduced opposite with English translations of the explanatory notes. It will be noted that the German observation balloon lines are referred to as a highly visible and convenient point for assembly after the *Staffel* completes a wave of attacks.

One of the strongest proponents of the *Schutzstaffeln* supporting the infantry was *Oblt.* Friedrich Lorenz *Ritter* von Krausser, the commanding officer of *Schusta 23b.* His recollections of the flights undertaken during the hard, defensive fighting that occupied the German Army in Flanders for most of 1917, appeared in Georg Paul Neumann's compilation, *"In der Luft unbesiegt."* It is presented here in order to show the various types of activities a typical *Schutzstaffel* undertook during this period. In addition, it reveals how the initiative of individual flyers contributed to developing the ground-attack role which became the central task of the *Schutzstaffeln.* Krausser relates:

"Bavarian *Schutzstaffel 23* was assigned to the Prussian *Flieger Abteilung 19* and was situated together with it at the airfield at Ingelmunster (Flanders) when I took it over on June 18, 1917. On the very same day the protection flights began. One or two airplanes from my *Staffel* always had to accompany an infantry contact or artillery spotter aircraft – a less than pleasant and thankful, but on the other hand dull and strenuous task. This was especially true when the aircraft to be protected were faster, as was the case with us. We had to pay very close attention if we didn't want to lose sight of our charge. Over the front, we had to allow ourselves to be properly beaten about the neck and shoulders by the English fighters, who mostly appeared in superior numbers. Our sluggish DFWs were no match for the Englishmen.

"'No! One can't call this a very nice business,' I said to myself after a few days. 'There must be some variety so that we can recover a bit from the endless monotony.'

"At first we tried systematic attacks on the enemy trenches. As soon as the 'work aircraft' – namely, our charge – had fired off his flare as a signal that one was dismissed, the former 'escorts' dove upon the nearest enemy trenches and sprayed them with hundreds of rounds from the machine guns from as low a height as possible – not above 300 meters, mostly below 100 meters. It was often quite amusing how the Tommies crawled into their dugouts and whirred around in their trenches like stirred-up ants. But they also fired upon us – and none too sparingly! Many of us still have a reminder of it. Myself included! Later we strengthened our attacks by dropping bombs and hand grenades. In appreciation of this, the English dropped bombs on our airfield quite often. Considerably more unpleasant was their sending fighter pilots to fasten upon our necks and having them lie in wait for us. This often led to heated scraps. We could not 'work' in peace as we had done previously.

"On July 2, 1917, the following remarkable occurrence took place: The pilot *Unteroffizier* Kornder and his gunner *Unteroffizier* Gieler, in their good old DFW C.V, were in the process of shooting up enemy trenches near Ypres with their machine guns when they were suddenly attacked by surprise by three English fighters. In a few seconds, before they could properly begin to defend themselves, the pilot had received two shots in his legs and the gunner a ricochet through his shin. The left rudder and elevator cables had been shot away. As a result, the aircraft could no longer be steered and began to turn in circles. The situation was quite precarious, since the three Englishmen gave no thought to easing up on their quarry.

"Then the badly wounded *Unteroffizier* Gieler clambered out of his seat and positioned himself upon the lower left wing, clinging to a strut. A single short fainting spell and he would be a goner! The air resistance created by the body of this man standing upon the wing caused the machine to fly straight. By means of a steep descent, the pilot was able to escape the enemy fighters and land his airplane in a cornfield behind our front without significant damage. Gieler still stood between the wings during the landing. Through this daring deed a valuable airplane and two even more valuable human lives were saved.

"In time the eternal nocturnal bombings by the English became quite discomfiting and we began to think about revenge. At first when I came to Flanders night-flying was forbidden. Why? That has remained unknown to me. Later it was permitted, probably due to the impudence of the English in this respect. So I said to myself, actually we could for once give those fellows over there a proper blasting with bombs by night. But not a single one of us had flown by night! That was the business of the bombing units. However, the idea would not leave me alone until one fine day I assembled my 12 'brothers' – a bunch of young non-commissioned officers from all parts of the Fatherland. Cautiously I touched upon the notion of whether one or the other of them might carry out a night-bombing flight voluntarily. They were immediately all afire. Brave fellows! How many of them gave up their young lives in Flanders?

"A fellow from Munich responded to my suggestion, 'That's right! Let's just toss a bomb over there as an eye-opener!' And a staunch Swabian, one of my best, offered: 'I'll be the first one there!' I refused this offer. I wanted to – had to – be the first one there. That was my obligation as the commander of the *Staffel*. Immediately, the necessary preparations were undertaken. I chose as a target the small town of Poperinghe, in which there always reigned an extraordinary amount of traffic. On August 5, 1917, at 10:25 p.m. the take-off began. We had eight bombs on board. Everything went smoothly. A fire was started. At 11:30 we were already home again. At midnight we were at it once more. Almost the entire *Staffel* was present. But now orientation was considerably more difficult, as ground-fog had accumulated in the meantime. However, Poperinghe was still to be found. The fire made a good beacon. But hardly was the first bomb away when all around searchlights lit up – I counted 14. Beneath us we saw the flashes of exploding shells. I unloaded my six bombs, four of which whizzed down into the town. I didn't see the others hit. And then we snuck our way through the probing searchlights.

"For myself, who saw this fireworks display for the first time from above, it was a rather entertaining spectacle. I had been enjoying the beautiful drama for quite some time but suddenly had no idea where we actually were. In addition, the ground-mist had become so thick that details could no longer be made out. 'So let's head down!' The altimeter indicated 800, 600, 400, 200 meters. Then almost right beneath us a white flare rose up. My first thought was, 'Maybe we're already over our own airfield.' I fired off the agreed-upon flare signal. The effect was surprising: we were received by a mad hail of machine gun and rifle fire. At first we were both dumbfounded. Then I quickly drew my flashlight out, took a somewhat closer look at my compass and saw, 'Holy cow! We're flying northwards instead of towards the east!' – 'Head around to the right!' I hollered to my pilot and yanked on my good Strunz' shoulder.

"'Hell! What if we wind up in Holland?' Pitch-black night, a dreadful mist, and no idea where we are! In the event of an emergency landing there'll be a real crack-up, because everywhere from out of the mist the tops of poplars peek encouragingly. But that's all one can see. Nice prospects! My main thought was, 'Just don't let yourself be captured! The fuel will still last for another hour. We won't go down any sooner than that.' And above all, 'Off to the east!' However, after a few minutes ambition grabbed me by the collar. Should I as *Staffelführer* and an old observer make an emergency landing because of poor navigation? No, that would be a fine scandal!

"First of all, I calmly considered our flight path up to this point and the time we had used up and came to the conclusion that we had to fly first toward the southeast and then after a few minutes head southward in order to at least arrive in the vicinity of our airfield. For about 15 minutes we cruised along when suddenly the beacons from our field appeared right in front of us. We quite nearly ran our noses right into them! You see? An old observer will find his way home even in night and fog! The landing went smoothly. It was 1:30 a.m. My little band stood nearly at full-strength upon the field. They had gotten a bit worried about the 'Old Man.'

"In the meantime the English counter-offensives had commenced in full fury. The 'protective' duties implied by the term *'Schutzstaffel'* were gradually pushed more and more into the background. The intervention in the ground battle as *'Sturmflieger'* – the direct support of the hard struggling infantry – became their main task entirely of its own accord. The name *'Sturmflieger'* came into being during the Battle of Flanders. Later the *Schutzstaffeln* received the official designation *'Schlachtstaffel.'* The *Schlachtflieger* as pilots and gunners were almost exclusively non-commissioned officers and of the lower ranks. Only the *Staffel* commander was an officer. But what sort of spirit was yet to be found in the crews at the end of the bloody year 1917 can be shown through a few examples.

"*Vizefeldwebel* Schäffer, a Württemberger, returns from a flight one day, climbs out of his crate, and reports to me. Then he stiffly turns, heads towards a bench, puts one of his feet on it, and begins to unwrap his puttee. I watch him without thinking anything about it. He pulls back his breeches and – there, everything is full of blood. 'Say Schäffer, what's going on?' I call out. And he answers in the purest Swabian, 'Nothing, *Herr Oberleutnant*, I think the swine got me a little bit.' He bares his knee. A ball of shrapnel is stuck in it – true, not very deeply, but nonetheless ...! But what is the fellow doing? I can't believe my eyes! Before I can prevent it, he has scratched out the ball with his fingers, which are all greasy and oily from the flight. Grinning, he holds it toward me and says, 'There, I've got it!'

"'Are you crazy, Schäffer? March to the auto and head immediately to the hospital!' He pleads, '*Herr Oberleutnant,* I'd like to stay. I don't need a hospital because of this little bit of scrap!' 'No, not a word! Go immediately to the hospital!' I have to go along, otherwise he'll run off. Finally, he's delivered, examined, and bound up. The wound is not at all harmless. After 14 days old Schäffer suddenly comes hobbling along on a crutch. I stand motionless. 'Where did you come from?'

'From the hospital.'

'Have you already been discharged from there?'

'No. I ran away from there, because I never did like it.'

'And did you walk here the entire four kilometers from the hospital?'

'Well, yeah. I want to start flying again.'

'Not a chance! That's not going to work out.'

'*Herr Oberleutnant*, it's fine.'

"And, in fact, it was fine.

"During an infantry support flight on July 31, 1917, two aircraft fly over the front at approximately 300 meters height in spite of rain and storm. Four kilometers behind the forwardmost English lines they come across marching infantry. First they are thrown into a state of confusion with bombs and then the Tommies scattering into every corner are attacked with machine guns from less than 100 meters height. Of course, the Englishmen don't put up with this for very long and defend themselves with rifles and machine guns. Soon the steel tubes of the stabilizer and elevator of one of the aircraft are hit. The steering controls respond poorly. But his comrade isn't finished and keeps attacking again and again. The rear-gunner of the lame aircraft also lets his weapon speak profusely. He silently agrees with his pilot not to start the return flight until their comrade has finished his attack. Both occupants of the badly damaged aircraft know precisely the danger they will face should the shot-up controls or stabilizer be completely destroyed by the strong air pressure. However this doesn't hinder them in their faithful perseverance. And God aids the courageous! They arrive safely at their home airfield.

"October 30, 1917. The day of a big battle! Of course, there is as always the usual rotten weather: storms, rain, clouds. We receive the mission of driving off the bothersome enemy infantry contact flyers in the vicinity of Passchendaele. We head out in a group of five. And, as often happens, upon our arrival at the front there are no infantry contact flyers at all to be seen. And we 'deep-sea researchers' can't do anything against the fighter aircraft flying at 5,000 to 6,000 meters height. We're only at 2,400 meters. But wait! Ah! Right there behind the enemy front a flight of enemy birds is cruising up and down. We head straight toward them – they are just about of equal strength – but they immediately head further back. There's nothing to do! We try to entice them by continuously flying back and forth behind the enemy front, always to the borders of our division sector. But even that doesn't attract them. We dive several times upon the enemy positions, fire with all our machine guns on the Tommies crouching in the shell-holes, going down low in the process so that the others can easily fall upon us. But that doesn't draw them either. 'Dull company!'

"We avenge ourselves in that we behave quite comfortably in the English sector. They continuously fly with us up and down as though they were our mirror-image. But upstairs we always have to be on our guard. From time to time my eyes glance over my little band. Suddenly one of them is missing. There were always five of us and now there are only four? With the best of intentions I can't account for any more than four. 'Where might the fifth one be?' I keep on the lookout, count again and again, and always come to the same result. Far on the other side fly the five or six Englishmen – I think they are Sopwiths – peacefully up and down. So no unpleasant surprise could have come from there

"But what is suddenly wrong with them over there? They're swirling around like a stirred up swarm of bees. I can count them exactly: there are six! Wait! One of them is detaching himself from the swirl of confusion and comes directly toward us. No, he is going down! Well, what could this mean? That's a German airplane? He comes through below us. Of course it's a German! I see him quite clearly now. Why, that's my missing fifth man! How did he get over there? What was going on? Everything is a mystery to me. Our man goes lower and lower, disappearing behind the German lines. We want to avenge ourselves against the Tommies and head directly for them. They again turn around. There's really nothing to be done with that bunch!

"After the landing I look for who's missing. This is quickly determined. While we're still standing together and discussing the incident, I am called to the telephone.

'*Unteroffizier* Thaufelder here,' a voice blares at me. 'What was wrong with you then?' 'Well, the constant flying back and forth became too boring for me and I became so angry at the five blasted Englishmen that I wanted to attack them. But they immediately shot up my entire crate and so we had to make an emergency landing near Roulers. The machine has to be dismantled.' So now I knew! What I didn't know was whether I should give the fellow a proper dressing down for his frivolous recklessness and his unauthorized actions or should I praise him because of his daring resolve and his spirited pluck. In reality I was glad, but I preferred not to show it. Otherwise everyone would have soon done whatever he wanted to do.

"A Difficult Day (September 20, 1917)

"For three days the English have been 'drumming,' so that in our quarters about 18 kilometers behind the front the window panes never cease rattling and trembling. An uninterrupted distant roar, like a wild surf which every couple of seconds is exceeded by a muffled explosion, resounds through the moist, rain-laden air. The earth is shaking, the houses are shaking, everything is vibrating. Our pulses are racing. When will it begin? If only the weather would improve! How might things stand up front? God, this is a miserable, wretched feeling when we must remain inactive in readiness during such a superhuman struggle. Have they in the end forgotten us?

"In the course of the 17th of September reassuring reports come in from the 121st Infantry Division, to which we are assigned. 'The Tommies are drumming away, but nowhere have attacks occurred, and no signs of such have yet been reported.' But such attacks will yet come. They are coming. But when? There is nothing more wretched than this uncertainty. Thus pass the 17th and 18th of September. The 19th is also almost over and the hell is still raging steadily. Steadily? No! From hour to hour the muffled rumbling increases, grows to a raging hurricane. What must the poor infantry be enduring up there? What superhuman hardships must they bear? If only one were able to – permitted to – help them! There is one consolation, our artillery will also not be inactive and will contribute their share in this hellish racket!

"The 19th of September has passed. In the night the uproar rages on and becomes louder! An explosion, a window pane in my room shatters onto the floor. I can no longer endure it in my bed. It is 4 a.m. A pitch-dark night. The rain drizzles, whipped by heavy gusts of wind. This is real Flanders battle weather! An uncertain feeling tells me, 'Today it begins!' Sitting on the edge of my bed, I hardly know what to do. Roust my men already? No point. Why should I? They could use the rest, if only they're more sharp. And that they are, I know it!

"Rrrrr! Rrrrr! Rrrrr! – *Donnerwetter!* That startled me! Yes, even the best of nerves will gradually be shot to hell! This damned telephone! 'What's up?' '*Flieger Abteilung 19* here. Duty officer. We must send out an infantry contact aircraft into the division sector at the break of day. I am requesting an escort for him. In addition, the division requests that a *Sturmflieger* be made available today, as the launch of the attack is expected.'

"'*Jawohl*, everything will be taken care of. It's now 4.30 a.m. It can get light in about an hour. At 5:45 the escort aircraft will stand by ready for take-off in front of your hangars. Good morning.' Quickly, get the duty log. Who's up first today? Aha, here it is. Stand-by for an escort flight on September 20th: No. 6. Crew: *Vizefeldwebel* Möhlenbeck and *Unteroffizier* Bitzer. Stand-by for a ground-attack flight: Aircraft Nos. 3, 4, and 5. Crews: etc. Reserve: Aircraft No. 2. Under repair: Aircraft No. 1. So, let's go! – Telephone: 'Is the airfield sentry there? Yes? Alert the *Staffel* immediately. All machines are to stand ready for take-off before the hangars at 5:30 a.m. All crew to assemble in Hangar 1 in full flight gear. Repeat the order! ... Good! Over!'

"Today there is something to do! Since 5 a.m. the torrent of fire has increased considerably. This has been going on since July 31st with only short interruptions. In spite of that the English advance only tentatively. Their attacks get stuck in the mud and blood. Yes, if only they didn't have German infantry facing them! At 5:15 everyone is already on the airfield. The motors of the five aircraft are running, spraying sparks in the darkness, and at times covering the roar of the barrage with their thunder. The mechanics are still busy fiddling around, the foreman swears and curses, the armorer with his assistants drags over machine guns and ammunition and as a test allows his spray of bullets to rattle away merrily at the rainy sky.

"Now to the crews in Hangar 1. They're all standing there, my 12 'brothers' with whom I've grown together, as only a frontline soldier can with his comrades. And yet we've only been together three months. But every one of them has once or more often dug the others out of the '*rue de merde,*' as one says at the front – to be sure, not very elegantly, but on the other hand all the more fittingly. I, too, have many of them to thank for saving my neck. Möhlenbeck and Bitzer report themselves ready for the flight. They haven't been with the *Staffel* for long, but I like them. They are calm, brave men who, sparing of words, fulfill their duty to the utmost. The one is Prussian, the other a Swabian from Bavaria. Thus they are paired in a small airplane, depend on one another, and have become faithful comrades. May it be so everywhere in the German Fatherland! Both receive their mission, climb into their aircraft, and taxi over to *Flieger Abteilung 19*, where they are to report to the infantry contact flyer. Bitzer waves one more time, then they disappear around the corner of the hangar. I never saw them again. The fate of flyers!

"The four remaining aircraft are ready. We wait. At 7 a.m. a message comes from the division, 'Large English attack in progress. Our forwardmost troops pressed back to the Wilhelm Line. This latter is in our hands.' Again we wait. New uncertainty. Then at 8:20 a.m. the telephone rattles. '121st Infantry Division here. The division immediately requires a *Sturmstaffel* for the support of a counter-thrust from the Wilhelm Line. The infantry has already taken up its position.' '*Jawohl!* In 20 minutes at the latest three aircraft will be over the Wilhelm Line.'

"Now things get lively. We're already wrapped up in our leather clothing. Quickly a short discussion of the situation and the order. 'Aircraft 3 and 5 fly behind me. I myself will lead in Aircraft 4. Upon my firing a flare signal the attack will begin with machine guns and hand grenades against everything to be seen on the English side of the line. *Hals und Beinbruch!*'

"Crash-helmet and goggles are put on quickly. No. 5 is the first to roar over the field. My aircraft, in the hands of the brave *Vizefeldwebel* Weidner, takes off last, but hardly one minute after the other two. *Pfui Teufel*, what weather we're having! It's raining in streams, the clouds are hanging down to 100 meters over the earth. Every five seconds we must wipe our goggles, for we can see nothing because of all the water. The rain whips against our faces, bringing tears to our eyes. We can't climb any higher than 100 meters because of the clouds. We fly over the rail-line from Iseghem to Roeselaere (Roulers) and from there along the railway to Ypres. There's nothing else to be found in our division sector with all the muck. Above our artillery positions the airplane is shaken back and forth. It hops and leaps; it rocks and bucks. We notice the pleasant proximity of the German shells fired which are racing with us toward the English. Every moment there are explosions below. We look and search and assume it is enemy return fire, as we are now already close to the front. But it is only the discharge of our own gallant guns.

"We continue at breakneck speed. Moorslede comes into sight – we're already over it. Below, enemy shells burst and smoke. Thick columns of smoke rise out of the earth from which reddish glowing flashes shoot up. A German ammo dump is blown to bits. To us it looks like a harmless fireworks display – and yet – how many a brave German artillerist may have lost his young life. Onward, onward. We see men nestled closely together in water- and mud-filled holes: German infantrymen. Incomparable patient sufferers. They stare upward with white faces. Individuals who recognize us as friends wave with caps and handkerchiefs. I wave back, 'Yes, you poor, brave fellows, we want to aid you as much as it lies within our feeble power to do so.' Onward, ever onward, and forward our bird speeds. We are in the desolate battle zone. Below there are flashes and explosions. The area is smoking and smoldering. Suddenly there is a thick darkness all around us. A low-hanging shred of cloud obscures our view downward. Through it!

"Ah! Look! What's that? Like a brightly colored butterfly an enemy infantry contact flyer decorated with cockades and streamers is flitting and swaying about. We almost rammed into him. He is so surprised by our emergence from the cloud that he forgets his flitting around and cuts and runs in a straight dive toward his rear lines. 'Weidner, we've got to haul him in!' I shout into my pilot's ears. He aims briefly and his forward-firing machine gun rattles away. Unfortunately, the Tommy was a faster airplane. The distance becomes greater and greater. We dive after him for all we're worth. My eyes are fixed on the foe. He goes lower and lower. Our altimeter indicates 50 meters height.

"Ahead of us and to our left is our Airplane No. 3. I can't locate Machine No. 5. Suddenly there is the sound of a hundred whips cracking in my ear. Almost simultaneously I see Aircraft No. 3 turn around in a steep curve to the left and dash over us in the direction of home. What's wrong? Did he lose his nerve? He disappears. Where are we anyway? *Donnerwetter!* Frezenberg is there below us – very familiar to all of us since the beginning of the Flanders battle. We can't follow the Tommy any further if we want to come back more or less intact.

"The sound like cracking whips becomes more intense – not exactly reassuring, as we know that it's machine gun and rifle fire intended for us. A few times there's already been a suspicious rustling sound in our 'crate', a sign that it's not just a bunch of bunglers shooting down there. By my estimate we're now about 5 kilometers behind the front – and only 50 meters high. If only something doesn't go wrong! I keep a look-out to see whether there isn't something to pounce on. Right, there's a battery, entirely in the open. And how it's firing away! It flashes again and again with the firing of each round. Just wait, friends. First, four hand grenades to calm then down. Then a hail of machine gun fire sends everyone below scurrying away to crawl into holes. They have no cover from us!

"The guns are silent. We turn around. The damned cracking is making me uneasy. It seems as though everyone who has a rifle is firing at us. It doesn't take long and then we hear 'boom' and again 'boom' in our machine. We both recognize the sound from experience. Now we've taken a hit. But where? We both listen anxiously to the engine. But it roars calmly and smoothly. That's the main thing. Otherwise the least we'll suffer is imprisonment, if they don't kill us outright. There's no time to look any further for where we've been hit. I have some shooting to do. 100, 150, 250 rounds. The ammunition belt is depleted. Weidner has 1000 rounds in his machine gun. Again and again he tips the aircraft forward and fires everything he's got. There's enough 'fodder.' Everything is full of Tommies. They're lying quite closely together in the shell-holes.

"Finally we're back again over Moorslede, our point of rendezvous. But I don't see any sign of our two companions. While circling, I load a new ammunition belt. Strain and excitement is making my whole body sweat, only – I don't know what it is – but my feet are freezing terribly. By chance I look down and – oh, what a fine kettle of fish! Fuel is just spilling all around in the airplane. I'm already ankle deep in it! So that's what the 'boom' was earlier. I shake Weidner's shoulder and yell at him: 'Hit in the main fuel tank!' He nods. He always just nods! Nothing gets him excited. I shout, 'Can we have another go at it?' He glances at the fuel gauge and again he nods. 'Okay, let's do it!' A vapor trail several meters long from the spraying fuel extends out behind us. Now if only a couple of sparks from the exhaust would mix with it! A cheerful prospect!

"My two companions have disappeared without a trace. Neither do I see any other aircraft. Again we fall upon the mass of Englishmen. Whenever we fire everyone runs and throws themselves down and horses bolt. My God, if only there were 20 or 30 of us, the attack would really make a bitter impression on them. But we are simply too weak. And again a belt of ammunition is exhausted. My armorer is indeed a stout fellow. Up to now not a single jam. On the return flight I see for the first time the infantrymen of our first line. They're hard to find. They are far and away nothing like the masses to be found over by the enemy. Here lie two or three. There lies a little group of four to five men. And yet they're holding up the giant enemy attacks. What a superhuman heroic accomplishment!

"But unfortunately they are no longer in the Wilhelm Line and I also can't detect any sign of a counter-attack in progress. Who knows what all has happened down there. It wouldn't be the first time that all plans and intentions were thrown into disarray at the last moment. The poor fellows down below wave at me, wave with whatever they have: helmets, rifles, caps, and handkerchiefs. Apparently they are gladdened by our presence and that fills me with a great sense of pride. I also wave to them as long as I can see them and then once again we are over Moorslede, i.e., what we still call 'Moorslede' because that's what it says on the map. In fact, it was nothing but desolate heaps of stone. The old game repeats itself: loading a new ammunition belt, a futile search for our comrades, and the question to Weidner whether we can 'have another go at it.' Again he nods!

"The fuel vapor, our faithful companion, trails as ever behind us. We dive upon the enemy a third time. Thank God the damned rain has eased up a bit. Now I can see better. Once more we swoop down to about 50 meters upon the infantry. Weidner and I fire away our ammunition down to the last round. But now it is high time for our return flight, otherwise we'll never come home again. It would be a shame if we were to crash our nicely shot-up airplane while making an emergency landing somewhere in a field of craters. We still have 25 liters of fuel and it's running out awfully quickly through the hole in the tank. With a strong tailwind we'll reach our airfield in ten minutes, where we can make a smooth landing. Here I find one of my two companions, Aircraft No. 5. They had always been close to me but had not participated in the third attack due to a lack of ammunition. Their crate reveals a fair number of honorable holes.

"To the crews of Aircraft 2 (which up to now was in reserve) and 5 I issue the order for an immediate attack on the English lying before and in the Wilhelm Line. Unfortunately, Weidner and I can no longer go along in our Machine No. 4. It looks bad. Aircraft 3 and 6 are missing. The latter can no longer be in the air as it has been out for considerably longer than three hours. Shortly after 9 a.m. Numbers 2 and 5 take off and return badly shot up, but safe and sound after an hour, having carried out several attacks. Both have to be dismantled and repaired. Now my *Staffel* is 'finished.' For me there remains nothing to do but order the speediest restoration of the three shot-up machines, report the condition of my *Staffel*, and then make inquires concerning the two missing aircraft. Unfortunately, this remains fruitless. Our concern is great.

"Finally, at 3 p.m. comes a report by telephone from the aerial gunner *Unteroffizier* Schwarz of Aircraft 3 that his pilot, *Unteroffizier* Jokisch, was hit in the middle of his chest at 50 meters right during the first attack. At the same time his engine and fuel tank were shot to pieces. In spite of this Jokisch landed the aircraft smoothly in a meadow near Dadizeele strewn with shell-holes – an all the more praiseworthy achievement, as the weather was also quite stormy and unfavorable for an emergency landing. Immediately after the landing he was brought to the corner field hospital at St. Eloi. The aircraft was hauled in already by afternoon. It had over 30 hits, including one in the fuel tank and three in the engine.

"Unfortunately, all inquires concerning Möhlenbeck and Bitzer remained fruitless. Only on the evening of September 24th did the news arrive that the missing Aircraft 6 lay completely wrecked in the field of craters near Westroosebeke, with the two occupants lying dead beside the ruins. After a lot of effort they were recovered on September 28 and transported home. Shortly after his departure on the morning of the 20th, the Iron Cross arrived for *Unteroffizier* Bitzer. As a result of the losses on September 20th, my *Staffel* withdrew from any participation in the defensive battles for eight days, as new aircraft were not available and the others needed to be patched up."

Krausser's description of his unit's activities in the latter half of 1917 amply demonstrates the determined spirit of the *Schutzstaffel* crews in the face of multiple hazards, be it enemy fighters, enemy ground fire, friendly fire, or even the weather. Their spirit was bolstered to a great extent by the sense of solidarity with the ground troops. Krausser describes how enemy fighters kept a respectful distance when encountering *Schusta* crews in numbers. However, another account is contained in the book *Wir Kämpfer im Weltkrieg*, compiled by Wolfgang Foerster and Helmuth Greiner. Entitled '*Schlachtflieger*,' written by a *Ltn.d.R.* Klinker, believed to be from *Schusta 8,* it reveals the perils encountered by individual, roving *Schlachtflieger* who come up against a superior force of enemy fighters:

"On September 25, 1917, 6:18 p.m., my pilot Heuser and I took off for an infantry support flight. At 3000 meters height we flew over the front and dropped our bombs on enemy positions about 400 meters west of Gerteaux-Ferme. Then we proceeded at a lower altitude in the direction of Pargny and then flew again toward the enemy near Fort Malmaison. Then I noticed four or five enemy single-seater fighters coming from the direction of Colombe-Ferme.

"My pilot Heuser immediately turned away from the front and went down to 300 meters. Approximately between the Basin and Monampteuil the enemy caught up to us and attacked our flank simultaneously from above and below. Although we'd descended toward the high ground between Monampteuil and Laval down to about 10 meters, two Spads still came below us from out of the ravines and hung behind us for awhile, firing continuously. I waited in vain for the aid of our flak or artillery.

"When the enemy had eased off, I gave my pilot the signal to climb higher and fly homewards. When we were about 500 meters high he shook his head and pointed with one hand at his chest. I noticed that he was wounded, gave him some encouragement, and indicated a spot for him to land – at which point I strapped myself in securely. Suddenly the machine climbed steeply and right after that the pilot slumped forward over the controls. I crept through the cabane struts, lay lengthwise over the fuselage, pulled back the throttle, and held the controls to keep the machine horizontal.

"The unconscious pilot had pushed the rudder to the left. The machine therefore swung toward the left and in the process slipped sharply now and again. Above the forest encampment near La Canotte, east of Mons, I again righted the machine somewhat in order to decrease our speed. The left wing struck a tree. The aircraft spun once and then hit the ground, whereby it was completely destroyed. The badly injured Heuser was able to be pulled from the machine by medics rushing to the scene and was immediately bandaged up. The crash occurred at approximately 6:50 p.m."

Opposite
Top left: *Oblt.* Eduard Wolfgang Zorer shown here early in his career as an observer with *Fl.Abt. 54* on the Eastern Front.

Top right: *Oblt.* Eduard Wolfgang Zorer as C.O. of *Schusta 7* with an Albatros C.III. It was with this unit and with his pilot, *Vzfw.* Josef Schleiffer, that he made the first low-level, close-in, infantry support flight that established the value of the tactic and ultimately led to the renaming of these units to *Schlachtstaffeln.*

Bottom: *Schutzstaffel* 2 taken early in 1917 while they were escorting *Fl.Abt. 222(A)*. The man sitting in the center is *Oblt.* Oskar Kuppinger. The others are not identified. Photo credit: Helge Dittmann.

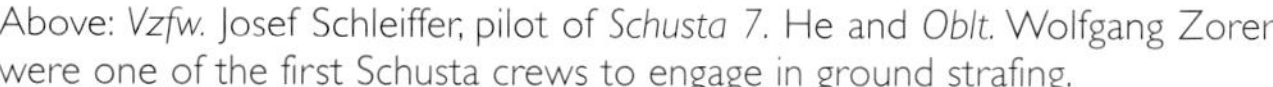

Above: *Vzfw.* Josef Schleiffer, pilot of *Schusta 7.* He and *Oblt.* Wolfgang Zorer were one of the first Schusta crews to engage in ground strafing.

Top right: *Vzfw.* Julius Tillmanns, pilot, served with *Schusta 2* from its inception until being posted to *KG 1, Kasta 3* on 26 June 1917.

Right: *Oblt.* Friedrich *Ritter* von Krausser who led *Schusta 23b* from 15 June 1917 to 1 February 1918.

Left: *Vzfw.* Fritz Strunz served as a pilot with *Schusta/Schlasta 23b* from the time it was formed until the end of the war, rather a unique career. Credit: UTD/HAC.

Below: The crew of *Uffz.* Robert Bitzer (G) and *Vzfw.* Gerhard Möhlenbeck (P) of *Schusta 23b* who were killed in action on September 20, 1917. The aircraft is a DFW C.V. Credit: UTD/HAC.

Below: The *Schuztstaffel 24b* Albatros C.VII C.1237 of *Uffz.* Wilhelm Miltner and *Vzfw.* Ferdinand Wens. They were shot down in flames and KIA on 25 May 1917. Photo credit: Walter Werner.

CHAPTER V

THE SCHUTZSTAFFELN STRIKE AT CAMBRAI (FALL 1917)

In the Fall of 1917 the *Schusta* participated in an attack that was imminently important, both because of its effect on the opposing British troops and in light of the *Schusta* slowly being transformed from escort duties to ground support duties. To quote from Gray and Thetford:

> "One of the first successful operations involving the Halberstadt CL.II was an attack on the Somme bridges at Bray and St. Christ on 6th September 1917. The Germans had been obliged to evacuate Péronne due to the success of heavy attacks by the British, and the concentration of British reserves on the west bank of the river had been spotted by reconnaissance aircraft. It was planned to attack these troops as they actually crossed the bridges, where it was estimated the greatest havoc might be wrought. Such indeed was the case – the attack was mounted by twenty-four Halberstadts and panic ensued, troops jumping over the parapets of the two bridges in their endeavor to escape the machine gun fire and grenades coming from the aircraft. The artillery troops and their horses farther in the rear were also attacked, and it was estimated the Halberstadts had disorganized the best part of a division. During the whole period the Halberstadts were assailed by only two Sopwith scouts, one of which was promptly shot down, the other then making off."

Although a thrilling report, it does contain a couple of factual errors which need to be corrected. First, the only aircraft downed by a two-seater crew was indeed a Sopwith, but at Woesten in the *4. Armee*. This was a *Schusta 10* crew and Woesten is a little north of both Poperinge and Ypres. Secondly, no *Schutzstaffel* was operating in *2. Armee* on this date. This was probably a *7. Armee Schusta,* possibly *Schusta 14*. Thus the attack by twenty-four aircraft was most likely six repeated attacks by four aircraft, four being the optimum number of aircraft that the *Schusta* commanders found they could effectively control in the air. Nevertheless, it goes to show just how effective a coordinated attack could be and how disrupting to the attacking enemy troops.

On 20 November, 1917, the British 3rd Army under the command of General Sir Julian Byng attacked the German *2. Armee* by surprise at Cambrai. The attack was spearheaded by the British Tank Corps led by Brigadier General Sir Hugh Elles. The corps consisted of 474 tanks of which 376 were battle tanks, with the rest holding various reserve/support capacity. In fact, being the first true test of tanks in battle, the Tank Corps had actually selected the Cambrai area as the ideal place in which to launch the attack. The ground before Cambrai, although somewhat undulating, was firm, hard and not pock-marked with shell craters nor did it consist of a muddy slime, as did the positions further north in Flanders. This tank attack was designed to be a mere trench raid, as the tanks had previously proven ineffective in the fighting in Flanders.

The English attack began at 6:30 in the morning with a short artillery barrage so as not to alert the Germans as to what was coming. The tanks moved out from their previously camouflaged positions and fell upon the German trenches. They quickly overran these and, with the infantry in close support, succeeded in penetrating the Hindenburg Line with a 5 mile advance over a 6 mile wide front. More enemy territory was captured in the first day than in all the previous fighting on the Somme and in Flanders.

The German *2. Armee* under the command of *General der Kavallerie* Georg von der Marwitz was taken totally by surprise, not only by the short one-half hour preparatory artillery barrage, not at all the norm for infantry attacks, but also by the appearance of so many attacking tanks. At this time *2. Armee* was divided into two *Gruppen*, *Gruppe Arras* to the NW under the command of *Generalleutant* Otto von Moser and *Gruppe Caudry* to the SE led by *General der Infanterie* Theodor *Freiherr* von Watter. The attack fell mainly upon the latter group. Orders immediately were sent out by *Kofl 2*, *Hptm.* Wilhelm Haehnelt, to the aviation units protecting these *Gruppen* to prepare to take off and repel the attack. Sadly, only two 'defensive' units were available to the *2. Armee*: *Jagdstaffel 5* at Boistrancourt led by *Oblt.* Richard Flashar and *Schutzstaffel 10* led by *Hptm.* Paul von Winckler stationed at Bertry. Low fog, mist and intermittent rain prevented either unit from being very effective in halting the British advance.

The British attack had been designed to be a mere raid, but was so successful that the British C-in-C, General Sir Douglas Haig, had visions of capturing Cambrai, and then turning his cavalry loose in the open country beyond. On the first day alone the Germans suffered the loss of over 8,000 prisoners, 123 guns and 281 machine guns. The Germans immediately called for reinforcements and *Schusta 19,* led by *Hptm.* Wilhelm Aschenborn, arrived on the evening of the 20th and settled in at Boussières. Also *Schusta 24b* (*Oblt.* Karl Schröder) was transferred on the 20th to Abscon in the *6. Armee*, but were then called on to support the *2. Armee.* German infantry reinforcements began arriving on the 22nd and *Jagdgeschwader Nr. I* (von Richthofen) flew in that evening and began flying sorties on the 23rd in support of the hard-pressed *Jasta 5*. By the 22nd *Schusta 12 (Oblt.* Johannes Missfelder) had come to support the *2. Armee. Schusta 27b* (*Oblt.d.R.* Sigmund Kreitmair) arrived on the 23rd, establishing residence at Bertry. Finally, on the 25th, *Schusta 1* under the command of *Oblt.* Eduard Seldner, *Schusta 5 (Oblt.* Ulrich von Schimony-Schimonsky), *Schusta 17 (Hptm.* Walter Mundt), and *Schusta 25b* (*Oblt.* Josef Rittmann) had come from the *4. Armee* to provide even more support.

By November 27th the British salient was 9 miles wide and 4 miles deep. However, also on the 27th the Germans began planning their counter-attack. Their plan called for attacking both flanks of the salient in the hope of trapping all the British within. The Germans launched this attack on the 30th. On this date, *Schusta 6* sent four aircraft from the *7. Armee* to assist *Schusta 25b*. Therefore, for the counter-offensive, as far as can be determined, at least eight *Schutzstaffeln*: *1, 5, 10, 12, 17, 19, 24b, 25b,* and *27b* were available. Additional reinforcements in the form of *Schusta 29b (Oblt.* Cornelius Vogeley) arrived at Caudry in the *2. Armee* on December 1st.

The attack began at 6:30 in the morning with an intense artillery barrage followed by the infantry assault at 7:00. By this time the British Tank Corps had pretty much been depleted. Just 63 fighting tanks remained serviceable and these were in the process of being withdrawn. In fact many tanks had already been entrained preparatory to their being returned to the rear. The attack was spearheaded in the northern part of *2. Armee* under a newly formed *Gruppe Busigny* under the command of *General der Infanterie* Hugo von Kathen.

The *Schusta* led the attack and were eminently successful. Capt. Geoffrey Dugdale of the 6th King's Somerset Light Infantry remarked: "The German aeroplanes were very active flying over our lines in large numbers, very low. They were shooting with machine guns at the troops on the ground, and I am quite sure this did more to demoralize our men than anything else." (From 'The Battle of Cambrai' by Bryan Cooper).

The *Schusta* were so successful in fact that the British convened an official Court of Inquiry on 21 January 1918 at Hesdin to examine the German success. It lasted a full nine days. The findings recorded the appearance of close-support aircraft in considerable numbers at altitudes lower than 100 feet, firing into both the front line trenches as well as the rear positions. The effect on morale was reported as being very great and facilitated the German success. British infantry seemed at a loss to counteract the performance of these low-flying aircraft. One witness even stated that firing on them produced no visible effect.

When the great Tank Battle of Cambrai finally ground to a halt on December 7, 1917, the British advance and retreat left the original front lines resembling a lopsided figure 8, with the Germans capturing the lower loop, and the British the upper. The total amount of land gained or lost was virtually nil. This 'mere trench raid' cost the British 44,207 casualties including over 6,000 prisoners, 103 field guns and howitzers and 55 heavier pieces. The price to the Germans was between 45,000 and 53,000 KIA, MIA or POW, 142 guns, 350 machine guns, and 70 trench mortars. It is estimated that over 10,500 men were captured. The known *Schusta* losses consisted of one gunner KIA and one crew taken POW. The *Schutzstaffeln* had shown what could be accomplished in a concentrated attack, and much more would follow in the year 1918.

Schutzstaffel 8 Christmas celebration, 1917. None of the men are identified. Photo credit: Marcus Pleyer.

The men of *Schutzstaffel 12* celebrating New Year's Eve, 1917.

Gefr. August Beckedorf a gunner with *Schusta 10* on the left and his pilot *Uffz.* Hermann Märzhäuser on the right prepare for a mission on 10 December 1917. The aircraft is a DFW C.V. Photo credit: Tobias Weber.

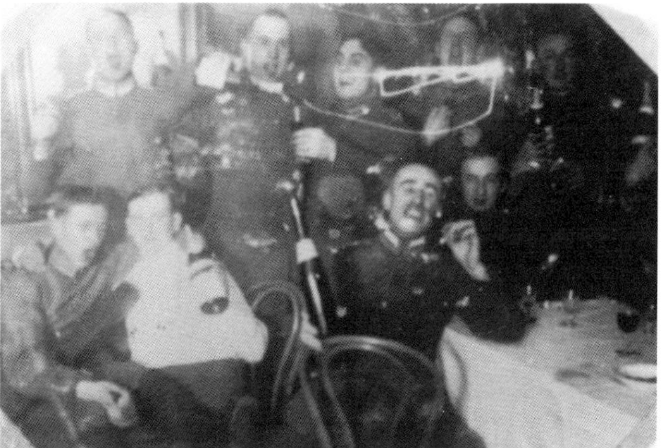

Schusta 12 at New Year's Eve, 1917. The wine was flowing pretty well! The white streak in the middle is a flaw in the original photograph.

Uffz. Otto Kutter and some of the men of *Schusta 8* in the winter of 1917/18.

Maria Aalter, the airfield of *Schusta 12*, and the crash of *Uffz*. Kruse and *Uffz*. Voigt in LVG C.V 3342/17 on 30 October 1917. Note the aircraft individual number (42) and that it is derived from the last two digits of the serial number (3342). This was common practice for *Schusta 12* at this time.

Gefr. Rudolf Schadt, a gunner with *Schusta 12*, taken during the winter of 1917.

Schutzstaffel 29b celebrating Christmas Eve, 1917. None of the men are identified. Photo credit: UTD/HAC.

PART II
THE SCHLACHTSTAFFELN

(MARCH 1918 TO NOVEMBER 1918)

CHAPTER VI

1918

The victory over the Russians, culminating in the signing of the Treaty of Brest-Litovsk on December 15, 1917, allowed over a million ground troops to be transferred to the Western Front in preparation for the Great March Offensive. Air units operating on the Eastern Front likewise were able to relinquish their equipment and personnel to bolster the *Luftstreitkräfte* in the West. Thus during the Spring of 1918 *Schusta 31b, 32-37,* and *38s* were formed from the disbanded *Flieger Abteilungen 47b, 4, 15, 21, 11, 25, 220(A)*, and *24s*, respectively. At the same time the '*Amerika Programme*' was in full swing the goal of which was to double the number of *Jagdstaffeln.*

The plan also called for increasing the number of aircraft of each *Schusta* from six to nine. This never occurred. The limited growth of the *Schusta* was no doubt due to the lack of available, trained gunners as well as the shortage of acceptable ground attack two-seaters, the Halberstadt and Hannover. In addition, many of the *Schusta* pilots desired a transfer to the more illustrious *Jagdstaffeln*. As fighter pilots they would also be relieved of the responsibility of ensuring the safety of the rear gunner. Examples abound, but to name merely three would include *Ltn.d.R.* Friedrich Hengst who transferred from *Schusta 3* to *Jasta 64w* in February 1918, *Gefr.* Erich Mix who went from *Schlasta 21* to *Jasta 54s*, and *Vzfw*. Willi Gabriel who left *Schlasta 15* for *Jasta 11*. The latter two transfers occurred in mid-May 1918. All three men scored victories while flying with their respective *Jagdstaffeln,* Hengst and Gabriel becoming aces.

Much preparation had to be done by the *Schusta* for the upcoming March offensive. For instance the crews needed to be trained, orientation flights carried out, and new tactics devised. An indication of this initial planning is presented by *Oblt.* Hugo Miller, at this time the commander of Bavarian *Schutzstaffel 25.* It appeared in *"Bayerische Flieger im Weltkrieg"*, compiled by Max Zeidelhack. His account also reveals the hazards occasionally involved even in simple orientation flights:

> "The first days of February had brought ice and snow. The little French children romped upon the frozen ponds in the park at the entrance to Lille and Roubaix. For some days thick fog had sentenced us to a life of inactivity. Before Hindenburg attacked, all of the *Staffel* commanders and their crews once more had to impress upon their memories the exact layout of the front from Ostend to Laon. Then they could reach their targets even in conditions hindering their orientation, such as fog and low-hanging clouds.
>
> "And then it was as though the weather suddenly offered us a hand. On this day – it was the 16th of February – not a single cloud obscured the horizon. So at 9 a.m. I gave the order that an orientation flight was to be carried out in the direction of Ostend. Two aircraft were to accompany me and they were to be manned by my best crews. *Vizefeldwebel* [Konrad] Dumpert and [Benekidt] Wölfle were to fly in the second aircraft and in the third machine were [Wilhelm] Dörfler and [Ludwig] Kraus.
>
> "We took off at 10 o'clock. At 900 meters height I signaled my pilot to fly in the direction of Warneton. The two others followed nicely. One aircraft was staggered to the right, the other to the left at 300 meters rearward. The ruins of Ypres shone brightly and in the background, beyond the high ground of Passchendaele and the flood plain, the blue sea greeted our eyes. Our gaze was spellbound in that direction. Only now and then did I glance backwards to make sure the other two machines

were following me. But, at first, my concern for them was unnecessary.

"It may have been a short distance beyond Staden that I once more turned to look for them. I couldn't see them. Perhaps the one crew had made an emergency landing and Dumpert, helpful as ever, had landed his machine beside them. But Ostend was not far off and I couldn't miss them there. There was neither an enemy nor a German aircraft to be seen. Only far out over the sea, above patrol ships, did a German seaplane circle at a low height. We were over Ostend. Directly below me, 4000 meters down, ships appeared like cockleshells as they lay at anchor. White foam was created by waves breaking upon the coast and far off in the haze lay the large enemy island.

"Our engine functioned flawlessly. We flew two circles. But all reconnoitering was in vain. The two aircraft didn't come into sight. Concern for them caused me to turn around. The flight proceeded over Thourout, Poelkapelle, and Wervicq. The landing at our field near Lille proceeded smoothly. The crew of Dörfler and Kraus came toward me and reported that unrectifiable jams in their machine guns had forced them to return. They knew nothing about the third crew. Just where could they be? Dumpert, the old, experienced pilot, would certainly have sent some sort of word to us.

"The afternoon passed and then evening approached. Then we became anxious. We were unable to get any sort of clarification from the information centers. Could Dumpert have made an attack on an observation balloon and been shot down in the process? He had also spoken of doing loops. The day before he had flown in crazy turns above the roofs of Lille. Everyone had stood still and stared upwards with apprehension. I still hadn't given him a reprimand for the breakneck display of daring. And I never would get a chance to do so.

"The entire *Staffel* already lay fast asleep. Then my telephone rang. 'Adjutant of the *Kommandeur der Flieger der Armee* here.' 'This is the commander of Bavarian *Schlachtstaffel 25*.' 'I would like to report to you that two Bavarian *Unteroffiziere*, according to their papers members of *Schlachtstaffel 25*, are lying dead about 800 meters behind the front line. You may recover the airplane and the deceased, which will be released by the *6. Armee*. My condolences.' The inconceivable had become a reality.

"A day of great sorrow dawned for us. The grieving faces of the crews greeted me in the morning as I left the airfield in a truck accompanied by two others. Our journey proceeded to Oost-Nieuwkerke via Roulers. We left the vehicle behind a half-destroyed house. From the church waved the Red Cross. All around was emptiness and desolation. No one in the first-aid station, which was set up in the aisle of the church, had seen the airplane crash. We left the village on foot. Shells landed in the vicinity. Perhaps the artillery could give us more information. Not quite an hour later we came to a concrete bunker. The artillery observation officer gave us the first bit of news. On the basis of his report regarding the crash of a German aircraft observed the previous morning, I came to the conclusion that the accident had been caused either by a broken cable or a steering malfunction.

"The corpses were supposed to be lying further up near the front near the dugout of the troop commander. It was a long distance away. The dangerous spots where shells were landing had to be covered at full speed. One shell-hole lay next to another across the landscape and there were no trenches leading to the front line. Far and wide not a single person could be seen. The first sign of human habitation was the remnants of a wall of a detached farmhouse. The path curved through a narrow gully and over a little undulation. Then a shot-up patch of brushwood with a heap of stones in front of it came into view. Close by it was the entrance to a barren dugout and in front of that on the righthand side the yellow fuselage of the missing machine was gleaming in the sunlight.

"The wings and the engine were stuck deep in the earth pointing toward the direction of the enemy. There was no doubt. Here my best crew had died a hero's death. The troop commander related that at the time of the accident very heavy fire had been falling on the position. The only cause he could think of was that the machine had entered the path of an enemy shell and had crashed as a result. We now held a short prayer over the bodies of the heroes, which had been brought to safety some time ago. On February 21st we buried them ceremoniously to the mournful airs of a Bavarian regimental band in a lovely park to the south of Tourcoing.

"Dumpert, my pride, our shining model, he who knew no rest, who feared no danger, the intrepid soldier, the faithful, honest friend. And Wölfle, who was bound to him by similar daring, who sought to measure his own bravery only against the most well-tested, his companion in peril and exploits. May both rest in peace! We have not forgotten them."

On February 20, 1918 the Chief of the General Staff of the Field Army issued an order governing the employment and duties of the *Schutzstaffeln.* First published in English in *The War in the Air*, Volume IV, by H.A. Jones, it so completely and succinctly defines the role of the *Schusta/Schlasta* during the remainder of 1918, that it is presented here in its entirety. (Since the original German document has yet to be discovered and to partially put it back into its original German context, for battle flights read *Schlachtstaffeln*, for battle flight groups read *Schlachtgruppen*, and for protective flights read *Schutzstaffeln*):

"I. Employment and Duties of Battle Flights

"1. The employment of low-flying aeroplanes on the battle-field and their co-operation in the fighting on the ground, by opening machine-gun fire or attacking with bombs and hand grenades, is particularly effective from the point of view of *morale*, both on our own and the enemy's troops.

"2. The systematic participation in the battle of massed flying formations (battle flights) against ground targets is of extreme importance.

"In the attack, battle aeroplanes fly ahead of and carry the infantry along with them, keeping down the fire of the enemy's infantry and barrage batteries.

"In the defense, the appearance of battle aeroplanes affords visible proof to heavily engaged troops that the Higher Command is in close touch with the front, and is employing every possible means to support the fighting troops. Confidence in a successful defence is thereby strengthened.

"The object of the *battle flights* is to shatter the enemy's nerve by repeated attacks in close formation and thus to obtain a decisive influence on the course of the fighting.

"They cause confusion to a considerable distance behind the enemy's front line, dislocate traffic and inflict appreciable losses on the reinforcements hastening up to the battle-field.

"3. Formations of *reconnaissance flights* should not be employed for the attack of ground targets, as this would be to the detriment of their special work of reconnaissance and observation.

"On the other hand, the contact-patrol machine, which, from the very nature of its duties, is compelled to fly low, will frequently find opportunities to employ its machine-gun against ground targets.

"*Bombing squadrons* are not suitable for low-flying work.

"The most important duty of *pursuit flights* is the engagement of the enemy's air forces. Nevertheless, as far as fighting in the air will allow, scouts must also participate in the battle, diving steeply and firing both their machine-guns on the enemy on the ground.

"4. *Battle flights* (formerly known as protective flights) are allocated the task of engaging ground targets in close formation. They consist of 6 machines; the commander of a battle flight is an officer.

"To obtain more permanent results in offensive operations on a large scale, several battle flights may be grouped to form a *battle-flight group.*

"5. The execution of a battle mission makes the fullest demands on the physical capabilities and will-power of a crew. Battle flights must devote themselves exclusively to their particular sphere of action. Tasks forming part of the duties of contact patrol or artillery machines must not be assigned to them simultaneously with their battle duties. On the other hand, battle aeroplanes are responsible for reporting to the proper quarters, immediately after landing, any definite observations made during their flights which may be of value to the Higher Command and to the artillery, e.g. the position of our own or the enemy's infantry in the battle zone.

"6. Battle flights should only be employed in *decisive* infantry actions. At other times, they can be employed as escorts to reconnaissance flights working with the infantry and artillery.

"II. Composition of Battle Flights and Battle-Flight Groups

"7. Decisive effect upon the enemy is obtained by the employment of a number of machines in close formation. The *fighting strength of a battle flight* must, therefore, not be less than four machines. The number that can be engaged simultaneously is limited by the possibility of manoeuvre under one command. More than six machines are difficult to control.

"8. Where several flights are concentrated to form a battle-flight group (three to six battle flights) operating on a single sector of attack (see para. 4), they should start from the same aerodrome.

"III. Employment of Battle Flights

"A. Attack

"9. In the attack, battle flights will be employed in force to destroy the enemy's forward infantry lines and harass his barrage batteries. In the battle flights, the higher command possesses a powerful weapon which should be employed at the *decisive* point of the attack. They are not to be distributed singly over the whole front of attack, but should be concentrated at decisive points. Less important sectors must dispense with the support of battle flights.

"10. Accurate *knowledge of the ground* is the first condition for the successful action of the battle flights. Above all, the crews must be familiar with their own forward battle zone, so as to avoid the possibility of firing on their own troops. Consequently, an attack upon the enemy's front line should be made by battle flights which have been flying for a considerable time in that particular sector.

"11. The decision as to *the moment at which to engage* battle flights is of particular importance. Engaged too soon they draw the enemy's attention to the point of attack; if too late, they become a danger to their own advancing troops. The greatest effect is obtained if the battle flights cross the front line at the same moment that the infantry advances to the attack (see para. 22).

"Special battle flights should be detailed to attack the enemy's barrage batteries.

"12. These battle flights should be placed under the command of *divisions,* to ensure their being engaged at the right moment. The question of a further decentralization (infantry brigade, infantry regiment) depends on how far in advance the division can fix zero hour.

"13. The *Corps* will retain a certain number of battle flights at its disposal for employment during the later stages of the battle in breaking up a fresh resistance or warding off counter-attacks. In these attacks, also, they must be engaged at the decisive point.

"In order to expedite the issue of orders, it will often be inadvisable to place flights under divisions. In this case, the flight will receive its instructions directly from the Corps.

"14. Finally, the *Army* requires a certain number of battle flights for harassing traffic in the enemy's back areas. These should operate, subsequent to the attack, against important roads, especially in cuttings, which are used by reinforcements and transport. Columns on the march, horsed transport columns and Staff cars offer remunerative targets. Furthermore, attacks combined with those of bombing squadrons should also be carried out on the enemy's aerodromes, head-quarters, traffic centres, and railway stations.

"15. During the enemy's *retreats*, the targets for battle flights will be the main routes of retirement.

"Better results are obtained by repeatedly attacking a single main road than by carrying out isolated attacks against a number of roads. The object must be to render retreat along a particular road impossible by day.

"B. Defense

"16. Although it is possible by careful preparation to employ battle flights in close co-operation with the infantry assault during our own offensive operations, it is difficult in a defensive battle to decide upon the correct time and place for their engagement. For defence, plans must be carefully thought out beforehand and all preparations systematically made for the concentration of a large force of battle flights.

"17. If the enemy's preparations indicate that the infantry attack is imminent, the battle flights must be held in combat readiness. Should the assembly position of the enemy's infantry, either in trenches or in shell holes, be located, the determined and relentless employment of the battle flights which have been held in readiness will impede the 'drive' of the enemy's attack, delay the latter, or break it up completely.

"18. Should the advance of the enemy's infantry from their trenches come in the nature of a surprise, the infantry battle, which will sway to and fro, will offer practically no opportunity for the co-operation of battle flights. In this case they will be kept in readiness at convenient aerodromes until the local reserves are engaged in counter-attacks, or until an organized counter-attack is made.

"For use in such attacks, battle flights will be placed under the orders of either the divisional commander of the battle sector or the commander of the infantry carrying out the counter-attack.

"As regards communications between battle flights and infantry, *see* para.22.

"IV. Allotment of Duties and Transmission of Orders

"19. The commander of the battle flight or of the battle-flight group receives *detailed orders* from the head-quarters to which he is attached. These will state the following:

"Exact position of our own and the enemy's front lines.

"Objective and sector of the attack.

"Nature of the preparatory phase.

"Method of attack.

"Zero hour.

"Targets specially allotted to the battle flight.

"20. It is essential that all battle flights should be *constantly informed* as to the situation; to facilitate this, the aerodromes where the battle flights are held in readiness must be close to Divisional Head-quarters. Direct telephonic communication with the Divisional or Corps Head-quarters from which orders are issued is absolutely necessary. It is particularly important for battle flights operating against forward targets to be thoroughly familiar with our own and the enemy's forward infantry positions. It will be advisable for a wireless station at the aerodrome to take in messages from the contact-patrol machine.

"21. Every battle flight will be given *one target* for each flight, for example, the enemy's front line in a definite area or the enemy's barrage batteries. If the position of our own front line is not exactly known, as, for instance, during rearguard actions, the enemy's batteries and not his infantry will be given as targets.

"22. The *time* for crossing our own front line in the case of targets close at hand should, whenever possible, be given by the watch. Watches must accordingly be synchronized. During open warfare or in counter-attacks, if the zero hour for the infantry attack is not ordered by the watch, the timely engagement of the battle flights will be arranged for by signals. A machine will fly over the command post of the commander of the attacking troops (regimental or battalion commander) and fire the light signals laid down by Army Head-quarters in order to demand the time at which the assault is to commence.

"Should there be no intention to assault within the next hour, the commander of the troops will lay out the signal 'No' (*see* table of visual signals). The machine will then inform its flight by wireless or by dropping a message on the aerodrome.

"The battle-flight commander must thenceforth keep in close touch with the situation by repeatedly sending out a fresh machine.

"If the assault is to take place in an hour's time or earlier, the signal 'Yes' will be laid out. The battle flight will then start, on receipt of the previously arranged wireless call or light signal, but will on no account cross the line of our own kite balloons. Immediately before the assault, the commander of the troops will give the signal 'We are about to advance' (see table of signals). The communication machine will then fly towards its formation and transmit this by light signal.

"23. The hour at which the battle flight will attack is to be *made known to the troops in the orders for the attack.* The infantry must be instructed to fire from time to time the light signals laid down by Army Head-quarters for indicating the position of the front line to the contact-patrol machine.

"24. In order to avoid confusion, firing of *further light signals* by battle flights over the lines is not permissible.

"25. When several battle flights form a *group*, they should not be employed simultaneously in line of flights, but in waves one behind the other.

"Each flight will repeat its attack several times and then be followed by the succeeding flight.

"The attack will be timed and the targets selected in such a manner that the enemy is continuously threatened at the *decisive* point of the battlefield.

"26. The lower battle machines fly, the greater the moral effect. For this reason, descents to 30-50 metres are advocated. In addition, the material effect against the enemy's front line is also increased by flying low. It has been proved that losses from anti-aircraft fire are not increased by flying very low. For the engagement of larger targets (for instance, reserves and batteries) a height of 400-500 metres is more favorable.

"V. Training

"27. Battle flights must make use of every opportunity to carry out *training behind the front* for their difficult task. The most important features of this training should be attacks in close formation, manoeuvre in single combat, observation of the flight leader and rapid concentration for a new attack. Each individual man must be completely master of his weapon; the machine-gunners must also be familiar with the use of hand grenades and bombs.

"Practice over the enemy's lines, so far as the enemy's anti-aircraft defence permits, offers the best opportunities of training in picking up targets quickly.

"Example of Method of Establishing Communications between the Troops and the Battle Flight.

"Communication Machines.	*Troops.*	*Battle Flight.*
"Flies over the Battle H.Q. of the commander of the troops, firing the signals laid down by Army Headquarters.		Has machines in readiness on the aerodrome.
	"The attack will take place in half an hour.	
"Sends a wireless message to the flight to start.	Lay out the signal 'Yes".	Starts and remains behind its own kite balloons.
	"The attack has been postponed for two hours.	
"Fires the agreed signal. for the battle flight	Lay out signal 'No'.	Returns to its aerodrome.
	"The attack will take place in 15 minutes.	
"Once more instructs the flight. to start, by wireless	Lay out signal 'Yes'.	Starts and remains behind its own kite balloons.
	"The attack will take place immediately.	
"Again fires the prearranged signal for the battle flight.	Lay out signal 'We are about to advance'".	Advances to attack.

Notwithstanding this new role assigned to the *Schutzstaffeln*,. it should be quickly pointed out that this did not negate their role as escort aircraft. Since the normal complement of a *Schusta* was six aircraft, and as four aircraft were the ideal ground support attacking formation, this still left two aircraft, one usually in reserve and the other as a protective aircraft. These escort flights continued to the end of the war, despite the preponderance of the *Schusta/Schlasta* aircraft being employed in an infantry support capacity.

Halberstadt Cl.II 14207/17 of *Schusta 2* and individually marked '3,' photographed at Ecly airfield in January 1918. It is purported to be the aircraft of *Vzfw.* Wilhelm Krake, a gunner with the unit.

Schlachtstaffel 2 at Bergnicourt, probably taken on 18 March 1918, the date upon which Galle left the unit. Left to right: *Ltn.d.R.* Otto Gawron, *Oblt.* Ernst Galle the C.O., *Ltn.d.R.* Mathias Jorissen, and *Ltn.d.R.* Kessler. Photo credit: Marcus Pleyer.

Hannover Cl.II of *Schlasta 12* in March 1918. The white/black/white diagonal stripes on the fuselage are the unit marking.

A mixed bag of *Schusta 15* and *Fl.Abt. 207(A)* crew, the unit they were escorting in March 1918. Huffzky is on the far left with Ehmann standing next to him. Warda is ninth from the left.

Halberstadt Cl.II 6348/17 marked '4' of *Schlachtstaffel 24b*. On the right the gunner, *Vzfw.* Franz Xaver Brandl with his pilot, *Vzfw.* Albert Hermann. The photo was taken in the Spring of 1918. Photo credit: Walter Werner.

A Hannover Cl.II marked with '6' in a white square caught in flight. Note the gunner waving at the photographer.

A crashed Halberstadt Cl.II. The *Schlasta* is not known.

A Halberstadt Cl.II. Neither the pilot nor his unit are identified.

CHAPTER VII

OPERATION MICHAEL

Operation Michael – *Der Tag* – was brilliantly conceived and executed by *Generalquartiermeister der OHL General der Infanterie* Erich Ludendorff and *Chef des OHL General-Feldmarschall* Paul von Beneckendoff und von Hindenburg. The attack was to be conducted by the *18. Armee* (*General der Infanterie* Oskar von Hutier), the *2. Armee* (*General der Kavallerie* Georg von der Marwitz), and the *17. Armee* (*General der Infanterie* Otto von Below). The attacking front was 75 km wide, stretching from the Oise in the south to the Scarpe in the north. Along this front were 64 divisions of specially trained storm troops. These men had been rehearsed in the new art of attacking: avoid confronting any strong points, and instead flow around them, similar to dumping water into a child's sand box, where the water flows around the high points (i.e., those which were well defended) and instead encompasses and fills the low spots. The second and third attacking waves, accompainied by the *Schutzstaffeln,* would be relied upon to nullify the resisting strong points.

The key to success lay in the very capable hands of *Oberstleutnant* Georg Bruchmüller, hereafter known as "*Durchbruch* (breakthrough) Müller" to the German troops. He was in overall charge of the 6200 artillery pieces facing the English, including 950 field batteries, 701 medium batteries, and 55 heavy batteries. Bruchmüller's plan was quite the contrary to those attacks previously attempted by either side. Instead of first bombarding the barbed wire, then the first line of trenches, then the second, and so on, trying to stay just ahead of the attacking infantry, his plan was to order all his batteries to begin shelling the enemy artillery to prevent counter battery fire. The lighter guns would then move backward to the second line of trenches, then the first line, and finally the wire. Meanwhile the heavier batteries raised their sights and began shelling the rear areas, thus preventing reinforcements from reaching the point of attack.

The German creeping barrage began at 4:40 AM and the massive artillery barrage at 4:45. It could be heard all the way across the channel in England. The attacking troops fell upon the British 5th (General Sir Hubert Gough) and 3rd (General Sir Julian Byng) Armies at precisely 9:45. Ludendorff's main objective was designed as a one-two punch: one, divide these two Armies destroying the British 5th Army in the process; two, capture Amiens, then turn northeast and roll up Arras. He felt that this would be sufficient to separate the British from the French Army, drive the British back to the channel ports and send the French back to the defense of Paris.

The *Luftstreitkräfte* were very well represented in Operation Michael. The aviation units included 49 *Flieger Abteilungen* and *Artillery Flieger Abteilungen*, 42 *Jagdstaffeln*, 4 *Bombengeschwader,* and 35 of the by then existing 38 *Schutzstaffeln*, almost 50% of the entire German Air Force serving on the Western front. The *Schusta* were arrayed, from south to north, or left to right as viewed from the German lines, as members of *Schlachtgruppen (Schlagru)* as follows: the *18. Armee* had at its disposal *Schlagru 1 (Schusta 8, 31b, 36, 38s)* and *Schlagru 2 (Schusta 7, 18, 37)* both under the command of *Oblt.* Walter Lackner, and *Schlagru 3 (Schusta 6, 32, 34)* and *Schlagru 4 (Schusta 2, 5, 20, 33)* under the command of *Oblt.* Werner Lange.

The bulk of the *Luftstreitkräfte* strength was concentrated in the *2. Armee*, including the *Schusta* with *Schlagru A (Schusta 10, 17, 22b)* C.O. *Hptm.* Zimmermann; *Schlagru B (Schusta 4, 15, 26b, 28b)* led by *Ritt.d.R.* Herrmann; *Schlagru C* under *Hptm.* Heinecke (*Schusta 11 and 30b*); and *Schlagru D (Schusta 12 and 23b)* under the command of *Oblt.* Johannes Missfelder. Finally, the *17. Armee* on the right wing of the attack was supported by *Schlagru A (Schusta 13 and 27b)* commanded by *Oblt.* Müller; *Schlagru B (Schusta 14, 19, 24b, 25b, 29b)* led by *Hptm.* Wilhelm Aschenborn; and *Schlagru C*

(Schusta 3, 9, and 16) under the command of *Oblt.* Hermann Ramdohr. For further clarity refer to Table I where the disposition of the *Schusta* are illustrated from north to south, as if reading a map:

Table I
Disposition of the *Schlachtgruppen* Operation Michael
(North to South)

Armee	*Schlagru*	Composition	*Schlagru Kommandeur*
	C	3, 9, 16	*Oblt.* Hermann Ramdohr
17.	B	14, 19, 24b, 25b, 29b	*Hptm.* Wilhelm Aschenborn
	A	13, 27b	*Oblt.* Müller
	D	12, 23b	*Oblt.* Johannes Missfelder
2.	C	11, 30b	*Hptm.* Heinecke
	B	4, 15, 26b, 28b	*Ritt.d.R.* Herrmann
	A	10, 17, 22b	*Hptm.* Zimmermann
	4	2, 5, 20, 33	*Oblt.* Werner Lange
18.	3	6, 32, 34	*Oblt.* Werner Lange
	2	7, 18, 37	*Oblt.* Walter Lackner
	1	8, 31b, 36, 38s	*Oblt.* Walter Lackner

The weather on the 21st was both favorable and unfavorable to the attacking German troops. The Somme River valley in the middle of the attacking *2. Armee* was completely enveloped in fog, which coupled with the mist and low clouds had a great effect on the battle. The weather was favorable for the attacking German infantry in that they suddenly appeared out of the mist and fog and quickly overran the British defensive formations. It was unfavorable in that the low clouds, mist and fog prevented the German *Jagdstaffeln* from taking off. The weather on the flanks was apparently better, as *Jasta 35b*, based in the *17. Armee,* reported an air victory at 9.00 hours. By way of contrast, in the *2. Armee* the *Schusta* were not even able to take off until around 10.30 hours, when they could fly under the low clouds as the fog lifted slightly. Thus the *Schlachtgruppen* could attack the British front lines as well as range far beyond them to attack reinforcements, artillery batteries, and reserve troops. The *Jagdstaffeln*, at least in the *2. Armee*, finally left the ground at 12.30 hours, when *Jage Nr. I* reported the destruction of two balloons at 12.55 and 13.10 hours.

The *Schutzstaffeln* performed admirably during this operation. Machine gunning and bombing the frontline trenches, including using hand grenades, they then attacked the rear positions and succeeded in preventing reinforcements from moving forward. The combined strength of the *Schusta* raised such havoc in the British lines that their withdrawal was inevitable. Coupled with the strength of the attacking storm troops, the British were forced to retreat.

The German offensive gained over 1200 square miles. More than 90,000 British were captured and vast quantities of stores plus more than 1000 guns were taken by the Germans. The British suffered 164,000 casualties, the French about 70,000. Yet, on 28 March 1918, only a week later, the attack suddenly came to a halt at Albert. Why? Due to the British blockade.

Having captured many supply depots, the Germany infantry had suddenly fallen upon stores that the blockade had prevented them from having during three long years of war. The British tins of bully beef and jam were pretty mundane for the average British soldier, but a Godsend to the common German infantryman. There was bread, real bread, not ersatz bread comprised of 80% sawdust; real coffee, not a mix of coffee and 50%-60% sawdust; cheese, eggs, hams, chickens, all of which were delicacies they had not experienced since 1915. These in addition to the French wines, champagnes, brandies, and cognacs were sufficient to halt the attack while the Germans indulged themselves in a literal feast! *Ltn.d.R.* Rudolf Binding wrote that he paused the infantry attack he was leading in order to polish his boots with real shoe polish. All this 'indulgence' while the main objective of Amiens with its cathedral spires was in sight. Therefore the extent of the British blockade begun in 1915 had a very telling effect on the German advance in March, 1918.

Due to their success during Operation Michael, the *Schutzstaffeln* were renamed *Schlachtstaffeln* on 27 March 1918, reflecting their new role as an infantry support weapon. However there was little they could do to spur their comrades on the ground to continue the attack. Some well-trained shock troops struggled on until 6 April, but for all practical purposes the attack had ceased by March 28th. The Germans had penetrated forty miles deep into the Allied lines. The German front had been extended, perhaps too far to defend, and thousands of their best storm troops had been lost. Furthermore over 70 divisons had been depleted. Worst of all the great breakthrough had not been achieved. Known *Schusta/Schlasta* losses during this operation amounted to 21 men KIA/KIC, 20 WIA/IIC, and another 5 taken POW. These include two C.O.s KIA and one WIA, Amann, Deetjen, and Henke. Although the numbers may seem small in comparison to the overall scope of events, this was the equivalent of almost 4 complete *Schlachtstaffeln* lost or over 10% of the initial attacking force.

The loss of three commanding officiers is particularly significant. It should be strongly emphasized that the *Schusta/ Schlasta* C.O.s, despite commanding crews mainly consisting of enlisted men, did not sit back and merely 'fly a desk.' They led by example. When he received an order to attack or defend, the C.O. led his unit over the battlefield. This is evident, for instance, in the previous accounts by Kuppinger, Zorer, Miller, and von Krausser. That they shared the dangers of the crews under their command is revealed by the number of *Schlasta* C.O.s lost during the fierce battles of 1918.

CHAPTER VIII

THE SPRING OFFENSIVE 1918: SCHLACHTFLIEGER REMINISCENCES

The 'Great Battle in France' launched by the Germans in March 1918 produced many post-war articles by the surviving participants. Two of these concerning *Schusta* flyers are presented below. The first was written by *Oblt.* Oskar Bechtle, the commander of *Schusta 2*, and published in *In der Luft unbesiegt* compiled by Georg Paul Neumann. One should note how closely Bechtle's command and orders followed the guidelines suggested by *Idflieg* and presented in the preceeding chapter:

"Forming up for Deployment

"March 1918. At corps headquarters the *Staffel* leaders' conference was just ending. With all due gravity, in no way dismissing the difficulties which the decisive breakthrough on the Western Front would bring to all branches of the service, each one repeated once again the nature of his operation and its execution. Each conveyed a confident undertone, an absolute trust in the success of the liberating decisive action. I could be satisfied with the mission assigned to my *Schlachtstaffel*. After long years of wearisome defense we could – fully conscious of our superiority – rush upon the enemy with the storming infantry in a manner previously seen only in cavalry attacks.

"And I could rely on my *Staffel*. That much was certain! I had exercised my maneuverable black-tailed two-seater Halberstadt behind the front daily in rigid formation flying for good reason. Every pilot, every gunner, had to have the feeling: no one can touch me when I am with the *Staffel* and stick close to the leading aircraft! In addition, we had a good supply of aircraft and three extra airplanes well hidden from sight in two old barns. They too could be made ready for flight within a few hours, if necessary. A 'flying convoy', composed of three of the best trucks with repair equipment, fuel, ammunition, and foodstuffs, was to immediately set itself in motion in the case of a change of airfields. The crews had firmly impressed upon their memories, with the aid of maps and photos, the area over which whey would fly.

"If only things would soon get started! The eternal rain and fog got on the nerves of us flyers. Finally, on the afternoon of March 20th, an automobile came to the farm bringing us the order announcing that the attack was to begin on the 21st. Now the reserve machines as well could be assembled and feverish activity set in. An hour before dawn the crews and mechanics stood at their aircraft. In every Halberstadt were two or three 12 1/2 kilo bombs and in addition as many hand grenades and as much machine gun ammunition as would fit. The pilot did not always make a happy face when the gunner tried to smuggle on yet a few more kilos of grenades behind his back, because during take-off the 'crate' could hardly lift off from the ground.

"The day couldn't decide whether to show itself. The rain-laden clouds hung down nearly to the dripping wet tents in which the aircraft were kept. And yet we should have been at our assembly point at Grougis a long time ago. There we were to join two more *Staffeln* to form a *'Schlachtgeschwader'*, which was to be at the disposal of the *Armee Hutier* advancing from the area of St. Quentin. Only after 8 o'clock did it get lighter. One more time the 160 hp Mercedes engines of all six aircraft are listened to attentively. Cost what it may, we all wanted to be underway in order to arrive in time for the attack.

"One aircraft after another entered the veil of mist at barely 50 meters, circling around the field until the lead airplane – recognizable by the white ring wrapped around the fuselage – took its place in their midst and flew off toward the south. Closely behind one another, like Indians on the warpath, they proceeded at a very low height along the tree-lined highway, anxiously following every curve in the path. Whoever strays here into the fog will get so thoroughly lost in this 'pea soup' that he won't be able to avoid crashing. There's the crossroads already right next to the assembly field. Now let's just figure out the right approach. A large bonfire, which the occupants of the airfield presumably lit to reveal the direction of the wind, should apparently make the landing easier for us. Flying toward it, all six of us landed close by, but the ground was so soft that once we'd barely set down we were already stuck in the mud above our axles.

"Upon closer inspection we then discovered that we had landed next to the actual airfield, which was playfully hiding in the fog above us upon the high ground. We allowed ourselves to be deceived by the fire set by the personnel of an ambulance detachment. Well, we got out again with the aid of horses. The mechanics sent out in advance had observed our landing with skepticism and feared some bad crashes. However, we left it to the commander of our sister *Staffel* to accomplish this. They landed in the fog amidst the third *Staffel* already there and in the process put several airplanes out of commission. So for us *Schlachtflieger* the offensive did not exactly have a successful beginning. Because of the thick fog, first of all, we couldn't think about deploying our aircraft. We had to attack in either *Staffel* or *Geschwader* strength in order to increase our effectiveness through the moral effect which a multitude of low-flying, firing aircraft brings about. But this effect would have been thoroughly lost if we were to find our way to the front individually – if at all.

"During the Infantry Assault

"Ill-tempered, we lay about in our autos or airplanes. The thunder of the artillery hardly found its way through to us in the thick, foul weather. Finally, toward 3 o'clock in the afternoon, when the sun began to wage a more successful battle against the fog, the telephone called out: 'Support for the infantry during the assault on Holnon Wood!' I was familiar with that area from earlier. Many a heavy gun lay hidden there. How that revived us! Hardly ten minutes later we were in the air, anxious concerning the situation of things, as no news had gotten through to us about conditions on the front. Only the area of the assault was indicated and it was left to us to inform ourselves concerning its progress. Therefore I had especially impressed upon my crews not to fire a shot until I had fired my signal flare as a sign to begin the attack. Under all circumstances we were to avoid disappointing our infantry through a mis-directed attack. On the contrary, they had to be swept along with us.

"Having arrived above St. Quentin, which was under isolated fire – especially in the vicinity of the cathedral – we groped our way northward in a sharp right turn. Everywhere below us were columns moving westward. Here and there we heard and felt at our 200 meters height the short barks of the discharging guns and discovered all around groups of our own artillery firing. So the attack could not have extended all that far. Thus we must proceed with twice as much caution. We flew up and down over our old positions, from which the troops waved to us. Then from the second enemy line came light signals. A German battalion commander laid out his square cloth signal there. Now we'd got the picture. Here and there were small groups advancing in fits and starts. Now we could venture the attack. Back once more in a curve. On their own everyone swung into line over our artillery and – huzzah – at the enemy!

"A signal flare over the forwardmost line, permitted the machine guns to open fire, and off we went at a slight downward angle toward the enemy at a speed of 180 kilometers per hour. The pilots opened up with their fixed machine guns making an emphatic 'tack tack' and, commencing the assault, strewed regular and tracer ammunition through the whirl of the propeller blades toward enemy territory. Finally, we also saw them. More quickly than anticipated, we arrived above the preparations which the English were making, hidden behind slopes and in large shell-holes. Down with the hand grenades, whose little black clouds of smoke appeared everywhere in and around the opposing shell-holes. No one was moving anymore down below.

"After a turn to the right the flexible machine gun was taken up by the rear gunner. How nicely the line can be swept with it so that one sees the mud spraying! What a joy to tickle some Tommies and put them through a few exercises around the terrain! We saw hardly any opposing fire. Back to our infantry, and two or three times the drama repeated itself. And then finally everyone had three powerful bombs on board which, as a finale, were unloaded in the last attack on groups of batteries located close to roads further back of the lines. For a long time during the return flight we saw the bright red glow of the piled up stocks of artillery ammunition we hit.

"Behind the Enemy Front

"The first day with its minimal opposition had made us confident. So we welcomed a *Geschwader* attack on the little town of Ham and its surrounding roads the next day with twice the joy. The infantry attack was making quick progress between the Somme and the Crozat Canal. This was favorable to our mission, as we could therefore arrive quickly and unnoticed at the rear of the enemy positioned north of the Somme. We felt proud to set out with the twenty graceful Halberstadts and grumpy Hannovers packed full of bombs, crossing the Crozat Canal over deserted encampments and burning sheds in the brilliant sunshine. We were hardly bothered at all by flak, let alone enemy aircraft.

"We approached Ham from the southwest at barely 600 meters height. One *Staffel* occupied itself with the railway station, the other the western exits, while mine, as the last, performed a follow-up attack. Like wild wasps the airplanes ahead of us dove upon their targets after dropping their bombs in order to lend a little more assistance with their machine guns. A truck-mounted anti-aircraft gun made a shy attempt to disturb them in their work. But our machine guns soon caused the gunner to take cover – and then it was our turn with our bombs and grenades. After the preceding thorough work by our sister *Staffeln*, there wasn't much traffic to be seen anywhere. But some kilometers northeast of the town there was a terrific bustle and therefore rich targets for us *Schlachtflieger*. First some trucks. Some hand grenades were placed nicely in front of the radiator, which burst quite effectively on the paved roadway. Cautiously the truck drivers made their way into the ditches, as the road was blocked by the halted column. Then we went back once more, flying along the road to 'spit' downward in the customary fashion with the flexible machine gun. Not a soul dared to move while my valiant *Staffel* brothers were tending to the neighborhood in a similar manner.

"Then we went back to the infantry which was just about to cross the Somme in the north between Artemps and St. Simon in order to get to the rear of the enemy, who was still fighting tenaciously before St. Quentin. Our eyes, now much better trained in observing the ground battle, recognized every detail. From the south, we joined in the battle and roamed along the enemy line with our machine guns making our presence felt in the most effective way. The infantry pressed forward one dash after another, but the opponent was firmly planted and didn't want to yield. My pilot was enthusiastic. When he noticed a troop of resting Englishmen, he drew a bead on them with his fixed machine gun although he hadn't a single round in it. I was afraid that he wanted to strike them dead with the undercarriage. Then a splintering in the varnished wood of the fuselage showed us that our opponent was still quite capable of putting up a fight. That sobered us up again and advised caution.

"With the last drum I put on my machine gun I could still support our evening attack at Fluquières. The flight back along the road to St. Quentin was unforgettable! Everywhere as far as the eye could see there was a forward movement; everywhere there were advancing columns of every branch of the army. Leaning out far over the side of the fuselage, we returned the waves of the troops. Just as we'd always dreamed, we could now work directly with the infantry, the branch of the service which has the greatest burden, and earn their visible gratitude. That satisfied us more than any medals.

"In the Advance

"The Roman Road runs as straight as an arrow from Vermand to Amiens. Near Brie it crosses the Somme not far from Péronne. Our infantry wanted to get to the other side before the evening and shortly beforehand we were supposed to clean up the area somewhat on the other side. So we contentedly flew along the Roman Road at 400 meters height in the evening sunlight. Far and wide there was nothing special to be seen other than brightly glowing fires and thick dirty clouds of smoke. For the most part the English seemed to have crossed over the marshy Somme, which glittered and gleamed before us.

"Then suddenly my neighboring aircraft whipped its tail three times. I glanced over – and look! – below us to the right were three peace-loving bearers of the cockade! They were flying obviously toward Germany – big, twin-engined Caudrons or something like that, probably dug up in haste out of necessity – apparently strange to the area and unsuspecting. Right away we turned around and headed after the three cumbersome Frenchmen, who were suddenly nabbed from above and below. Immediately two of them put their tails up out of fear and made an emergency landing. A cloud of dust revealed that they wound up in a pile of matchwood. The third attempted to sneak away, but two of us had gotten above and behind him and, with the flexible machine gun sticking out above the upper wing, calmly shot up his motor amongst other things so that he, trailing a steep plume of smoke, quickly set down in the marshes on the banks of the Somme.

"There were still three tanks in Brie. A bomb was dropped on the road next to them for safety's sake, but they were not brought out of their apparent eternal slumber. While flying over the Somme, strong artillery fire compelled us to carry out a more cautious reconnaissance. Our opponent was still sitting well-hidden on the opposing heights, including many infantry, as the nasty gunfire showed, which as a *Schlachtflieger* we generally noticed only when the burst splinters in the middle of the airplane. But we weren't so easily diverted from our mission. North of Villers Carbonnel, we got hold of a column and set it in motion. Further to the south we disrupted firing artillery positioned in the open. The whole bank of the river became lively, especially because our own artillery lovingly embraced this area.

"Strangely enough, our opponent once more was withdrawing here. With empty machine gun ammunition drums and empty bomb holders, we headed back to the old airfield which already was located all too far to the rear. In the meantime, I had planned to pay a visit to the former English airfield at Guizancourt, which was allotted to us for the advance. One of our own batteries still stood firing on its western edge. But since the landing cross left behind by the English looked especially enticing, I made an intermediate landing and while I was at it, immediately gave the artillery commander a report concerning the situation on the banks of the Somme.

"The first thing in the morning on the following day the whole crew landed happily and smoothly at the new airfield. Of course, we were especially interested in how it was equipped. The hangars were burned. Under the broken wooden frames, some charred Bristol Fighters were still standing. We were disappointed by the uninhabitable, wind-blown corrugated tin barracks, but all the more pleasantly moved by the supplies of fuel and oil we encountered. Soon our 'flying convoy' also arrived with ammunition and tents. So close behind the front, we were twice as ready for battle and were able to effectively spoil the enemy's withdrawal in the shelterless waste of the Somme region in often repeated attacks. We were now assigned to a shock division with which we could cooperate superbly in close contact and with whom we were even in wireless communication.

"Enemy pilots were now showing up again individually. Then upon being contacted through wireless by the division, three Halberstadts always took off. They were especially suited for this purpose because of their maneuverability and heavy machine gun armament. But after his heavy losses amongst flying personnel, our opponent had become very hesitant in the air.

"One especially nice day for us here was the capture of Rozières, where we were able to appear upon call at the most critical moment and set upon the enemy infantry, which had taken shelter in the houses and afterwards wanted to steal away unseen behind the village. We were also able to report this withdrawal in a timely fashion by dropping a message to our artillery. To the south of Caix a bomb struck limbering English artillery. The day after we were able personally to observe the frightful effect upon the target.

"Defensive Battles

"Again a change of airfields while advancing! It was a rather small field of stubble, the lodgings of a former prison where a few days previously our German comrades had been forced by the French to fill in the old trenches from the Somme battles. The advance had come to a standstill. Nearly within our grasp was Amiens, to a good extent ruined, toward which two white roads strove from St. Quentin and Roye. Behind it lay the sea, at a distance only dimly perceived and yet was all the more yearned for. The infantry was fighting a difficult battle along and on the other side of the Avre. We still had two *Staffeln* and had set up an advanced landing ground as far forward as possible. We assembled there every day whether the sun was shining or, as was usually the case, it was pouring rain. The defenses from the ground and in the air had become substantially stronger.

"Daily on a three division front we had to engage in stubborn individual defensive combats or accompany reconnaissance aircraft as protection on flights lasting for hours. Again and again, attack preparations were our main target, for which hand grenades proved themselves to be an especially suitable weapon. We now also recognized the presence of the French in their preparations by their blue uniforms.

"There was in addition another interesting field of activity. On the western slopes of the Avre Valley our infantry was sticking firm. Close at their backs the swampy little river lay under constant artillery fire, which by day cut off any sort of connection to the rear. Then flyers provided at times the only means of contact. We always brought along cans of rations in order to drop them to the troops. And reports which flew down from the airplanes in sandbags with black-white-and-red streamers brought the troops and leaders clarification and much relief from anxiety. Above all, the frontline troops saw that they hadn't been forgotten – a psychological support which shouldn't be underestimated!

"During the constant misty weather we had to stay at very low altitudes, usually under 200 meters, so that we were not spared severe losses. For example, the leader of our sister *Staffel* took off for a strafing mission with the two aircraft which remained left to him and soon thereafter came back alone. The two others collided during an air combat with enemy Spads and crashed. So of the entire *Staffel* there remained tragically only the lead aircraft. A quarter of an hour later the lone *Staffel* commander joined us and flew during the most difficult attacks on the Forest of Castel. This was the fulfillment of duty to the last and one can hardly imagine a more difficult test of nerves!

"But our own *Staffel* wasn't spared losses. Several kilometers on the other side of the lines, in Allie-sur-Noye, rail traffic had been reported. We were supposed to disrupt it. We saw the futility of the undertaking, as our four remaining aircraft, which were not equipped to carry heavy bombs, were not capable of causing any significant disruption of the rail traffic. In addition, it was in the broad daylight of the afternoon, when defensive attacks by the enemy could ensue with the sun at their backs. But thoughts of the infantry, who must be encouraged to see low-flying aircraft heading far over to the enemy, provided a counterweight to our reservations. With a north wind blowing, we approached the railway. Of course there was no train to be seen far and wide. So our bombs were dropped in the little town. Then wild anti-aircraft and machine gun fire opened up along the entire route home. While flying over the lines I saw one of my Halberstadts speed steeply toward the earth. Whether it was on our side or the other side of the lines could no longer be determined.

"We landed badly shot-up and not exactly in a happy mood. This was only improved on the next morning when the missing and lightly wounded pilot reported himself. Shot down by the enemy infantry, he had just made it back to our lines. He had been able to pull his badly wounded gunner out of the burning airplane and bring him back during the night with the aid of the infantry.

"My faithful pilot caught it soon thereafter. He was an elementary school teacher from Saxony, always eager to attack, who smuggled his own personal bomb on his seat each flight and even when he'd fired off all his ammunition was not satisfied. We were once again over our favorite little woods near Grivesnes, from which almost daily attacks by the French broke out, at barely 100 meters height. I had just dropped my last hand grenade when there was a cracking and splintering all around such as I'd never experienced before. The aircraft reared up and my pilot went with me off and away toward France. Only after I'd shaken him thoroughly several times did he wake up and I happily waved him back toward the front. Upon my inquiry as to whether he'd been wounded, he held up his bloody right hand and yelled into my ear, 'I think so!'

"During the return flight he insisted that I drop a report and only after this had taken place did he fly the entire stretch back to our home field, refusing to land at the advanced field. Of course, it was not exactly a text-book landing. Hardly had the machine come to a standstill when my hearty old L [*Vzfw.* Landmann] jumped out and wanted to proudly count the hits in the crate. But then everything spun around him. During the examination it was determined that he'd suffered a gunshot wound which had passed entirely from his left hip to his right shoulder. With this severe wound he had still summoned the energy for the long return flight!

"Not long afterwards, during a defensive flight which we had to undertake in pairs in the most severe rainy weather at less than 100 meters height, a machine gun round from the ground also put a temporary end to my frontline service. But the *Staffel* recovered with new deeds in the great successful attacks between the Aisne and the Marne. After the defensive battles on the Avre that was the best tonic, as offensive battles provide the *Schlachtflieger* above all with the most successful and therefore the most satisfactory employment. In that respect he is closely related to the cavalryman of earlier days."

While *Schusta 2* was busy attacking Ham and enemy infantry in the vicinity of St. Quentin on the *18. Armee* front, in the *2. Armee* sector the crews of *Schusta 30b* were having an equally busy time. The Bavarian *Staffel* lost one of its members, pilot *Uffz.* Franz Xaver Mall, who was wounded and taken prisoner. His gunner, *Feldwebel* Franz Mülberger, managed to escape capture and "tell the tale" of his close call. His account was written by an unknown author and published in "*Flieger an allen Fronten*" compiled by Friedrich Schilling. It should be noted that it contains a certain element of propaganda and is most likely in error because it refers to American troops. No Americans were deployed against the German offensive in March 1918. These were no doubt British troops:

> "The deployment of *Schlachtstaffeln* – which with machine guns, bombs, and grenades brought relief and aid to our own troops, but confusion and losses to our enemy – were part of our daily bread in the great spring offensive of 1918 in France. On March 22, 1918 the engines of *Schlachtstaffel 30b* thundered away at barely thirty or forty meters above the torn-up battlefield. In close formation they rained machine gun fire and grenades upon the rows of enemy defenders.
>
> "At this low altitude every man on the ground, every steel helmet, and the colors of the uniforms denoting friend or foe could be clearly distinguished from our planes. The

men from our own defensive positions waved joyfully toward their helpers in the air. Those on the other side no doubt cursed up a storm because their own flyers weren't on hand right at this moment. Even in the best of circumstances, the influence on the morale of the ground troops brought by low-level attack aircraft was always greater than the material effect of their armament. The machine gun fire from the ground rattled against the armored crates like peas against the side of a tin bathtub. It didn't, however, cause any damage, which increased the enemy infantry's feeling of powerlessness against the *Schlachtflieger.*

"The *Staffel* roared around in wonderful closed formation, the lead aircraft up front recognizable by his streamer. Then suddenly the machine on the left flank of the closed attack formation peeled off. Some gunners of the neighboring aircraft continued to gaze after it. The *Staffel* had already roared onward. The battle completely absorbed the attention of the airplane crews. Losses in the air are just as inevitable as they are on the ground.

"The aircraft falling out of formation had been hit in the engine by artillery fire. The engine went 'blubb, blubb' and stood still, as though it had been smashed with an axe. At the same time flames shot out of the carburetor. The pilot, *Unteroffizier* Mall, tried to turn off the ignition. Too late! The crate was already on fire! Just barely flattening out in time, he was still able to put the burning plane down on a meadow off to one side, not far from the edge of a village. By then the machine was completely ablaze. At the last moment the pilot and gunner jumped out and escaped burning to death. Mall yelled to his gunner, *Feldwebel* Mülberger, that he was wounded.

"*Piu! Piu! P-i-u-u!!* The rifle-fire from the enemy infantry whistled right past their heads. They threw themselves down and searched for cover. Mülberger's leg was grazed twice. A close call! But the wounds didn't interfere with his complete freedom of movement. They made some more dashes and hit the deck. Again they got up and made a run for it, bullets whizzing past their ears. But they did reach cover once more. They headed for the village. There they expected to find shelter and a hiding-place amongst the houses. They reached the first shot-up house. A little bit behind it was a tiny hut in reasonable shape, a former English mess. Mülberger hid the badly bleeding Mall, weary after running, in a narrow room. He then searched for a second hiding-place for himself.

"Then the American riflemen came after him. So he was off running like mad in a zig-zag amongst ruins, around them, over them, and through a maze of huts. So much crisscrossing! The Americans were always behind him. Sometimes they lost sight of him, then they tracked him down again and the hunt continued. Now he'd shaken them off again. He stopped briefly to catch his breath. He didn't have much time. He heard them again to the rear, calling out and cursing. Quick as lightning he threw himself down flat behind a heap of loose rubble and debris. With both of his hands he scraped together some loose debris and covered his entire body with it. He lay undisturbed for about two hours.

"What now? They were searching the vicinity for him with a dog, first nearer, then farther off. He didn't come out in any event for fear of being discovered. It was a good thing that the mongrel either had a bad nose or a chronic cold. Anyway, they didn't find him. The concern for his wounded pilot finally drove Mülberger out of his nice hiding place. He began searching for Mall. But, oh hell! The band of soldiers ferreted him out and for a little while chased after him and somehow drove him into a cul-de-sac with no way out. And now...? Hands up! It was all over. He'd been caught.

"An officer and a sergeant interrogated him and threatened him when he refused to answer. So he told them a fairy tale. A guard was supposed to transport him to the rear. Off to prison! Behind barbed wire! For Mülberger that was absolutely unthinkable. In the village an unarmed infantryman joined both of them. 'You lout! In an altercation with this guard here you would just needlessly get in the way,' the German grumbled inaudibly between his teeth. The three of them left the village, the two Americans nonchalantly plodding along, the German closely scrutinizing his surroundings and waiting for a favorable moment to run off. They walked across tortuous terrain with many shell craters between which there were remnants of bushes.

"Mülberger, a strapping, muscular fellow, was just waiting to make a surprise attack. He casually cast a sidelong glance through narrowed eyes at his escorts. 'Confound it! I'll deal with you two slouches!' Then the unarmed escort stumbled for a second. Get him! A powerful shove from Mülberger sent him head over heels into a deep shell crater. At the same instant a large fist landed between the eyes of the armed guard so that a rainbow of green, red, and violet lights danced before his pupils. Before he could view the world in natural colors again, unshoulder his rifle, and fire it, the prisoner had already disappeared into the landscape. A couple of futile shots rang out after him.

"Like a weasel, he snuck toward the shot-up village of Bernes, remaining watchful as a head stag, and when everything appeared safe to him he crawled into a deserted hut, the roof of which had been torn up by shellfire. He then pulled a couple of ragged old sacks over himself and lay as quiet as a mouse. Then the sun set over this long day. Up to now no one had come looking for him. He listened intently, awaited complete darkness, and gradually began thinking about the march home. During the night he crept forward up to a short distance from the enemy lines. Heavy fire from both sides across the entire landscape restrained him from making an attempt at a breakthrough.

"The heavy German barrage fire indicated to him preparations for a new attack. So he crawled back into his hiding place and waited. To his joy, the German attack soon gained ground. He saw fleeing Americans. Again he waited. And finally he saw the first German shock troops. He had been liberated!

"Mülberger reported to the nearest battalion adjutant, requested some men to search for Mall, and then set out to help his lost comrade. In vain they searched everywhere in and around the village. Mall remained missing. He was probably found by the enemy and dragged off as a prisoner. After forty-eight hours the plucky gunner Mülberger landed alone at the *Staffel.*"

Mülberger fared better than his pilot on this day, escaping capture with only a slight wound. However, in the end Mall was the more fortunate of the two. About two months later, on May 21, 1918, Mülberger was killed in a crash during a practice flight.

Opposite
Top: Hannover Cl.II (Rol.) 669/18. Note that the "stripes" on the fuselage are merely the shadows of the wing struts. The Roland built Hannover Cl.II aircraft were only used at the *FEA* and the *Fliegerschulen*.

Bottom: Hannover Cl.V, a superb aircraft, it would have replaced the Hannover Cl.III and Cl.IIIa machines in 1919.

Right: Crashed Halberstadt Cl.II from an unknown unit. Credit: Reinhard Kastner.

Below: Hannover Cl.II 9288/17. The unit is not identified.

CHAPTER IX

OPERATION GEORGETTE

Operation Georgette, considerably scaled down by Ludendorff from the original Operation St. George, was launched on 9 April 1918. Known to the Germans as the Battle of the Lys and to the Allies as the Battle of Armentières, it was primarily commenced by the *6. Armee* (*General der Infanterie* Ferdinand von Quast) and supported on the right wing by the *4. Armee* (*General der Infanterie* Friedrich Sixt von Arnim). *Oberstleutnant* Georg Bruchmüller again brought his artillery to bear on the enemy positions, employing the same tactics and enjoying the same success as he had in Operation Michael.

The *6. Armee* was supported by (from left to right) *Schlachtgruppe A (Schlasta 3* and *19*) at Faumont led by *Hptm.* Wilhelm Aschenborn, *Schlagru B (Schlasta 16* and *29b*) at Tourmignies commanded by *Ritt.* Jürgen *Frhr.* von Zobel, *Schlagru C (Schlasta 9* and *21*) led by *Oblt.* Friedrich-Carl Hanesse and based at Houplin, and *Schlagru D (Schlasta 24b* and *25b*) commanded by *Oblt.* Hugo Miller and stationed at Ronchin. This distribution is illustrated in Table II. The *Schlasta* used the same tactics which had proven so successful during The Great Battle of France, namely, attacking enemy strong points with machine guns, grenades, and bombs. They were also to harass the rear enemy positions, prevent reinforcements from coming up, clear roads of traffic, and generally do everything possible to support the infantry.

Table II
Disposition of the *Schlachtgruppen* Operation Georgette
(North to South)

Armee	*Schlagru*	Composition	*Schlagru Kommandeur*
	D	24b, 25b	*Oblt.* Hugo Miller
6.	C	9, 21	*Oblt.* Friedrich-Carl Hanesse
	B	16, 29b	*Ritt.* Jürgen von Zobel
	A	3, 19	*Hptm.* Wilhelm Aschenborn

As with Operation Michael, Ludendorff planned on a one-two punch. The 'left' hook was designed to capture Armentières and the strategically high point of Mont des Cats. The 'right' jab was to launch the *4. Armee* against the French army and capture the 159 meter high Mt. Kemmel. The capture of these two heights would allow the Germans to shell the channel ports of Dunkirk and Calais and possibly force the British to entirely evacuate France.

Bruchmüller's artillery barrage on the *6. Armee* front began at 4:15 on the morning of April 9th, between Armentières and the La Bassée Canal. At 7:00 the bombardment shifted to the trenches and strong points. Besides high explosive shells, the Germans also employed mustard and phosgene gas shells. Nine German divisions attacked at 8:45, again through a thick mist, falling mainly on the Portuguese 2nd Division, which bore the full brunt of the attack. The Portuguese could do little 'but take off their shoes and run,' according to General Sir

Douglas Haig. During the next few days, the Germans were able to capture Armentières and the British abandoned Passchendaele, but they were unable to take the Mont des Cats.

The *4. Armee* attack on Mount Kemmel began on 25 April 1918 and was successfully completed by the 29th. For this assault the *Schlasta* had been redeployed as follows: *Schlagru A (Schlasta 1, 14, 21,* and *28b, Oblt.* Emil Ziegler gen Stege) at Heule, *Schlagru B (Schlasta 10, 23b, 26b,* and *30b, Oblt.d.R.* August Ertl) at Bisseghem, *Schlagru C (Schlasta 3, 13, 19,* and *29b, Hptm.* Wilhelm Aschenborn) at Ingelmunster, and *Schlagru D (Schlasta 9, 12, 16, 24b,* and *25b, Oblt.* Johannes Missfelder) at Linselles. Table III presents these from north to south, again as if reading a map.

The French holding Mt. Kemmel experienced the Bruchmüller 'artillery train' for the first time – a rather rude awakening. The attack extended from Bailleul to the coast and therefore also fell upon the Belgian 2nd Army. The *Schlasta* again lived up to their new designation and were instrumental in the capture of Mt. Kemmel. However, known *Schlasta* losses during all of Operation Georgette amounted to 8 killed, 13 wounded or injured, and 6 taken prisoner. These included one C.O. KIA (Ramdohr) and two WIA (Baumann and Müller). Again, these 27 casualties were the equivalent of over two complete *Schlasta*, losses which the Germans were finding increasingly difficult to replace.

Table III
Disposition of the *Schlachtgruppen* Battle of Mount Kemmel
(North to South)

Armee	*Schlagru*	Composition	*Schlagru Kommandeur*
	C	3, 13, 19, 29b	*Hptm.* Wilhelm Aschenborn
4.	A	1, 14, 21, 28b	*Oblt.* Emil Ziegler gen Stege
	B	10, 23b, 26b, 30b	*Oblt.d.R.* August Ertl
	D	9, 12, 16, 24b, 25b	*Oblt.* Johannes Missfelder

Surviving documents housed at the Military Archive in Munich detail orders issued by *Armee Oberkommando (AOK) 4* with respect to the deployment of the *Schlachtstaffeln* in the attack on Mount Kemmel. These consist of a summaary report dated June 10, 1918 with attachments written prior to the launching of the attack (April 21 and 24) and during the course of the battle (April 28). They well illustrate the methodical approach in the order and timing of ground attacks and the specification of when leaders of *Schlasta* formations were to use their own discretion in conducting 'free operations' *(Freie Schlacht).* Wireless telegraphy became an important means of maintaining communication as telephone lines were severed by artillery fire. For this reason, wireless codes such as those found in Attachment 4 were issued.

German military leaders paid close attention to the effectiveness of these new tactics, especially with respect to their effect on the morale of the enemy groundtroops. This is shown in an additional appended document (Attachment 7) with a summary of prisoners' statements as well as *General* Ludendorff's concluding comments. Note that even in these "official" German documents the term *Schlachtgeschwader* is used repeatedly when, in fact, the correct term is *Schlachtgruppe:*

Kommandeur der Flieger A.O.K. 4
Army Headquarters, 10 June 1918
Special Aviation Report No. 18

Activity of Aerial Units During the Attacks of the *4. Armee* in April 1918

Preparation for the Taking of the Kemmel Heights. 18.-24.4.18

Air superiority remained in our hands thanks to the fully satisfactory equipment of the *4. Armee* with aerial forces for the Kemmel attack. On 22.4 a further nine *Schlachtstaffeln* and six *Jagdstaffeln* were supplied to the *Armee*. By way of army orders their deployment was fundamentally regulated.

The Kemmel Battle 25.4 – 29.4.1918
With the storming infantry the four *Schlachtgeschwader* of the *Armee* carried out a united attack against the village of Kemmel, Kemmel Hill, and Dranoetre. The yielding enemy infantry was attacked from the rear with the armament aboard the aircraft. According to balloon and troop reports, enemy batteries which were attacked ceased fire. Over 60,000 machine gun rounds were fired, 700

mortar grenades and numerous bombs were dropped. With the further progress of the attack, considering the misty weather conditions which hampered unified deployment, the *Schlachtstaffeln* were granted full freedom of operation.

In individual attacks up to points deep within the enemy rear areas, villages and roads filled with columns of enemy troops were engaged in battle. The enemy ground defenses, apparently scattered by the masses of aircraft deployed, were surprisingly minimal so that various *Schlachtstaffel* commanders characterized the attack on 25.4 as the easiest since the beginning of the German spring offensive. Just how insignificant the enemy resistance was is best shown by the fact that a *Schlachtstaffel* advanced up to the region of Steenvorde, over 10 km. behind the enemy frontlines, attacked English columns there, and returned without losses.

The attack was to be continued on 26.4 to Vlamertingen and Reninghelst, but it did not develop because of strong counterattacks which the enemy carried out on both sides of the road from De Kleit to Kemmel with fresh troops. In spite of low clouds individual *Infanterieflieger* succeeded in establishing contact with the forward line. Individual ground attack aircraft pressed forward up to Poperinghe and Elverdinghe at a height of 80-200 meters and attacked lively traffic composed of marching columns on the roads behind the enemy front. One aircraft did not return. Enemy flyers did not show themselves.

On 27.4 heavy ground mist prevented any sort of aerial activity until late afternoon. Only toward the evening did six ground attack aircraft engage in the embittered struggles around Vormezeele. In spite of heavy flak and machine gun defenses, others attacked enemy railway stations, camps, and marching columns with 10,000 rounds of machine gun fire and 200 bombs.

The continuation of the attack in the Kemmel area was pushed back to 29.4. In contrast to the attacks on 25.4, our ground attack aircraft had to suffer under very heavy anti-aircraft fire. Of the 48 aircraft of the *Schlachtgeschwader* assigned to the X. R.K. alone, 17 had been rendered more or less unserviceable by midday. In spite of this all of the *Schlachtgeschwader* made multiple concentrated assaults on the trenches occupied by the enemy, nests of batteries around Dickebusch, and traffic in the area of Dickebusch – Reninghelst, with a total of 66,000 rounds of machine gun fire, 35 mortar grenades, 500 kg. of bombs, and hand grenades.

(signed) Wilberg
[*Hptm.* Hellmuth Wilberg]

Attachment 3)
Armee Oberkommando 4 Armee H.Q. 21.4.18
Re: Georgette

Army Orders
for the Deployment of Aerial Forces
for the Attack of the XVIII. and X. R.K.
Deployment of *Schlachtflieger*

7. For *Schlachtflieger* units in the first assault, the following targets will be especially suitable for attack:

a) Enemy batteries still firing.
b) Sweeping with fire the slopes which flank the advance of our infantry, upon which one can assume with certainty the presence of numerous machine gun nests.
c) Sweeping with fire folds in the terrain located to the rear which are suitable for the assembly of reserves which cannot be effectively engaged by our own artillery.

The first continuous attack formation of *Schlachtflieger* may fly over the forward line only by 7:05 a.m. and only by 6:50 a.m. on the left wing of the XVIII. R.K. during the attack, which will commence at 6:45 a.m. Otherwise the instructions in army order Ia/b Kofl. 307/April for deployment are applicable.

8. In the night before the attack, columns of troops heading toward the front are to be illuminated with flares and scattered with machine gun fire at the same time gas shells are fired.

9. *Schlachtstaffel 24b* (G.R.K.) will be placed at the disposal of the XVIII. R.K. for the day of the attack. On the day of the attack it is to stand ready for take off beginning at 6:45 a.m. on the airfield at Heule and in the evening will return to its home airfield.

(signed) Wilberg
[*Hptm.* Hellmuth Wilberg]

Attachment 4)
Gruppenführer der Flieger Nr. 3 Korps H.Q., 24.4.1918
Strictly Confidential!

Operational Order No. 4 for the Attack of the XVIII. R.K. (Instructions for the Deployment of the *Schlachtgeschwader*)

1. Unified Deployment During the 1st Attack.
Both *Geschwader – Schlachtgeschwader A (Oblt.* Ziegler gen. Stege) with *Staffeln 1, 14, 21,* and *28b*, and *Schlachtgeschwader C (Hauptmann* Aschenborn) with *Staffeln 3, 13, 19,* and *29b* – will be deployed simultaneously at two focal points of the battle with the *49. Reserve Division* upon obtaining a closer agreement with this unit. Orders concerning the targets will follow via telephone.

Deployment of the individual *Geschwader* is to proceed in two waves, which are to follow one another in intervals of 2-3 minutes. The strength of the two waves and formations is to be left to the *Geschwader* commanders. The assembly of the *Geschwader* is to take place far enough behind the lines that it is not noticed by the enemy. According to further directions by the *Geschwader* commander, *Geschwader C* is to assemble and fly northward along the line Meenen-Waasten-Meesen [Menen-Warneton-Messines] and *Schlachtgeschwader A* south of this line. The timing of the approach flight is to be calculated in such a way that the forward line is flown over only 5 minutes after the infantry begins its advance in order to prevent under all circumstances alerting the enemy prematurely. In my opinion, where no special circumstances exist, both waves are to be of equal strength, each accordingly about two *Schlachtstaffeln* strong.

The first wave is to attack the rear trenches and shellholes up to the infantry positions within the line of barrage fire and the expected machine gun nests, namely on the flanking slopes, from a very low altitude. They will circle to the right above the target and turn to the right to assemble and approach again.

The second waves will fly over the first waves engaged in battle and – likewise from a very low altitude – attack with bombs and machine guns the battery nests lying to the rear, batteries seen to be firing, and reserves being sent forward. After exhausting their ammunition, both waves are to return to their fields, prepare once again for take off, and rest.

2. Deployment at the *Staffel* and Perhaps Individual Level During the Further Course of the Battle
As soon as the battle is in flux, the *Geschwader* will be granted general freedom of operation (*"Freie Schlacht").* However, on each day of battle a reserve of 2 *Staffeln* will be placed at my disposal. They will be made available on the first day of attack (25.4) by *Schlachtgeschwader C* and on the second day of attack by *Schlachtgeschwader A*. Further orders will follow on a case to case basis. In the event of accruing losses, the aircraft are to be assembled into new *Staffeln.*

The point at which free operation is granted will be communicated to the *Geschwader* via telegraph or telephone. From this point on, one *Schlachtstaffel* is to take off every two hours for free operation, to wit in the following sequence, each providing one *Staffel*:

Schlachtgeschwader A
" *A*
" *C*
" *A*
" *A*
" *C.*

On the next day this will occur in the reverse order *(C,C,A,C,C,A)*. The establishment of targets will follow according to free selection insofar as no special movements of enemy troops or combat areas are indicated.

For reports via wireless the following signals apply:

Wavelength = 250.
a b f = Call signal.
d d = End signal.
a b e = *Schlachtgeschwader A* is herewith to receive orders for deployment.
b b e = *Schlachtgeschwader B* is herewith to receive orders for deployment.
c b e = *Schlachtgeschwader C* is herewith to receive orders for deployment.
z w ü = Targets are left to the *Staffeln.*
g e s = Uniform deployment of *Geschwader.*
e s t = Individual deployment of the *Staffeln* ("free operation").
s r a = Deployment will ensue in combat area a.
s r b = Deployment will ensue in combat area b.
s r c = Deployment will ensue in combat area c.
b o w = Deployment for dropping bombs will ensue for (location or target).
- - - = Time of deployment (according to copy book).
- - - = Area of deployment (according to copy book)
- - - = Target for deployment (according to copy book).
(The division into "combat areas" will be conveyed via telephone or will be regulated in advance via daily operational orders.)

3. Deployment as Bombing Formations in the Closer Combat Sector of the *Korps*
The *Geschwader* must be prepared to be deployed in bombing attacks from a medium altitude against closer lying traffic junctions, command posts, unloading points, and railway stations. Notification will be via W.T.

(signed) Baer
[*Hptm.* Gerhard Baer]

Attachment 6)
General Command *X. Reserve Korps Korps H.Q.* 28.4.1918
Korps Orders
for the Deployment of Aircraft

2. Deployment of *Schlachtflieger*
On 29.4 at 6:15 a.m. are to stand ready for take off: *Schlachtgeschwader B* at Bisseghem airfield. *Schlachtgeschwader D* at Linselles airfield.

The *Schlachtgeschwader* are to attack individually in two waves in two engagements beside one another; each rendezvous one *Schlachtstaffel. Schlachtgeschwader B* is to fly over the forward line at 6:45 a.m. Accordingly the take off is to be regulated precisely by the *Geschwader* commander. *Schlachtgeschwader D* is to attack 1/2 hour later at 7:15 a.m.

Take off and Approach
The first attack must under all circumstances take place in uniform fashion. The approach for attack against the contour line De Kleit – Scherpenberg – Roter-Berg is to ensue from the south of Ploegsteert Wood. Take off only in a westerly direction. After returning the *Schlachtflieger* are to immediately submit a report to *Grufl 7 [Hptm.* Bruno Zühlke] about their flight and the situation encountered.

Targets for Attack
The forward enemy lines are not to be fired upon in order not to endanger our own storming infantry. The forward assembling aircraft are to attack the enemy lines and the heights between De Kleit and Roter-Berg, similarly enemy batteries still firing, reserves, and camps. The *Schlachtgeschwader* approaching at 7:30 is to launch a uniform attack against enemy artillery. Further targets for this *Geschwader* are the reserves marching toward the battlefield. Later deployment of the *Geschwader* is to follow according to special orders depending upon the situation. After returning from each flight the *Geschwader* is to immediately be readied again for take off.

Attachment 7)
Inspectorate of Prison Camps Muenster, 31.5.1918
in the Area of the *VII. Armee*
Korps Abt.1b.
No. 3628 N.D. Confidential.

Re: Effect of German *Schlachtflieger*
According to the statements of French prisoners captured at the end of April at Kemmel, the manner of attack of our *Schlachtflieger* around Mount Kemmel was seriously detrimental to the resistance of the enemy troops. The prisoners (especially those of the 22nd and 30th Infantry Regiments) relate that the second line and approaching roads were greatly disturbed for days by a large number of low-flying aircraft. Apart from the effect of bombing on morale, the supply of provisions was severely endangered so that in the end the columns could no longer advance and the troops themselves had to retrieve the provisions from some distance. The attacks on the troops occupying the 1st line by *Infanterieflieger* and *Schlachtflieger* have a great moral effect. The losses from these attacks were fairly insignificant, but the feeling of helplessness in the face of these attacks created confusion among the soldiers. The prisoners say that at times artillery fire did not bother the troops as much as fire from the low-flying aircraft.

Chief of the General Staff G.H.Q., 8.6.18
of the Army
Ic No. 8322 op.
The interrogation of prisoners shows that the enemy has suffered as much from the effects of our *Schlachtflieger* as have our own troops through the attacks of enemy flyers. The statements further prove the importance of a methodical deployment of our *Schlachtflieger* for attacks with machine guns, bombs, and hand grenades.

(signed) Ludendorff

Oblt. Johannes Missfelder served as C.O. of *Schusta 12* from 7 June 1917 to 24 April 1918 when he was permanently installed as *Schlagru D (Schlasta 9, 12, 16*, and *24b*).

Hannover Cl.II 13274/17 at *AFP 4* in Gent photographed in April/May 1918. This is probably a *Schlagru D* aircraft.

Above: A *Schlasta 26b* Halberstadt Cl.II. The crew is not identified. This unit participated in Operation Georgette.

Uffz. Fritz Rittershofer and his unknown gunner while serving with *Schusta 16*. His unit was also involved in Operation Georgette.

CHAPTER X

OPERATION BLÜCHER

Having been successful in the north, primarily against the British in capturing a large amount of territory, many prisoners, artillery pieces, machine guns, and stores, yet unsuccessful in achieving a decisive break through, Hindenburg and Ludendorff switched their emphasis and planned an assault on the French. Called Operation Blücher by the Germans and the Battle of the Chemin des Dames by the Allies, it was spearheaded by the *7. Armee* (*General der Infanterie* Max von Boehn), supported by the *1. Armee* (*General der Infanterie* Fritz von Below) on the left and the *18. Armee* (von Hutier) on the right. Consisting of 25 divisions with another 15 divisions in reserve spread along a 25 mile front, the German attack commenced on 27 May 1918. The primary objective was to capture the heights of the Chemin des Dames, then pull their artillery forward and be in a position to bombard Paris.

At 1:00 Bruchmüller unleashed his usual savage artillery bombardment, consisting of 3,719 guns of 1,158 batteries. However the French, having learned valuable lessons from the earlier battles conducted in 1918, had essentially abandoned their first and second front line trenches, leaving only a few sacrificial machine gun emplacements to man them. The bulk of the French infantry was stationed in their third line trench system and the communication trenches. Thus the German infantry met little resistance during their initial advance.

At 3:40 the storm troops went over the top. The *Schlachtstaffeln* detailed to support the *7. Armee* in this attack consisted of *Schlagru A (Schlasta 1, 8, 10, 14*, and *21)* led by *Oblt.* Emil Ziegler gen Stege, based at Eppes, *Schlagru B (Schlasta 23b, 26b, 28b*, and *30b*, *Oblt.d.R.* August Ertl at Ebouleau and Montigny-le-Franc), and *Schlagru C (Schlasta 5, 20, 32, 33*, and *37*, *Oblt.* Werner Lange) stationed at St. Erme. The *1. Armee* had *Schlagru 1 (Schlasta 2, 7, 22b*, and *31b)* commanded by *Oblt.* Walter Lackner, based at Alincourt and Tagnon at its disposal. The *18. Armee* was supported by *Schlagru 3 (Schlasta 6, 18, 34, 35*, and *38s*) at Dury led by *Ritt.* Herrmann, but assigned to *Gruppe Liesse* in the *7. Armee*. These dispositions are illustrated in Table IV, once again from north to south.

Table IV
Disposition of the *Schlachtgruppen* Operation Blücher
(North to South)

Armee	*Schlagru*	Composition	*Schlagru Kommandeur*
18.	3	6, 18, 34, 35, 38s	*Ritt.* Herrmann
	C	5, 20, 32, 33, 37	*Oblt.* Werner Lange
7.	B	23b, 26b, 28b, 30b	*Oblt.d.R.* August Ertl
	A	1, 8, 10, 14, 21	*Oblt.* Emil Ziegler gen Stege
1.	1	2, 7, 22b, 31b	*Oblt.* Walter Lackner

The Germans captured the Chemin des Dames within the first few hours of the initial attack and proceeded to push forward. They crossed the Aisne River, then by the next day had crossed the Vesle and were headed toward the Marne, with Paris just ahead. On the first day alone, the Germans advanced 12 miles, and within the next few days captured Soissons, Fere-en-Tardenois, and extended their drive over 50 miles deep. By May 28 they had advanced as far as Château Thierry in the south and Villers-Cotterêts in the west.

Although the apex was growing, the base was relatively stagnant, producing a perfect trap for the Allies to conduct a counter-attack on the flanks and cut off the head. This they did on 30 May. The British and French fell upon both sides of the German advance, and shortly thereafter the American 2nd Division halted the German advance at Château Thierry on June 1st. The German infantry struggled on until the 4th, when Ludendorff realized the attack had came to naught.

Known *Schlachtstaffeln* losses incurred during Operation Blücher in the *1., 7.,* and *18. Armeen* during this attack consisted of 11 men killed in action, including two *Schlasta* commanders (Cleinow and Winsloe), 10 men wounded in action and an additional 8 men taken prisoner a total of 29 men and again equivalent to more than two complete *Schlasta* lost in action.

One particularly successful attack by a *Schlachtstaffel* during this battle was cited by the commanding General of the *Luftstreitkräfte*, *Generalleutnant* Ernst von Hoeppner in his book, *Deutschlands Krieg in der Luft*: "Also this time enemy aerial reconnaissance did not succeed in detecting our attack preparations. Thanks to thorough preparation, the deployment of our aircraft went off smoothly. Also in the air the enemy was surprised by our massive deployment. His countermeasures were so insignificant that the aircraft of all units had abundant opportunity to attack ground targets. Already on the second day of the battle one of our *Jagdstaffeln* took possession of the large enemy accommadations at Magneux, after shortly beforehand a *Schlachtstaffel* used bombs and machine gun fire to force a French *Escadrille* in the process of taking off to quickly vacate the field."

The unit which achieved this coup was *Schlachtstaffel 37* commanded by *Ltn.d.R.* Holbeck. His account of the attack was compiled by Wolfgang Foerster and Helmuth Greiner in "*Wir Kämpfer im Weltkrieg 1914-1918*" titled, '*Bericht des Leutnant Holbeck, führer der Schlachtstaffel 37, über einen Angriff gegen den französischen Flughafen Magneux am 27 Mai 1918*," (Report of *Ltn.* Holbeck, Leader of *Schlachtstaffel 37*, Concerning an Attack against the French Airfield of Magneux on May 17, 1918):

"The *Staffel* took off at one o'clock in the afternoon on May 27, 1918 to attack enemy columns which had been reported withdrawing on the roads leading from the north of Fismes. During the first approach we were able to detect large marching columns on the roads from Baslieux to Fismes and from Blanzy to Fismes and to attack them effectively with hand mortars and machine guns. Since the great amount of traffic in Fismes itself as well as on the roads lying further to the south promised rewarding targets, the attack was continued further to the south and in the process we flew over the enemy airfield at Magneux.

"In front of the numerous hangars on the northern part of the airfield were standing about eight to ten aircraft of various types. Four of them were just taking off when the *Staffel*, approaching from the west at a height of about 400 meters, dove to the attack. Amidst the fire from our fixed machine guns two airplanes landed again, whereby a Spad two-seater crashed next to a hangar on the western edge of the field. The numerous trucks on the field raced away at a high speed. Everyone standing in the vicinity of the aircraft ran away and were fired upon with the flexible machine guns. More than 30 hand mortars and light bombs were dropped on hangars and barracks from a height of 30 to 50 meters to excellent effect.

"Defensive fire from apparently sunken machine guns was very heavy. Almost all the aircraft received hits in the fuselage and wings. One machine gunner was wounded in the thigh. After an attack lasting nearly half an hour we set upon the return flight. After our infantry had reached the line Courville-Jonchery we immediately inspected the area and were able just a few days later to ask remaining infantrymen and civilians about the impression made by the *Staffel's* attack. The following was determined.

"Already nervous about the disconcerting reports of the enemy's disposition, the French *escadrille* completely lost its head during the unexpected low-level attack. After the first hits on the hangars and barracks, crews and mechanics left the aircraft behind and drove away on the already heavily laden trucks. Most of the hangars and aircraft revealed hits from machine gun bullets. Three hangars and five barracks received direct hits from hand mortars.

"The Spad two-seater which had been forced to land again lay on the western edge of the field and was half burned. Machine guns and ammunition were also found. The bloody losses amounted to 17 men, amongst them an NCO of Infantry Regiment 21 and several mechanics. One mechanic was apparently struck by a machine gun bullet while turning a propeller and lay before his machine.

Because of the *Staffel's* attack, the entire airfield together with its equipment was preserved from destruction and a French *escadrille* was weakened by bloody losses and robbed of the majority of its aircraft."

Following Operation Blücher the *Luftstreitkräfte* had an opportunity to evaluate the effects of the *Schlachtstaffeln* on ground operations. Although their losses were high in terms of both men and material, they had been successful in raising the morale of and providing support for the German infantry. The tactical effects of their low-level attacks were in general excellent and occasionally decisive. So, despite the difficulties involved in trying to maintain supplies of replacement aircraft and personnel to the existing units, an attempt was made to make these units even more effective.

A plan was prepared by *Kogenluft* (von Hoeppner) which proposed increasing the number of *Schlasta* from thirty-eight to sixty units, each with six machines and crews. This would provide 360 aircraft and crews to support the needs of the *Armee* during offensive and defensive battles. To facilitate the air-ground support operations, the sixty *Schlasta* were to be grouped into ten *Schlachtgeschwader*, each with six *Schlasta* of six aircraft and crews. The plan was submitted to General Ludendorff on 8 June 1918 for approval. This development and reorganization was to commence on 1 July 1918 and to be completed by 1 April 1919.

As a result of the aviation training schools' and the German aircraft and equipment industries' inability to achieve the requirements of this expansion program, *Kogenluft* revised this plan of 28 July 1918, reducing the demands for personnel and equipment by only increasing the number of *Schlasta* by two. However, to meet the needs of the *Armee* for 360 aircraft and crews, *Kogenluft* ordered that the aircraft and crew strength be fulfilled. This was to be accomplished by increasing the aircraft and crew strength from six to nine in each *Schlasta*. He further ordered that the establishment of the ten *Schlachtgeschwader* be completed, but with four *Schlasta* instead of six.

During the last five months of the war, the aircraft and personnel strengths were increased as the availability of crews and aircraft permitted. No new *Schlasta* nor *Schlachtgeschwader* were established by the end of war. Thus *Kogenluft's* plan went unfulfilled, and the *Schlachtgruppen* continued to be temporary formations that were established to meet the tactical needs of the *Armeen* during the battles of 1918.

To illustrate the lack of available air crew, the reader need only examine the rosters of the ten Bavarian *Schlasta* at the end of the war, for which good numerical data is known. These ten *Schlasta* had on their rolls a total of 76 pilots and 77 gunners, or an average of 7.6 pilots and 7.7 gunners, clearly not the nine of each which would be required to man nine aircraft.

"Fill 'er up and check the oil." A Halberstadt Cl.II being refueled. Although bearing an interesting marking of a two-color band narrowly edged in white, this is not believed to be a *Schusta* aircraft as no individual identification number is visible. Photo credit: Reinhard Kastner.

Above: This Halberstadt has performed a head stand (*Kopfstand*). The lack of an individual aircraft number would indicate this is not a *Schusta* aircraft. Photo credit: Reinhard Kastner.

Top left: *Ltn.d.R.* Karl Cleinow was the C.O. of *Schlasta 1* from 1 January 1918 until he was killed in action on 2 June 1918 at Chaudun.

Left: *Schlasta 2 Vzfw.* Rolf Steinvorth and *Vzfw.* Otto Gawron, May 1918.

Below: A Halberstadt Cl.II of an unknown unit but with a similar two-color band edged with narrow white stripes as shown in the previous photos. Photo credit: Reinhard Kastner.

CHAPTER XI

OPERATION GNEISENAU-YORCK

Because of the amount of territory captured by the Germans during Operations Michael and Blücher, two large sacs had been punched into the Allied lines. As Barrie Pitt described the front, it was "in general outline not unlike that of a rather untidily filled brassiere." The first sac encompassed St. Quentin to the north; the second involved the capture of the Chemin des Dames. Therefore a French salient extended into the German lines anchored at Compiègne and Villers Cotterêts. Ludendorff sought to eliminate this salient by launching Operation Gneisenau-Yorck, known to the Allies as the Battle of the Matz. Again designed as a one-two punch, the *18. Armee* (von Hutier) was to attack in the north on 9 June, 1918, with the objective of capturing Compiègne (the right jab). The *7. Armee* (von Boehn) was to attack the next day from the south with the aim of capturing Villers Cotterêts (the left hook). By eliminating this salient and straightening the line, the Germans would be a mere 40 miles from Paris extended along a broad front.

The *18. Armee* was supported by *Schlagru 1 (Schlasta 2, 7*, and *31b)* under *Oblt.* Walter Lackner at Villeselve, *Schlagru 2 (Schlasta 6, 18, 34, 35,* and *38s)* led by *Ritt.* Herrmann based at Dury, and *Schlagru 3 (Schlasta 3, 13, 19,* and *29b)* just recently arrived from the *4. Armee* and under the command of *Oblt.* Helmut Bühling. In addition the *2. Armee* sent its *Schlagru 1 (Schlasta 4, 11, 15,* and *17)* under the command of *Hptm.* Erich Sonntag based at Cappy to assist the *18. Armee* on both the 9th and the 11th of June. The *7. Armee* employed *Schlagru Staabs (Schlasta 1, 8, 10, 14,* and *21)* headed by *Oblt.* Emil Ziegler gen. Stege and based at La Pavillon Ferme, *Schlagru Winckler (Schlasta 23b, 26b, 28b,* and *30b)* led by *Oblt.d.R.* August Ertl and headquartered at Montigny-le-Franc with the composite units also stationed at Ebouleau north of Montaigu and Monthussart Ferme, and *Schlagru Wichura (Schlasta 5, 20, 32, 33,* and *37)* under the command of *Oblt.* Werner Lange and based at Raperie Ferme. These are shown in Table V.

Table V
Disposition of the *Schlachtgruppen* Operation Gneisenau-Yorck
(North to South)

Armee	*Schlagru*	Composition	*Schlagru Kommandeur*
	3	3, 13, 19, 29b	*Oblt.* Helmut Bühling
18.	2	6, 18, 34, 35, 38s	*Ritt.* Herrmann
	1	2, 7, 31b	*Oblt.* Walter Lackner
	Wichura	5, 20, 32, 33, 37	*Oblt.* Werner Lange
7.	Winckler	23b, 26b, 28b, 30b	*Oblt.d.R.* August Ertl
	Staabs	1, 8, 10, 14, 21	*Oblt.* Emil Ziegler gen Stege

Bruchmüller's barrage began early on the morning of June 9. The *18. Armee* troops, composed of 13 divisions with 9 in reserve, attacked along a 7 mile front and by 11:00 had advanced over 6 miles and nearly halfway to Compiègne. The next day they crossed the River Matz in the north. Also on the 10th the *7. Armee* attacked with 11 divisions along a 6 mile front in the south. However, the French resistance stiffened in the afternoon of the 10th. The French then launched a counter-attack on the 11th and Ludendorff called off Operation Gneisenau-Yorck on the 12th. Neither objective had been attained.

Since the entire battle only lasted from June 9-12, *Schlasta* losses were quite modest. *Schlachtstaffel 13* had one crew taken POW at Villers Bocage on the 9th (*Gefr.* Kuesler and *Vzfw.* Müllenbach), and *Ltn.d.R.* Becker of *Schlasta 10* had been lightly injured on the 10th. On the 11th, one *Schlasta 17* crew (*Uffz.* Conze and *Flg.* Busch) was killed by Flak fire, falling at Le Ployon, one *Schlasta 20* crew (*Uffz.* Karnapke and *Gefr.* Schlüssler) was killed at Soissons, and one *Schlasta 3* crew (*Uffz.* Arnold and *Uffz.* Held) was killed over Compiègne. Still, a total loss of nine men in four days of fighting indicates just how perilous ground support could be to the attacking *Schlasta* crews.

This *Schlachtstaffel 31b* Hannover Cl.II 13282/17 of *Vzfw.* Karl Peez (P) and *Gefr.* Michael Lang (G) was downed on 2 May 1918. It is shown here in British hands.

Another photograph of the *Schlasta 13* Halb. Cl.II 15342/17, which was captured by the British.

Below: The *Schlachtstaffel 13* Halberstadt Cl.II 15342/17 taken POW on 9 June 1918. The unit markings of black and white stripes and the individual aircraft number displayed in Roman numeral format are clearly seen.

Another photo of the *Schlasta 13* Halberstadt Cl.II 15342/17. Note that in the photos of this aircraft the cross form continues to change. The Balken Crosses have been added and the Maltese crosses modified by the British.

Halberstadt Cl.II of *Schlasta 2*, displaying the unit marking of a white fin and rudder and white number aft of the cross and black tail planes. These markings were used after April/May 1918.

CHAPTER XII

A GUNNER WITH SCHLASTA 15: JOHANNES HOHMANN (MAY 30 - JULY 7, 1918)

Although the *Idflieg* directive specified that *Schlachtstaffeln* were to be 'concentrated at decisive points of the battle,' not all *Schlasta* were engaged at the focal point of each offensive. Such was the case of *Schlachtgruppe 1 (Schlasta 4, 11, 15* and *17)* under the command of *Hptm.* Erich Sonntag, which did not participate in either Operation Blücher nor Operation Gneisenau-Yorck, being located during this period at Cappy in *2. Armee.* The unit did, however, briefly support the *18. Armee* on June 9th and 11th during the latter battle.

An account by the gunner Johannes Hohmann, who served with *Schlasta 15*, reveals that this period was anything but quiet for his unit. In addition to ground-attack duties, the *Schlasta* retained the role of escorting reconnaissance aircraft and conducting bombing missions. Hohmann found himself in heated aerial battles with enemy fighters, at times in company with *Schlasta 15's* ace gunner Gottfried Ehmann. Hohmann's story was published in *Unsere Luftstreitkräfte 1914-18* by Walter von Eberhardt:

"A Bombing Show

"The situation created by the tactical conditions required special adjustments for night-time flying. The *Bombengeschwader* were deployed at greater distances, while we *Schlachtstaffeln* had to work the territory close behind the front together with the *Fliegerabteilungen.* The crews of *Schlachtstaffel 15* were awaiting their first mission in the mess. Of course, for us *Schlachtflieger* it was not a particularly pleasant feeling to join the 'night moths.' There were especially big undertakings in store for May 30, 1918. The *Bogohls* were deployed at Abbeville, while we *Schlachtstaffeln* and *Fliegerabteilungen* were given the mission of hindering the advance of the enemy reserve troops through the destruction of the railway junction at Bacouel southwest of Amiens.

"A bright night seemed to allow hope for a successful 'show.' Finally, at 4:10 the *Staffel* took off in short intervals and flew directly from Cappy via Hamel to the front. Already over Villers-Bretonneux the machines of the *Bogohl*, which were on the return flight, came toward us. Without resistance we succeeded in flying toward Amiens and dropping bombs on the railway concentration from a height of 600 meters.

"After the effects had been determined satisfactorily and we had set upon the return flight, a hellish anti-aircraft fire commenced. In addition, the countless searchlights became active and two of these fellows caught our Halberstadt from both sides. We now sat above the sea of houses in Amiens, turning relentlessly. With machine gun fire we succeeded in putting one of the searchlights out of action and we escaped the other one through skillful turns. Now our orientation was taken up again, but – oh horrors! – in the meantime the morning mist so familiar to those who had flown over the Somme had set in and had spread a gray blanket over the landscape. So the watchword was: northeast! Now and again one recognized a highway and the Somme.

"Because of the wild turns our supply of fuel and been greatly diminished and we pushed through the blanket of mist, spotting a Red Cross ground marker as well as a large group of trees before us. The crate passed over it and we searched onward. In the meantime, continuous rocket flares ascended from the mist and we likewise fired off flare cartridges in order to draw the attention of our comrades to our desperate situation. For us it was a matter of descending now, cost what it may, for it could no longer be determined where we were located after flying through the fog. Beneath us we had spotted tents and initiated a landing. While the machine was still rolling, soldiers stormed out of the barracks who by the way of their clothing closely resembled the British. We had decided to take off again, when it became known to us through shouting and waving that it was a German unit.

"After we had clambered out of the machine we shook hands and both of us used only the one expression: 'the damned bombing show.' Our comrades of *Jagdstaffel 5* hosted us in the well-known manner of aviators. After we had submitted a report by telephone to our *Staffel* of our emergency landing only about 2 km. from the airfield, we flew back. The success of the undertaking met with corresponding losses. Almost all of the machines had to make an emergency landing as a result of the fog and in the process were in part badly damaged. However, the following day saw us all at work again.

"The Treacheries of an Instructional Flight

"On the 5th of June 1918 the *Staffel* again received new crews and we old hands had the pleasant task of taking on the baptism of fire with the young novices. *Artilleriefliegerabteilung 207* required protection for the ranging of batteries. Two machines of *Schlasta 15* took off. We flew over Morcourt, Hamel, and Warfusée-Abancourt in a continual flight back and forth. It was difficult flying with the new people. Because at one moment we found ourselves at 1000 meters and then again at 500 meters over the artillery aircraft. My comrade nosed his machine down homeward again, because it was impossible for him to carry out his protection duties. My Halberstadt found itself again at a great distance from the machine to be protected. Three SE5s used this moment to attack us by surprise. Before I succeeded in directing my pilot again, bullets were already smacking into the machine and threads of phosphorous hissed through the wings and about our heads.

"I still succeeded in putting a drum of my special ammunition in front of the fellows' noses. After they made several spirited attacks, the three SE5s dove toward their lines. I used the momentary rest to put on a new drum and to orient my pilot toward the work aircraft located beneath us. In the meantime we found ourselves again in the vicinity of the aircraft we were to protect, when again a flight of SE5s appeared (it was a squadron of the so-called 'Anti-Richthofen Wing') and disturbed my pilot's equilibrium. Consequently my pilot flew as straight as an arrow and dove the machine to an extreme degree. Through this manoeuver I was forced to shoot my 'spray can' straight in the air so that the Tommies would notice that there was still life in the crate.

"Two SE5s attacked with extreme daring and I succeeded in getting one of them in a burst from my machine gun. He took his leave with a nice dive. His comrade gave us a thorough peppering and likewise disappeared after I had served him up a good series of bursts. My pilot, as I now was able to determine, had been wounded in the face and legs. And I had to summon all my energy, in that I bent far over my gun-mount, to show him the direction toward the airfield and furthermore to indicate to him that he should throttle back and prepare to land.

"We were now in the vicinity of our airfield and I pressed on both his shoulders so that he would begin to land. Without easing up on the gas, he buzzed toward the middle of the field and ran the machine into the ground at full throttle. While I flew out in a high arc, my comrade hung in the harness like a bent rose. Everyone came rushing over, as each of them thought the machine would be burning. But that didn't happen.

"I brought my pilot to the nearest field hospital. My honorable old Halberstadt No. 4 was done in. My single solace was the certainty of having carried out my mission and returning with an important report of newly discovered battery positions by Lamotte.

"My Special Shows

"Through long-range reconnaissance enemy reserves and columns had been discovered in an extraordinarily wide area before the *18. Armee* near Magnelay and Coivrel. The Supreme Army Command had decided to cause unrest amongst these troops through the consolidation of several battle formations. My *Schlachtstaffel* took off on June 9, 1918 for the airfield at Curchy, where the units were to assemble. Several *Staffeln* had already shown up before us and now began once again the period of waiting which was so unpleasant for us flyers. It is a period of tense stand-by.

"Finally, in the afternoon the order to take off was passed on with the mission of attacking the above-mentioned reserves. The actual forward thrust of our infantry did not take place in our sector, but rather further to the south. The goal of the day was to be the Matz Valley. Our corps had the mission of securing the flank by bringing the first line forward. The *Schlachtgeschwader* took off in short intervals and flew a southwesterly course via Roye. The rail line and road led directly toward Montdidier, which already lay under heavy artillery fire.

Now a southerly course, along the rail line. The junction near Domfront was soon recognized. It was a sublime feeling to see three *Staffeln* flying toward the target in close formation. And wherever one looked, above and below us, were flights from *Jagdstaffeln*, who had taken on the task of protecting us.

"The artillery and flak batteries fired like mad between the row of approaching *Schlachtstaffeln*. The village of Dompierre, the first point of attack, was reached. Three fragmentation bombs whizzed downward. Next, Godenvillers received a load. And now began the work of the machine guns. Both villages were repeatedly approached and the access roads and trenches brought under heavy fire. One machine gun nest, which was especially bothersome, was attacked from a height of 5 meters and silenced. The crews fled into the dug-outs. These attacks were continuously repeated. It was a source of satisfaction for us to be able to help our fighting comrades in the infantry here.

"A travelling column on the road from Magnelay to Coivrel was approached at a very low level and destroyed. The village of Tricot stood in brilliant flames. But now it was time to withdraw because the air was filled with enemy fighter pilots. This successful day was able to be fought without any losses on our side and we returned to our home field satisfied.

"However on the 11th of June we were once again requested and took off for the collection point at Curchy. We sat in the mess in intense anticipation and whiled away the time until relief would come with the order to take off. A comrade from *Staffel 11* played one gramophone record after another incessantly and with great enthusiasm. Another group occupied themselves with games of chess. But above all this was the expectant question: What is going on at the front and when can we come to the aid of our advancing comrades?

"The British prepared an attack in order to withdraw their forwardmost line. The rear trenches were filled with reserves and especially at the afore-mentioned junction it was swarming with replacement troops. Low-hanging clouds forced us to fly at a very low height. Before Montdidier the French and British threw up a wall of flak which perhaps in its own way was without equal. However, 20 machines roared resolutely into this inescapable hell. Next to me a machine of *Staffel 11* was knocked down by a direct hit. It was the comrade who a half hour before had cheered us with his gramophone music. [Note: it is believed this is actually a *Schlasta 17* crew who were KIA at Le Ployron this date.]

"The defenses around Godenvillers appeared to have reckoned upon our coming. Because a hellish concert commenced as we plunged down in line of battle formation upon the enemy reserves. While my comrades still flew at them several times, I was forced to fly back due to a defective cartridge. After the removal of the jam I waved to my pilot. He was enthusiastic about the fact that we could now both run the show alone.

"Apparently no one had guessed that another outsider would appear. Because we succeeded in reaching the enemy reserves without encountering any defensive fire. Machine on its nose and down on the surprised opponent. Before they were properly conscious of the fact that they had a Halberstadt in front of them, we fired over 700 rounds into the surprised troops and dropped six fragmentation bombs in a large munitions column stopping at the edge of a woods near Magnelay. The onsetting confusion and panic revealed the effect of our surprise attack.

"Now the last drum of ammunition was put on for aerial combat and we headed in the direction of home. In the meantime it had already become dark and not a single German flyer was to be seen. A squadron of Breguet bombing 'barges' were headed in the same direction at a few hundred meters' distance, somewhat higher than we. A flight which was accompanying the bombing 'barges' attempted from time to time to disturb my return flight through attacks. However, the short salvoes from my machine gun forced them to turn back.

"Finally I spotted two Albatroses above me and could think about orientation, which up to this point my pilot had been carrying out. Over Roye we set upon the road which led to Nesle. After a rather long roaming about we landed in complete darkness on our airfield at Curchy. We had already been reported as lost. During the return flight of the *Schlachtgeschwader* the crash of a burning plane had been observed and it had been presumed that the same was our machine. After delivering the report we received a reprimand because of our separation from the *Geschwader*. However, this was balanced out by a special mention which followed a short time afterward. All the devils of the world could not have prevented us from carrying out our mission in spite of the jam.

"There wasn't a long rest afterward, for in the meantime a report came in that the British were planning an advance and for this purpose had deployed formations of tanks which had assembled on the edge of the woods at the well-known junction of Godenvillers. The weather was radiant. Above us droned the *Jagdstaffeln* in order to prevent possible surprises from above. At the front reigned a degree of activity such as we had rarely seen before. The flak batteries sent up a great fireworks display to us in the form of an aerial barrage. But we also pressed on through this wall of fire and descended upon the eastern rim of the woods near Magnelay, where some of the tanks were located. In addition, the wood was full of troops. A *Schlachtflieger* rarely chanced upon such good targets.

"Now I was again forced by a bad gun jam to break off the attack and then once more approached the target alone, in spite of the flight of Sopwith Camels situated above me. The fellows in no way disturbed me in my work. Only when I once more dove upon six tanks and sprinkled the same with mortar grenades and machine gun fire did they come staggering down. My good old pilot, an East Prussian, wanted in spite of that to approach the tanks again. I had to hold him back, because the Sopwiths' machine guns were now hammering away. But they didn't seem to have too much pluck, because I was still able to quite calmly put on my drum of special ammunition. However, since more flights of enemy aircraft caught our attention, we put our nose down in all modesty – that is, down to a very low altitude – toward our front lines. The flight followed us a short distance, but otherwise behaved quite decently. Less pleasant was the continuous ground fire. With a not inconsiderable number of hits we landed tardily at the assembly field, where once more there was a reproach awaiting us. In any event, the mission had been carried out as ordered.

"A Protection Flight with Obstacles

"Our neighbor on the airfield, *Abteilung 207*, requested protection for the ranging of artillery. Mission: ranging batteries onto the crossroads south of Fouilloy. The weather was deplorable. Our engines struggled against the strong wind and the machines were tossed to and fro like balls in a game of catch. We flew in the triangle Cerisy, Hamel, and Warfussée-Abancourt. After we had already circled around several times, the well-ranged flak battery of Corbie forced us into a sharp turn from which our dear Halberstadt did not come out. Now we spun involuntarily. Several times my brave pilot tried to pull the machine out. But everything was in vain. We were still 600 meters high and so he had a lot of time to get out of it.

"Due to the sudden spin I was still hanging in the ring mounting, as I had been busy drawing in changes in enemy positions. We smiled at one another in the mirror and when I pointed to the altimeter the East Prussian Reck shrugged his shoulders in resignation and at the same time raised both his arms up, wherewith he wanted to tell me that the stick was standing in the corner and that our bird should just get it out of its system.

"The flak batteries shot at us like mad because we presented such a nice target for them in our flat spin. Our comrade of 207 in the meantime had finished his mission and had to fly home because of important reports. At 200 meters height I pointed out to my pilot in all seriousness that he should now think about righting the machine. But in spite of all good attempts at persuasion our Halberstadt did not react. The lines came closer and closer and we could make out the crews who were already taking cover, since we could roar into the ground at any moment.

"Finally, at 80 meters height we succeeded in putting the machine on its nose and bringing it into a normal flight attitude. To the consternation of the flak batteries of Corbie, we had been saved. Out of gratitude and in recognition of the extraordinary efforts which they had made to shoot us down, we flew toward the battery and bid farewell in our own way by dropping fragmentation bombs and firing 400 rounds from the machine gun. Everybody was of course astonished when we came roaring back, because in the meantime our crash as a result of anti-aircraft fire had already been reported.

"The Birthday Flight

"On the night of June 23 to 24, 1918 we were sitting in the dug-out because enemy bombers were making serious efforts to flatten our field at Cappy. No one thought about sleeping before midnight as it concerned offering best wishes to a comrade on his 20th birthday. However, since the new day would probably be waiting for us with special demands, one after the other lay on his side. Around 6 o'clock we were quite roughly awakened by the orderly, as we had to prepare for a photographic reconnaissance flight. After consultation with the crew of the *Abteilung* machine we took off in order to photograph the nest of enemy positions west of Hill 104 up to Blagny-Tronville.

"The clear weather had also brought the enemy fighter squadrons to their feet and they were flying barrage patrols at every altitude. Over Péronne we climbed in a spiral up to 4800 meters and headed directly toward the target. The heavy enemy activity however forced us to fly further to the south of Hangard. We succeeded in approaching unnoticed; only now and then was there the bark of a flak battery.

"The final approach began when four Spads appeared as unexpected guests and attempted to separate us through short haphazard bursts of fire. Finally we were relieved by the flare from the *Abteilung* machine, which signalled the end of the mission. Then it dove in the direction of home, while I at this point could take on aerial combat. The Spads had gotten above us and dove to within 200 meters of us. My pilot, probably unnerved by my great calm, already began to fly a zig-zag course in order to make it more difficult for the fellows to hit us. My supposition that it couldn't be particularly spirited lads was justified, as they maintained a discreet distance. I therewith directed my pilot to fly straight and with the 'spray can' under my arm I waited for that which might yet follow.

"This sort of attack no longer seemed to suit the squadron commander – distinguished by streamers – as he dove upon us, without however firing in the process. At a distance of about 100 meters I made my machine gun ready for firing and wanted to send him a salvo, but my 'spray can' only responded with single shots. Even today I regret not having a camera in order to at least capture the fellows in a photograph. The Spads seemed to find themselves in the same state, as now and then I saw the tracers around my machine. I made use of this refined behavior to change my lock and besides that thoroughly oiled my machine gun.

"After completion of this task my pilot received his agreed-upon signal: machine on its nose and downward. The Spads chased after us and attempted to force us toward the front. A further dive brought us out of their vicinity and I now gave them the works. Circling around us, they often tried to shoot us down, however in the meantime a *Staffel* of Fokker triplanes and biplanes (D7) hurried on over and shot us out of the situation. We were rescued and left the remaining work to our comrades who specialized in that field.

"To the Aid of the Infantry

"The *Staffel* felt it had already been put out of action, since hour by hour we were expecting marching orders to another *Armeegruppe*. At the front the battle was raging in full swing. The British were doing everything they could to break through our line near the village of Hamel. On July 4, 1918 everything was in a high state of alert. The weather was very suitable for ground-strafing. Low-hanging clouds prevented any sort of insight into enemy movements. After a long wait we were finally relieved by the order to take off. After heavy artillery preparation the British had pushed back our line, taken the village of Hamel as well as the wood near Hamel, and extended the line over the Wuthen ravine.

"In order to prevent a further thrust, or to bring the advance to a halt, our side initiated a counter-thrust. And we had the mission of providing it with effective support. Besides our *Staffel*, *Schlachtstaffeln 4* and *17* came roaring along. The village of Hamel was approached and the northwest part, where heavy troop concentrations were to be found, was brought under machine gun fire.

"Strong activity in the air hindered our attack to an extraordinary extent, because the British had likewise deployed ground-attack aircraft which were supposed to stop the counter-thrust by our infantry. The Spads and Sopwiths attempted by flying around in a loose fashion to break up our orderly ground-attack. Our infantry was located below us and stormed through the Wuthen ravine. We prevented this disruption by the enemy ground-attack aircraft by flying a blockade in line-abreast formation.

"Warfusée-Abancourt and Hamel lay under heavy artillery fire. In spite of all resistance we repeated our attacks in close order formation until we had thoroughly exhausted our supply of ammunition. On the return flight we were convinced that this would be only the beginning of further difficult battles. Our infantry had settled in again and on the next day, July 5, 1918, all flying units were in the highest state of alert in order to prevent the enemy from gaining any insights into our rear area. Barrage patrols were carried out in alternating order. My *Staffel* took off at 9:35 a.m. and we flew along the Somme up to the area of Hangard Wood.

"Already on the approach a flight of British single-seater fighters appeared over Amiens, which however left us unmolested. The *Staffel* flew in the form of an arrow staggered upward, on the left flank our ace, Ehmann, while I had taken over the right. But already during the second approach the Tommies, who could fly much higher than we, hung onto us. Our lead machine seemed not to have noticed any of this because it led us further toward Villers-Bretonneux.

"In vain I attempted through flare signals to make my lower-flying comrades aware of the danger. But with the exception of Ehmann, no one took any notice of it. From the attack of the Sopwith Camels we could see that we were faced by some spirited lads and that here offense was the best defense. Our attack naturally required separation from the rest of our comrades, who strove homeward undisturbed. The attack was so keen and effective that I succeeded in drawing close to Ehmann.

"But now more enemy fighter squadrons arrived and attacked firing from all sides, so that in a few minutes my elevator and rudder were shot to pieces. My comrade Ehmann fastened onto a Spad two-seater and disappeared with him into the depths. I too was forced to give up the unequal battle and to clear a path through the pack of enemy fighters toward our front. Closely pursued and shot up, I tried to dive homeward and saw the Spad two-seater, which Ehmann was working on, crash out of control. It was his 8th victory.

"Another machine from the *Staffel*, which had observed our struggle and had rushed to our aid, had to make an emergency landing badly shot about in the artillery line after shooting down a Sopwith Camel. Our little aerial combat in the end developed into an aerial battle in which about 80 machines from both sides participated. Four Sopwith Camels in particular impeded my return flight through continuous spirited attacks. I had shot away my last drum of ammunition when two Fokker triplanes and one Pfalz single-seater intervened surprisingly and I gained a little breathing room in order to be able to leave the combat arena with a badly damaged machine and without ammunition. On the return flight we met yet more *Jagdstaffeln* which were striving to support the front.

"We succeeded in reaching the field and submitting a report. The mission had been carried out; however, two of our machines were stuck at the front as a result of emergency landings, as Ehmann too had to make an emergency landing due to a hit in the engine in further aerial combats. On this day three Englishmen were brought down by *Schlachtstaffel 15*. Our comrades who had returned early with the leading aircraft were amazed by our experience and the related developments.

"Our aerial blockade denied the enemy an insight in our area of deployment. On the other hand we couldn't prevent the British from pushing in our line by surprise after a terrible barrage. Every means of transmitting reports was cut off and so we received the honorable mission of determining the position of the new forward line in company with an AEG infantry support aircraft from *Abteilung 207*. Calm was reigning on the front after these difficult battles when we roared off at 5:20 a.m. on July 6th. The *Abteilung* machine, which was equipped with armored plating, was flying at a very low altitude, while I with my swifter Halberstadt carried out protection duties higher up. Hazy weather conditions prevented any sort of long-range visibility, so one had to maintain surveillance in a state of high tension in order to avoid surprises.

"After we had worked over the territory several times at continuously varying altitudes we were able to recognize to our great joy various friendly troops who had established themselves in shell-holes, completely surrounded. Lying in the craters, they made themselves known by waving steel helmets and ground-sheets and requested more ammunition by indicating the ammunition boxes. We should have gladly shaken the hands of our comrades, for such a heroic battle shook us up all the more, as for the time being we could only give them moral support. Naturally the British tried to disturb our work through heavy ground-fire, which at times was so vociferous that it rose above the roar of the 160 h.p. Mercedes. Flying above us, a flight of five Sopwith Camels succeeded in closing in on us by surprise. The ambush certainly would have succeeded had we not been alerted to the danger by the fire of our encircled comrades. The faithfulness of comrades!

"I immediately waved to my pilot and we dove with a roar upon the enemy pack so that the work aircraft could carry out its mission. The Sopwiths, in spite of the Indian-like painting on their fuselages – usually the outward sign of elite pilots – dove homeward and assembled again over the Forest of Blangy. After they had regained altitude they tried once more to have a go at us. In order to make up for the first failed attempt, they employed a new tactic in that the flight commander maintained his altitude and waited for me to change drums while the remaining aircraft dove firing, one after the other, put their machines on their noses a short distance from my horizontal stabilizer, and disappeared. This maneuver was repeated, as the changing of my drum was completed with the close cooperation of my pilot and the flight leader constantly missed his opportunity. In the meantime our *Abteilung* machine continued flying along the line and didn't allow itself to be disturbed in the slightest by the presence of the Sopwiths. At this point I attempted to draw the aerial combat toward our front, as I had in the meantime discovered that there was a German captive balloon near Proyart which would require protection from us. But it was in vain. The British seemed to have recognized my plan and cut off my return flight. There was nothing left for me to do but to once more go over to the attack.

"Now everything hung in the balance and only cold-bloodedness could help us succeed. It was remarkable that up to this point they hadn't molested my work aircraft in any way, yet with all the greater daring they attempted to shoot us down through continuous individual attacks. My salvoes were extremely well-aimed, as I only fired when they approached within 100 meters. Concerned about my consumption of ammunition, I kept a desperate look out for our fighter planes. But no German machine was to be seen.

"In the meantime I determined that our work aircraft had completed its mission and headed on a course for home. Immediately I tried to close with the machine in order to afford better protection. At the same moment the five Sopwiths dropped down on me in order to prevent our linking up. One attacked with such determination that I thought he wanted to bring me down by ramming me. I swept him with my last drum of special ammunition, so that his machine was completely enveloped. The shots hit above his undercarriage and the middle of his fuselage. The anticipated effect occurred. He disappeared in a dive into the depths, almost ripping off my elevator in the process. A long stream of smoke indicated to me that he was burning. In spite of the great danger my pilot turned around and yelled to me: 'Shot down!' The trail of smoke disappeared vertically in the direction of Hamel-Bouyencourt. The remaining four prevented me from determining more closely the point of impact. I continued the air combat up to my last round of machine gun ammunition and, after my pilot experienced a jam, had to dive homeward. A further attempt to fly back was prevented by the appearance of 12 SE5s. After landing we discovered a large number of hits in the machine. Amongst other things, my final ammunition drum had been shot through several times and the belt was hanging down in individual pieces. However, on the same afternoon we took off afresh for a photo-reconnaissance flight."

Vzfw. Friedrich Huffzky and *Vzfw.* Gottfried Ehmann in their Halberstadt Cl.II of *Schlasta 15*. Photo credit: Johan Ryheul.

Schlasta 15 Halberstadt Cl.II. *Vzfw.* Hilsbein (G) on the left and *Uffz.* Willi Gabriel (P) on the right. The unit marking is a white fuselage band aft of the cross and just before the white individual aircraft identification number.

A Halberstadt Cl.II of *Schlasta 15* marked '2.' The white fuselage band was the unit marking.

CHAPTER XIII

LETTERS HOME: EXPERIENCES OF A SCHLASTA COMMANDER

Schlasta 15's airfield at Cappy during the spring of 1918 has been described as "a depressing location ... damp, bleak, and twelve miles from the nearest town of significance. Years of war had pulverized the landscape and a pall of death hung in the air. Pockmarked like a desolate moonscape with craters and littered with the wreckage of incessant bombardment, Cappy was seemingly removed from the rest of the world ..." [Baker, 1990, 107].

Conditions were not much better at the airfield of *Schlasta 11*, another unit belonging to *Schlagru 1*. It was located near Haplincourt – or at least the ruins where Haplincourt once stood – about eight miles north of the "significant" town referred to above, Peronne.

Schlasta 11's commander for most of April to mid-June 1918 was a tall, blonde former cavalry officer by the name of Caspar Kulenkampff-Post. Hailing from the Hanseatic town of Bremen in northwest Germany, he had joined the *Schleswig-Holsteinsches Ulanen-Regiment Nr. 15* before the war's outbreak and took part in the very first offensive actions of the conflict. His boundless energy and offensive spirit distinguished him in these early engagements. Beginning with the rank of *Fahnenjunker*, he advanced quickly to *Fähnrich* and then *Leutnant* by October 1914.

The spirit of the charge carried over to his subsequent activity in the air service. Flying first as an observer – for a time with a certain Hermann Göring – and then as a pilot in *Feldflieger Abteiling 25* in the Verdun region, Kulenkampff-Post was not content merely to carry out reconnaissance duties, but rather sought out aerial combat at every opportunity and practiced his future trade with frequent attacks on enemy ground positions. Kulenkampff-Post then transferred to *Flieger Abteilung 261(A)Lb* at Cambrai, which shortly thereafter moved south to Ecly. Here his continued excellent performance earned him not only a high decoration, the *Hausorden von Hohenzollern*, but also his first independent command in the air. He was entrusted with the unit's *Reihenbild* detachment equipped with serial cameras and operating the most advanced Rumpler high-altitude design available. During short range reconnaissance missions, the detachment was accompanied by *Schutzstaffel 2*. The leadership experience Kulenkampff-Post gained with the *Reihenbildzug* in his charge did much to help him prepare for his subsequent role as the commander of *Schlachtstaffel 11*.

Kulenkampff-Post's energetic nature is reflected as well in the abundant correspondence he produced during the war years. Following are excerpts from letters to his parents beginning in the days immediately prior to arrival at his new command. For understandable reasons, there are no detailed descriptions of his hectic combat activity – both against ground targets and pugnacious members of the RAF – but his "reports" from the front well illustrate the living conditions of a *Schlachtstaffel* operating in the Somme region during this period and the various difficulties a *Schlasta* commander had to contend with, both in the air and on the ground. These lines also reveal an enthusiastic and aggressive nature which obviously inspired the crews under his command and made him well suited to this, his ultimate role in the conflict.

> Ecly, 31.3.18
>
> "It's done. In a few days your son will be the proud commander of a *Schlachtstaffel*. Yesterday I flew over to old *Herr* Hähnelt, upon which he immediately took me aboard. The matter is still passing through the *Kogen* and then I'll move. A *Schlachtstaffel* is probably the nicest thing one can have. Up there but a single voice reigns over one's choice occupation.

"The main purpose is to engage in the infantry's struggle from an extremely low altitude of 10-100 meters. Perhaps fodder for your son! One has 6 decent two-seater fighters. You can believe that I am thoroughly happy. The impressions of the battlefield up there – I was on the Peronne front – are so powerful that 1914 seems like a war game in comparison. It can hardly be expressed in words what a tremendous amount of material has been assembled there and for the time being is lying around unattended.

"On the roads an auto can make its way through the piles of munitions only with difficulty. The dead Englishmen lie to the right and left next to their cannons, tanks, and machine guns which no one has been able to salvage yet. Millions of wonderful wool blankets are lying in the trenches. The hospitals are full of first-class bandages and piles of the most lovely linens. Every common barracks is furnished with nice solid materials. There are food provisions which have been lying in supply depots for many weeks. The food is of a quality which is unknown to our stomachs, which have experienced rationing, both qualitatively and quantitatively. In short, it's a booty which suffices to equip militarily and provide for an entirely modern army. Accommodations are relatively good. Everyone is housed in English barracks and tents.

Ecly, 4.4.18

"To put you at ease, let it be reported that at the moment I am leading a peaceable existence. The weather is bad and I am waiting daily for my transfer. But since it's going through the *Kogen*, it is of course taking years. In the meantime in my little two-seater fighter I am fervently practicing the so-called '*Schlaffeln*', i.e., ground-attack flying, much to the terror of peacefully marching columns, comfortably grazing calves, or pretty village maidens working in the fields.

"Leave is of course quite out of the question, for myself supposedly for a fairly long time. I must honestly say that I don't have the slightest desire to go on leave. On the contrary, I'm angry that I don't have anything to do these days, because it's clear that the war is drawing to a close. But it's equally clear that one wants to and is able to accomplish as much as possible there. If only I could roar at the head of my *Staffel*. Geyer recently said grinning, '*poor English!*' [*Hptm.* Hugo Geyer was *Kommandeur der Flieger* of the *1. Armee*. His mock sympathy for the British groundtroops, which he expressed in English, would seem to indicate his confidence in the spirit and ability of the new commander of *Schlachtstaffel 11*.]

"Here in Ecly it's all over. It's a big laugh how in a year one becomes an enfranchised member of the village. *Oh Monsieur Kuli part, oh c'est dommage!* [Oh *Monsieur* Kuli is leaving, oh that's too bad!] 'Mr. Kuli' or 'Mr. Kulicke' are my acquired names here. The Champagne is not overly beautiful, but the region I am heading to next defies all description. It is the old Somme terrain, artfully beautified by our previous year's Siegfried operation and touched up by the current offensive. A tree is as rare as red deer in Zebu's Sottrum hunt and there is less unpoisoned water than in the Sahara Desert. ['Zebu', derived from Zebaoth, was an affectionate nickname for the author's father.]

Written 5.4.18

"My address is: Commander of *Schlachtstaffel 11, II. Armee.* I'm taking off immediately.

4.4.18 (sic) Haplincourt near Bapaume

"After a 48-hour trip I have arrived safely at my new field of activity. Sumptuous luxury and flowing riches and blinding beauty reign here. 1. Quarters with two crews in a corrugated tin barracks in which one can determine from one's resting place (not exactly a bed), without using the windows or doors, if the weather is good or bad. 2. Bed: old English stretcher with English coats, which incidentally beginning today will be used as hanging mats. 3. Food: field kitchen. 4. Water: no problem, i.e. rain in torrents.

"But it's war and the business is loads of fun for me, especially since I've landed in a gang of 14 splendid young fellows. All of them are *Unteroffiziere* and *Feldwebel*, apparently with great ambition and a lot of passion. There indeed reigns a rough, but comfortable tone. In any event I believe I can accomplish something with the bunch.

"There's nothing to say for the landscape! Before the front door one stumbles over English machine guns and coats, then falls into a trench, rips one's pants in a tangle of barbed wire, and then is perhaps on what one used to call a road. There one finds the view blocked by a tank or some other such furniture and then recognizes from a sign that the village of Haplincourt once must have stood here. A road sign together with the position of the sun further informs us that we're located southeast of Bapaume. Otherwise it would probably be easier to get one's bearings in the Gobi Desert.

"As a spoiled aviator one can hardly imagine such living conditions anymore. We all hope that we'll move soon to a nice area. The parting from the *Abteilung* in Ecly was properly done, especially because I flew away in the morning after the celebration and had to return because of the rain. As a result we celebrated again. The hardships of this world war are terrible. The next evening saw me looking for accommodations in Le Cateau in the pouring rain at 3 a.m. And last night the English, by means of welcome, seemed to offer everything they had in the way of bombs and machine gun fire. It was a rosy racket.

"The *Gruppenführer der Flieger* unfortunately is not German, but rather a *bvarisch*-speaking Bavarian. But he seems very nice. You can imagine that I am thoroughly satisfied to once again be sitting in the middle of things. It's an established fact that the war is always the most endurable where it is the thickest. Steinhäuser and Wolff with *Staffel* Richthofen are lying close by. I will visit them in the near future. In the meantime Steinhäuser has shot down a whole bunch. Because of the rain everything is swimming and the shellholes are becoming dangerous waterfalls. I am living on a slope and the waves are breaking on the barracks, which provides a delightful lullaby.

"Sometimes I feel like it's 1914 again in terms of the scantiness in all vital functions. But it's going wonderfully and that's the main thing. I'm just waiting frantically for good weather in order to be able to dive with fervor upon the louts ... If you can again send some things, do so. I am grateful for anything which tastes good or bad, as we have in fact barely enough to fill ourselves here.

11.4.18

"In terms of flying things are enormously interesting. I have already undertaken two ground attack flights with my *Staffel* at the extremely low height of 50 meters. It went marvelously. My crews are made up of quite devilish fellows who keep together nicely and attack steadily. I think one must restrain oneself to some extent. Off-duty it is of course difficult to enjoy oneself with so many *Unteroffiziere*, but it's going quite well. I'm living with 3 officer candidates, nice fellows, in a barracks. Each has his own corner where he lies and sticks his pictures on the corrugated tin. A fat oven in the middle replaces the cozy, but terribly impractical, English fireplace. The louse-box is guarded by 4 rat traps which do their duty most outstandingly. The worst thing is the way home in the evening, probably the most dangerous thing in the whole war. Unfortunately we no longer belong to Major Hähnelt, but our new superiors are likewise thoroughly decent people with whom one can work.

18.4.18

"I am doing well. I am flying a lot, even in bad weather. The fellows are staying together nicely, so that four of us held up quite well against 20 Englishmen. Only one was wounded and in the end Richthofen carved our way out quite nicely. Unfortunately my best crew was shot down from the earth during a ground-attack flight. He fell from our midst like a partridge dropping out of a covey. Otherwise we're freezing here in the lousy corrugated tin barracks and hope to move to Flanders. [The lost crew was *Vzfw.* Eduard Müller and *Vzfw.* Wilhelm Elschenbroich who were killed on April 12 over Aveluy Wood, north of Albert. The identity of the wounded man has yet to be discovered.]

21.4.18

"I have an extremely reasonable *Grufl*, to whom one can make all manner of suggestions ... The last days we've been mainly dropping bombs and are now starting to work at night also. It's going brilliantly by the bright light of the moon. This morning we took off in the darkness and dropped our 'eggs' entirely without disturbance. I'm now regularly flying 2 or 3 times a day, because it's still worth it here.

"Otherwise life is unpleasant. But I must laugh in the morning when with chattering teeth I unwrap my 4 saddle blankets and see my dirty body and think back on the luxurious encampment and the daily bath at Ecly ... When one wakes up at night, one is lost, because one can't get back to sleep again as a result of the cold, not to mention that systematic bombardment over a period of time does not increase one's comfort or improve the airfield. This is an old English practice field for tanks, is anything but nice, and requires acrobatic landing skills.

"I hardly have a chance to get any work done. Oddly, the *Schlachtstaffel* doesn't have an adjutant, while I must do all the unfortunately considerable paperwork alone because of a stupid *Feldwebel* and a yet more stupid office *Unteroffizier.*

"I will now probably get 50 Englishmen and will then have a barracks built for me. These mass billets are somewhat troublesome for an old *Staffel* commander, especially when one has bomb-shy people who can't stand the crashing and who must always respond with a rather long stroll.

Haplincourt, 24.4.18

"We've been doing well during the last days and in several aerial combats showed the old Englishman a thing or two. Unfortunately none tumbled down. On the other hand I unfortunately lost a crew again yesterday afternoon, dead. Such a thing is always horrible, but it can't be avoided ...

Flying agrees with me splendidly. I am in better form than ever and I thoroughly pester my boys with flying. When one participates in everything oneself, then one can also demand everything. [The crew killed on April 23 most likely fell to ground fire. They were *Vzfw.* Ernst Henze and *Sgt.* Hans Engel.]

27.4.18

"I'm building a stylish barracks for myself. From three old English barracks a living *château* is being assembled for the *Herr Staffelführer.* When several sleep together everyone disturbs each other. I especially disturb the others since with constant wickedness I only receive the orders at three in the morning.

"Do I have anything to do with Richthofen? Not in the least. I am with *Schlachtstaffel 11.* A *Jagdstaffel* engages in pursuit while we take part in the battle below. Our task consists largely of giving the fellows on the other side a case of nerves. If you consider that I already managed in peacetime through my purely negative behavior to have an unpleasant effect on the nerves of my old father and charming mother, then how much easier must it be, and what substantially greater effect may one expect, if one catches the enemy from a very low height in crates furnished with 6 bombs and machine guns. By the way, we are also doing well upstairs. We were recently praised in corps orders, as five of us energetically drove 6 Sopwiths far back on the other side of the lines. That Richthofen fell on the other side is infinitely regrettable and painful for the German air service, which needs such people. But if one had kept Richthofen from flying and merely let him serve as an instructor, the usefulness of it would have become illusory within a month, because within this short span of time the situation changes so substantially that one must be in the midst of it in order to have a say in the matter.

30.4.18

"Fog, rain, and storm cause one to doubt whether it is in fact spring already and above all, whether aviation is to be considered a pleasure. With rain-specked goggles and dripping wings it is decidedly not so. Especially since the light planes are tossed around barbarically in stormy weather, which is sometimes a bit ticklish when flying in close formation and requires great alertness. Yesterday we twice set off shakily in lousy weather. Among other things, I achieved a direct hit in a densely packed village. I think many a Tommy had a damned awful time of it.

"I now have a colossal number of crews, I think 15 or 16 men, who are being drilled for a large battle and are in part quite good. I always fly alternately with individual gunners. In difficult situations I of course fly with old experienced gunners. My fellows have now built me a palace, much better than what I wanted. It has a proper wooden roof, there are hardly any drafts and the rain doesn't leak through, so I can again put up wallpaper. It has been built into the ground as proof against splinters of shrapnel. Should the sun shine again, I will have a photograph taken of it.

4 May 1918

"Business is fine, one cannot complain about too little flying. We had a big celebration 5 times the day before yesterday, 3 times yesterday, and last night because it was supposedly going to rain today. Wrong. Radiant sunshine. Yesterday morning there was a wonderful picture of flying! About 50-60 German airplanes met one another by chance and flew in fine order, so that we literally swept the whole front clear.

"In the end I got a fairly firm hold on a Tommy two-seater and°when I had to let him go, because he didn't catch fire, I found myself all alone far over the other side of the lines and unpleasantly low. But making use of some clouds we snuck back home.

"One has the most comical experiences. The day before yesterday I had dismissed the *Staffel* after a bombing raid and am flying back alone and arrive over the airfield at 1500 meters suspecting nothing. Just as I am about to land a Sopwith shoots me up from close range and, indeed, so thoroughly that I could hardly avenge myself. Rather I had to save my skin by spinning down. Those fellows are quite cheeky.

"At the moment we're getting into the thick of it upstairs, which is very profitable. Yesterday I was the object of such intense ovations from my crews that it was embarrassing. In any event, the fellows will fly with me even if it's to the moon! And that is also a fine form of protection.

6 May 1918, Haplincourt

"Several bits of supposedly good news for you. 1. In the near future we will have a so-called closed season, insofar as there will be less frequent and more reserved flying and 2. there is a justified prospect that the suspension of leave for flyers will be lifted. I would then come to Landruh for 2-3 days. ["Landruh" refers to the property owned by the writer's father in Bremen.]

"I will try to get Rompe, who is still wounded in Germany, as an adjutant. People are now gradually noticing that that is necessary. This confounded paperwork. [*Ltn.* Rompe was a former observer in *RHBZ 1* under Kulenkampff-Post and had been lightly WIA on 21 March 1918.]

10 May 1918, Haplincourt
"The day before yesterday in the afternoon I picked up *Hauptmann* Cranz and we flew to Ecly. A fabulous celebration and directly from this we got into the airplane and flew back again to Haplincourt in thoroughly miserable weather. I took E. along back, who wants to apply for a position in an *A.O.K. Abteilung.* He was perhaps astonished at the carnage here. Yesterday afternoon I took him along for a bombing show and it was as if the old Mr. Englishman had unpacked everything for Ebelt. It all cut loose already directly over the airfield. As soon as one had dealt with one formation, the second came along. In any event we got the worst of it – as a matter of exception, thank God – and had to land again with our bombs! [The mention of Ebelt's name was an apparent oversight, as he'd previously been referred to simply as 'E'.]

14 May 1918, Haplincourt
"In the morning one is so furious with the Tommy, who makes such a racket at night, that one must somehow vent oneself there. Otherwise we're conducting exercises with rest battalions. In short, one is preparing for a world war.

"The vegetation is a month behind here. The grass is 5 cm. high and the trees are just beginning to turn green. The oven is blazing on merrily. The world war is absolutely horrible! Our decent *Grufl* has left again, but has apparently been replaced by one who is even more decent. I always have luck in that respect. Less so with store directors, who in spite of all our attempts at persuasion and the kindest words don't fork out our provisions. That is fairly irksome! One can't fill oneself with groats, sugar, and a slice of canned meat per day. But that's all a transition and since we don't adhere to closed seasons and shoot a lot of hares and hens we are getting along alright.

Haplincourt, 17 May 1918
"I'm now having several air combats daily. We have a reputation as a wild group of brawlers, with the result that another *Gruppe* has requested us. Business is a lot of fun, especially since I have an adjutant and only need to concern myself with paperwork for 1/2 hour per day.
"Yesterday evening I was at a cozy celebration with *Hauptmann* B. Right after that I had a delightful scrap with 6 Englishmen over Albert. One lives and enjoys ... One has enough to eat here, but dried vegetables, groats, peas, peas, groats, dried vegetables, etc., etc.

Whitsunday 1918, Haplincourt
"A glorious Whitsunday with a radiant sun and cooling wind could almost make one forget the war, if one didn't have to stand by on the field ready for take off and now and again get awakened by English bombers. And since I have just been decisively woken up by 68 bombs here in the surrounding area, I am taking hold of the opportunity and the pen in order to inform you that I can think of nicer Whitsuntide celebrations than this promises to be. This can in no way be altered by the 'Sirinnien' which Stossig has plucked for me in massive quantities. Nor the fact that at noon today there will be proper roast (R-O-A-S-T) with proper asparagus (A-S-P-A-R-A-G-U-S) with Schultheiss beer instead of the too expensive *Bowle*. This also can in no way be changed by the memory that Whitsundays in Landruh were always blessed with a horrible profusion of music ... Concerning the regrettable fact that everything has now changed so much for me, I can only be consoled to some extent by the conviction that you will make much better use of the most splendid Whitsunday weather than I, who in the course of the day with the aid of some bombs will probably transport a few more Englishmen into the better world to come. I can still picture times in which I didn't want to kill a beetle. [Stossig was the name of Kulenkampff-Post's orderly.]

21 May 1918, Haplincourt
"For some days we have had a crazy hot spell without thunderstorms. One pants like a young dog and yet has no water for bathing. One flies with old vigor. Once again I have just had one out of a formation of 7 in front of me, pursued him all the way down, and when I was just about to sear him with a final burst, I get a good peppering from above. That's the way things go in aerial combat. Significantly more negative are prospects for leave.

25 May 1918, Haplincourt
"There is not much to report aside from the fact that I applied for leave at the beginning of June. Whether I will receive it seems quite doubtful. But an attempt has been made. Life here passes quickly and uniformly. Flying, sleeping, eating, flying.

28.5.1918, Haplincourt
"This is perhaps a joyful surprise for you, the big attack on the Aisne, less happy for the French, who must be completely surprised. The old *Herr* Hindenburg seems to

know his profession. Here we're again flying untiringly in fairly turbulent weather. I am now the proud possessor of 9 crates! I am by all means hoping to be able to be sitting on the train enroute to Bremen on Sunday. At the moment the request is with the *A.O.K.* Let's hope for the best. We're now building a dreamlike beautiful mess with a living room, dining room, and veranda. [Kulenkampff-Post was on leave from June 1 – 8.]

12 June 1918
"After an exhausting trip and a stylish day in Brussels I arrived seven hours late in Cambrai, precisely where a Mr. Bomb Splinter went right through my auto. Nothing new here. We have been sent into action again. Weather just as in Bremen, everything dry. My stand-in was wounded during my leave, shot in the chest, but has had a good bit of luck and is in no mortal danger. [The identity of this acting commander has not been determined.]

16 June 1918
"Business here is now going splendidly with enough Englishmen and nice air combats. The day before yesterday I forced one to land on the other side of the lines, but it hasn't been confirmed due to lack of witnesses on the ground. Today within an hour we had aerial combats with five different formations. I didn't receive a single hit! At the end of the week I'll probably go to Ecly for two days and Saturday for over eight days in Brussels. Besides that, in this time I should become an *Oberleutnant*, which will hopefully influence your respect for me in a favorable manner.

19 June 1918
"My dear parents! Your Landruh hearts would laugh here today, because it's pouring in streams and if we had peas here they would simply have to grow. This weather is highly displeasing to me, as I 1. wanted to go to Ecly and 2. could accomplish a tremendous amount in the nights with a full moon. Nothing can be done about it! On the other hand we have a nice new mess. Yesterday I was in Valenciennes and the vicinity and amongst other things saw many interesting captured aircraft. Give my regards to my stout brothers."

Caspar Kulenkampff-Post's letter of the 19th was the last he would write to his parents. On the following day, while flying to Ecly to visit some of his former comrades in *Fl.Abt. 261(A)Lb,* he suffered a fatal accident as a result of a 'propeller defect.' Two months previously he offered some words intended to console his parents in the event of his death. He wrote: "Today death as an individual phenomenon has lost its horror, where daily thousands of young people fall, especially when one has seen out here how human lives at times lose value when compared to values which previously seemed insubstantial to us. If an old person dies, then his life is fulfilled and therefore it isn't sad. But how much more has a young German who has sacrificed his life for the Fatherland made full use of his life. Not sorrow, but pride is in order and I know quite well – and this is really comforting for me – that you will feel the same thing should I fall."

A crashed Halberstadt Cl.II of *Schlasta 11*. Note the unit marking on the fuselage of four black and three white bands. This is thought to be the fatal crash of *Oblt.* Caspar Kulenkampff-Post and *Flg.* Wladsilaus Pockladerki on June 20, 1918, at Ecly. Photo credit: Greg VanWyngarden.

CHAPTER XIV

OPERATION FRIEDENSTURM

Operation Friedensturm (Peace Offensive) was launched by the Germans on 15 July, 1918. It was spearheaded by the *1. Armee* (now under the command of *General der Infanterie* Bruno von Mudra) and the *7. Armee* (*General der Infanterie* Max von Boehn), supported on the left flank by the *3. Armee* (*Generaloberst* Karl von Einem gen. von Rothmaler) and the *9. Armee* (*General der Infanterie* Fritz von Below) on the right. The *9. Armee* had been formed on July 5th expressly for this attack from those remaining troops which could be spared from the Eastern Front. The primary objective was to capture Reims, the secondary objectives being the capture of Châlons and Epernay, and then to occupy as much French territory as possible. By this date Hindenburg and Ludendorff realized the war was lost. With the introduction of America and her masses of troops and industrial back-up, the only remaining prospect for the German high command was to capture and occupy as much of France as possible, in the hope of gaining more favorable terms at the bargaining table.

Since literally entire volumes have been written about this battle, known to the Allies as the Second Battle of the Marne, the emphasis here will focus on the *Schlasta*. The units supporting the attack were assembled into *Gruppen* as follows: *3. Armee*, *Schlagru 1 (Schlasta 5, 20, 33*, and *37*) under the command of *Oblt*. Werner Lange, based at Briey and Annoux, and *Schlagru 2 (Schlasta 7, 22b, 23b, 26b, 35,* and *36*) at Le Chesne commanded by *Oblt*. Walter Lackner, although *Schlasta 22b* did not arrive until the 18th; *1. Armee, Schlagru J (Schlasta 4, 15, 24b,* and *25b*) based at St. Loup under the command of *Oblt.d.R.* Franz Albertshauser, and *Schlagru 2 (Schlasta 28b, 30b 31b,* and *32*) commanded by *Oblt.d.R.* August Ertl at Tagnon, although *Schlasta 28b* and *30b* did not arrive until the 18th, settling in at l'Ecaille; *7. Armee*, *Schlagru A (Schlasta 1, 8, 10, 14*, and *21*), *Oblt.* Emil Ziegler gen Stege at Eppes and *Schlagru B (Schlasta 3, 13, 19,* and *29b*) at Mont Notre Dame, *Oblt.* Helmut Bühling; and *9. Armee*, *Schlagru 3 (Schlasta 6, 18, 34,* and *38s*), *Oblt.* Friedrich-Carl Hanesse at Dury. Thus, 31 of the 38 *Schlasta,* or almost 82% of the available units, were involved in the attack. These dispositions are shown in Table VI, below.

Table VI
Disposition of the *Schlachtgruppen* Operation Friedensturm
(North to South)

Armee	*Schlagru*	Composition	*Schlagru Kommandeur*
9.	3	6, 18, 34, 38s	*Oblt*. Friedrich-Carl Hanesse
7.	B	3, 13, 19, 29b	*Oblt*. Helmut Bühling
	A	1, 8, 10, 14, 21	*Oblt*. Emil Ziegler gen Stege
1.	2	28b, 30b 31b, 32	*Oblt.d.R.* August Ertl
	J	4, 15, 24b, 25b	*Oblt.d.R.* Franz Albertshauser

3.	2	7, 22b, 23b, 26b, 35, 36	*Oblt.* Walter Lackner
	1	5, 20, 33, 37	*Oblt.* Werner Lange

At 1:10 in the morning of the 15th, *Oberstleutnant* Georg Bruchmüller's artillery opened the attack by using the same tactics he had previously employed. By 2:30 the first German storm troopers had begun to cross the Marne. However, the French were again using an 'elastic defense,' which essentially relied on a few, admittedly sacrificial, machine gun emplacements in the first and second line trenches, with the majority of their troops stationed substantially further back. Thus, the artillery barrage was not nearly so successful as it had proved to be against the English earlier in the year. Bruchmüller and the German high command had not learned the lesson of Operation Blücher back in late May when attacking the French.

Furthermore, unbeknownst to the Germans, the French were planning their own offensive to commence on July 18th. The German attack, therefore, although furious, amounted to little more than three days of advance. Not only was Reims not captured, but the attack was halted when the Supreme Allied Commander, Field Marshal Ferdinand Foch counter-attacked on the 18th and drove the Germans back to the Vesle River. Known *Schlasta* losses over the three days amounted to 12 men either killed, wounded, injured or taken prisoner, again the equivalent of a complete unit being wiped out. As events would prove, Operation Friedensturm was the last offensive the Germans would launch during World War I. The *Schlasta* were now placed into a reactive rather than a proactive role. Since the German Army was clearly on the defensive following July 18, the *Schlasta* were in a defensive posture also and shuttled hither and yon, more or less at the whim of higher command, in a desperate attempt to negate ever successful Allied attacks, like 6-year-olds chasing a soccer ball around the pitch.

On 18th July *Schlagru B (Schlasta 5, 20, 33,* and *37)* left the *3. Armee* and arrived at Seringes in the *7. Armee*. They were to remain there until the 28th when they moved to St. Loup in the *1. Armee* and rejoined *Schlasta 35.* By 29 July, 1918, at the height of the defensive battle of Reims, the *Schlasta* had been reorganized into the following *Gruppen: 3. Armee, Schlagru 2 (Schlasta 7, 22b, 23b,* and *36)* stationed at Le Chesne under the command of *Oblt.* Lackner; *1. Armee, Schlagru J(2) (Schlasta 4, 15, 24b,* and *25b)* soon (1 August 1918) to be commanded by *Oblt.* Erhardt Egerer, and *Schlagru B (Schlasta 5, 20, 33, 35,* and *37), Oblt.* Lange, St. Loup; *7. Armee, Schlagru A (Schlasta 1, 8, 10, 14,* and *21*), *Oblt.* Ziegler, at Eppes and *Schlagru B (Schlasta 28b, 30b, 31b,* and *32), Oblt.d.R.* Josef Gramp, at Montaigu; and *9. Armee, Schlagru 3 (Schlasta 6, 18, 34,* and *38s)* at Toulis, *Oblt.* Hanesse. This is illustrated in Table VII, below.

All of these dispositions were due to the French offensive begun on the 18th. Known *Schlasta* losses in the four *Armeen* under discussion, *1., 3., 7.,* and *9.*, during this defensive battle, 18 July until 7 August, 1918, consisted of 14 KIA, 10 WIA, 1 KIC, 4 POW, and 4 IIC, a total of 33 losses or over 2 complete units. These losses also include one C.O., *Oblt.d.R.* Franz Albertshauser of *Schlasta 24b* who was severely WIA on the 20th. His loss once again reinforces the fact that the *Schusta/ Schlasta* commanders were not desk-bound warriors, but led their crews into battle and led by example.

Table VII
Disposition of the *Schlachtgruppen* Reims Defensive Battle
(North to South)

Armee	*Schlagru*	Composition	*Schlagru Kommandeur*
9.	3	6, 18, 34, 38s	*Oblt.* Friedrich-Carl Hanesse
7.	B	28b, 30b, 31b, 32	*Oblt.d.R.* Josef Gramp
	A	1, 8, 10, 14, 21	*Oblt.* Emil Ziegler gen Stege
1.	B	5, 20, 33, 35, 37	*Oblt.* Werner Lange
	J(2)	4, 15, 24b, 25b	*Oblt.* Erhardt Egerer
3.	2	7, 22b, 23b, 36	*Oblt.* Walter Lackner

Schlachtstaffel 21 in July 1918. From the left there are three Halberstadt Cl.II, then the Halbertstadt Cl.IV of the C.O., *Oblt.* Hans Ebel, and finally another Halberstadt Cl.II.

Schlasta 23b Halberstadt Cl.II number'5' and the crash of *Vzfw.* Ludwig Thaufelder when he hit a hangar during a test flight.

Hannover Cl.II of *Schusta 19*. Note that the black and white wheel covers came from its predecessor unit Ks S.2. The crew is not identified.

A mixed bag of Hannover Cl.II, Halberstadt Cl.II and Cl.IV of *Schlasta 5* (with the red/white fuselage stripe) and *Schlasta 20* (with the white arrow) as unit markings. They were part of *Schlagru 1* and later *Schlagru B*.

CHAPTER XV

THE BATTLE OF AMIENS, AUGUST 8, 1918

The distribution of the *Schlasta* on 7 August as shown in Table VIII is evidence that the German Army and therefore the *Luftstreitkräfte* were totally unprepared and taken by surprise by the British attack on 8 August 1918. The majority of the *Schlasta* were situated in the *7.* and *1. Armeen*, resisting the French counter attacks following the failed Operation *Friedensturm*.

The British attack, known as the Battle of Amiens to the Allies and 'the black day of the German Army' to Ludendorff, initially fell upon the *2. Armee* (General von der Marwitz) which only had *Schlasta 17* under the command of *Ltn.d.R.* Friedrich Geiger based at Bouvincourt. This was the only true defensive air unit that the *2. Armee* could use for infantry support. An immediate call for assistance was sent out by *Kofl 2*, Major Wilhelm Haehnelt, and by the afternoon of the 8th, both the *17. Armee* and the *7. Armee* responded.

The *17. Armee* sent three aircraft each from *Schlasta 11* and *27b* (a portion of *Schlagru 2, Hptm.* Sonntag) where they settled in at Nurlu. The *7. Armee* provided all of *Schlagru A (Schlasta 1, 8, 10, 14*, and *21, Oblt.* Ziegler) and they located at Curchy. Both groups returned to their respective *Armeen* that evening, but they provided some amount of infantry support for *Schlasta 17.*

Table VIII
Disposition of the *Schlachtstaffeln* on August 7, 1918
(North to South)

Armee	*Schlagru*	Composition	*Schlagru Kommandeur*
4.	D	9, 16	*Oblt.d.R.* Hermann Schulz
6.	2	3, 13, 19, 29b	*Oblt.* Helmut Bühling
7.	2	11, 27b	*Hptm.* Erich Sonntag
2.	-	17	
18.	-	12	
9.	3 -	6, 18, 26b, 34, 38s 7	*Oblt.* Friedrich-Carl Hanesse

7.	A	1, 8, 10, 14, 21	*Oblt.* Emil Ziegler gen Stege
	B	28b, 30b, 31b, 32	*Oblt.d.R.* Josef Gramp
	C	5, 20, 33, 35, 37	*Oblt.* Werner Lange
1.	J	4, 15, 24b, 25b	*Oblt.* Erhardt Egerer
	B	2, 22b, 23b, 36	*Oblt.d.R.* Ludwig Männer

By the 9th the British attack had broadened to include the German *18. Armee* (*General* von Hutier) and *Kofl 18*, *Hptm.* Alfred Streccius, also put out a call for assistance to aid *Schlasta 12,* the lone *Schlasta* in the *18. Armee.* Once again the *7. Armee* forwarded *Schlagru A*, this time taking up residence at Guizancourt in the *18. Armee*. The *18. Armee* also received reinforcements from the *1. Armee* in the form of *Schlasta 2* and *22b* which relocated to Villeselve as part of *Schlagru B*. In addition, the *9. Armee* provided *Schlasta 7* to support the *18. Armee*, and their *Schlagru 3 (Schlasta 6, 18, 34*, and *38s, Oblt.* Hanesse), to assist the *2. Armee*, arriving at Bouvincourt, while the *6. Armee* forwarded their *Schlagru 2 (Schlasta 3, 13, 19*, and *29b*, *Oblt.* Helmut Bühling), which established themselves at the airfield of Nurlu.

By the 10th of August, *Oblt.d.R.* Josef Gramp had led *Schlagru A (Schlasta 28b, 30b, 31b*, and *32*) from the *7. Armee* to the airfield at Athies to reinforce the *2. Armee.* Things finally began to sort themselves out by the 11th, by which time *Schlagru J (Schlasta 4, 15, 24b,* and *25b*, *Oblt.* Egerer) from the *1. Armee* and reinforced by *Schlasta 35* from the *7. Armee*, joined the fray and arrived at airfield Athies NW in the *2. Armee.* By this date the *2.* and *18. Armeen* had increased their number of *Schlasta* from two (*Schlasta 12* and *17*) on 7 August 1918, to nineteen. The majority of them resided in *2. Armee,* which was facing the brunt of General Sir Douglas Haig's attack. Clearly the 'soccer ball' was in bounds and being widely chased across the pitch. This was not the last time during 1918 that such a rapid redeployment of the *Schlachtstaffeln* would be undertaken.

The disposition of the *Schlachtstaffeln* for August 8, 9, 10, and 11-12, for just the *2.* and *18. Armeen,* are presented in Tables IX – XII. As a footnote it might be added that although the German Army was being driven back, the *Luftstreitkräfte* recorded 184 victories between 8th and 12th August, as given in the *Nachrichtenblatt*, including four by *Schlasta* crews. Clearly they were not a defeated air force. However, on the debit side of the ledger, those *Schlachtstaffeln* resisting the British assault lost at least 23 men either KIA, KIC, WIA, IIC, or POW between the 8th and the 22nd of August, including three commanding officiers, *Ltn.d.R.* Friedrich Geiger who was KIA and *Oblt.* Gustav Bauer and *Oblt.* Helmut Bühling, who were WIA.

Table IX
Disposition of the *Schlachtstaffeln* on August 8, 1918 in the *2.* and *18. Armeen*
(North to South)

Armee	*Schlagru*	Composition	*Schlagru Kommandeur*
2.	2	11, 27b	*Hptm.* Erich Sonntag
	-	17	
	A	1, 8, 10, 14, 21	*Oblt.* Emil Ziegler gen Stege
18.	-	12	

Table X
Disposition of the *Schlachtstaffeln* on August 9, 1918 in the *2.* and *18. Armeen*
(North to South)

Armee	*Schlagru*	Composition	*Schlagru Kommandeur*
	-	27b	
	2	3, 13, 19, 29b	*Oblt.* Helmut Bühling
2.	-	17	
	3	6, 18, 34, 38s	*Oblt.* Friedrich-Carl Hanesse
	-	12	
18.	A	1, 8, 10, 14, 21	*Oblt.* Emil Ziegler gen Stege
	B	2, 22b	*Oblt.d.R.* Ludwig Männer

Table XI
Disposition of the *Schlachtstaffeln* on August 10, 1918 in the *2.* and *18. Armeen*
(North to South)

Armee	*Schlagru*	Composition	*Schlagru Kommandeur*
	-	17	
	2	3, 13, 19	*Oblt.d.R.* Jaspers
2.	3	6, 18, 34, 38s	*Oblt.* Friedrich-Carl Hanesse
	B	28b, 30b, 31b, 32	*Oblt.d.R.* Josef Gramp
	-	12	
18.	A	1, 8, 10, 14	*Oblt.* Emil Ziegler gen Stege
	B	2, 22b	*Oblt.d.R.* Ludwig Männer

Table XII
Disposition of the *Schlachtstaffeln* on August 11 and 12, 1918 in the *2.* and *18. Armeen*
(North to South)

Armee	*Schlagru*	Composition	*Schlagru Kommandeur*
	2	11, 27b	*Hptm.* Erich Sonntag
	2	13, 19	*Oblt.d.R.* Jaspers
2.	-	17	
	3	6, 18, 34, 38s	*Oblt.* Friedrich-Carl Hanesse
	J	4, 15, 24b, 25b, 35	*Oblt.* Erhardt Egerer
	-	12	
18.	B	2, 22b	*Oblt.d.R.* Ludwig Männer

The *Schlachtstaffel 10* crew of *Gefr.* August Beckedorf, G, and *Vzfw.* Binnewald, P, at Eppes in August 1918. Their aircraft is a Halberstadt Cl.IV. Photo credit: Tobias Weber.

Ltn.d.R. Friedrich Geiger was the C.O. of *Schlachtstaffel 17* from 3 April 1918 until he was KIA on 22 August 1918.

Opposite
Top: *Schlasta 14* in late March or early April 1918. Standing 5th from the left is the C.O. *Oblt.* Emil Ziegler gen Stege, sitting directly below him is *Vzfw.* Wimmer (P), and on the far right, leaning against the balustrade, is *Uffz.* H. Kamrath (P). Photo credit: Tobias Weber.

Bottom: The Halberstadt Cl.II "Friedel" of *Schlasta 35* crewed by *Ltn.d.R.* Müller-Friedel on the left and his pilot, *Vzfw.* August Matthies, August 1918.

CHAPTER XVI

THE BRITISH KEEP THE PRESSURE ON

Following the Battle of Amiens, Generals Foch and Haig met to discuss where the next British blow should fall. There was a slight disagreement, as Foch wanted the British attack to be directed against the Roye-Chaulnes position but Haig wished to extend his offensive front northward, between the Somme and the Scarpe. Marschal Foch eventually agreed and he left the meeting in a happy frame of mind as the British were at least willing to continue their attacks. This decision fit nicely into Foch's 'master strategic plan' to win the war in the West which was, rather crudely paraphrased, "attack, attack, everywhere attack."

Accordingly, the British continued to exert pressure on the German lines, conducting the Battle of Bapaume on 23 August against the German *17. Armee* (General Otto von Below), the Battle of the Scarpe on 26 August against the German *2. Armee* (General von der Marwitz), the Battle of Péronne which the Australians under the command of General Sir John Monash captured on 1 September, and the Battle of the Drocourt-Quéant Line on 2nd September which was captured by the Canadians led by Lt.General Sir Arthur Currie and which broke through the Hindenburg Line. Although not quite as dramatic as the German offensive of 21 March, the British slowly retook all that portion of France that had been previously captured by the Germans. The disposition of the *Schlachtstaffeln* on 23 August 1918 is illustrated in Table XIII. Known *Schlasta* losses in defense of these continuing British attacks, from 23 August until 11 September, 1918, amounted to 6 men KIA, 2 taken POW, 11 either WIA or IIC. In addition, the *Schlasta* suffered the loss of two commanding officers, *Ltn.d.R.* Hugo Sillus killed and *Oblt.* Wilhelm Gebhardt wounded in action.

These successful attacks were rapidly followed by the Battle of the Canal du Nord on September 27 against the German *2. Armee*, the Battle of Cambrai-St. Quentin from the 8th to the 10th of October, the Battle of Flanders led by the Belgians beginning on 14 October, the Battle of the Selle River between the 17 and the 25 of October, and finally the Battle for Maubeuge beginning on 1st November and continuing right up to the end of war. Overall these attacks fell on the German *4., 6., 17., 2.,* and *18. Armeen*. The *Schlachtstaffeln* were unable to do much in the way of halting the German retreat, and from 12 September through the end of the war those units supporting these Armies lost 21 men either KIA, WIA, IIC, or taken POW. These included one *Schlasta* C.O., *Hptm.* Erich Sonntag, who was killed on 1st October 1918.

The *Schlachtstaffeln* were hampered by a shortage of crews, aircraft, and fuel – problems that would plague them throughout the remainder of the war. They were also subjected to constant airfield changes as the Germans continued their retreat. Additionally, the *Schlasta* were finding it was much more difficult to defend than to attack. The halcyon days of March – June 1918 were over, and although the *Schlachtgruppen* were now being formed for strictly defensive purposes, lacking knowledge of precisely where and when the next attack would fall, was decidedly deleterious to them in performing any useful function in support of the infantry. They were left with merely having to retreat with the rest of the German Army.

Table XIII
Disposition of the *Schlachtstaffeln* on August 23, 1918
(North to South)

Armee	*Schlagru*	Composition	*Schlagru Kommandeur*
4.	-	16	
6.	-		
17.	J	4, 15, 24b, 25b	*Oblt.* Erhardt Egerer
	2	9, 11, 27b	*Hptm.* Erich Sonntag
	A	1, 8, 10, 14	*Oblt.* Emil Ziegler gen Stege
2.	2	3, 13, 19, 29b	*Oblt.d.R.* Jaspers
	-	17	
18.	3	6,12,18,26b,34,38s	*Oblt.* Friedirch-Carl Hanesse
9.	-	7	
7.	C	5, 20, 33, 35, 37	*Oblt.* Werner Lange
	-	21	
	B	28b, 30b, 31b, 32	*Oblt.d.R.* Josef Gramp
1.	B	2, 22b, 23b, 36	*Oblt.d.R.* Ludwig Männer

CHAPTER XVII

THE BATTLE OF ST. MIHIEL, SEPTEMBER 12-16, 1918

The distribution of the *Schlachtgruppen* and their composition as of September 1, 1918, are shown in Table XIV. It should be noted that no units were stationed to the South of the *1. Armee*, i.e. the *3. Armee, 5. Armee, AAC, 19. Armee, AAA,* nor *AAB.* Clearly the Germans were still defending the *17.* and *2. Armeen* against British attacks and the *9.* and *7. Armeen* against French attacks. No threat was anticipated from the Americans.

Table XIV
Disposition of the *Schlachtstaffeln* on September 1, 1918
(North to South)

Armee	*Schlagru*	Composition	*Schlagru Kommandeur*
4.	-	16	
6.	-	12	
	J	4, 15, 24b, 25b	*Oblt.* Erhardt Egerer
17.	2	11, 27b	*Hptm.* Erich Sonntag
	A	1, 8, 10, 14	*Oblt.* Emil Ziegler gen Stege
2.	2	3, 13, 19, 29b	*Oblt.* Helmut Bühling
	-	17	
18.	-		
9.	3	6, 18, 26b, 34, 38s	*Oblt.* Friedrich-Carl Hanesse
	-	7	
	-	21	
7.	B	28b, 30b, 31b, 32	*Oblt.d.R.* Josef Gramp
	C	5, 20, 33, 35, 37	*Oblt.* Werner Lange
1.	B	2, 22b, 23b, 36	*Oblt.d.R.* Ludwig Männer

Yet, almost exactly two weeks later, this was the very sector that General John. J. 'Blackjack' Pershing led the American Army in an attack on the St. Mihiel salient. The American attack fell mainly on *AAC* (*General der Infanterie* Georg Fuchs), but extended on the left and right to the *19. Armee* (*Generaloberst* Felix Graf von Bothmer) and the *5. Armee* (*General der Artillerie* Max von Gallwitz). On September 6, 1918 *Schlagru B (Schlasta 5, 20, 32*, and *37*) under the command of *Oblt.* Lange had been relocated to Anoux-le-Grange in *AAC*, in an attempt to repel this upcoming attack, but to no avail. One rather experienced *Schlasta 20* crew was taken POW during an orientation flight from their new airfield on the 6th, but this was the only loss inflicted on *Schlagru B* during the battle.

It should be further noted that since the French counter attack on July 18th, and the complete stoppage of Operation *Friedensturm*, the *Schlachtstaffeln* had not received any detailed orders or instructions from *Kogenluft* as to how they were to use their aircraft in a completely defensive role. Nothing like the instructions prior to March 21, 1918 had been transmitted to the units. Thus, the *Schlachtstaffel* commanders were pretty much left to their own devices as to how to best use their aircraft in a strictly defensive posture.

By September 16th the St. Mihiel salient was completely eliminated and General Pershing directed his attention further north.

Above: In the foreground Hannover Cl.II of *Schusta 12*. In the background Halberstadt Cl.II of *Schusta 23b*. The photo was taken in March 1918 when these units were components of *Schlagru D*.

Below: Hannover Cl.IIIa 13369/17 marked 6 of *Schlasta 20* was downed on 6 September 1918. The crew of *Uffz.* Paul Weisser (P) and *Uffz.* Wilhelm Scharg (G) were captured. The aircraft is shown here on display in the town square of Nancy.

Above: *Uffz.* Paul Weisser (P) on the far right while serving with *Feld Flieger Abteilung 6* in the Fall of 1916. The visible sleeve patches represent *Feld Flieger Abteilung 33* and *24*. All three units served in Flanders during this time. Weisser was taken POW on September 6, 1918, while serving with *Schlasta 20*. Photo credit: Frank Garove. Below: *Gefr.* Wilhelm Krieger a pilot with *Schlasta 29b* in front of his Halberstadt Cl.II at St. Aubert airfield by Cambrai on 22 September 1918. Photo credit: Marcus Pleyer.

CHAPTER XVIII

THE BATTLE OF THE MEUSE-ARGONNE, SEPTEMBER 26 - NOVEMBER 11, 1918

General Foch and General Pershing agreed that the next battle would be fought in the Meuse-Argonne, but for this attack Pershing was insistent that it be an all-American affair. Foch reluctantly agreed. Pershing was now faced with the task of extricating 300,000 American troops from the St. Mihiel sector 25 miles south of Verdun, moving them 60 miles to the northwest, combining them with an additional 300,000 American troops, withdrawing 220,000 French troops, and preparing a 24 mile wide assault front between the western edge of the Argonne forest and the Meuse River.

Here he would be faced by the German *3. Armee* (*Generaloberst* Karl von Einem gen. von Rothmaler) and the German *5. Armee* (*General* von Gallwitz), comprising only 5 divisions but with a further 15 divisions in reserve, which could be expected to reach the battlefront within three days. Pershing's right wing would also attack the troops of *Armee Abteilung C (General* Georg Fuchs).

The distribution and composition of the *Schlachtgruppen* along the entire Western Front on 26 September 1918 is presented in Table XV. The *5. Armee* had at its disposal *Schlagru 2 (Schlasta 3, 13, 19, 29b, Oblt.* Bühling) located at Preutin, and *Schlagru B (Schlasta 5, 20, 21, 33, Oblt.* Bruno Zipplies), stationed at Thonne-le-Près. The *3. Armee* contained *Schlagru 3 (Schlasta 2, 22b, 23b, Oblt.d.R.* Sigmund Kreitmair) at Autrecourt and *Schlagru B (Schlasta 6, 18, 34, 38s, Oblt.* Friedrich-Carl Hanesse), probably at Le Chesne, but confirmation is lacking. *Armee Abteilung C* was supported by *Schlagru 1* (*Schlasta 26b* and *37, Oblt.d.R.* Konrad Hoffmann), based at Anoux-le-Grange.

Table XV
Disposition of the *Schlachtstaffeln* on September 26, 1918
(North to South)

Armee	*Schlagru*	Composition	*Schlagru Kommandeur*
4.	-	16	
6.	-		
	S	9, 11, 27b	*Hptm.* Hugo Weingarth
17.	J	4, 15, 24b, 25b, 35	*Oblt.* Friedrich von Krausser
2.	-	17	
18.	-	12	

7.	-	7	
1.	B	30b, 31b, 32	*Ritt.d.R.* Julius Bossert
3.	B	6, 18, 34, 38s	*Oblt.* Friedrich-Carl Hanesse
	3	2, 22b, 23b	*Oblt.d.R.* Sigmund Kreitmair
5.	B	5, 20, 21, 33	*Oblt.* Bruno Zipplies
	2	3, 13, 19, 29b	*Oblt.* Helmut Bühling
AAC	1	26b, 37	*Oblt.d.R.* Konrad Hoffmann
19.	2	28b, 36	*Oblt.* Oskar Baumann
AAA	A	1, 8, 10, 14	*Oblt.* Emil Ziegler gen Stege

To demonstrate just how effectively the *Schlasta* performed during this battle, the following is a letter written by the *3. Armee* commander *Generaloberst* Karl von Einem gen von Rothmaler to his wife dated September 29, 1918. It is contained in the book *"Ein Armeeführer erlebt den Weltkrieg"* compiled by Junius Alter, translation courtesy of Hannes Täger. "*Prinz* Eitel Friedrich was attacked by incredibly strong masses of Americans who were bravely rushing forward. Then our *Schlachtgeschwader* (sic) appeared which flung itself with bombs and machine guns on the Americans who scattered away in wild flight. We immediately reported that the Americans would not hold their ground against attacking aircraft." It is suspected that the attacking air group was *Schlagru 3* composed of Schlasta *2, 22b*, and *23b* under the command of *Oblt.d.R.* Sigmund Kreitmair.

However, things did not always go so smoothly for the German *Schlasta,* as seen by this report of *Oblt.d.R.* Konrad Hoffmann, the commander of *Schlasta 26b*. He, along with his pilot *Vzfw.* Ludwig Müller, was shot down by American ground fire and forced to land between the lines on October 3, 1918. His account appeared in the *Nachrichtenblatt der Luftstreitkräfte*, Nr. 34, 17 October 1918:

> "With the approval of the *Komandeur der Flieger* ___ I undertook a voluntary ground-attack flight with 6 aircraft at 4:30 in the afternoon. Very heavy traffic, especially involving motorized columns on the road from Montfaucon to Gercourt and Montfaucon to Dannevoux, was thoroughly attacked with mortar grenades, small bombs and machine guns. When the *Staffel* attacked a second time amid heavy flak and machine gun fire, my aircraft received several hits by machine gun bullets in the main fuel tank and fuel lines, among other places, at a height of about 200 meters.
>
> "The engine cut out, but while we were descending northward past the Forest of Septsarges, it jumped from time to time to almost full revs. I sought to diminish the extremely heavy fire from countless machine guns upon our aircraft, now at about 50 meters height, by firing off a full roll of ammunition alternately from right to left. In the meantime, through skillful climbing and diving as the engine again ran for seconds at a time, my pilot succeeded in getting over Nantillois in the direction of the Forest of Ogen. However, flying at only a few meters height, we didn't manage to get over this wood. We turned to the left and made a smooth landing.
>
> "Immediately fired upon heavily by machine guns from enemy positions, we ran to a distance of 50 meters from the aircraft and lay flat on the ground in a shallow depression, awaiting the dawn amid machine gun fire and rounds of artillery fire bursting nearby. After crawling for a lengthy period of time in a northerly direction, where, judging by the enemy artillery fire, we supposed our own troops were located, we reached the forward posts around 7:00. With their help, the aircraft was pulled from the forward perimeter to the back of Hill 253 under the cover of darkness.
>
> "Since we still had some reserve fuel and assumed we could effect a temporary repair to the damaged fuel line, we decided to repair the aircraft at dawn, create a new strip for take-off by filling up the shell holes, and reach the nearest airfield. We stayed overnight in a barracks in the Cunel Woods. The preparatory fire for the enemy attack on October 4th, which began around 11:00

at night and increased to a considerable extent in the morning, made an approach to the aircraft impossible. As the attack gained ground to the left of us and an encirclement of the Cunel Woods was feared, we attempted a breakthrough around 9:00 that morning through the heavy box-barrage and came back safe and sound through the village of Romange and the zone of harassing fire via Remonville. On the afternoon of October 5th we finally returned to the *Staffel.*

"With the consent of the *Flivo* of the ___ Infantry Division, the troop commander promised me that he would recover the machine guns and instruments, which were impossible to take along during the extremely strenuous march back through the zone of fire, and destroy the aircraft, which had already received about 30 hits before the landing. It seems worthy of note that in the forward line I was able to detect even among the officers a striking ignorance of both our own and enemy types of aircraft. It is maintained by them that the newer form of crosses are very difficult to recognize compared to the older form. For this reason, our own aircraft are often fired upon. No one knows anything about the white rudders."

During the next six weeks, or over the length of the battle, the *5. Armee* would be reinforced by *Schlasta 26b*, joining *Schlagru 2* on 6 October, and *Schlasta 32* would briefly reinforce *Schlagru B* between the 23rd and the 29th of October. Finally on October 29th the *3. Armee* was supported by a new *Schlagru B* composed of *Schlasta 7, 18, 32, 34,* under the command of *Oblt.* Ernst Bonatz. The original *Schlagru B* under the command of Hanesse, had been relocated to the *7. Armee,* renamed *Schlagru 3* and was now comprised of *Schlasta 6, 12, 23b*, and *38s*. Refer to Tables XVI-XIX for further clarification of the *Schlachtgruppen* composition and their movements during this time frame. *Schlasta* losses in the *3.* and *5. Armeen* during the Battle of the Meuse-Argonne amounted to at least 25 men: 4 KIA, 10 WIA/IIC, and 11 taken POW. *Schlasta 20* was especially hard hit, losing four crews between 2-10 October, 1918, although each of the other three units of *Schlagru B* also suffered losses during the first week of October 1918.

The American fighter squadrons, notably the 1st Pursuit Group comprised of the 27th, 94th, 95th, and 147th Aero Squadrons, instituted a policy of flying one low patrol, 400-600 meters or approximately 1200-1800 feet, which put them at an excellent height advantage to dive on the still lower flying *Schlasta* aircraft. Of course these low patrols were protected from any marauding *Jagdstaffeln* flights by higher flying patrols, roughly 10,000 feet or above.

The interested reader is encouraged to consult the two excellent books on the history of the 94th and the 95th USAS Squadrons by Charles Woolley, *The Hat in the Ring Gang* and *The First to the Front*. These low flying American patrols accounted for at least four and possibly seven of the *Schlasta* aircraft mentioned above.

Table XVI
Disposition of the *Schlachtstaffeln* on October 9, 1918
(North to South)

Armee	*Schlagru*	Composition	*Schlagru Kommandeur*
4.	J	9, 16, 24b, 25b	*Oblt.* Friedrich von Krausser
6.	-		
17.	S	4, 11, 15, 27b, 35	*Hptm.* Hugo Weingarth
2.	A	1, 8, 10, 14, 17	*Oblt.* Emil Ziegler gen Stege
18.	-	12	
7.	B	6, 7, 18, 34, 38s	*Oblt.* Friedrich-Carl Hanesse
1.	B	30b, 31b, 32	*Ritt.d.R.* Julius Bossert
3.	3	2, 22b, 23b	*Oblt.d.R.* Karl *Ritter* von Gruny

5.	B 2	5, 20, 21, 33 3, 13, 19, 26b, 29b	*Oblt.* Bruno Zipplies *Oblt.* Helmut Bühling
AAC	-	37	
19.	2	28b, 36	*Oblt.* Oskar Baumann

Table XVII
Disposition of the *Schlachtstaffeln* on October 17, 1918
(North to South)

Armee	*Schlagru*	Composition	*Schlagru Kommandeur*
4.	J	9, 24b, 25b	*Oblt.* Friedrich von Krausser
6.	-		
17.	S -	4, 11, 15, 27b 16, 35	*Hptm.* Hugo Weingarth
2.	A	1, 8, 10, 14, 17	*Oblt.* Emil Ziegler gen Stege
18.	-	6, 12	
7.	B	7, 18, 34, 38s	*Oblt.* Friedrich-Carl Hanesse
1.	B	30b, 31b, 32	*Ritt.d.R.* Julius Bossert
3.	3	2, 22b, 23b	*Oblt.d.R.* Karl *Ritter* von Gruny
5.	B 2	5, 20, 21, 33 3, 13, 19, 26b, 29b	*Oblt.* Bruno Zipplies *Oblt.* Helmut Bühling
AAC	-	37	
19.	2	28b, 36	*Oblt.* Oskar Baumann

Table XVIII
Disposition of the *Schlachtstaffeln* on October 23, 1918
(North to South)

Armee	*Schlagru*	Composition	*Schlagru Kommandeur*
4.	J	9, 24b, 25b	*Oblt.* Friedrich von Krausser
6.	-		

17.	S A	4, 11, 15, 27b 8, 10, 16, 35	*Hptm.* Hugo Weingarth *Oblt.* Emil Ziegler gen Stege
2.	A	1, 14, 17	*Hptm.* Hermann Krüger
18.	3	6, 12, 23b, 38s	*Oblt.* Friedrich-Carl Hanesse
7.	B	7, 18, 34	*Oblt.* Ernst Bonatz
1.	B	30b, 31b	*Ritt.d.R.* Julius Bossert
3.	-		
5.	B 2	5, 20, 21, 32, 33 3, 13, 19, 26b, 29b	*Oblt.* Hans Ebel *Oblt.* Helmut Bühling
AAC	-	37	
19.	2	2, 22b, 28b, 36	*Oblt.d.R.* Karl *Ritter* von Gruny

Table XIX
Disposition of the *Schlachtstaffeln* on October 31, 1918
(North to South)

Armee	*Schlagru*	Composition	*Schlagru Kommandeur*
4.	J	9, 24b, 25b	*Oblt.* Friedrich von Krausser
6.	-		
17.	S A	4, 11, 15, 27b 8, 10, 16, 35	*Hptm.* Hugo Weingarth *Oblt.* Emil Ziegler gen Stege
2.	A	1, 14, 17	*Hptm.* Hermann Krüger
18.	-		
7.	3	6, 12, 23b, 38s	*Oblt.* Friedrich-Carl Hanesse
1.	B	30b, 31b	*Ritt.d.R.* Julius Bossert
3.	B	7, 18, 32, 34	*Oblt.* Ernst Bonatz
5.	B 2	5, 20, 21, 33 3, 13, 19, 26b, 29b	*Oblt.* Hans Ebel *Oblt.* Helmut Bühling
AAC	-	37	
19.	2	2, 22b, 28b, 36	*Oblt.d.R.* Karl *Ritter* von Gruny

Above: A Halberstadt Cl.II of *Schlasta 15* captured by the French on 13 October 1918. The crew of *Sgt.* Kuchenbacher (P) and *Sgt.* Otto Becker (G) were taken prisoner at Solesmes.

Right: *Oblt.* Hugo Weingarth as an observer with *Fl.Abt. 256(A)*. In October 1918, as a *Hptm.*, he would be named C.O. of *Schlagru S (Schlasta 4, 11, 15* and *27b*).

Opposite

Top: A Halberstadt Cl.II of *Schlasta 21* marked '3' captured by American forces on 2 October 1918. It was crewed by *Uffz.* Max Niemann (P) and *Vzfw.* Rudolf Kolodzicj (G). It is painted in what would appear to be red/yellow bands. A close inspection will reveal the black fuselage with white stripes beneath the colored bands.

Bottom: *Schlachtstaffel 3* Hannover Cl.IIIa 3885/18 captured on October 3, 1918. German prisoners are pushing the aircraft under the trees to camouflage it from overhead observation. The crew is not known.

CHAPTER XIX

DEMOBILIZATION

When the "War to End All Wars" finally ground to a halt on November 11, 1918, it didn't take the *Luftstreitkräfte* long to demobilize their air units. Based on those known dates for the Bavarian *Schlachtstaffeln*, demobilization occurred within two weeks following the cessation of hostilities. The exact dates for the Prussian units are not, as yet, known. However, through the diligent research of Jörg Mückler, the locations of the demobilization of the remaining *Schlachtstaffeln* are provided. It is assumed that these also occurred in late November 1918.

PART III

EQUIPMENT OF THE SCHUTZSTAFFELN/ SCHLACHTSTAFFELN

CHAPTER XX

THE AIRCRAFT OF THE SCHUTZSTAFFELN

In January 1917, with the conversion of the *Kasta* to *Schusta*, the units retained their aircraft, personnel, and equipment, as well as their traditions and unit markings. They started a new *Kriegstagabuch* (War Diary). This chapter describes the aircraft that were transferred to the *Schusta* and those that were later issued in 1917.

Each *Schusta* was equipped with six two-seat, single engine, armed C Class aircraft, assigned with the role of flying escort and protection for the C Class aircraft of the *Flieger Abteilungen*, performing their reconnaissance or photographic duties, or escorting the artillery-spotting C Class aircraft of the *Artillerie Flieger Abteilungen.* The *Schusta* flew aircraft with identical performance characteristics and fighting abilities of the aircraft they were escorting.

While almost all of the C Class aircraft used by the *Schusta* had bomb carrying capabilities, they did not normally engage in these activities, but on some occasions did perform such missions. They were armed with a fixed, synchronized, forward firing machine gun, generally a Maxim lMG 08 machine gun controlled by the pilot. The ammunition containers usually held 500 rounds of 7.92mm ammunition. The gunner had an air cooled Parabellum Modell 14 on the wooden turret of the LVG Franz Schneider design, or a variation of the Schneider turret, which was mounted on top of the fuselage over the rear seat. The gunner typically had three drums of 250 rounds per drum, one on the gun and two or three in spare drum racks.

Most aircraft crews were enlisted men and the gunner was, as a rule, the aircraft commander. There were a few instances where an officer was the pilot with an enlisted gunner, and in these cases the pilot would be in command.

The observer/gunner had a wireless radio for receiving and sending Morse code, a trailing wire antenna, maps with various colored pencils, a flare pistol, colored flares to be used for signaling, and a battery-operated signal light with a pistol grip for the same purpose.

In most of the C Class aircraft, there were internal racks for carrying light bombs, and heavier carriers mounted externally under the fuselage with a capacity up to 50 kg bombs. In some machines, there was an internal rack installed in the observer's cockpit that held four 12.5 kg P.u.W. bombs stored horizontally, one above. These bombs could be dropped in train or one at a time by the gunner. On the belly of the fuselage was a spring loaded trap door that opened with the weight of the bomb.

The Original Aircraft

The *Kasta* turned over to the newly organized *Schusta* their aircraft, which were of the types Albatros C.III, C.V, C.VI, C.VII, LFG Roland C.II, and Rumpler C.I. The *Schusta* known to be equipped with these aircraft are as follows:

Alb. C.III: *Schusta 19, 21*
Alb. C.V: *Schusta 27b*
Alb. C.VI: *Schusta 7, 19, 20, 21*, and *27b*
Alb. C.VII: *Schusta 4, 17, 19, 20, 23b, 24b,* and *27b*
Roland C.II: *Schusta 2, 6, 11, 15, 20, 21, 26b, 27b*, and *28b*
Ru. C.I: *Schusta 1, 2, 3, 4, 17,* and *21.*

The characteristics of these aircraft are described below.

Albatros C.III

The Albatros C.III was a two seat armed biplane second generation C Class general purpose reconnaissance/bomber that entered service with the *Fliegertruppe* in February 1916 and served to August 1917. The number of Albatros C.III

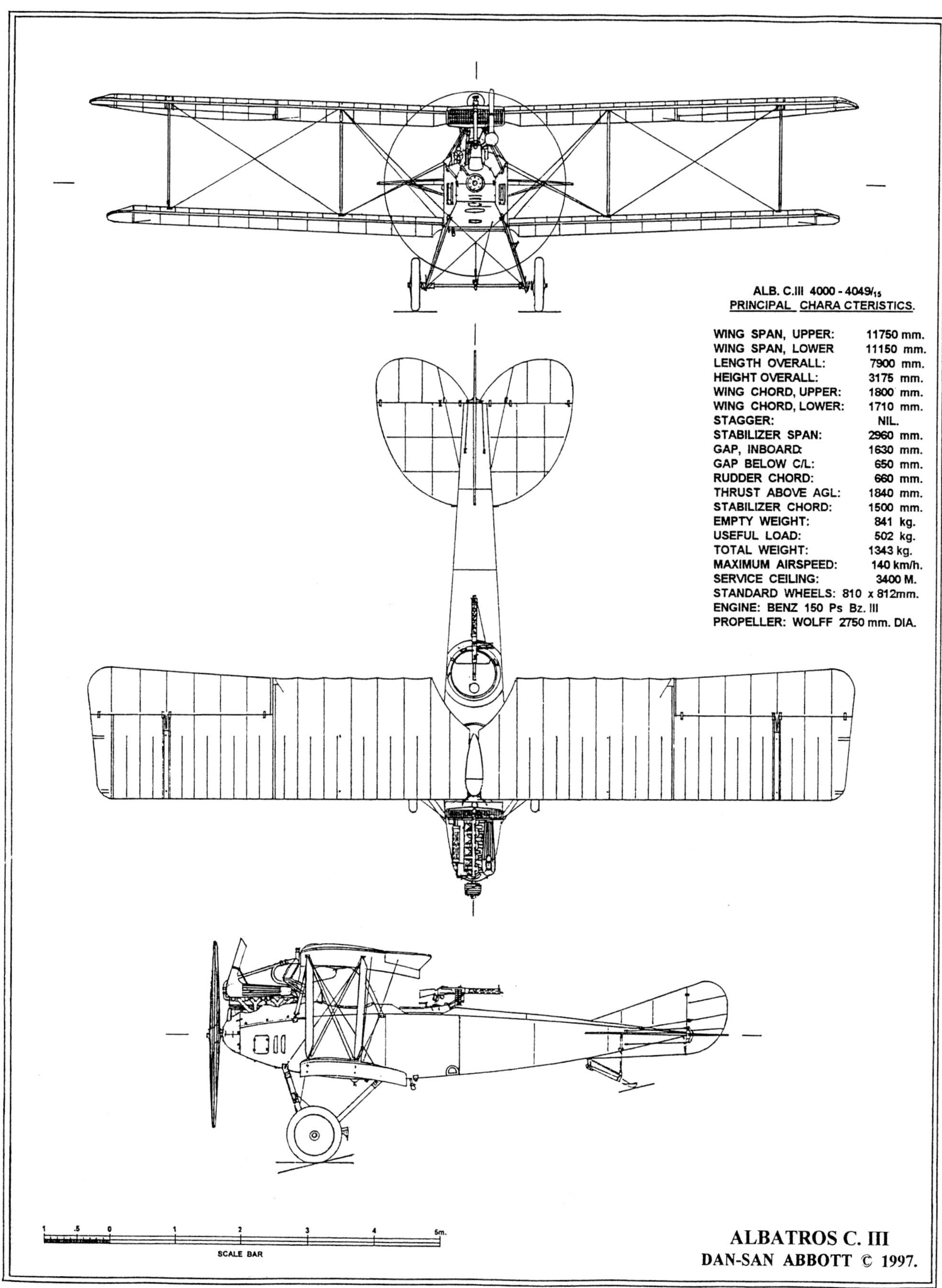
ALB. C.III 4000 - 4049/15
PRINCIPAL CHARACTERISTICS.
WING SPAN, UPPER: 11750 mm.
WING SPAN, LOWER 11150 mm.
LENGTH OVERALL: 7900 mm.
HEIGHT OVERALL: 3175 mm.
WING CHORD, UPPER: 1800 mm.
WING CHORD, LOWER: 1710 mm.
STAGGER: NIL.
STABILIZER SPAN: 2960 mm.
GAP, INBOARD: 1630 mm.
GAP BELOW C/L: 650 mm.
RUDDER CHORD: 660 mm.
THRUST ABOVE AGL: 1840 mm.
STABILIZER CHORD: 1500 mm.
EMPTY WEIGHT: 841 kg.
USEFUL LOAD: 502 kg.
TOTAL WEIGHT: 1343 kg.
MAXIMUM AIRSPEED: 140 km/h.
SERVICE CEILING: 3400 M.
STANDARD WHEELS: 810 x 812mm.
ENGINE: BENZ 150 Ps Bz. III
PROPELLER: WOLFF 2750 mm. DIA.
1 .5 0 1 2 3 4 5m.
SCALE BAR
ALBATROS C. III
DAN-SAN ABBOTT © 1997.

aircraft employed at the front reached a peak of 354 aircraft in August 1916.

It was of wooden construction with a minimal number of steel fittings, having a birch plywood covered fuselage and fabric covered wings and tail surfaces. It was first ordered in November 1915. Deliveries began in January 1916 and were completed around the end of September 1916. Those that served in the *Schutzstaffeln* were of the later production in 1916.

They were powered with either the 160 Ps Mercedes D.III or the 150 Ps Benz Bz.III engine. The upper wingspan measured 11,750mm and the lower 11,150mm. The fuselage length was 7900mm and the height was 3175mm. It had an empty weight of 851 kg and the useful load was 502 kg bringing the total weight to 1353 kg. The aircraft had a service ceiling of 3400 meters and a maximum speed of 140 km/hr. The Albatros C.III could stay aloft for four hours at a speed of 135 km/hr and had a range of 540 kilometers. Its bomb capacity was 60 kg.

The Albatros C.III was also built by the subsidiary of the Albatros Werke, Ostdeutsche Albatros Werke (OAW), Schneidemühl, and by the Bayerische Flugzeug Werke (BFW) in München. The Albatros and BFW-built Alb. C.III machines were finished with a shellacked and copal varnished plywood fuselage and lower fin, resulting in a warm straw color. The fabric surfaces were clear doped and given a coat of waterproofing varnish, making the wings somewhat translucent and lending them a pale beige color when covered with unbleached linen or a yellowish white color for bleached linen. The struts, cowlings, and metal parts were painted a light grey color. The early OAW-built Alb. C.III machines were finished in the same manner as the Albatros-built C.III aircraft. The camouflage scheme for the Albatros C.III was applied in conformance with a direct order issued by the *Inspektion der Fliegertruppen* (*Idflieg),* Inspectorate of Military Aviation in July 1916. Accordingly, 100 Alb. C.III (OAW), serial numbers C.2274 - 2373/16, were camouflaged in the Terrain/Sky Scheme of deep green, light green, and burnt sienna on the top and side surfaces, with pale blue for the under surfaces of the wings, fuselage, and tailplane. All other parts, struts, cowlings, radiator, plumbing, and fittings were painted a light grey color.

There were more than 3400 Alb. C.III aircraft built, including those constructed in 1917 and 1918 as trainers. The Alb. C.III served with *Schusta 19* and *21*. They were withdrawn from *Schusta* service after April 1917.

Albatros C.V

The Albatros C.V was of the third generation of C Class aircraft and was fitted with the new 220 Ps geared Mercedes D.IV in-line eight cylinder engine. *Idflieg* placed the production order with the Albatros Werke in March 1916 for 200 Alb. C.V, and later reduced the total to 75 machines. Serial numbers C.1175 - 1224/16 and C.1251 - 1275/16 were built by OAW. The Alb. C.V was a fast airplane for the C Class, with a maximum airspeed of 170 km/hr (105.4 mph). It is most likely that it was the 1917 redesigned and improved version of the Alb. C.V that were delivered to the *Schutzstaffeln* in March 1917. An example of a unit known to have been equipped with this aircraft is *Schusta 27b*. Albatros received an order from *Idflieg* for 50 Alb. C.V in January 1917, serial numbers C.1371 - 1420/17. The redesigned Alb. C.V had all control surfaces balanced and the formerly raked angular wing tips were given an elliptical form on the lower wing.

All the Alb. C.V aircraft in this production order were camouflaged in the Terrain/Sky Scheme. The colors used by Albatros were pale greenish grey, olive green, and rust brown on the upper surfaces of the wings, tailplane, and rudder. The undersurface of the wings, tailplane, and wheel covers were pale sky blue. The fuselage and fin were covered with birch plywood and were shellacked and varnished producing a warm straw color. All the struts, spinner, cowlings, and fittings were painted light grey.

The Albatros C.V had an upper wingspan of 12,620mm, while the lower measured 12,120mm. The overall length was 8950mm and the height was 3450mm. The empty weight was 1069 kg and the useful load 561 kg, so that the total combined weight came to 1630 kg. The aircraft's maximum airspeed at sea level was 170 km/hr. The service ceiling was 5200 meters. The C.V had a flight duration of 3.25 hours at a speed of 150 km/hr. Mounted in front of the pilot was a 7.92mm caliber Maxim IMG 08 with 500 rounds of ammunition. The observer manned a 7.92mm Parabellum Modell 14 *Luftgekühlt* (air-cooled) machine gun mounted on an LVG Franz Schneider wood turret. The bomb capacity was 200 kg. The Albatros C.V served with *Schusta 27b* and was withdrawn after March 1917.

Albatros C.VI

In May 1916 the Albatros Werke received an order from *Idflieg* for seventy-five Alb. C.VI, serial numbers C.1775 - 1849/16. The airframe was identical to the Alb. C.III except for minor dimensional differences so that the engine compartment could be fitted with the 180 Ps Argus As.III engine. The upper wingspan of the Albatros C.VI measured 11,700mm and the lower span 11,150mm. The length was 7900mm. All other dimensions were the same as those of the Alb. C.III. The empty

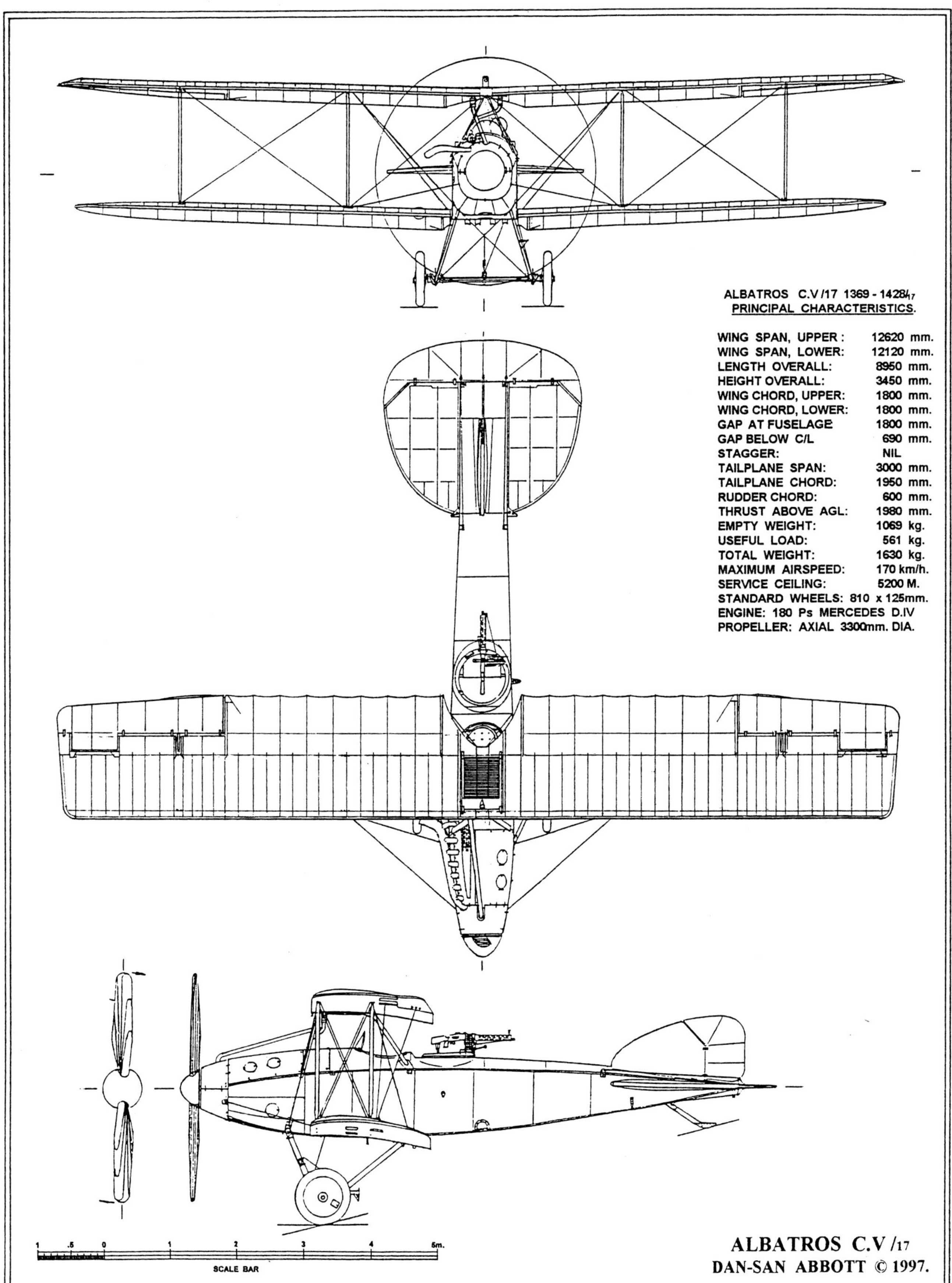
ALBATROS C.V/17 1369 - 1428/17
PRINCIPAL CHARACTERISTICS.
WING SPAN, UPPER: 12620 mm.
WING SPAN, LOWER: 12120 mm.
LENGTH OVERALL: 8950 mm.
HEIGHT OVERALL: 3450 mm.
WING CHORD, UPPER: 1800 mm.
WING CHORD, LOWER: 1800 mm.
GAP AT FUSELAGE 1800 mm.
GAP BELOW C/L 690 mm.
STAGGER: NIL
TAILPLANE SPAN: 3000 mm.
TAILPLANE CHORD: 1950 mm.
RUDDER CHORD: 600 mm.
THRUST ABOVE AGL: 1980 mm.
EMPTY WEIGHT: 1069 kg.
USEFUL LOAD: 561 kg.
TOTAL WEIGHT: 1630 kg.
MAXIMUM AIRSPEED: 170 km/h.
SERVICE CEILING: 5200 M.
STANDARD WHEELS: 810 x 125mm.
ENGINE: 180 Ps MERCEDES D.IV
PROPELLER: AXIAL 3300mm. DIA.
1 .5 0 1 2 3 4 5m.
SCALE BAR
ALBATROS C.V /17
DAN-SAN ABBOTT © 1997.

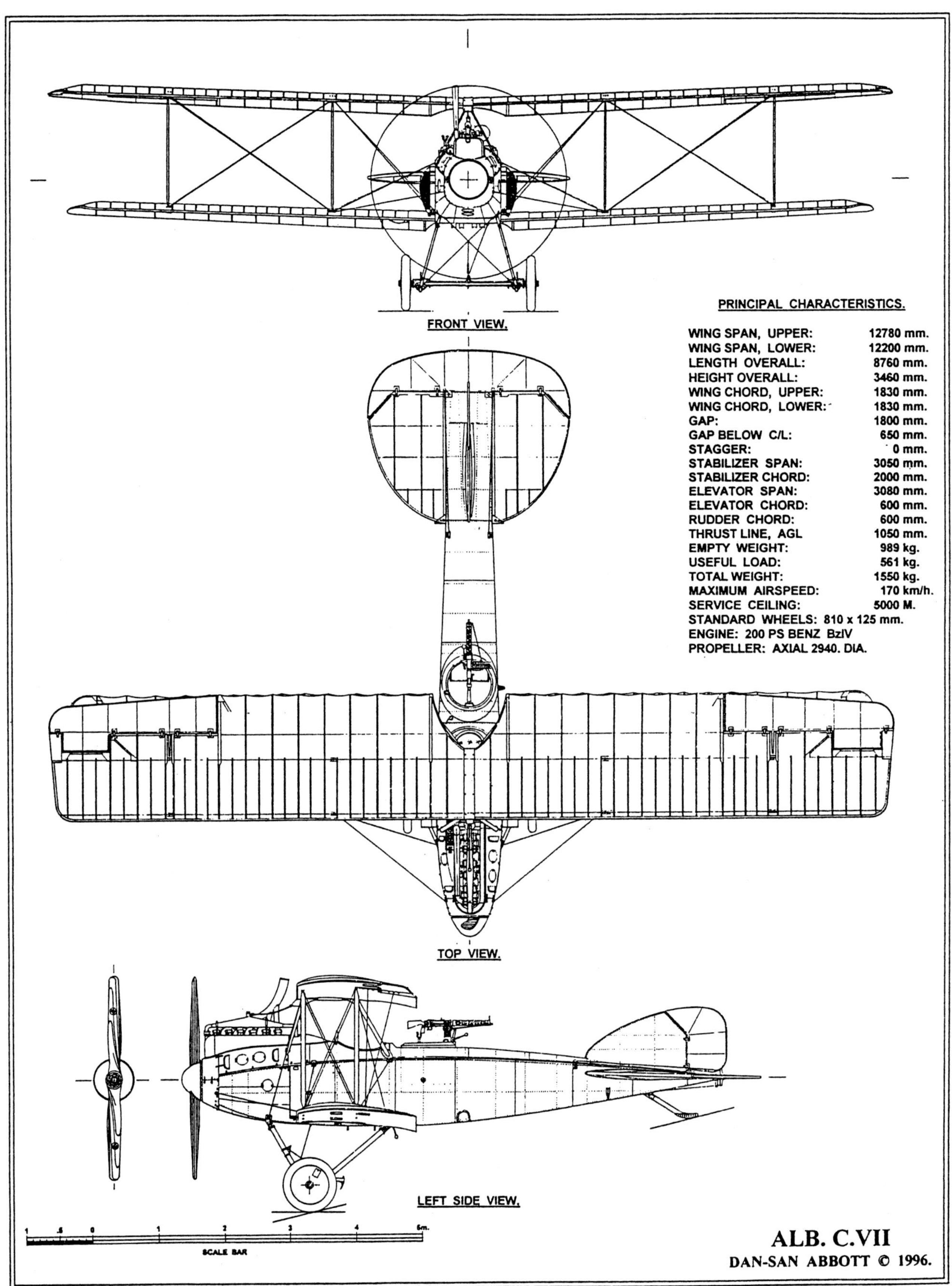
FRONT VIEW.
PRINCIPAL CHARACTERISTICS.
WING SPAN, UPPER: 12780 mm.
WING SPAN, LOWER: 12200 mm.
LENGTH OVERALL: 8760 mm.
HEIGHT OVERALL: 3460 mm.
WING CHORD, UPPER: 1830 mm.
WING CHORD, LOWER: 1830 mm.
GAP: 1800 mm.
GAP BELOW C/L: 650 mm.
STAGGER: 0 mm.
STABILIZER SPAN: 3050 mm.
STABILIZER CHORD: 2000 mm.
ELEVATOR SPAN: 3080 mm.
ELEVATOR CHORD: 600 mm.
RUDDER CHORD: 600 mm.
THRUST LINE, AGL 1050 mm.
EMPTY WEIGHT: 989 kg.
USEFUL LOAD: 561 kg.
TOTAL WEIGHT: 1550 kg.
MAXIMUM AIRSPEED: 170 km/h.
SERVICE CEILING: 5000 M.
STANDARD WHEELS: 810 x 125 mm.
ENGINE: 200 PS BENZ BzIV
PROPELLER: AXIAL 2940. DIA.
TOP VIEW.
LEFT SIDE VIEW.
1 .5 0 1 2 3 4 6m.
SCALE BAR
ALB. C.VII
DAN-SAN ABBOTT © 1996.

weight was 830 kg and the useful load was 513 kg, for a combined weight of 1343 kg. The aircraft had a service ceiling of 4000 meters. At sea level its maximum airspeed was 145 km/hr. The flight duration was 3.2 hours at 140 km/hr. The armament was the same as the Alb. C.III, but it had a maximum bomb load of 100 kg. The Alb. C.VI was finished identical to the Alb. C.III aircraft. The Alb. C.VI served with *Schusta 27b* and was withdrawn from service after April 1917.

Albatros C.VII

The Alb. C.VII was in production simultaneously with the Alb. C.V. The initial order of 200 machines was divided between by the Alb. C.V and Alb. C.VII, of which 125 were the Alb. C.VII, with serial numbers C.1225 - 1250/16 and C.1276 - 1374/16. The Alb. C.VII was powered with the in-line six cylinder 200 Ps Benz Bz IV engine. The Alb. C.VII became the workhorse for the *Fliegertruppe*, and was used on all fronts during 1916-18. The aircraft served in *Fl.Abt., Fl.Abt.(A), Kasta*, and *Schusta* with good results. It was stable and easy to fly.

The upper wings of the Albatros C.VII had a span of 12,780mm and the lower wingspan was 12,200mm. The aircraft's length was 8760mm and its height 3460mm. The empty weight was 989 kg and the useful load was 561 kg. The combined weight was therefore 1550 kg. The Alb. C.VII had a maximum airspeed of 170 km/hr and its service ceiling was 5000 m. It had an endurance of 3.3 hours at 165 km/hr. The armament consisted of one synchronized 7.92mm caliber Maxim lMG 08 machine gun with 500 rounds of ammunition for the pilot and, mounted on a LVG Schneider wood turret for the gunner, a 7.92mm caliber Parabellum Modell 14 machine gun with three drums of 250 rounds of ammunition per drum in the rear cockpit. The bomb load 200 kg.

The total production of the Alb. C.VII from the Albatros Werke, Ostdeutsche Albatros Werke, and Bayern Flugzeug Werke was approximately 781 machines – 281 built by Albatros, 350 by OAW, and 150 by BFW. All the machines were delivered in the Terrain Camouflage Scheme, except for the initial production order of BFW.

Albatros used five different patterns of pale greyish green, olive green, and rust brown on the upper surfaces of the wings, tailplane, and rudder, with pale sky blue under surfaces. The plywood fuselage and fin were shellacked and varnished resulting in a warm straw yellow. All metal parts were painted light grey.

The Alb. C.VII (OAW) were camouflaged in two patterns with slight variations in light green, deep green, and burnt sienna on the upper surfaces of the wings, tailplane, and rudder. The under surfaces of the wings, tailplane, and wheel covers were pale blue. The plywood surfaces of the fuselage and fin were shellacked and varnished presenting a warm straw color. The spinner, cowlings, struts, and all fittings were pale grey.

The first order of BFW-built Alb. C.VII (BFW), C.3000 - 3074/16, were finished in the Sky Camouflage Scheme with clear doped fabric surfaces of yellowish white with shellacked and varnished plywood and fin in a straw-yellow. All metal parts were light grey. With the second order for twenty-five Alb. C.VII (BFW), C.7000 - 7024/16, BFW introduced an all-over banded pattern camouflage of deep greyish green and brown on all upper and side surfaces and sky blue on the under surfaces.

The Albatros C.VII equipped several *Schutzstaffeln* upon their conversion from the *Kampfstaffeln*. Among these were *Schusta 4* and *21* to April 1917, *Schusta 17* to February 1917, *Schusta 19, 20,* and *23b* to at least February 1917 and *Schusta 24b* and *27b* to May 1917.

LFG Roland C.II

The Roland C.II was the *Fliegertruppe* "hot rod" of 1916 for a C Class reconnaissance and light bomber aircraft. It was fast, in fact, as fast as most contemporary fighter aircraft of the time. It was maneuverable, with large control surfaces and with ailerons on the upper wings only. The Rol. C.II was a radical design with the fuselage filling the gap between the wings. The Roland engineers were very inventive, and produced a structure that was both light and streamlined which gave the Rol. C.II, powered with the new 160 Ps Mercedes D.III engine, a good turn of speed. The aircraft was nick-named *Walfisch* (Whale) for its rotund fuselage. The Rol. C.II was ordered by *Idflieg* after having demonstrated its superior performance over other C Class machines then in service. *Idflieg* ordered 50 Rol. C.II, serial numbers C.4413 - 4462/15, on 23 December 1915. This was followed by a second order in March 1916 for 25 aircraft, numbers C.999 - 1023/16.

After having passed its type tests in February 1916, production deliveries commenced. The *Walfisch* entered service with the *Fliegertruppe* in March 1916, and equipped the *Fl.Abt., Fl.Abt.(A), Kasta*, and *Schusta*, and served with distinction until June 1917. It was an airplane which when flown by a good pilot performed excellently, but a novice would have his hands full. The Roland C.II had upper wings spanning 10,300mm, while the lower wing had a span of 10,030mm. The length of the aircraft was 7700mm and the height 2860mm. Its empty weight was 789 kg and he useful load 520 kg, for a total weight of 1309 kg. Its bomb load was 100 kg. The service ceiling was 4500 meters. The *Walfisch* had a flight duration of 5.5 hours and its range was 825 km. Its armament consisted of one synchronized forward firing,

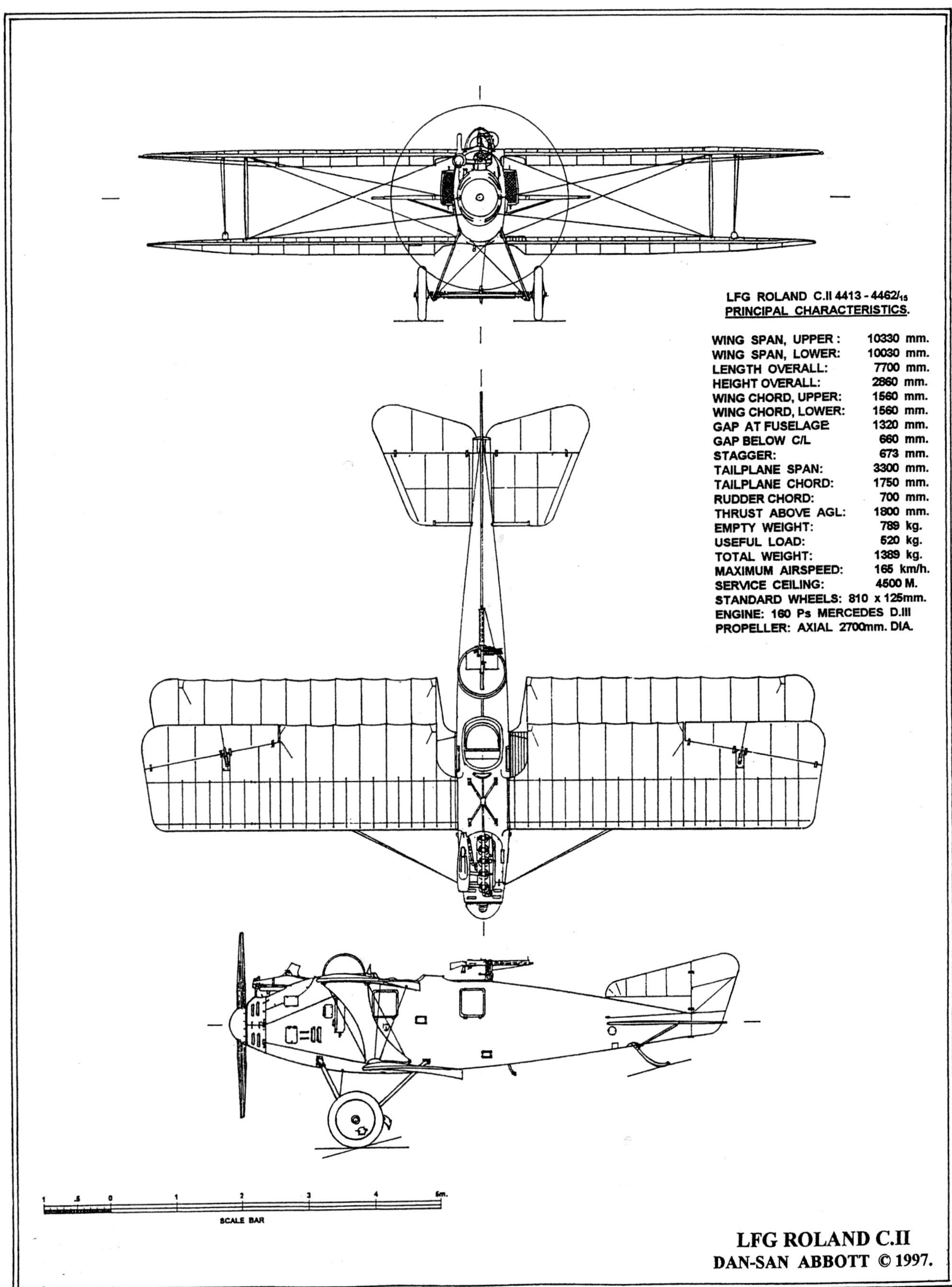
LFG ROLAND C.II 4413 - 4462/15
PRINCIPAL CHARACTERISTICS.
WING SPAN, UPPER : 10330 mm.
WING SPAN, LOWER: 10030 mm.
LENGTH OVERALL: 7700 mm.
HEIGHT OVERALL: 2860 mm.
WING CHORD, UPPER: 1560 mm.
WING CHORD, LOWER: 1560 mm.
GAP AT FUSELAGE 1320 mm.
GAP BELOW C/L 660 mm.
STAGGER: 673 mm.
TAILPLANE SPAN: 3300 mm.
TAILPLANE CHORD: 1750 mm.
RUDDER CHORD: 700 mm.
THRUST ABOVE AGL: 1800 mm.
EMPTY WEIGHT: 789 kg.
USEFUL LOAD: 520 kg.
TOTAL WEIGHT: 1389 kg.
MAXIMUM AIRSPEED: 165 km/h.
SERVICE CEILING: 4500 M.
STANDARD WHEELS: 810 x 125mm.
ENGINE: 160 Ps MERCEDES D.III
PROPELLER: AXIAL 2700mm. DIA.
1 .5 0 1 2 3 4 5m.
SCALE BAR
LFG ROLAND C.II
DAN-SAN ABBOTT © 1997.

fixed Maxim 7.92mm lMG 08 machine gun for the pilot and mounted in the gunner's cockpit on a LVG Schneider wood turret was a 7.92mm Parabellum Modell 14 machine gun.

LFG redesigned the aileron control system and made some improvements to lighten the airframe, and reduced the lower wing-span. The span of the lower wing was shortened to 9600mm and the empty weight decreased to 714 kg. The reduced useful load was 500 kg providing a new total weight of 1214 kg. These changes occurred in a production order for 100 Rol. C.II machines numbers C.1600 - 1699/16. Modification began with aircraft serial number C.1664/16, and the designation was changed to Rol. C.IIa. LFG Roland received two orders from *Idflieg* for 40 LFG Rol. C.IIa, serial numbers C.2700 - 2739/16, and some unknown quantity, most likely 40 serial numbers C.2800 - 2839/16. The machines in these two orders incorporated the last alteration, an enlarged fin and rudder, to improve the directional control. With this modification, the empty weight was altered to 764 kg, the useful load to 520 kg, and total weight became 1284 kg.

Idflieg awarded a license agreement to Linke-Hofmann A.G. of Breslau, a manufacturer of railway carriages and rolling stock. The first order was in July 1916, for twelve Rol. C.IIa (LiHo), serial numbers C.1851 - 1862/16. A second order was awarded in September 1916, for forty more, serial numbers C.3624 - 3663/16. Both orders were for the initial Rol. C.IIa with the original style fin and rudder.

The Rol. C.II machines in the first two orders were painted in the Sky Camouflage Scheme of pale bluish white all over. Commencing with the third order, LFG Roland introduced their Terrain/Sky Camouflage Scheme of chestnut brown and light greyish green on the top and side surfaces and pale bluish white on the under surfaces. Linke-Hofmann painted the aircraft in both orders on the top and side surfaces, burnt sienna and pastel greyish green and bluish white on the under surfaces. The fin and rudder were painted white.

Assuming all orders were completed, LFG Roland built 139 Rol. C.II machines and 168 Rol. C.IIa aircraft were made by both manufacturers. The Rol. C.II or C.IIa served with *Schusta 2, 6, 11, 15, 17, 21, 24b, 26b, 27b* and *28b*. By June 1917 all Rol. C.II aircraft had been withdrawn from the front and replaced with improved new designs.

Rumpler C.I

The Rumpler C.I was one of the few aircraft that remained in production from its maiden flight to the end of the war, first as a combat aircraft and later as a trainer. It was derived from the Rumpler B.I, a pre-war unarmed reconnaissance aircraft. The Rumpler engineers paid close attention to details and designed a superb aircraft as a reconnaissance-light bomber. It was powered with the new 160 Ps Mercedes D.III or the 150 Ps Benz Bz.III. The Ru. C.I demonstrated a very good airspeed of 152 km/hr at sea level and a very good rate of climb that surpassed the *Idflieg* requirements. It so impressed *Idflieg* that in July 1915 they awarded the Rumpler-Werke GmbH an order for fifty Ru. C.I, C.393 - 442/15. Other orders followed in July 1915 for 42 Ru. C.I, C.1025 - 1066/15, and then 20 more, C.1580 - 1599/15. In October 1915, Rumpler-Werke received their fourth order for fifty-one more, serial numbers C.1836 - 1886/15. The last order in 1915 was for 150 Ru. C.I, C.4515 - 4664/15. The first order in 1916 for the Ru. C.I was for fifty Ru. C.I, C.50 - 99/16 in January 1916. The last order that Rumpler-Werke received for the Ru. C.I was in March 1916, for 150 Ru. C.I, C.1125 - 1174/16 and C.2600 - 2699/16.

A Roland C.II *Walfisch* of an unknown *Schutzstaffel* that has seen better days. Crew, unit and date are all unknown.

All of the production Ru. C.I aircraft thereafter were of license manufacture. The first order went to the Hannoversche Waggonfabrik AG, which produced 200 as combat aircraft. These were designated as Ru. C.Ia(Han), with serial numbers C.4600 - 4799/16. All of the Hannoversche built Ru. C.Ia aircraft were powered with the 180 Ps Argus As.III engine. All Ru. C.I machines ordered after this were for the trainer version only and production continued into 1918.

The service ceiling was 5000 meters. The upper and lower wingspans measured 12,150mm and 10,040mm, respectively. The C.I had a length of 7850mm and a height of 3060mm. The empty weight of 793 kg and useful load of 540 kg brought the aircraft's total weight to 1333 kg. The armament was one fixed forward firing synchronized Maxim lMG 08 with 500 rounds of 7.92mm caliber ammunition operated by the pilot, and one Parabellum Modell 14 and three drums each of 250 rounds operated by the gunner in the rear cockpit. The bomb load was 100 kg.

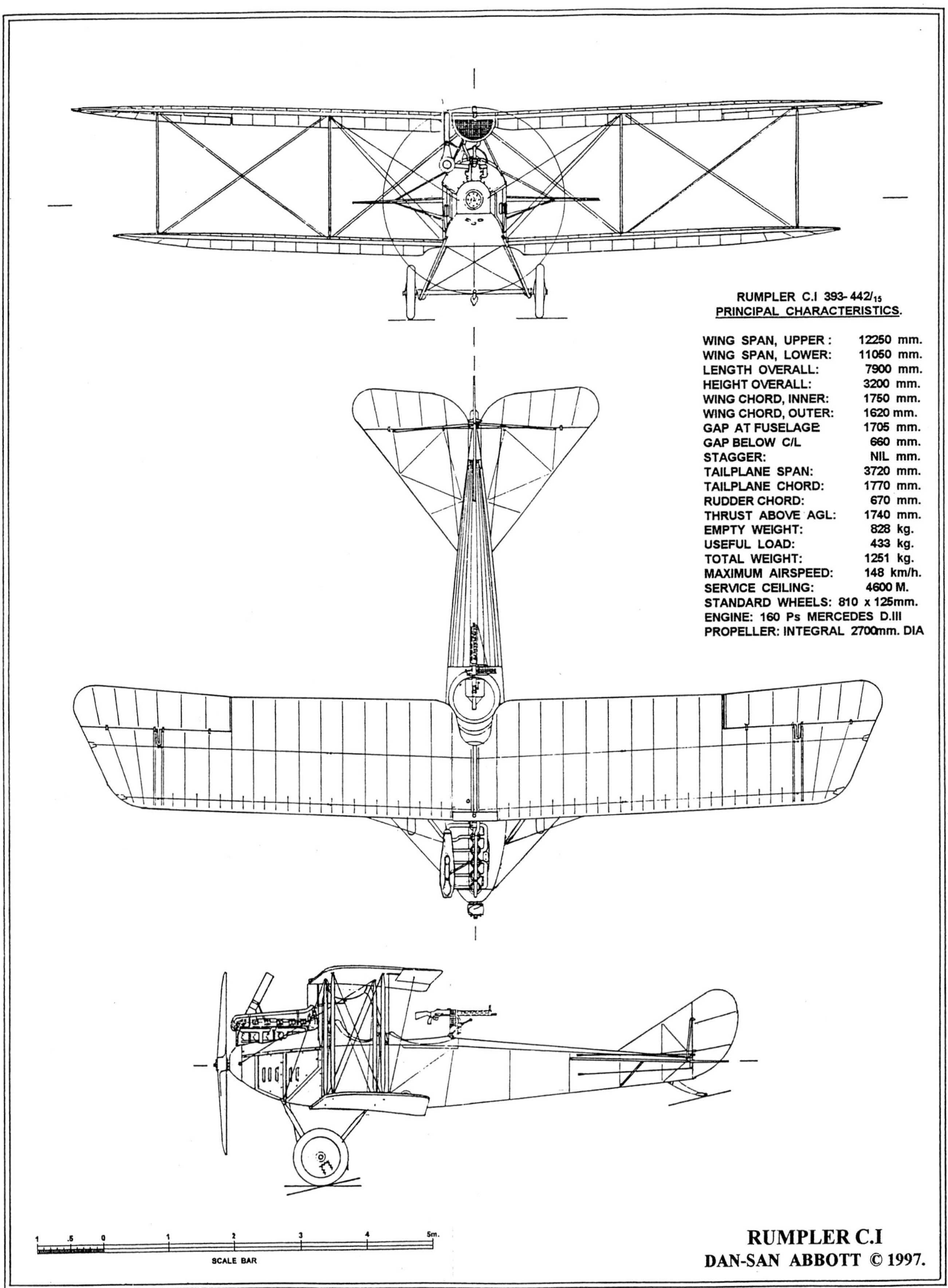
RUMPLER C.I 393-442/15
PRINCIPAL CHARACTERISTICS.
WING SPAN, UPPER: 12250 mm.
WING SPAN, LOWER: 11050 mm.
LENGTH OVERALL: 7900 mm.
HEIGHT OVERALL: 3200 mm.
WING CHORD, INNER: 1750 mm.
WING CHORD, OUTER: 1620 mm.
GAP AT FUSELAGE: 1705 mm.
GAP BELOW C/L: 660 mm.
STAGGER: NIL mm.
TAILPLANE SPAN: 3720 mm.
TAILPLANE CHORD: 1770 mm.
RUDDER CHORD: 670 mm.
THRUST ABOVE AGL: 1740 mm.
EMPTY WEIGHT: 828 kg.
USEFUL LOAD: 433 kg.
TOTAL WEIGHT: 1251 kg.
MAXIMUM AIRSPEED: 148 km/h.
SERVICE CEILING: 4600 M.
STANDARD WHEELS: 810 x 125mm.
ENGINE: 160 Ps MERCEDES D.III
PROPELLER: INTEGRAL 2700mm. DIA
1 .5 0 1 2 3 4 5m.
SCALE BAR
RUMPLER C.I
DAN-SAN ABBOTT © 1997.

The Ru. C.I aircraft of the first order, serial numbers C.393 - 442/15, were finished in a Sky Camouflage Scheme of overall yellowish white, of translucent clear doped and varnished fabric surfaces with all other parts of the aircraft painted to match the fabric surfaces. All Ru. C.I aircraft ordered in 1915 were finished in the same scheme. Commencing with the first 1916 order for fifty, serial numbers C.50 - 99/16, the Ru. C.I were camouflaged in a translucent overall bluish white on the fabric and other parts painted to match. The fore and aft plywood panels on the fuselage were in a natural shellac varnish finish.

All the Hannoversche Waggonfabrik-built Ru. C.Ia machines were camouflaged in the Terrain/Sky Scheme of sprayed reddish brown and light greyish green with very pale blue under surfaces. Delivery of the Ru. C.Ia began in November 1916. The Ru. C.I equipped *Schusta 1, 2, 3, 4, 6, 14, 16*, and *21*. By May 1917 all Ru. C.I aircraft had been replaced with either the AEG C.IV, Albatros C.VII, or the DFW C.V.

CHAPTER XXI

REPLACEMENT AIRCRAFT

In early 1917, new and improved C Class machines began to arrive at the front. As they became available, they replaced lost or damaged aircraft in the *Schutzstaffeln*. As production of these new aircraft began to fill the pipeline, units began to convert over to the new types. The first to arrive was the Aviatik C.III.

Aviatik C.III

In March 1917 *Schusta 8* was re-equipped with the Aviatik C.III (Av. C.III). In April 1916 *Idflieg* had placed an order with Automobil und Aviatik A.G. of Leipzig-Heiterblick for twenty-five Aviatik C.III, serial numbers C.1750 - 1774/16. A second order with Aviatik was placed in July 1916 for an additional twenty-five Av. C.III aircraft. The Av. C.III was a cleaned-up and slightly smaller version of the Av. C.I. It was of all wooden construction with fabric covering and had a streamlined nose tapering into a spinner. The upper span was 11,800mm and the lower span, 10,200mm. It had an overall length of 8080mm and the height was 2950mm. It was powered with a 170 Ps Mercedes D.IIIa engine. It had an empty weight of 980 kg, which with a useful load of 360 kg brought the aircraft total weight to 1340 kg. Its maximum airspeed was 160 km/hr at sea level. The Aviatik C.III had a flight duration of three hours and its service ceiling was 4500 meters. Its armament consisted of two Parabellum Modell 14, 7.92mm caliber machine guns positioned on Geyer steel tubular rails mounted on both sides of the front gunner's cockpit. This was a less than satisfactory arrangement and was a major shortcoming of the design of this aircraft. The design flaw was quickly corrected and the gunner's cockpit was moved to the rear with the machine guns mounted on a wood Schneider turret. There was no capacity to carry bombs.

All Av. C.III aircraft were finished in the Sky Camouflage Scheme of clear doped and varnished linen fabric with all struts, spinner, cowlings, plywood paneling, and metal parts painted yellowish white to match the fabric surfaces. The Av. C.III service life was short with *Schusta 8*, and they were replaced with the superb DFW C.V by May 1917.

AEG C.IV

In April 1917 *Idflieg* began issuing the AEG C.IV to the *Schusta*. In some cases they replaced the older machines. In other cases they served as replacements for lost or severely damaged aircraft. This was also a second generation aircraft powered with the 160 Ps Mercedes D.III engine on the early orders and the improved 170 Ps D.IIIa engine on all subsequent orders. The AEG C.IV was a product of the Allgemeine Elektrizitäts Gesellschaft, AEG (General Electric Company) located at Henningsdorf, near Berlin. AEG was established in 1910 when it set up the *Flugtechnische Abteilung* (Flight Technical Department). AEG designed and manufactured a series of biplane designs, the AEG B types that culminated in the C.I to C.III single engine biplane and leading to the successful AEG C.IV and G Class twin engine bombers.

The AEG C.IV was unique in that the airframe was constructed entirely of welded steel tubing, except for the wing ribs and the leading edge of the main wing panels, which were wood. The only other wood in the airframe was the rear plywood turtle-deck and the floors in the front and rear cockpits. The entire aircraft was covered with linen fabric and had aluminum cowlings on the engine bay. The main fuel tank was under the pilot's seat and the reserve tank in the upper center-section.

The armament of the AEG C.IV was comprised of the synchronized Maxim lMG 08, 7.92mm caliber machine gun for the pilot, mounted on the right side of the engine, with the Parabellum Modell 14 air-cooled machine gun for the gunner, mounted on an AEG track in the rear gunner's cockpit. On the right side of the gunner's cockpit on the floor was a rack for stowing horizontally four 12.5 kg P.u.W. bombs that could be dropped individually, or in train through the belly of the aircraft. The upper wingspan of the AEG C.IV measured 13,000mm and the lower 12,500mm. It had a length of 7200mm and a height of 3300mm. The aircraft had an empty weight of 800 kg and a useful load of 520 kg. The total weight was therefore 1320 kg.

The total production of the AEG C.IV by the Allgemeine Elektrizitäts Gesellschaft was 495 aircraft. An order for 200 was placed in March 1916, serial numbers C.1024 - 1123/16 and in October, a further 100 were ordered with serial numbers C.6575 - 6674/16. Two hundred and eighty three AEG C.IV machines were ordered in 1917. In April a batch of 100 were produced, serial numbers C.1700 - 1799/17, followed in May by 100 more, C.4800 - 4899/17. July saw an order for 75 aircraft, serial numbers C.7050 - 7124/17. Finally, in December 1917 an order was placed for eight "tropical prepared" aircraft with unknown serial numbers. The tropical AEG C.IV had an enlarged capacity radiator installed in order to deal with the higher temperatures experienced in the Middle East. Twenty-five machines of this order, serial numbers C.7100 - 7124/17, were designated the AEG C.IV v.R., *verlängerter Rumpf* (lengthened fuselage). The fuselage was lengthened by inserting a 600mm bay forward of the tailplane. This was done to improve the landing characteristics and handling of the AEG C.IV. Pilots had found that the short fuselage made the AEG C.IV difficult to land and this resulted in numerous landing accidents. The final order was for twelve additional tropical prepared AEG C.IV, serials C.1100 - 1111/18.

The Fokker Flugzeugwerke G.m.b.H. was awarded a contract in January 1917 to produce the AEG C.IV under license as the AEG C.IV (Fok.). They were to be used as training aircraft. The order was for 200 AEG C.IV (Fok.), serial numbers C.240 - 439/17. Because of the shortfall of the 160 Ps Mercedes D.III engines, these Fokker- built machines were to be powered with the 180 Ps Argus As III. To keep Fokker Werke busy, *Idflieg* placed a second order in June 1917 for 200 additional AEG C.IV (Fok.) training aircraft, serial numbers C.6500 - 6699/17. However, only 100 of these machines were built, C.6500 - 6599/17, and the production of the remaining order was canceled in favor of committing the Fokker production capability to the Fokker DR.I.

The camouflage finish of the AEG C.IV of the first order, C.1024 - 1123/16, was in the Terrain Camouflage Scheme of greyish green and raw sienna on the top and side surfaces in a sprayed interlocking irregular pattern, with a pastel greyish blue on the under surfaces. However part of this order, approximately twenty-five AEG C.IV machines, in the serial number range of C.1099 - 1123/16, were delivered with clear doped and varnished fabric surfaces in a greyish yellow color. The matte black Iron Crosses were painted on square flat white cross fields.

The second order of the AEG C.IV aircraft, serial numbers C.6575 - 6674/16, were camouflaged in the same manner, colors, and irregular patterns as the first order. During the course of production, the white cross fields were eliminated and were replaced by a 50mm wide border surrounding the Iron Crosses. This occurred between C.6590 and 6674/16. All Iron Crosses subsequently were surrounded with a 50mm wide white border.

Commencing with at least AEG C.IV 6602/16, a third color was added to the Terrain Camouflage Scheme. It is thought to be greyish ruby and that this change in the camouflage scheme coincided with *Idflieg* directive Flz. A. 3356263, which required elimination of the red and red-brown colors from the camouflage schemes and the substitution of lilac for those colors. The change was the result of German pilots mistaking German aircraft for Allied Powers aircraft and shooting them down. It is believed that the AEG C.IV camouflage colors were greyish green, dark green, and greyish ruby.

For the third order, serial numbers C.1700 - 1799/17, a fourth color was added to the Terrain Camouflage Scheme on the top and side surfaces. This is thought to be lilac added to greyish green, dark green, and greyish ruby. The under surfaces were pastel blue. The fourth order, AEG C.IV, C.4800 - 4899/17, and the fifth order, C.7050 - 7124/17, reverted to a two-color Terrain Scheme for the upper and side surfaces. The two colors were greyish green and lilac with pastel blue under surfaces.

Fokker Flugzeugwerke had developed their own Terrain Camouflage Scheme, which was olive brown paint applied in light to dark streaking on the top and side surfaces. On the top surfaces the streaking was slightly diagonal on the wings, diagonal on the top of the fuselage and tailplane, vertical on the sides of the fuselage and fin and crosswise on the rudder. The under surfaces were painted sky blue with a varnish top coat which, because of its yellowish cast, resulted in a color shift to turquoise.

Schusta 6 and *7* received the AEG C.IV in June 1917, *Schusta 12* in July, *Schusta 13* in May, while *Schusta 24b* received the AEG C.IV in April 1917 and turned them in for DFW C.V aircaft. *Schusta 27b* used AEG C.IV machines alongside the DFW C.V from June to September. The AEG C.IV was issued to *Schusta 37* in February 1918 as initial equipment and were replaced in March by the Halb. Cl.II.

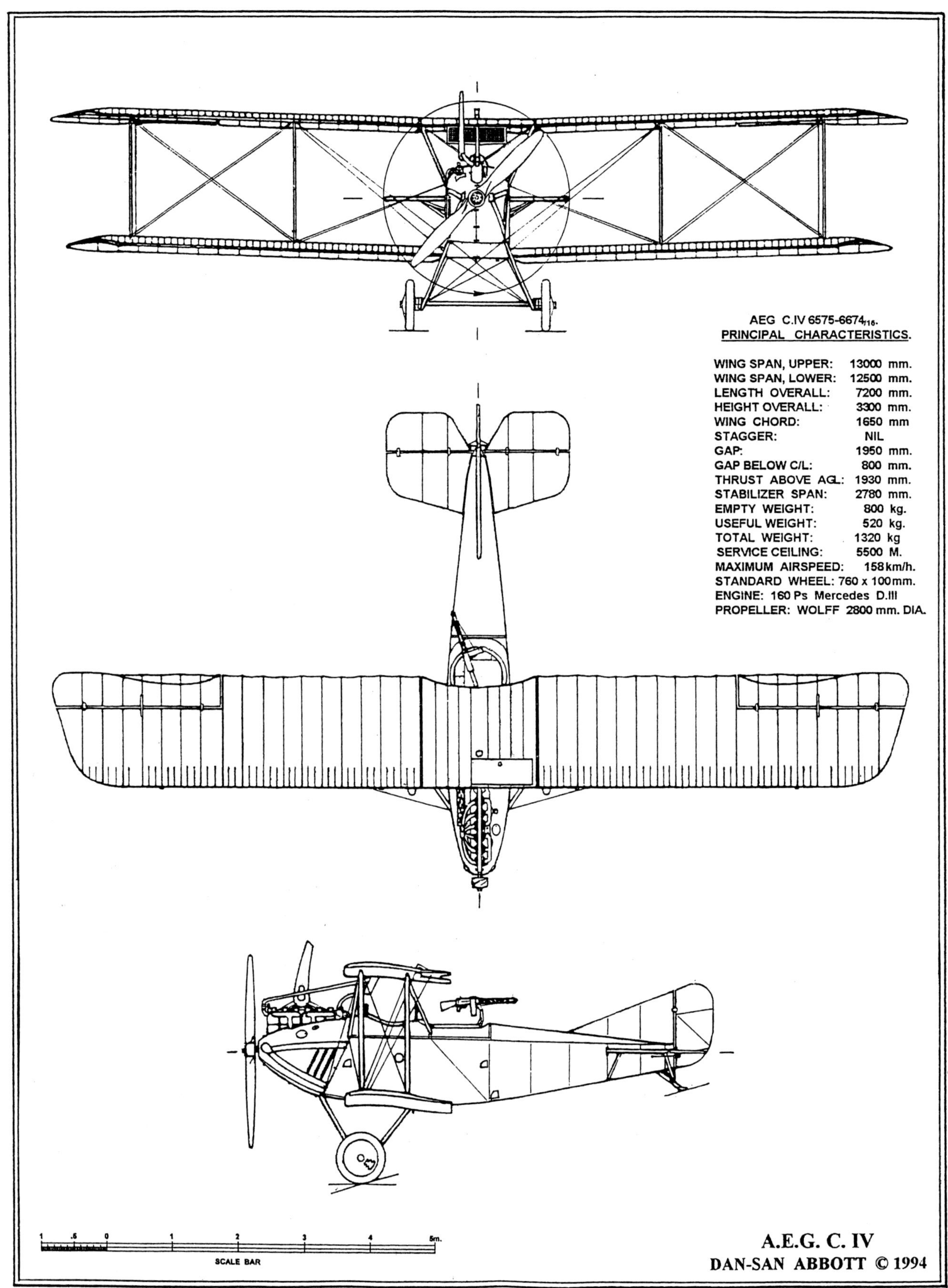
AEG C.IV 6575-6674/16.
PRINCIPAL CHARACTERISTICS.
WING SPAN, UPPER: 13000 mm.
WING SPAN, LOWER: 12500 mm.
LENGTH OVERALL: 7200 mm.
HEIGHT OVERALL: 3300 mm.
WING CHORD: 1650 mm
STAGGER: NIL
GAP: 1950 mm.
GAP BELOW C/L: 800 mm.
THRUST ABOVE AGL: 1930 mm.
STABILIZER SPAN: 2780 mm.
EMPTY WEIGHT: 800 kg.
USEFUL WEIGHT: 520 kg.
TOTAL WEIGHT: 1320 kg
SERVICE CEILING: 5500 M.
MAXIMUM AIRSPEED: 158 km/h.
STANDARD WHEEL: 760 x 100mm.
ENGINE: 160 Ps Mercedes D.III
PROPELLER: WOLFF 2800 mm. DIA.
1 .5 0 1 2 3 4 5m.
SCALE BAR
A.E.G. C. IV
DAN-SAN ABBOTT © 1994

DFW C.V

Also in April 1917, one of the very best C Class aircraft to see service with the *Luftstreitkräfte* was issued to the *Schusta*, the DFW C.V. The DFW C.V was designed by the Deutsche Flugzeug Werke G.m.b.H. (DFW) of Lindenthal by Leipzig. The Deutsche Flugzeug Werke built a number of aircraft of their design for the *Fliegertruppe,* most notably the DFW B.I, known as the "Flying Banana" because of the crescent-shaped wings. The real success came for DFW when Willy Sabersky-Müssigbrodt designed the T-29. The prototype was test-flown in May 1916. After the type tests were conducted at Adlershof, some minor corrections were incorporated during the period 3-4 August 1916, and it was accepted for front line service. The Deutsche Flugzeug Werke received its first contract on 6 August 1916 for sixty DFW C.V (T-29) aircraft, serial numbers C.3300 - 3359/16, which included the three prototype test aircraft, C.3300 - 3302/16. Because of its very good performance, *Idflieg* committed the DFW C.V with the 200 Ps Benz Bz.IV engine to large scale production. In September 1916, DFW was awarded the second contract for forty DFW C.V, serial numbers C.3400 - 3439/16. These differed from the original DFW C.V in that the bluff shaped nose was redesigned with an elegant nose and spinner. DFW received in October 1916 an order for 240 DFW C.V aircraft, serial numbers C.4800 - 5039/16.

In October 1916, *Idflieg* placed the first of many orders to other German aircraft manufacturers to build the DFW C.V under license. The first, Luft-Verkehrs Gesellschaft m.b.H. (LVG), Johannisthal near Berlin, received an order for 250 LVG C.VI, serial numbers C.5040 - 5289/16. The aircraft's designation was changed on 28 March 1917 to DFW C.V (LVG). A second order was awarded in October 1916 to the Halberstädter Flugzeugwerke G.m.b.H. (Halb) of Halberstadt for 75 Halb. C.I, numbers C.5750 - 5824/16. On 19 February 1917, the designation was changed to DFW C.V (Halb). A third order to license-build the DFW C.V went to Automobil und Aviatik A.G. (Av) of Leipzig-Heiterblick for 150 Av. C.VI, numbers C.5825 - 5974/16. As with the other two license manufacturers, the Aviatik-built DFW C.V was given a modified designation and was changed to DFW C.V (Av) on 20 December 1916. A second order for 50 LVG C.VI, C.7650 - 7699/16, was given to Luft-Verkehrs Gesellschaft also in October 1916. The final order in 1916 was to Deutsche Flugzeug-Werke for 100 DFW C.V aircraft, serial numbers C.9000 - 9099/16. Thus the total number of DFW C.V machines ordered from the parent company in 1916 amounted to 440 aircraft. The number of license-built machines of this type were 300 from LVG and 75 from Halberstädter Flugzeugwerke. This brought the year's total of DFW C.V aircraft ordered to 815.

In 1917 the production of the DFW C.V accelerated with five orders awarded to Deutsche Flugzeug Werke. The first order was for one hundred fifty in January, serial numbers C.750 - 899/17. In April 1917, the second order was for 150, serial numbers C.4578 - 4727/17. This was followed in May with the third order for 200, C.6000 - 6199/17. In July, *Idflieg* placed its fourth order with DFW for another 200 machines, serial numbers C.7750 - 7949/17. The final order to DFW was placed in October 1917 for 300 training versions of the DFW C.V with the 185 Ps NAG C.III engine. The serial numbers were C.17000 - 17299/17. The total orders to DFW in 1917 were 1000 aircraft.

Aviatik received four orders from *Idflieg* for a total of 550 DFW C.V (Av) aircraft. The first order was awarded in January 1917 for 100 machines, serial numbers C.100 - 199/17. The second order was in February for 100 aircraft, C.2000 - 2099/17. In April 1917 *Idflieg* placed a third order with Aviatik for 200 DFW C.V (Av), serial numbers C.3800 - 3999/17. The final order to Aviatik for 1917 from *Idflieg* occurred in July for 150 machines, C.6900 - 7049/17. In February 1917 LVG received its final order for the DFW C.V for 100 aircraft, serial numbers C.2100 - 2199/17. LVG would be devoting its design efforts and very large production facilities to their new project, the LVG C.V.

The Halberstädter Flugzeugwerke was a small firm and lacked the capacity to produce aircraft in the numbers of DFW and LVG and as a consequence received only small orders. In February, *Idflieg* gave Halberstädter an order for twenty-five DFW C.V (Halb), C.2500 - 2524/17, followed with a second order in April 1917 for a quantity of 50, serial numbers C.3378 - 3427/17. At this time Halberstädter Flugzeug-Werke was at work on their new two-seat fighter that would very soon go into production as the Halberstadt Cl.II. These two orders were to keep the Halberstädter staff and workers busy during the interim period between flight and acceptance testing the Halb. Cl.II and waiting for the production orders.

Total DFW C.V production for 1917 was 1725 aircraft. All future production would be done by DFW and Aviatik. The production of the DFW C.V would continue at this pace to the end of the war at DFW and Aviatik. DFW received six orders totaling 950 machines and Aviatik got orders for 600 DFW (Av) machines. Of the total of 3955 DFW C.V aircraft ordered, not all orders were completed at war's end. Probably 200-250 DFW C.V aircraft that were ordered were not built. The DFW C.V was truly a remarkable machine and was the most produced aircraft during the war. The performance was so good that it was able to serve as a high altitude reconnaissance machine, a day and night bomber, artillery spotter, escort aircraft, air-ground support, and a personnel transport in the fighter units. The DFW operated on all fronts with the German Army. The 1918 production did not contribute to the *Schusta* operations prior to 27 March 1918 and the *Schlasta* after that date.

The large scale of production and the licensing of the DFW C.V to other manufacturers resulted in a variety of camouflage schemes. Following is a brief discussion of the different patterns applied by each of the various firms producing the aircraft.

The first few aircraft were finished with clear doped and varnished linen surfaces with the plywood-covered fuselage, cowlings, and struts painted to match in a yellowish white to a pale yellow. About serial number C.3310/16, the upper and side surfaces were painted a myrtle green with the bottom surfaces clear doped and varnished. The belly of the fuselage and struts were painted yellowish white to pale yellow to match the fabric under surfaces. This camouflage scheme was used on the production orders 1 and 2 through serial number C.3439/16. The matte black Iron Crosses were painted on flat white cross fields on the top of the upper wing, both sides of the fuselage and rudder. Plain matte black Iron Crosses were painted under the lower wings without white cross fields on the first two orders.

Commencing with the third order, C.4800 - 5039/16, DFW introduced a new Terrain Scheme of dark green and light brown. During the course of production of the third order, to comply with a directive from *Idflieg*, DFW eliminated the white cross fields and painted a white border, 50mm wide, surrounding the Iron Cross for all the crosses except those painted on the under side of the lower wings. This went into effect around serial number C.4895/16.

A major change occurred with the fourth order, C.9000 - 9909/16. The aircraft were painted an overall light grey with dark grey struts and wheel covers. With the fifth order, C.750 - 899/17, DFW again changed their camouflage to a two-color scheme of dull green and light olive on the upper and side surfaces. The under surfaces of the fuselage belly and struts were painted to match the pale yellow clear doped and varnished linen under-sides of the wings and tailplane. With the sixth order, C.4578 - 4727/17, DFW again altered their camouflage scheme to an overall dark myrtle green, with the struts and fuselage under surfaces painted pale yellow to match the clear doped and varnished under sides of the wings and tailplane. The seventh order was for 200 DFW C.V, serial numbers C.6000 - 6199/17, with still another change in the camouflage scheme, which now reverted back to the fifth order pattern. However, the fuselage colors were reversed, with the dull green forward on the fuselage and the light olive on the rear fuselage and empennage.

The eighth order in July 1917 was for 200 aircraft, C.7750 - 7949/17, and there was introduced a total departure from DFW previous camouflage schemes. They adopted the practice developed by Fokker of a darker color streaked over a lighter color, possibly dark dull bluish grey over lighter bluish grey. The streaking was chord-wise on the wings and vertical on the sides of the fuselage. Other machines in this order were doped deep green, brown, and purple. The underside colors were warm straw. The last order DFW received in 1917 for the DFW C.V was in October for 300 DFW C.Vc, serial numbers C.17000 - 17299/17. The DFW C.Vc differed from the standard DFW C.V in that it was powered with the 185 Ps NAG C.III engine and was used for training purposes only. The DFW C.Vc were painted all white. In 1918 DFW began using four-color printed fabric applied span wise on the wings. The seam was approximately 1300mm from the leading edge of the wing.

LVG received an order from *Idflieg* for 250 LVG C.VI, serial numbers C.5040 - 5289/16. These were painted in the LVG pattern of greyish green and chestnut brown with pale green undersides. This pattern remained in use throughout the first order. With the second order for 50 DFW C.V (LVG), C.7650 - 7699/16, a third color was added and the forward fuselage was painted greyish magenta. With the third order for 100 DFW C.V (LVG), C.2100 - 2199/16, the greyish magenta supplanted the greyish green on the wing tips and the right half of the tailplane. In the later half of the production, the greyish magenta was added to the upper and lower main plane on the inboard ends to the third rib from the wing roots. The under surfaces and struts were pale green.

Aviatik und Automobil was awarded a license contract to build 150 Av C.VI, serial numbers C.5825 - 5974/16, and these were later designated DFW C.V (Av). Aviatik used a two-color scheme of dark green and chestnut brown in a sprayed interlocking pattern on the top and side surfaces. The bottom surfaces were clear doped and varnished producing a warm straw color. With the later 1917 order, Aviatik adopted a light and dark greyish green scheme with clear doped undersides. For the July 1917 order for 150 DFV C.V (Av), C.6900 - 7049/17, Aviatik added mauve to their sprayed camouflage scheme on the top and side surfaces with clear doped undersides. With the March 1918 order for 150 DFW C.V (Av), C.2150 - 2299/18, Aviatik covered the wings and tail surfaces with four-color lozenge printed day pattern fabric, the dark pattern being on the top surfaces and the lighter pattern on the under surfaces. The fuselage was camouflaged in dark green and mauve, the rudder was white, and the struts light grey.

Halberstädter received an order for 25 Halb C.I aircraft in February, serial numbers C.2500 - 2524/17, followed by another order in April 1917 for 50, serial numbers C.3378 - 3427/17. These were unusual because Halberstädter covered the top surfaces with the lighter five-color fabric normally used

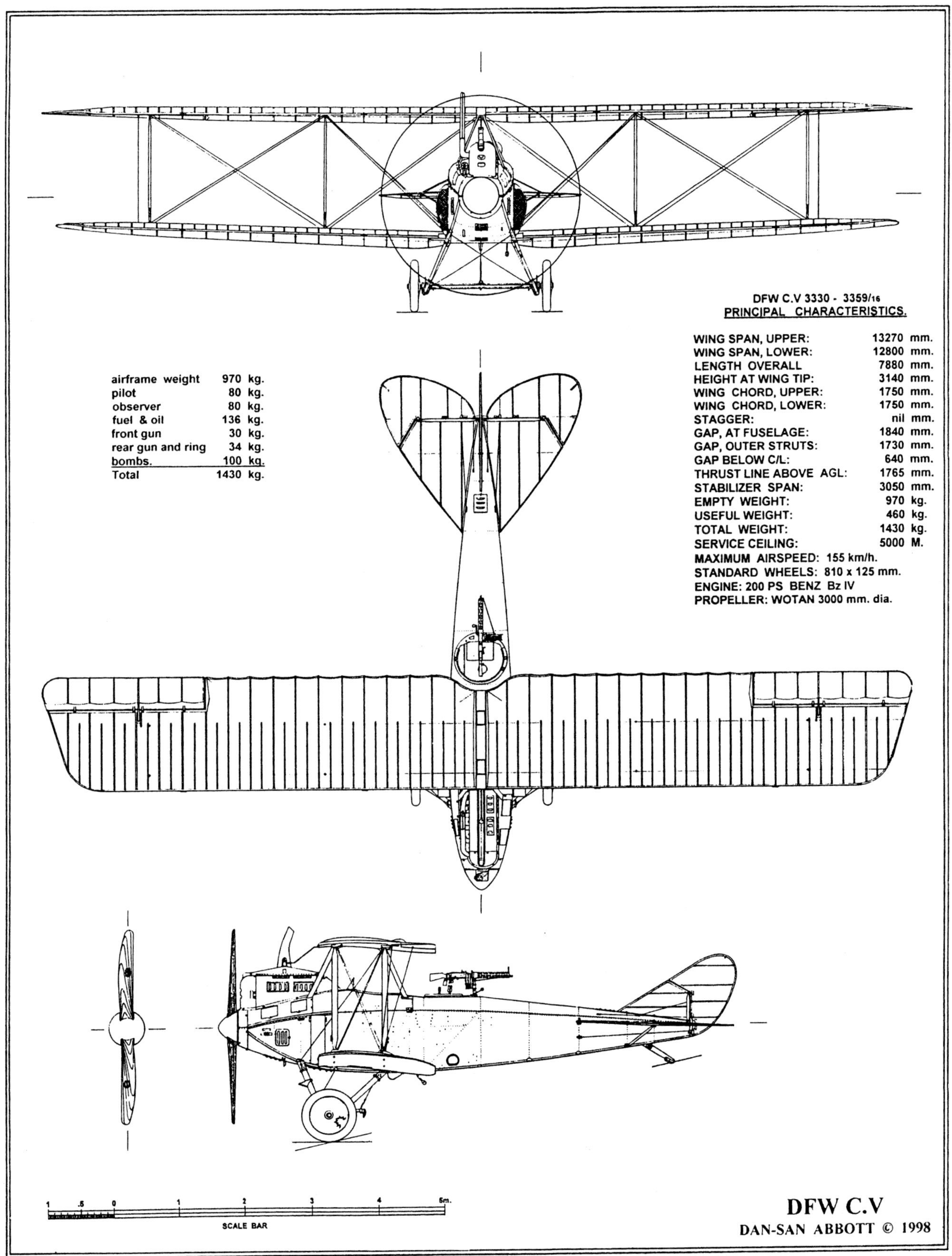

DFW C.V 3330 - 3359/16
PRINCIPAL CHARACTERISTICS.
WING SPAN, UPPER: 13270 mm.
WING SPAN, LOWER: 12800 mm.
LENGTH OVERALL 7880 mm.
HEIGHT AT WING TIP: 3140 mm.
WING CHORD, UPPER: 1750 mm.
WING CHORD, LOWER: 1750 mm.
STAGGER: nil mm.
GAP, AT FUSELAGE: 1840 mm.
GAP, OUTER STRUTS: 1730 mm.
GAP BELOW C/L: 640 mm.
THRUST LINE ABOVE AGL: 1765 mm.
STABILIZER SPAN: 3050 mm.
EMPTY WEIGHT: 970 kg.
USEFUL WEIGHT: 460 kg.
TOTAL WEIGHT: 1430 kg.
SERVICE CEILING: 5000 M.
MAXIMUM AIRSPEED: 155 km/h.
STANDARD WHEELS: 810 x 125 mm.
ENGINE: 200 PS BENZ Bz IV
PROPELLER: WOTAN 3000 mm. dia.
airframe weight 970 kg.
pilot 80 kg.
observer 80 kg.
fuel & oil 136 kg.
front gun 30 kg.
rear gun and ring 34 kg.
bombs. 100 kg.
Total 1430 kg.
1 .5 0 1 2 3 4 5m.
SCALE BAR
DFW C.V
DAN-SAN ABBOTT © 1998

for the lower surfaces. The undersides were instead covered with plain linen which was a warm straw color. The fuselage was painted in a pattern matching the colors of the top and side surfaces.

The DFW C.V was constructed of wood with a minimal amount of steel fittings. All the struts were streamline steel tubing. The fuselage was framed in wood and covered with molded panels of plywood. The wings were of wood construction with two hollow spars and built up ply ribs and were covered with bias panels of linen fabric laid at 45° to the leading edges of the wings and tail. The tail surfaces were metal framed with wood ribs and bias covered with linen fabric. The main fuel tank was in the forward cockpit and the pilot's seat was attached to it. The 200 Ps Benz Bz.IV engine cylinders were enclosed in aluminum cowlings. The pilot was provided with a Maxim lMG 08 machine gun mounted on the top cowl to the right of the engine cowlings. The gunner had a Parabellum Modell 14 machine gun mounted on a LVG Schneider wood turret on the rear cockpit. In the gunner's cockpit mounted on the right side was a bomb rack for four 12.5 kg P.u.W. bombs. On the bottom of the fuselage were aluminum spring loaded doors through which the bombs could be released. The gunner was provided with a map case, a rack for flares, and flare pistol and a hole in the floor for installation of a photographic camera.

The DFW C.V had an upper wingspan of 13,270mm and a lower span of 12,800mm. The overall length measured 7880mm and the height was 3140mm. The wheels were 810mm X 125mm with a 55mm X 160mm hub. The aircraft's empty weight was 990 kg and its useful load was 515 kg, yielding a combined weight of 1505 kg. Its service ceiling was 5000 meters and its maximum airspeed was 155 km/hr at sea level.

Beginning in March 1917 the DFW C.V aircraft were issued to the *Schutzstaffeln*. The first to receive the DFW C.V was *Schusta 17*, followed by *7, 13,* and *19* in April. In May *Schusta 4, 7, 24b*, and *27b* were equipped with the DFW C.V. June 1917 would find the DFW C.V aircraft with *Schusta 11, 12, 23b,* and *30b*. In July 1917, the DFW C.V was issued to *Schusta 9* and *28b*. In October 1917 the DFW C.V was on the inventory list of *Schusta 25b. Schusta 5, 9, 16, 19*, and *22b* were wholly or partially equipped with the DFW C.V. In December 1917, the DFW C.V was still on the strength of *Schusta 5*. The DFW C.V began to be phased out in November 1917 and were being replaced by the Halberstadt Cl.II and the Hannover Cl.II aircraft in December 1917.

LVG C.IV

In May 1917, the LVG C.IV was issued to the *Schutzstaffeln* and served at least with *Schusta 7* and *27b*. The LVG C.IV

LVG C.VI in Allied hands (most likely US) after the war. This type of aircraft supplied some of the *Schlasta* during 1918. Credit: The Lafayette Foundation.

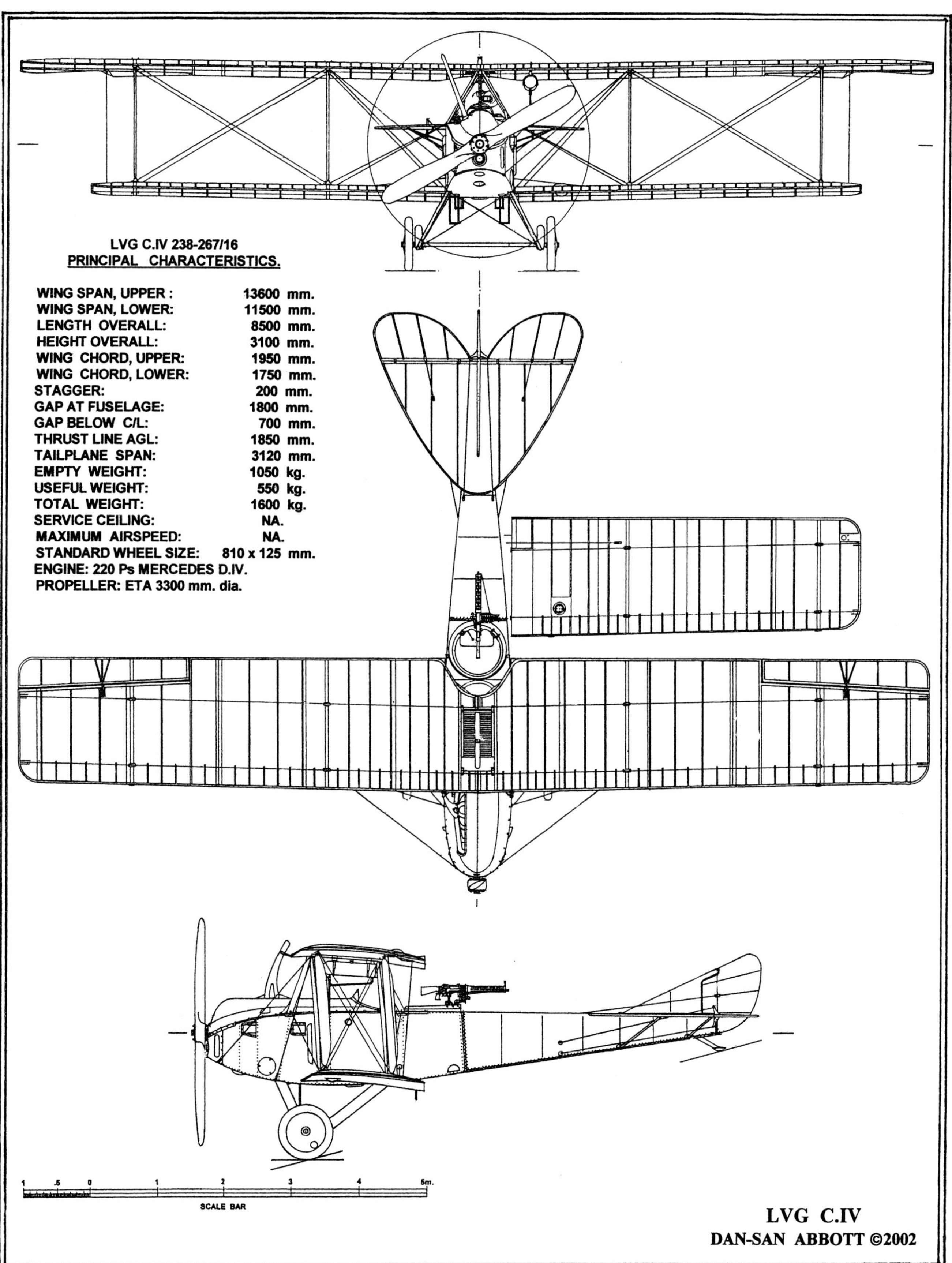
LVG C.IV 238-267/16
PRINCIPAL CHARACTERISTICS.
WING SPAN, UPPER : 13600 mm.
WING SPAN, LOWER: 11500 mm.
LENGTH OVERALL: 8500 mm.
HEIGHT OVERALL: 3100 mm.
WING CHORD, UPPER: 1950 mm.
WING CHORD, LOWER: 1750 mm.
STAGGER: 200 mm.
GAP AT FUSELAGE: 1800 mm.
GAP BELOW C/L: 700 mm.
THRUST LINE AGL: 1850 mm.
TAILPLANE SPAN: 3120 mm.
EMPTY WEIGHT: 1050 kg.
USEFUL WEIGHT: 550 kg.
TOTAL WEIGHT: 1600 kg.
SERVICE CEILING: NA.
MAXIMUM AIRSPEED: NA.
STANDARD WHEEL SIZE: 810 x 125 mm.
ENGINE: 220 Ps MERCEDES D.IV.
PROPELLER: ETA 3300 mm. dia.
1 .5 0 1 2 3 4 5m.
SCALE BAR
LVG C.IV
DAN-SAN ABBOTT ©2002

was an enlarged redesign of the LVG C.II, fitted with the new in-line eight cylinder 220 Ps Mercedes D.IV engine. This huge powerplant required an increase in wing area to carry its 410 kg of weight – an increase over the 268 kg of the 160 Ps Mercedes D.III engine of the LVG C.II and C.III designs of 1915. With the Mercedes D.IV being geared, the huge 3300mm diameter propeller turned at a slow 910 rpm, while the crankshaft turned at 1400 rpm. The reduction gearing raised the propeller shaft which permitted the engine to be buried in the fuselage with the top of the engine below the line of the turtle-deck. Aluminum cowling panels covered the top and front of the engine. The forward fuselage sides and bottom were covered with plywood. The wings, rear fuselage, and empennage were covered with linen fabric.

The upper wingspan of the LVG C.IV was 13,600mm and the lower wingspan measured 12,000mm. The length of the aircraft was 8500mm and its height was 3100mm. The empty weight was 1050 kg (2310 lbs) and its useful load was 550 kg (1210 lbs), the gross weight thus amounting to 1600 kg (3520 lbs).

Armament on the LVG C.IV was one fixed forward firing Maxim lMG 08 machine gun mounted on the right side of the forward fuselage and the engine. A Modell 14 Parabellum flexible machine gun was mounted on a Schneider wood turret over the rear cockpit. Under the fuselage were four bomb racks with a total capacity of 70 kilograms (154 lbs). While the specific performance of the LVG C.IV is not known, it would be reasonable to assume the performance was similar to that of the Albatros C.V, which was also powered by the 220 Ps Mercedes D.IV engine, and because both aircraft were nearly identical in size and weight.

Idflieg ordered the six prototype LVG C.IV aircraft, serial numbers C.4389 - 4394/15, in December 1915. Production orders followed in February 1916 for 30 LVG C.IV, C.238 - 267/16, and also an additional 80, C.288 - 367/16. In March 1916, the LVG Köslin factory received an order for 40 LVG C.IV, serial numbers C.408 - 447/16. In September 1916, LVG received their final order for the LVG C.IV for 70 aircraft, serial numbers C.4340 - 4409/16. The total purchased by *Idflieg* was 226 LVG C.IV aircraft. *Idflieg* delivered to LVG 235 Mercedes D.IV engines.

The initial six aircraft were painted a very pale blue-grey. Subsequent production aircraft were painted in the Terrain Camouflage Scheme of greyish green and rust brown; the under surfaces were painted a pale sky blue. Matte black crosses were painted on white cross fields. In May 1917, *Schusta 7, 9,* and *27b* were issued the LVG C.IV. The aircraft served with these *Schusta* for an unknown period.

AGO C.IV

Ago Flugzeugwerke G.m.b.H. was founded in 1912 at Berlin-Johannisthal. The company was small and grew slowly with a relatively small production capacity. Ago had built a small number of twin boom single engine pusher machines, the Ago C.I and C.II, that saw limited service in 1915 with the *Fliegertruppe.* Ago made a final attempt to improve the Ago C.II twin bay configuration with a smaller single bay, twin boom, pusher engine, Ago C.III. The Ago C.III did not go into production.

The Swiss engineer August Haefeli was replaced by Gabriel Letsch who then designed a single engine tractor one and one-half bay biplane, the Ago C.IV. The Ago C.IV was an interesting design with the leading and trailing edges tapering toward the wing tips and the front and rear spars converging at the wing tip. The ailerons were only on the upper wing panels. The front spar was a single-bay configuration with one interplane strut without interplane wire bracing. The rear spar was two-bay, with two wire braced struts. This form of wing design, tapering in chord and thickness, only complicated its manufacture, and would increase its manufacturing cost. The wings were covered with fabric. The engine cooling airfoil radiator was set into the right upper wing panel and the auxiliary fuel tank was in the upper left wing panel. The upper wing panels were joined to a trestle of streamlined steel struts.

The fuselage was constructed of four longerons with vertical and horizontal distance wood struts and was cross-braced with wire. The forward half of the fuselage was covered with plywood sheet and the rear covered with fabric. The 220 Ps Benz B.IV six cylinder engine was housed in the nose with aluminum spinner and cowlings covering the nose and upper fuselage.

The fuel tank was situated in the pilot's forward cockpit, and upon it was the pilot's seat. The pilot's synchronized forward-firing machine gun was mounted on a trestle above the forward turtle-deck and positioned to fire over the top of the engine. Ammunition consisting of cartridge and belt chutes were led from containers into the fuselage.

The rudder was the "comma" type without a fin. The ample size stabilizer and elevator were mounted on top of the rear fuselage. The empennage was fabric covered. The undercarriage struts were of steel tube and faired with wood to a streamline shape. The ash tail skid was shod with steel. The observer's rear cockpit was surrounded with a gun ring on which was mounted a Parabellum Modell 14 machine gun.

The Ago C.IV displayed excellent performance with an airspeed at sea level of 190 km/hr, and a rate of climb of 32 minutes to 4000 meters. This was better than contemporary German and Allied fighters. After the required type tests and modification to improve the wing attachment structure, in June

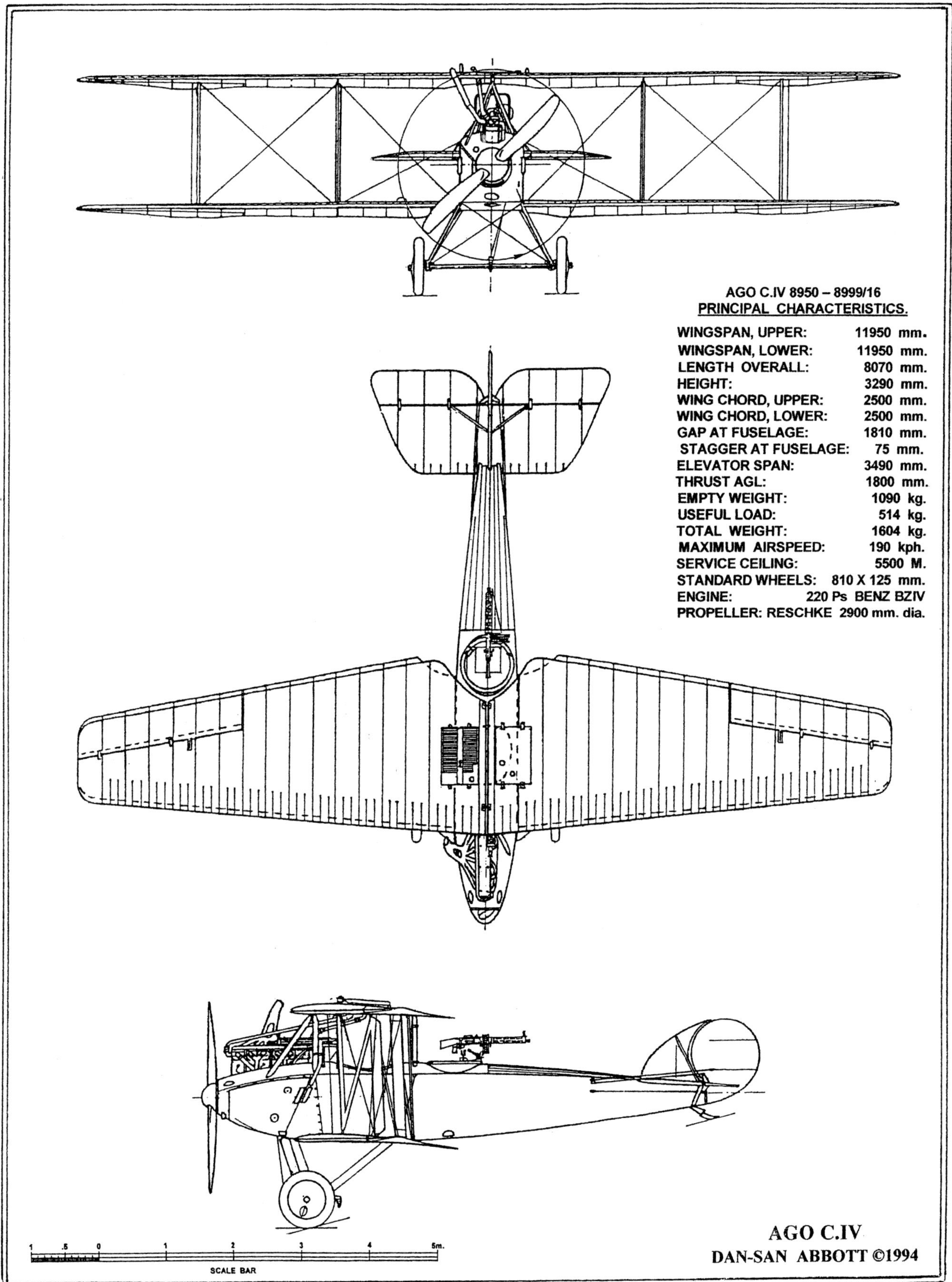
AGO C.IV 8950 – 8999/16
PRINCIPAL CHARACTERISTICS.
WINGSPAN, UPPER: 11950 mm.
WINGSPAN, LOWER: 11950 mm.
LENGTH OVERALL: 8070 mm.
HEIGHT: 3290 mm.
WING CHORD, UPPER: 2500 mm.
WING CHORD, LOWER: 2500 mm.
GAP AT FUSELAGE: 1810 mm.
STAGGER AT FUSELAGE: 75 mm.
ELEVATOR SPAN: 3490 mm.
THRUST AGL: 1800 mm.
EMPTY WEIGHT: 1090 kg.
USEFUL LOAD: 514 kg.
TOTAL WEIGHT: 1604 kg.
MAXIMUM AIRSPEED: 190 kph.
SERVICE CEILING: 5500 M.
STANDARD WHEELS: 810 X 125 mm.
ENGINE: 220 Ps BENZ BZIV
PROPELLER: RESCHKE 2900 mm. dia.
1 .5 0 1 2 3 4 5m.
SCALE BAR
AGO C.IV
DAN-SAN ABBOTT ©1994

1916, *Idflieg* awarded Ago an order for twenty-four Ago C.IV, serial numbers, C.2740 - 2763/16.

In September 1916, *Idflieg* placed a license order with Waggonfabrik Josef Rathgeber, of München-Moosach for ten Ago C.IV (Rat), serial numbers C.3714 - 3723/16. In October 1916, under license, *Idflieg* ordered 250 Ago C.IV (Schül) from Luftfahrzeugbau Schütte-Lanz of Mannheim-Rheinau, the airship manufacturer. Two follow-on orders were awarded to Ago in November 1916. The first was for twenty-four Ago C.IV, C.3600 - 3623/16, and the second for fifty Ago C.IV, C.8950 - 8999/16. In February 1917, Ago received another order for fifty machines, Ago C.IV C.1521 - 1570/17. The final order was issued in May 1917 for 100 Ago C.IV, serial numbers C.5575 - 5674/17. However, only sixty-four machines of this order were completed, with the balance of the order canceled in October 1917.

Ago began deliveries in December 1916, with eight Ago C.IV machines listed at the front on 31 December 1916. Shortly after these arrived at the front, landing accidents began to occur caused by fuselages breaking aft of the observer's cockpit. This failing was corrected in January 1917, but then flying accidents began to occur as the result of side slipping. This was rectified with the addition of the fin to increase the side area.

Further changes were made to the machine, with redesigned lower wing panels that included ailerons. The final change was the elimination of the two outer interplane struts which were replaced by a single "N" strut.

The front line inventory increased to 25 on 28 February 1917, then dropped to one on 30 April 1917. After the completion of the modifications to the Ago C.IV, the inventory on 30 June 1917 was nineteen machines, of which some were issued to *Schusta 25b*. In July 1917 *Schusta 9* and *12* received the Ago C.IV machines. In August 1917 the Ago C.IV were issued to *Schusta 5*. By September 1917, the Ago C.IV had disappeared from front service with the *Schutzstaffeln*.

The Ago-built Ago C.IV machines were camouflaged in dark green, light green, and rust brown on the upper and side surfaces, with sky blue undersides. The finish was spray painted with diffused edges.

Albatros C.X

During the summer of 1916, the Albatros Werke G.m.b.H. engineers designed a new airframe to the *Idflieg* requirements for a new reconnaissance light bomber to be powered by the Mercedes Daimler 260 Ps Mercedes D.IVa engine. The design formula followed that of the Albatros C.V and C.VII, but the new model was to be a little larger with slightly less wing area to cope with the increased power of the 260 Ps D.IVa. The upper wingspan was 14,360mm, and the lower span was 12,900mm. The overall length was 9150mm and the height was 3400mm.

The wings were of a new plan form, with raked tips on both planes. They were framed in wood with plywood covering the leading edges to the front spar. The upper wing panels had tapered ailerons with balanced inset and small tapered airlerons were incorporated as well in the lower wing tips. An airfoil radiator was mounted on the cabane struts, being positioned between the upper wing spars.

The fuselage was constructed in accordance with previous practice at the Albatros firm. The structure consisted of six light longerons and a series of formers. Built-up plywood-covered formers were used in the forward half of the fuselage and also in the empenage, the latter being necessary to carry the tail assembly loads. Light formers were used for the aft mid fuselage. The fuselage frame and vertical fin were covered with birch plywood. The upper turtle-deck over the observer's and pilot's cockpits was covered with molded plywood.

The tailplane stabilizer was identical to those used on the Albatros C.V and C.VII, framed in wood and covered with linen fabric. The Mercedes D.IVa engine cylinders protruded above the fuselage turtle-deck, the top of the fuselage and nose being composed of aluminum cowling panels while the propeller hub was covered with an aluminum spinner.

The wings were framed in wood. The ailerons, elevator, and rudder were framed in steel tubing and covered chord-wise with linen fabric. All struts were made of streamlined profile steel tubing. The pilot had either a single synchronized Maxim lMG 08 or the lMG 08/15. The observer's cockpit was fitted with the Franz Schneider wood gun ring upon which a single Parabellum Modell 14 lMG was mounted. Racks were installed under the fuselage for four 12.5 kg P.u.W. bombs.

The empty weight of the Albatros C.X was 1050 kg and it had a useful load of 618 kg. The total weight was therefore 1668 kg. Maximum airspeed was 175 km/hr and the service ceiling was 5000 meters. The climb to 1000 meters took 5 minutes and it could attain an altitude of 5000 meters in 55 minutes.

Upon completion of the required load testing at Adlershof and its acceptance for front line use, *Idflieg* ordered 100 Alb. C.X machines, serial numbers C.2900 - 2999/16. With Albatros committed to production of the Alb. D.II and D.III fighter aircraft, *Idflieg* placed license orders with four other firms to produce the Albatros C.X.

In November 1916 Ostdeutsche Albatroswerke G.m.b.H., Schneidemühl, received an order for 147 Alb. C.X (OAW), C.5828 - 6074/16. OAW received type test approval on Alb. C.X (OAW) C.5828/16 on 28 February 1917. In December 1916 Luft Fahrzeug Gesellschaft m.b.H. (Roland), in Charlottenburg, was awarded a license order for 100 Alb. C.X

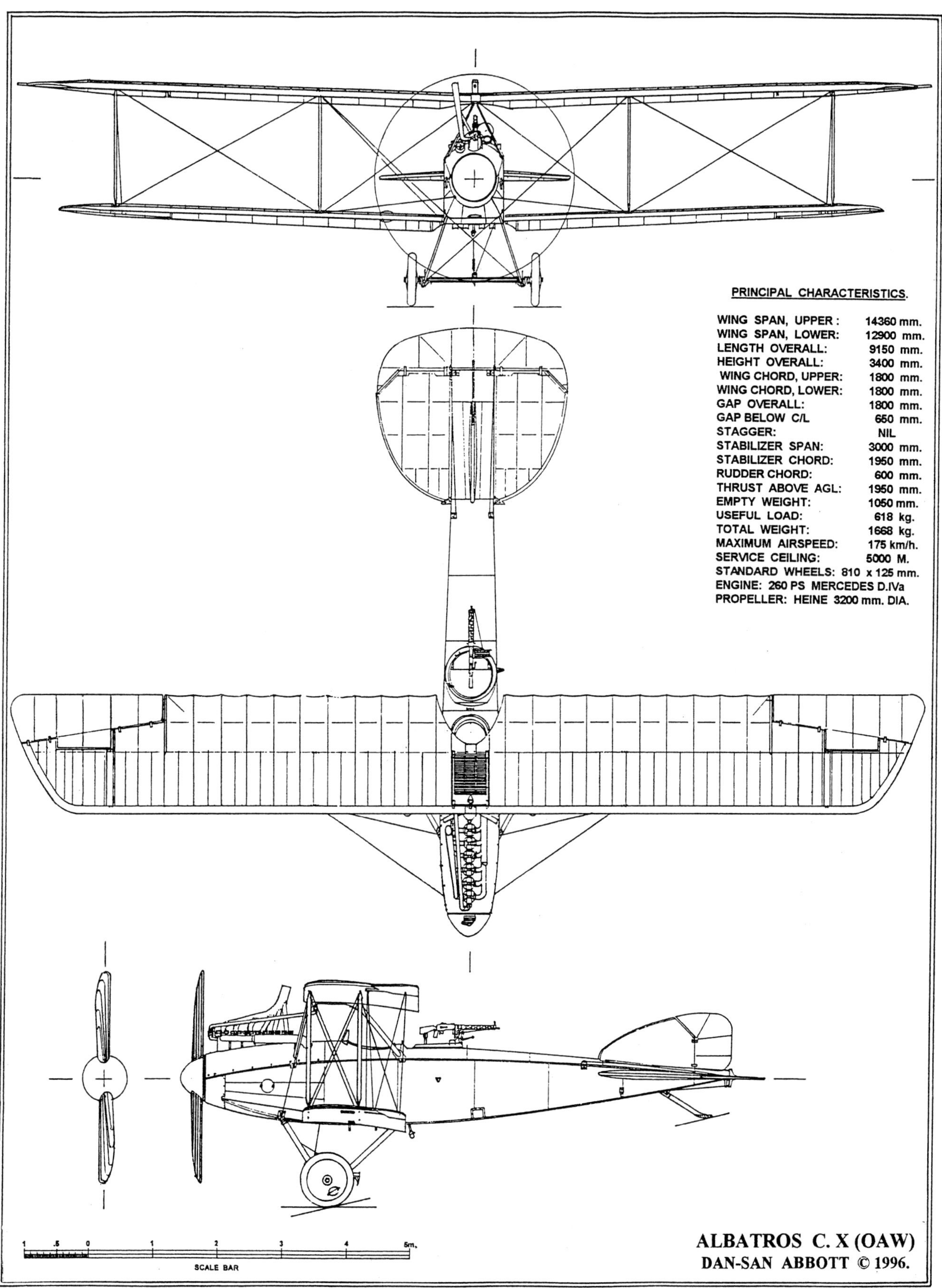
PRINCIPAL CHARACTERISTICS.
WING SPAN, UPPER : 14360 mm.
WING SPAN, LOWER: 12900 mm.
LENGTH OVERALL: 9150 mm.
HEIGHT OVERALL: 3400 mm.
WING CHORD, UPPER: 1800 mm.
WING CHORD, LOWER: 1800 mm.
GAP OVERALL: 1800 mm.
GAP BELOW C/L 650 mm.
STAGGER: NIL
STABILIZER SPAN: 3000 mm.
STABILIZER CHORD: 1950 mm.
RUDDER CHORD: 600 mm.
THRUST ABOVE AGL: 1950 mm.
EMPTY WEIGHT: 1050 mm.
USEFUL LOAD: 618 kg.
TOTAL WEIGHT: 1668 kg.
MAXIMUM AIRSPEED: 175 km/h.
SERVICE CEILING: 5000 M.
STANDARD WHEELS: 810 x 125 mm.
ENGINE: 260 PS MERCEDES D.IVa
PROPELLER: HEINE 3200 mm. DIA.
1 .5 0 1 2 3 4 5m.
SCALE BAR
ALBATROS C. X (OAW)
DAN-SAN ABBOTT © 1996.

(Rol), C.6834 - 6933/16. On June 5th, LFG "Roland" received type test approval on Alb. C.X (Rol) C.6834/16 and the aircraft was released for production. The third license order was placed with Bayerische Flugzeug Werke A.G. München on 20 December 1916, for fifty Alb. C.X (Bay), C.7725 to 7774/16. A contingency order of 300 more machines of this type was placed with Bayerische Flugzeug Werke, but they were never built. Bayerische Flugzeug Werke received type test approval on 21 February 1917. In December 1916, a second order was awarded to OAW for 100 Alb. C.X (OAW), C.9200 – 9299/16. The fourth and last license was awarded to Linke-Hofmann Werke Aktiengesellschaft, Breslau for fifty Alb. C.X (Li), C.8300 to 8349/16. The machines of this order were scheduled to be used in training units. Linke-Hofmann received type test approval on 14 July 1917. It is assumed that none of these machines were ever issued to the *Schutzstaffeln.*

The *Fl.Abt.* and *Fl.Abt.(A)* began to receive the Alb. C.X in April 1917. The front inventory on 30 April 1917 was seventy, on 30 June this was increased to ninety-eight. The following months saw a steady decline in the number of Alb. C.X aircraft at the front, amounting to forty-seven on 31 August, twenty-six on 31 October, and eleven on 31 December 1917. The last listing of the Alb. C.X was four machines on 28 February 1918. It is known that at least *Schutzstaffel 5* had some quantity of Alb. C.X in their inventory in September 1917 and that these were replaced by the DFW C.V in November 1917.

The camouflage schemes, colors, and patterns used on the Alb. C.X and Alb. C.X (OAW) were the same as those employed on the Alb. C.VII and Alb. C.VII (OAW). In addition, OAW introduced a scheme of two shades of mauve in the late production batch carrying serial numbers C.9200 - 9299/16. LFG "Roland" used a three-color camouflage scheme of dark green, light green, and brown, in asymmetrical bands, with sky blue undersides. Bayerische Flugzeug Werke used a three-color camouflage scheme of light green, dark green, and brown applied in diagonal bands on the wings and fuselage, with lateral bands on the tailplane, and sky blue under surfaces. Linke-Hofmann also used three colors of brown and dark green on the fabric surface covered with blotches of light green. The under surfaces were sky blue. The fuselage and fin were shellacked and varnished birch plywood of a warm straw yellow color.

Rumpler C.IV

As better C Class aircraft were deployed with the *Flieger Abteilungen,* the *Schutzstaffeln* that flew protection for them had to be equipped with aircraft of equal performance. It was during the latter half of 1917 that these more powerful machines began to be utilized with the *Schusta.* One of the very best was the Rumpler C.IV, with its superior high altitude performance. This was a photo-reconnaissance machine which could reach a ceiling of 6800 meters and had a maximum airspeed of 175 km/hr at sea level. The Ru. C.IV could climb to 5000 meters in thirty minutes.

In the summer of 1916, *Idflieg* ordered 50 Rumpler C.III aircraft, serial numbers C.1863 to 1912/16. Within this order, serial numbers C.1874, 1895, and 1912/16 were built as Rumpler C.IV prototypes powered with the 260 Ps Mercedes D.IVa engine. Ru. C.IV 1912/16 was used in the type tests at Adlershof and the Rumpler C.IV received approval on 1 December 1916.

With the promising performance of the Ru. C.IV, pending acceptance of the type tests, *Idflieg* issued an order to the Rumpler Werke G.m.b.H. in September 1916 for 150 Ru. C.IV, serial numbers C.6675 - 6824/16. Also in September a second order for 100 Ru. C.IV, C.8200 - 8299/16, was placed. In November 1916, *Idflieg* ordered 150 Ru. C.IV machines, serial numbers C.8400 - 8549/16. Commencing with serial number C.8500/16, the spinner was eliminated and the new nose cowling was installed on all subsequent Ru. C.IV and variants: Ru. C.V, Ru. C.IV Rubild (Ru. C.VI), and the Ru. C.IV Rubild Mb (Ru. C.VII). The next order for the Ru. C.IV was in February 1917 for 100 Ru. C.IV, C.1420 - 1519/17. There were further orders for the Ru. C.IV and variants throughout 1917 and 1918.

On 10 February 1917, Rumpler Werke received type test approval and commenced production. First deliveries were made in April 1917. On 30 April 1917, 24 Ru. C.IV machines were listed in front line units. Deliveries continued at about 100 aircraft per month from Rumpler. On 30 June 1917, 122 Ru. C.IV aircraft were listed in front line units. The listing peaked at 257 Ru. C.IV at the front on 31 August 1917 and then declined to 225 on 31 October 1917. By 31 December 1917 the total Ru. C.IV machines at the front dropped to 228 and this further decreased so that by 28 February 1918 there were only 161 at the front. The numbers at the front then increased to 187 on 30 April 1918. The number of Ru. C.IV aircraft at the front dropped to 182 on 30 June 1918 and decreased yet further to 110 Ru. C.IV machines on 31 August 1918. The superb high-flying Ru. C.VII, with the 240 Ps Maybach Mb.IV engine, began to fill the shoes of the Ru. C.IV in mid-1918.

The Ru. C.IV machines were built under license by Bayerische Rumpler Werke A.G., Augsburg, which was awarded three orders: November 1916 for 50 Ru. C.IV (Bayru), C.8900 - 8949/16, February 1917 for 100, C.2750 - 2849/17, and 200 in July 1917, serial numbers not available. The Ru. C.IV (Bayru) machines were powered with the Basse und Selve BuS.IVa 300 Ps engine.

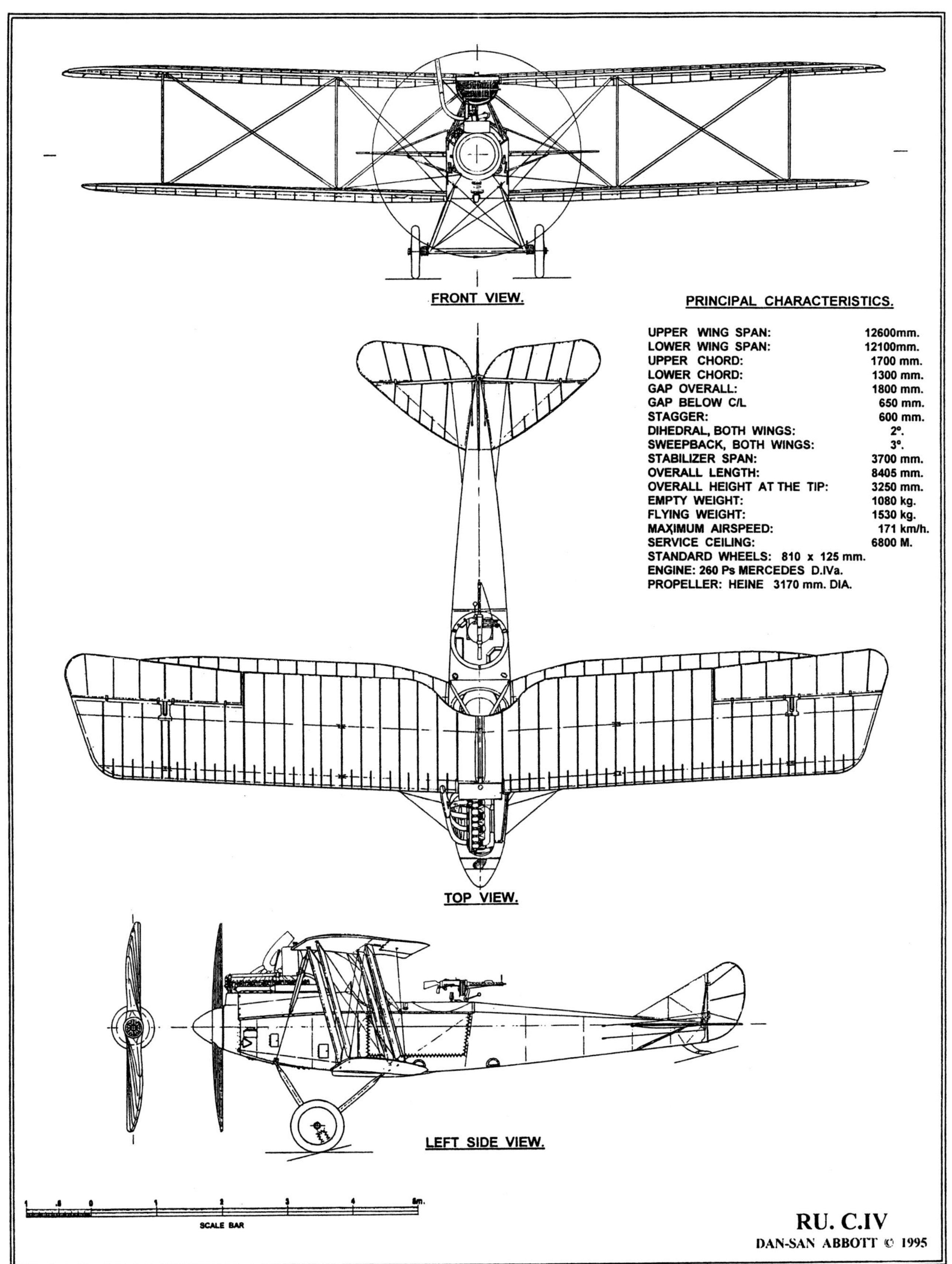
FRONT VIEW.
PRINCIPAL CHARACTERISTICS.
UPPER WING SPAN: 12600mm.
LOWER WING SPAN: 12100mm.
UPPER CHORD: 1700 mm.
LOWER CHORD: 1300 mm.
GAP OVERALL: 1800 mm.
GAP BELOW C/L 650 mm.
STAGGER: 600 mm.
DIHEDRAL, BOTH WINGS: 2°.
SWEEPBACK, BOTH WINGS: 3°.
STABILIZER SPAN: 3700 mm.
OVERALL LENGTH: 8405 mm.
OVERALL HEIGHT AT THE TIP: 3250 mm.
EMPTY WEIGHT: 1080 kg.
FLYING WEIGHT: 1530 kg.
MAXIMUM AIRSPEED: 171 km/h.
SERVICE CEILING: 6800 M.
STANDARD WHEELS: 810 x 125 mm.
ENGINE: 260 Ps MERCEDES D.IVa.
PROPELLER: HEINE 3170 mm. DIA.
TOP VIEW.
LEFT SIDE VIEW.
SCALE BAR
RU. C.IV
DAN-SAN ABBOTT © 1995

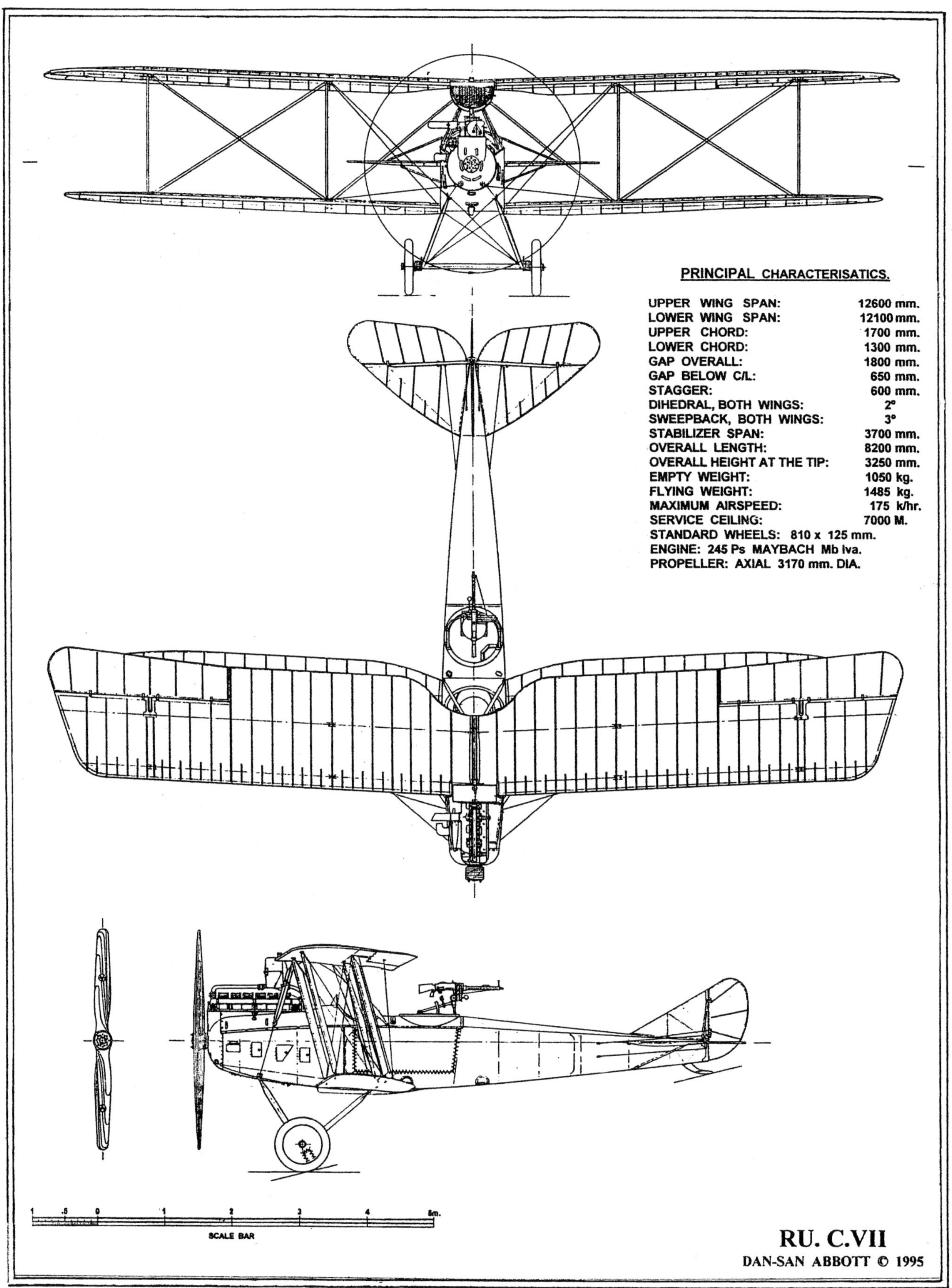
PRINCIPAL CHARACTERISATICS.
UPPER WING SPAN: 12600 mm.
LOWER WING SPAN: 12100 mm.
UPPER CHORD: 1700 mm.
LOWER CHORD: 1300 mm.
GAP OVERALL: 1800 mm.
GAP BELOW C/L: 650 mm.
STAGGER: 600 mm.
DIHEDRAL, BOTH WINGS: 2°
SWEEPBACK, BOTH WINGS: 3°
STABILIZER SPAN: 3700 mm.
OVERALL LENGTH: 8200 mm.
OVERALL HEIGHT AT THE TIP: 3250 mm.
EMPTY WEIGHT: 1050 kg.
FLYING WEIGHT: 1485 kg.
MAXIMUM AIRSPEED: 175 k/hr.
SERVICE CEILING: 7000 M.
STANDARD WHEELS: 810 x 125 mm.
ENGINE: 245 Ps MAYBACH Mb Iva.
PROPELLER: AXIAL 3170 mm. DIA.
1 .5 0 1 2 3 4 5m.
SCALE BAR
RU. C.VII
DAN-SAN ABBOTT © 1995

The Pfalz Flugzeug Werke, Speyer am Rhein, received two orders to build the Ru. C.IV (Pfal.), 150 in October 1916, serial numbers C.7500 - 7649/16, and 150 in January 1917, serial numbers in question.

The Rumpler C.IV had an upper wingspan of 12,660mm and the lower span measured 12,100mm. The overall length was 8405mm and the height was 3250mm at the wing tip. It had an empty weight of 1080 kg and a useful load of 450 kg. Its flying weight was therefore 1530 kg.

The first order, serial numbers C.6675 - 6824/16, were painted in a two-color camouflage of dark green and brown on the upper and side surfaces with the undersides of the wings, fuselage, tailplane, all struts, and wheel covers a very pale blue. Commencing with the second order the Terrain camouflage was changed to three top and side colors: dark green, light green, and brown with very pale blue undersides, struts, and wheel covers. Starting with serial number C.1420/17, purple was substituted for the brown in the top and side three-color camouflage scheme. The scheme was changed again with Ru. C.IV (Rubild) 8250/17 to a two-color scheme of dark green and violet on the top and side surfaces with the pale blue undersurfaces, struts and wheel covers.

The Basse und Selve Ru. C.IV (Bayru) aircraft were covered with five-color printed fabric. The Pfalz-built Ru. C.IV (Pfal.) were spray painted in dark green and brown. In September 1917, a few Ru. C.IV aircraft served with *Schusta 5* and *27b.* Some Ru. C.VII machines were on strength with *Schusta 29b* in February 1918.

Albatros C.XII

The last Albatros design to serve with the *Schutzstaffeln* was the Albatros C.XII. It was a refinement of the Alb. C.X design, a very elegant machine with a streamlined fuselage, oval in cross-section. The change in cross-section resulted in loss of side area, which required the addition of the lower fin and enlargement of the upper fin to provide adequate directional stability. The spade handle tailplane plan form was changed to an oval shape with a higher aspect ratio. The Albatros C.XII retained the wing design of the Alb. C.X. Although it was a more streamlined design with the 260 Ps Mercedes D.IVa engine, there was no improvement in maximum airspeed of 175 km/hr. However, the rate of climb was improved and the Alb. C.XII reached 5000 meters in 45 minutes and had a service ceiling of 5500 meters. The upper wingspan was 14,370mm, and the lower span 13,010mm. The overall length was 8850mm and the height 3400mm. The empty weight was 1021 kg and useful load 618 kg, for a total weight of 1639 kg.

In December 1916, Albatros Werke received an order for 23 Alb. C.XII aircraft, serial numbers C.9300 to 9322/16. In January 1917, after successfully passing the type tests, *Idflieg* awarded Albatros Werke G.m.b.H. (the name changed to Albatros Gesellschaft für Flugzeugunternehmungen m.b.H. on 3 March 1917) a second order for 200 Alb. C.XII, C.1000 to 1199/17.

License orders were placed with OAW for 100 Alb. C.XII (OAW), C.1200 - 1299/17. On 26 June 1917, OAW received type test approval on Alb. C.XII C.1200/17. In February 1917,

Albatros C.XII 1109/17 armed with two bombs. This type of aircraft equipped at least *Schusta 22b*. This particular aircraft was on the strength of *Fl.Abt. 218(A)* in the fall of 1917. Photo Credit: Terry Phillips.

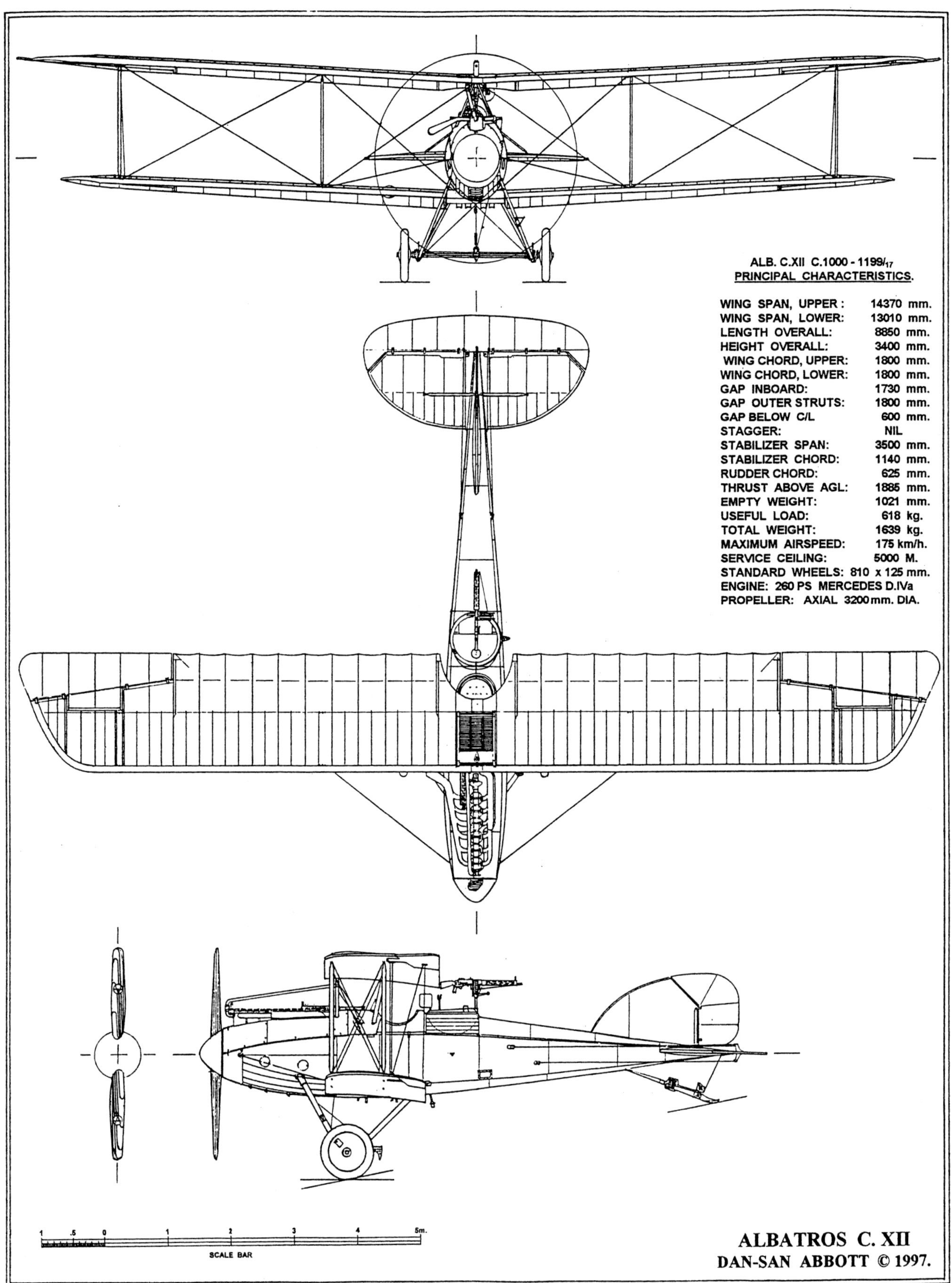
ALB. C.XII C.1000 - 1199/17
PRINCIPAL CHARACTERISTICS.
WING SPAN, UPPER : 14370 mm.
WING SPAN, LOWER: 13010 mm.
LENGTH OVERALL: 8850 mm.
HEIGHT OVERALL: 3400 mm.
WING CHORD, UPPER: 1800 mm.
WING CHORD, LOWER: 1800 mm.
GAP INBOARD: 1730 mm.
GAP OUTER STRUTS: 1800 mm.
GAP BELOW C/L 600 mm.
STAGGER: NIL
STABILIZER SPAN: 3500 mm.
STABILIZER CHORD: 1140 mm.
RUDDER CHORD: 625 mm.
THRUST ABOVE AGL: 1885 mm.
EMPTY WEIGHT: 1021 mm.
USEFUL LOAD: 618 kg.
TOTAL WEIGHT: 1639 kg.
MAXIMUM AIRSPEED: 175 km/h.
SERVICE CEILING: 5000 M.
STANDARD WHEELS: 810 x 125 mm.
ENGINE: 260 PS MERCEDES D.IVa
PROPELLER: AXIAL 3200 mm. DIA.
1 .5 0 1 2 3 4 5m.
SCALE BAR
ALBATROS C. XII
DAN-SAN ABBOTT © 1997.

Idflieg ordered 200 Alb. C.XII (Bay), C.1800 - 1999/17, and on 5 May 1917, Bayerische Flugzeug Werke received type test approval on Alb. C.XII (Bay) C.1802/17.

Albatros began deliveries in June 1917, and by 30 June 1917, 41 Alb. C.XII machines were in the inventory of the front line *Fl.Abt.* and *Fl.Abt.(A)*. The front inventory lists show that on 31 August 1917 there were 93 Alb. C.XII, dropping to 92 on 31 October 1917, and 66 in December 1917. The Alb. C.XII were used by front line units to at least 31 August 1918, when 15 were listed at the front.

The Albatros Werke employed a three-color camouflage scheme of dark green, light green, and brown on the upper surfaces. The under surfaces of the wings and tailplane were sky blue and the rudder was painted the same as the center color of the tailplane. This scheme was used on the first order and the first half of the second order. In the second half of the second order, Albatros changed to a two-color scheme on the fabric upper surfaces of dark green and light green with sky blue under surfaces. The plywood surfaces of the fuselage, upper and lower fins were shellacked and varnished, resulting in a straw yellow color.

OAW followed their previous patterns, but used mauve in place of the sienna brown. Bayerische Flugzeug Werke changed their scheme to two colors of light green and mauve on the upper fabric surfaces, with sky blue fabric under surfaces. Fuselages were varnished on Alb. C.XII (OAW) and Alb. C.XII (Bay) machines. In November 1917, *Schusta 22b* was issued some Alb. C.XII aircraft which served along with the DFW C.V and Halb. Cl.II. As of this writing, none have been found listed after that date.

LVG C.V

Luftverkehrsgesellschaft m.b.H. (LVG), Berlin-Johannisthal, was founded in 1910 by Arthur Müller, a far-sighted financier. He owned the land at Johannisthal, southeast of Berlin, which would become the heart of the German aviation industry and location of the major aircraft manufacturers AGO Flugzeugwerke, Albatros Werke, Jeannin Flugzeugbau, Luft Torpedo Gesellschaft, Nationale Flugzeugwerke, Rumpler Werke, and Luftverkehrsgesellschaft. Also belonging to him was the property of Adlershof, where *Idflieg* headquarters and base of operations were located. The LVG factory was founded with 13,329 square meters and a staff of 30 workers. By 1918, this factory had grown to 42,026 sq.m. and personnel of 3520 workers and staff. In floor area and number of workers, LVG was number one of the German aircraft factories. To the end of the war, LVG built 5640 aircraft and was second only to Albatros, which had built 6242 aircraft at its Johannisthal factory. With this large, modern plant LVG was able to produce large quantities of aircraft each month. In 1917, 70 machines were manufactured per month. The beginning of 1918 saw over 150 machines being produced per month. By March 1918, *Idflieg* had committed LVG to delivering 200 aircraft per month. These monthly commitments were exceeded only by Albatros and Pfalz Flugzeugwerke at 230 machines per month.

Franz Schneider, a Swiss engineer, was responsible for the aircraft designs up to the LVG C.IV. Then he lost the confidence of Arthur Müller, left LVG, and later formed his own company. With the departure of Franz Schneider, LVG was committed to the manufacture of other aircraft under license: the Alb. D.II (LVG), Gotha G.IV (LVG), and the DFW C.V (LVG).

Wilhelm Sabersky-Müssigbrodt, the designer of the DFW C.V, was sent to LVG to assist in setting up production lines and procedures for the building of the DFW C.V (LVG) at the request of *Idflieg* as part of the licensing agreement with DFW. Willy Sabersky-Müssigbrodt impressed the directors at LVG and was hired as the Technical Director of LVG. He was soon at work on the design of the LVG D.XV, which had its roots in the design of the DFW C.V. By 24 December 1916, the LVG D.XV with the 200 Ps Benz Bz.IVa engine was unveiled and had shown very good flight characteristics and performance. It was an improved DFW C.V, as one would expect in a succession of designs. The LVG D.XV was designated the LVG C.V and submitted to *Idflieg* for tests and evaluation. Between 22 and 28 March 1917, the machine was subjected to type tests. Upon completion of a long list of required changes, corrections, and inclusion of some equipment required by *Idflieg*, the LVG C.V was approved for production on 12 April 1917. This same month, a contract was awarded to LVG for 200 LVG C.V aircraft, serial numbers C.3200 - 3377/17 (178) and C.4556 - 4577/17 (22).

A contract for 500 LVG C.V machines, C.9400 - 9899/17, was awarded in August 1917, followed in November 1917 with an order for 250 LVG C.V, 14403 - 14652/17. In December 1917, *Idflieg* ordered 150 LVG C.V, C.15815 - 15946/17. A further order was placed in February 1918 for 100 machines, C.1000 - 1099/18 and the last order in March 1918 was for 50 LVG C.V, C.1750 - 1799/18.

The LVG C.V had an upper wingspan of 13,260mm and a lower wingspan of 12,830mm. The aircraft's overall length was 8070mm and the height was 2950mm. The empty weight was 966 kg and the disposable load was 530 kg, bringing the flying weight to 1496 kg. Its maximum airspeed at sea level was 170 km/hr. The LVG C.V had a service ceiling of 5000 meters and it could climb to a height of 4000 meters in 35 minutes. It had a flight duration of 3.5 hours. The LVG C.V was armed with a synchronized Maxim 08 lMG firing through the propeller mounted to the right side of the engine and a Parabellum Modell 14 mounted on a Haussmann Gun Ring on the observer's cockpit. The rear cockpit had an internal bomb rack for four 12.5 P.u.W. bombs. The observer's cockpit was also fitted for the installation of photographic equipment.

Deliveries began to arrive in early August and by 31 August 1917, 98 LVG C.V machines were reported at the front. This figure rose to 219 by 31 October and 446 by 31 December 1917. By 28 February 1918, the front inventory listing was 504, and peaked at 565 on 30 April 1918. The LVG C.VI began to replace the LVG C.V at the front and on 30 June 1918, the front inventory was 312 and dropped to 133 on 31 August 1918. The LVG C.V continued to serve in the *Fl.Abt.* and *Fl.Abt.(A)* until the end of the war.

LVG employed from serial number C.3200/17 through C.15964/17, a two-color Day Terrain camouflage scheme on the upper surfaces of the wings, tailplane, and rudder of a light mossy-green and pale lilac with pale green undersides. The plywood fuselage, undercarriage, and interplane struts were shellacked and varnished resulting in a straw yellow color. The cowlings, louvers, access doors, radiator, fittings, and cabane struts were painted in light grey.

In November 1917, *Schusta 1, 9, 11, 15, 27b,* and *30b* were issued the LVG C.V, which served in diminishing numbers with the *Schusta*, until the end of April 1918, when they were replaced by the Halberstadt and Hannover Cl types.

CHAPTER XXII

INTRODUCTION OF THE TWO-SEAT FIGHTER

In an effort to improve the performance of the C Class aircraft, *Idflieg* issued a design specification in September 1916 for the new lightweight C Class two-seat aircraft. The requirements limited the engines to 160 to 180 Ps and stipulated that the weight of these aircraft were to be 250 kg lighter than the standard C Class aircraft. The aircraft manufacturers selected by *Idflieg* to design and provide prototype machines to these requirements were: Halberstädter Flugzeugwerke G.m.b.H., Halberstadt, and Hannoversche Waggonfabrik A.G., Hannover-Linden.

Halberstädter Flugzeugwerke G.m.b.H. was founded on 9 April 1912 as Deutsche Bristol Werke G.m.b.H. in Halberstadt v.d. Thekenbergen. The flying school, *Halberstädter Fliegerschule G.m.b.H.*, was situated at Thekenbergen and the factory site in Halberstadt.

Halberstädter Flugzeugwerke G.m.b.H. was a relatively small aircraft manufacturer with limited production capabilities. In 1916 Halberstädter Flugzeugwerke had a factory space of 5140 square meters with 307 workers and staff. In 1917 the factory had grown to 6340 square meters and 967 employees. The monthly production rate in 1917 was 80 to 90 aircraft. In 1918 the factory expanded to 8020 square meters and 1499 workers and staff. By March 1918, the monthly aircraft production had risen to 100 aircraft and was scheduled at that rate throughout 1918.

The Halberstädter Flugzeugwerke had produced under license the two-seat Fokker M.8, which was designated the Halb. A.1, and the DFW C.V, as previously discussed in the DFW C.V section. Halberstädter Flugzeugwerke also produced original designs by *Dipl-Ing* Karl Theis, the Halb. B.I, Halb. D.I, D.II, D.III, and D.V single-seat fighter aircraft. These latter machines had gone into limited series production and served well in the early *Jagdstaffeln* in late 1916 and early 1917. These first generation Halberstadt D Class machines were small, lightweight and very maneuverable single-seat fighter aircraft. The unsuccessful design in this series, the Halb. D.IV, would become the model for the very successful Halberstadt Cl.II.

Halberstadt Cl.II

The Halberstädter Flugzeugwerke received a contract in November 1916 from *Idflieg* for three prototype aircraft, Halb. C.II C.9901 to 9903/16, to meet the requirement for a two-seat, single engine, armed, lightweight C Class biplane with the Mercedes D.III 160 Ps engine. *Dipl-Ing* Karl Theis met the challenge with the design of an aircraft which was small in C Class terms.

The one-piece upper and lower wingspans were 9400mm and the overall length was 7320mm. The engine was covered with a close fitting aluminum cowling. The fuselage was constructed with fretted plywood formers joined with four longerons and covered with molded birch plywood skin. The wings were of wood construction with fabric covering. The center-section was also of wood construction, but covered with plywood. The empennage had a frame of steel tubing. Streamlined steel tubing was used for all struts. The aileron actuation was by means of steel tubes running through the upper wing aft of the rear spar with a curved crank linked to the controls in the pilot's cockpit. The elevator and rudder controls were cables that ran through the fuselage and were operated with the control stick and rudder bar.

The pilot and gunner sat in a communal cockpit separated by a common bulkhead. The pilot's seat was fastened to a fuel tank with a capacity of 128 liters. Mounted above and behind the gunner was a wooden machine gun ring that was supported by six struts. After the introduction of the Halb. C.II in April 1917 and during subsequent testing it was determined the

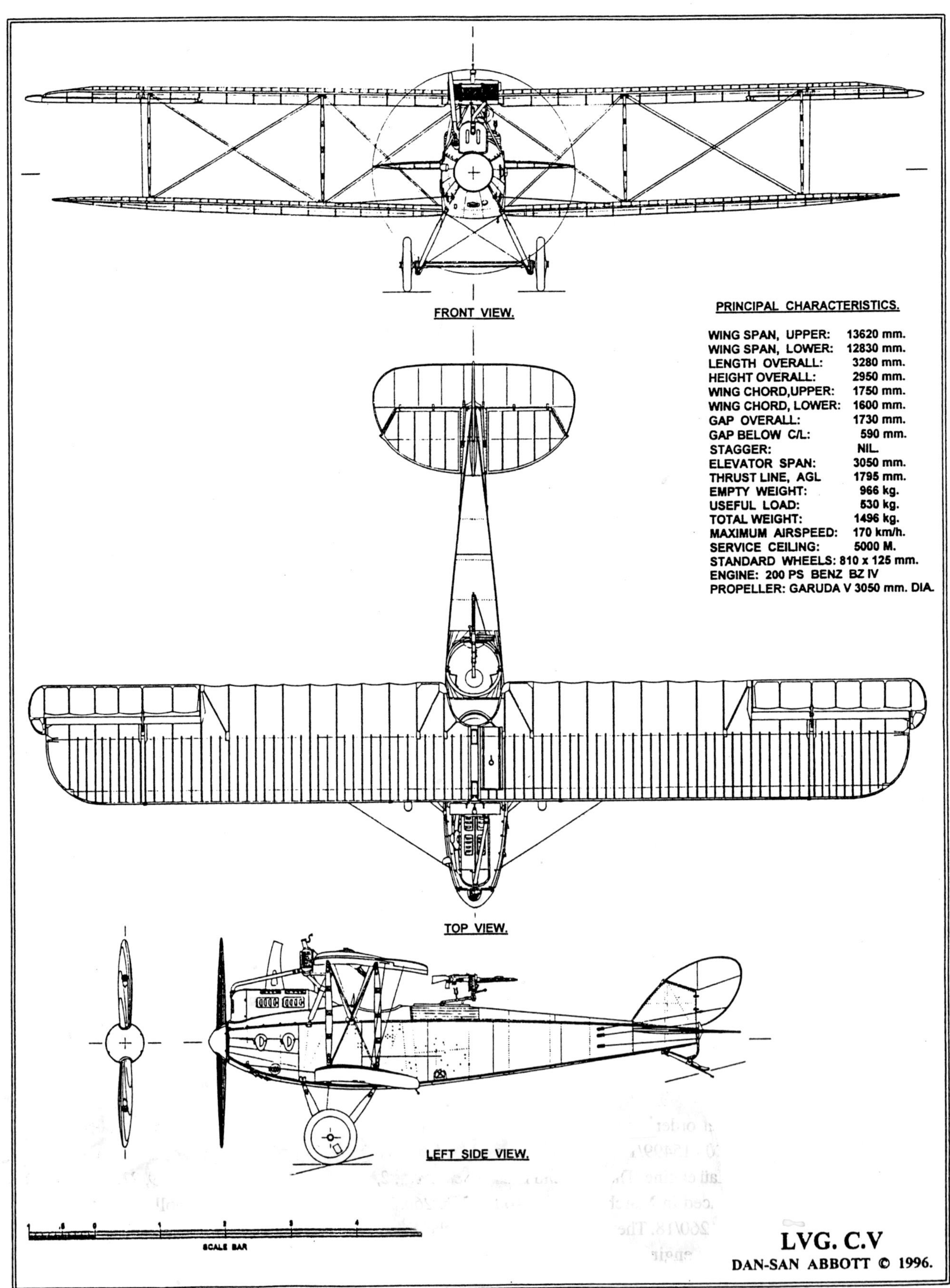
FRONT VIEW.
PRINCIPAL CHARACTERISTICS.
WING SPAN, UPPER: 13620 mm.
WING SPAN, LOWER: 12830 mm.
LENGTH OVERALL: 3280 mm.
HEIGHT OVERALL: 2950 mm.
WING CHORD,UPPER: 1750 mm.
WING CHORD, LOWER: 1600 mm.
GAP OVERALL: 1730 mm.
GAP BELOW C/L: 590 mm.
STAGGER: NIL.
ELEVATOR SPAN: 3050 mm.
THRUST LINE, AGL 1795 mm.
EMPTY WEIGHT: 966 kg.
USEFUL LOAD: 530 kg.
TOTAL WEIGHT: 1496 kg.
MAXIMUM AIRSPEED: 170 km/h.
SERVICE CEILING: 5000 M.
STANDARD WHEELS: 810 x 125 mm.
ENGINE: 200 PS BENZ BZ IV
PROPELLER: GARUDA V 3050 mm. DIA.
TOP VIEW.
LEFT SIDE VIEW.
SCALE BAR
LVG. C.V
DAN-SAN ABBOTT © 1996.

machine needed more wing area to improve handling and altitude performance.

The upper wingspan was increased to 10770mm and the lower span to 10650mm. The fuselage length was reduced to 7300mm. The construction of the upper wing was changed from one piece to three panels. With all these changes, the empty weight increased from 701 kg to 773 kg. The useful load was decreased from 370 kg to 360 kg. In this form, after the completion of the type tests and acceptance on 7 May 1917, the production aircraft emerged and was designated the Halb. Cl.II. In May 1917 *Idflieg* awarded Halberstädter Flugzeugwerke a contract for 100 Halb. Cl.II aircraft, serial numbers C.2825 to C.2924/17. A second order was placed in June 1917 for 100 Halberstadt Cl.II machines, serial numbers C.5675 to 5774/17. The production aircraft up to about C.2924/17 were powered with the 170 Ps Mercedes D.IIIa engine. From about Cl.II C.5675/17, they were equipped with the 180 Ps Mercedes D.IIIaü.

The camouflage finish of this first order was as follows: The upper surface of the wings, tailplane, fin, rudder, and wheel covers were covered with the light lower pattern five-color lozenge printed fabric. The undersides of the wings and tailplane were covered with plain unbleached linen fabric. The fabric covering was applied to the wings at a 45o angle to the leading edge of the wing panels, running outboard from the leading edge toward the wing tips. The rib tapes were all cut strips of the lozenge fabric on the top surfaces and plain fabric on the bottom surfaces.

The fuselage and center-section were painted in the fabric colors of light blue, rose, light violet, greenish grey, and ocher. The irregular polygon patterns were sprayed with merging edges and the whole over-sprayed in a splatter of light blue flecks. The bottom of the fuselage and center-section were the straw yellow of the varnished plywood. All the struts were painted light grey.

Idflieg issued a third order to Halberstädter Flugzeugwerke in June 1917 for an additional 100 Cl.II aircraft, serial numbers C.6300 to 6399/17. With this order, the machines were powered by the 180 Ps Mercedes D.IIIaü engine. In October 1917 Halberstädter Flugzeugwerke received the fourth order for 200 Halb. Cl.II machines, serial numbers C.14200 to 14399/17. The aircraft of this order were also powered with the Mercedes D.IIIaü engine. In November 1917 Halberstädter Flugzeugwerke received the fifth [illegible] for [illegible] Halb. Cl.II machines, serial numbers C.1530[illegible]17. [illegible]e too were powered with the Mercedes D.II[illegible] [illegible] and final order for the Halb. Cl.II was [illegible] for [illegible] aircraft, serial numbers C.1161 [illegible] were powered with the 200 Ps Mercedes D.II[illegible]

All of these aircraft from the second and subsequent orders were covered with the five-color lozenge printed linen fabric, the dark pattern on the upper surfaces on the wing panels, tailplane, fin rudder, and wheel covers. The under surfaces of the wings and tailplane were covered with the lighter lower surface printed five-color fabric. The fabric colors were applied to the wings, tailplane, fin, and rudder at a 45o angle, to the leading edge on the wings and to the stern post on the empennage.

In February 1918 *Idflieg* awarded a contract to Bayerische Flugzeug Werke A.G. for 100 Halb. Cl.II (BFW) machines, serial numbers C.700 to 799/18, which were to be powered with the 180 Ps Mercedes D.IIIaü engine. Deliveries were to commence in March 1918 with 20 aircraft and 40 were to follow in April 1918. A second order was awarded in April 1918 for a further 200 Halb. Cl.IIa (BFW), serial numbers C.2800 to 2999/18, to be powered with the 180 Ps Argus As.III engine. Deliveries for this order amounted to 60 in April, 80 in May and 60 in June 1918.

The Halb. Cl.II (BFW) machines were delivered with five-color printed fabric, the dark pattern on the upper surface of the wings, tailplane, fin, rudder, and wheel covers. The fabric covers were made in panels with the joining seams parallel to the ribs. The light five-color pattern was used on the undersurface of the wings and tailplane. Cut strips of matching printed fabric were used for rib tapes. The plywood-covered portions were clear varnished, resulting in a straw yellow color. Metal work, struts, and cowlings were light grey.

Deliveries of the Halberstadt Cl.II began during August 1917 to the *Armee Flugpark 4 (AFP 4)*, Army Air Park 4, and to *AFP 5*. By 31 August 1917, fifteen Halb. Cl.II aircraft were listed in the *Front Bestand* (front inventory) of aircraft at the front. On 31 October 1917, 65 Halb. Cl.II aircraft were listed and by 31 December 1917 the total had risen to 170 Halb. Cl.II machines.

In September 1917, *AFP 4* began to issue the Halb. Cl.II to *Schutzstaffeln 19, 23b, 25b,* and *27b*. *AFP 5* also began to equip *Schusta 22b* with the Halb. Cl.II. By the end of December 1917, *AFP 2, 4, 5, 6* and *Schusta 1, 2, 5, 9, 10, 11, 12, 13, 17, 19, 22b, 23b, 24b, 25b, 26b, 27b*, and *28b* were equipped with this machine. Each *Schusta* had six Halb. Cl.II machines and *AFP 2, 4, 5,* and *6* held in reserve at their bases three of this type for each *Schusta* in their *Armee*. The strength of the Halb. Cl.II at the front on 28 February 1918 was 224. By 20 March 1918, the Halb. Cl.II equipped either partially or completely *Schusta 1* [illegible], *5, 9, 10, 11, 12, 13, 15, 17, 19* *21, 22b, 23b, 24b,* [illegible] *27b, 28b, 29b, 35,* and *37*. Following the equipage of the *Schlachtstaffeln*, Halb. Cl.II aircraft, when available, were issued to the *Fl.Abt.* and *Fl.Abt.A* and the *Jagdstaffeln* as personnel transport. On 30 April 1918, there were 342 Halb.

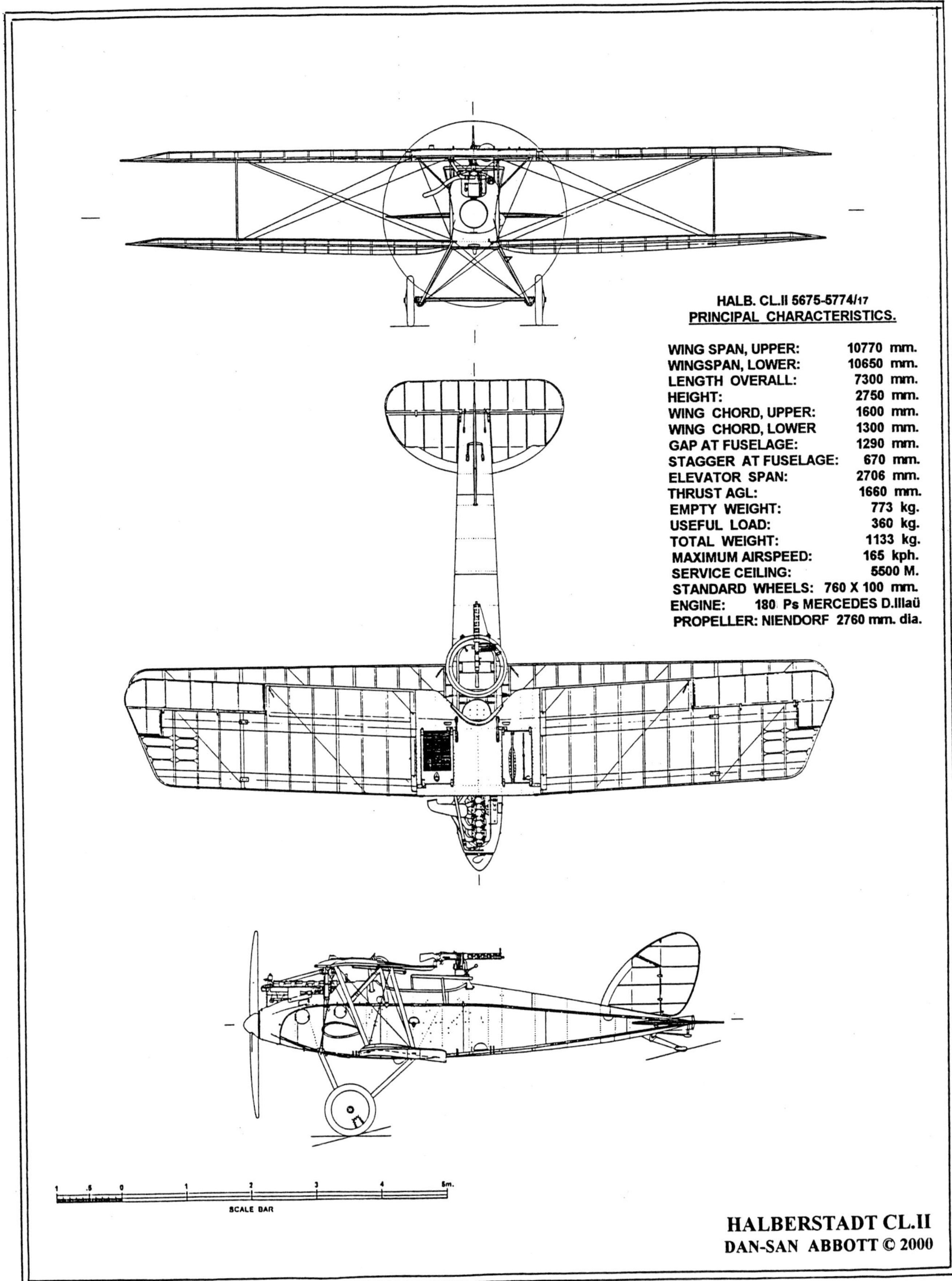
HALB. CL.II 5675-5774/17
PRINCIPAL CHARACTERISTICS.
WING SPAN, UPPER: 10770 mm.
WINGSPAN, LOWER: 10650 mm.
LENGTH OVERALL: 7300 mm.
HEIGHT: 2750 mm.
WING CHORD, UPPER: 1600 mm.
WING CHORD, LOWER 1300 mm.
GAP AT FUSELAGE: 1290 mm.
STAGGER AT FUSELAGE: 670 mm.
ELEVATOR SPAN: 2706 mm.
THRUST AGL: 1660 mm.
EMPTY WEIGHT: 773 kg.
USEFUL LOAD: 360 kg.
TOTAL WEIGHT: 1133 kg.
MAXIMUM AIRSPEED: 165 kph.
SERVICE CEILING: 5500 M.
STANDARD WHEELS: 760 X 100 mm.
ENGINE: 180 Ps MERCEDES D.IIIaü
PROPELLER: NIENDORF 2760 mm. dia.
1 .5 0 1 2 3 4 5m.
SCALE BAR
HALBERSTADT CL.II
DAN-SAN ABBOTT © 2000

Cl.II aircraft at the front, on 30 June 1918, there were 311. On the last reporting date, 31 August 1918, the total number of Halb. Cl.II listed at the front amounted to 175 aircraft. By this time the Halb. Cl.IV was superseding the Halb. Cl.II.

A Halberstadt Cl.II marked 2 of an unknown unit. Credit: Reinhard Kastner.

The *Schutzstaffel 15* crew of *Uffz.* Warda, in the center adjusting his goggles, and *Uffz.* Ehmann on the right. Their aircraft is a Halberstadt Cl.II.

Unknown crew and *Schlasta*. The aircraft is a Halberstadt Cl.II. Photo credit: Marcus Pleyer.

Hannoversche Waggonfabrik A.G.

Hannoversche Waggonfabrik A.G. was an old established firm that had been founded in 1871. The company built rolling stock and passenger carriages. In 1915, at the suggestion of *Idflieg*, a *Flugzeugbau* (Aircraft Division) was established by Hannnoversche Waggonfabrik in Hannover-Linden. The first products of the Hannoversche Flugzeugbau were propellers. Later Hannover undertook the repair of military aircraft for *Flieger Ersatz Abteilung 5 (FEA 5)*, Aviation Replacement Section 5, located at Hannover. Having proved their abilities, *Idflieg* awarded Hannover a contract to manufacture under license, 24 Aviatik C.I aircraft, with the designation Han. C.I, serial numbers C.1951 to 1974/15. In 1916 Hannover received four further orders for the Han. C.I, which amounted to a total of 146 aircraft, now designated Aviatik C.I (Han).

In September 1916 Hannover received an order from *Idflieg* for 300 Rumpler C.Ia (Han), serial numbers C.4500 - 4799/16. In October 1916 Hannover received an order for 30 Halb. D.II (Han) aircraft, D.800 - 829/16.

In September 1916 Hannover was able to acquire the services of *Dipl-Ing* Hermann Dorner as Chief Engineer. He had worked for the *Prüfanstalt und Werft* under *Idflieg*. Prior to this, Dorner had been the Director of Engineering for Deutsche Flugzeugwerke G.m.b.H., Leipzig. He was just what

Hannover needed, an expert engineer with the knowledge and ability to design aircraft with reduced weight to meet the requirements of the new lightweight C Class machines. Hannover initiated their 'in house' design as a private venture, without financial support from *Idflieg*. However, they were required by *Idflieg* to use the 180 Ps Argus As.III engine in their design. *Dipl-Ing* Hermann Dorner produced the Hannover Type 3a, which was completed in late March or early April 1917.

Idflieg was impressed with the flying characteristics of the Hannover Type 3a and in April or May 1917 awarded Hannoversche Waggonfabrik a contract for three prototype machines which were to undergo type tests and flight evaluation. These three aircraft, with type designation Han. Cl.II, were powered by the 180 Ps Argus As.III engine and bore the serial numbers C.4500 - 4502/17. The three prototypes were delivered in July 1917 and were type tested and approved for front line use on 21 July 1917. In the same month, *Idflieg* ordered 200 Han. Cl.II aircraft, serial numbers C.9200 to 9399/17, powered with the Argus. In anticipation of the contract, the Hannoversche Waggonfabrik Abteilung Flugzeug commenced production of the Cl.II. By August they were able to start their deliveries.

Hannover Cl.II

The production models Han. Cl.II differed from the prototype Hannover Type 3a in that the lower wingspan was reduced from 11,200mm to 11,170mm on the production machines. The upper wingspan of 12,950mm and the overall aircraft length of 7800mm remained the same. The height was increased from 2750mm to 2860mm on the production machines. The upper and lower tailplane plan form of the Hannover Type 3a were somewhat rectangular, while those of the Han Cl.II were rounded on the leading edges. The control cables were situated mid-span on the ailerons, but were moved to the inboard end on the production aircraft. The aircraft empty weight changed from 773 kg to 775 kg and useful load from 360 kg to 380 kg, with the respective overall weight being 1133 kg for the Hannover Type 3a and 1155 kg for the Han. Cl.II production machines. The maximum airspeed at sea level was 165 km/hr (103 mph), 160 km/hr (100 mph) at 2000 m and 145 km/hr (90.6 mph) at 4000 m.

The Hannover Cl.II was a docile aircraft with excellent flying and handling characteristics, and a ceiling of 7500 m (24,600 ft). With this superb high altitude performance it would fly with the *Fl.Abt.* that operated with the German Army and Army Corps Headquarters in performing strategic and operational reconnaissance and aerial photography. It would also serve with the *Fl.Abt.A* that operated with the *Armee Korps*, directing artillery fire and performing tactical battlefield reconnaissance. However, the primary function of the Han. Cl.II would be in service with the *Schutzstaffeln* flying escort duties, protecting C Class type aircraft flying missions for the *Fl.Abt.* and *Fl.Abt.A.*

Dipl-Ing Dorner had paid close attention to the small details in the design of this Han. Cl.II machine. The fuselage, 1400mm deep, almost filled the gap between the wings, and was constructed of ten light formers joined on four longerons, covered with molded 1.6mm birch plywood skin, over which was placed linen fabric. Metal fittings and hardware were at a minimum and those that were there served as attachments of internal fittings, combat equipment, struts, tails, and wings. The design was clean and simple with great care taken in weight reduction and streamlining. Aluminum cowlings enclosed the nose and the sides of the engine compartment. Aluminum doors provided access to the engine for servicing. A circular fuel tank of 140 liters was mounted below the seat in the pilot's compartment.

A 7.92 Maxim lMG or lMG 08/15 machine gun was mounted on the top right side of the fuselage for the pilot. A wooden turret of the Franz Schneider type was located on top of the fuselage over the observer's cockpit for a Parabellum lMG 14 machine gun. In this cockpit were fittings for attaching a photographic camera, wireless radio equipment, trailing antenna, map case, folding table, flare pistol, and canvas belt for colored flares and sockets for an electrically heated flying suit.

The wings were constructed of two spars, with fretted plywood ribs and milled leading edges and wing tips. The trailing edge of the upper wing panel was a wood strip. That of the lower wing was wire. The center-section was framed in wood and covered with 1.6mm thick plywood and then covered with linen fabric. A reserve fuel tank of 35 liters was situated on the left center between the spars and on the right center was a radiator of 40 liters capacity. The 180 Ps Argus As.III(O) engine, manufactured under license by the firm of Adam Opel, Rüsselsheim, provided the power for the Han. Cl.II.

The wings, tailplanes, rudder, and wheel covers of the Han. Cl.II, C.9200 - 9399/17 were covered with light five-color lozenge pattern printed fabric usually used for the lower surfaces. The under surfaces of the wings and tailplane were covered with plain linen fabric. Rib tapes were cut strips of matching fabric. The fuselage, fin, center-section, and struts were painted in colors matching the printed fabric, which were, ocher, green, rose, light violet, and blue. The lozenges painted on the fuselage were irregular polygons about the same size as those of the printed fabric at the rear of the fuselage and fin. They were distinct, with sharply defined edges. As the lozenges progressed forward they became larger and at about mid fuselage had doubled in size and the edges became diffused

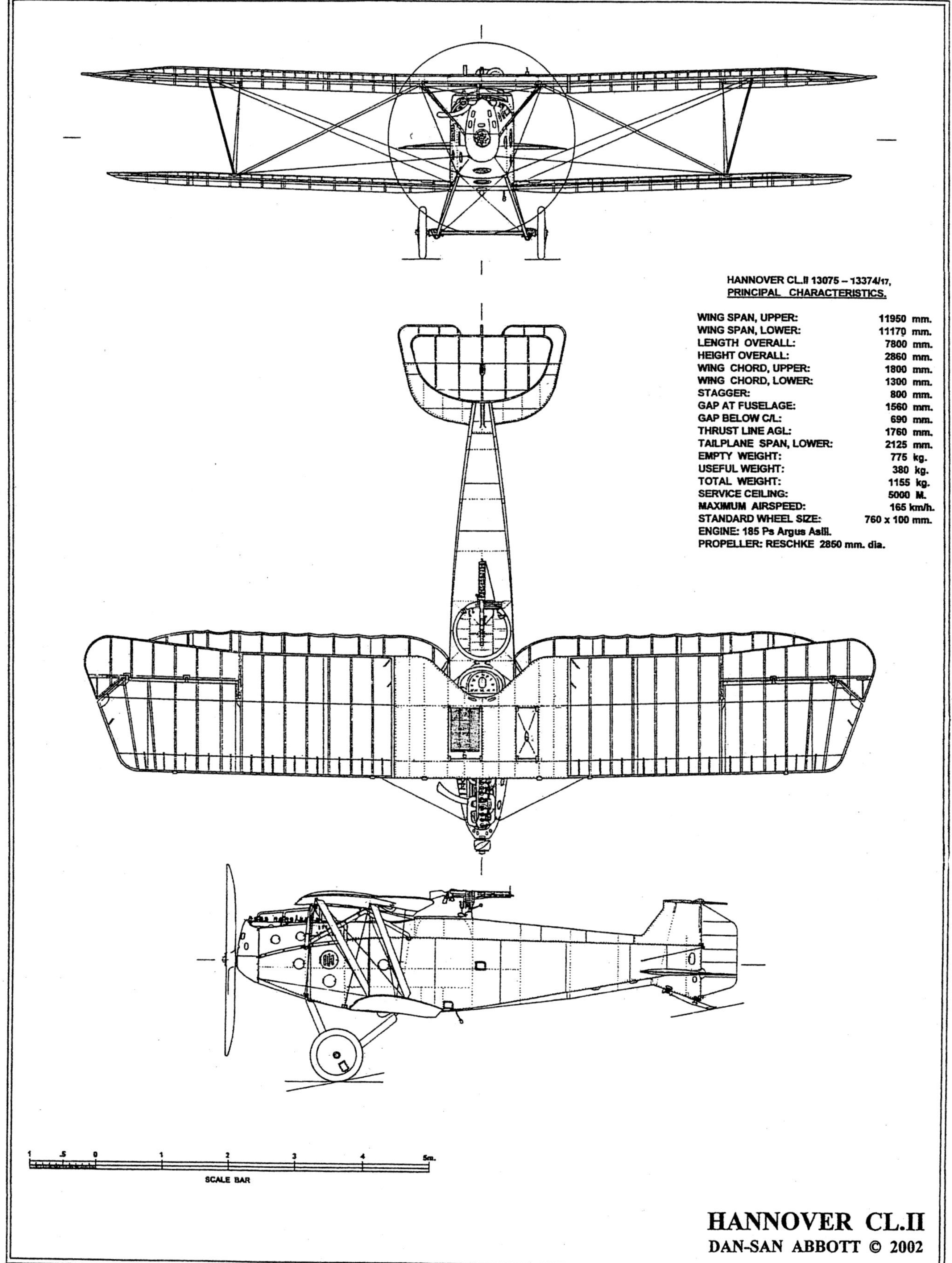
HANNOVER CL.II 13075 – 13374/17,
PRINCIPAL CHARACTERISTICS.
WING SPAN, UPPER: 11950 mm.
WING SPAN, LOWER: 11170 mm.
LENGTH OVERALL: 7800 mm.
HEIGHT OVERALL: 2860 mm.
WING CHORD, UPPER: 1800 mm.
WING CHORD, LOWER: 1300 mm.
STAGGER: 800 mm.
GAP AT FUSELAGE: 1560 mm.
GAP BELOW C/L: 690 mm.
THRUST LINE AGL: 1760 mm.
TAILPLANE SPAN, LOWER: 2125 mm.
EMPTY WEIGHT: 775 kg.
USEFUL WEIGHT: 380 kg.
TOTAL WEIGHT: 1155 kg.
SERVICE CEILING: 5000 M.
MAXIMUM AIRSPEED: 165 km/h.
STANDARD WHEEL SIZE: 760 x 100 mm.
ENGINE: 185 Ps Argus AsIII.
PROPELLER: RESCHKE 2850 mm. dia.
1 .5 0 1 2 3 4 5m.
SCALE BAR
HANNOVER CL.II
DAN-SAN ABBOTT © 2002

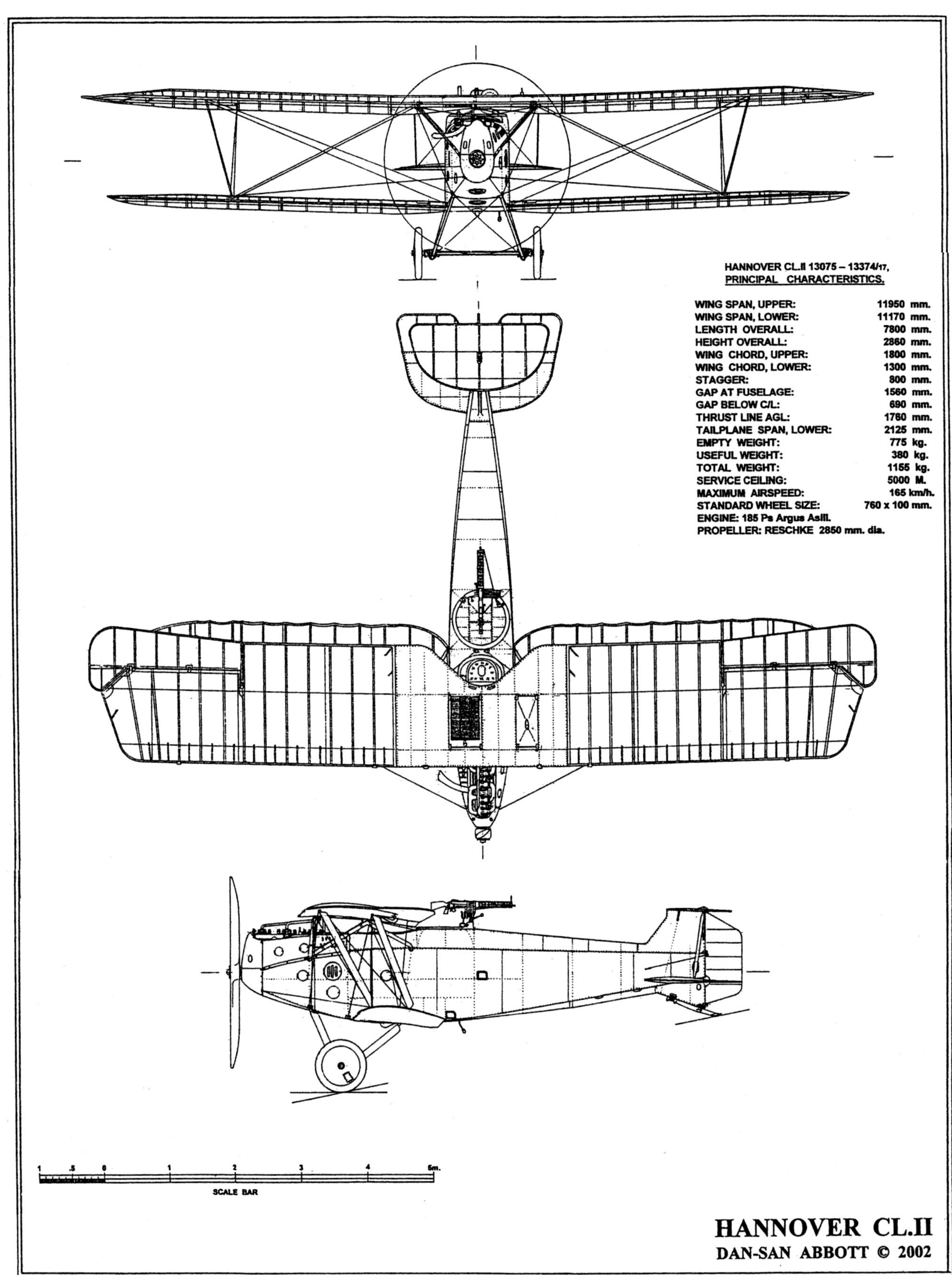
HANNOVER CL.II 13075 – 13374/17,
PRINCIPAL CHARACTERISTICS.
WING SPAN, UPPER: 11950 mm.
WING SPAN, LOWER: 11170 mm.
LENGTH OVERALL: 7800 mm.
HEIGHT OVERALL: 2860 mm.
WING CHORD, UPPER: 1800 mm.
WING CHORD, LOWER: 1300 mm.
STAGGER: 800 mm.
GAP AT FUSELAGE: 1560 mm.
GAP BELOW C/L: 690 mm.
THRUST LINE AGL: 1760 mm.
TAILPLANE SPAN, LOWER: 2125 mm.
EMPTY WEIGHT: 775 kg.
USEFUL WEIGHT: 380 kg.
TOTAL WEIGHT: 1155 kg.
SERVICE CEILING: 5000 M.
MAXIMUM AIRSPEED: 165 km/h.
STANDARD WHEEL SIZE: 760 x 100 mm.
ENGINE: 185 Ps Argus AsIII.
PROPELLER: RESCHKE 2850 mm. dia.
SCALE BAR
HANNOVER CL.II
DAN-SAN ABBOTT © 2002

with the colors merging together. The lozenges painted on the center-section were large and of a size found on the mid-fuselage.

A second order was awarded to Hannoversche Waggonfabrik in September for 300 Han. Cl.II, C.13075 - 13374/17. Two design changes had occurred that were incorporated into this order. Wire braced interplane struts were installed between the upper and lower tailplane and the aileron balance area was increased, which would reduce the control force. All the aircraft in the second order incorporated these two changes. The addition of the tailplane struts were retrofitted to the first production order, but they were not fitted on all of the Han. Cl.II machines. It appears the change was made only in the front line units. The camouflage and finish of the second order was identical to the first order.

In 1917, Hannoversche Waggonfabrik Abteilung Flugzeugbau was a medium-size factory with a production capacity of 60 to 70 aircraft per month. By year's end, Hannoversche Waggonfabrik had delivered 250 Han. Cl.II aircraft. Deliveries of this machine were made to the *Luftstreitkräfte* and by 31 August 1917, 15 Han. Cl.II were listed on the front inventory lists. These 15 machines were probably delivered to *AFP 4* and *AFP 7* and were then issued to *Schusta 3, 6, 12,* and *30b*. By 31 October 1917, 65 Han. Cl.II machines were noted as being at the front. By 31 December 1917, 162 Han. Cl.II were listed at the front. The front total for 28 February 1918 peaked at 295 machines. After that the number of Han. Cl.II aircraft declined to 249 on 30 April 1918, 72 on 30 June, and 31 on the last recorded date, 31 August 1918.

On 26 January 1918 as part of the *Amerika Programme*, eight *Schutzstaffeln* were created from *Fl.Abt. 47b(Lb), Fl.Abt. 4, Fl.Abt. 15, Fl.Abt. 21, Fl.Abt. 11, Fl.Abt. 25, Fl.Abt.(A) 220, and Fl.Abt. 24s*, which had been transferred from the Eastern Front. The *Flieger Abteilungen* after conversion became, respectively, *Schusta 31b, 32, 33, 34, 35, 36, 37,* and *38s*. These new *Schusta* were re-equipped with the Halb. Cl.II or Han. Cl.II aircraft.

While the following list is not complete and does not indicate the actual months the conversion to the Hannover Cl.II, Cl.III and Cl.IIIa took place by the various units, it does serve as a guide. By January 1918, *Schusta 17, 25b*, and *27b* were partially equipped with Hannover Cl.II aircraft. In February *Schusta 30b* had converted to the Han. Cl.II. By 20 March 1918, *AFP 2, 17,* and *18* held in reserve Han. Cl.II aircraft for *Schusta 12, 17, 22b, 24b, 25b, 30b, 34,* and *38s* which were equipped with this two-seat fighter.

On 27 March 1918 the *Schutzstaffeln* were renamed *Schlachtstaffeln (Schlasta)* Battle Flights, more in keeping with their new offensive role. In April 1918, *Schlasta 16* converted to the Han. Cl.II. During May *Schlasta 6, 13,* and *31b* were equipped with Han. Cl.II machines. In August 1918, *Schlasta 7, 10,* and *20* had converted to Han. Cl.II aircraft. By September *Schlasta 33* had made the change.

Deliveries of the last Han. Cl.II scheduled in 1918 by *Idflieg* were as follows: January, 80; February, 70; March, 35; April, 45; and May, 20. However, of the 500 Han. Cl.II machines ordered, only 439 were delivered. On 1 March 1918 there was a fire at the factory and 61 machines were destroyed. As deliveries of the Han. Cl.II were completed, production of the Han. Cl.III had begun.

Hannover Cl.II 13080/17 from an unknown unit. It's marked with a sort of funky 'reddy kilowatt' personal insignia. Photo credit: Terry Phillips.

Hannover Cl.II 13130/17 in French captivity. It has been painted in the French five color camouflage and was photographed at Le Bourget airfield just outside Paris. Credit: The Lafayette Foundation.

Hannover Cl.III

In December 1917, *Dipl-Ing* Dorner had started a redesign of the Han. Cl.II powered with the 180 Ps Mercedes D.IIIaü engine. He had reduced the size and weight of the new machine, now designated Han. Cl.III, while maintaining an almost identical appearance. The upper span was shortened from 11,950mm to 11,700mm. This was accomplished by cutting the span of the center-section 200mm and the overhang portion of the upper main panels 25mm each. The lower overall wingspan was decreased 180mm from 11,200mm to 11,020mm. This was done by narrowing the fuselage width 50mm and each wing panel by 65mm. The upper and lower wing chords remained the same. The fuselage length was shortened 170mm. The overall height was lowered 50mm, from 2800mm to 2750mm, on the Han. Cl.III. The empty weight was significantly lessened from 775 kg to 741 kg. The change from the Argus As.IIIa to the 180 Ps Mercedes D.IIIaü accounted for 20 kg in engine weight of the overall 34 kg weight reduction. The useful load was decreased from 380 kg on the Han. Cl.II to 340 kg on the Han. Cl.III to further improve the flight performance of the new machine.

The ceiling of the Han. Cl.III was 7000 meters. The maximum airspeed was 165 km/hr at 2000 meters. The rate of climb was improved, attaining 3000 meters in 19.0 minutes. *Idflieg* placed an order with Hannoversche Waggonfabrik in late December 1917 for 200 Han. Cl.III aircraft, prototype and production machines, serial numbers C.16000 - 16199/17.

The prototype passed the structural tests at Adlershof on 23 February 1918 and production of the Han. Cl.III commenced. In March 1918 Hannoversche Waggonfabrik was to start delivery of 65 Han. Cl.III machines along with 35 Han. Cl.II aircraft. Due to the acute shortage of the 180 Ps Mercedes D.IIIaü engine, the production of the Han. Cl.III stopped in April 1918 with the eightieth machine, serial number C.16079/17. The remaining machines on the order were completed as Han. Cl.IIIa aircraft with the Argus As.IIIa(O).

The wings, upper tailplane, lower elevators, rudder, and wheel covers were covered with four-color, dark pattern lozenge printed fabric on the upper surfaces and the lighter lower surface pattern on the under surfaces of the wing, upper tailplane, and lower elevators. Plain fabric strips were used for rib tapes.

The fuselage, lower stabilizer, center-section, and all struts were painted with lozenges in colors matching the printed fabric. The lozenges on the empennage were approximately the same size as the printed fabric and were sharply defined, and as they progressed forward to mid-fuselage, were about doubled in size. The adjoining edges of the lozenges were diffused with the colors merging into each other.

Deliveries to the front line units began in March 1918 and by 30 April 1918, 51 Han. Cl.III machines were listed in the *Front Bestand.* On 30 June 1918, 67 Han. Cl.III aircraft were listed with front units. On the last posting of 31 August 1918, the total had dropped to 29 machines at the front. The following units are known to have been equipped in whole or in part with the Han. Cl.III: *Schlasta 5, 16,* and *24b* in May, *Schlasta 12* in June, *Schlasta 10* in August and *Schlasta 20* and *33* in September 1918.

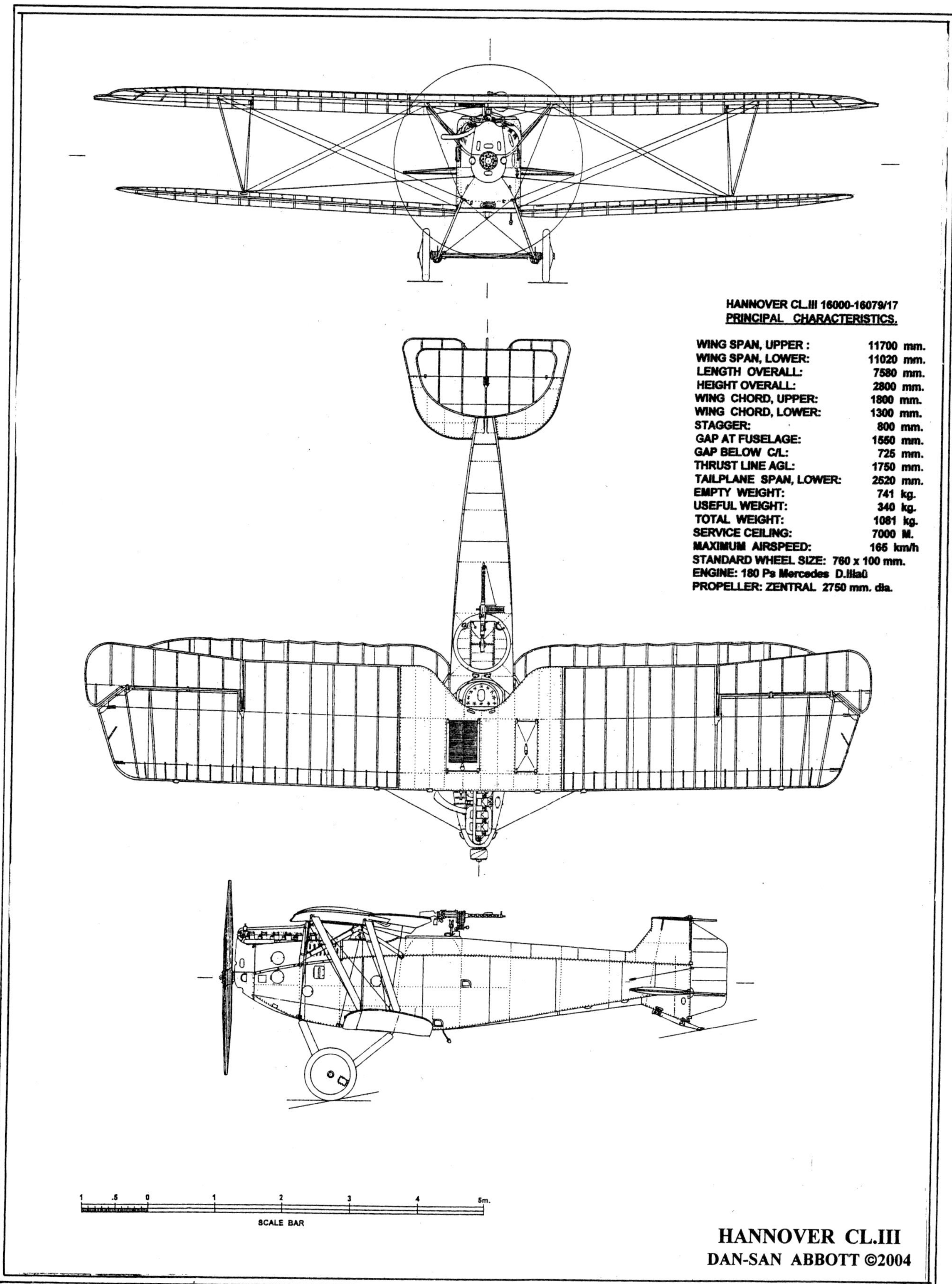
HANNOVER CL.III 16000-16079/17
PRINCIPAL CHARACTERISTICS.
WING SPAN, UPPER : 11700 mm.
WING SPAN, LOWER: 11020 mm.
LENGTH OVERALL: 7580 mm.
HEIGHT OVERALL: 2800 mm.
WING CHORD, UPPER: 1800 mm.
WING CHORD, LOWER: 1300 mm.
STAGGER: 800 mm.
GAP AT FUSELAGE: 1550 mm.
GAP BELOW C/L: 725 mm.
THRUST LINE AGL: 1750 mm.
TAILPLANE SPAN, LOWER: 2520 mm.
EMPTY WEIGHT: 741 kg.
USEFUL WEIGHT: 340 kg.
TOTAL WEIGHT: 1081 kg.
SERVICE CEILING: 7000 M.
MAXIMUM AIRSPEED: 165 km/h
STANDARD WHEEL SIZE: 760 x 100 mm.
ENGINE: 180 Ps Mercedes D.IIIaü
PROPELLER: ZENTRAL 2750 mm. dia.
1 .5 0 1 2 3 4 5m.
SCALE BAR
HANNOVER CL.III
DAN-SAN ABBOTT ©2004

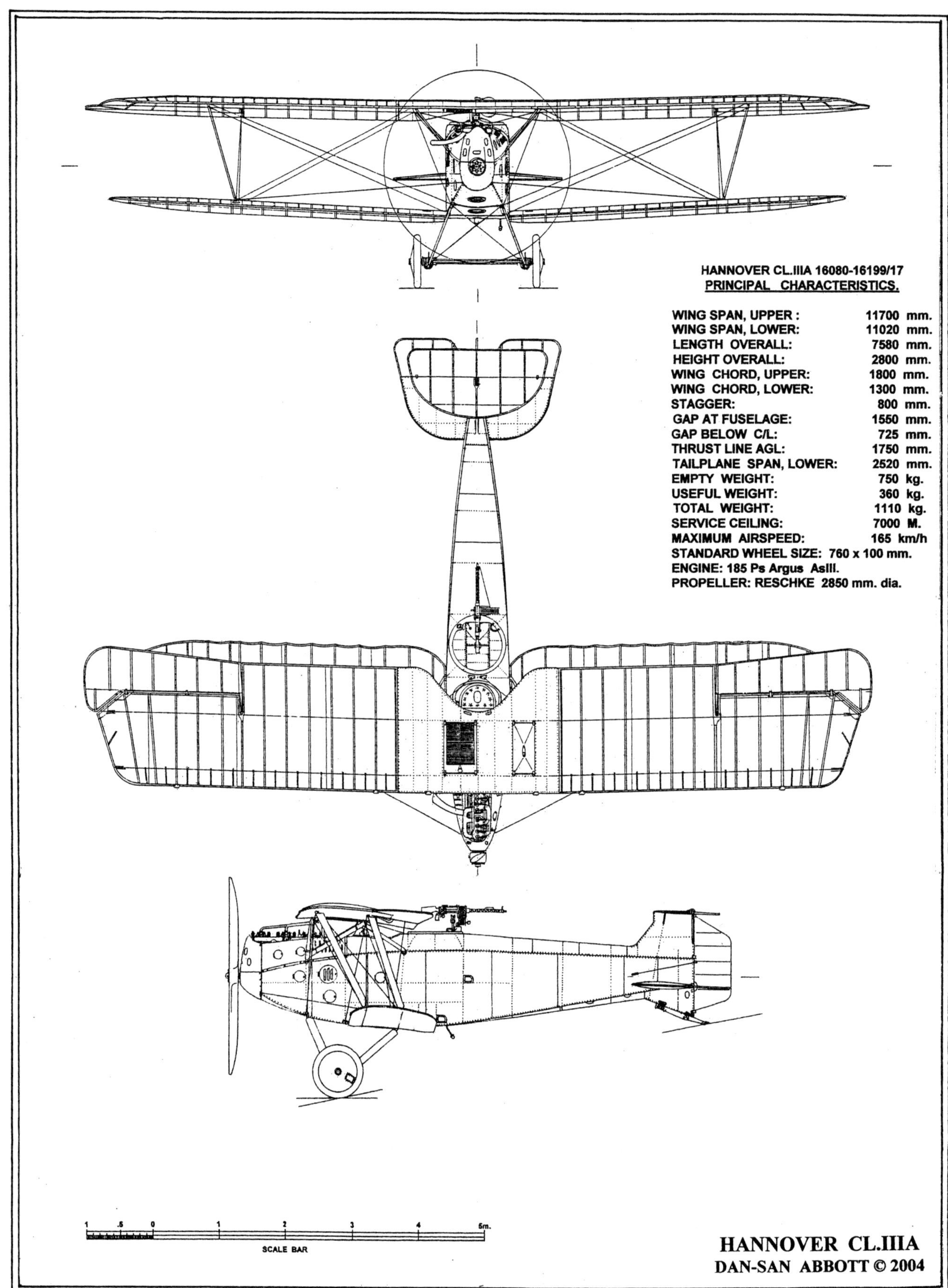
HANNOVER CL.IIIA 16080-16199/17
PRINCIPAL CHARACTERISTICS.
WING SPAN, UPPER : 11700 mm.
WING SPAN, LOWER: 11020 mm.
LENGTH OVERALL: 7580 mm.
HEIGHT OVERALL: 2800 mm.
WING CHORD, UPPER: 1800 mm.
WING CHORD, LOWER: 1300 mm.
STAGGER: 800 mm.
GAP AT FUSELAGE: 1550 mm.
GAP BELOW C/L: 725 mm.
THRUST LINE AGL: 1750 mm.
TAILPLANE SPAN, LOWER: 2520 mm.
EMPTY WEIGHT: 750 kg.
USEFUL WEIGHT: 360 kg.
TOTAL WEIGHT: 1110 kg.
SERVICE CEILING: 7000 M.
MAXIMUM AIRSPEED: 165 km/h
STANDARD WHEEL SIZE: 760 x 100 mm.
ENGINE: 185 Ps Argus AsIII.
PROPELLER: RESCHKE 2850 mm. dia.
1 .5 0 1 2 3 4 5m.
SCALE BAR
HANNOVER CL.IIIA
DAN-SAN ABBOTT © 2004

Hannover Cl.IIIa

Due to the critical situation and the demands for the Mercedes D.IIIaü and the D.IIIaüv engines for fighter aircraft and the Halberstadt Cl.II, production of the Han. Cl.III was stopped at the eightieth machine, serial number C.16079/17. With serial number C.16080/17, production resumed as the Han. Cl.IIIa. This aircraft differed from the Han. Cl.III in the incidental details required for the installation of the Opel manufactured Argus As.IIIa(O) engine. Dimensionally and structurally, both aircraft were identical, however the weight increased with the Argus engine. The empty weight of the Han. Cl.IIIa was 750 kg, the disposable load was 360 kg and the flying weight was 1110 kg, an increase of 29 kg over the Han. Cl.III. The big change was in maximum airspeed, 165 km/hr at sea level, and the ceiling was 7500 meters. The performance was better than the Han. Cl.III.

Following completion of the first production order, *Idflieg* placed an order in April 1918 for 200 Han. Cl.IIIa aircraft, C.2600 - 2799/18. In May 1918 another order was placed with Hannover Waggonfabrik for 100 Han. Cl.IIIa machines, serial numbers C.3800 - 3899/18. This was followed in June by an order for 100 more, with serial numbers C.6950 - 7049/18. A final order was awarded to Abteilung Flugzeugbau of Hannoversche Waggonfabrik in September 1918 for fifty Han. Cl.IIIa machines, serial numbers C.12620 - 12669/18. The production capacity of the Abteilung Flugzeugbau in 1918 was ninety aircraft per month. Manufacture of the Han. Cl.IIIa continued to the end of the war with a total of 573 machines completed by war's end. One hundred Han. Cl.IIIa aircraft were finished after the war.

Deliveries began to reach the front in March 1918 and by 30 April 1918, 109 Han. Cl.IIIa machines were listed there. On 30 June 1918, the number had increased to 159 and on the last bimonthly report, 31 August 1918, there were 233 Han. Cl.IIIa aircraft listed with front line units. The Han. Cl.IIIa had replaced, for the most part, the Han. Cl.II and Cl.III machines with the *Schlachtstaffeln*. The Han. Cl.IIIa was a very good all-around aircraft and was also used by the *Flieger Abteilungen* serving with the various *Armee Ober Kommandos (AOK)* and *Armee Korps (AK)*, performing strategic and operative reconnaissance and aerial photography. It was also deployed with the *Flieger Abteilungen (Artillerie)* in battlefield photo reconnaissance and artillery direction. However it gained its fame as a *Schlachtflugzeug* with the *Schlasta*. Those units known to be wholly or partially equipped with the Hannover Cl.IIIa commencing in August 1918 were: *Schlachtstaffeln 3, 7, 9, 16, 20, 24b, 33, 34*, and *38s*.

The camouflage scheme changed slightly with the production of the Han. Cl.IIIa. The four-color printed fabric of the Han. Cl.III was replaced by the five-color day pattern printed fabric, the dark patterned fabric on the upper surfaces of the wing panels, upper tailplane, lower elevator, and the wheel covers. The lighter five- color pattern lower surface fabric was used to cover the undersides of the wing panels, upper tailplane, and the lower elevators. The rib tapes were natural color cut strips of linen, approximately 25mm wide. The rudder was covered with natural color fabric and painted white. The fuselage, fin, lower stabilizer, and the upper wing center-section were painted in five colors mimicking the printed fabric colors. These five dark colors were painted on the sides and top of the fuselage, stabilizer, center-section, and all struts. The five lighter printed fabric colors were painted on the undersides of the fuselage, stabilizer, and the center-section.

Albatros J.I

To assist the *Schlachtstaffeln* in the Battle of the Lys, which was to commence on 9 April 1918, *Idflieg* had issued to *Schlasta 1* and *28b* a few Albatros J.I armored single-engined biplanes. This class of machine was developed to fill the requirement for the low-altitude battlefield reconnaissance missions of the *Infantrieflieger (Ifl.)* Infantry Flyer. Their purpose was to fly over the battlefield at very low altitudes and determine the location of the advancing forces by the color of their uniforms and to mark the location of the front lines on sector maps with colored pencils. Accomplishing this task required the crews to fly at altitudes of 50 meters or less over the battlefield. The Alb. J.I aircraft were normally issued to *Flieger Abteilungen* assigned to support the *AOK* or *AK*. The Alb. J.I was issued to *Schlasta 28b* in April 1918, to *Schlasta 17* and *Schlasta 21* in May 1918. In June 1918 these machines were issued to *Schlasta 36*. *Schlasta 17* was issued Alb. J.I 710/17 with the gunner's cockpit armed with a 20mm Becker Flugzeug Kanone, Typ 2. There is little information available on the success of the experiment with the Becker 20mm aircraft cannon.

The Alb. J.I was a derivation of the Alb. C.XII. The fuselage was redesigned into a rather boxy affair of typical Albatros construction using built-up plywood-covered frames in the forward fuselage and light wood frames in the aft portion, all secured with four primary longerons and two light stringers on the sides of the fuselage. The entire fuselage and upper and lower fins were covered with molded birch plywood panels. The central part of the fuselage, with the pilot's and observer's cockpits – which included the fuel tank under the pilot's seat – were encased on the sides and bottom in 5mm thick chrome nickel steel plates bolted to the fuselage frame. This 5mm steel plate would provide protection against small arms fire from enemy ground forces. The top of the fuselage and the nose were covered with removable aluminum panels.

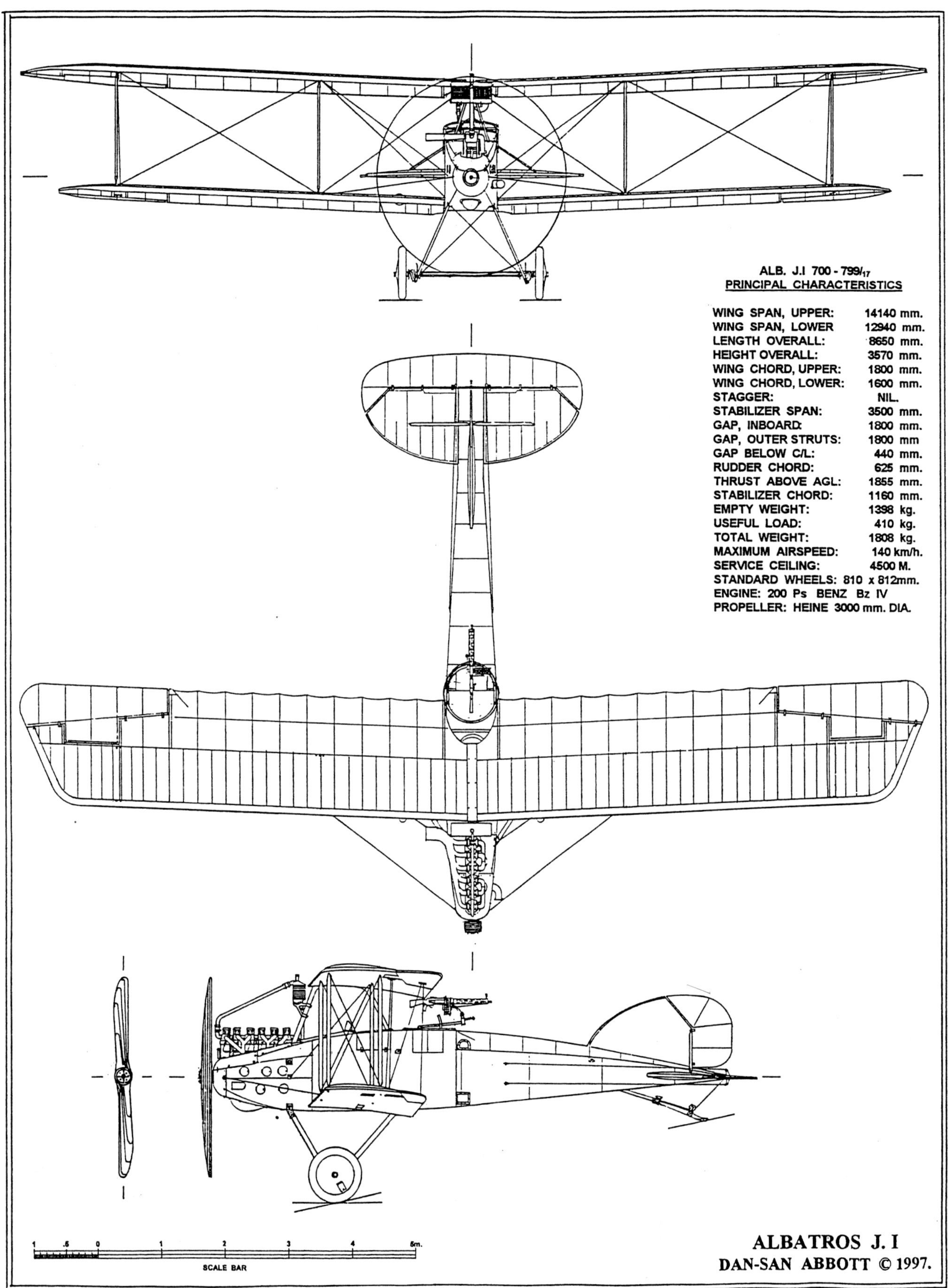
ALB. J.I 700 - 799/17
PRINCIPAL CHARACTERISTICS
WING SPAN, UPPER: 14140 mm.
WING SPAN, LOWER 12940 mm.
LENGTH OVERALL: 8650 mm.
HEIGHT OVERALL: 3570 mm.
WING CHORD, UPPER: 1800 mm.
WING CHORD, LOWER: 1600 mm.
STAGGER: NIL.
STABILIZER SPAN: 3500 mm.
GAP, INBOARD: 1800 mm.
GAP, OUTER STRUTS: 1800 mm
GAP BELOW C/L: 440 mm.
RUDDER CHORD: 625 mm.
THRUST ABOVE AGL: 1855 mm.
STABILIZER CHORD: 1160 mm.
EMPTY WEIGHT: 1398 kg.
USEFUL LOAD: 410 kg.
TOTAL WEIGHT: 1808 kg.
MAXIMUM AIRSPEED: 140 km/h.
SERVICE CEILING: 4500 M.
STANDARD WHEELS: 810 x 812mm.
ENGINE: 200 Ps BENZ Bz IV
PROPELLER: HEINE 3000 mm. DIA.
1 .5 0 1 2 3 4 5m.
SCALE BAR
ALBATROS J. I
DAN-SAN ABBOTT © 1997.

The Alb. J.I was powered with the 200 Ps Benz Bz.IV six-cylinder engine. The weight of the armor plate approximating 490 kg (1078 lbs) denigrated the performance considerably. The Alb. C.XII wings were modified to fit the Alb. J.I and were swept 2.5o. The tailplane was identical to the Alb. C.XII assembly.

The maximum airspeed at sea level was 140 km/hr, the ceiling was 4500 meters and the climb to 4000 meters took 55 minutes. The upper wingspan was 14,140mm and the lower span was 12,940mm. Its overall length was 8650mm and the height 3570mm. The aircraft's empty weight was 1398 kg and its useful load 410 kg, amounting to a gross weight of 1808 kg.

In May 1917 *Idflieg* placed an order with Albatros for three test aircraft and twenty-five Alb. J.I, 400 - 427/17. Production aircraft were subject to acceptance of the type test results on the test and evaluation prototypes. A second order was awarded in July 1917 for fifty Alb. J.I, 700 - 749/17. A third order was issued in 1917 for twenty-five Alb. J.I, 750 - 774/17. In September 1917, *Idflieg* approved the Alb. J.I for production. Deliveries commenced with 37 of these aircraft listed in the front inventory for 31 December 1917. On February 28, 1918, there were 42 listed. This dropped to 33 on 30 April 1918 but then increased to 51 on 30 June 1918. With deliveries of the Alb. J.II, the number of Alb. J.I at the front decreased to 16 machines on 31 August 1918.

With the July 1917 order, J.I aircraft numbered 700 - 749/17, the nose of the fuselage was redesigned and the spinner eliminated and replaced with a bowl-shaped cowling finishing off the nose.

There were several camouflage schemes employed on the first production order of the Alb. J.I. The first (J.I 415/17) was an irregular pattern of diagonally sloped areas of dark green, light green, and mauve on the upper surfaces of the wings and tailplane, with the rudder generally painted light green. The undersides of the wings, tailplane, and wheel covers were sky blue. The plywood fuselage was shellacked and varnished. All struts, cowlings, access doors, fittings, and the armor plates were painted light grey. A second scheme (Alb. J.I 417/17) was a two-color symmetrical pattern of dark green and light green with the undersurfaces and fuselage finished as before.

The third scheme (Alb. J.I 707/17) commenced with the second order of J.I, 700 - 749/17, where a five-color printed fabric covered the wings, tailplane, and rudder. The dark day pattern was used on the upper surfaces of the wings and tailplane, with the light five-color pattern on the under surfaces of the wings, tailplane, and rudder. The wheel covers were painted dark green. The fuselage, struts, etc. were finished as before.

The fourth scheme was a return to the second two-color pattern with the upper colors reversed. The final scheme was a two-color diagonal banding of the wings, tailplane, and fuselage in greyish strawberry red and pale beige. The fin and rudder were white, with the under surfaces of the wings, fuselage and tailplane sky blue.

There is evidence of another pattern of two upper and two lower colors. At least one Albtros J.I was painted all over with beige with greyish ruby in an irregular and random foliage pattern on all upper and side surfaces. The undersides of the wings, fuselage, and tailplane in an overall pale sky blue with an irregular and random foliage pattern of aurora, a greyish pink. The serial number is unknown.

Halberstadt Cl.IV

The Halberstadt Cl.IV was the last wartime design to reach operational service with the *Schlachtstaffeln.* The Halberstadt Cl.IV was a development of the Halb. Cl.II. The design of the Halb. Cl.IV commenced in late 1917 with the prototype machine first flown in February 1918. The Halberstädter engineers wanted to improve the design of the Cl.II in its performance and handling through weight reduction and careful attention to streamlining and detail. While the wings were essentially the same design and construction as the Halb. Cl.II, the fuselage and empennage were completely new. The agility of handling was achieved through the design of the shorter fuselage with the length reduced from 7300mm on the Cl.II to 6539mm for the Cl.IV. The upper wingspan was 10,742mm and the lower span 10,584mm. The height of the Cl.IV increased to 3060mm. More significantly, the empty weight was reduced from 773 kg to 720 kg, which would improve the performance of the Cl.IV over the Cl.II. The useful load was 340 kg and the flying weight, 1060 kg. Maximum airspeed remained the same at 165 km/hr, but the ceiling was increased from 5100 meters for the Cl.II to 6000 meters for the Cl.IV.

After the initial flight tests at the Halberstädter Werke, the prototypes were delivered to Adlershof for type tests in early March 1918. The tests were conducted beginning 5 March and the Halb. Cl.IV was approved for front line use and production on 27 March 1918. *Idflieg* awarded a production contract in May 1918 for 150 Halb. Cl.IV aircraft, C.4600 - 4749/18. Deliveries were scheduled at 100 Halb. Cl.IV per month commencing in June 1918. That month a second order was issued to the Halberstädter Werke for 200 Halb. Cl.IV, C.5779 - 5969/18, followed in August 1918 for 200 more of this type with tentative serial numbers of C.6390 - 6589/18.

To support the production program of the Halberstadt Cl.IV, a license contract was awarded in July 1918 to LFG Roland for 150 Halb. Cl.IV (Rol), C.8050 - 8199/18. The

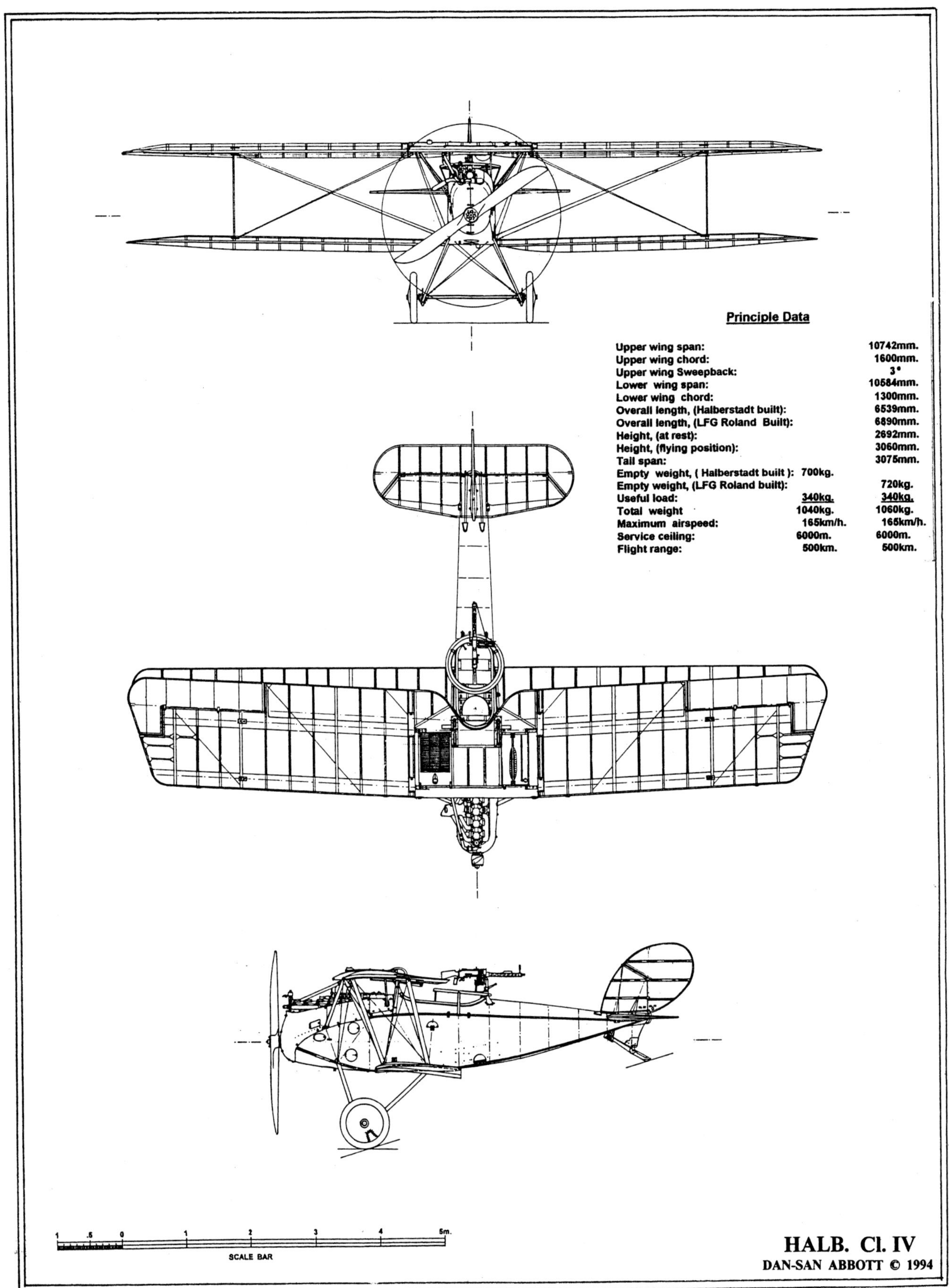
Principle Data
Upper wing span: 10742mm.
Upper wing chord: 1600mm.
Upper wing Sweepback: 3°
Lower wing span: 10584mm.
Lower wing chord: 1300mm.
Overall length, (Halberstadt built): 6539mm.
Overall length, (LFG Roland Built): 6890mm.
Height, (at rest): 2692mm.
Height, (flying position): 3060mm.
Tail span: 3075mm.
Empty weight, (Halberstadt built): 700kg.
Empty weight, (LFG Roland built): 720kg.
Useful load: 340kg. 340kg.
Total weight 1040kg. 1060kg.
Maximum airspeed: 165km/h. 165km/h.
Service ceiling: 6000m. 6000m.
Flight range: 500km. 500km.
1 .5 0 1 2 3 4 5m.
SCALE BAR
HALB. Cl. IV
DAN-SAN ABBOTT © 1994

engineers at Halberstädter were directed by *Idflieg* to lengthen the fuselage to improve its directional stability. The change was incorporated in the contract to LFG Roland, but that was held in abeyance for Halberstädter-built Cl.IV machines pending flight evaluation of the Roland built Halb. Cl.IV aircraft. The Roland machines differed in that they had longer fuselages with an overall length of 6890mm. Deliveries were to commence with 80 in August and 100 per month thereafter. A second order was issued to LFG Roland in August 1918 for 200 Halb. Cl.IV (Rol), C.9400 - 9599/18. On 30 June 1918, 41 Halb. Cl.IV were listed in the front inventory, increasing to 136 on 31 August 1918.

Halberstadt Cl.IV production aircraft wings, tailplane, and wheel covers were covered with five-color day lozenge printed fabric. The dark pattern was used on the upper surface of the wings, tailplane, and wheel covers and the light pattern on the bottom surface of the wings and tailplane. The fabric was applied to the wings at 45o to the leading edge and span-wise to the tailplane. The rib tapes were cut strips approximately 25mm wide in matching five-color fabric. The fin and rudder were covered with plain linen fabric and painted white. The struts and fittings were pale water green. The fuselage and the plywood parts of the center-section were painted in large irregular polygons about 600mm in diameter and purple, dark green, dark blue, and brown in color.

The LFG Roland-built Halb. Cl.IV (Rol) were covered with the same five-color printed fabric as the Halberstadt-built Halb. Cl.IV. The fuselage was painted in four colors, front to rear, purple, light brown, dull green, and greyish blue. The center-section and struts were purple.

The Halb. Cl.IV arrived at the front in June and initially were used as replacements for the Halb. Cl.II. As they more became available, the Halb. Cl.IV were issued to the various *Schlasta.* At least *Schlasta 4, 5, 6, 9, 13, 21, 27b,* and *31b* are known to have been partially or completely equipped with the Halb. Cl.IV.

CHAPTER XXIII

THEY ARRIVED TOO LATE

From the last months of 1917 through 1918, six German manufacturers were designing and developing new aircraft to the requirements of *Schlachtflugzeuge* as established by *Idflieg*. The designs of these new machines consisted of either improvements on existing aircraft then in production or new designs by new participants that were a leap forward in aircraft design and construction.

Albatros C.XIII

The failure of the Albatros Gesellschaft für Flugzeugunternehmungen m.b.H. (the name had been changed on 2 March, 1917) to be able to design *Schlachtflugzeug* acceptable to *Idflieg* is of interest. Albatros had made an attempt in 1917 with the Alb. C.XIII in the Cl Class category, and it appeared to be a good design. The two-seat Albatros C.XIII (Cl.XIII) was a redesign of the successful single-seater fighter Albatros D.Va. The plywood-skinned oval-shaped streamlined fuselage filled the gap between the wings, much like that of the Hannover Cl.II. The nose was finished off with an aluminum spinner and enclosed a 180 Ps Mercedes D.IIIaü engine. The pilot's cockpit was positioned below the cutout in the trailing edge of the upper wing, with the gunner's cockpit immediately aft and almost level with the trailing edge of the upper wing. It would have offered a very good field of fire for the gunner. The overall length was 7800mm, only 500mm longer than the Albatros D.Va. The upper and lower wings were enlarged versions of the D.Va. The upper wingspan measured 10,000mm. Its height was 2710mm. The aircraft's empty weight was 700 kg, and the disposable load 360 kg, bringing the total weight to 1060 kg. Maximum airspeed of the C.XIII was 165 km/hr at sea level. It could climb to 1000 meters in 4 minutes and reached 5000 meters in 47 minutes. Its armament was one synchronized Maxim lMG 08 forward-firing machine gun and a Parabellum Modell 14 lMG on the gun ring around the gunner's cockpit. It is not known what caused *Idflieg* to reject the machine. The performance of the Albatros C.XIII was as good or better than that of the Halb. Cl.II and the Han. Cl.IIIa. With an empty weight of 700 kg, it was lighter than the Alb. D.Va. It is possible that its structure may have failed the load tests as required in the type tests.

BFW Cl.I

Bayerische Flugzeug Werke A.G. of München was in license production of the Halb. Cl.II aircraft. Their engineering staff attempted to design a two-seater fighter in the Cl Class. These efforts resulted in the BFW Cl.I two-seat airplane which was completed in April 1918. The BFW Cl.I was powered by a 160 Ps Mercedes D.III engine set in a slab-sided box-like fuselage with a circular nose radiator. The fuselage tapered to a small knife-edge at the rear. The sides of the fuselage were covered with plywood forward of the rear cabane struts, with aluminum cowlings above and below the engine. Plywood sheet covered the top to the rear end of the fuselage and the bottom of the fuselage to the rear landing gear legs. Linen fabric covered the four sides of the fuselage.

The wing tips were raked and of unequal span and covered with linen fabric. The wings were not staggered. They were set aft of the engine and were supported by steel streamline "N" cabane struts and outward sloping "I" interplane struts. They were braced with a single landing and flying wire on each side. The pilot's cockpit was located aft of the cabane struts below the upper wing. The gunner's cockpit was equipped with a Hausmann Gun Ring and was immediately behind the pilot's cockpit, offering a good field of fire. The empennage was of cantilever construction without wire bracing.

BFW Cl.II and Cl.III

The prototype BFW Cl.I was completed in April 1918. After test flights with the 160 Ps Mercedes D.III engine, it was found to be under-powered. After the engine was changed to a 175 Ps Man III, made by Maschinenfabrik Augsburg-Nürnberg, Augsburg, the BFW Cl.I was designated BFW Cl.II. The upper wing was moved forward slightly to correct the center of gravity. A radiator expansion tank was installed over the engine.

It emerged from the BFW factory in standard day camouflage covered with five-color printed lozenge fabric in May 1918 and was evaluated by *Idflieg* and found lacking. The BFW Cl.II was returned to the factory and the engine was replaced with the 200 Ps Benz Bz.IV six-cylinder engine. Following the changes the machine was designated the BFW Cl.III and sent to Adlershof for evaluation. The BFW Cl.III failed to measure up to the design requirements and consequently was dropped.

Zeppelin Cl.I

The aircraft of the Zeppelin Werke Lindau G.m.b.H. designed by Claudius Dornier were unusual inasmuch as they were metal framed and covered with aluminum sheet. The design, development work, and prototype construction were done at the Lindau facility on the Bodensee (Lake Constance).

The Zep. Cl.I design was completed at the end of 1917, with the prototype completed and flight tested in March 1918. The two- panel upper wingspan was 10,500mm, and the lower span was 8970mm. The wing tips were raked on both upper and lower wings. The overall length was 7420mm and the height 2760mm. It had an empty weight of 730 kg and a disposable load of 340 kg, yielding a gross weight of 1070 kg. The rectangular cross-section fuselage was constructed entirely of aluminum with aluminum sheet covering the frames and longerons. The pilot's seat was located behind the engine, under the upper wing trailing edge cut-out. The gunner's cockpit was immediately behind the pilot's cockpit. The 180 Ps Mercedes D.IIIaü engine was set in the nose with removable nose and top cowling panels. An airfoil radiator was installed in the root of the right upper wing panel. Four cabane struts were constructed integral to the fuselage and seemed to grow from it like horns. The wing spars and ribs were fabricated from aluminum sheet in a conventional manner with linen fabric covering. Aluminum framed ailerons were on the upper wing attached to auxiliary aluminum spars. Cantilever horizontal and vertical tail surfaces were aluminum-framed and covered with linen fabric.

Based on preliminary flight tests and results of the type test at Adlershof, *Idflieg* awarded a contract to Zeppelin Werke on 26 March 1918 for 300 Zep. Cl.I. *Idflieg,* on a contingency basis, set deliveries to commence with 15 by the end of April 1918, 60 in May, and 75 aircraft per month in June, July and August 1918. Production of the Zep. Cl.I was to be undertaken at Zeppelin Werke G.m.b.H., Staaken bei Spandau. Performance problems arose in that the maximum airspeed was only 162 km/hr and the service ceiling was 5000 meters. Therefore *Idflieg* reduced the order to 200 Zep. Cl.I, and later further reduced the quantity to 100 and finally to 50 of these machines. The serial numbers were probably C.1820 – 1869/18, and of these, C.1820 to 1828/18 are known to have been built. There is no evidence they were ever used at the front.

The Zep. Cl.I was returned to Staaken for further development and emerged as the Zep. Cl.II in August 1918. The radiator was changed to a flat square shape and moved forward to the nose. The length was increased to 7460mm. A slight improvement was made in the maximum airspeed to 165 km/hr and the service ceiling was raised to 5300 meters. This level of performance was totally inadequate and the Zep. Cl.II program was terminated.

Junkers-Fokker Werke A.G.

Junkers & Co., Dessau, was the manufacturer of all-metal aircraft starting in 1915. Junkers was in reality an engineering company and they were unable to produce aircraft in quantity. Junkers & Co. had designed an all-metal aircraft, company designation J4, in late 1916 as an *Infanterieflieger (Ifl),* armored infantry aircraft used to fly at low altitudes over the battle to determine the location of the front lines. The J4 was an all-metal, two-seat, cantilever sesquiplane, powered with the 200 Ps Benz Bz.IV engine. The forward half of the fuselage was constructed of 5mm thick steel plate to protect the crew and engine. The rear half was made of riveted aluminum tubing and covered with linen fabric. The wings and empennage were constructed with aluminum tube framing and covered with corrugated aluminum sheet. In November 1916 *Idflieg* ordered three prototypes, Junk. J.I 425 – 427/17. The first prototype, Junk. J.I 425/17, flew on 28 January 1917. In March 1917, after some modifications improving the design, *Idflieg* ordered 50 J4 machines now designated Junk. J.I 100-149/17. On 7 May 1917 the Junk. J.I 425/17 was approved for production following type test approval.

The '*Amerika Programme*' plan required doubling the monthly production of aircraft and engines but delivery was slow at Junkers & Co., with only two machines built in August. Major Hugo Wagenführ of *Idflieg* believed that Anthony Fokker could help Professor Hugo Junkers in better managing their aircraft production. After discussions with Junkers and Fokker, both of whom thought well of the suggested merger, Junkers Fokker Werke A.G. (Jfa) was established on 20 October 1917 in Dessau. Junkers & Co. (Jco) would continue to design new aircraft and Junkers-Fokker Werke would be the manufacturer. The production of the Junk. J.I was turned over to the Junkers-Fokker Werke with a total order of 283 by *Idflieg*. Of these 184 were delivered by 31 October 1918. After the war, production continued and stopped after 227 Junk. J.I machines were manufactured. Of these, 215 were built by Junkers-Fokker Werke A.G. Even though the Junkers-Fokker Werke had greatly improved deliveries of the Junk. J.I, *Idflieg* was unimpressed with the production efforts of the firm and looked for a solution to the problem.

Junkers Cl.I

In July 1917 Jco had designed the J7, a new single-seat, single-engine, low-wing monoplane. It was first flown in September 1917. With the successful flight tests of the J7, Prof. Junkers decided to develop a two-seat version of the J7, the J8. During this period of designing and construction of the J7 and J8, *Idflieg* became concerned with the huge delays in production of the Junk. J.I. Delivery in August 1917 consisted of the two remaining prototype machines *Idflieg* had ordered in November 1916. Three months after the first flight of the J7, the J8 flew on 10 December 1917. Further time was spent in developing and modifying the J7 as well as the J8 with Anthony Fokker assisting by doing flight testing and making suggestions in improving their flight characteristics. Fokker wanted to acquire the manufacturing license for both the J7 and J8 for the Junkers-Fokker Werke.

In February 1918 the J7 and the J8 had been submitted to *Idflieg* for flight tests. *Idflieg* was impressed and three prototypes were ordered for type testing. The prototype J8 and two additional J8 built by Jco were delivered to *Idflieg* in March 1918 and were designated J8I, J8II, and J8III. A fourth J8 was built by Jco and retained by Jco for experimental flight tests. J8II was used for the structural testing at Adlershof and J8III was used for flight evaluation test and first flew on 6 May 1918. The J8 received type test approval in May 1918.

Fokker wanted the J8 to be produced by Junkers-Fokker Werke and as a result of negotiations, Prof. Junkers retained the J7 and J8 designs and the modified two machines, J7 and J8 became the J9 and J10, respectively, and these were licensed to Junkers-Fokker Werke for production.

Idflieg had placed an order with Junkers-Fokker Werke for ten Junkers Cl.I, 1800-1809/18. Junk. Cl.I 1800/18 made its first flight on 4 May 1918. *Idflieg* then placed additional orders in June for twenty Junk. Cl.I; ten were awarded to Jco and ten to Jfa. The probable serial numbers were C.1850 - 1869/18. Jfa received an order in October for twenty Junk. Cl.I, 12600 - 12619/18, and this was followed with another order for ten Junk. Cl.I, 12920 - 12929/18.

After a less than satisfactory relationship with Prof. Junkers, negotiations were held between the two and Junkers purchased Fokker's shares in the Junkers-Fokker Werke A.G. Anthony Fokker withdrew from the partnership in August 1918. The Junkers-Fokker Werke was dissolved and the assets were taken over by Junkers & Co.

Of the forty-four Junk. Cl.I machines built by Junkers & Co. and Junkers-Fokker Werke, eight were delivered by November 1918, two by Jco in August and six in November by Jfa/Jco. All the remaining machines ordered by *Idflieg* were delivered after the war. None of these eight aircraft were to see front line service during the war.

Idflieg was not satisfied with the production efforts of Junkers & Co. and Junkers-Fokker Werke and had decided to seek a production license for the Linke-Hofmann Aktiengesellschaft, Breslau, which had established a *Flugzeugbau* in 1916. This effort apparently failed, as there are no records of *Idflieg* ordering any Junk. Cl.I machines from Linke-Hofmann.

The Junkers Cl.I was a huge advance in aircraft design and construction, well ahead of all other aircraft manufacturers. The low-wing monoplane configuration was a step into the future. The all-metal construction made the aircraft virtually weatherproof and only 7 kg heavier than the Halb. Cl.IV. The empty weight of the Junkers Cl.I was 735 kg and its disposable load was 410 kg, its takeoff weight thus amounting to 1145 kg. Its maximum airspeed was 190 km/hr at sea level. The aircraft could climb to an altitude of 1000 meters in 3 minutes, 54 seconds. It could reach 3000 meters in 14 minutes and the climb to 5000 meters took 30 minutes. Its service ceiling was 8000 meters.

Eliminating the aileron overhang of the J8, the configuration was designated the J10 and was given the military designation Junk. Cl.I. The span was 12,200mm. Its length was 7900mm and height 3100mm. The power was provided by a 180 Ps Mercedes D.IIIaü engine fully enclosed with removable corrugated aluminum cowlings. The armament consisted of two synchronized forward-firing lMG 08/15 machine guns, and the gunner had a single Parabellum Modell 14 lMG mounted on a circular metal turret. Junk. Cl.I were camouflaged in pale mossy green and pale mauve on the upper and side surfaces with very pale bluish white on the under surfaces. The rudder was painted white.

Hannover Cl.V

Following in the succession of designs emanating from the Hannoversche Waggonfabrik Abteilung Flugzeugbau was the Han. Cl.V, a large machine with a wingspan of 12,500mm, a length of 7800mm. It was powered by the 245 Ps Maybach Mb.IVa engine. It was designed for high altitude performance. Five of these machines were built during 1918. It is not documented that any served with front line units.

In 1918 *Idflieg* issued a specification for Cl two-seat fighter powered with the BMW IIIa engine with the type tests requirements of the single-seat fighter. *Dipl-Ing* Hermann Dorner responded with a remarkable aircraft that was relatively small for a two-seater, light and yet strong enough to meet the strength requirements of a fighter. The design was a winner, the Han. Cl.V, a small two-seat biplane fighter powered with the 185 Ps BMW IIIa engine. In September 1918 *Idflieg* issued a contract to Hannoversche Waggonfabrik for 100 Han. Cl.V C.9600 - 9699/18. A second order was also issued in September for 50 Han Cl.V C.9850 - 9899/18.

The first prototype, Han. Cl.V 9800/18, appeared with the biplane tail and a one-piece upper wing spanning 10,560mm, an overall length of 7100mm and height of 2900mm. The third prototype, Han. Cl.V 9802/18, reverted to a conventional empennage and the upper wingspan was reduced to 10,490mm. It had an empty weight of 720 kg, a disposable load of 360 kg, its gross weight thus totalling 1080 kg.

The fuselage was constructed of lightweight built-up formers with four longerons and a light stringer on the side centerline of the fuselage. The main former branched out from above the upper longerons to form the base of the cabane struts. The cabane struts of the former were faired fore and aft with wood ribs, as were the leading and trailing edges. The fuselage, cabane struts, fin, and stabilizer were covered with birch plywood. A radiator much like the Fokker D.VII fighter was mounted in the nose, above the upper longeron in front of the engine. A three-piece aluminum cowling with multiple louvers covered the engine.

The pilot's cockpit was immediately behind the engine compartment containing the flight and engine controls. The pilot's seat was mounted on a frame above the fuel tank. Located above the cowling in front of the pilot's cockpit were two lMG 08/15 machine guns with ammunition stored in an aluminum container placed forward of the main bulkhead. The gunner's cockpit was separated from the pilot's cockpit by a light built-up former. A wide web sling provided a seat for the gunner. A wood gun ring was mounted on the gunner's cockpit and installed on the ring was a single Parabellum Modell 14 lMG.

The undercarriage consisted of wood-faired steel tubes with standard 760 X 100mm wheels covered by five-color printed fabric. The ailerons, elevators, and rudder were framed in steel tubing and covered with printed fabric. The wings were of two box spar construction with fretted plywood ribs and auxiliary ribs between each main rib from the leading edge to just aft of the front spar. The trailing edges of the wings were braided wire. The upper wing was one-piece, with the ailerons mounted on an auxiliary spar. The ailerons were operated by a torque tube that ran through the wing aft of the rear spar and linked to the controls with a bell-crank and small section steel tubes. The interplane "I" struts were framed in wood and covered with birch plywood. Steel fittings were fastened at the ends of the struts, attaching these to the wing spars. The wing cellule and undercarriage were wire braced.

The performance of the Hannover Cl.V was very good and compared well with the Fokker D.VII that it was tested against. Maximum airspeed was 185 km/hr at 2000 meters altitude. The Hannover Cl.V climbed to 1000 meters in 3 minutes and 18 seconds. It reached 4000 meters in 15 minutes and 5000 meters in 25 minutes and 42 seconds. The service ceiling was 9000 meters (29,520 feet). Production most probably commenced in early October 1918 and by the armistice, 46 machines had been delivered. An additional 57 were delivered after the war.

The upper and lower wings, ailerons, elevator, and wheels were covered with five-color lozenge printed fabric. The fabric was applied to the wings chord-wise and span-wise to the ailerons and elevators. The ribs and edges of the wings, ailerons, and elevators were taped with narrow, natural colored, linen tape. The rudder was painted white. The fuselage, fin, undercarriage, cabane struts, and interplane "I" struts were stained with purple, brown, dark green, and dark blue and finished with a waterproofing coat.

Halberstadt Cls.I

Halberstädter Flugzeugwerke responded to the *Idflieg* specification for a C Class battle aircraft with a lightened smaller successor to the Halberstadt Cl.IV, the Cls.I, also powered with the 180 Ps Mercedes D.IIIaü engine. The Halb. Cls.I was a small, single-engine, single-bay, two-seat biplane. Armament consisted of two forward-firing synchronized 08/15 lMG and a single Parabellum Modell 14 lMG mounted on a wood turret for the gunner. The fuselage was identical to that of the Halb. Cl.IV, but shorter. The one-piece upper wing spanned 9700mm, the aircraft's overall length was 6950mm and the height was 3050mm. The empty weight was 682 kg and the disposable load was 420 kg, bringing the maximum takeoff weight to 1102 kg. The maximum airspeed was 185 km/hr at sea level. The climb rate was 36 minutes to 4500 meters.

Idflieg ordered three prototype Halberstadt Cls.I aircraft in February 1918, serial numbers C.1797 - 1799/18. A second order was awarded in February for what is believed to be 100 Halb. Cls.I 2000 to 2099/18. The prototypes were delivered to Adlershof in September 1918 for type tests and evaluation. It is not known if they were produced beyond the test aircraft.

The prototype aircraft were covered with five-color, day pattern, lozenge fabric. Cut strips of the five-color printed fabric were used for rib and peripheral taping. The fuselage was stained and varnished in the same manner as the Halb. Cl.IV. The struts were painted water green. This was the last Cl Class aircraft to be evaluated and tested by the engineers at Adlershof at Johannisthal during the war.

Deliveries and Supplies

After acceptance test flights at the aircraft factory by *Luftstreitkräfte* pilots assigned to the *Bauaufsicht* (Inspection Office), the aircraft would be disassembled and loaded on railway flatcars. When the train was made up and with destination instructions from *Idflieg*, delivery would be made to the designated *Armee Flugpark*. After 8 February 1918, the aircraft, engines, parts, and supplies were transported to *Fliegerdepot Nord, Maubeuge (Adam)*, (Aviation Depot North, Maubeuge, Adam). This supplied air units for the northern front, occupied by the *4., 6., 17., 2., 18., (9.), 7., 1.*, and *3. Armeen*. On the southern front *Fliegerdepot Süd, Saarbrücken (Eva)*, (Aviation Depot South, Saarbrücken, Eva) similarly supplied the *5., AAC, 19., AAA, and AAB Armeen*. The Aviation Depots made the distribution of aircraft, engines, and equipment to the various *Armee Flug Parke* (Army Air Parks). When the machines were received at the *AFP*, they would be reassembled and then test flown by the *AFP* test pilots. The course of these events took about ten days to two weeks time. The front unit would be notified that their new aircraft had arrived and the number available for pickup. The pilots of the unit would fly in their old aircraft to the *AFP*, turn them in, take delivery of their new machines, and fly them back to their airfield. Each unit had held in reserve at the *AFP* three machines of the type with which they were equipped.

For example, in August 1918 *Schlachtstaffel 5* was equipped with three Halberstadt Cl.II and three Halberstadt Cl.IV aircraft. *AFP 7* would have three machines of both types in reserve for this unit. *Schlasta 5* had assigned personnel for duty at *AFP 7* to maintain these reserve machines. This would be the case for all the aviation units assigned to any *Armee*. For example, on 1 August 1918, the *7. Armee* had 25 *Flieger Abteilungen*, 18 *Jagstaffeln*, 3 *Bombenstaffeln*, and 14 *Schlachtstaffeln*, for a total of 60 units. *AFP 7* should have seventy-five C Class reconnaissance aircraft, fifty-four D Class fighters, nine G Class twin-engine bombers, and forty-two Cl Class two-seat fighters, or a total of 180 aircraft in reserve. A°total of 240 personnel (four from each unit) would be assigned to maintain all these aircraft. Pilots and crews awaiting assignment to front line units were encouraged to fly these aircraft to improve their proficiency.

Spare parts such as wings, ailerons, tails, struts, wheels, tailskids, propellers, radiators, engines, nuts, bolts, fabric, dope, paint, and all the sundry things needed to maintain the units in the field would be held in reserve for each unit in the *Armee*. Subordinate to the *AFP* were *Parkstaffeln* (Park Flights) and *Tankstellen* (Fueling Stations) that were established in each *Armee Korps* between the front units and the *AFP*. The *Parkstaffeln* maintained stores that would be required quickly and or daily, including propellers, ammunition, wheels, and some spare parts that might be needed. The *Tankstelle* held in store water, fuel, and oil reserves. The *AFP* assigned the personnel. Pick up of supplies, parts, water, and fuel were made daily by personnel assigned those duties at each *Schlasta*.

From the beginning of the war delivery of engines did not match the manufacture of aircraft. To 1 November 1918, 41,012 engines were delivered and 47,931 aircraft for a deficit of 6919 engines. It would be considered a normal ratio of engines to aircraft at 2:1, however the ratio was 0.86:1. *Idflieg* attempted to resolve this problem by establishing an engine repair, overhaul, and modification facility, the *Motor-Instandsetzungwerkstatt Warschau* (Motor Reparation Work Shop, Warsaw) in April 1917. Worn-out and/or damaged engines were shipped there to be rebuilt or modernized. Some engines were returned to the original or license manufacturer for rebuilding or repair. These engines would be brought up to the latest standard. This aircraft engine repair facility was moved to Brussels, Belgium, on 5 January 1918 and was renamed *Flug-Motorenwerkstätte Brüssel* (Aircraft Motors Workshop, Brussels). The primary product was rebuilt Mercedes D.III engines.

CHAPTER XXIV

AIRCRAFT ENGINES

In order to identify aircraft powerplants, *Idflieg* established a system of engine codes with two to four components. First, a two- or three-letter abbreviation designated the design/manufacturer. The second component was a Roman numeral indicating the performance ranges. One additional element was a lower case letter appended to the Roman numeral (a, b, etc.) to indicate successive versions within that performance range. Finally, a letter code was appended in parenthesis if the actual manufacturer were other than the design/manufacturer. For example, "As.IIIa(O)" would indicate the following: As: Argus Motoren-Gesellschaft is the design/manufacturer, III: 150-200 Ps performance range, a: second version within this performance range, (O): Opel is the actual manufacturer. Ps (*Pferdestärke*) is a measure of engine horsepower, where 1.0 HP equals 1.014 Ps. The engine manufacturers were:

Ad	Adlerwerke vorm.h. Klever, A.G. Frankfurt am Main.
As	Argus Motoren-Gesellschaft m.b.H., Reinickendorf-Berlin.
BMW	Bayerische Motoren Werke, München.
Bus	Basse und Selve, Altona.
Bz	Benz & Cie., Mannheim.
B	Reinhold Becker, Horgen bei Zurich.
C	Deutsche Motorenbau G.m.b.H. (Conrad), Marienfelde.
D	Daimler Motoren Gesellschaft, Stuttgart-Untertürkheim.
Dz	Gasmotorenfabrik Deutz, Köln-Deutz.
Goe	Gandenberger'sche Maschinenfabrik, proprietor G.Goebel, Darmstadt.
Gü	Güldner Motoren Gesellschaft, Aschaffenberg.
Kg	Gebrüder Körting, Körtingsdorf-Hannover.
Man	Maschinenfabrik Augsburg-Nürnberg A.G., Nürnberg.
Mb	Motorenbau G.m.b.H., Friedrichshafen.
Nag	Nationale Automobil Gesellschaft, Oberschöneweide.
O	Adam Opel, Rüsselsheim.
Rie	L.A. Riedinger Maschinen Fabrik, Augsburg.
Rp	Rapp Motoren Werke G.m.b.H., München.
Sh	Siemens & Halske A.G., Siemensstadt-Berlin.
St	Stoewer-Werke A.G., Stettin.
Sw	Otto Schwade & Co., Erfurt.
U,UR	Motorenfabrik Oberursel A.G., Oberursel.
Un	Union Werke A.G., Mannheim.

The listing of performance ranges were:

0	under	80 Ps
I		80-100 Ps
II		100-150 Ps
III		150-200 Ps
IV		200-300 Ps
V		300-400 Ps
VI		400-500 Ps
VII	over	500 Ps

The most important of these aircraft engine manufacturers was Daimler Motoren-Gesellschaft, which made the Mercedes engine. Of the 41,012 engines made by the German aircraft engine industries up to the end of the war, Daimler Motoren Gesellschaft built 19,240 engines. Of these the Mercedes D.III series was the most important, with 11,670 built, comprising 28.4 percent of all the engines made. The following sections detail the powerplants of aircraft equipping the *Schutzstaffeln* and *Schlachtstaffeln.*

Mercedes D.III Series

The Daimler Mercedes D.III engine evolved from the six cylinder 100 Ps Mercedes D.I engine of 1913 with a bore of 120mm and a stroke of 140mm. The cylinders were cast in pairs, two valves per cylinder, and operated by a gear-driven overhead camshaft. Dual ignition was provided by two Bosch ZU-6 magnetos. The crankcase was aluminum. The dry weight of the Mercedes D.I was 190 kg. In 1914 Daimler introduced the 120 Ps Mercedes D.II with the bore increased to 125mm and the stroke increased to 150mm. Various improvements were made, such as enclosing the cam tower and gears, but otherwise the engine was essentially the same as the D.I. The dry weight was 210 kg.

In 1915 Daimler engineers developed the 160 Ps Type Fl466 six-cylinder engine that, after type test approval on 15 December 1915, became the 160 Ps. Mercedes D.III engine. The water pump was moved from the bottom of the lower crankcase of the D.I and D.II to the middle of the cam tower. The valve train was the same as the D.I and D.II. Dual ignition was by two Bosch ZU-6 magnetos.

Whereas the D.I and D.II cylinders were paired, in the D.III the cylinders were individual. Steel water jackets were welded to the machined steel cylinders. An overhead camshaft operated single intake and exhaust valves. The compression ratio was 4.5:1. Carburization to the engine was through openings in the lower forward crankcase to dual throat carburetors to dual intake manifolds, fore and aft, each feeding to three cylinders on the left side of the engine. The D.III engine was rated at 160 Ps at 1400 rpm. The dry weight of the D.III engine was 275 kg.

In February 1917 Daimler engineers made an improvement to the Mercedes D.III by increasing the compression ratio to 4.64:1 that increased the power output to 170 Ps. The improved engine was designated the Mercedes D.IIIa. Changes were made to the lower crankcase, relocating the oil pump and the water pump. The engine dry weight was 300 kg. Delivery of the Mercedes D.IIIa engines began in June 1917. In July 1918 Daimler made improvements to the D.IIIa engine, which included increasing the bore to 145mm and the compression ratio to 5.73:1. These resulted in the Mercedes D.IIIaüv engine rated at 180 Ps at 1400 rpm and 240 Ps at 1600 rpm.

The 160 Ps Mercedes D.III was also built under license by Nationale Automobil Gesellschaft, D.III (Nag), and L.A. Riedinger, who built the 170 Ps Mercedes D.IIIa (Rie) and 180 Ps D.IIIaüv (Rie). The demand for the Mercedes D.III engine and the variants exceeded the production capabilities of Daimler, Nationale Automobil, and L.A. Riedinger. With the information available, the production of the D.III engines in 1915 amounted to 783. During 1916 there were 2379 engines built, in 1917, 1604 D.III engines and 2644 D.IIIa engines for a total of 4248 manufactured. In 1918 to 1 November, Daimler built 4260 D.IIIaü and D.IIIaüv engines which were delivered:

Year	*Engines Built*	*Aircraft Ordered*	*Balance*
1915	783	830	-155
1916	2379	1955	+269
1917	4248	5047	-530
1918	4260	4553	-823
Total	**11670**	**12,385**	**-715**
to 1 Nov 1918			

It became apparent that the demand exceeded production of the Mercedes D.III engine. The situation was somewhat rectified in April 1917 with the establishment of the *Motor-Instandsetzungwerkstatt* in Warsaw, Poland, which was later moved to Brussels in January 1918, and renamed *Flug-Motorenwerkstatt Brüssel.* The above table only deals with new aircraft and does not account for the need for spare engines to replace damaged or worn engines in field units. As the 1915 and 1916 C class aircraft were replaced with 1917 machines using the Benz Bz.IV, Mercedes D.IV, or D.IVa, about 1800 Mercedes D.III were freed for use in the Cl and D Class machines of 1917.

During 1918 the lack of availability of the Mercedes D.IIIa and later series became critical and affected deliveries of aircraft. This situation caused *Idflieg* to stop production of the Hannover Cl.III at the eightieth aircraft of which 300 were ordered with the Mercedes D.IIIa engine, as the engine was not at hand. When production was resumed on this order, the designation was changed to Hannover Cl.IIIa, powered with the As.IIIa(O) engine.

The Mercedes 160 Ps D.III powered the Albatros C.III, Roland C.II, Rumpler C.I, and AEG C.IV. Mercedes 170 Ps D.IIIa engines were used in late AEG C.IV and the Aviatik C.III aircraft. The Mercedes 180 Ps D.IIIaü engine was used in the Halberstadt Cl.II and Hannover Cl.III. The Halberstadt Cl.IV aircraft used the 200 Ps Mercedes D.IIIaüv.

Mercedes D.IV

In order to gain more power, Daimler engineers had used the cylinders from the D.III six-cylinder engine and designed the F-1468, an in-line eight cylinder engine to provide a more powerful engine for the second generation of C Class aircraft. The Type F1468 was rated at 220 Ps at 1100 crankshaft rpm. The propeller shaft was geared, with the crankshaft turning at the rated 1400 rpm, and spur gears turning the propeller shaft at 910 rpm, which produced 230 Ps. The bore and stroke were the same as the Mercedes D.III engine, however the compression was increased to 4.73:1. The dual ignition spark was delivered to each cylinder by two Bosch HL8 magnetos. Two Mercedes twin jet carburetors provided the fuel mixture to the cylinders through two intake manifolds, each delivered to four cylinders. The engine dry weight was 420 kg.

Daimler received type test approval on 20 December 1915 and F-1468 became the Mercedes D.IV engine. During 1915 and 1916 Daimler manufactured 424 D.IV engines. In 1915 *Idflieg* issued a specification for a two-seat reconnaissance-bomber powered with the 220 Ps Mercedes D.IV engine. Four aircraft manufacturers responded to the *Idflieg* specification: AEG with the AEG C.V, Albatros Werke with the Albatros C.V, Kondor Flugzeugwerke G.m.b.H. in Essen, and LVG with the LVG C.IV. After flight-testing and evaluation, *Idflieg* selected the Albatros C.V and the LVG C.IV for production and orders were placed.

Mercedes D.IVa

Following the completion of the design of the Mercedes D.IV, Daimler engineers were immediately at work on an engine, the F-1686, of greater power for the third generation of C Class reconnaissance/bomber and G Class twin-engine bombers. F-1686 was a six cylinder, in-line, direct drive engine with a single overhead cam, and with four valves per cylinder. The bore was 160mm and the stroke 180mm. The compression ratio was 4.94:1. The F-1686 was rated at 260 Ps at 1400 rpm. The dry weight of the F-1686 was 410 kg. Type test approval was granted in June 1916, the engine was designated the 260 Ps Mercedes D.IVa, and approved for production.

The 260 Ps Mercedes D.IVa became the second most important engine delivered from Daimler. Daimler built 4550 Mercedes D.IVa engines from June 1916 to the end of October 1918. The delivery was between 150 and 180 engines per month. The Mercedes D.IVa engine powered the Rumpler C.IV, Albatros C.X, and Albatros C.XII used by the *Schutzstaffeln* and many other German C and G Class aircraft.

Benz Bz.III

In 1914 Benz & Cie. of Mannheim, Germany, had introduced the Benz type F-F. This was an in-line, six-cylinder engine with overhead valves. The bore was 130mm and the stroke 180mm. Intake and exhaust valves were push rod actuated. Each cylinder was provided with dual ignition with two Bosch ZH-6 magnetos. The Benz type F-F was rated at 150 Ps at 1200 rpm. Upon approval of *Idflieg* it was designated the 150 Ps Benz Bz.III. This engine developed 160 Ps at 1400 rpm. The compression ratio was 4.5:1.

The cylinders were cast iron with steel water jackets welded on the cylinders. Two Benz carburetors provided fuel to the engine through two induction manifolds, which branched into three ports each and were mirror images. The water pump was at the rear base of the engine. The dry weight of the engine was 250 kg. From 1914 to 1 November 1918, 2024 engines were built. The 150 Ps Benz Bz.III engine was used on many early aircraft, but in regard to the *Schusta* aircraft, some of the production orders of the Albatros C.III and Rumpler C.I used the 150 Ps Bz.III engine. The color of the engines was aluminum.

Benz Bz.IV

In late 1915 the engineers at Benz began work on a new 200 Ps engine for the third generation of C Class aircraft. Benz & Cie. received type test approval in February 1916 for the 200 Ps Benz Bz.IV engine. The engine was produced in large quantities with 7124 manufactured and delivered by 1 November 1918. This engine powered the AGO C.IV, Albatros C.VII, Albatros C.XV, Albatros J.I, Albatros J.II, DFW C.V, Junkers J.I, LVG C.V, and the LVG C.VI.

The Benz Bz.IV was rated at 200 Ps at 1250 rpm and 200 Ps at 1400 rpm. This was a six cylinder in-line engine with two intake and two exhaust valves per cylinder. The bore was 145mm and the stroke was 190mm. The overhead valves were push rod operated. The two mirror-image intake manifolds were similar to the manifolds on the Benz Bz.III engine. Air induction to the engine was achieved through holes in the lower crankcase to the two Benz carburetors. There were two spark plugs per cylinder with electrical impulses delivered from two Bosch ZH-6 magnetos. The cylinders were cast iron with welded steel water jackets. The water pump was situated above the magnetos at the rear of the engine. The crankcase was aluminum. The dry weight of the engine was 385 kg. The engine was of aluminum color with black baked enamel on the cylinders and induction manifold.

Argus As.III

The 180 Ps Argus As.III engine was designed in 1915 by Argus Gesellschaft m.b.H. and developed 180 Ps at 1400 rpm. The engine was a success and *Idflieg* needed large quantities quickly. In order to produce the Argus As.III engine in the large numbers needed for the planned aircraft production, *Idflieg* arranged with Argus Gesellschaft m.b.H. Reinickendorf-Berlin (834 As.III engines) to place license manufacturing orders with six engine companies. They were: Gasmotoren-Fabrik-Deutz (252 As.III Dz) at Köln-Deutz, Güldner Motoren Gesellschaft at Aschaffenburg, Maschinenfabrik Augsburg-Nürnburg Flugmotoren Werke (252 As.III Man) at Augsburg, Adam Opel (1863 As.III O) at Rüsselheim, Stoewer Werke A.G. (406 As.III St.) at Stettin, and Seebacher Maschinegesellschaft m.b.H. (149 As.III Be). The total number of As.III engines built and delivered as of 1 November 1918 was 3385 versus the 3756+ which were ordered.

The As.III engines and license-built engines, notably the As.III(O) built by Opel, were the powerplants for the Albatros C.VI, Hannover Cl.II, and Hannover Cl.IIIa. The Argus As.III had six in-line cylinders, set 18mm off center to the right of the center of the crankshaft. This engine had overhead valves, two per cylinder, operated by push rods. The bore was 145mm and the stroke was 160mm. The compression ratio was 4.75:1. Each cylinder had two spark plugs with ignition from two Bosch ZH-6 magnetos. The water pump was at the bottom rear of the lower crankcase. Two German Zenith carburetors provided the mixture through two induction manifolds, each to three cylinders. The dry weight was 290 kg. The cylinders were grey with an aluminum crankcase.

Argus As.IIIa

In late 1916 Argus Motoren-Gesellschaft improved the engine power by increasing the bore to 148mm and the stroke to 165mm. This As.IIIa engine was rated at 220 Ps at 1450 rpm. The engine dry weight increased to 325 kg.

CHAPTER XXV

WEAPONS

In early 1915 the Class A monoplanes and Class B biplanes were given defensive armament in the form of a light machine gun, fixed on a swivel mounting for the observer. While this was an interim move, it led to establishing a new design category of Class C, the armed, two-seat, single-engine biplane. With this new C Class the seating of the pilot and the observer were reversed with the pilot in the front seat and the observer in the rear seat providing him a better field of view. Only the observer was armed with a swivel- mounted Parabellum Modell 14, 7.92mm caliber, air-cooled light machine gun.

Franz Schneider, engineer for LVG, had designed a circular wood turret with a parallelogram arrangement of steel tubes to effect elevation of the gun which could be moved laterally on a yoke and the entire turret was able to rotate 360°. This Schneider Machine Gun Ring became the standard and was used by most German aircraft manufacturers. Some builders made their own variations on the Schneider Gun Ring.

Parabellum

In early 1911, Karl Heinemann joined the Deutsche Waffen und Munitionsfabriken (DWM) in Berlin. In his previous work, Heinemann had developed a reputation in the design of automatic weapons. Shortly after joining D.W.M. he was given the design task to improve the Maxim Machine Gun 08. The result of his endeavors was accepted by the German Army and Navy as the Parabellum Modell 14, 7.92mm caliber. The firing rate was 700 rounds per minute. The Parabellum MG Modell 14 was water-cooled and weighed 11 kg empty and 12.8 kg with the water jacket full. The overall length of the weapon was 1250mm. It was belt-fed and had provisions to mount an ammunition box on the right side of the receiver. The belt was fed straight through the receiver and exited on the left side, while the empty cartridge cases were ejected from the bottom.

In late 1914, the Parabellum MG Modell 14 was selected for aircraft use. The water jacket was slotted to air cool the barrel and the modified machine gun weighed 9.5 kg. In this form the Parabellum was designated lMG Modell 14, 'l' meaning *luftgekühlt*, i.e., air-cooled. This modified Parabellum arrived at the front in January-February 1915.

The Parabellum ammunition belts were made of light hemp webbing 25mm wide. Spaced metal clips were folded over the two plies of webbing and each clip was secured with two hollow rivets. The riveted metal clips were spaced along the two plies of webbing, thus forming pockets to hold the cartridges. These were retained in the pockets only by friction. The 250-round ammunition belt was wound around a steel drum (*Trommel*). Usually each aircraft would have two drums in reserve in racks in the gunner's cockpit and one on the machine gun. The drum axle sat in a retainer on the right side of the receiver case.

The ammunition was fed into the right side of the receiver case, and the empty belt was ejected out the left side and into the airstream. The empty belt could have posed a problem for the observer/gunner, whipping about and possibly striking him. The empty cartridge cases were ejected from the bottom of the breech and most likely into the airstream, some probably falling into the observer's cockpit.

In 1917 Deutsche Waffen und Munitionsfabriken made some modifications to the Parabellum Modell 14, reducing the diameter of the slotted jacket and adding a carrying handle. In this configuration the weapon became the Parabellum Modell lMG 14/17. This version was issued to the *Schusta* and other units in mid-1918. It was fitted with a ring sight on the fore barrel and an adjustable, folding rear sight on top of the receiver. The lMG Modell 14 was finished dull black. In 1918 a good number of the *Schlasta* machine gunners were

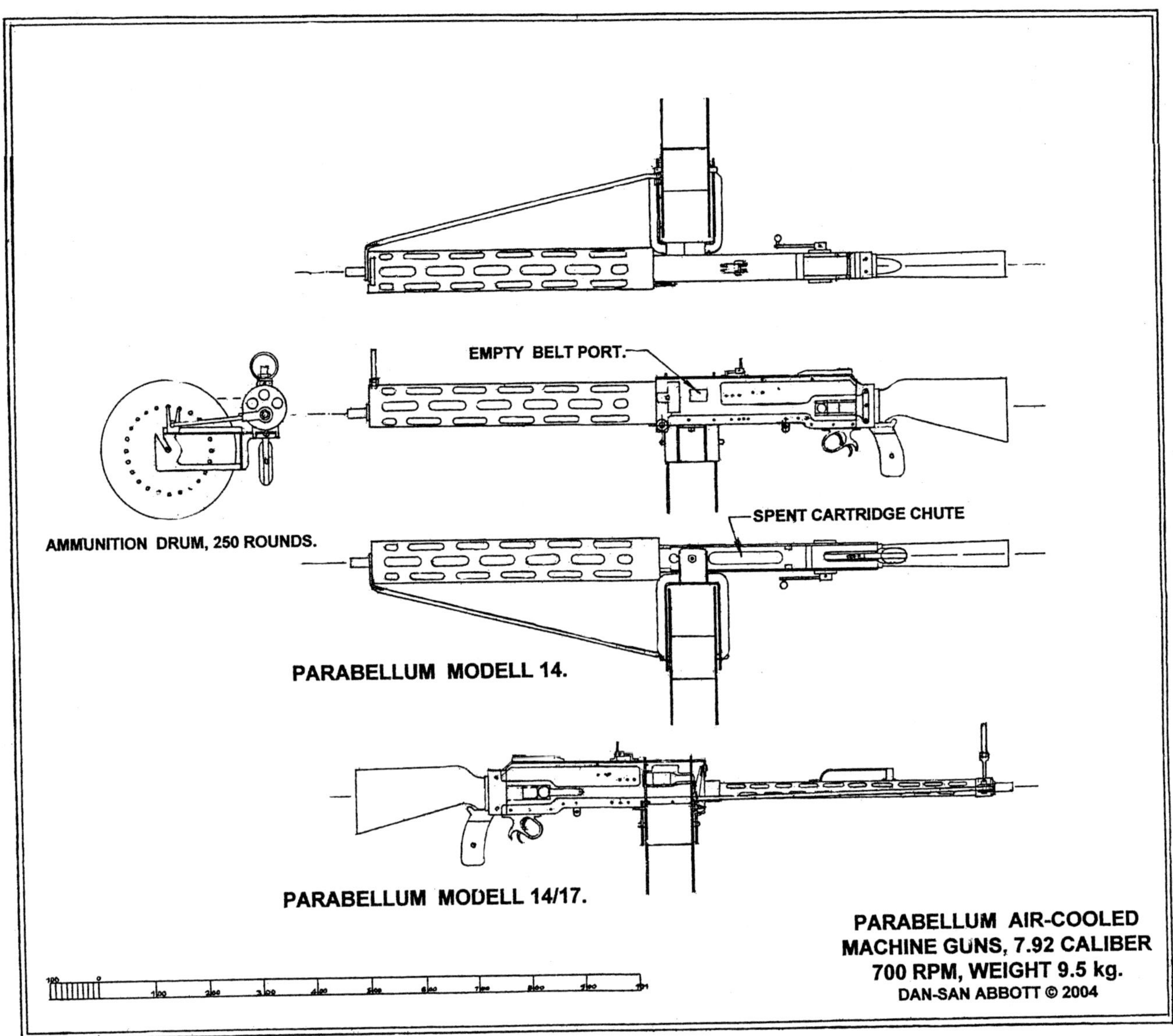

using an Oigee telescopic sight on the Modell IMG 14/17 to facilitate aiming at ground targets.

Saulnier-Garros Deflector Wedges

Raymond Saulnier had conceived of a mechanical synchronization system in April 1914. When tested, the system was semi-successful, the engine was run at 1200 rpm and the shots were well grouped. With variation in rpm the grouping of the shots moved. The tests failed when a few shots exhibited unusual firing times and shot the propeller. This was caused by the lack of uniformity in loading the cartridges. The system was rejected. In order to save the device, Saulnier then removed the linkage to the synchronizer and installed deflector plates on the rear of the propeller blades in line with the machine gun muzzle. The war then commenced and the French Army retrieved the Hotchkiss machine gun, stopping any further testing.

Roland Garros, a pre-war pilot, had entered the French *Aviation Militaire* in August 1914 joining his unit *Escadrille M.S. 26* at Verdun. When *Escadrille M.S. 26* moved to Dunkerque, Roland obtained permission from his commanding officer to go to the *Société des Aéroplanes Morane-Saulnier* at Villacoublay to work on the Saulnier system. Garros explained to Raymond Saulnier that he thought he could help with the bullet deflector device and got Saulnier's permission to try.

Roland Garros had brought his mechanic Jules Hue with him from *Escadrille M.S. 26*. In their first attempt during a static firing trial the propeller failed and resulted in the destruction of a Morane H aeroplane. Jules Hue acquired a

Morane Type L and restructured the Hotchkiss machine gun mount, added a groove on both sides of the deflectors and improved the reinforcing rods. The groove cut into each deflector plate gave direction to the deflected bullets. It was static-tested, firing over 1,000 rounds with no problems. After the static test Roland Garros did flight- firing tests with the deflector system. While Garros has generally been given sole recognition for this achievement, the credit should be distributed among three individuals. Raymond Saulnier conceived of the deflector system, Jules Hue perfected the system, and Garros worked with both men to develop and perfect it.

On 1 April 1915 Roland Garros scored his first victory over a German aircraft over Westkapelle. His second victory came on 15 April 1915 between Ypres and Armentières and the last during the morning of 18 April 1915, shooting down an Albatros near Langemarck. That afternoon Garros flew a Morane Type L, MoS.3 parasol monoplane of *Escadrille M.S.26* on a mission to bomb the railway station at Courtrai. His engine was hit by ground fire and stopped. He was forced to land in the German lines near Ingelmunster and became a prisoner. After landing he attempted to burn his machine, with only limited success. The German military authorities took charge of the aircraft remains, including the 80 hp LeRhône engine, propeller, and Hotchkiss machine gun.

The engineers at *Idflieg* attempted to copy the deflector system without success. During a test the copied propeller disintegrated, destroying the test set-up. As a result of this failure of the copied propeller, it was decided around mid-May 1915 to seek outside help. *Hptm.* Förster of *Idflieg* invited Anthony Fokker, Director of the Fokker Aeroplane G.m.b.H. (the first company, Fokker Aviatik G.m.b.H., was dissolved on January 1, 1915 and was reorganized as Fokker Aeroplanebau G.m.b.H.) to come to Döberitz to see the bullet deflection system and discuss the problem. On 16 May 1915 a representative of the Pfalz Flugeugwerke was also asked to come to Döberitz to discuss the problem.

Fokker *Stangensteuerung* System

The credit for inventing the first synchronization device which allowed a machine gun to fire between the rotating blades of an aircraft propeller has often been given to Anthony Fokker. This was based to a good extent on the following dubious account by the Dutch aircraft manufacturer, according to which the revolutionary device was created by him with remarkable speed: "I returned to Schwerin by train with a Parabellum machine gun under my arm and also ammunition. Then within 48 hours I had designed, static tested, and flight tested the Fokker *Stangensteuerung* (push rod control) on Fok. M5K and returned to Döberitz with the Fok. M5K with the machine gun installed ready for trial testing before *Idflieg* officials."

It is much more likely that Heinrich Lübbe, Fritz Heber, and Leimberger had completed the *Stangensteuerung* system design before *Hptm.* Förster invited Fokker to come to Döberitz. Heinrich Lübbe was a watchmaker by trade and would have understood timing sequences between the engine and the machine gun. He later became the director of the Flugzeug Waffen Fabrik in Reinickendorf, Berlin.

The operation of the Fokker *Stangensteuerung* was described by A.R. Weyl in his biography of Anthony Fokker titled, *Fokker: The Creative Years:* "The advantages of a synchronizing mechanism were fairly obvious: the airscrew could retain its efficient shape; the airscrew shaft was not subjected to irregular flexural hammering by bullets striking the deflector plates; no ammunition was wasted; and the rate of fire could be high. The synchronizing mechanism that evolved at Schwerin, chiefly by Lübbe, Heber and Leimberger, was similar in principle to Franz Schneider's gear. It consisted of a simple linkage of cams and push rods between the oil-pump drive of the Oberursel and the gun trigger, and was called *Stangensteuerung* (push rod control). It was mounted on an improvised firing stand and tested until it worked; it then required only a means of starting and stopping it at will, and this was designed and embodied in the mechanism."

The synchronizing system was installed on the single-seat monoplane Fokker M5K, *Werkenummer* 216 (Fok. E.1/15). The installation would have simply involved welding clips and brackets to the welded steel tubular fuselage. Aluminum ammunition and empty belt boxes were fabricated with the necessary belt guides and were installed. The assembly was tested and adjusted until it worked properly. This modified Fokker M5K was taken to Döberitz a few days later for trials. After these successful trials *Idflieg* adopted the Fokker *Stangensteuerung*. The aircraft was designated the Fokker M5K/MG and *Idflieg* placed orders for the immediate delivery of the modified monoplane. The Fokker designation is M = *Militär*, 5 = fifth model, K = *kurz* (short wing span, 8950mm, 6750mm length), MG = *Maschinengewehr* (machine gun). After it was approved for use at the front by *Idflieg* (without type tests), it was designated Fok. E, the "E" standing for "Eindecker" or "monoplane," this becoming the standard designation for armed single-seat monoplanes. The prototype Fok. M5K/MG was demonstrated on 23 May 1915 at Stenay in the German 5. *Armee* for the Crown Prince. At the request of Major Friedrich Stempel, *Stab Offizier der Flieger 6*, (Staff Officer of the 6th Army), the Fok. M5K was sent to Douai in the German *6. Armee* for demonstration flights.

Initially there was trouble with the synchronizing system being driven off the oil pump drive. The system was re-engineered with a steel plate cut into the cam drive and mounted on the propeller rear hub flange. This system became the standard and was used until the *Zentralsteuerung* system was adopted in December 1916.

Until December 1916, all synchronizing systems were manufactured at the Fokker factory at Schwerin and systems were furnished to all German aircraft manufacturers. Albatros Werke G.m.b.H. at Johannisthal worked in cooperation with Herr Hetzke had developed the Albatros-Hetzke synchronizer. The Albatros Werke used this system on their new Albatros D.I and D.II fighters. The Albatros-Hetzke system was a mechanical system. This had disturbed *Idflieg,* as they felt it would complicate deliveries and also the training of unit armorers with duplicate systems. *Idflieg* thought the new Fokker system was superior to the Albatros-Hetzke mechanical synchronizer. There was a concern in *Idflieg* that with Fokker having a monopoly of the *Zentralsteuerung* system, he might take advantage of other manufacturers by delaying deliveries. It was decided that Fokker could own the Flugzeug Waffen Fabrik (Aircraft Weapons Company), but he could not act as the Managing Director. Heinrich Lübbe was appointed Director of the newly established armament firm and the factory was set up in a former gramophone company building in Reinickendorf near Berlin that *Idflieg* had secured for that purpose. Fokker had to promise *Idflieg* that he would not interfere with the management of, or cause delays in, their production of the *Zentralsteuerung* machine gun synchronizers. By agreeing with the demands of *Idflieg*, Anthony Fokker gained a subsidiary of Fokker Flugzeugwerke G.m.b.H. (which had undergone a name change in December 1915 from the Fokker Aeroplanebau) with a monopoly and guaranteed orders. This situation existed to the end of the war. Production of the *Stangensteuerung* system was stopped and all weapons work was transferred to Flugzeug Waffen Fabrik in Reinickendorf.

Fokker *Zentralsteuerung*

The *Zentralsteuerung* used flexible steel shafts encased in a flexible housing driven off the camshaft inter-connected with a clutch. When the trigger was pushed, it pulled a Bowden cable, which engaged the dogs on the flexible shafts with the dogs on the synchronized drives. Thus engaged, the flexible shaft rotated, turning the cam on the trigger motor mounted at the forward base of the receiver. As the trigger motor rotated twice in each revolution, the lobe on the cam engaged and pushed a spring-loaded pin, which in turn pushed the trigger, thus allowing the gun to fire only when the propeller blades were clear of the gun. This *Zentralsteuerung* system became the standard of the *Luftstreitkräfte.* The Flugzeug Waffen Fabrik designed clutch motor synchronizers for all engine installations on all aircraft under the management and direction of Heinrich Lübbe.

The development of the synchronized machine gun, enabling the gun to fire between the propeller blades without damaging them, led to C Class reconnaissance aircraft being fitted with the *Stangensteuerung* system and a forward firing machine gun in May 1915. After December 1915 all C Class and later D aircraft were fitted with the *Zentralsteuerung* system.

Maxim 08 Machine Gun

Only a few Fokker M5K machines were equipped with the Parabellum Modell lMG 14 machine gun. *Idflieg* considered the Maxim 08 machine gun, which weighed 17.5 kg, to be a more reliable weapon. The Maxim was to be modified in the manner of the Parabellum, air-cooled with a fretted jacket. The modification of the Maxim 08 machine guns was accomplished at the Fokker factory at Schwerin. The modified machine gun became the Maxim lMG 08. The Fokker Flugzeugwerke removed all parts of the Maxim 08 machine gun that were not required in the aircraft installation, replacing the water jacket with a fretted jacket to air cool the barrel. On the early installation of Fokker and Pfalz E types, the guns were equipped with a forward Gate sight. The first installation of the lMG 08 was on Fokker M5K, *Werkenummer* 258, later designated Fok. E.11/15. It was a 7.92mm caliber and weighed 15.5 kg. The lMG 08 equipped most of the Class C and Cl aircraft even into 1918.

The lMG 08 was belt loaded and fed to the left side of the receiver and exited from the right side. The belt was made of hemp webbing, 60mm wide, with the edge folded over 17 to 18mm and sewn with two rows of stitching 10mm apart. The two plies were joined with the folded edges facing each other and held together with spaced metal clips on both sides with each spacer secured by three hollow rivets. The finished belt was 42 to 43mm wide. The gap between the spacers formed pockets for the cartridges which were retained in the pockets only by friction. The aircraft belt did not have the third 65mm long spacer of the ground used version. Most aircraft belts had a 500 round capacity and these weighed 12.5 kg. The empty cartridge cases were ejected from a tube on the front of the receiver below the fretted jacket.

Ammunition and empty belt boxes were made from aluminum sheet often with plywood bottoms. Ammunition feed chutes were also made of aluminum sheet, generally with a hinged access door to facilitate loading the machine gun, and located on the right side of the receiver. The empty belt box was mounted in front of or behind the ammunition box. Belt

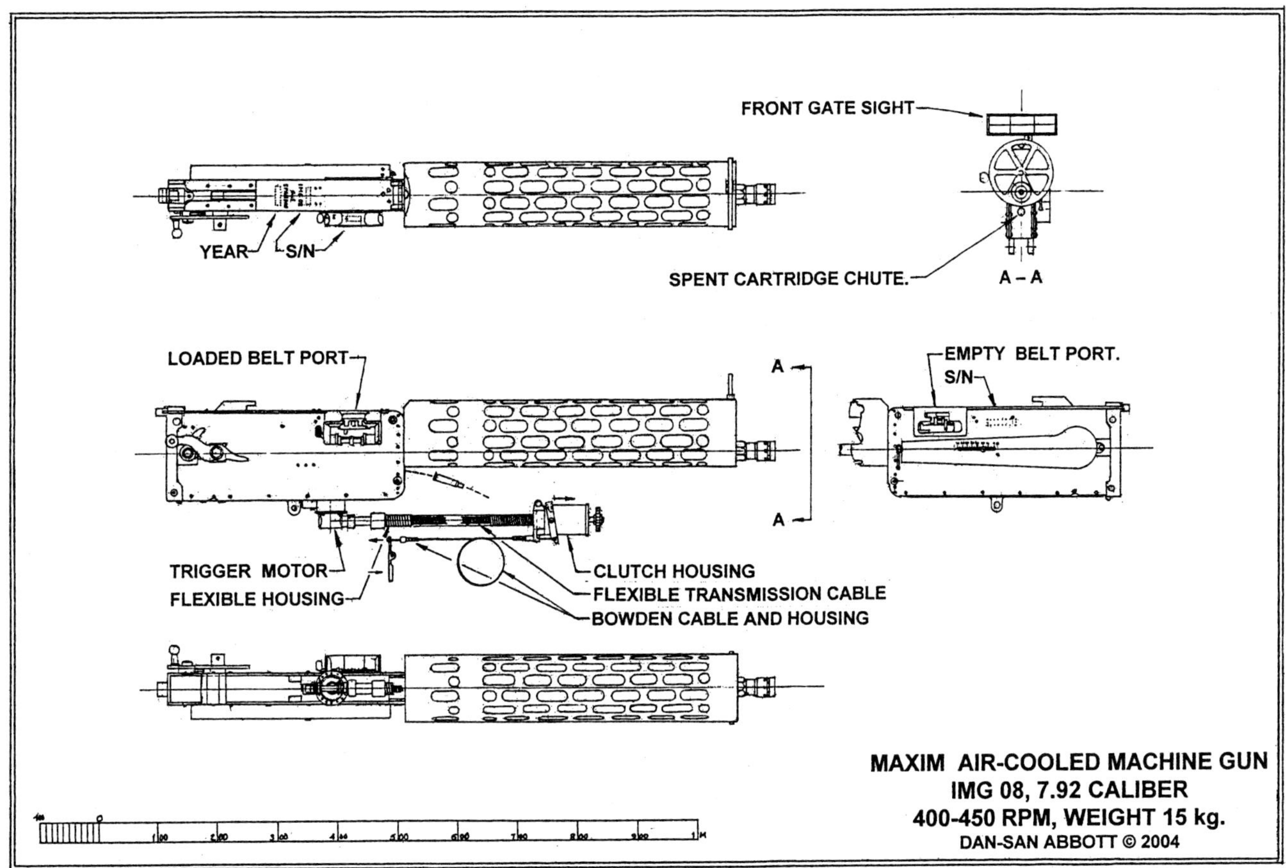

exit chutes were made of aluminum sheet or tubing and would lead the empty belt from the machine gun. Expended cartridges exited into a curved tube about 30mm in diameter which led through the bottom of the fuselage and the empty cartridges exited the tube into the free airstream below the fuselage. Machine gun ammunition boxes and chutes weighed about 3 or 4 kg.

Machine gun mountings were generally fabricated of steel tubing with steel fittings or brackets. Mountings and fixtures weighed approximately 3.5 kg. The Bowden trigger control wires were encased in a flexible steel housing. The forward end of the Bowden housing was attached to the trigger mechanism on the *Stangensteuerung*, or to a clutch on the gear housing of the *Zentralsteuerung* system. The aft end was clipped to the control column and fixed to the push or pull triggers on the control column handgrip.

Air-Cooled LMG 08/15

A revised version of the Maxim 08 machine gun had been developed by *Oberst* von Merkatz and was designated LMG 08/15. It was standardized in 1915 for the Germany Army. The LMG 08/15 weighed 19.5 kg with full water jacket. This was less than the Maxim 08, which weighed 26.5 kg with a full water jacket. The changes in the LMG 08/15 involved reducing the wall thickness of the receiver from 4 to 3mm and eliminating the top rear and bottom front. The jacket diameter was changed from 109 to 89mm.

In 1916 *Idflieg* had decided to modify the LMG 08/15 for use on aircraft. The water jacket was removed and replaced with a fretted jacket and all parts not needed were removed. With these changes the weight decreased to 12.3 kg. It had a rate of fire of 400-500 rounds per minute and the modified aircraft weapon became the lMG 08/15.

The lMG 08/15 air-cooled aircraft machine guns, 7.92mm caliber, were manufactured at the Königlich Gewehr und Munitionsfabrik, Spandau Berlin (Royal Gun and Munitions Factory, Spandau). The lMG 08/15 machine gun was referred to as a "Spandau" because of the place of manufacture, the Spandau arsenal. The lMG 08/15 machine guns were shipped to the Waffen Flugzeug Fabrik to have the synchronizer gear installed. The assemblies were then shipped to the aircraft manufacturers.

The lMG 08/15 incorporated the 25mm wide ammunition belt. The 40mm aluminum tubular belt chutes used on the lMG 08/15 would not permit the use of the Maxim 08 42mm wide cartridge belt with the 65mm long spacer. The lMG 08/15

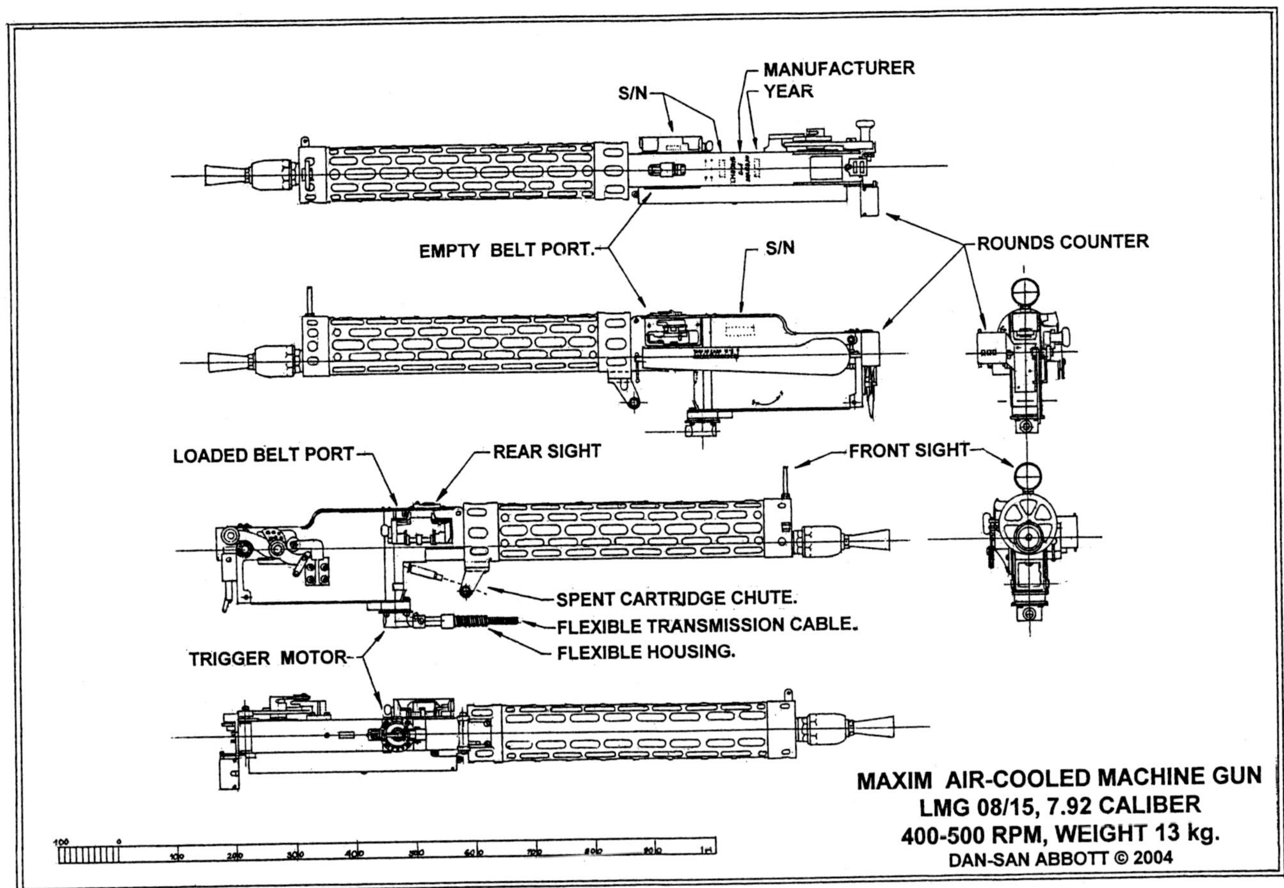

aircraft machine guns were delivered to the aircraft factories and initially were restricted for single seat fighters only. The heavier lMG 08 were used on all other types of aircraft. Later in 1918 the lMG 08/15 were specified as the forward firing synchronized machine guns on Class C and Cl aircraft.

Ammunition

The ammunition used on the Parabellum Modell 14 lMG 08 and the lMG 08/15 was the 1905 standard 7.92 x 57 caliber service ball ammunition based on the *Patrone S* (Cartridge S). The *Patrone S* had a diameter of 8.14mm and has a pointed end. "S" is an abbreviation for *spitz*, pointed. It was for use on bores with deeper rifling such as the Modell 98 Mauser service rifle and Maxim machine guns. The bullet jacket was coppered sheet steel with a lead core. The bullet weight was 10 grams. For identification, the bullet had a black primer annulus.

Another type of ammunition used was the armor piercing *Patrone* SmK. SmK is an abbreviation for *spitz mit Stahlkern*, which means "pointed with a steel core." The bullet consisted of a coppered sheet steel jacket with soft lead filler over a pointed tempered steel core 6mm in diameter and 29.8mm in length. The bullet weight was 11.55 grams. It was identified by a red primer annulus. This bullet was used for piercing and damaging the aircraft engine as well as fuel and oil tanks.

The armor-piercing tracer *Patrone* SmKL'spur cartridge was brought out in 1916. The bullet weighed only 10.15 grams. *L'spur* was an abbreviation for *Leuchtspur*, which means "tracer." The jacket was coppered sheet steel with a hard pointed steel core 15.6mm long and 5.9mm in diameter, set over a capsule of illuminating composition and an igniter 6.1mm in diameter and 13mm long. The cartridge was identified with two markings, the black bullet tip and the red primer annulus. Because of the lightweight of the *Patrone* SmKL'spur, it was the general practice to mix them with the *Patrone* SmK cartridges in the belt to take advantage of the striking power of the heavier SmK bullet. There were two *Patrone* SmKL'spur bullets tried out before a satisfactory bullet was standardized.

In 1916 the *Patrone* PrL, a phosphor tracer or incendiary bullet, was developed for attacks on enemy kite balloons. This bullet was copied from the British incendiary bullet. The coppered steel jacket encased white phosphorus, which was sealed in the bullet with hardened lead. The bullet weight was 10.3 grams. The identity marking of the *Patrone* PrL cartridge was entirely black including the primer annulus. When using the *Patrone* PrL ammunition pilots were given a card which stated they were under orders to use this ammunition to shoot down observation balloons. This ammunition was loaded in one of the machine guns and could not be used against aircraft. In the summer of 1918 there were several incidents of auto-ignition of the *Patrone* PrL ammunition in Fokker D.VII aircraft in several *Jadgstaffeln*. To minimize the overheating of the ammunition containers, the pilots removed the upper engine cowlings, thereby reducing the heat in the forward fuselage.

The *Luftstreitkräfte* introduced in late 1918 the *Patrone* F armor-piercing incendiary cartridge for use against aircraft, the 'F' meaning *Flugzeug*, aircraft. The coppered steel jacket enclosed white phosphorus and a tempered armor-piercing steel core sealed with lead. The phosphorus did not ignite until the jacket was ruptured after striking the enemy aircraft. The cartridge was not to be used against observation balloons. The identity markings were a black bullet and a red primer annulus.

Ammunition belts would have a mixed load of cartridges, such as four *Patrone* SmK, one *Patrone* SmKL'spur and then repeat until the belt was full. On balloon attacks, one machine gun would have a normal loading sequence and the other machine gun would be loaded with *Patrone* PrL incendiary ammunition. Because of the auto-ignition problem with the *Patrone* SmKL'spur ammunition, its use was discontinued in late 1918 and *Patrone* F was used instead. The cartridge cases were 57mm long, made of either brass or lacquered sheet steel on all of the above types. Because of shortages of brass late in the war, cartridge cases were made of sheet steel and lacquered as a rust preventative.

Signal Pistol

Colored flares were used for giving signals from the *Kettenführer* (flight leader) to other pilots in his formation or from a pilot in the formation to alert the group of an enemy attack. The flares were red, white, and green star shells. Prior to the mission the different colors would be assigned codes, such as: red, attack; white, re-assemble; or green, return to base. The color codes would be changed daily. Every *Staffel* would be issued 27mm flare pistols, one for each aircraft. To meet operational requirements, the *Armee Flugpark* issued red, white, and green flares in sufficient quantities to meet the daily needs of the field units.

The 27mm star shell cartridge was made like a shotgun shell, a brass base with heavy paper jacket. The overall length was 170mm and they were 27mm in diameter. The flare pistol was single action and single cartridge. The frame was hinged to facilitate loading, and the barrel was 175mm long. On the bottom of the handgrip was a ring for the attachment of the lanyard. The pistols were generally stowed in a pocket in the gunner's cockpit. Flare cartridges were often stored in a webbed band with multiple pockets on the turtle-deck aft of the gunner's cockpit. In other cases the cartridges would be placed in a rack on the outside of the fuselage below the machine gun ring.

Bombs

The C Class aircraft used by the *Schusta* in 1917 generally had an internal bomb-rack in the gunner's cockpit. This rack could hold four 12.5 kg *P.u.W.* bombs *(Prüfanstalt und Werft der Fliegertruppe),* Test Establishment and Workshop of the Flying Troops. Some of the *Schusta* aircraft could also install bomb gear under the fuselage and have the capability of carrying two to four 50 kg *P.u.W.* or one to two 100 kg *P.u.W.* bombs in addition to the four smaller bombs in the gunner's cockpit. When *Idflieg* drafted the C light specification, the bombing requirement was omitted. *Idflieg* did not want to compromise the performance of the two-seater attack fighter by carrying bombs.

During 1917 there were instances where the *Schutzstaffeln* engaged in bombing attacks. The bombs used were the 12.5 kg, 50 kg, and 100 kg. *P.u.W.* There were also 300 kg and 1000 kg *P.u.W.* bombs, but these were used on the G and R Class bombers. The *P.u.W.* bombs were designed in 1915 by the *Prüfanstalt und Werft* in cooperation with Goerz und Friedenau, the manufacturers of the bomb sights. The *P.u.W.* bombs were aerodynamically superior to the earlier Carbonit cast iron bombs designed by the *Artillerie Prüfungs Kommission (APK)* in 1912-1913. The *P.u.W.* bombs had tails with the incidence built-in, which induced the bomb to spin. The spinning action armed the nose fuse and improved the bomb's flight and trajectory, making the *P.u.W.* bombs more accurate.

The nose fuse was provided with a safety pin that passed through the fuse body that prevented the fuse from being armed. The safety pin was a length of hard wire with a loop at one end. When the bomb was mounted on the bomb rack, either internal or external, the bomb was positioned with the safety pin loop facing up. A piece of wire was secured to the safety pin loop and the other end was fastened to the bomb rack. When the bomb was released and fell away, the arming wire extracted the safety pin freeing the fuse. The tail fins induced the bomb to rotate. After a specific of rotations of the bomb, the nose fuse would be armed. The larger bombs, 100 kg, 300 kg, and 1000 kg had two fuses, a nose and rear end fuse, each with an arming wire. The superb aerodynamic shape of the *P.u.W.* bombs gave the bomb greater penetration of the target.

The 12.5 kg *P.u.W.* came in three categories: normal fragmentation bomb, painted light grey; attack fragmentation bomb, painted yellow; and the night bomb, painted white. The attack bomb had greater incidence in the fins which caused the bomb to spin at a higher rate. The faster spin would arm the bomb quicker, permitting it to be delivered at a lower altitude. The night fragmentation bomb had a light built into the afterbody for the purpose of allowing the observer to see where the bomb exploded. The 12.5 kg fragmentation bombs were 750mm long and 90mm in diameter. The fuse was brass, the bomb body was machined steel, the conical afterbody and the three fins were sheet steel. There were also 12.5 kg incendiary bombs which were 850mm in length and 140mm in diameter. These were painted black, but their construction was the same as the other 12.5 kg bombs.

The 50 kg *P.u.W.* high explosive demolition bombs were 1700mm long and 180mm in diameter. The bombs contained 23 kg of high explosive. The forebody was machined steel, the center was sheet steel and the rear of the bomb was machined steel. The conical tail and three fins were sheet steel. The nose fuse was made of brass. The fins were bent to induce spinning that armed the nose fuse. These bombs were painted pale blue.

The 100 kg *P.u.W.* high explosive demolition bombs were 1900mm long and 120mm in diameter. The bomb contained 60 kg of high explosive. The fore and rear bodies were machined steel. The center body, conical shaped rear body, and the four tail fins were sheet steel. As with the other *P.u.W.* bombs, the tail fins were bent to induce spinning and this action

An unknown German flyer with rather maniacal eyes holding an armful of *P.u.W.* bombs. Note the distinctive bent fins. The two larger bombs are 50 kg which were carried by the *Schutzstaffeln.* Photo Credit: Terry Phillips.

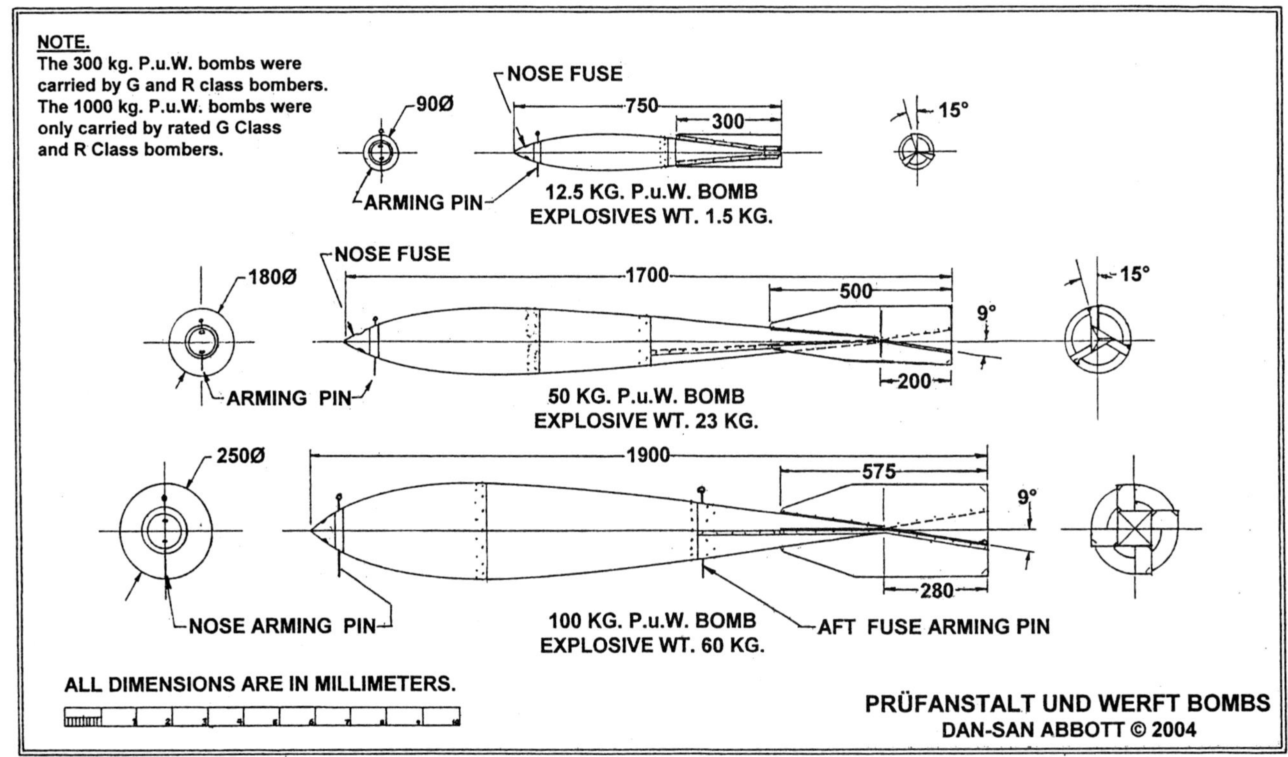

armed the nose and tail fuses. This bomb was also painted pale blue.

The *P.u.W.* bombs were carried level in the aircraft in a steel tubular internal rack holding four 12.5 kg bombs, one above the other. The bombs could be sequenced to drop one at a time or could be released in a salvo. The external racks were made of steel tubing, rectangular in shape, bolted to the fuselage structure for each size of the bomb. The bombs were held in individual bomb racks with cable slings fixed on one side of the two semi-circular cradles and connected to a release device on the opposite side of the cradle. The two slings were joined with a connecting cable. When the gunner operated the release, it opened the retaining jaws of the device, loosened the slings, and the bomb fell away.

Stielhandgranate

The *Stielhandgranate*, stick hand grenade, or more commonly *Kartoffel Stampfer,* "potato masher" hand grenade, was used by the crews of the Halberstadt Cl.II beginning in September 1917, and later by the Hannover Cl.II. The stick grenade was used for low level attacks on allied ground forces with great affect. The stick grenade had a 5 1/2 second fuse. The high explosive charge weighed 165 grams and the total weight of the grenade was 480 grams. The overall length was 356mm, the length of the grenade can was 75mm, and the diameter of the can was 60mm. To operate the stick grenade, the gunner would unscrew the cap on the end of the wooden handle and remove the *Abreisszünder* (rip detonator) safety cord arming lanyard porcelain bead and pull. This action would ignite the match in the fuse. The gunner then had 5 1/2 seconds to throw the grenade before it exploded.

The *Schlasta* gunners in 1918 began to bundle six grenade heads without handles on one stick grenade and tape the heads together, making one large explosive. These were called *Die Teufel Faust*, "the Devil's fist." The center grenade with the handle would be armed by pulling on the safety lanyard and the Devil's fist would be thrown. When the center grenade exploded the shock of the explosion would set off the other six grenades. The Devil's fist was stowed on the floor in the gunner's cockpit and each one weighed approximately 2.6 kg.

The *Schlasta* aircraft would have to fly very low over the enemy forces, less than 45 meters above the ground, for the grenade to be effective, because of the 5 1/2 second delay. Using the grenade above that altitude would result in an air burst. The effective range was about 25 meters. A standard load on a Halberstadt Cl.II or Hannover Cl.II would be around 10 potato masher grenades stored in an open top box on each side of the fuselage. The *Luftstreitkräfte* grenade body and caps were painted light grey. Standard infantry stick grenades and caps were painted dark green. The handles were natural varnished wood.

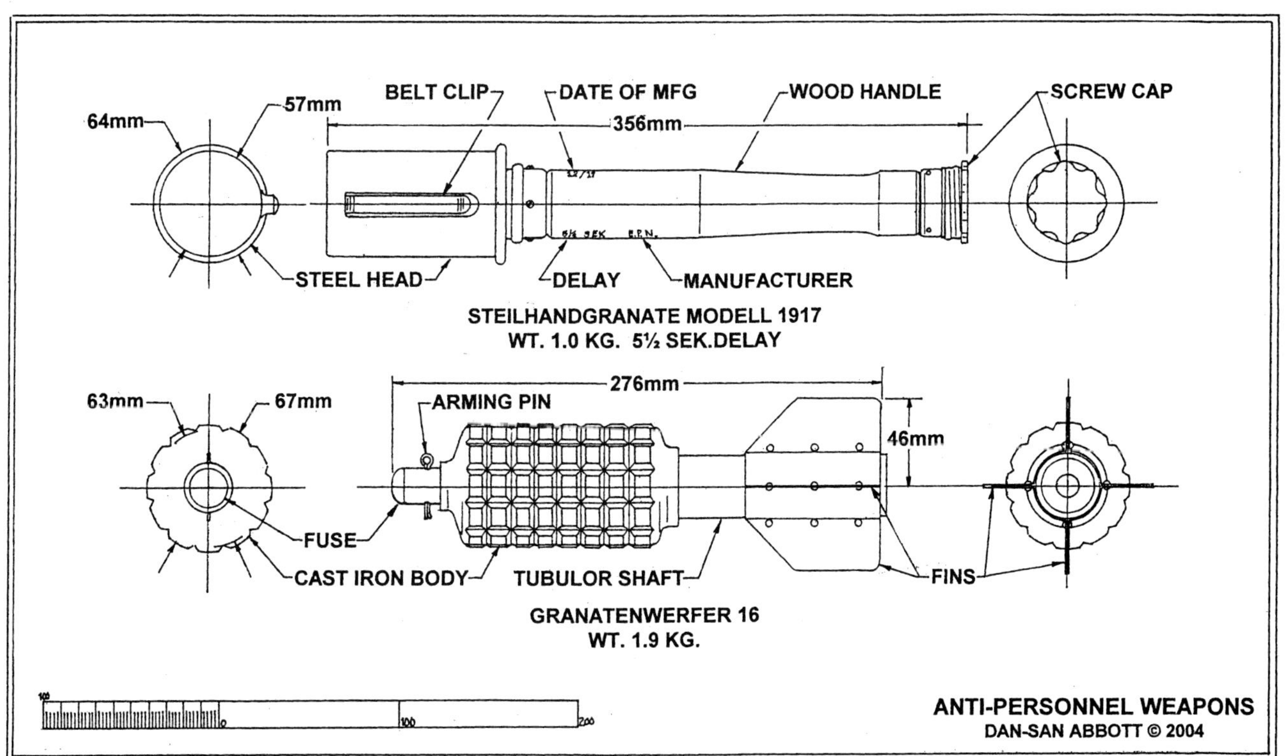

Granatenwerfer 1916

The *Granatenwerfer 16* grenade launcher was also known as the "Priester Minenwerfer," named for a Hungarian priest who conceived the device. Each infantry company was issued two *Granatenwerfer 16* mortars and they were operated by a two-man mortar crew. The weapon would be used by inserting a blank cartridge in the Priest mortar grenade tail. The grenade tail tube was then inserted on the mortar barrel. When the firing lanyard was pulled it released the mortar firing pin which struck the primer on the cartridge. The cartridge fired and propelled the grenade 300 to 500 meters. The use of the Priest mortar grenade by the gunners of the *Schlachtstaffeln* did not require the launcher. The grenade was stored on a rack on the side of the fuselage. The nose contact fuse projected through a hole in the rack and was secured to the rack with the fuse safety pin. The normal load was four or five grenades on both sides of the fuselage near the gunner's cockpit. To release the grenades, the gunner removed the safety pin and the grenade fell away. Or he could remove the safety pin and throw the grenade. There was no time-delay fuse on the Priest mortar grenade only a contact fuse. This made the Priest grenade safer to use and did not require the crew to fly at very low altitudes.

When striking the ground the grenade would rebound into the air and explode a fraction of a second later. The grenade weighed 1.85 kg. The body was cast steel; the tail tube and fins were steel. The grenade was 325mm long and 80mm in diameter. The span of the tail fins was 110mm. The infantry Priest grenades were painted dark green, and the *Luftstreitkräfte* grenades were light blue. *Granatenwerfer 16* were manufactured by Stock und Cie., A.G. Marienfeld, Berlin, as well as several other munitions companies.

Fliegermaus

Fliegermaus, "Flyer's mouse," was the nickname given to the 1 kg fragmentation bomb. The *Fliegermaus* was 150mm long and 45mm in diameter. The weight of the fuse was 0.37 kg, the weight of the explosive was 0.080 kg. The total weight was therefore 1.025 kg. Removing the safety wire from the end of the fuse armed the bomb. On contact with an object the bomb would explode. The *Fliegermaus* was used to some extent in 1916 and 1917. It was replaced with the stick hand grenade in 1917.

PART IV

UNIT MARKINGS OF THE SCHUTZSTAFFELN/ SCHLACHTSTAFFELN AIRCRAFT

UNIT MARKINGS OF THE SCHUTZSTAFFELN/SCHLACHTSTAFFELN AIRCRAFT

While the markings of the *Jagdstaffeln* have been fairly well documented, the *Schusta* and *Schlasta* have not. There has been a general lack of information on these formations and knowledge of unit markings has been even more sparse. Since the beginning of this project several years ago, an extensive search has been made for every piece of data on the identity of these units and their markings.

Some of the units have been identified from the organization of the *Schlachtgruppen* by knowing its composition and, by eliminating the known *Schlasta,* the unknowns have been identified. Documented data on unit markings have also aided in determining some of the unknown units. Photographs of thirty of the *Schusta/Schlasta* have been located. Photographs of seven other units have been obtained and one, *Schlasta 7*, has been identified but not confirmed. The remaining six remain as unidentified units. Therefore the unit markings presented here are based on photographs and documentation and are not merely "guessed at." The camouflage and markings of the *Schusta* and *Schlasta* are a culmination of sixty-plus years of study and research of the German *Fliegertruppe* and the later *Luftstreitkräfte*.

Plate 1. ***(page 185)***

Schusta/Schlasta 1.

Schusta 1 was equipped with the Ru. C.I in January 1917. Later in December 1917 it was issued the Halb. Cl.II. In April *Schlasta 1* had in its inventory the Halb. Cl.II, LVG C.V, and one Alb. J.I. The unit markings are unknown.

Schusta/Schlasta 2.

Schusta 2 was equipped with the Rol. C.II and Ru. C.I in January through April 1917. By January 1918, it began to receive the Halb. Cl.II aircraft. *Oblt.* Oskar Bechtle, the *Schustaführer*, adopted the black empennage for the unit marking. Aircraft were marked with white arabic numerals 1 to 6 with a stop. *Oblt.* Bechtle's Halb. Cl.II was machine number 4 and had a white band forward of the fin. When the *Idflieg* directive came out, the unit changed the cross form and painted the fins and rudders on all aircraft white. Bechtle was wounded on 24 April 1918 and there are no data nor photographs available after that date.

Schusta/Schlasta 3.

Schusta 3 had the Ru. C.I aircraft in January 1917. There is no further information regarding this unit until Han. Cl.III 3885/18 was shot down on October 3, 1918.

Schusta/Schlasta 4.

Schusta 4 had on strength in January 1917 the Alb. C.VII and the Ru. C.I. In May 1917, *Schusta 4* was issued the DFW C.V. Nothing else has been found on *Schlasta 4* until October 1918 when it was reported that it was equipped with the Halb. Cl.II and Halb. Cl.IV machines. There is no known photograph of this unit.

Schusta/Schlasta 5.

The first available information regarding *Schusta 5* is in August 1917, at which time the unit had AGO C.IV aircraft in their inventory. In September 1917, *Schusta 5* received Alb. C.X and Ru. C.IV aircraft to replace them. These machines were replaced with DFW C.V airplanes in November. Intelligence data reports in May 1918 have *Schlasta 5* equipped with the Halb. Cl.II machines. A photograph of a *Schlasta 5* line-up with Halb. Cl.II shows the red and white horizontal stripe along the fuselage side center line, commencing just forward of the horizontal stabilizer leading edge and ending about one meter short of the nose. The two Halb. Cl.II aircraft have numbers three and six visible in red outlined in white bisecting the red/white fuselage stripe. The fuselage cross on number six is the variation ordered by *Idflieg* on 15 May 1918 which dates the photograph between 15 May and 4 June 1918 when the next cross change occurred.

During this period *Schlasta 5* was commanded by *Oblt.* Bruno Zipplies who instituted the unit marking. While there is no evidence detailing the color of the dark stripe on the *Schlasta 5* aircraft, in the photographs it appears to be slightly lighter than the black of the fuselage cross. A set of three photographs, taken on 10 August 1918 at Chivres-en-Laonnois airfield, show the final known *Schlasta 5* markings. At this time the unit had Halb. Cl.II with individual aircraft numbers of 4, 5, and 6 and Halb. Cl.IV machines marked 1, 2, and 3. The *Staffelführer*, *Ltn.* Hans-Joachim Rath's Halb. Cl.IV, number 1, has, in addition to the unit marking, a white turtle-deck. By 2 October 1918, *Schlasta 5* was fully equipped with the Halb. Cl.IV.

Plate 2. ***(page 186)***

Schusta/Schlasta 6.

Intelligence reports state that *Schusta 6* was equipped with the LFG Roland C.II in January 1917. Photographs confirm that by June 1917 *Schusta 6* was re-equipped with the AEG C.IV and the unit marking was an elongated geometric form in black, bordered in white. By May 1918, *Schusta 6* had been issued Han. Cl.II machines. The only marking in use at this time were the white numbers 1-6 painted on both sides of the fin. On 14 April 1918, *Oblt.* Jürgen Lüdeke was named *Schlastaführer*. As his original regiment was the 17th Brunswick Hussars, he took the Hussar Totenkopf (death's head) as the *Schlasta 6* insignia and a yellow pennant as his personal marking. The colors of his home of Brunswick are red and yellow. The individual aircraft identity were the numbers 1 through 6 painted on the fins of the machines.

Oblt. Jürgen Lüdeke was joined by his younger brother Günther in September 1918. On his arrival *Ltn.* Günther Lüdeke was given a Halb. Cl.II, which he adorned with a red and yellow diagonal sash as his personal marking. Later in October *Ltn.* Günther painted a broader red and yellow sash on his Halb. Cl.IV. *Schlasta 6* was fully equipped in October 1918 with the Halb. Cl.IV and carried the Totenkopf to war's end.

Schusta/Schlasta 7.

Schusta 7 inventory in April 1917 consisted of a mix of machines including Alb. C.VI, DFW C.V, and Ru. C.I. The following month they had DFW C.V and LVG C.IV aircraft. In June they were fully equipped with the AEG C.IV aircraft. Unfortunately there are no known photographs of these machines. In fact there is no information until 9 August 1918, when *Schlasta 7* was reported to have Han. Cl.IIIa machines. With some photographs of an unknown *Schlasta* equipped with Han. Cl.IIIa at hand, and through a process of elimination, it has been possible to identify the aircraft in these photos as *Schusta 7*. However, this premise needs to be confirmed. *Schlasta 7* markings are a white diagonal band around the fuselage aft of the gunner's cockpit sloping forward to the bottom of the fuselage. Aircraft markings are white numerals 1 to 6 painted on the Han. Cl.IIIa sides aft of the fuselage cross.

Schusta/Schlasta 8.

Very little information is available on *Schusta 8*. The Summaries of Air Intelligence report that in April 1917 *Schusta 8* was equipped with the Aviatik C.III and in June 1917 DFW C.V aircraft replaced the Av.C.III machines. The DFW C.V aircraft carried white numerals 1 to 6 for aircraft identification painted on the sides of the fuselage. In July 1917 the *Staffel* symbol was a black 'W' on the side painted on a white band forward of the cross. The black aircraft identity numbers 1 to 6 were painted on a white field on the side of the fuselage. On 9 May and 28 July 1918, *Schlasta 8* had Halb. Cl.II machines in their inventory. There are no known photographs available of these aircraft in *Schlasta 8* markings.

Schusta/Schlasta 9.

In July 1917, *Schusta 9* had on hand AGO C.IV, DFW C.V, and LVG C.IV aircraft. By November 1917 LVG C.V aircraft replaced the AGO C.IV and the LVG C.IV machines. In December 1917, *Schusta 9* was fully equipped with Halb. Cl.II aircraft. *Ltn.* Hans Deetjen, the *Staffelführer*, adopted the new *Staffel* design of two white bands, separated with a narrower black band painted on the four sides of the fuselage aft of the cross and white wheel covers. White numerals 1-6 were painted on the fuselage sides centered below the cockpits. About mid-October 1918, *Schlasta 9* began to receive Halb. Cl.IV aircraft in replacement of damaged Halb. Cl.II machines.

Plate 3. ***(page 187)***

Schusta/Schlasta 10.

The first information available on *Schusta 10* is in December 1917 at which time they were equipped with LVG C.V machines. In 1918 there are two citations, 30 April when the *Staffel* had Halb. Cl.II aircraft and 8 August when it was reported to be equipped with Han. Cl.III machines. There are two photographs of a *Schlasta 10* Halb. Cl.II completely devoid of any unit or personal markings. The Iron Cross insignia would indicate the photo was taken before 17 March 1918. Most likely, *Schlasta 10* received their Halb. Cl.II in February in preparation for Operation Michael which commenced on March 21, 1918.

Schusta/Schlasta 11.

The first known aircraft of *Schusta 11* was the DFW C.V reported in May 1917. The LVG C.V was on hand with *Schusta 11* in October and November 1917. By 31 December transition to the Halb. Cl.II had been completed. During the transition to the Halb. Cl.II, a photograph was taken of five Halb. Cl.II and the two remaining LVG C.V aircraft. Five of the six aircraft were marked with double white banding separated with what is presumed to be a narrower black band. It could have been dark blue, dark green, or red. On the under side of the lower wings was a chevron in narrow black and white stripes, running from the inner leading edge to the trailing edge, terminating at the trailing edge near the rear cross arm. One LVG C.V had the double white fuselage band forward of the cross; the second LVG C.V had the double bands fore and aft of the cross (illustrated on Plate 3.), however this machine only had the black chevron under the lower wing. Three of the four Halb. Cl.II were marked with the banding and the black and white chevrons under the lower wing. One Halb. Cl.II had no unit markings at all. One of the Halb. Cl.II had the double white banding fore and aft of the cross. Another had the double banding aft of the cross and the third had triple white banding aft of the cross. It is thought that the banding served as the unit marking with the individual aircraft identity number.

Recently another photograph was obtained, showing the fatal crash of *Oblt.* Caspar Kulenkampff-Post on June 20, 1918. The cross has the 150mm wide border which has been over-painted in the light color of the front and rear portions of the fuselage. While the color is not specifically known, the tonal value matches light blue, so this color was chosen. Halb. Cl.II machines were reported to equip *Schlasta 11* in August 1918 and most probably served as the aircraft of the unit until the end of the war.

Schusta/Schlasta 12.

In June 1917, DFW C.V were reported on strength of *Schusta 12*. In July the aircraft complement was a mix of AGO C.IV, AEG C.IV, and DFW C.V machines. By September, the AGO C.IV machines had been withdrawn and returned to *AFP 4*. The AEG C.IV and the DFW C.V aircraft only carried black aircraft identity numbers 1 to 6 painted on the sides of the fuselage. In October 1917, *Schusta 12* turned in their AEG C.IV and DFW C.V machines and were issued LVG C.V as replacement aircraft. At this time the 1 to 6 identity numbers were replaced with new identity numbers consisting of the last two digits of the aircraft serial number. For example, LVG C.V 3342/17 used 42 as the aircraft identity number. When in early 1918 *Schusta 12* converted to the Halb.Cl.II the practice of using the last two digits of the serial was continued.

In preparation for the forthcoming Battle of France, Operation Michael, *Schusta 12* was issued Han. Cl.II machines and with these aircraft the *Staffelführer*, *Oblt.* Johannes Missfelder, adopted new *Staffel* markings of a double white diagonal banding separated by a broader black band, which wrapped around the fuselage at the trailing edge of the right-hand lower wing, diagonally over the fuselage and terminating at the lower left longeron just forward of the left stabilizer. White numerals 1-6 were painted on the fuselage sides below the gunner's cockpit. In June 1918, *Schlachtstaffel 12* was converted to the Han. Cl.III. After *Oblt.* Missfelder was transferred to *Schlachtgruppe D* on 23 April 1918, little is known of the markings of *Schlasta 12.*

Plate 4. ***(page 188)***

Schusta/Schlasta 13.

In April 1917, *Schusta 13* was reported to be equipped with LVG built DFW C.V aircraft. In the following month they were using AEG C.IV machines. No other report exists on *Schusta 13* until March 1918, now designated *Schlasta 13*, when it had on strength Halb. Cl.II and LVG C.V aircraft. On 9 June 1918, an RE 8 of No. 3 Sqn. RFC brought down Halb. Cl.II 15342/17, crewed by *Gefr.* Kuesler and *Vzfw.* Müllenbach, in British lines. The Halb. Cl.II machine had a black and white tailplane with a grey fin and rudder, which are thought to be the unit marking. The aircraft number was a black Roman numeral III edged in white. On 23 August 1918, a Halb. Cl.IV was captured and the crew interrogated. They stated that *Schlasta 13* had a mixed complement of Halb. Cl.II and Halb. Cl.IV aircraft. The sole marking was a red Roman numeral V edged in white. Without additional confirmation, the empennage marking on Halb. Cl.II 15342/17 are considered the crew's personal marking. On 24 September 1918, an intelligence report stated that *Schlasta 13* had on its strength LVG C.VI aircraft.

Schusta/Schlasta 14.

The only information on *Schusta/Schlasta 14* is dated 24 April 1918, when it was reported the unit was equipped with Halb. Cl.II aircraft.

Schusta/Schlasta 15.

In January 1917, when *Kasta 39* was converted into *Schusta 15*, the crews brought with them their LFG Roland C.II aircraft, which they continued to fly until at least March 1917. By June of that year, *Schusta 15* was re-equipped with the DFW C.V (LVG). The DFW C.V machines were turned in and *Schusta 15* were issued Halb. Cl.II aircraft at least by March 1918, and continued to fly these aircraft until the end of the war. By 4 October 1918, *Schlasta 15* had in its inventory some Halb. Cl.IV machines to complement the Halb. Cl.II aircraft.

The unit marking in March 1918 was a white band immediately aft of the fuselage cross, with black individual aircraft numbers 1 to 6 aft of the white band. At some date prior to May 1918, the individual aircraft marking was changed to bold white numbers 1 to 6 aft of the white fuselage band.

Plate 5. ***(page 189)***

Schusta/Schlasta 16.

Upon formation, *Schusta 16* was issued the equipment of its predecessor, *Kasta 40*, the Ru. C.I aircraft. The next report was in November 1917, when *Schusta 16* was equipped with DFW C.V and LVG C.V machines. By 9 April 1918 *Schlasta 16* was flying Han. Cl.II machines. In May it was confirmed that *Schlasta 16* was now using Han. Cl.III aircraft. On 17 July 1918 a report stated *Schlasta 16* had been issued the LVG C.V. The last report on 4 October 1918 states that *Schlasta 16* had Halb. Cl.II and Han. Cl.IV machines in its inventory. This seems doubtful inasmuch as the Han. Cl.IV was not put into production. Most likely these were Han. Cl.IIIa machines which were in production at the Hannoversche Waggonfabrik at the time.

A report from *Kofl 4*, dated 14 August 1918, provides information on the markings of *Schlasta 16*. It states, "The body is camouflaged, yellow nose and rear fuselage band with numbers 1 to 6." This can be confirmed on Han. Cl.II machines in photographs as early as March 1918 and is illustrated on Plate 5 as of May 1918.

Schusta/Schlasta 17.

On formation *Schusta 17* had in inventory a mix of Alb. C.VII and Rol. C.II machines. By March 1917, *Schusta 17* had been issued DFW C.V aircraft to replace the Alb. C.VII machines. By April 1917, *Schusta 17* was completely equipped with the DFW C.V aircraft, which were replaced by the Halb. Cl.II machines in December 1917. On 28 January, the Han. Cl.II were listed in the aircraft inventory of *Schusta 17.*

Idflieg had prepared several Alb. J.I airplanes with the Becker Cannon in the observer/gunner cockpit. These machines were issued to a few *Schlasta*, including *Schlasta 17* and four other *Schlasta,* for evaluation. The serial number of the Alb. J.I issued to *Schlasta 17* is known to be Alb. J.I 734/17, however no photograph of this specific aircraft has been discovered. A photograph of Alb. J.I 738/17 is available. It is assumed by the closeness of the serial numbers that the camouflage scheme of Alb. J.I 734/17 and Alb. J.I 738/17 are the same. Since the unit marking of *Schlasta 17* is not known, none are illustrated. The camouflage of the Alb. J.I aircraft is included to show its interesting scheme.

Schusta/Schlasta 18.

No information nor photograph of *Schusta/Schlasta 18* aircraft or dispositions is known to exist.

Schusta/Schlasta 19.

On formation *Schusta 19* had the Alb. C.VI and Alb. C.VII and by April 1917 was issued the DFW C.V. In September 1917, they received the LVG C.V to supplement the DFW C.V aircraft. *Schusta 19* began receiving the Halb. Cl.II two-seater fighter as replacements during November. By the end of December 1917, *Schusta 19* was issued the Han. Cl.II to supplement the Halb. Cl.II. Whether *Schusta 19* continued with the Han. Cl.II is in doubt. A report in May 1918 lists only the Halb. Cl.II in the inventory of the unit. When *Schusta 19* was formed from *Sonder Staffel II*, they brought with them the unit markings of the light blue nose or spinner, black and white wheel covers, and white numerals 1 to 6. These markings are depicted in the profile views of the Han. Cl.II and Halb. Cl.II machines.

Schusta/Schlasta 20.

When *Schusta 20* was formed, it took over the aircraft of its predecessor *Sonder Staffel I,* a mix of Alb. C.VI and Alb. C.VII airplanes. What aircraft were received between January 1917 and 8 August 1918 is not known. On the later date, *Schlasta 20* was equipped with Han. Cl.II and Han. Cl.IIIa machines, which it deployed to the end of the war. On 18 October 1918, *Schlasta 20* had at least one Halb. Cl.II on hand. There are several photographs of Han. Cl.II and Han. Cl.IIIa machines identified as *Schlasta 20* aircraft with the white arrow on both sides of the fuselage and a white nose. Individual aircraft were marked with white numbers 1 to 6 on the fuselage sides forward of the white arrow. Two of these are illustrated on Plate 5.

Schusta/Schlasta 21.

In January 1917, *Schusta 21* had on hand a mix of Alb. C.III and Alb. C.VI. In February 1917, the LFG Roland C.II and Ru. C.I had replaced the Alb. C.III. In April 1917, the Alb. C.VII aircraft arrived and replaced the Alb. C.VI, LFG Roland C.II, and Ru. C.I machines. There is no information of the aircraft type used by *Schlasta 21* until March 1918, when the unit deployed Halb. Cl.II and Han. Cl.II aircraft. In May 1918, *Schlasta 21* had one Alb. J.I on hand to supplement the Halb. Cl.II aircraft in its inventory.

Plate 6. *(page 190)*

There is no specific information about the Alb. J.I sent to *Schlasta 21*, but it is illustrated to show one of the interesting Alb. J.I camouflage schemes. The serial number is left off the fin, however it would have been in the J.700 - 799/17 order. By July 1918, *Schlasta 21* began to receive Halb. Cl.IV machines and had two on hand. On 18 October 1918, the Halb. Cl.IV had supplemented the Halb. Cl.II aircraft in *Schlasta 21*. The markings of *Schlasta 21* in July 1918, were horizontal black stripes 150mm wide and 100mm wide white stripes along the length of the fuselage with white spinners. Black individual aircraft numbers 1 to 6 were painted on the forward base of the white fin and rudder. *Oblt.* Hans Ebel, the *Schlastaführer,* had his machine painted in the reverse of the other machines with 150mm white and 100mm black stripes with a white tailplane. No individual aircraft identification was displayed on the fin.

Schusta/Schlasta 22b.

Little is known about what type aircraft *Schusta 22b* was equipped with until September 1917, when they had DFW C.V machines. In November 1917, they were issued Alb. C.XII while they were transitioning to Halb. Cl.II machines and replacing the DFW C.V aircraft. In December 1917, the transition to Halb. Cl.II was complete. The Halb. Cl.II was used by *Schlasta 22b* at least until May 1918. No information about the type of aircraft nor the markings of *Schlasta 22b* to the end of the war has been uncovered.

Schusta/Schlasta 23b.

In January 1917, *Schusta 23b* was formed from *KG 6/Kasta 32*, receiving its equipment and enlisted personnel, and bringing with it the Alb. C.VII with their white aircraft numerals on a blue diamond. The DFW C.V replaced the Alb. C.VII aircraft at some date prior to June 1917. The DFW C.V continued to serve in *Schusta 23b* until at least October 1917. The DFW C.V machines were replaced by the Halb. Cl.II by November 1917. In March 1918, a mix of Halb. Cl.II and the Han. Cl.II comprised the equipment of *Schlasta 23b*. In addition to the white number on a blue diamond on the sides and top of the fuselage, six white bands spanning the full rib space in width at the upper main plane wing root were added. These were also adjacent to both sides of the Iron Cross on the upper wing. The bands were also added to the lower wings forming a four lateral border for the crosses. After March 1918, no information is available regarding aircraft types or the markings used by *Schlasta 23b*.

Schusta/Schlasta 24b.

Unlike *Schusta/Schlasta 23b,* every make of aircraft used by this unit from its creation in January 1917 is documented. *Schusta 24b* brought with it six Rol C.II aircraft from *KG 6/ Ks 35* and its unit marking, a blue number, one to six, in a white diamond to identify each aircraft. By April 1917, *Schusta 24b* was issued AEG C.IV and Alb. C.VII to replace the Rol C.II machines. In May 1917, the AEG C.IV were replaced by the DFW C.V and they became the sole equipment of *Schusta 24b*. By November 1917, the DFW C.V aircraft had been replaced by LVG C.V, Han. Cl.II, and Halb. Cl.II machines. As the Halb. Cl.II became more available they replaced the LVG C.V airplanes in the *Schusta 24b* inventory.

Plate 7. *(page 191)*

A mix of Halb. Cl.II and Han. Cl.II continued to serve *Schlasta 24b* to May 1918 when they were issued Han. Cl.III as a substitute for the Han. Cl.II machines. In September 1918, *Schlasta 24b* received Halb. Cl.IV and LVG C.VI as replacement aircraft. In the waning months of the war, *Schlasta 24b* received the Han. Cl.IIIa machine as an update to the Han Cl.III. *Schlasta 24b* flew a mix of Han. Cl.IIIa, Halb. Cl.II, and Halb. Cl.IV machines to the end of the war.

The unit marking was changed in late February 1918, when the entire empennage was painted white with a 100mm wide blue band around the fuselage on the leading edge of the white empennage. Sometime late in the war, the blue band was dispensed with, but they retained the white empennage along with the white diamond and blue numbers as the unit marking.

Schusta/Schlasta 25b.

Little is known about *Schusta 25b* from its date of formation until June 1917, at which time it was equipped with AGO C.IV aircraft. At least by October 1917, *Schusta 25b* was flying the DFW C.V, which was replaced with LVG C.V, Han. Cl.II, and Halb. Cl.II machines. As more Halb. Cl.II became available, the LVG C.V aircraft were returned to *AFP 6*. *Schusta 25b* operated with the Halb. Cl.II from December 1917 to at least February 1918. No information regarding unit or aircraft marking is known. Unconfirmed markings exist for *Schlasta 25b* near war's end. A Belgian officer found a Halb. Cl.II crashed near a small village near Deinze. Stationed at Deinze at the end of the war was *Schlachtgruppe J* consisting of *Schlasta 9, 24b,* and *25b*. As the markings of *Schlasta 9* and

24b are known, that leaves *Schlasta 25b* as the likely unit. The Belgian officer recorded the markings and his grandson, Frederic Liefferinckx, has graciously provided them.

Schusta/Schlasta 26b.

When *Schusta 26b* was formed in January 1917, it was equipped with the Rol. C.II aircraft. From that date until January 1918, nothing is known of its aircraft nor markings. In January 1918, the *Staffelführer, Oblt.* Benedikt Schmalschläger, had the noses of their Halb. Cl.II painted red with flames trailing along the fuselage. The identification marking was a white number 1 to 6 painted on a red disc. *Oblt.* Schmalschläger was transferred out on 23 February 1918, and *Oblt.d.R.* Konrad Hoffmann replaced him as *Staffelführer* and remained until the end of the war. It is not known if the 'flame markings' were retained under *Oblt.* Hoffmann. *Schlasta 26b* continued to fly operations with the Halb. Cl.II until at least June 1918.

Plate 8. ***(page 192)***

Schusta/Schlasta 27b.

All the aircraft types with which *Schusta 27b* flew combat missions are known from January 1917 to August 1918. Upon formation *Schusta 27b* was equipped with the Rol. C.II and brought with it the markings of its former unit, *KG 6/Ks 36*, the black chevron and aircraft numbers 1 to 6. *Schusta/Schlasta 27b* retained these markings to as late as August 1918. The unit operated with the Rol. C.II until May 1917, when they were issued Alb. C.VII and DFW C.V aircraft. During June 1917, the AEG C.IV replaced the Rol. C.II and the Alb. C.VII and *Schusta 27b* used the DFW C.V and AEG C.IV until September 1917. These two aircraft were replaced with Ru. C.IV and Halb. Cl.II aircraft. While it is known that *Schusta 27b* had the Ru. C.IV, no photo has been located, and as a result no illustration of this aircraft is presented in the *Schusta 27b* unit markings. During the time the unit was stationed at Oostkamp airfield, the unit and aircraft markings were changed to white. In addition, grotesque demons were added as individual markings on the forward side of the fuselage. Halb. Cl.II number 1 was the "dogs of war" painted in black on the forward sides of the fuselage. The pilot or gunner has added his girlfriend's name, "Anni", forward of the tailplane. In November 1917, the Ru. C.IV machines were replaced with the Han. Cl.II. Han Cl.II 9256/17 number 5 has a stylized dragonfly in black on the sides of the fuselage.

A new unit marking was instituted in December 1917. The rudder and rear edge of the fuselage was painted white. Sometime before March 1918, the white-black-white band was added aft of the fuselage cross, and the individual aircraft number was moved forward on the fuselage sides between the wings. The tailplane was painted in white and black stripes. The fin and rudder were white. The girlfriend's name was then painted in white and positioned aft of the fuselage band.

Plate 9. ***(page 193)***

***Schusta/Schlasta 27b* (continued).**

A further change occurred when *Schlasta 27b* received the Halb. Cl.IV. With its very short rear fuselage, the aircraft number 2 was moved about 300mm and the girlfriend's name, "Brünhilde", was placed between the chevron and the aircraft number.

Schusta/Schlasta 28b.

When *Schusta 28b* was formed, it was issued the Rol. C.II. The aircraft illustrated was flown by *Oblt.* Eduard Schleich. It was without forward armament. By July 1917, *Schusta 28b* was equipped with DFW C.V machines. The aircraft shown was built by Automobil und Aviatik A.G. It was painted entirely dark green on the top and side surfaces. The name "Betty" is painted in white under the pilot's cockpit. By March 1918, *Schlasta 28b* had been issued Halb. Cl.II aircraft. These had the nose painted light blue and the rudder white. While the cross changes are evident, it appears that *Schlasta 28b* received this Halb. Cl.II prior to the *Idflieg* directive of 17 March 1918, ordering the change of the Iron Cross to the Balken Cross. In April *Schlasta 28b* had been one of the *Schlasta* to receive the ground support Alb. J.I aircraft. Unfortunately, no photo of their Alb. J.I has been located.

Schusta/Schlasta 29b.

This is another unit for which there is scant information or photographs. One photo shows a crashed DFW built DFW C.V with two narrow white bands around the fuselage aft of the gunner's cockpit. These white bands are presumed to be the unit marking of *Schusta 29b*. Along with the DFW machines, *Schusta 29b* had Rumpler C.VII aircraft in their inventory. In September 1918, they were equipped with the Halb. Cl.II.

Schusta/Schlasta 30b.

There are a few photographs of *Schlasta 30b* taken at Inchy airfield in March 1918. They are line-up pictures which show all the Han. Cl.II machines of this unit. While the color band and aircraft number could be either red or Prussian blue, it is thought they were actually black. The aircraft were numbered 1 to 6 in large numbers on the sides of the gunner's cockpit.

Schusta/Schlasta 31b.
The blue markings painted on the upper nose cowl and the white and blue diagonal stripe painted on the fuselage sides below the gunner's cockpit are the unit markings. There are no individual aircraft markings painted on the sides of Han. Cl.II 13282/17.

Plate 10. ***(page 194)***

***Schusta/Schlasta 31b* (continued).**
In May 1918, *Schlasta 31b* was also equipped with Halb. Cl.II and carried unit markings similar those displayed on the Han. Cl.II aircraft. The spinner is painted blue.

Schusta/Schlasta 32.
The only information on *Schlasta 32* is that the unit was equipped with the Han. Cl.II on 17 June 1918.

Schusta/Schlasta 33.
Schlasta 33 was identified in a series of photographs taken on 10 August 1918 where two of the three *Schlasta* were known. The other units present were *Schlasta 5* and *Schlasta 20.* There was a single Halb. Cl.II in the group of photographs and by enlarging the photo it is possible to discern unconfirmed markings of this *Schlasta 33* Halberstadt. The spinner and the aircraft identification number are white, as well as the fin and rudder. Immediately aft of the fuselage cross are green and white bands encircling the fuselage. In September 1918, *Schlasta 33* was reported to have the Han. Cl.III aircraft in their inventory.

Schusta/Schlasta 34.
In May 1918, *Schlasta 34* was equipped with Han. Cl.II aircraft. The unit markings were diagonal black and white bands enclosing the top and sides of the fuselage, terminating at the lower longeron. The aircraft identity number was painted in white on both sides of the upper fin. In August 1918, *Schlasta 34* was equipped with Han. Cl.III machines. The fuselage crosses were over-painted, moved forward, and re-painted on the sides of the fuselage below the gunner's cockpit. The location, style, and colors of the unit markings and aircraft identification number remained the same.

Schusta/Schlasta 35.
In August 1918, the Halb. Cl.II aircraft of *Schlasta 35* had green-white-green-white diagonal bands painted on the fuselage just forward of the vertical fin. The fin and rudder were white with the aircraft identity number painted on both sides of the vertical fin. On the *Schlasta 35* machine of the *Schlastaführer Ltn.* Müller-Friedel, his name "Friedel", was painted in white below the pilot's cockpit.

Schusta/Schlasta 36.
The only information available on *Schlasta 36* is that in May 1918 it was equipped with the Halb. Cl.II and Han. Cl.II. In June 1918, they were outfitted with the Halb. Cl.II and Albatros J.I. No data is at hand regarding markings or colors.

Schusta/Schlasta 37.
When *Schusta 37* was established it was equipped with the AEG C.IV. In March 1918, it received Halb. Cl.II aircraft. The illustration of the AEG C.IV aircraft is for the purpose of showing this machine initially used by the unit. No information is available on markings or colors.

Schusta/Schlasta 38s.
On 23 March 1918, Han. Cl.II 13199/17 was shot down and captured. The information about this machine, its colors and markings, are taken from an Air Ministry report. There is no further information with regard to this unit.

Plate 11. ***(page 195)***

Schusta/Schlasta 7.
This was a late identification and is illustrated on this plate. Two photographs have been found of the Han. Cl.IIIa and one of the Halb.Cl.II. In these photographs, both aircraft have identical markings. The diagonal white band is the unit marking, and the white numbers are the individual aircraft markings. In the single photo of the Halb. Cl.II the spinner is painted white. The unit identification remains unconfirmed.

The Halb. Cl.II and Halb. Cl.IV illustrated as *Schusta V* to *Schusta Z* are unidentified units and are shown to request the reader's assistance in identification. Please contact the authors if you have any information.

Plate 12. ***(page 196)***

The illustrated Halb. Cl.II is from the first production order for 100 Halb. Cl.II, serial numbers C.2825 to C.2924/17. It is covered with the lighter under surface printed fabric on the tops of the wings, tailplane, rudder, and wheel covers. The under sides of the wings and tailplane are covered with plain linen fabric, applied to the wings at a 45o angle to the line of flight. It is quite evident *Schlachtstaffel 27b* received its Halb. Cl.II before *Idflieg* issued the 17 March 1918 directive changing the Iron Cross insignia to the Balken Cross. The Iron Cross has been painted over with grey paint.

This machine is from a much-published photo of the line-up of *Schlasta 27b*. Aircraft number 2 "Brünhilde" was in the foreground of the line-up. The unit markings were the black and white tailplane stripes, the fuselage band, the white chevron on the sides of the fuselage, wing stripes, and wheel covers. The aircraft were identified in *Schlasta 27b* with the white numbers 1 to 6 and later in 1918, 1 to 9. The personal markings were the girlfriend's names painted in white aft of the fuselage band.

Plate 13. ***(page 197)***

Halb. Cl.II 5720/17 was from the second production order and was probably delivered mid to late July. This Halb. Cl.II was most likely issued to *Schusta 21* in late 1917. The unit markings carried on *Schusta 21* or *Schlasta 21* before July 1918 are unknown. When received by the unit, the upper surface of the wings, tailplane, fin, rudder, and wheel covers of Halb. Cl.II 5720/17 were covered with the five-color dark upper pattern. The under sides of the wings and tailplane had the five-color light pattern. The fuselage top and sides and the top surface of the center-section were stippled with colors to match the dark pattern five-color fabric. The under side of the center-section was stippled in the colors of the light five-color printed fabric.

By July 1918, *Schlasta 21* painted the fuselage in 150mm wide black and 100mm wide white longitudinal stripes. The fin and rudder were painted white with a stylized and "leaning" numeral 3 on both sides of the fin. The Balken Crosses had been modified to Latin Crosses with 150mm wide white borders on the sides only. The wing crosses were full chord. At some later date, probably in August or September 1918, *Oblt.* Hans Ebel, the *Führer* of *Schlasta 21*, changed the markings of the unit from the black and white stripes to red and yellow bands on the fuselage and red and yellow stripes on the tailplane, with all-yellow wings and wheel covers. The yellow and red bands did not quite mask the black and white fuselage stripes. On 2 October 1918, Halb. Cl.II 5720/17 was flown by *Uffz.* Max Niemann with his gunner, *Vzfw.* Rudolf Kolodziej, when they were shot down and captured.

Plate 14. ***(page 198)***

The Halb. Cl.II illustrated on Plate 14 is from the second production batch, serial numbers C.5675 to 5774/17. It was probably delivered to *Schusta 23b* in October or November 1917. The upper surface of the wings, tailplane, fin, rudder, and the wheel covers were covered with the dark pattern five-color printed fabric. The under sides of the wings and tailplane were covered with the five-color light patterned fabric. The rib tapes were cut strips of matching colors of the dark printed fabric. The fabric was applied to the wings at a 45o angle to the line of flight. The fuselage and center-section were stippled in colors matching the printed fabric, dark on the top and sides of the fuselage and center-section and the light colors on the under side of the center-section. The belly of the fuselage was shellacked and varnished birch plywood. The cowlings, struts, and metal fittings were light grey.

The *Schusta 23b* unit marking was a blue diamond with white numbers 1 to 6 centered on the diamond, painted aft of the cross on the sides of the fuselage and on the turtle deck above the cross. By March 1918, *Schlasta 23b* added six white stripes, 250mm wide, painted on the upper surface of the top wing, on each side of the Iron Cross, and at the wing panel inner ends. On the under side of the lower wing panel, 4 stripes, 250mm wide, were painted on each side of the Iron Crosses.

Plate 15. ***(page 199)***

In July 1918, *Schlasta 21* had four Halb. Cl.II and two Halb. Cl.IV aircraft on strength. *Oblt.* Hans Ebel, the *Schlastaführer*, had one of the Halb. Cl.IV machines, but his aircraft did not carry an identification number. The other Halb. Cl.IV carried a leaning number six on both sides of the fin and against the edge of the fin. The fuselage was striped like the Halb. Cl.II (see Plate 5). *Oblt.* Ebel had painted the stripes on his Halb. Cl.IV the opposite of the other aircraft, the white stripes were 150mm wide and the black stripes were 100mm wide. The tailplane carried the same stripes as the fuselage. By October 1918, *Schlasta 21* was completely equipped with the Halb. Cl. IV.

Plate 16. ***(page 200)***

This color plate illustrates the Hannover Cl.II aircraft from the first production order for 200 Han. Cl.II, serial numbers C.9200 – 9399/17 placed with the Hannoversche Waggonfabrik A.G. in July 1917. Characteristic of all Han. Cl.II, the aircraft were covered with the light pattern five-color printed linen fabric on the top of the wings, upper elevators, upper tailplane, rudder, and wheel covers. The under side of the wings, lower elevators, and the lower tailplane were covered with plain linen fabric. The rib tapes covering the stitching of the fabric to the ribs were cut strips of the light pattern printed fabric on the upper surfaces of the wings, lower elevators, and upper tailplane. The under surfaces were taped with plain linen fabric strips. The fuselage, lower stabilizer, and center-section were spray-painted in the colors of the printed fabric in large irregular hexagons that diminish in size toward the rear of the fuselage to the size of the lozenges that are printed on the fabric. The lozenges are sharp edged on the rear fuselage forward of the empennage and include the upper and lower fins and the lower stabilizer. All the struts were painted in the camouflage colors.

These machines were assigned to *Schusta 12* around late December 1917. In March 1918, the *Staffelführer Oblt.* Johannes Missfelder adopted the white-black-white running diagonal band from the bottom longeron aft of the trailing edge of the lower right wing up and over the rear turtle-deck and ending at the bottom longeron just forward of the left lower stabilizer. The individual aircraft were numbered 1 to 6 painted in white on the sides of the fuselage below the gunner's cockpit. *Schlasta 12* flew the Han. Cl.II until June 1918 when they began to receive the Han. Cl.III aircraft.

Plate 17. ***(page 201)***

Han. Cl.II 13274/17 was photographed at *AFP 4* at Gent. The white empennage is thought to be a *Schlagru D* marking, as all units in the *Gruppe* had white displayed on the empennage of their aircraft. The white 4 is the individual aircraft marking. The black and white pennant may be a personal marking. This machine was from the last production order for Han. Cl.II aircraft. All the Han. Cl.II machines were covered and camouflaged in the same manner, with the light five-color pattern on the upper surfaces with natural linen fabric on the under surfaces.

Plate 18. ***(page 202)***

With the introduction of the Han. Cl.III, having the 180 Ps Mercedes D.IIIaü engine, Hannover Waggonfabrik changed the fabric to the four-color printed fabric, dark on the top surfaces and the four-color light pattern on the under surfaces. All the crosses were altered by over-painting the wide white border of the Balken Cross and extending the arms of the crosses to full chord or full depth of the fuselage. *Schlachtstaffel 9*, for most of 1918, was equipped with Halb. Cl.II and Cl.IV aircraft. In September 1918, *Schlasta 9* had all three aircraft. As with *Schlasta 25b*, *Schlasta 9* had a white fin and rudder as the *Schlachtstaffelgruppe* identification. The white-black-white band was the unit marking which was repeated on the upper wing. The white 5 painted on the sides of the fuselage below the gunner's cockpit is the aircraft identity marking.

Plate 19. ***(page 203)***

Hannover Waggonfabrik again changed the camouflage to five-color medium dark pattern for the upper surfaces and wheel covers. The under surfaces were covered with the five-color printed fabric. Rib taping was with natural linen fabric. The fuselage, fins, and stabilizer were camouflaged in colors approximating the colors of the five-color printed fabric. The *Schlasta 20* markings were the white arrow on both sides of the fuselage and the white nose cowlings. The black crosses on the white nose were added by mechanics of the 94 Sqn. USAS after the aircraft had been captured. The white 4 is the aircraft identity number.

The yellow diagonal stripes on the top of the center-section were a warning device to the gunner to aid him from shooting into his own propeller. This machine had been attributed to Captain E.V. Rickenbacker and Lt. Reed Chambers, however, it was really brought down by anti-aircraft fire. For a complete discussion about the capture of this aircraft see Appendix VII.

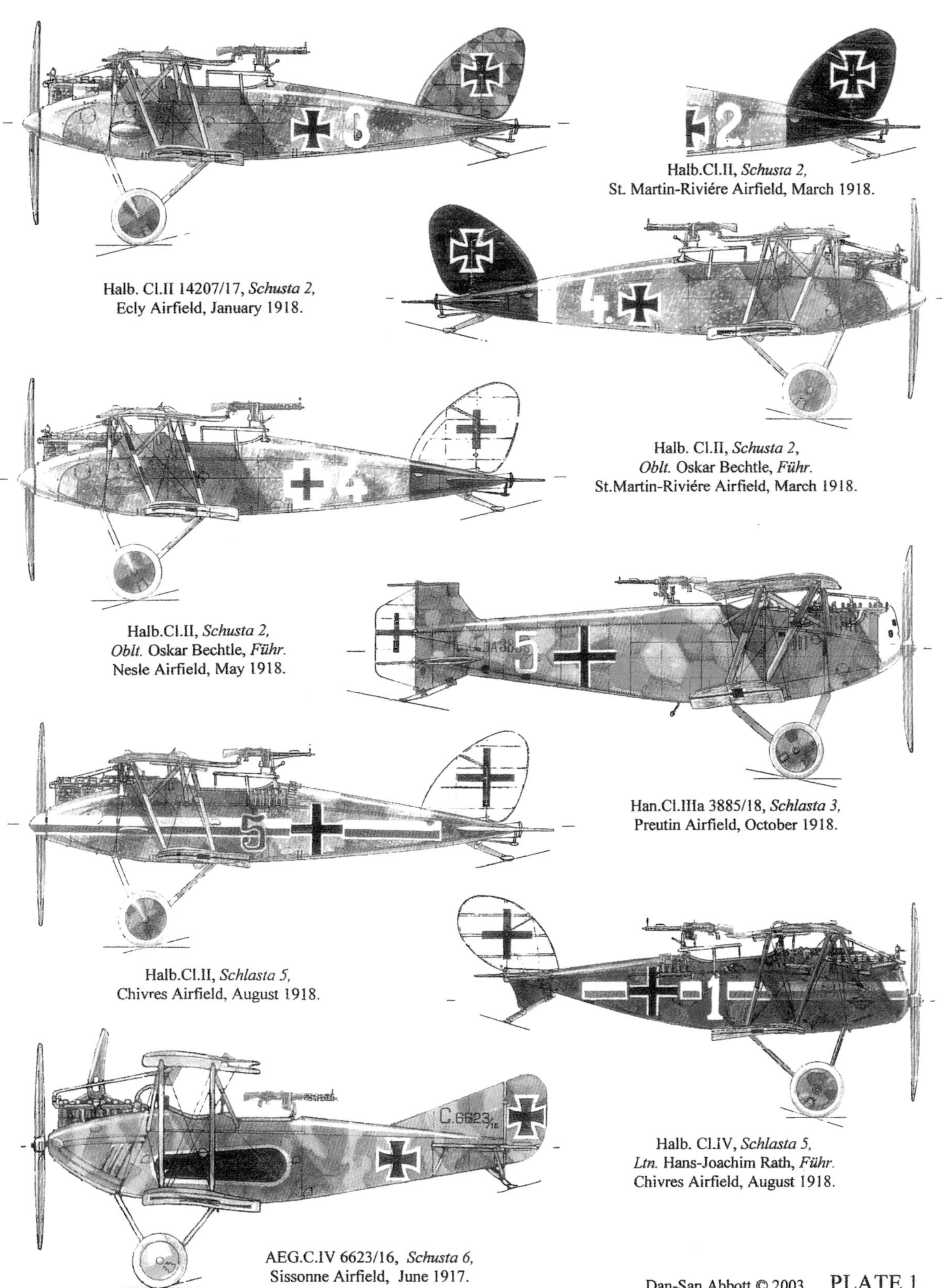

Halb. Cl.II 14207/17, *Schusta 2,*
Ecly Airfield, January 1918.

Halb.Cl.II, *Schusta 2,*
St. Martin-Riviére Airfield, March 1918.

Halb. Cl.II, *Schusta 2,*
Oblt. Oskar Bechtle, *Führ.*
St.Martin-Riviére Airfield, March 1918.

Halb.Cl.II, *Schusta 2,*
Oblt. Oskar Bechtle, *Führ.*
Nesle Airfield, May 1918.

Han.Cl.IIIa 3885/18, *Schlasta 3,*
Preutin Airfield, October 1918.

Halb.Cl.II, *Schlasta 5,*
Chivres Airfield, August 1918.

Halb. Cl.IV, *Schlasta 5,*
Ltn. Hans-Joachim Rath, *Führ.*
Chivres Airfield, August 1918.

AEG.C.IV 6623/16, *Schusta 6,*
Sissonne Airfield, June 1917.

Dan-San Abbott © 2003 PLATE 1.

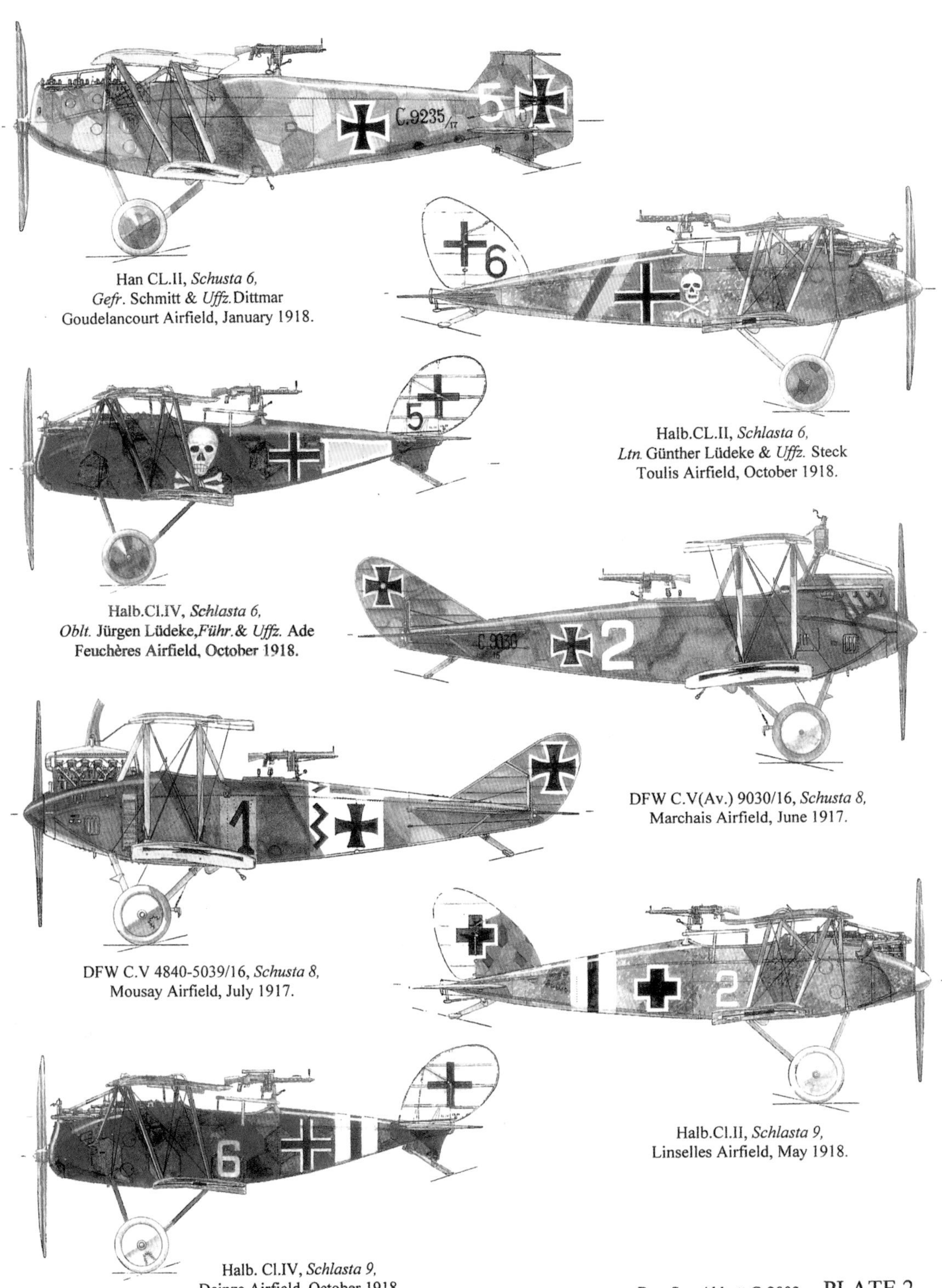

Han CL.II, *Schusta 6,*
Gefr. Schmitt & *Uffz.*Dittmar
Goudelancourt Airfield, January 1918.

Halb.CL.II, *Schlasta 6,*
Ltn. Günther Lüdeke & *Uffz.* Steck
Toulis Airfield, October 1918.

Halb.Cl.IV, *Schlasta 6,*
Oblt. Jürgen Lüdeke,*Führ.*& *Uffz.* Ade
Feuchères Airfield, October 1918.

DFW C.V(Av.) 9030/16, *Schusta 8,*
Marchais Airfield, June 1917.

DFW C.V 4840-5039/16, *Schusta 8,*
Mousay Airfield, July 1917.

Halb.Cl.II, *Schlasta 9,*
Linselles Airfield, May 1918.

Halb. Cl.IV, *Schlasta 9,*
Deinze Airfield, October 1918.

Dan-San Abbott © 2003 PLATE 2.

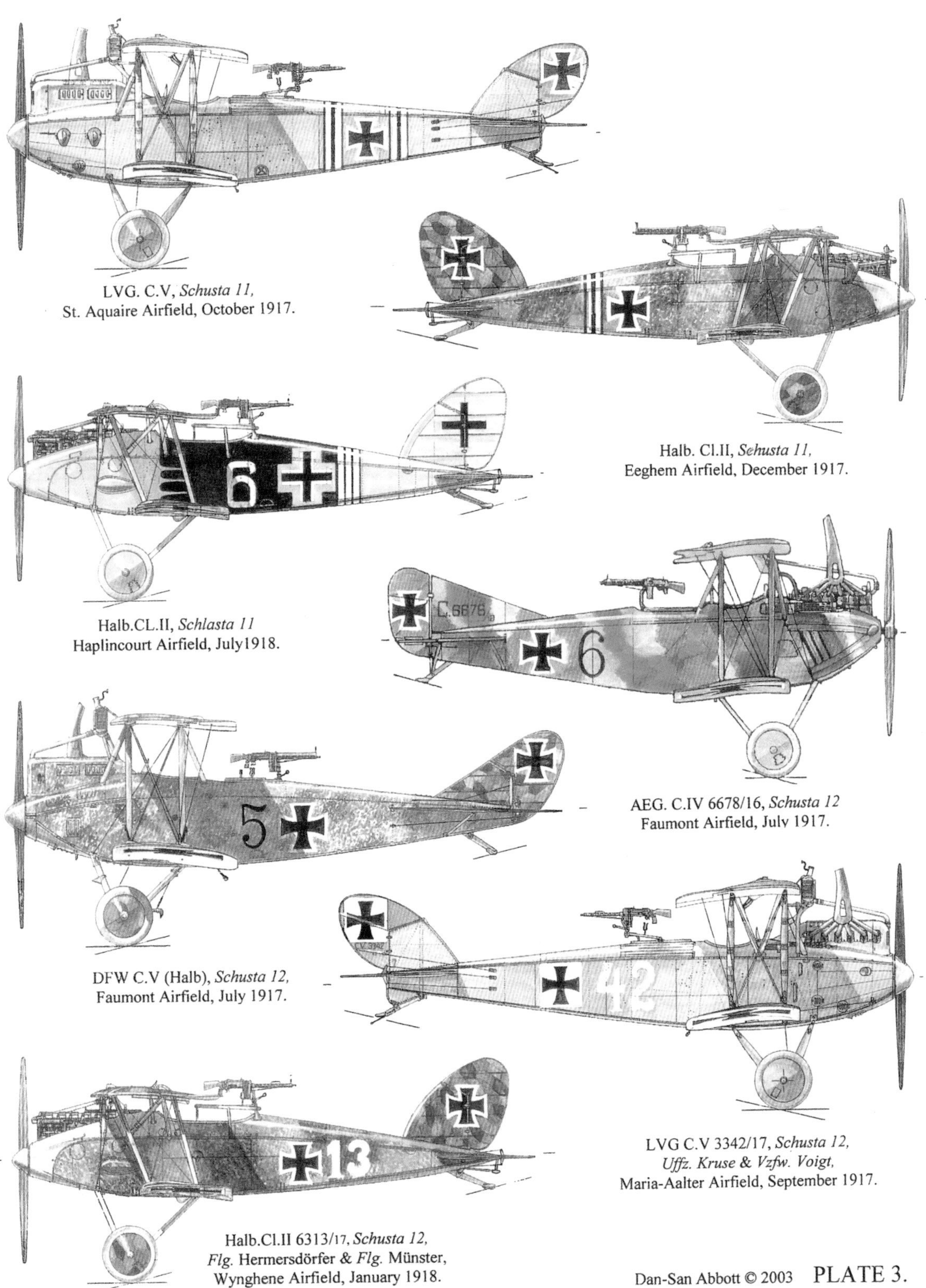

LVG. C.V, *Schusta 11*,
St. Aquaire Airfield, October 1917.

Halb. Cl.II, *Schusta 11*,
Eeghem Airfield, December 1917.

Halb.CL.II, *Schlasta 11*
Haplincourt Airfield, July1918.

AEG. C.IV 6678/16, *Schusta 12*
Faumont Airfield, July 1917.

DFW C.V (Halb), *Schusta 12*,
Faumont Airfield, July 1917.

LVG C.V 3342/17, *Schusta 12*,
Uffz. Kruse & *Vzfw.* Voigt,
Maria-Aalter Airfield, September 1917.

Halb.Cl.II 6313/17, *Schusta 12*,
Flg. Hermersdörfer & *Flg.* Münster,
Wynghene Airfield, January 1918.

Dan-San Abbott © 2003 PLATE 3.

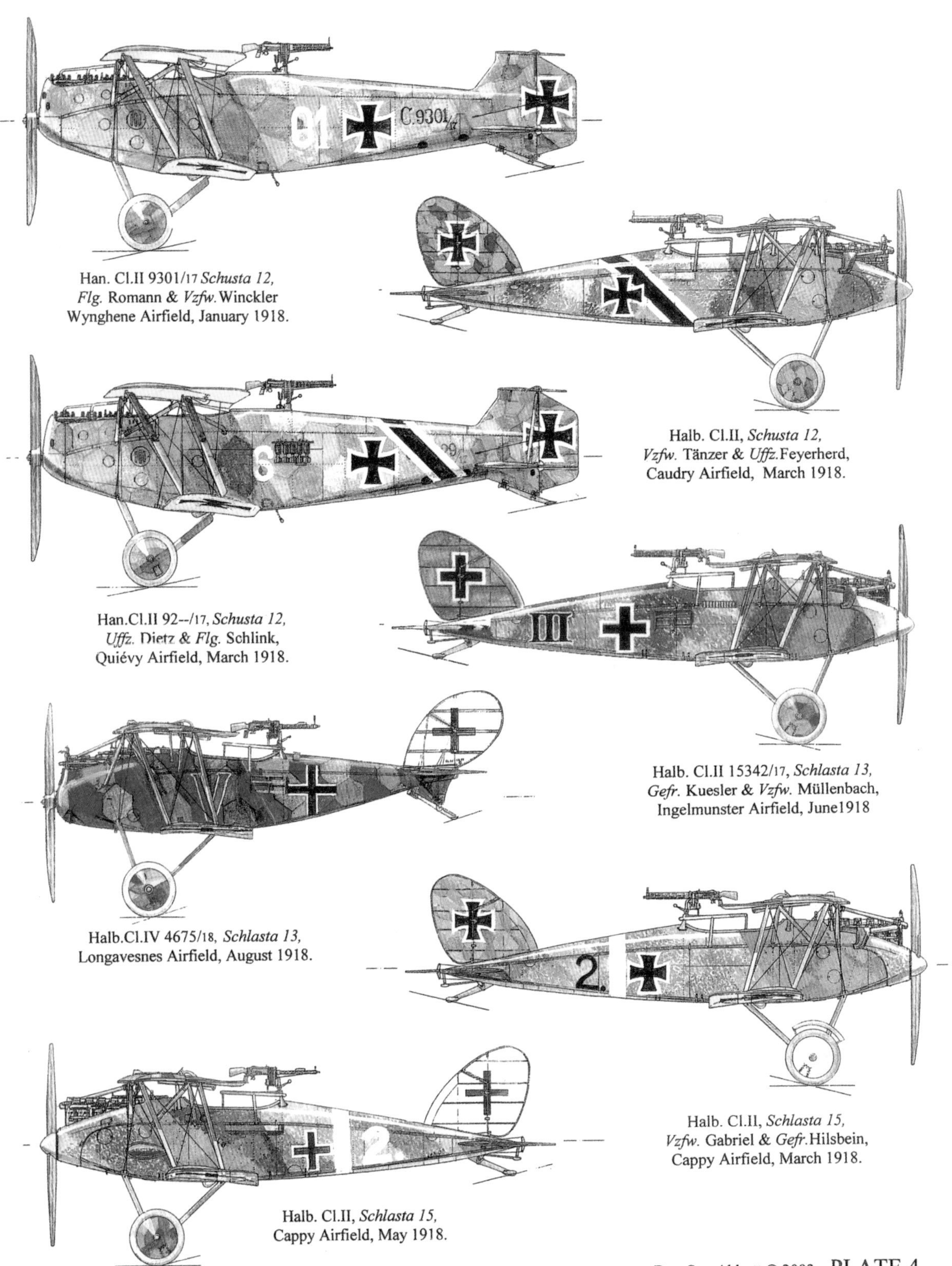

Han. Cl.II 9301/17 *Schusta 12*, *Flg.* Romann & *Vzfw.* Winckler Wynghene Airfield, January 1918.

Halb. Cl.II, *Schusta 12*, *Vzfw.* Tänzer & *Uffz.* Feyerherd, Caudry Airfield, March 1918.

Han.Cl.II 92--/17, *Schusta 12*, *Uffz.* Dietz & *Flg.* Schlink, Quiévy Airfield, March 1918.

Halb. Cl.II 15342/17, *Schlasta 13*, *Gefr.* Kuesler & *Vzfw.* Müllenbach, Ingelmunster Airfield, June1918

Halb.Cl.IV 4675/18, *Schlasta 13*, Longavesnes Airfield, August 1918.

Halb. Cl.II, *Schlasta 15*, *Vzfw.* Gabriel & *Gefr.* Hilsbein, Cappy Airfield, March 1918.

Halb. Cl.II, *Schlasta 15*, Cappy Airfield, May 1918.

Dan-San Abbott © 2003 PLATE 4.

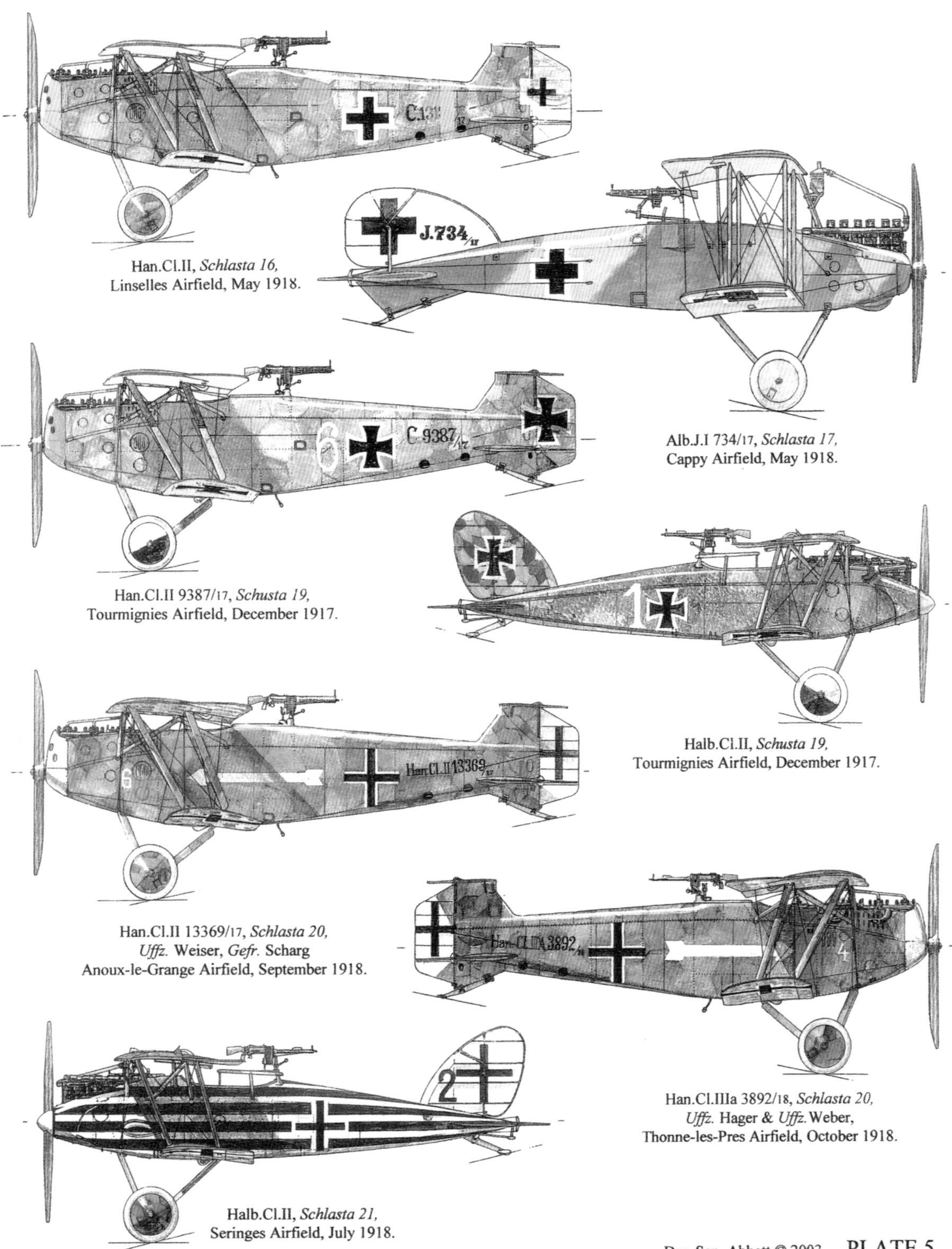

Han.Cl.II, *Schlasta 16,*
Linselles Airfield, May 1918.

Alb.J.I 734/17, *Schlasta 17,*
Cappy Airfield, May 1918.

Han.Cl.II 9387/17, *Schusta 19,*
Tourmignies Airfield, December 1917.

Halb.Cl.II, *Schusta 19,*
Tourmignies Airfield, December 1917.

Han.Cl.II 13369/17, *Schlasta 20,*
Uffz. Weiser, *Gefr.* Scharg
Anoux-le-Grange Airfield, September 1918.

Han.Cl.IIIa 3892/18, *Schlasta 20,*
Uffz. Hager & *Uffz.* Weber,
Thonne-les-Pres Airfield, October 1918.

Halb.Cl.II, *Schlasta 21,*
Seringes Airfield, July 1918.

Dan-San Abbott © 2003 PLATE 5.

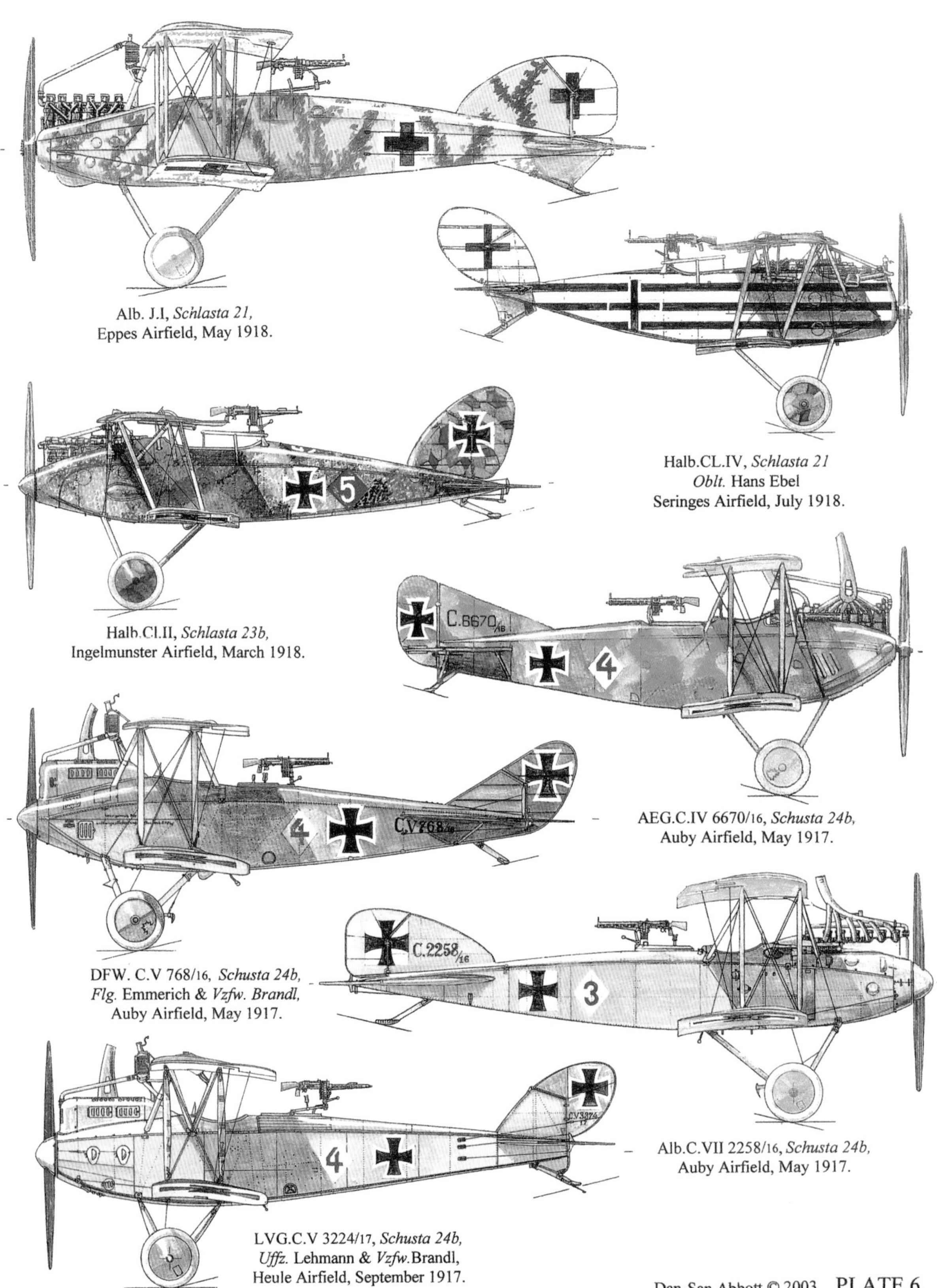

Alb. J.I, *Schlasta 21*, Eppes Airfield, May 1918.

Halb.CL.IV, *Schlasta 21* *Oblt.* Hans Ebel Seringes Airfield, July 1918.

Halb.Cl.II, *Schlasta 23b*, Ingelmunster Airfield, March 1918.

AEG.C.IV 6670/16, *Schusta 24b*, Auby Airfield, May 1917.

DFW. C.V 768/16, *Schusta 24b*, *Flg.* Emmerich & *Vzfw. Brandl*, Auby Airfield, May 1917.

Alb.C.VII 2258/16, *Schusta 24b*, Auby Airfield, May 1917.

LVG.C.V 3224/17, *Schusta 24b*, *Uffz.* Lehmann & *Vzfw.*Brandl, Heule Airfield, September 1917.

Dan-San Abbott © 2003 PLATE 6.

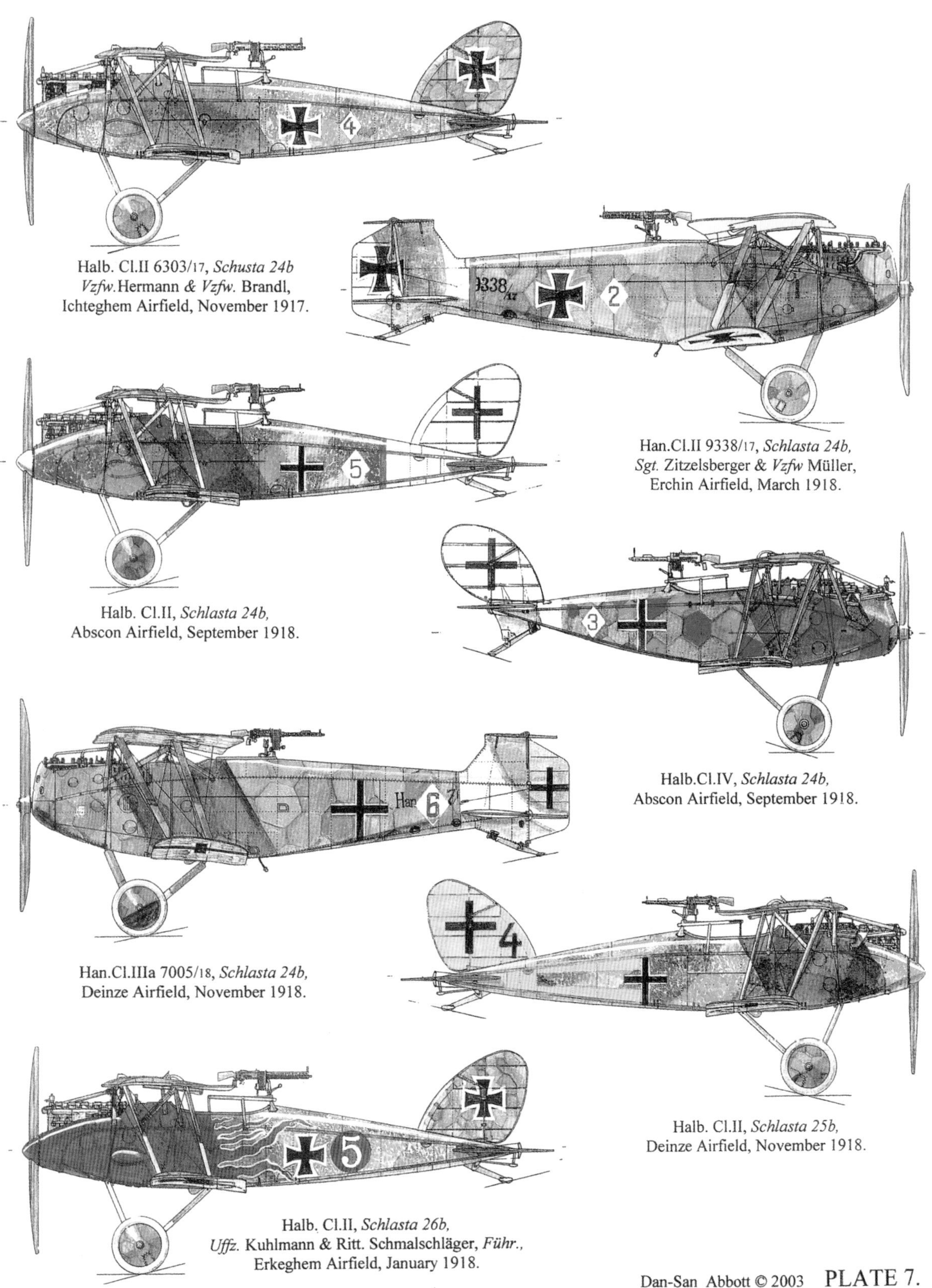

Halb. Cl.II 6303/17, *Schusta 24b*
*Vzfw.*Hermann & *Vzfw.* Brandl,
Ichteghem Airfield, November 1917.

Han.Cl.II 9338/17, *Schlasta 24b,*
Sgt. Zitzelsberger & *Vzfw* Müller,
Erchin Airfield, March 1918.

Halb. Cl.II, *Schlasta 24b,*
Abscon Airfield, September 1918.

Halb.Cl.IV, *Schlasta 24b,*
Abscon Airfield, September 1918.

Han.Cl.IIIa 7005/18, *Schlasta 24b,*
Deinze Airfield, November 1918.

Halb. Cl.II, *Schlasta 25b,*
Deinze Airfield, November 1918.

Halb. Cl.II, *Schlasta 26b,*
Uffz. Kuhlmann & Ritt. Schmalschläger, *Führ.,*
Erkeghem Airfield, January 1918.

 PLATE 7.

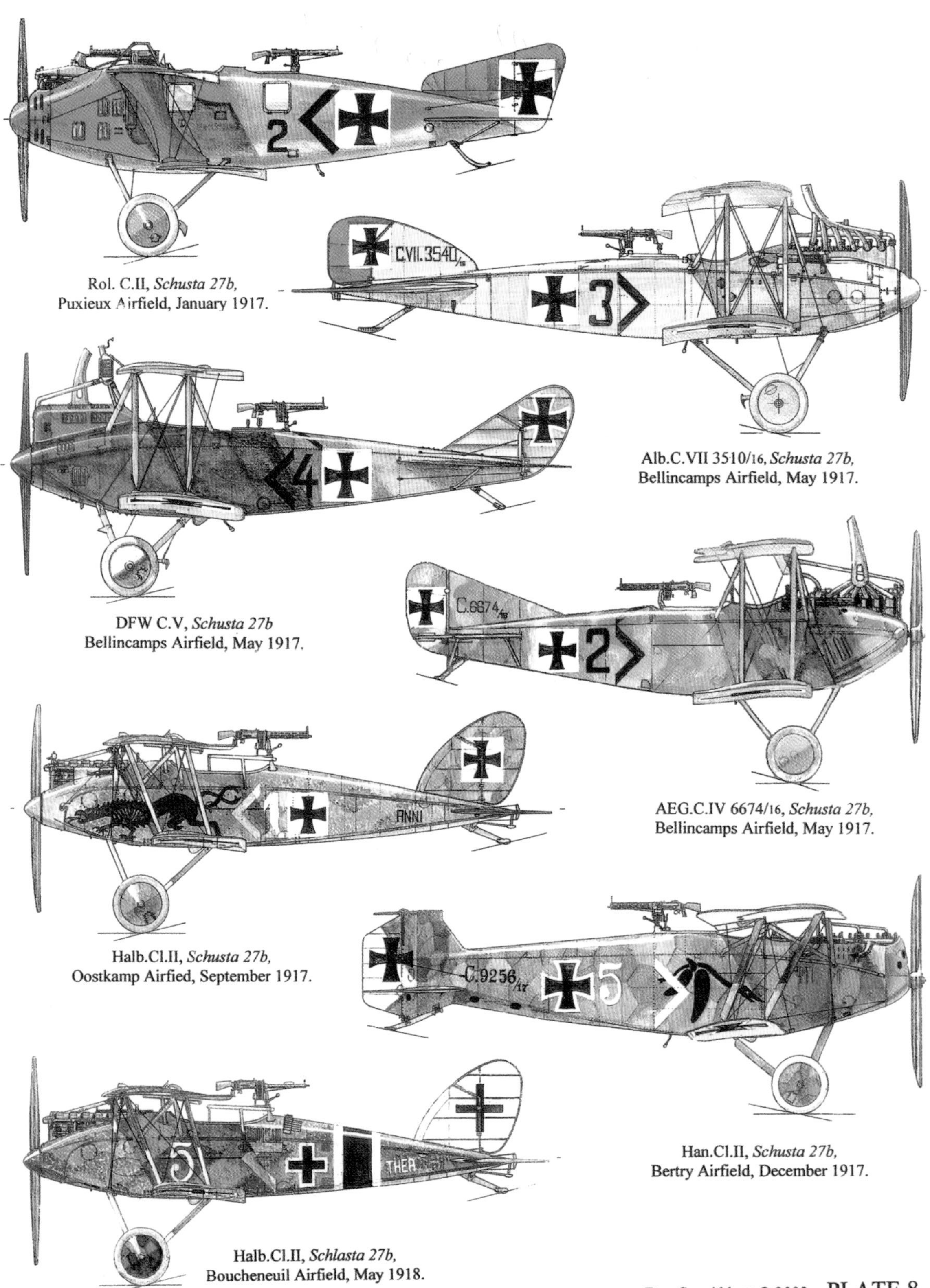

Rol. C.II, *Schusta 27b,*
Puxieux Airfield, January 1917.

Alb.C.VII 3510/16, *Schusta 27b,*
Bellincamps Airfield, May 1917.

DFW C.V, *Schusta 27b*
Bellincamps Airfield, May 1917.

AEG.C.IV 6674/16, *Schusta 27b,*
Bellincamps Airfield, May 1917.

Halb.Cl.II, *Schusta 27b,*
Oostkamp Airfied, September 1917.

Han.Cl.II, *Schusta 27b,*
Bertry Airfield, December 1917.

Halb.Cl.II, *Schlasta 27b,*
Boucheneuil Airfield, May 1918.

 PLATE 8.

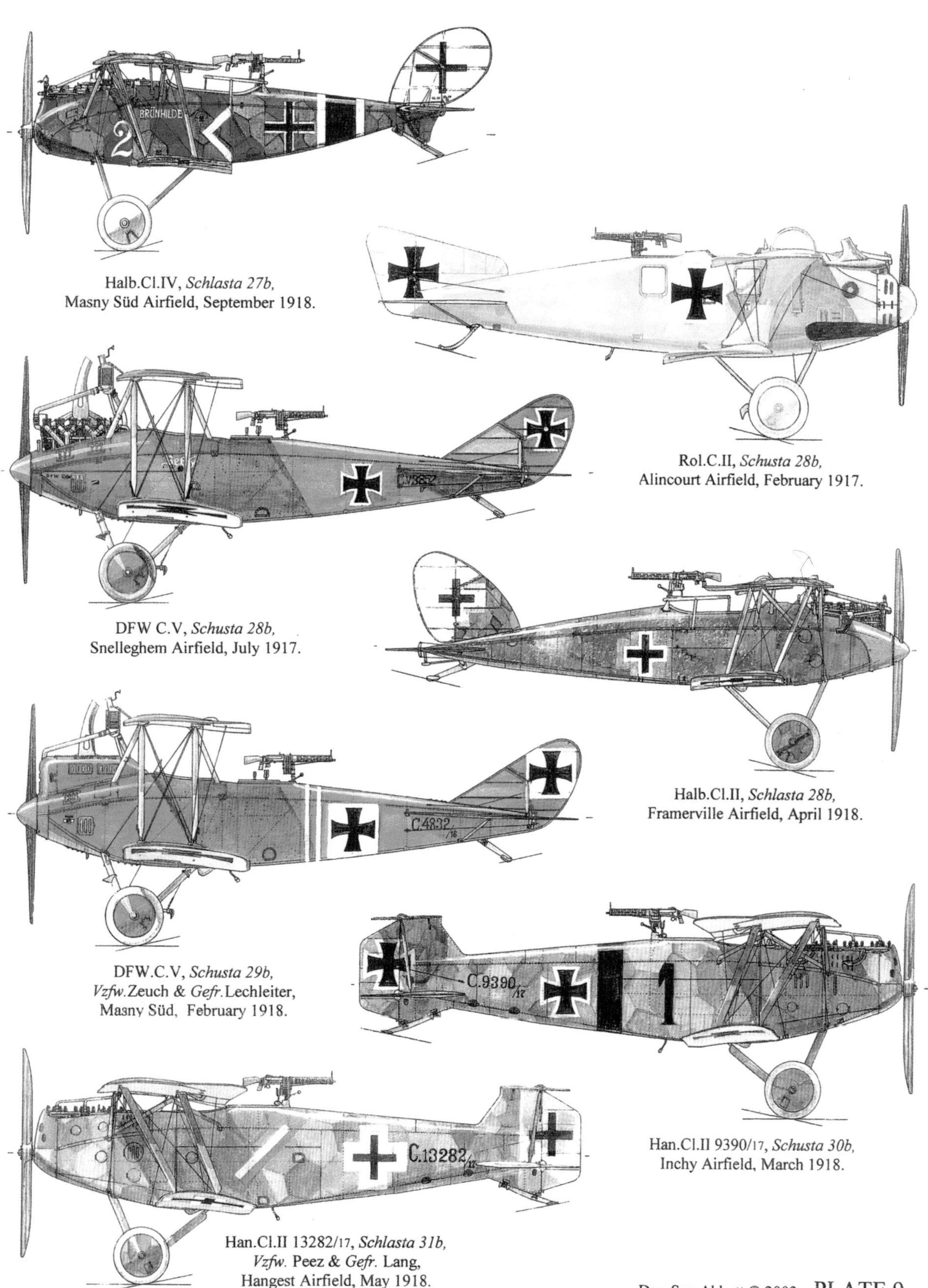

Halb.Cl.IV, *Schlasta 27b,*
Masny Süd Airfield, September 1918.

Rol.C.II, *Schusta 28b,*
Alincourt Airfield, February 1917.

DFW C.V, *Schusta 28b,*
Snelleghem Airfield, July 1917.

Halb.Cl.II, *Schlasta 28b,*
Framerville Airfield, April 1918.

DFW.C.V, *Schusta 29b,*
*Vzfw.*Zeuch & *Gefr.*Lechleiter,
Masny Süd, February 1918.

Han.Cl.II 9390/17, *Schusta 30b,*
Inchy Airfield, March 1918.

Han.Cl.II 13282/17, *Schlasta 31b,*
Vzfw. Peez & *Gefr.* Lang,
Hangest Airfield, May 1918.

Dan-San Abbott © 2003 PLATE 9.

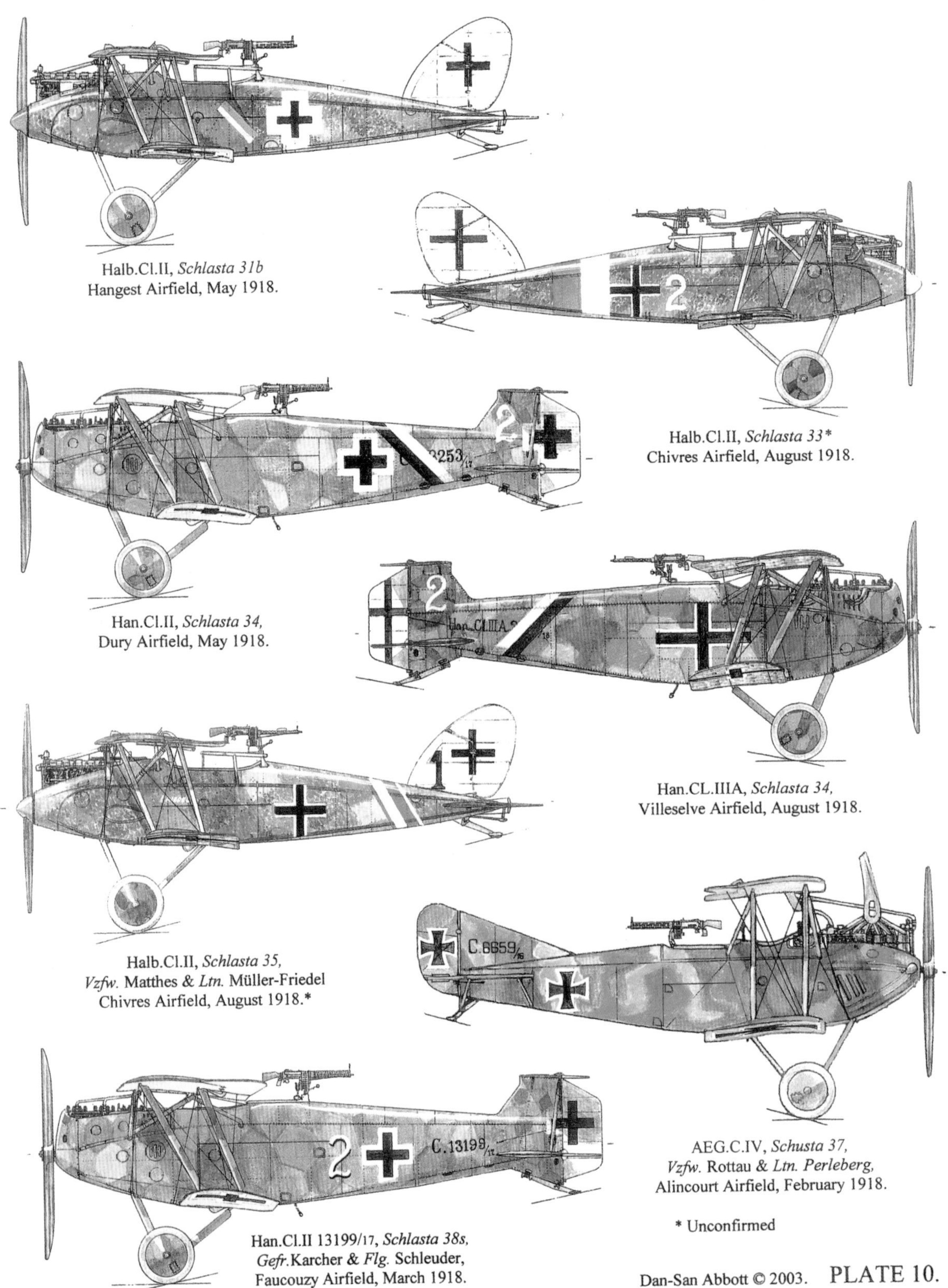

Halb.Cl.II, *Schlasta 31b*
Hangest Airfield, May 1918.

Halb.Cl.II, *Schlasta 33**
Chivres Airfield, August 1918.

Han.Cl.II, *Schlasta 34,*
Dury Airfield, May 1918.

Han.CL.IIIA, *Schlasta 34,*
Villeselve Airfield, August 1918.

Halb.Cl.II, *Schlasta 35,*
Vzfw. Matthes & *Ltn.* Müller-Friedel
Chivres Airfield, August 1918.*

AEG.C.IV, *Schusta 37,*
Vzfw. Rottau & *Ltn. Perleberg,*
Alincourt Airfield, February 1918.

Han.Cl.II 13199/17, *Schlasta 38s,*
*Gefr.*Karcher & *Flg.* Schleuder,
Faucouzy Airfield, March 1918.

* Unconfirmed

 PLATE 10.

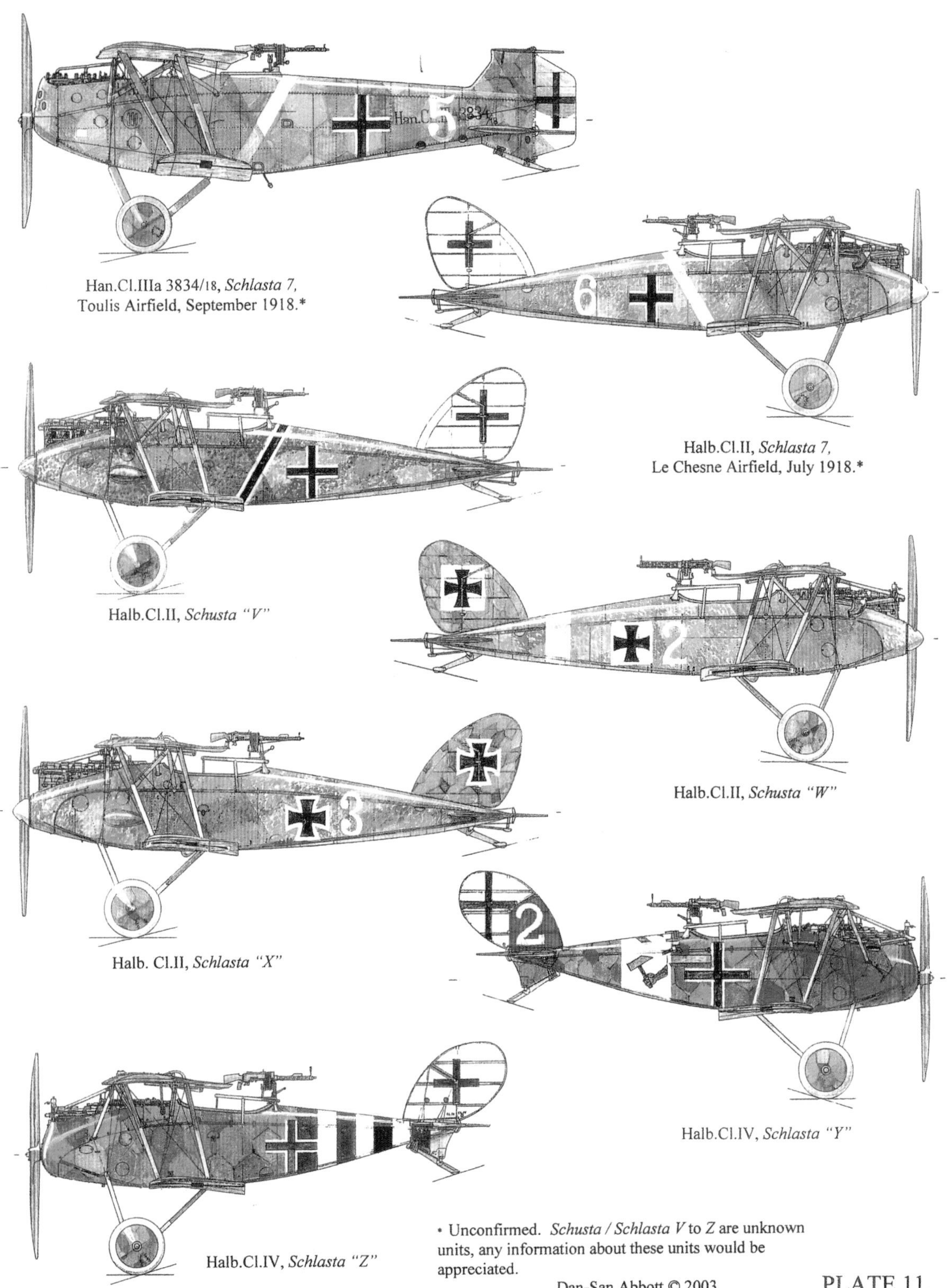

Han.Cl.IIIa 3834/18, *Schlasta 7*, Toulis Airfield, September 1918.*

Halb.Cl.II, *Schlasta 7*, Le Chesne Airfield, July 1918.*

Halb.Cl.II, *Schusta "V"*

Halb.Cl.II, *Schusta "W"*

Halb. Cl.II, *Schlasta "X"*

Halb.Cl.IV, *Schlasta "Y"*

Halb.Cl.IV, *Schlasta "Z"*

• Unconfirmed. *Schusta / Schlasta V* to *Z* are unknown units, any information about these units would be appreciated.

PLATE 11.

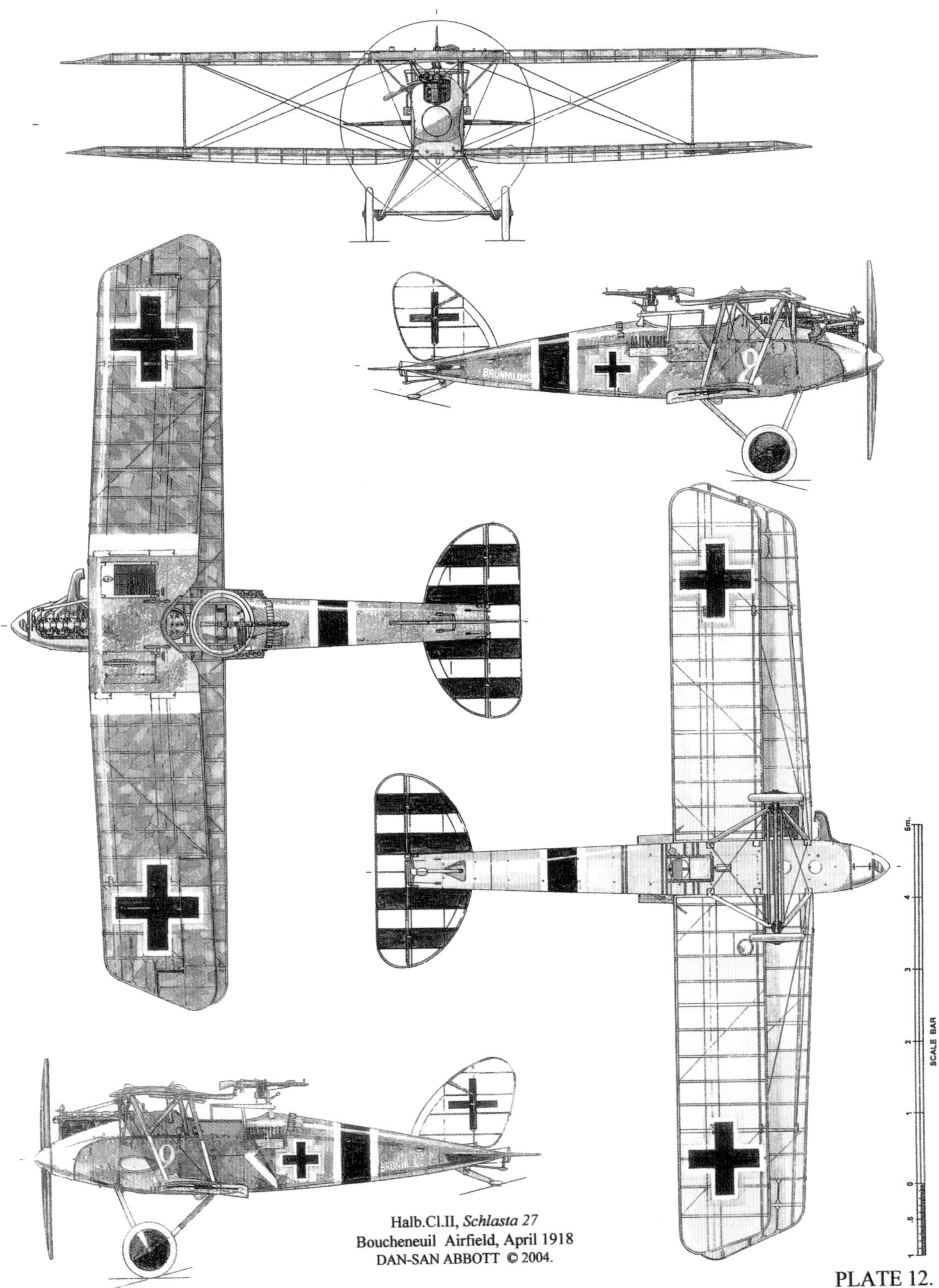

Halb.Cl.II, *Schlasta 27*
Boucheneuil Airfield, April 1918
DAN-SAN ABBOTT © 2004.

PLATE 12.

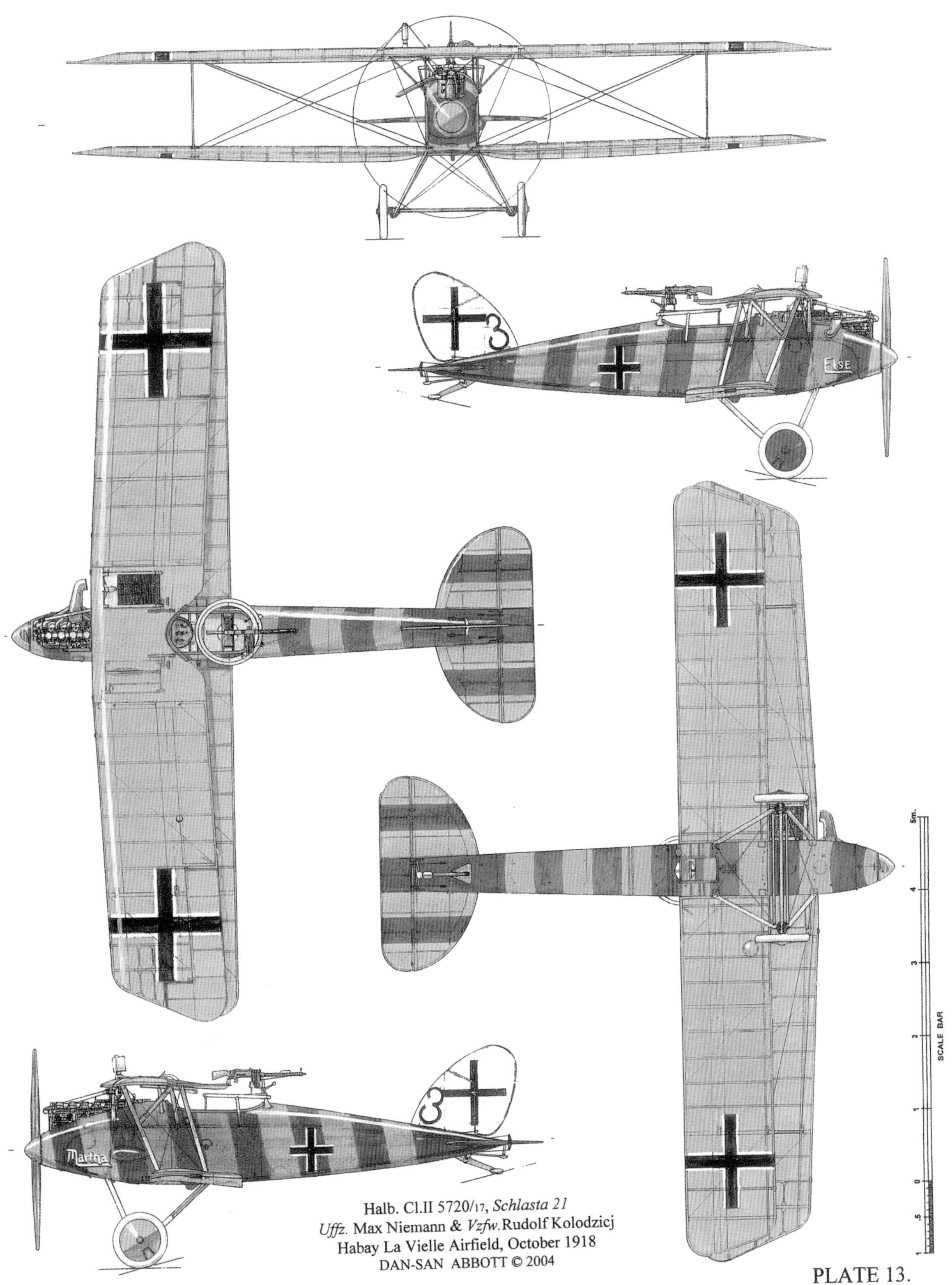

Halb. Cl.II 5720/17, *Schlasta 21*
Uffz. Max Niemann & *Vzfw.* Rudolf Kolodzicj
Habay La Vielle Airfield, October 1918
DAN-SAN ABBOTT © 2004

PLATE 13.

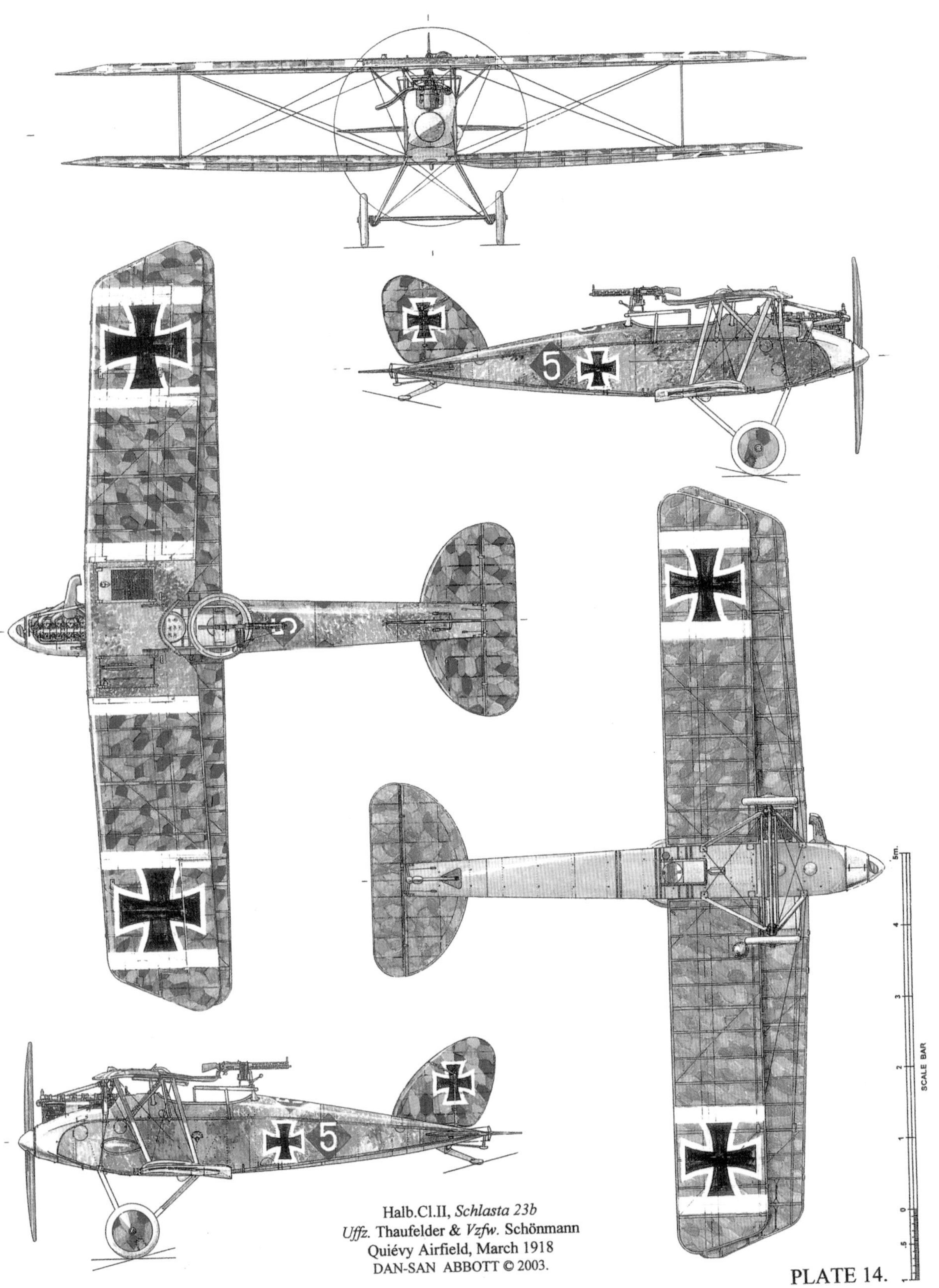

Halb.Cl.II, *Schlasta 23b*
Uffz. Thaufelder & *Vzfw.* Schönmann
Quiévy Airfield, March 1918
DAN-SAN ABBOTT © 2003.

PLATE 14.

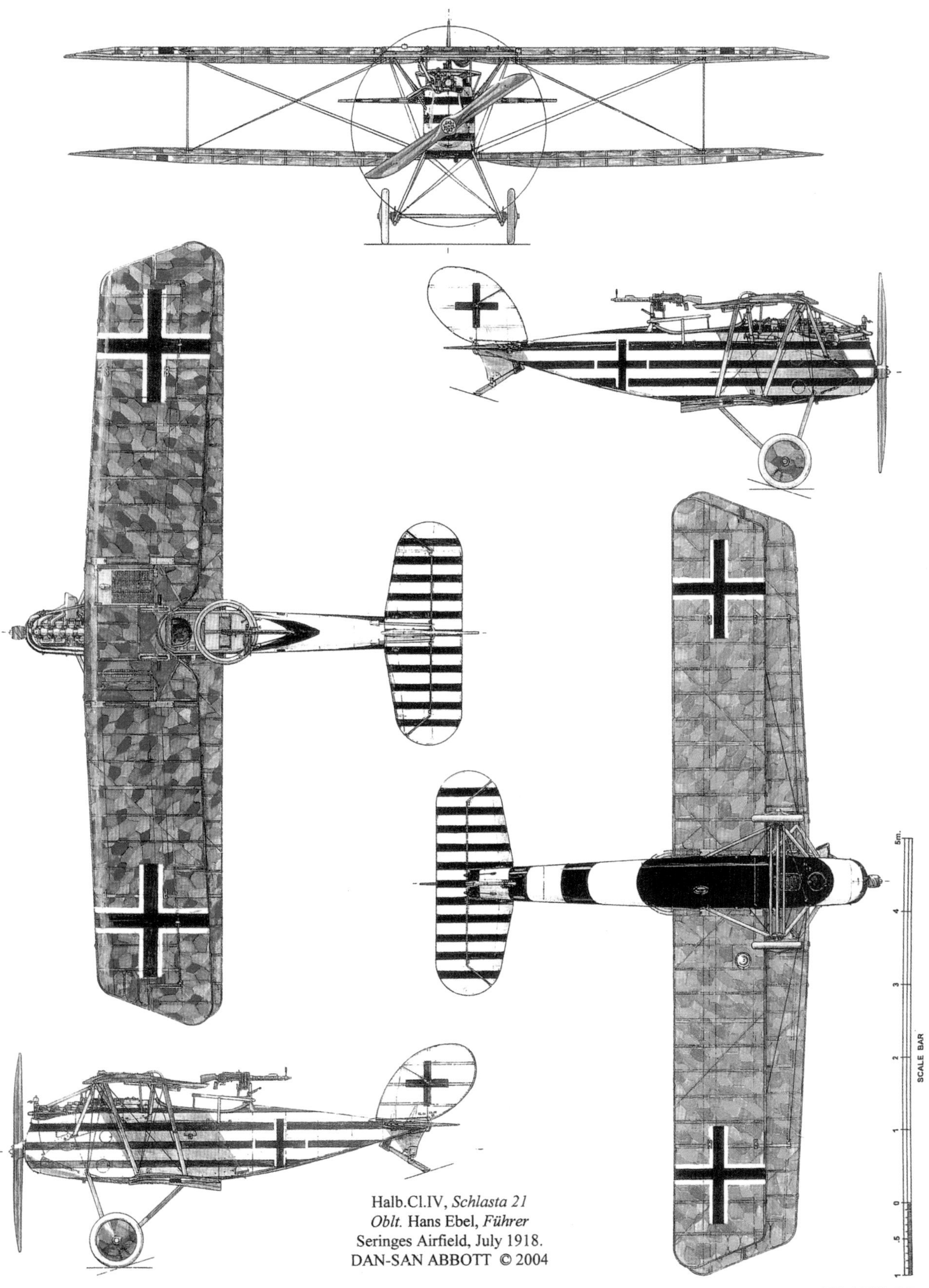

Halb.Cl.IV, *Schlasta 21*
Oblt. Hans Ebel, *Führer*
Seringes Airfield, July 1918.
DAN-SAN ABBOTT © 2004

PLATE 15.

Han.Cl.II, *Schlasta 12*
Uffz. Schlink & *Uffz. Dietz*
Quiévy Airfield, March 1918
DAN-SAN ABBOTT © 2003.

PLATE 16.

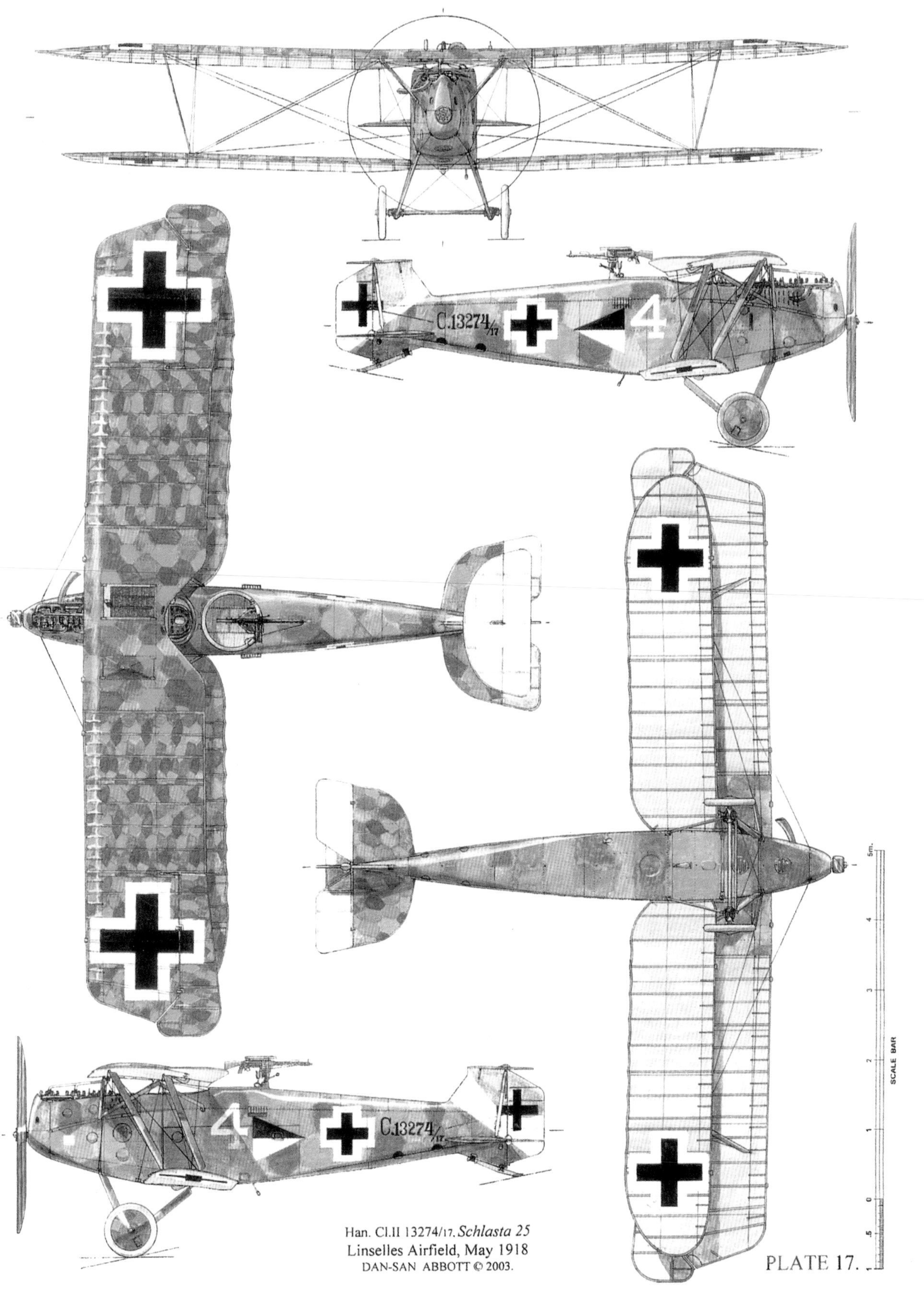

Han. Cl.II 13274/17. *Schlasta 25*
Linselles Airfield, May 1918
DAN-SAN ABBOTT © 2003.

Han. Cl.III 16087/17. *Schlasta 9*
Masny Süd Airfield, September 1918
DAN-SAN ABBOTT © 2003.

PLATE 18.

Han. Cl.IIIa 3892/18. *Schlasta 20*
Uffz. Hager & *Uffz.* Weber
Thonne-les- Pres Airfield, October 1918
DAN-SAN ABBOTT © 2003.

PART V

UNIT DETAILS OF THE SCHUTZSTAFFELN/ SCHLACHTSTAFFELN

UNIT DETAILS OF THE SCHUTZSTAFFELN/SCHLACHTSTAFFELN

This section presents the rosters, airfields, and combat logs for each of the *Schusta/Schlasta* for 1917-1918. The ten Bavarian units are almost 100% complete with respect to the rosters, including the mechanics and other ground crew. The remaining twenty-eight units are not nearly as complete, primarily because the required information is just not available:

Abbreviations Used in the Unit Rosters

AFP	*Armee Flugpark*
AKP	*Armee Kraftpark*
AOK	*Armee Ober Kommando*
Artllry	*Artillerie*
b	Bavarian unit
BG X/Y	*Bombengewschwader X/Bombenstaffel Y*
BS	*Beobachter Schule*
DOW	Died of Wounds
Dschgd	Discharged from Military Service
EOW	End of War
FA	*Flieger Abteilung*
FAA	*Flieger Abteilung (Artillerie)*
FBLA	*Flieger Bomben Lehr Abteilung* at Frankfurt a.d. Oder
FEA	*Flieger Ersatz Abteilung*
FnkSch	*Flieger Funker Schule*
FS	*Flieger Schule*
GS	*Geschwader Schule*, either Paderborn or Freiburg
Grufl	*Gruppenführer der Flieger*
Hosp.	Hospital
IIC	Injured in a crash
Infntry	*Infanterie*
Inj.	Injured
Js	*Jagdstaffel*
JsSch I	*Jastaschule I* at Valenciennes
JSch II	*Jastaschule II* at Nivelles
KEA	*Kraft Ersatz Abteilung*
KG X/Y	*Kampfgeschwader X/Kampfstaffel Y*
KIA	Killed in action
KIC	Killed in a crash
KnBtln	*Bavarian Konstruktion Battalion*
Kofl	*Kommandeur der Flieger*
Küst	*Küsten Artillerie Staffel*
KWP	*Kraftwagon Park*
LSO	*Luft Schütz Offizier*
lt.	Lightly
M FA	*Marine Flieger Abteilung*
MFJ	*Marine Feld Jagdstaffel*
Mrds Wk	Mercedes Werke
POW	Taken Prisoner of War
s	Saxon unit
SEE	*Seeflugstation*
SGp	*(Schlagru) Schlachtstaffel Gruppe*
Ss	*Schutzstaffel/Schlachtstaffel*
sv.	Severely
vS	von Strantz
w	Württemberg unit
WIA	Wounded in Action

Royal Prussian *Schutzstaffel 1*

Pilot/Gunner	Type	From Unit	From Date	To Date	To Unit
Vzfw. Eugen Bader	P			18Apr17	KIA
Vzfw. Wilhelm Blum	P		(Jul17)	12Oct17	FA 26
Flg. Borkowski	G	AFP 4	12Oct17		
Uffz. Brank	G	AFP 4	12Oct17		
Flgmstr. Moritz Brenner	P	MFJ I	11Aug17	16Aug17	MFJ I
Uffz. Konrad Brendle	P			13Sep17	JsSch I
Ltn.d.R. Karl Cleinow, C.O.	O	Idflieg	1Jan18	2Jun18	KIA
Vzfw. Valentin Dietrich	P			15Aug17	KIA
Uffz. Drinda	P	AFP 4	20Dec17		
Sgt. Heinrich Dung	G	AFP 4	9Mar18	18Jul18	KIA
Uffz. Franzen	G	AFP 4	10Jan18	24Feb18	AFP 4
Pion. Karl Gütz	G	AFP 4	8Aug17		
Vzfw. Emil Haas	P	KG 3/13	1Jan17	(May17)	KG 3/16
Vzfw. Havel	P			13Nov17	WIA,lt.
Offz.Stv. Franz Hermann				9Apr17	KIA
Vzfw. Wilhelm Hillner	P		(Jun17)	24Feb18	AFP 4
Uffz. Jarnaczak	G	AFP 4	10Jan18		
Vzfw. Jüchser	G		(Jun17)	19Oct17	AFP 4
Vzfw. Kaempfer	P	AFP 4	26Feb18	9Mar18	AFP 4
Vzfw. Kaempfer	P	AFP 4	16Apr18		
Vzfw. Kapatsch	G			15Aug17	WIA,sv.
Flg. Littmann	G	AFP 4	19Oct17		
Vzfw. Franz Maschke	P			23Feb18	KIC
Gefr. Karl Müller	G	AFP 4	12Oct17	3Jan18	BG 4/19
Uffz. Muschen	P	AFP 4	24Feb18		
Vzfw. Hans Naumann	G			12Oct17	AFP 4
Flg. Nolte	P	AFP 4	12Oct17		
Gefr. Paetzmann	P	FA 40	14Sep17		
Uffz. Pagemann	P	AFP 4	24Feb18		
Pion. Lorenz Pichler	P	AFP 1	13Jun17	11Jul17	Ss 26b
Uffz. Pohl				30May18	IIC,sv.
Flg. Renson	G	AFP 4	21Sep17	(Oct17)	
Flg. Paul Richter	P	KG 3/14	1Jan17	14Dec17	FEA 11
Pion. Sebastian Ritzinger	G	AFP 1	13Jun17	11Jul17	Ss 26b
Gefr. Schmidt	G	AFP 4	21Dec17	15Feb18	AFP 4
Flg. Schmidt	G	AFP 4	24Feb18		
Gefr. Schmitz	G	AFP 4	23Dec17	27May18	WIA,lt.
Vzfw. Schmückler	G		(May17)		
Vzfw. Schubert	G			23Feb18	IIC,sv.
Oblt. Eduard Seldner, C.O.	O	KG 3/13	1Jan17	20Dec17	AFP 6
Vzfw. Smoltczyk	G		(Aug17)	9Mar18	AFP 4
Sgt. Fritz Stegmeyer (+ 6Jun18)	P	AFP 4	27Sep17	2Jun18	WIA,sv.
Oblt. Thiemann, C.O.			Jun18	EOW	
Gefr. Tracinski	P	AFP 4	20Jan18	14May18	Js 57
Uffz. Hermann Uhe	P	AFP 4	4Nov17	10Dec17	KIA
Uffz. Ferdinand Vieth	P	AFP 4	21Dec17	20Jan18	AFP 4
Vzfw. August Wagner	P		(Aug17)	22Jan18	JSch II
Flg. Wedekind	G	AFP 4	21Sep17	13Nov17	FEA 12
Vzfw. S. Wieczorek	G	AFP 4	29Oct17	10Dec17	POW
Gefr. Wiltberger	P			3Sep18	IIC
Flg. Otto Ziegert	P			18Jul18	KIA

Schutzstaffel/Schlachtstaffel 1 Airfields

From	To	Location	*Schlachtgruppe* Affiliation	*Armee*
1Jan17	(31Jan17)	Ribécourt	Escort for FA 210(A)	1
(Feb17)	5Mar17	1		

5Mar17	16Apr17	Le Thour	Escort for FA 286(A)b	7
16Apr17	24Jun17	Le Thour	Escort for FA 286(A)b	1
24Jun17	(10Jul17)	Vlisseghem	Escort for M FA I	4
(Jul17)				6
(Aug17)	20Nov17	Desselghem		4
20Nov17	25Nov17			6
25Nov17	20Dec17	Neuvilly, E. Caudry	Escort for FA 263(A)	2
20Dec17	1Jan18	Heule-Watermill	Escort for FA 8	4
1Jan18	19Feb18	Neuvilly		2
19Feb18	(25Apr18)	Heule	Escort for FA 8	4
(25Apr18)	(17May18)	Heule	SGp A (Ss 1,14,21,28b) C.O. *Oblt.* Emil Ziegler gen Stege	4
(27May18)		Eppes	SGp A (Ss 1,8,10,14,21) C.O. *Oblt.* Emil Ziegler gen Stege	7
(9Jun18)	(25Jun18)	La Pavillon Ferme	SGp Staabs (Ss 1,8,10,14,21) C.O. *Oblt.* Emil Ziegler gen Stege	7
(15Jul18)	18Jul18	Seringes	SGp A (Ss 1,8,10,14,21) C.O. *Oblt.* Emil Ziegler gen Stege	7
18Jul18	(29Jul18)	Eppes	SGp A (Ss 1,8,10,14,21) C.O. *Oblt.* Emil Ziegler gen Stege	7
(3Aug18)			SGp A (Ss 1,8,10,14,21) C.O. *Oblt.* Emil Ziegler gen Stege	17
	8Aug18	Eppes	SGp A (Ss 1,8,10,14,21) C.O. *Oblt.* Emil Ziegler gen Stege	7
8Aug18	8Aug18	Curchy	SGp A (Ss 1,8,10,14,21) C.O. *Oblt.* Emil Ziegler gen Stege	2
8Aug18	10Aug18	Eppes	SGp A (Ss 1,8,10,14,21) C.O. *Oblt.* Emil Ziegler gen Stege	7
10Aug18	11Aug18	Guizancourt	SGp A (Ss 1,8,10,14) C.O. *Oblt.* Emil Ziegler gen Stege	18
11Aug18	12Aug18	Guizancourt	SGp A (Ss 1,8,10,14,21) C.O. *Oblt.* Emil Ziegler gen Stege	18
12Aug18	22Aug18	Eppes	SGp A (Ss 1,8,10,14,21) C.O. *Oblt.* Emil Ziegler gen Stege	7
22Aug18	25Sep18	Bouchain	SGp A (Ss 1,8,10,14) C.O. *Oblt.* Emil Ziegler gen Stege	17
25Sep18	7Oct18	Bühl	SGp A (Ss 1,8,10,14) C.O. *Oblt.* Emil Ziegler gen Stege	AAA
7Oct18	21Oct18	Croix-les-Rouveroy	SGp A (Ss 1,8,10,14,17) C.O. *Oblt.* Emil Ziegler gen Stege	2
21Oct18	31Oct18	Croix-les-Rouveroy	SGp A (Ss 1,14,17) C.O. *Hptm.* Hermann Krüger	2
31Oct18	EOW	Trazegnies	SGp A (Ss 1,14,17) C.O. *Hptm.* Hermann Krüger	2

Royal Prussian *Schutzstaffel 1*

1Jan17	*Schutzstaffel 1* is created from KG 3/Ks 13 by KM Nr.1425.16.g.A.7.L. of 1Jan17.
9Apr17	*Offz.Stv.* Franz Hermann is KIC at Le Thour. Uncertain if he was a flying member of the unit.
18Apr17	*Vzfw.* Eugen Bader, P, is KIA over Montcornel.
3May17	*Vzfw.* Haas-n/c, *Vzfw.* Schmückler-n/c, Einsitzer, 12.45, La Neuvillett
20Jul17	*Vzfw.* Blum-1, *Vzfw.* Jüchser-1, Sopwith Camel, NW Slype #N.6360, Naval 6, F/Cdr. G.G. Maclennan, KIA
15Aug17	*Vzfw.* Valentin Dietrich, P, is KIA and *Vzfw.* Kapatsch, G, is WIA,sv. over Middelkerke during air combat.
26Aug17	*Vzfw.* Wagner-zLg, *Vzfw.* Smoltczyk-zLg, Sopwith 1, 12.00, Westende Bad, Pup #A.6184, 54 Sqn. RFC, 2/Lt. S.J. Schooley, OK
13Nov17	*Vzfw.* Havel, P, is WIA,lt. during air combat.
10Dec17	*Uffz.* Hermann Uhe, P, is KIA over Cambrai by ground fire and *Vzfw.* S. Wieczorek, G, is WIA and taken POW.
23Feb18	*Vzfw.* Franz Maschke, P, is KIC and *Vzfw.* Schubert, G, is IIC,sv. in a crash landing at Lichtervelde.
27Mar18	*Schutzstaffel 1* is renamed *Schlachtstaffel* 1 by KM Nr. 5126.18.A.7.L.IV.C. of 27Mar18.
27May18	*Gefr.* Schmitz, G, is WIA,lt. over Missy by ground fire.
27May18	An unidentified *Schlachtstaffel 1* crew is reported being taken POW at Crugny in LVG C.II 3871/16 following air combat.
30May18	*Uffz.* Pohl is IIC,sv.

2Jun18	*Sgt.* Fritz Stegmeyer, P, is WIA,sv. and *Ltn.d.R.* Karl Cleinow, O, is KIA at Chaudun during an air combat. Stegmeyer DOW on 6Jun18 at Crecy sur Serre.
18Jul18	*Flg.* Otto Ziegert, P, and *Sgt.* Heinrich Dung, G, are KIA at Neuilly.
3Sep18	*Gefr.* Wiltberger, P, is IIC.
Nov18	*Schlachtstaffel 1* is demobilized at FEA 7, Braunschweig.

Above: Some of the men of *KG 3/Kasta 13* before the unit was renamed *Schutzstaffel 1* on 1 January 1917. It is not known if the fellows in the 'coal shuttle' helmets were members of the unit or just visiting infantry men.

Right: *Vzfw.* Wilhelm Hillner was a pilot with *Schusta 1* during 1917 before being transferred to *BG 3.*

Below: *Flugzeugmeister* Moritz Brenner was a Marine pilot who briefly served with the Army unit *Schutzstaffel 1* in August 1917. The photo was taken while he was serving with *MFJ 1* and shows his Albatros D.V fighter aircraft. Photo credit: Aaron Weaver.

Royal Prussian *Schutzstaffel 2*

Pilot/Gunner	Type	From		To	
		Unit	Date	Date	Unit
Oblt. Oskar Bechtle, C.O.	O	AFP 4	18Mar18	24Apr18	WIA
Blumenkamp	P		(Apr18)		
Vzfw. Hans Bowski	P	KG 3/14	1Jan17	Feb17	JsSch I
Ltn.d.R. Franz Brandt	P	KG 3/14	1Jan17	11Mar17	Js 19
Uffz. Büge	P		(Apr17)		
Uffz. Johannes Diekhaus	G			20Jan18	KIC
Gefr. Georg Feltz	G			20Apr18	KIA
Oblt. Ernst Galle, C.O.	P	Ss 25b	30Jun17	18Mar18	AFP 4
Ltn.d.R. Otto Gawron	G	FEA 10	Apr17	EOW	
Oblt.d.R. Otto Hafner, OzbV	O	Ss 9	1Jun18	30Jun18	SGp 3
Oblt. Friedrich-Carl Hanesse, C.O.	P	Ss 9	1Jun18	30Jun18	SGp 3
Gefr. Albert Hentschel	P			9Dec17	KIA
Gefr. Hoess	P			20Apr18	WIA,lt.
Gefr. Hoesterey	G			24Mar18	WIA,lt.
Vzfw. Mathias Hubert Jorissen	G	Ss 25b	20Sep17	(Mar18)	
Ltn.d.R. Mathias Hubert Jorissen	G		(Mar18)		
Vzfw. Kessler	P		(Jul17)	3Sep17	
Ltn.d.R. Kessler	P		(Mar18)	13May18	Js 12
Klar	P		(Mar18)	26Apr18	
Vzfw. Wilhelm Krake	G		(Jan18)	(Aug18)	
Oblt. Oskar Kuppinger, C.O.	O	KG 7/41	1Jan17	26Jun17	KG 1/3
Vzfw. Landmann	P		(Jan18)	22Apr18	WIA,sv.
Uffz. Richard Mann			(Dec17)		FEA 1
Ltn.d.R. Kurt Monnington	P	FA 67	23Jan17	3Jun17	AFP 7
Uffz. Hugo Moning				31Jul17	KIA
Uffz. Alfred Niemz	P	AFP 18	Jun18	Sep18	JSch II
Vzfw. Wilhelm Oesterreicher	P	AFP 18	Apr18	29Sep18	Js 32b
Uffz. Paulus	G		('18)		
Uffz. Richard Piez	P	KG 3/14	1Jan17		KEST 3
Gefr. Georg Post	G	AFP 7	17Jun17		Ss 18
Gefr. Prüser				6Jun18	WIA,lt.
Vzfw. Karl Reisberg	P		(Apr17)	3Jan18	BG 3/13
Uffz. Max Rossbach			('17)		Ss 18
Vzfw. Scheller	P			30Mar17	Js 19
Gefr. Christian Schiller	P			20Jan18	KIC
Uffz. Theodor Seffzig	P	FA 13	10Mar17	12Aug17	AFP 4
Uffz. Solecki	P		(Feb18)	31Mar18	
Uffz. Steinberg	G			13Aug18	WIA
Vzfw. Bruno Steinfeld				31Jul17	KIA
Vzfw. Rolf Steinvorth	P		Apr18	3Jul18	KIC
Vzfw. Teigeler					
Vzfw. Julius Tillmanns	P	KG 7/41	1Jan17	26Jun17	KG 1/3
Vzfw. Hermann Vichlein			('17)	(Jan18)	

Schutzstaffel/Schlachtstaffel 2 Airfields

From	To	Location	*Schlachtgruppe* Affiliation	*Armee*
1Jan17		Cantaing	Escort for FA 204(A)	1
(31Jan17)	Mar17	Lörchingen	Escort for FA 238(A), 281(A)	AAA
Mar17	Apr17	Cerny les Bucy	Escort for FA 222(A)	7
Apr17	12May17	Notre Dame de Liesse	For FA 255(A)s	7
12May17	9Jun17	Chéry les Pouilly	For FA 277(A)	7
9Jun17	16Jun17	Iseghem		4
16Jun17	15Aug17	Notre Dame de Liesse	For FA 255(A)s	7
15Aug17	19Aug17	Preutin	Escort for FA 207(A)	5
19Aug17		Stenay	Escort for FA 274(A)	5
(Sep17)	16Oct17	Preutin		5

16Oct17	26Nov17	Toulis	Escort for FA 209(A)	7
26Nov17	(Jan18)	Jametz	Escort for FA 36, FA 209(A)	5
(4Jan18)	(23Jan18)	Ecly	Escort for FA 212(A), 261(A)Lb	1
	19Feb18	St. Loup by Alincourt	For FA 212(A)	1
19Feb18	18Mar18	Bergnicourt	Escort for FA 212(A), 248(A)	1
18Mar18	23Mar18	St. Martin-Riviére	SGp 4 (Ss 2,5,20,33) C.O. *Oblt.* Werner Lange	18
23Mar18		Guizancourt	SGp 4 (Ss 2,5,20,33) C.O. *Oblt.* Werner Lange	18
(9Apr18)		Erches	SGp 4 (Ss 2,5,20,33) C.O. *Oblt.* Werner Lange	18
(25Apr18)	19May18	Erches	SGp 1 (Ss 2,7,31b) C.O. *Oblt.* Walter Lackner	18
19May18	(6Jun18)	St. Loup	SGp 1 (Ss 2,7,22b,31b) C.O. *Oblt.* Walter Lackner	1
(9Jun18)		Villeselve	SGp 1 (Ss 2,7,31b) C.O. *Oblt.* Walter Lackner	18
(3Jul18)		St. Loup		1
(15Jul18)	3Aug18	Villeselve		18
4Aug18	9Aug18	St. Loup	SGp B (Ss 2,22b,23b,36) C.O. *Oblt.d.R.* Ludwig Männer	1
9Aug18	9Aug18	Villeselve	SGp B (Ss 2,22b) C.O. *Oblt.d.R.* Ludwig Männer	18
10Aug18	10Aug18	St. Loup	SGp B (Ss 2,22b,23b,36) C.O. *Oblt.d.R.* Ludwig Männer	1
10Aug18	12Aug18	Villeselve	SGp B (Ss 2,22b) C.O. *Oblt.d.R.* Ludwig Männer	18
13Aug18	9Sep18	St. Loup	SGp B (Ss 2,22b,23b,36) C.O. *Oblt.d.R.* Ludwig Männer	1
9Sep18	17Sep18	St. Loup	SGp B (Ss 2,22b,23b,36) C.O. *Oblt.d.R.* Sigmund Kreitmair	1
17Sep18	28Sep18	Autrecourt	SGp 3 (Ss 2,22b,23b) C.O. *Oblt.d.R.* Sigmund Kreitmair	3
28Sep18	19Oct18	Autrecourt	SGp 3 (Ss 2,22b,23b) C.O. *Oblt.* Karl *Ritter* von Gruny	3
19Oct18	EOW	Diffenbach-lès-Puttelange	SGp 2 (Ss 2,22b,28b,36) C.O. *Oblt.* Karl *Ritter* von Gruny	19

Royal Prussian *Schutzstaffel 2*

1Jan17	*Schutzstaffel 2* is created from KG 3/Ks 14 by KM Nr.1425.16.g.A.7.L. of 1Jan17.
31Jul17	*Uffz.* Hugo Moning and *Vzfw.* Bruno Steinfeld are KIA over Cerny les Bucy.
9Dec17	*Gefr.* Albert Hentschel, P, is KIA at Jametz.
20Jan18	*Gefr.* Christian Schiller, P, and *Uffz.* Johannes Diekhaus, G, are KIC at Ecly during a practice flight.
25Jan18	*Vzfw.* Krake-n/c, Spad, Trois-Puits, S. Reims
24Mar18	*Gefr.* Hoesterey, G, is WIA,lt. by a Flak splinter while in a Halberstadt Cl.II.
27Mar18	*Schutzstaffel 2* is renamed *Schlachtstaffel 2* by KM Nr.5126.18.A.7.L.IV.C. of 27Mar18.
20Apr18	*Gefr.* Hoess, P, is WIA,lt. and *Gefr.* Georg Feltz, G, is KIA at Morisel. They were forced to land between the lines.
22Apr18	*Vzfw.* Landmann, P, is severely WIA over Grivesnes Wood and to hospital.
24Apr18	*Oblt.* Oskar Bechtle, O and C.O., is WIA,sv. by ground fire and to hospital.
3May18	*Uffz.* Steinvorth-1, *Ltn.d.R.* Gawron-1, Breguet 14B2, Thory #1457, Esc. Br.111, M.d.L. J. Charnet,KIA & Sgt. A. Teissedre,KIA
19May18	An unknown *Schlasta 2* pilot is IIC,sv. at St. Loup by Alincourt.
6Jun18	*Gefr.* Prüser is WIA, lt. during air combat.
3Jul18	*Vzfw.* Rolf Steinvorth, P, is KIC at St. Loup by Alincourt during a practice flight.
4Aug18	*Uffz.* Niemz-1, *Vzfw.* Krake-1, Spad 2, 18.50, Reims
13Aug18	*Uffz.* Steinberg, G, is WIA.
Nov18	*Schlachtstaffel 2* is demobilized at *Militär Fliegerschule* Hundsfeld (Breslau)

Above: *Vzfw*. Otto Gawron, left, and his pilot *Vzfw*. Reisberg of *Schusta 2*.

Below: A line-up of *Schusta 2* Halberstadt Cl.II aircraft exhibiting the unit marking of a black tail group.

Top: Halberstadt Cl.II aircraft possibly of *Schlasta 2*. The aircraft in the foreground displays the white number 3 aft of the fuselage cross.

Above: A *Schlasta 2* Halberstadt Cl.II with the white number 4 aft of the cross. The unit marking now consists of a white fin and rudder with white number, and a black tail plane. These markings were used after April/May 1918.

Right: *Schlachtstaffel 2*, *Vzfw.* Otto Gawron and *Vzfw.* Rolf Steinvorth in their Halberstadt Cl.II. Photo credit: Marcus Pleyer.

Uffz. Otto Gawron while serving with *Fl.Abt. 226(A)* prior to his being posted to *Schusta 2*. Photo credit: Marcus Pleyer.

Im Felde, Juli 1918.

Am 3. Juli starb infolge Absturzes mit dem Flugzeug den Heldentod der

Flugzeugführer

und Vizefeldwebel der Reserve

Rolf Steinvorth

Ritter des Eisernen Kreuzes I. u. II. Kl. und des Bulgarischen Tapferkeitsordens IV. Kl., Inhaber des Flugzeugführer-abzeichens.

Ein tüchtiger Soldat, schneidiger Flieger und braver Kamerad ist mit ihm aus unserer Mitte gerissen, der, wo und wann es von ihm verlangt wurde, stets sein Bestes hergab.

Sein Andenken wird in der Staffel unvergesslich bleiben.

Hanesse,

Oberlt. u. Führer einer Schlachtstaffel.

The obituary of *Vzfw.* Rolf Steinvorth and signed by his old C.O., *Oblt.* Friedrich-Carl Hanesse of *Schlasta 2*. Steinvorth was KIC on 3 July 1918 whereas Hanesse had 'officially' left the unit on the 1st. Photo Credit: Immo Frese.

Royal Prussian *Schutzstaffel 3*

Pilot/Gunner	Type	From		To	
		Unit	Date	Date	Unit
Uffz. Albert Arnold	P	AFP 4	18May18	11Jun18	KIA
Otto Busch					
Ltn.d.R. Criege	O	KG 3/15	1Jan17	(Mar17)	
Vzfw. Ernst Diez				16Feb17	KIA
Walter Fick	P				
Gefr. Alfred Frantz	P	AFP 7	Jun17		
Oblt. Heinz Funke-Münster, C.O.	O	BG 3/15	21Oct18	EOW	
Gefr. Berthold Guthmann	G			27Sep17	WIA
Vzfw. Franz Hamann				16Feb17	KIA
Oblt. Otto Hartmann, C.O.	O	KG 3/15	1Jan17	24Apr17	AFP 1
Uffz. Hartmann	P		(Apr18)	29May18	FEA 9
Uffz. Walter Held	G		(Apr18)	11Jun18	KIA
Flg. Wilhelm Heissenberg	P	AFP 4	19May18	22May18	KIA
Flg. Emil Hellwig	P	Ss 28b	24Apr18	30May18	AFP 4
Vzfw. Friedrich Hengst	P	KG 3/15	1Jan17	6Feb18	Js 64w
Ltn.d.R. Fritz Herder			(Jul18)		
Flg. Hildebrandt	G			18Aug18	IIC,sv.
Oblt.d.R. Jaspers, C.O.	O		(Jul18)	Oct18	
Ltn. Jung					

Uffz. Julius Kickhefel	G		(May18)	10Sep18	+ i.Kr.
Offz.Stv. Willy Kern	P	FA 256A	20May18		
Gefr. Fritz Koehler	G		(May18)	(Jul18)	
Uffz. Mathias Konz	G	AFP 4	27May18	7Aug18	KIA
Flg. Otto Krämer	P	AFP 4	29May18	2Aug18	+ i.Kr.
Flg. Hermann Lange			(Nov17)		
Gefr. May	G	KG 3/15	1Jan17	(May17)	
Uffz. Richard Mehrow	P	AFP 4	30May18	EOW	
Vzfw. Mikeler	G			17May18	FA 26
Uffz. Heinrich Moje	P			18Aug18	KIC
Gefr. Emil Morlock	P	Ss 28b	24Apr18		
Vzfw. Ludwig Panzer	G	AFP 7	30Jul17	21May18	IIC
Vzfw. Peters	G		(Apr18)	(Jun18)	
Feldw. Erich Pust			(Apr17)		
Vzfw. Richter	P	KG 3/15	1Jan17		
Ltn. Julius Graf von Soden	O	KG 3/15	1Jan17	(Mar17)	
Hptm. Scheffer, C.O.			Apr17	May18	
Gefr. Schneider	P			19May18	AFP 4
Uffz. Karl Tegtmeier	P			7Aug18	KIA
Vzfw. Thiel	P	KG 3/15	1Jan17	24Jan17	Js 2
Feldw. Tretow-Rostock	P		(Apr17)	17Apr18	WIA
Trupke	P				
Pion. Peter Weber	G	AFP 4	30May18	30May18	AFP 4
Werkmstr.Stv. Robert Werner	M			10May18	KIA
Uffz. Ernst Wiehle	P	FS West	7Feb17	9Sep17	Posted

Schutzstaffel/Schlachtstaffel 3 Airfields

From	To	Location	*Schlachtgruppe* Affiliation	*Armee*
1Jan17	(31Jan17)	St. Olle by Cambrai	Escort for FA 239(A)	1
(Mar17)	23Mar17	Dercy-Mortiers	Escort for FA 277(A)	7
23Mar17				2
(7Jun17)	(Aug17)			7
12Aug17	29Aug17			3
29Aug17	(Aug17)			5
(Sep17)				5
(31Oct17)				7
(Nov17)	(Dec17)	Dercy-Mortiers	Escort for FA 277(A)	7
(1Jan18)	14Mar18	Joppecourt	Escort for FA 205(A)	5
14Mar18	21Mar18	Dorignies	Escort for FA 205(A)	17
21Mar18	25Mar18	Dorignies	SGp C (Ss 3,9,16) C.O. *Oblt.* Hermann Ramdohr	17
25Mar18	28Mar18	Epinoy	SGp C (Ss 3,9,16) C.O. *Oblt.* Hermann Ramdohr	17
28Mar18	9Apr18	Pont de la Deule	SGp C (Ss 3,9,16) C.O. *Oblt.* Hermann Ramdohr	17
9Apr18	24Apr18	Faumont Süd	SGp A (Ss 3,19) C.O. *Hptm.* Wilhelm Aschenborn	6
24Apr18	17May18	Ingelmunster	SGp C (Ss 3,13,19,29b) C.O. *Hptm.* Wilhelm Aschenborn	4
17May18	3Jun18	Ingelmunster	SGp 2 (Ss 3,13,19,29b) C.O. *Hptm.* Wilhelm Aschenborn	4
4Jun18	9Jul18	Bonneuil Ferme	SGp 3 (Ss 3,13,19,29b) C.O. *Oblt.* Helmut Bühling	18
10Jul18	29Jul18	Mont Notre Dame	SGp B (Ss 3,13,19,29b) C.O. *Oblt.* Helmut Bühling	7
30Jul18	9Aug18	Liéramont	SGp 2 (Ss 3,13,19,29b) C.O. *Oblt.* Helmut Bühling	6
9Aug18	9Aug18	Nurlu	SGp 2 (Ss 3,13,19,29b) C.O. *Oblt.* Helmut Bühling	2
9Aug18	11Aug18	Liéramont		6
12Aug18	18Aug18	Harbourdin	SGp 2 (Ss 3,13,19) C.O. *Oblt.d.R.* Jaspers	2

18Aug18	23Aug18	Longavesnes	SGp 2 (Ss 3,13,19) C.O. *Oblt.d.R.* Jaspers	2
23Aug18	26Sep18	St. Vaast	SGp 2 (Ss 3,13,19,29b) C.O. *Oblt.d.R.* Jaspers	2
26Sep18	6Oct18	Preutin	SGp 2 (Ss 3,13,19,29b) C.O. *Oblt.* Helmut Bühling	5
6Oct18	21Oct18	Preutin	SGp 2 (Ss 3,13,19,26b,29b) C.O. *Oblt.* Helmut Bühling	5
21Oct18	31Oct18	Mercy-le-Haut	SGp 2 (Ss 3,13,19,26b,29b) C.O. *Oblt.* Helmut Bühling	5
1Nov18	EOW	Stenay	SGp 2 (Ss 3,13,19,26b,29b) C.O. *Oblt.* Helmut Bühling	5

Royal Prussian *Schutzstaffel 3*

1Jan17	*Schutzstaffel 3* is created from KG 3/Ks 15 by KM Nr.1425.16.g.A.7.L. of 1Jan17.
16Feb17	*Vzfw.* Ernst Diez and *Vzfw.* Franz Hamann are KIA over Villers au Flos.
11Mar17	*Vzfw.* Hengst-1, *Ltn.d.R.* Criege-1, Vickers #A.5443, 10.40, Beugny FE 2b, 23 Sqn. RFC, 2/Lt. A. Holden,POW & 2/AM A.G. Walker,POW
16Apr17	*Uffz.* Wiehle-1, *Gefr.* May-1, Spad, SE Corbeny Spad S.7 #1178, Esc. N.48, S/Lt. P. de Larminat, MIA
27Sep17	*Gefr.* Berthold Guthmann, G, is WIA.
27Mar18	*Schutzstaffel 3* is renamed *Schlachtstaffel 3* by KM Nr.5126.18.A.7.L.IV.C. of 27Mar18.
11Apr18	*Vzfw.* Tretow-Rostock-1, *Vzfw.* Peters-1, Camel, Steenwerck
12Apr18	*Uffz.* Hartmann-1, *Uffz.* Held-1, Engl. 2, Neuve-Chapelle
17Apr18	*Feldw.* Tretow-Rostock, P, is WIA by ground fire.
10May18	*Werkmstr.Stv.* Robert Werner, M, is KIA at Kortyrk.
21May18	*Vzfw.* Ludwig Panzer, G, is IIC and to hospital.
22May18	*Flg.* Wilhelm Heissenberg, P, is KIA at Gent.
11Jun18	*Flg.* Krämer-1, *Vzfw.* Peters-2, Spad 1
11Jun18	*Uffz.* Alfred Arnold, P, and *Uffz.* Walter Held, G, are KIA over Compiègne.
30Jul18	*Uffz.* Mehrow-zLgzw, *Gefr.* Koehler-zLgzw, S.E. 5, 10.50, N. Bethune
2Aug18	*Flg.* Otto Krämer, P, dies at Lille.
7Aug18	*Uffz.* Kurt Tegtmeier, P, and *Uffz.* Mathias Konz, G, are KIA over Lestrem during air combat.
18Aug18	*Uffz.* Heinrich Moje, P, is KIC at Haubourdin and *Flg.* Hildebrandt, G, is IIC,sv.
10Sep18	*Uffz.* Julius Kickhefel, G, dies in hospital at Crailsheim, Germany.
3Oct18	An as yet unidentified *Schlasta 3* crew is shot down in aerial combat and taken POW between Véry and Cheppy in Hannover Cl.IIIa 3885/18.
Nov18	*Schlachtstaffel 3* is demobilized at FEA 7, Braunschweig.

Royal Prussian *Schutzstaffel 4*

Pilot/Gunner	Type	From		To	
		Unit	Date	Date	Unit
Uffz. Kurt Ahrens	P			1Jun18	KIC
Ltn.d.R. Bader	O		(May18)		
Uffz. Reinhold Bendlin	P	AFP 4	10Sep17	26Jan18	KIC
Gefr. Biller	G	AFP 4	21Sep17	(Nov17)	
Ltn.d.R. Paul Billik	P	FEA 4	1Jan17	26Mar17	Js 12
Uffz. Ebert	G		(Feb17)	(Jun17)	
Vzfw. Eichler	G	AFP 4	13Sep17	20Oct17	IIC,lt.
Vzfw. Eldner	P			29Jan18	WIA,sv.
Ltn.d.R. Josef Figulla	O		(Apr17)		FA 26
Vzfw. Gossen	P			1Dec17	AFP 4
Werkmstr. Heidrich	M			20Feb18	IIC,sv.
Flg. Hellwig	P		(Jun17)		
Uffz. Herdam	P			20Oct17	IIC,lt.
Ritt.d.R. Herrmann, C.O.			(Aug17)	23Apr18	Ss 12
Pion. Ludwig Herrndobler	P	AFP 4	29Jun17	13Jul17	Ss 26b
Gefr. Herwig	P	AFP 4	29Aug17	10Sep17	FEA 5
Uffz. Paul Höschel	G			1Jun18	KIC

Flg. Holm	G		(Aug18)	(Sep18)	
Uffz. Isenbach	P		(Sep18)	(Oct18)	
Oblt. Max Jüngling, C.O.			(Sep18)	13Oct18	Idflieg
Hptm. Otto Kadelke, C.O.	O	KG 3/16	1Jan17	26Feb17	FA 7
Uffz. Kern	P		(Feb18)		
Vzfw. Kirchner	P			20Feb18	IIC,sv.
Ltn.d.R. Bernhard Knake	O	KG 3/16	1Jan17	(Mar17)	
Gefr. Kuhne	G	AFP 4	31Aug17	(Dec17)	
Vzfw. Ewald Liersch	G			26Jan18	IIC
Vzfz. Michael Lüderitz	P		(Mar17)	Jun18	JsSch I
Vzfw. Gerhard Masolyn	G	AFP 4	29Aug17	6Apr18	KIA
Ltn.d.R. Karl Meierdirks	O	KG 3/16	1Jan17	(Feb17)	
Uffz. Matthias Meinberg	P			19Feb18	WIA,sv.
Uffz. Müller	P		(Aug18)	(Sep18)	
Uffz. Heinz Orth	P		(May17)		
Vzfw. Ostermann	P			25Aug17	POW
Vzfw. Wilhelm Pannes	P			13Oct17	AFP 4
Uffz. Parschau	G			31Aug17	AFP 4
Uffz. Parschau	G	AFP 4	21Sep17	20Nov17	AFP 8
Uffz. Kurt Petzinna	P	FFA 46	Jan17	31Jan17	KS Pdbn
Vzfw. Friedrich Pieper	G			7Jul17	KIA
Vzfw. Simon Pinczower	G	KG 3/16	1Jan17	(Feb17)	
Ltn.d.R. Platt	O	KG 3/16	1Jan17		
Uffz. Paul Podbiol	P			14Aug17	WIA
Gefr. Pollack	G	AFP 4	25Oct17	27Oct17	FS IV
Ltn.d.R. Werner Roloff	O	Ss 16	6Jun18	EOW	
Oblt.d.R. Werner Roloff, C.O.	O		16Oct18	EOW	
Ltn.d.R. Hans Rusche	O	KG 3/16	1Jan17	(Feb17)	FA 25
Oblt.a.D. Scheibler	P	KG 3/16	1Jan17	26Feb17	Ss 4
Oblt.a.D. Scheibler, C.O.	P	Ss 4	26Feb17	(Mar17)	
Vzfw. Anton "Toni" Schmitz	P	KG 3/16	1Jan17	(May17)	JsSch I
Uffz. Franz Schnitt	P			7Jul17	KIA
Vzfw. Arthur Schorisch	P	KG 3/16	1Jan17	5Mar17	Js 12
Uffz. Willi Scholz	P			6Apr18	KIA
Uffz. Schrey	G			25Aug17	POW
Uffz. Slater	G			14Aug17	SD,OK
Uffz. Slotha	G	AFP 4	31Aug17	27Oct17	Ss 10
Uffz. Steinert	G			19Feb18	WIA,sv.
Uffz. Karl Theodor Steudel	P	KG 3/16	1Jan17	Jun17	JsSch I
Uffz. Steveif	G		(Mar17)		
Uffz. Willy Thoerner	P	AFP 4	23Aug17	26Aug17	WIA
Ltn.d.R. Tod, OzbV	O	FA 211A	11Jun18		
Vzfw. Ulber	G			22Aug17	Ss 19
Vzfw. Wagner	G		(Feb18)		
Flg. Wilhelm Walter	P	KG 3/16	1Jan17	(Mar17)	
Feldw. Weiss	G		(Feb17)	7Sep17	AFP 4
Uffz. Wels	G		(Feb17)		
Vzfw. Willy Wenck	P	FA 258A	23Jul17	4Sep17	Ss 11
Ltn.d.R. Willy Wenck	P	Ss 11	9Sep17	(May18)	
Vzfw. Reiner Wirtz	P	KG 3/16	1Jan17	14Feb17	KS Pdbn
Ltn.d.R. Albert Zander	O	KG 3/16	1Jan17	3Apr17	KG 3/13

Schutzstaffel/Schlachtstaffel 4 Airfields

From	To	Location	*Schlachtgruppe* Affiliation	*Armee*
1Jan17	(31Jan17)	Cagnicourt	Escort for FA 45b, FA 256(A)	1
Feb17	23Mar17	Abscon	Escort for FA 45b	1
23Mar17	9Jun17	Douai	Escort for FA 288(A)b	6
9Jun17	24Aug17	Bisseghem	Escort for FA 256(A)	4
24Aug17	25Nov17	Wynghene	Escort for FA 256(A)	4
(1Jan18)	10Mar18	Bertry	Escort for FA 202(A)	2
10Mar18	21Mar18	Bertry	SGp B (Ss 4,15,26b,28b) C.O. *Ritt.d.R.* Herrmann	2

21Mar18	3Apr18	Bertry	SGp B (Ss 4,15,26b,28b) C.O. *Ritt.d.R.* Herrmann	2
4Apr18	9Apr18	Bertry	SGp B (Ss 4,11,15) C.O. *Ritt.d.R.* Herrmann	2
9Apr18	19Apr18	Herbécourt	SGp B (Ss 4,11,15) C.O. *Ritt.d.R.* Herrmann	2
19Apr18	12May18	Cappy	SGp A (Ss 4,11,15,17,22b) C.O. *Hptm.* Zimmermann	2
12May18	9Jun18	Cappy	SGp 1 (Ss 4,11,15,17) C.O. *Hptm.* Zimmermann	2
9Jun18	9Jun18	Curchy	SGp 1 (Ss 4,11,15,17) C.O. *Hptm.* Erich Sonntag	18
9Jun18	11Jun18	Cappy	SGp 1 (Ss 4,11,15,17) C.O. *Hptm.* Erich Sonntag	2
11Jun18	12Jun18	Curchy	SGp 1 (Ss 4,11,15,17) C.O. *Hptm.* Erich Sonntag	18
12Jun18	6Jul18	Cappy	SGp 1 (Ss 4,11,15,17) C.O. *Hptm.* Erich Sonntag	2
7Jul18	10Jul18	Assevillers	SGp J (Ss 4,15,24b,25b) C.O. *Oblt.* Franz Albertshauser	2
11Jul18	10Aug18	St. Loup	SGp J (Ss 4,15,24b,25b) C.O. *Oblt.* Erhardt Egerer	1
11Aug18	12Aug18	NW Athies	SGp J (Ss 4,15,24b,25b,35) C.O. *Oblt.* Erhardt Egerer	2
13Aug18	20Aug18	St. Loup	SGp J (Ss 4,15,24b,25b,35) C.O. *Oblt.* Erhardt Egerer	1
21Aug18	1Sep18	Beuvry	SGp J (Ss 4,15,24b,25b) C.O. *Oblt.* Erhardt Egerer	17
2Sep18	8Sep18	Abscon	SGp J (Ss 4,15,24b,25b,35) C.O. *Oblt.* Erhardt Egerer	17
9Sep18	3Oct18	Abscon	SGp J (Ss 4,15,24b,25b,35) C.O. *Oblt.* Friedrich von Krausser	17
3Oct18	13Oct18	Marly	SGp S (Ss 4,11,15,27b,35) C.O. *Hptm.* Hugo Weingarth	17
13Oct18	18Oct18	Nouvelles	SGp S (Ss 4,11,15,27b) C.O. *Hptm.* Hugo Weingarth	17
18Oct18	EOW	NW St. Simphorien	SGp S (Ss 4,11,15,27b) C.O. *Hptm.* Hugo Weingarth	17

Royal Prussian *Schutzstaffel 4*

1Jan17	*Schutzstaffel 4* is created from KG 3/Ks 16 by KM Nr.1425.16.g.A.7.L. of 1Jan17.
11Jan17	*Vzfw.* Arthur Schorish, P, and *Ltn.d.R.* Karl Meierdirks, O, crashland Rumpler C.I 4554/15. The aircraft is destroyed, they are OK.
16Apr17	*Ltn.d.R.* Figulla-1, *Uffz.* Steudel-1, Sopwith #A.3322, 8.10, by Douai, Bristol F.2a, 48 Sqn. RFC, 2/Lt. H.D. Davies,POW & 2/ Lt. R.S.L. Worsley,POW
7May17	*Uffz.* Orth-1, Engl. a/c, by Douai
1Jun17	*Flg.* Hellwig-1, *Uffz.* Ebert-1, Nieuport 17, W. Rouvroy #N.3029, Naval 6, Sqn/Cdr. C.D. Breese, WIA
7Jul17	*Uffz.* Franz Schnitt, P, and *Vzfw.* Friedrich Pieper, G, are KIA at Kokuit during an air combat. They fall in flames.
14Aug17	*Uffz.* Paul Podbiol, P, is WIA and *Uffz.* Slater, G, is shot down, OK, as a result of an air combat.
25Aug17	*Vzfw.* Ostermann, P, and *Uffz.* Schrey, G, are MIA and taken POW.
26Aug17	*Uffz.* Willy Thoerner, P, is WIA during air combat.
10Sep17	*Vzfw.* Lüderitz-1, *Feldw.* Weiss-1, Sopwith, 18.45, N. Schaapbalie
20Oct17	*Uffz.* Herdam, P, and *Vzfw.* Eichler, G, are IIC,lt. during a landing.
8Nov17	*Uffz.* Bendlin-1, *Gefr.* Kuhne-1, Spad, 17.00, Steenbecque
26Jan18	*Uffz.* Reinhold Bendlin, P, is KIC and *Vzfw.* Ewald Liersch, G, is IIC at Bertry.
29Jan18	*Vzfw.* Eldner, P, is WIA,sv. at Bertry during air combat.
19Feb18	*Uffz.* Kern-1, *Vzfw.* Wagner-1, 12.10, Spad, Metz en Couture
19Feb18	*Uffz.* Matthias Meinberg, P, and *Uffz.* Steinert, G, are severely WIA during air combat.
20Feb18	*Vzfw.* Kirchner, P, and *Werkmstr.* Heidrich, M, are IIC, sv. at Bertry while on a check out flight.
27Mar18	*Schutzstaffel 4* is renamed *Schlachtstaffel 4* by Km Nr.5126.18.A.7.L.IV.C. of 27Mar18.
6Apr18	*Uffz.* Willi Scholz, P, and *Vzfw.* Gerhard Masolyn, G, are KIA over Amiens.

6May18	*Ltn.d.R.* Wenck-1, *Ltn.d.R.* Bader-1, S.E. 5a
6May18	*Ltn.d.R.* Wenck-2, *Ltn.d.R.* Bader-2, S.E. 5a
1Jun18	*Gefr.* Kurt Ahrens, P, and *Uffz.* Paul Höschel, G, are KIC at Moislains.
29Sep18	*Ltn.d.R.* Roloff-1, *Uffz.* Isenbach-1, 2 Seater, 16.16, Park la Folie an der Kanalbrucke
Nov18	*Schlachtstaffel 4* is demobilized at FEA 7, Braunschweig.

Vzfw. Anton Schmitz (P) served with *KG 3/Ks 16* before this unit was renamed *Schusta 4*. Since the photo is undated it is not clear with which formation it was taken, despite his sleeve patch. Credit: Terry Philipps.

Royal Prussian *Schutzstaffel 5*

Pilot/Gunner	Type	From		To	
		Unit	Date	Date	Unit
Flg. Ackermann	P			28May18	POW
Gefr. Paul Bäumer	P	AFP 2	22Feb17	26Feb17	AFP 1
Uffz. Hans Becker	P	AFP 1	28Feb17	1Aug17	AFP 6
Gefr. Walter Behm	G			8Mar18	KIA
Flg. Betscher	G	AFP 4	2Oct17		
Uffz. Biesenbach	P			22Dec17	POW
Uffz. Robert Bitzer	G	AFP 1	20Jun17	25Jul17	AFP 6
Uffz. Anton Bode	G			22Dec17	KIA
Vzfw. Fritz Böttcher	P			30Mar18	KIA
Gefr. Johannes Bogdan	G			19Aug17	KIC
Vzfw. Engel	G	AFP 4	26Oct17		
Uffz. Arno Fischer	P			25Jan18	KIC
Uffz. Josef George	P			19Aug17	KIC
Uffz. Max Greiner			(Jan18)		
Uffz. Kurt Gross	G	Ss 26b	11Nov17	25Jan18	KIC
Vzfw. Paul Groll	P		(Jun17)		
Vzfw. Fritz Hankner	G			23Nov17	FEA 8
Vzfw. Fritz Hankner	G		(Mar18)	2Oct18	POW
Pion. Paul Heinze	G	Ss 24b	28Oct17	(Nov17)	
Vzfw. Paul Holtmann	P		(May18)	2Oct18	POW
Uffz. Janning	P		(Apr17)		
Flg. Jeschke	G			28May18	POW
Vzfw. Hans Erich Kauffmann	G		(Jun17)		AFP 4
Sgt. Richard Kostanski	M			15May18	KIA
Uffz. Lemke	P			15Nov17	FEA 8
Vzfw. Kurt Liehr	G		(Jun17)	(Jan18)	
Gefr. Heinrich Lüders				2Oct18	WIA,lt.
Uffz. August Matthies	P		(Jan18)		Ss 35
Flg. Gustav Maurer	G	AFP 1		10Apr18	KIA
Vzfw. Martin Meinke	G		(Jan18)	30Mar18	KIA
Flg. Kaspar Mink	M			12Mar17	Died
Vzfw. Müller	P	AFP 4	26Oct17	(Nov17)	
Uffz. Nitzkowski	P		(Jun17)		
Vzfw. Otto Pelz	P	KG 3/17	1Jan17	24Feb17	KsSch P
Uffz. Peter	G			29Jan18	WIA
Ltn. Hans-Joachim Rath, C.O.	P	Idflieg	18Jun18	EOW	
Uffz. Reich	P	AFP 4	15Nov17		
Uffz. Walter Reimers	G		(Apr17)	20Jul17	KIA
Sgt. Ernst Schild (+ Nov18)	G	Ss 14		EOW	
Oblt. Ulrich von Schimony-Schimonsky, C.O.	O	Ss 18	25Apr17	12Dec17	BS Köln
Gefr. Karl Schott	G	AFP 4	26Oct17	13Nov17	Ss 13
Oblt. Arthur Schreiber, C.O.	O	Js 40s	9Dec17	14Apr18	AFP 18
Ltn.d.R. Herbert Schröder	P	KG 3/17	1Jan17	26Jan17	Js 1
Gefr. Willi Sellenböhmer	P			8Mar18	KIA
Oblt. Walter Sommé, C.O.	P	KG 3/17	1Jan17	Mar17	Ss 11
Ltn. Ernst Frhr. von Stenglin	P	KG 3/17	1Jan17	19Jan17	Js 1
Ltn.d.R. Fritz Thiede	P	KG 3/17	1Jan17	Oct17	JsSch I
Vzfw. Kurt Ungewitter	P	Alb Wrk	('17)	May18	AFP 18
Uffz. Walter Frhr. von Wangenheim	P			10Apr18	KIA
Flg. Weibeler	G		(May18)		
Ltn. Weinschenk, Stv. C.O.				21Oct18	SGp B
Oblt. Bruno Zipplies, C.O.	O	Js 69	14Apr18	15May18	Ss 20

Schutzstaffel/Schlachtstaffel 5 Airfields

From	To	Location	*Schlachtgruppe* Affiliation	*Armee*
1Jan17	(31Jan17)	Anneux	Escort for FA 213(A), 259(A)	1
(Feb17)	16Apr17	Sévigny	Escort for FA 226(A)s	7
(22Apr17)	19Jun17		Escort for FA 226(A)s	1
19Jun17	Aug17		Escort for FA 264(A)	6
Aug17		Ichteghem		4
(Sep17)	19Oct17		Escort for FA 264(A)	6
19Oct17	25Nov17	Ichteghem	Escort for FA 264(A)	4
25Nov17	(Dec17)	Le Cateau		2
(22Dec17)	(Mar18)	Seboncourt	Escort for FA 264(A)	18
(8Mar18)	21Mar18	Seboncourt	SGp 1 (Ss 2,5,20) C.O. *Oblt.* Werner Lange	18
21Mar18		Seboncourt	SGp 4 (Ss 2,5,20,33) C.O. *Oblt.* Werner Lange	18
(9Apr18)		Omiécourt	SGp 4 (Ss 2,5,20,33) C.O. *Oblt.* Werner Lange	18
(14Apr18)	(15May18)	Hangest-en-Santerre	SGp 4 (Ss 5,20,32,33) C.O. *Oblt.* Werner Lange	18
27May18	6Jun18	St. Erme	SGp C (Ss 5,20,32,33,37) C.O. *Oblt.* Werner Lange	7
(9Jun18)	(25Jun18)	Raperie Ferme	SGp Wichura (Ss 5,20,32,33,37) C.O. *Oblt.* Werner Lange	7
11Jul18	18Jul18	Anoux	SGp 1 (Ss 5,20,33,37) C.O. *Oblt.* Werner Lange	3
18Jul18	28Jul18	Seringes	SGp B (Ss 5,20,33,37) C.O. *Oblt.* Werner Lange	7
29Jul18		St. Loup	SGp B (Ss 5,20,33,35,37) C.O. *Oblt.* Werner Lange	1
7Aug18	1Sep18	Chivres-en-Laonnois	SGp C (Ss 5,20,33,35,37) C.O. *Oblt.* Werner Lange	7
2Sep18	6Sep18	Briey	SGp B (Ss 5,20,32,37) C.O. *Oblt.* Werner Lange	5
6Sep18	15Sep18	Anoux-le-Grange	SGp B (Ss 5,20,32,37) C.O. *Oblt.* Werner Lange	AAC
16Sep18	26Sep18	Briey	SGp B (Ss 5,20,21,26b,33) C.O. *Oblt.* Bruno Zipplies	5
27Sep18	13Oct18	Thonne-les-Prés	SGp B (Ss 5,20,21,33) C.O. *Oblt.* Bruno Zipplies	5
13Oct18	23Oct18	St. Mard, Virton	SGp B (Ss 5,20,21,33) C.O. *Oblt.* Bruno Zipplies	5
23Oct18	29Oct18	Louppy-sur-Loison	SGp B (Ss 5,20,21,32,33) C.O. *Oblt.* Hans Ebel	5
29Oct18	2Nov18	St. Mard, Virton	SGp B (Ss 5,20,21,33) C.O. *Oblt.* Hans Ebel	5
2Nov18	EOW	Habay-la-Vieille	SGp B (Ss 5,20,21,33) C.O. *Oblt.* Hans Ebel	5

Royal Prussian *Schuztstaffel 5*

1Jan17	*Schutzstaffel 5* is created from KG 3/Ks 17 by KM Nr.1425.16.g.A.7.L. of 1Jan17.
13Mar17	*Flg.* Kaspar Mink, M, dies at Montcornet.
16Apr17	*Uffz.* Janning-1, *Gefr.* Reimers-1, Nieuport, St. Thierry, NW Reims Nieuport 23 #2827, Esc. N.75, Cpl. J. Canivet-Lagrange, MIA
1Jun17	*Uffz.* Nitzkowski-1, *Vzfw.* Liehr-1, Spad 1, Berry au Bac Spad S.7, Esc. N.75, Sgt. C. Durand, KIA
15Jun17	*Uffz.* Groll-1, *Vzfw.* Kauffmann-1, Spad, Cormicy
20Jul17	*Uffz.* Walter Reimers, G, is KIA at Chérisy.
19Aug17	*Uffz.* Josef George, P, and *Gefr.* Johannes Bogdan, G, are KIC at Contiches.
22Dec17	*Uffz.* Biesenbach, P, is taken POW and *Uffz.* Anton Bode, G, is KIA over St. Quentin during air combat in a DFW C.V.
3Jan18	*Uffz.* Ungewitter-zLg and *Vzfw.* Liehr-zLg, D.H. 4, St. Quentin F.2b #A.7229, 48 Sqn. RFC, Lt. K.R. Park,OK & Lt. J.H. Robinson,OK

9Jan18	*Uffz.* Ungewitter-1, *Vzfw.* Meinke-1, Bristol F.2b, 12.00, Nauroy #C.4816, 48 Sqn. RFC, Capt. A.W. Field,KIA & 2/Lt. W.S. Smith,KIA
25Jan18	*Uffz.* Arno Fischer, P, and *Uffz.* Kurt Gross, G, are KIC at Montbréhain at 11.00 hours.
29Jan18	*Uffz.* Peter, G, is WIA during air combat.
18Feb18	*Vzfw.* Ungewitter-2, *Vzfw.* Meinke-2, D.H.
8Mar18	*Gefr.* Willi Sellenböhmer, P, and *Gefr.* Walter Behm, G, are KIA over Magny la Fosse during air combat.
27Mar18	*Schutzstaffel 5* is renamed *Schlachtstaffel 5* by KM Nr. 5126.18.A.7.L.IV.C. of 27Mar18.
30Mar18	*Vzfw.* Fritz Böttcher, P, and *Vzfw.* Martin Meinke, G, are accidently KIA over Folies by German Flak fire.
10Apr18	*Uffz.* Walter *Frhr.* von Wangenheim, P, and *Flg.* Gustav Maurer, G, are KIA over Merville aux Bois. As an interesting historical footnote, Walter Herbert *Frhr.* von Wangenheim was born on 19 April 1895 at Narre Warren, Victoria, Australia.
15May18	*Sgt.* Richard Kostanski, M, is KIA at Hangest-en-Senterre.
28May18	*Flg.* Ackermann, P, and *Flg.* Jeschke, G, are taken POW W. of Dampleux at 09.30 hours,
31May18	*Sgt.* Holtmann-1, *Flg.* Weibeler-1, 2 Seater
2Oct18	*Vzfw.* Paul Holtmann, P, and *Vzfw.* Fritz Hankner, G, are taken POW at Véry W. Montfaucon at 17.30 hours in a Halberstadt after being shot down in aerial combat.
2Oct18	*Gefr.* Heinrich Lüders is WIA,lt. by ground fire.
Nov18	*Schlachtstaffel 5* is demobilized at FEA 7, Braunschweig.

Above: The men of *Schusta 5* in 1917. The C.O., *Oblt.* Ulrich von Schimony-Schimonsky, is on the far left. Fifth from the left is *Vzfw.* Karl Ungewitter.

Opposite
Top: Halberstadt Cl.II, Cl.IV and Hannover Cl.II of *Schlasta 5*. Note the unit marking of a red and white fuselage stripe.

Bottom: A poor copy but important as it clearly illustrates the *Schlasta 5* unit marking on this Halberstadt Cl.II individually marked '6'. The crew is unidentified.

Royal Prussan *Schutzstaffel 6*

Pilot/Gunner	Type	From		To	
		Unit	Date	Date	Unit
Vzfw. Hans Ade	P	GS Pdb	(Jul17)	EOW	
Uffz. Hermann Auersch	P			25Feb17	KIA
Uffz. Fritz Bartholomäi	G		(Jul17)	31Jul17	KIA
Uffz. Brendel	P	AFP 9	17Aug18		
Uffz. Johann Bucher	G	Ss 23b	10Sep18		
Uffz. Capellen	G		(Oct17)		
Oblt. Rudolf Hermann Carl				31Jul17	WIA,sv.
Collmann von Schatteburg, C.O.	P			2Aug17	DOW
Uffz. Dittmar	P		(Jan17)	5Jan17	IIC,sv.
Uffz. Dittmar	P		(Jan18)	16Jul18	POW
Offz.Stv. Dreier	G		(Jan17)		
Vzfw. Willy Engler	G	KG 3/18	1Jan17	15Feb17	FEA 9
Ltn.d.L. Julius Erb	O	KG 3/18	1Jan17	(Jan17)	KG 4
Flg. Engelbert Esser	G	AFP 7	10May17	21May17	AFP 7
Offz.Stv. Fleischer	G		(Jan17)		
Uffz. Walter Graaf	P			19May18	KIA
Uffz. Graupner	G		(Jun17)		
Vzfw. Rudolf Grief	G			16Mar18	KIA
Ltn. Hartfiel	P	Js 8	30May18		
Flg. Haussmann	G		(Sep17)		
Sgt. Christian Hofele	G			19May18	KIA
Uffz. Hellmuth Krätzschmer	P		Aug17	1Dec17	JsSch I
Gefr. Lichtenberg			(Sep18)		
Ltn. Günther Lüdeke	P	GS Pdrb	17Sep18	EOW	
Oblt. Jürgen Lüdeke, C.O.	O	FA 254A	14Apr18	EOW	
Uffz. Richard Ludwig	G		(Jan17)	25Feb17	KIA
Ltn.d.R. Wilhelm Ernst Maser, Stv CO	P	FA 293Ab		5Nov17	FA 293Ab
Oblt. Herbert Massalsky, C.O.	O	KG 3/18	1Jan17		
Gefr. Meyer			(Sep18)		
Uffz. Michael	G			16Jul18	POW
Uffz. Nickel	P		(Jan17)		
Uffz. Niehaus	P		(Jan17)		
Vzfw. Noack	P		(Jan17)		
Hptm. Ernst Nordmann, Stv. C.O.	O	FA 234A	Aug17	Sep17	FA 234A
Uffz. Frank Oppenheimer	G	AFP 7	23Apr17	7May17	AFP 7
Offz.Stv. Hermann Patberg	P	AFS Ost	18Feb17	EOW	
Uffz. Paul Pfeiffer	P	KG 3/18	1Jan17	2Feb17	KS Pdbn
Uffz. Rössler	P		(Jan17)		
Vzfw. Fritz Schlüter	P		(Sep17)	3Sep18	KIA
Offz.Stv. Johann Schmid	P	Ss 23b	10Sep18		
Gefr. Schmitt	G		(Jan17)	5Jan17	IIC,sv.
Gefr. Schmitt	G		(Jan18)		
Uffz. Julius Schneider			(Apr18)		
Sgt. Schütze	G			21Jul18	IIC,sv.
Oblt. Schuster, C.O.			(Mar17)	Mar18	
Feldw. Schwarz	G		(Jan17)		
Vzfw. Max Seiwert	G			3Sep18	KIA
Uffz. Karl Steck	G		(Sep18)	EOW	
Gefr. Kurt Steinecke			(Apr17)		
Uffz. Teicke	G		(Jul17)		
Vzfw. Karl Weckerle	P	Ss 23b	10Sep18		
Vzfw. Adolf Wiegand	P			2May18	KIA
Vzfw. Xaver Zollinger	P			16Mar18	KIA
Uffz. Zorn	G		(Jan17)		

Schutzstaffel/Schlachtstaffel 6 Airfields

From	To	Location	*Schlachtgruppe* Affiliation	*Armee*
1Jan17		Graincourt	Escort for FA 3	1
(31Jan17)	Mar17	Villers les Cagnicourt	For FA 201(A)	1
Mar17	(Apr17)	Goudelancourt	Escort for FA 234(A)	7
(7Jun17)	15Aug17	Sissonne	Escort for FA 234(A)	7
15Aug17	16Oct17	Jametz	Escort for FA 36	5
16Oct17	30Nov17	Goudelancourt	Escort for FA 234(A)	7
30Nov17		AOK 7 sent 4 a/c to *2. Armee* to assist Ss 25b in the ground attack in the Vendhuille-Epehy area (Cambrai tank battle counter attack). They returned to *7. Armee* that same day, although one a/c was FTL 10 km. SW of Le Cateau.		
30Nov17	Jan18	Goudelancourt	Escort for FA 234(A)	7
Jan18				18
(Feb18)				18
(16Mar18)	(24Mar18)	Grougis	SGp 3 (Ss 6,32,34) C.O. *Oblt.* Werner Lange	18
4Apr18	Dury		SGp 3 (Ss 6,8,18,32) C.O. *Oblt.* Kurt Messow	18
(9Apr18)	14Apr18	Roye	SGp 3 (Ss 6,8,18,32) C.O. *Oblt.* Kurt Messow	18
14Apr18	(25Apr18)	Roye	SGp 3 (Ss 6,18,34)	18
(27May18)		Dury	SGp 3 (Ss 6,18,34,35,38s) C.O. *Ritt.* Herrmann	18
6Jun18	(24Jun18)	Dury	SGp 2 (Ss 6,18,34,35,38s) C.O. *Ritt.* Herrmann	18
(1Jul18)		Dricourt	SGp 3 (Ss 6,7,18,34,38s) C.O. *Oblt.* Friedrich-Carl Hanesse	3
15Jul18		Dury	SGp 3 (Ss 6,18,34,38s) C.O. *Oblt.* Friedrich-Carl Hanesse	9
(28Jul18)	3Aug18	Toulis	SGp 3 (Ss 6,18,34,38s) C.O. *Oblt.* Friedrich-Carl Hanesse	9
4Aug18	8Aug18	Toulis	SGp 3 (Ss 6,18,26b,34,38s) C.O. *Oblt.* Friedrich-Carl Hanesse	9
9Aug18	12Aug18	Bouvincourt	SGp 3 (Ss 6,18,34,38s) C.O. *Oblt.* Friedrich-Carl Hanesse	2
13Aug18	16Aug18	Toulis	SGp 3 (Ss 6,7,18,26b,34,38s) C.O. *Oblt.* Friedrich-Carl Hanesse	9
16Aug18	28Aug18	Villeselve	SGp 3 (Ss 6,12,18,26b,34,38s) 18 C.O. *Oblt.* Friedrich-Carl Hanesse	
28Aug18	18Sep18	Toulis	SGp 3 (Ss 6,18,26b,34,38s) C.O. *Oblt.* Friedrich-Carl Hanesse	9
18Sep18	6Oct18		SGp B (Ss 6,18,34,38s) C.O. *Oblt.* Friedrich-Carl Hanesse	3
6Oct18	13Oct18	Toulis	SGp B (Ss 6,7,18,34,38s) C.O. *Oblt.* Friedrich-Carl Hanesse	7
13Oct18	18Oct18	Landrecies		18
18Oct18	EOW	Feuchères	SGp 3 (Ss 6,12,23b,38s) C.O. *Oblt.* Friedrich-Carl Hanesse	7

Royal Prussian *Schutzstaffel 6*

1Jan17	*Schutzstaffel 6* is created from KG 3/Ks 18 by KM Nr.1425.16.g.A.7.L. of 1Jan17.
5Jan17	*Uffz.* Dittmar, P, and *Gefr.* Schmitt, G, are IIC,sv. in a crash landing of Rol C.II 1663/16.
25Feb17	*Uffz.* Hermann Auersch, P, and *Uffz.* Richard Ludwig, G, are KIA at Denain.
17Jun17	*Uffz.* Patberg-1, *Uffz.* Graupner-1, Spad, S. Craonne
28Jul17	*Uffz.* Tiecke-1, *Uffz.* Bartholomäi-1, Spad, Jumigny, Aisne Spad S.7 #401, Esc. N.73, Lt. A. Duellin, WIA,sv.
31Jul17	*Oblt.* Rudolf Collmann von Schatteberg, P and C.O., and *Uffz.* Fritz Bartholomäi, G, are shot down at Arancy. Bartholomäi is KIA, Collmann von Schatteberg DOW 2Aug17 at Liesse.
30Sep17	*Gefr.* Schlüter-1, *Flg.* Haussmann-1, Spad, by Malancourt
29Oct17	*Uffz.* Ade-1, *Uffz.* Capellen-1, Spad, by Pinon-Vauxaillon

16Mar18	*Vzfw*. Xaver Zollinger, P, and *Vzfw*. Rudolf Grief, G, are KIA over Bellenglise in air combat.
27Mar18	*Schutzstaffel 6* is renamed *Schlachtstaffel 6* by KM Nr. 5126.18.A.7.L.IV.C. of 27Mar18.
2May18	*Vzfw*. Adolf Wiegand, P, and *Ltn.d.R*. Paul Kallweit, O of Fl.Abt.206(A), are KIA over Montdidier during an air combat.
19May18	*Uffz*. Walter Graaf, P, and *Sgt*. Christian Hofele, G, are KIA over Montdider.
16Jul18	*Uffz*. Dittmar, P, and *Uffz*. Michael, G, are taken POW.
21Jul18	*Sgt*. Schütze, G, is IIC,sv.
3Sep18	*Vzfw*. Fritz Schlüter, P, and *Vzfw*. Max Siewert, G, are KIA over Anizy le Château.
Nov18	*Schlachtstaffel 6* is demobilized at *Werk Fliegerschule* Schwerin.

Above: A few of the men of *Schutzstaffel 6* in 1917. Names and the location are not known. Photo credit: Johan Ryheul.

Right: *Oblt*. Jürgen Lüdeke on the left and *Ltn*. Günther Lüdeke on the right. The Lüdeke brothers belonged to the *Braunschweigisches Husaren-Regiment Nr. 17* (Death's Head); thus they are both wearing Hussar uniforms. The aircraft is Jürgen's Halb. Cl.IV, individually marked number 5. The photo was taken at Toulis airfield in the *7.Armee* during October 1918. Photo credit: Marton Szigeti.

Right: Karl Steck and Günther Lüdeke in their Halb. Cl.IV. Clearly the *Schlasta 6* unit marking originated with the brother's previous connection with *Braunschweigisches Husaren-Regiment Nr. 17 Totenkopf* (Death's Head). Photo credit: Marton Szigeti.

Royal Prussian *Schutzstaffel 7*

Pilot/Gunner	Type	From		To	
		Unit	Date	Date	Unit
Gefr. Georg Andreae			(Jun18)		
Offz.Stv. Hans Basch	P	KG 5/25	1Jan17	3Apr17	KG 3
Gefr. Beckhorst	G	AFP 4	22Aug17		
Vzfw. Karl Berger	P		(Apr17)	(May17)	
Sgt. Paul Beschow	P	KEST 4b	16Aug17	13Sep17	AFP 4
Vzfw. Joachim Graf von Beissel und Gymnich	P	KG 5/25	1Jan17	8Jan17	Js 22
Uffz. Blobel	G		(Jan18)	23Mar18	POW
Ltn. Max Böhme			('17)		
Uffz. Arthur Brodbeck	P	AFP 4	19Oct17	1Dec17	KIA
Uffz. Eugen Brodbeck	P	AFP 4	22Nov17	(May18)	
Uffz. Max Bröll	P			12Jul17	WIA,lt.
Uffz. Max Bröll	P			13Oct17	FA 33
Ltn. Hans Denkewitz	P			18Mar17	Js 36
Uffz. Evers	P			16Oct17	FEA 11
Uffz. Helmuth Fever	P			17Aug18	POW
Flg. Andreas Graf	P	AFP 6	15May17	30May17	Hosp.
Flg. Andreas Graf	P	Hosp.	1Jul17	6Jul17	AFP 4
Gefr. Heinz von Guerard	P	AFP 4	18Dec17	3Jan18	KIA
Uffz. Hacke	P		(Jan18)	23Mar18	POW
Offz.Stv. Harnke	P	KG 5/25	1Jan17		
Vzfw. Hayne	P	AFP 4	22Aug17	26Aug17	AFP 4
Uffz. J. Heidelberg	P	FA 258A	13Sep17		
Offz.Stv. Hans Hinsch	P	KG 5/25	1Jan17	1Apr17	Js 11
Hptm. Hermann Horn, Stv. C.O.	O	FA 233A	28Apr17	12May17	FA 233A
Uffz. Kaiser					
Vzfw. Fritz Kellner	G			9Aug18	KIA
Uffz. Alfred Kind	G		(Apr17)	Jun17	KG 1/1
Uffz. Kluge	P			23Aug17	AFP 4
Ltn.d.R. Hanns Koch, OzbV	O	KG 5/25	1Jan17	(Apr17)	Flak
Ltn. Mark Albrecht von Köster	O			Aug18	Ss 34
Flg. Emil Kratzer	G	Ss 30b	8Oct17	(Jul18)	
Flg. Kümmerer	G			31Jul17	WIA
Offz.Stv. Erdmann Kupske				17May18	KIA
Oblt. Walter Lackner, C.O.	O	Ss 20	31Jan18	9Aug18	Kofl 9
Ltn. Gottfried von Langen	P		(Apr17)	Jun17	KG 1/1
Ltn.d.R. Aristides Fritz Müller	P			28May17	Js 36
Vzfw. Adolf Niess	P	FA 13	18Mar17	1May17	AFP 6
Uffz. Wilhelm Niess	G		(Mar17)	2May17	KIA
Vzfw. Pohlmann	P	AFP 4	20Sep17		
Ltn. Max Prechter	O	KG 5/25	1Jan17		
Uffz. Karl-Wilhelm Rabe	G	AFP 9	12Aug18	17Aug18	POW
Ltn.d.R. August Raben	P	KG 5/25	1Jan17	17Feb17	JsSch I
Uffz. Fritz Reiner	G	AFP 4	11Nov17	3Jan18	WIA,sv.
Uffz. Fritz Reiner	G			11Apr18	KIA
Gefr. Rommel	P		(Mar17)		
Ltn. Heinrich Sänger	O	KG 5/25	1Jan17	20Feb17	AFP 1
Feldw. Sauer	G		(Apr17)	(May17)	
Flg. Schäfer	P	AFP 4	28Sep17	12Nov17	IIC,sv.
Uffz. Schafmeister	P			22Aug17	FEA 7
Vzfw. Josef Schleiffer	P	KG 5/25	1Jan17	Jul17	KG 1/1
Flg. Scholz	P	AFP 4	30Aug17	(Sep17)	
Flg. Schumann	P	AFP 4	22Nov17		
Gefr. Schoop	P			7Apr17	POW
Vzfw. Seifert	P		(Apr17)	2May17	WIA,sv.
Uffz. Ewald Sirrenberg	G	AFP 4	21Sep17	1Dec17	KIA
Vzfw. Trumpf	P			9Aug18	WIA,sv.
Flg. Karl Udert				17May18	KIA
Vzfw. Unvericht	G		(Mar17)	(Mar18)	

Ltn. Viereck	O	KG 5/25	1Jan17	19Jan17	Idflieg
Gefr. Gustav Waschkau	P			11Apr18	KIA
Vzfw. Weber	P		(Mar17)		
Uffz. August Werkmeister	P			13Sep17	AFP 4
Vzfw. Adolf Wucherer	G	AFP 4	21Sep17	13Nov17	Ss 10
Oblt. Eduard Wolfgang Zorer, C.O.	O	KG 5/25	1Jan17	28Apr17	Leave
Hptm. Eduard Wolfgang Zorer, C.O.	O	Leave	12May17	13Jun17	Leave

Schutzstaffel/Schlachtstaffel 7 Airfields

From	To	Location	*Schlachtgruppe* Affiliation	*Armee*
1Jan17	26Feb17	Villers-Outréaux	Escort for FA 233(A)	1
26Feb17	3Jun17	Douai Petit Cuincy	Escort for FA 233(A)	6
3Jun17	17Oct17	Heule	Escort for FA 33	4
17Oct17	25Nov17	Moorsele	Escort for FA 33	4
25Nov17	1Dec17	Masny Süd		6
1Dec17		Masny Süd	Escort for FA 293(A)b	6
(1Jan18)	(Feb18)			18
(21Mar18)	(24Mar18)	Lesquielles-St. Germain	SGp 2 (Ss 7,18,37) C.O. *Oblt.* Walter Lackner	18
(4Apr18)	(9Apr18)	Villeselve	SGp 2 (Ss 7,31b,34,37) C.O. *Oblt.* Walter Lackner	18
(25Apr18)		Villeselve	SGp 1 (Ss 2,7,31b) C.O. *Oblt.* Walter Lackner	18
(27May18)		Alincourt	SGp 1 (Ss 2,7,22b,31b) C.O. *Oblt.* Walter Lackner	1
(6Jun18)	(9Jun18)	Villeselve	SGp 1 (Ss 2,7,31b) C.O. *Oblt.* Walter Lackner	18
(1Jul18)		Dricourt	SGp 3 (Ss 6,7,18,34,38s) C.O. *Oblt.* Friedrich-Carl Hanesse	3
(15Jul18)	18Jul18	Le Chesne	SGp 2 (Ss 7,23b,26b,35,36) C.O. *Oblt.* Walter Lackner	3
18Jul18	3Aug18	Le Chesne	SGp 2 (Ss 7,22b,23b,26b,36) C.O. *Oblt.* Walter Lackner	3
4Aug18	8Aug18	Le Chesne		3
9Aug18	13Aug18	Marle		9
13Aug18	16Aug18	Marle	SGp 3 (Ss 6,7,18,26b,34,38s) C.O. *Oblt.* Friedrich-Carl Hanesse	9
16Aug18	(1Sep18)	Marle		9
(12Sep18)		Grandlup-et-Fay	SGp B (Ss 7,28b,30b,31b,33) C.O. *Oblt.d.R.* Josef Gramp	7
(26Sep18)	6Oct18	Toulis		7
6Oct18	13Oct18	Toulis	SGp B (Ss 6,7,18,34,38s) C.O. *Oblt.* Friedrich-Carl Hanesse	7
13Oct18	18Oct18	Toulis	SGp B (Ss 7,18,34,38s) C.O. *Oblt.* Friedrich-Carl Hanesse	7
18Oct18	29Oct18		SGp B (Ss 7,18,34) C.O. *Oblt.* Ernst Bonatz	7
29Oct18	EOW		SGp B (Ss 7,18,32,34) C.O. *Oblt.* Ernst Bonatz	3

Royal Prussian *Schutzstaffel 7*

1Jan17	*Schutzstaffel 7* is created from KG 5/Ks 25 by KM Nr.1425.16.g.A.7.L. of 1Jan17.
16Mar17	*Vzfw.* Weber-1, *Gefr.* Unvericht-1, F.E. 2b, 17.00, Arras-Neuville #7693, 25 Sqn. RFC, 2/Lt. R.N.L. Munro,WIA & Sgt. C.H. Nunn,OK
16Mar17	*Gefr.* Rommel-1, *Flg.* Niess-1, F.E. 2b, 17.00, Arras-Neuville
7Apr17	*Gefr.* Schoop, P, and *Ltn. Hupe*, O of Fl.Abt. 233(A), are taken POW in Rumpler C.I 2606/16.
24Apr17	*Hptm.* Eduard Wolfgang Zorer, O, and *Vzfw.* Josef Schleiffer, P, strafe trenches at Gavrelle. This is the first recorded use of Schutzstaffeln aircraft as ground attack units.

2May17 — *Vzfw*. Siefert, P, is WIA,sv. and *Uffz*. Wilhelm Niess, G, is KIA in DFW C.V (LVG) 5178/16 over Gavrelle near Bailleul during air combat.

12Jul17 — *Uffz*. Max Bröll, P, is WIA,lt. during air combat.

31Jul17 — *Flg*. Kümmerer, G, is WIA by ground fire.

12Nov17 — *Flg*. Schäfer, P, is severely IIC in a crash landing and to hospital.

1Dec17 — *Uffz*. Arthur Brodbeck, P, and *Uffz*. Ewald Sirrenberg, G, are KIA over La Capelle.

1Jan18 — *Uffz*. Hacke-1, *Uffz*. Blobel-1, D.H. 4, N. Gricourt

3Jan18 — *Gefr*. Heinz von Guerard, P, is KIA and *Uffz*. Fritz Reiner, G, is WIA,sv. over Senerczy Ferme during air combat.

23Mar18 — *Vzfw*. Hacke, P, and *Uffz*. Blobel, G, are taken POW at Champien following air combat.

27Mar18 — *Schutzstaffel 7* is renamed *Schlachtstaffel 7* by KM Nr. 5126.18.A.7.L.IV.C. of 27Mar18.

11Apr18 — *Gefr*. Gustav Waschkau, P, and *Uffz*. Fritz Reiner, G, are KIA over Golancourt.

17May18 — *Flg*. Karl Udert and *Offz.Stv*. Erdmann Kupske are KIA at Beaufort-en-Santerre. Uncertainty exists as to who was the pilot and who was the gunner.

9Aug18 — *Vzfw*. Trumpf, P, is WIA,sv. and *Vzfw*. Fritz Kellner, G, is KIA over Mons-en-Chaussée in Hannover Cl.IIIa 2729/18 while on a mission to support the 18th Army. Trumpf takes to his parachute.

17Aug18 — *Uffz*. Helmuth Fever, P, and *Uffz*. Karl-Wilhelm Rabe, G, are taken POW.

Nov18 — *Schlachtstaffel 7* is demobilized at FEA 1, Altenburg.

Above: Hannover Cl.IIIa marked 5 and 6 of *Schlachtstaffel 7*. Note the unit marking of a white diagonal fuselage band and white numbers aft of the cross.

Below: Halberstadt Cl.II with a badly bent tail. The white diagonal band forward of the cross identifies this as a *Schlasta 7* aircraft, phtographed in late 1918. Credit: Reinhard Kastner.

Royal Prussian *Schutzstaffel 8*

Pilot/Gunner	Type	From		To	
		Unit	Date	Date	Unit
Uffz. Kurt Andres	P		Sep17	(Oct17)	Ss 19
Vzfw. Bischoff	G		(May18)		
Vzfw. Karl Christ	P	KG 5/26	1Jan17	May17	KG 2/7
Uffz. Albert Dinse				20Oct18	+ i.Kr.
Uffz. Eisenbeisser	G		(May17)		
Vzfw. Ernsemann	P		(Aug17)	(Apr18)	
Offz.Stv. Willy Fiebig				11Dec17	KIA
Offz.Stv. Daniel Frick				11Dec17	KIA
Gefr. Heinrich Haase	P		(May18)	5Jun18	Js 21s
Gefr. Hall	P			27May18	WIA
Vzfw. Albert Haussmann	P	KG 5/26	1Jan17	12Apr17	AFP C
Vzwachtm. Wilhelm Helmus (+ 31May)	G			30May18	WIA,sv.
Vzfw. Heuser	P		(Sep17)	25Sep17	WIA,sv.
Ltn.d.R. Klinker	O		(Sep17)	25Sep17	SD, OK
Gefr. Thomas Krenciessa	P			EOW	
Uffz. Otto Kutter (DOW 13Jun18)	G		('17)	9May18	WIA,sv
Uffz. Langer	G		(Aug17)	(Apr18)	
Uffz. Wilhelm Lüning			(Mar18)		
Oblt. Kurt Messow, C.O.	O		(Apr17)	14Apr18	
Gefr. Meischner	P			2Sep18	IIC,lt.
Gefr. Meischner	P		2Sep18		
Gefr. Christian Meyer	G			28Jul18	POW
Uffz. Helmut Michael	P			28Jul18	POW
Ltn. Otto Müller	O	KG 5/26	1Jan17		FA 24s
Flg. Josef Reuber (+ 24Apr17)	P			12Apr17	WIA,sv.
Vzfw. Karl Waldemar Ritscherle	G	AFP 7	16Apr17	7Jan18	FEA 1
Flg. Sachmann	G			21Mar18	IIC,sv.
Uffz. Schäfer	P		(May18)		
Vzfw. Emil Schäpe	P	KG 5/26	1Jan17	15Feb17	Js 5
Hptm.d.R. Eberhard von Seel, C.O.	P	KG 5/26	1Jan17		KG 4/19
Uffz. Willi Karl Franz Sonnenberg	P		(Apr18)	2May18	WIA,POW
Gefr. Arthur Gustav Stolz	G			2May18	WIA,POW
Oblt. Thesing, C.O.			21May18	Oct18	
Vzfw. Fritz Weber	P		(Mar17)	9Apr18	Js 44s
Flg. Paul Weiss	G			12Apr17	KIA
Oblt. Hans Wrede, C.O.	O		21Oct18	EOW	

Schutzstaffel/Schlachtstaffel 8 Airfields

From	To	Location	*Schlachtgruppe* Affiliation	*Armee*
1Jan17	(31Jan17)	Bellicourt	Escort for FA 205(A)	1
(Feb17)				7
(Mar17)		Sissonne	Escort for FA 205(A)	7
(Mar17)		St. Aquaire		7
(Apr17)				AAC
(Apr17)		Cohartille	Escort for FA 212(A)	7
(Apr17)	(May17)	Sissonne	Escort for FA 205(A)	7
(Jun17)		Marchais		7
(Jul17)	15Aug17	Mousay		7
15Aug17		Stenay	Escort for FA 249(A)	5
(Sep17)	(1Oct17)	Liesse		7
(Oct17)		St. Aquaire	Escort for FA 216(A)w	7
(Nov17)	(Feb18)	Notre Dame de Liesse	For FA 216(A)w	7
	21Mar18	Estouilly		18
21Mar18	(24Mar18)	Puisieux	SGp 1 (Ss 8,31b,36,38s) C.O. *Oblt.* Walter Lackner	18

(9Apr18)	14Apr18	Sept Fours, NW Rethonvillers	SGp 3 (Ss 6,8,18,32) C.O. *Oblt.* Kurt Messow	18
14Apr18	(25Apr18)	Sept Fours	SGp 2 (Ss 8,37,38s) C.O. *Ritt.* Herrmann	18
(3May18)	27May18	Sept Fours		18
27May18	6Jun18	Eppes	SGp A (Ss 1,8,10,14,21) C.O. *Oblt.* Emil Ziegler gen Stege	7
6Jun18	(25Jun18)	La Pavillon Ferme	SGp Staabs (Ss 1,8,10,14,21) C.O. *Oblt.* Emil Ziegler gen Stege	7
15Jul18	(29Jul18)	Eppes	SGp A (Ss 1,8,10,14,21) C.O. *Oblt.* Emil Ziegler gen Stege	7
(3Aug18)		Herin	SGp A (Ss 1,8,10,14,21) C.O. *Oblt.* Emil Ziegler gen Stege	17
	7Aug18	Eppes	SGp A (Ss 1,8,10,14,21) C.O. *Oblt.* Emil Ziegler gen Stege	7
8Aug18	9Aug18	Curchy	SGp A (Ss 1,8,10,14,21) C.O. *Oblt.* Emil Ziegler gen Stege	2
9Aug18	10Aug18	Guizancourt	SGp A (Ss 1,8,10,14,21) C.O. *Oblt.* Emil Ziegler gen Stege	18
10Aug18	11Aug18	Guizancourt	SGp A (Ss 1,8,10,14,21) C.O. *Oblt.* Emil Ziegler gen Stege	18
11Aug18	22Aug18	Eppes	SGp A (Ss 1,8,10,14,21) C.O. *Oblt.* Emil Ziegler gen Stege	7
22Aug18	25Sep18	Bouchain	SGp A (Ss 1,8,10,14) C.O. *Oblt.* Emil Ziegler gen Stege	17
25Sep18	7Oct18	Bühl	SGp A (Ss 1,8,10,14) C.O. *Oblt.* Emil Ziegler gen Stege	AAA
7Oct18	21Oct18	Croix-les-Rouveroy	SGp A (Ss 1,8,10,14,17) C.O. *Oblt.* Emil Ziegler gen Stege	2
21Oct18	EOW		SGp A (Ss 8,10,16,35) C.O. *Oblt.* Emil Ziegler gen Stege	17

Royal Prussia *Schutzstaffel 8*

1Jan17	*Schutzstaffel 8* is created from KG 5/Ks 26 by KM Nr.1425.16.g.A.7.L. of 1Jan17.
12Apr17	*Flg.* Josef Reuber, P, and *Flg.* Paul Weiss, G, are shot down at Cohartille. Weiss is KIA, Reuber is WIA and DOW 24Apr17 at Sissone.
3May17	*Uffz.* Weber-1, *Uffz.* Eisenbeisser-1, Spad 1, Ville au Bois either GC 14 C.O. Capt. R. Massenet Royer de Marancour, WIA or Esc. N.15, M.d.L. L. de Diesbach de Belleroche, WIA
20Aug17	*Vzfw.* Ernsemann-1, *Uffz.* Langer-1, Caudron, Höhe 304 Esc. C.13, Cpl. M. Chabert,KIA & Capt. A. Hubert,KIA
25Sep17	*Vzfw.* Heuser, P, is WIA,sv. and *Ltn.d.R.* Klinker, O, is OK when they are attacked by 5 Spads in the region of Monampteil and eventually crash land at La Canotte, near Mons-en-Laonois.
1Oct17	*Uffz.* Andres-1, *Vzfw.* Ritscherle-1, Spad, SE Fort Malmaison Spad S.7 #4245, Esc. N.124, Sgt. A.C. Campbell, KIA
8Nov17	*Vzfw.* Weber-2, *Vzfw.* Ritscherle-2, Spad, Prethes Thierny
11Dec17	*Offz.Stv.* Willy Fiebig and *Offz.Stv.* Daniel Frick are KIA at Notre Dame de Liesse.
23Dec17	*Vzfw.* Weber-3, *Vzfw.* Ritscherle-3, Sopwith 2, Chaillevois Esc. Sop.251, Brig. Baron,POW & Asp. Rebut,POW
21Mar18	*Flg.* Sachmann, G, is IIC,sv.
27Mar18	*Schutzstaffel 8* is renamed *Schlachtstaffel 8* by KM Nr.5126.18.A.7.L.IV.C. of 27Mar18.
12Apr18	*Uffz.* Sonnenberg-1, *Uffz.* Kutter-1, Breguet, Maignelay-Tricot Esc. Br.111,
12Apr18	*Vzfw.* Ernsemann-2, *Vzfw.* Langer-2, Spad, 17.50, Ferrières
2May18	*Uffz.* Willi Sonnenberg, P, and *Gefr.* Arthur Stolz, G, are WIA and taken POW.
3May18	*Gefr.* Haase-1, *Vzfw.* Bischoff-1, Spad S.7, 16.57, S. Gratibus Esc. Spa.84, S/Lt. O. Demeuldre, MIA
9May18	*Uffz.* Otto Kutter, G, is WIA, sv. over Montdider in a Halberstadt Cl.II. He DOW 13Jun18 in hospital at Stuttgart. *Uffz.* Schäfer, P, is OK.
27May18	*Gefr.* Hall, P, is WIA,sv. by ground fire SE of Sermpise.
30May18	*Vzwachtmstr.* Wilhelm Helmus, G, is WIA,sv. at Ploisy by ground fire. He DOW 31May18.
28Jul18	*Uffz.* Helmut Michael, P, and *Gefr.* Christain Meyer, G, are shot down and taken POW at Villers-le-Fère in a Halberstadt Cl.II.
2Sep18	*Gefr.* Meischner, P, is WIA,lt. with a bruising shot. He remains with the unit.

20Oct18	*Uffz.* Albert Dinse dies at Erquelinnes. Unknown if he is a flying or ground crew member of the unit. The date on his tombstone in the Langemark Germany Military Cemetary is 17Oct18.
Nov18	*Schlachtstaffel 8* is demobilized at *Flieger Bomben Lehr Abteilung*, Frankfurt an der Oder.

Opposite
Top: The men of *Schutzstaffel 8, Uffz.* Otto Kutter is on the far left. The man standing in the center might be the C.O. but if so, his identity is not known. Credit: Marcus Pleyer.

Bottom: Some of the men of *Schlachtstaffel 8. Uffz.* Otto Kutter, G, is standing on the far left. The man seated in the middle might be the C.O., *Oblt.* Kurt Messow, as he appears to be wearing at his neck the Knight's Cross of the St. Heinrich Order awarded from Saxony, but confirmation is lacking. Photo credit: Marcus Pleyer.

Right: The victory of *Uffz.* Kurt Andres and *Vzfw.* Karl Ritscherle, *Schusta 8*, on 1 October 1917. Their victim was the American pilot *Sgt.* Andrew Courtney Campbell of the *Lafayette Escadrille, N.124*.

Ltn.d.R. Karl Ritscherle wearing both a pilot's and a gunner's badge. No doubt this is a post-war photograph. Ritscherle, as a *Vzfw.*, served as a gunner in *Schutzstaffel 8* from 16 April 1917 to 7 January 1918, gaining three confirmed victories with the unit.

Uffz. Otto Kutter, a gunner with *Schlasta 8*, peering into the gunner's cockpit of a Breguet 14B2 from *Escadrille Br.107*. Kutter did not down this particular aircraft but he did claim a Breguet on April 12, 1918.

An Albatros C.V and an unknown crew of *Schusta 8*. Photo credit: Marcus Pleyer.

Royal Prussian *Schutzstaffel 9*

Pilot/Gunner	Type	From		To	
		Unit	Date	Date	Unit
Pion. Bruno Allert	G	Ss 26b	27Apr18	10May18	Ss 26b
Gefr. Archut	G	AFP 4	(Jun18)		
Flg. Bahrdt	G	FA 213A	19Jun18		
Uffz. Otto Bandel				2May17	KIA
Flg. Becker				25Apr18	WIA
Uffz. Beilicke		AFP 4	18Oct17		
Vzfw. Boehme	G		(Mar17)		
Ltn.d.R. Heinrich Bongartz	P	KG 5/27	1Jan17	11Mar17	Js 36
Uffz. Brandstetter	G	AFP 4	24Aug18	28Aug18	AFP 4
Uffz. Brandstetter	G	AFP 4	3Oct18		
Gefr. Brockjan	P			24Aug18	FTL,IIC
Gefr. Brunnel	P	AFP 4	14Jun18	3Aug18	ArtKodo
Uffz. Dannemann	P			13Oct17	FEA 1
Ltn. Hans Heinrich Deetjen, C.O.	O	FA 284A	Mar18	28Mar18	WIA,KIC
Gefr. Franz Dutkowski	G	AFP 4	1Jun18	12Jun18	AFP 4
Flg. Eichel	G	AFP 4	15Aug18	28Aug18	AFP 4
Vzfw. Wilhelm Erlewein	P		(Jan18)		JsSch I
Flg. Füssgen	G	FA 8	(May18)	19Jun18	FA 8
Gefr. Füssgen	G	FA 256A	3Aug18	23Aug18	IIC,sv.
Vzfw. Hermann Geissler	P	AFP 4	15Oct17	24Mar18	KIA
Gefr. Gotthardt	G	AFP 4	24Aug18		
Gefr. Grimm	G			19Jun18	FA 213A
Oblt.d.R. Otto Hafner, OzbV	O	FA 225A	27May18	31May18	Ss 2
Oblt. Friedrich-Carl Hanesse, C.O.	P	FA 225A	1Apr18	31May18	Ss 2
Uffz. Hennies	P	AFP 4	15Oct17		
Flg. Friedrich Hupp	P			11Jul17	KIC
Vzfw. Keicher	P		(Apr18)	18Aug18	IIC
Vzfw. Klempien	G			19Jul17	WIA,lt.
Vzfw. Klempien	G		19Jul17	15Aug17	WIA
Gefr. Klopfer	G	FA 8	16Jun18		
Oblt. Wilhelm Köckler, C.O.	O	AFP 5	15Oct17	1Jan18	FEA 10
Uffz. Otto Köhler			26Feb18		
Hptm. Komorowski, C.O.	P			12Oct17	FEA 11
Uffz. Georg Kratz	G			11Jul17	KIC
Oblt.d.R. Lantzius, C.O.	O	Namur	('18)		
Ltn.d.R. Lebrecht, OzbV	P	Js 7	17Jun18	20Aug18	Js 7
Vzfw. Franz Mann	P			28Mar18	WIA,KIC
Ltn.d.R. Theodor Mayer	P	KG 5/27	1Jan17	16Apr17	AFP 3
Vzfw. Willy Michaelis				2May17	KIA
Flg. Okerk	P			23Aug18	IIC,sv.
Gefr. Ollesch	P	AFP 4	(Jun18)		
Oblt. Curt Pflugbeil, C.O.	P	KG 5/27	1Jan17	20Jun17	KG 4/23
Vzfw. Pietsch	G			31May18	AFP 4
Vzfw. Pohland	G	AFP 4	18Oct17	10Nov17	AFP 4
Vzfw. Ractsch	P	KG 5/27	1Jan17		
Uffz. Georg Rohde	G	Ss 28b	19Oct17		
Vzfw. Georg Salzmann	G			24Mar18	KIA
Uffz. Schad	P	FA 13	27Apr18		
Ltn.d.R. Albert Schade, OzbV	P	Idflieg	15Aug18		
Uffz. Karl Scheerer	G	AFP 4	27Apr18	15Aug18	FA 250A
Oblt.d.R. Hermann Schulz, C.O.	O		Jun18	EOW	
Uffz. Schulz	G	KG 5/27	1Jan17		
Vzfw. Schumacher	G		(Apr18)	17Apr18	WIA
Vzfw. Kurt Skerath	G	AFP 4	18Oct17		FEA 12
Vzfw. Karl Stapel	P			23Feb18	KIC
Ltn.d.R. Stephan, OzbV	O	AFP 4	20Aug18	26Aug18	Ss 16
Flg. Stössel	P	AFP 4	28Aug18		
Gefr. Stryzewski	P			8Jun18	JSch II
Gefr. Stryzewski	P	JSch II	28Jun18	19Aug18	WIA

Uffz. Oskar Traulsen	G	AFP 4	12Nov17	23Feb18	KIC
Gefr. Uckert	P	Ss 12	3Aug18		
Gefr. Wolfgramm	P	AFP 4	28Aug18		

Schutzstaffel/Schlachtstaffel 9 Airfields

From	To	Location	*Schlachtgruppe* Affiliation	*Armee*
1Jan17		Vendhuille	Escort for FA 237(A)	1
(31Jan17)	Feb17	Mörchingen	Escort for FA 228(A)	AAA
Feb17	16Apr17	St. Loup	Escort for FA 245(A)	3
16Apr17	19Jun17	St. Loup	Escort for FA 245(A)	1
19Jun17	(15Aug17)	Ascq by Lille		6
6Sep17	27Oct17	Ascq by Lille	Escort for FA 240(A)	6
27Oct17	24Nov17	Ingelmunster	Escort for FA 238(A)	4
24Nov17	(23Feb18)	Faumont Süd	Escort for FA 235(A), 244(A)s	6
10Mar18	21Mar18	Neuville sur l'Escaut	Escort for FA 235(A)	6
21Mar18	25Mar18	Dorignies	SGp C (Ss 3,9,16) C.O. *Oblt.* Hermann Ramdohr	17
25Mar18	28Mar18	Epinoy	SGp C (Ss 3,9,16) C.O. *Oblt.* Hermann Ramdohr	17
28Mar18	9Apr18	Pont de la Deule	SGp C (Ss 3,9,16) C.O. *Oblt.* Hermann Ramdohr	17
9Apr18	12Apr18	Houplin	SGp C (Ss 9,21) C.O. *Oblt.* Friedrich-Carl Hanesse	6
12Apr18	18Apr18	Linselles	SGp D (Ss 9,12,16,24b) C.O. *Oblt.* Johannes Missfelder	4
18Apr18	30Apr18	Linselles	SGp D (Ss 9,12,16,24b,25b) C.O. *Oblt.* Johannes Missfelder	4
30Apr18	(9Jun18)	Linselles	SGp D (Ss 9,12,16,24b) C.O. *Oblt.* Johannes Missfelder	4
15Jul18		Linselles	SGp D (Ss 9,16) C.O. *Oblt.d.R.* Hermann Schulz	4
(29Jul18)		Linselles	SGp D (Ss 9,12,16) C.O. *Oblt.d.R.* Hermann Schulz	4
(7Aug18)	22Aug18	Linselles	SGp D (Ss 9,16) C.O. *Oblt.d.R.* Hermann Schulz	4
22Aug18	24Sep18	Abscon	SGp 2 (Ss 9,11,27b) C.O. *Hptm.* Erich Sonntag	17
24Sep18	7Oct18	Masny Süd	SGp S (Ss 9,11,27b) C.O. *Hptm.* Hugo Weingarth	17
7Oct18	13Oct18	Oudenaarde	SGp J (Ss 9,16,24b,25b) C.O. *Oblt.* Friedrich von Krausser	4
13Oct18	23Oct18	Oudenaarde	SGp J (Ss 9,24b,25b) C.O. *Oblt.* Friedrich von Krausser	4
23Oct18	EOW	Deinze	SGp J (Ss 9,24b,25b) C.O. *Oblt.* Friedrich von Krausser	4

Royal Prussian *Schutzstaffel 9*

1Jan17	*Schutzstaffel 9* is created from KG 5/Ks 27 by KM Nr.1425.16.g.A.7.L. of 1Jan17.
21Mar17	*Uffz.* Theodor Mayer, P, and *Vzfw.* Boehme, G, are forced to land, unharmed, following air combat.
2May17	*Uffz.* Otto Bandel and *Vzfw.* Willy Michaelis are KIA over Reims.
11Jul17	*Flg.* Friedrich Hupp, P, and *Uffz.* Georg Kratz, G, are KIC at Cuincy by Douai in LVG C.IV 4362/15.
19Jul17	*Vzfw.* Klempien, G, is WIA,lt. remains with the unit.
15Aug17	*Vzfw.* Klempien, G, is WIA by ground fire and to hospital.
23Feb18	*Vzfw.* Karl Stapel, P, and *Uffz.* Oskar Traulsen, G, are KIC at Rosières, St. Amand.
24Mar18	*Vzfw.* Hermann Geissler, P, and *Vzfw.* Georg Salzmann, G, are KIA at Évin by Leforest.
27Mar18	*Schutzstaffel 9* is renamed *Schlachtstaffel 9* by KM Nr.5126.18.A.7.L.IV.C. of 27Mar18.
28Mar18	*Vzfw.* Franz Mann, P, and *Ltn.* Hans Heinrich Deetjen, O and CO, are WIA and then subsequently KIC on their airfield at Pont de la Deule.
17Apr18	*Vzfw.* Keicher-1, *Vzfw.* Schumacher-1, Sopwith D.D, Pardelles

17Apr18	*Vzfw*. Schumacher, G, is WIA over Pardelles in this combat.
25Apr18	*Flg*. Becker is WIA.
18Aug18	*Vzfw*. Keicher, P, is IIC in a crash landing and to hospital.
19Aug18	*Gefr*. Stryzewski, P, is WIA during air combat, shot in the left thigh, and to hospital.
23Aug18	*Flg*. Okerk, P, and *Gefr*. Füssgen, G, are IIC,sv.
24Aug18	*Gefr*. Brockjan, P, is IIC,lt. during a forced landing.
Nov18	*Schlachtstaffel 9* is demobilized at FEA 14, Halle a.d. Salle.

Above: A Halberstadt Cl.II of *Schlasta 9*, indentified by the white/black/white fuselage band, crashed in a shell hole. Details are lacking.

Below: A derelict Halberstadt Cl.II fuselage from *Schlasta 9*. The unit marking was a white/black/white fuselage band which is clearly seen.

Royal Prussian *Schutzstaffel 10*

Pilot/Gunner	Type	From		To	
		Unit	Date	Date	Unit
Vzfw. Bauschke	P		(May17)	18Nov17	AFP 13
Uffz. August Beckedorf	G	Ss 24b	9Oct17	26Aug18	Leave
Uffz. August Beckedorf	G	Leave		8Sep18	EOW
Ltn.d.R. Wilhelm Becker	P		(May18)	10Jun18	IIC,lt.
Ltn.d.R. Behne	O			27Oct17	AFP 4
Flg. Biegelsack	G	AFP 4	27Oct17		
Vzfw. Binnewald	P		(May18)	(Aug18)	
Flg. Felix Bockenmühl	G			2May17	KIA
Vzfw. Brandner	G	AFP 4	21Sep17	13Nov17	FEA 12
Vzfw. Walter Richard Braun	P	KG 5/28	1Jan17	29Aug17	AFP 4
Vzfw. Bulla	G			30Oct17	FEA 12
Oblt.d.R. Wilfried Eberhard *Frhr.* von Cornberg, C.O.	O			21Oct18	EOW
Vzfw. Dehne	G		(Jul17)	27Oct17	AFP 4
Gefr. Adolf Döll	P			19Jul18	WIA,sv.
Uffz. Eydner	P	AFP 4	27Sep17		
Gefr. Fischbach	P	FA 13	20Apr18		
Vzfw. Kurt Gerschel	P			29Dec17	KIA
Uffz. Gilger	P		(Jan18)		
Flg. Albert Karzmarek	G			22Apr17	KIA
Vzfw. Wienand Kerzmann	P		(Jul17)	15Sep17	FA 40
Gefr. Heinrich Kielmann				21Jul18	KIA
Uffz. Gustav Krause	P	AFP 6	3Jul17	9Dec17	AFP 2
Uffz. Latzig				8Aug18	WIA,lt.
Uffz. Lehnert	G	AFP 4	27Oct17	29Dec17	POW
Oblt. Lerche, C.O.	O		11Mar18	Apr18	
Uffz. Liebnitz	G	AFP 4	7Oct17	19Jul18	WIA,sv.
Uffz. Heinrich Lins	G		(May18)	14Sep18	KIA
Flg. August Lüders				12Nov18	+ i.Kr.
Uffz. Hermann Märzhäuser	P	AFP 4	16Sep17	(Dec17)	FEA 2
Ltn. Hans-Georg von der Marwitz	P	KG 5/28	1Jan17	Mar17	JsSch I
Vzfw. Friedrich Matthies	P	KG 5/28	1Jan17	3Jan17	AFP 5
Uffz. Mau	P	AFP 4	1Sep17	14Sep17	Ss 21
Uffz. Mau	P	Ss 21	15Sep17	24Sep17	AFP 4
Gefr. Paul Meinke	G	AFP 4	21Sep17	1Dec17	KIA
Vzfw. Georg Münch	G		(Apr17)		FEA 7
Gefr. Franz Müller (DOW 26Oct18)				23Oct18	WIA,sv.
Uffz. Ernst Noerthen	G		(May17)	(Dec17)	
Uffz. Horst Rath	P		(Apr17)		
Ltn. Rath, Stv. C.O.	P	FA 217A	18Nov17	10Dec17	Ss 25b
Ltn. Rath	P	Ss 25b	17Dec17	Jan18	AFP 2
Uffz. Artur Roesler	G		(May17)	3Nov17	KIA
Uffz. Satajek	G		(Jan18)		
Uffz. Felix Schilf	P		(Jan17)	2May17	KIA
Vzfw. Alfred Schmidt	P	AFP 4	2Oct17	24Oct17	Ss 16
Ltn.d.R. Wilhelm Schmohl	O	AFP 4	23Apr18	25May18	AFS II
Flg. Karl Schott	G			Oct17	AFP 4
Ltn.d.R. Ferdinand Schulz	P		(Nov17)		
Uffz. Karl Schulz	P			22Apr17	KIA
Gefr. Kurt Seidel	P		(May17)	2Oct17	AFP 4
Uffz. Slotha	G	Ss 4	27Oct17	28Jul18	WIA
Vzfw. Speer	P			30Apr18	POW
Ltn. Trippmacher	O	KG 5/28	1Jan17	May17	KG 2/11
Hptm. Uma, C.O.			Apr18	May18	
Vzfw. Max Willmann	P	AFP 4	23Oct17	(Dec17)	
Hptm. Paul von Winckler, C.O.	P			18Nov17	FA 217A
Hptm. Paul von Winckler, C.O.	P	FA 217A	Jan18		
Uffz. Konstantin Winkler	P	AFP 2	19Dec17	28May18	WIA
Ltn. Karl Winsloe, C.O.	O	BG 3/13	21May18	28May18	KIA

Gefr. Robert Wirth	P		(Sep17)	20Apr18	JsSch I
Oblt. Heinz-Hellmuth von Wühlisch, C.O.	P	FA 32	10Dec17	23Jan18	AFP 2
Vzfw. Adolf Wucherer	G	Ss 7	13Nov17	17Nov17	AFP 4

Schutzstaffel/Schlachtstaffel 10 Airfields

From	To	Location	*Schlachtgruppe* Affiliation	*Armee*
1Jan17	(31Jan17)	Gouy	Escort for FA 286(A)b	1
(Feb17)	27Jun17	Ebouleau	Escort for FA 201(A)	7
27Jun17	20Jul17	Ascq by Lille		6
20Jul17	18Sep17	Aertrycke	Escort for FA 231(A)	4
18Sep17	15Nov17	Ichteghem	Escort for FA 217(A)	4
15Nov17	(10Dec17)	Escaufourt	Escort for FA 32, 217(A)	2
(Jan18)	(11Mar18)	Bertry	Escort for FA 32, 217(A)	2
(21Mar18)		Escaufourt	SGp A (Ss 10,17,22b) C.O. *Hptm.* Zimmermann	2
(9Apr18)		Caix	SGp A (Ss 10,17,22b) C.O. *Hptm.* Zimmermann	2
(12Apr18)		Heule	SGp B (Ss 10,23b,26b,30b) C.O. *Oblt.d.R.* August Ertl	4
24Apr18	17May18	Bisseghem	SGp B (Ss 10,23b,26b,30b) C.O. *Oblt.d.R.* August Ertl	4
(27May18)		Eppes	SGp A (Ss 1,8,10,14,21) C.O. *Oblt.* Emil Ziegler gen Stege	7
(6Jun18)	(25Jun18)	La Pavillon Ferme	SGp Staabs (Ss 1,8,10,14,21) C.O. *Oblt.* Emil Ziegler gen Stege	7
15Jul18	(29Jul18)	Eppes	SGp A (Ss 1,8,10,14,21) C.O. *Oblt.* Emil Ziegler gen Stege	7
(3Aug18)		Aubry	SGp A (Ss 1,8,10,14,21) C.O. *Oblt.* Emil Ziegler gen Stege	17
7Aug18	8Aug18	Eppes	SGp A (Ss 1,8,10,14,21) C.O. *Oblt.* Emil Ziegler gen Stege	7
8Aug18	9Aug18	Curchy	SGp A (Ss 1,8,10,14,21) C.O. *Oblt.* Emil Ziegler gen Stege	2
9Aug18	10Aug18	Guizancourt	SGp A (Ss 1,8,10,14,21) C.O. *Oblt.* Emil Ziegler gen Stege	18
10Aug18	11Aug18	Guizancourt	SGp A (Ss 1,8,10,14) C.O. *Oblt.* Emil Ziegler gen Stege	18
11Aug18	22Aug18	Eppes	SGp A (Ss 1,8,10,14,21) C.O. *Oblt.* Emil Ziegler gen Stege	7
22Aug18	25Sep18	Bouchain	SGp A (Ss 1,8,10,14) C.O. *Oblt.* Emil Ziegler gen Stege	17
25Sep18	7Oct18	Bühl	SGp A (Ss 1,8,10,14) C.O. *Oblt.* Emil Ziegler gen Stege	AAA
7Oct18	21Oct18	Croix-les-Rouveroy	SGp A (Ss 1,8,10,14,17) C.O. *Oblt.* Emil Ziegler gen Stege	2
21Oct18	EOW		SGp A (Ss 8,10,16,35) C.O. *Oblt.* Emil Ziegler gen Stege	17

Royal Prussian *Schutzstaffel 10*

1Jan17	*Schutzstaffel 10* is created from KG 5/Ks 28 by KM Nr.1425.16.g.A.7.L. of 1Jan17.
5Jan17	*Ltn.* von der Marwitz-1, Farman, by Hospital Ferme, Nähe Bouchavesnes Esc. F.218, Lt. de Joyet, WIA
25Jan17	*Ltn.* Trippmacher-1, *Uffz.* Schlif-1, Vikers D.D., Combles
15Apr17	*Uffz.* Rath-1, *Gefr.* Münch-1, Farman, by Oulcher Wood Esc. F.71, M.d.L. A. Wang, WIA
22Apr17	*Uffz.* Karl Schulz, P, and *Flg.* Albert Karzmarek, G, are KIA over Oulcher Wood at 18.30 hours.
2May17	*Uffz.* Felix Schilf, P, and *Flg.* Felix Bockenmühl, G, are KIA over Ailles at 20.35 hours.
25May17	*Flg.* Bauschke-1, *Uffz.* Roesler-1, Spad, E. Craonne

27May17	*Flg*. Seidel-1, *Gefr*. Noerthen-1, Spad, zw. Craonne & Winterberg
16Jun17	*Gefr*. Seidel-2, *Uffz*. Roesler-2, Spad, Jumigny, Aisne Spad S.7, Esc. N.23, Lt. A. Laplace, KIA
7Jul17	*Vzfw*. Kerzmann-1, *Vzfw*. Dehne-1, Sopwith 1, Bullecourt Pup #N.6462, Naval 9, F/S/Lt. J.C. Tanner, DOI
6Sep17	*Uffz*. Seidel-3, *Uffz*. Roesler-3, Sopwith, 8.50, N. Woestin
23Sep17	*Gefr*. Wirth-1, *Uffz*. Noerthen-2, Sopwith, Boesinghe S.E.5a, #B.557, 60 Sqn. RFC, 2/AM H.H. Bright, KIA
23Sep17	*Gefr*. Wirth-2, *Uffz*. Noerthen-3, Sopwith, Pypegaale
3Nov17	*Uffz*. Artur Roesler, G, is KIA by ground fire over Dickebusch.
1Dec17	*Gefr*. Paul Meinke, G, is KIA over Ossus-Wals, Vendhuille.
18Dec17	*Uffz*. Märzhäuser-1, *Gefr*. Beckedorf-1 a/c, W. Hesbécourt
23Dec17	*Vzfw*. Willmann-1, *Uffz*. Noerthen-4, Spad 1, 14.30, S. St. Emilie Spad S.7, Esc. Spa.65, Brig. Augier, WIA
29Dec17	*Vzfw*. Kurt Gerschel, P, is KIA and *Uffz*. Lehnert, G, is taken POW at Gonnelieu in an LVG C during air combat.
28Jan18	*Uffz*. Gilger-1, *Uffz*. Satajek-1, Sopw. Camel, 13.30, Hargicourt
10Mar18	*Uffz*. Hermann Märzhäuser, P, is KIC at Konitz, West Prussia on a practice flight while at FEA 2, Schneidemühl.
27Mar18	*Schutzstaffel 10* is renamed *Schlachtstaffel 10* by KM Nr. 5126.18.A.7.L.IV.C. of 27 Mar18.
30Apr18	*Vzfw*. Speer, P, is taken POW and *Flg*. Anton Zimmermann, G, Schlasta 28b, is WIA and and taken POW at Dickebusch following air combat in a Halberstadt Cl.II. Zimmermann DOW 1May18.
27May18	*Uffz*. Binnewald-1, *Gefr*. Lins-1, Salmson, Serches
27May18	*Uffz*. Binnewald-2, *Gefr*. Lins-2, Balloon
28May18	*Uffz*. Konstantin Winkler, P, is WIA and *Ltn*. Karl Winsloe, O and C.O., is KIA over Arcy-St. Restitue by ground fire.
10Jun18	*Ltn.d.R*. Wilhelm Becker, P, is IIC,lt.
19Jul18	*Gefr*. Adolf Döll, P, and *Uffz*. Liebnitz, G, are WIA,sv. in air combat.
21Jul18	*Gefr*. Heinrich Kielmann is KIA over Mont de Soissons.
28Jul18	*Uffz*. Slotha, G, is WIA by ground fire.
8Aug18	*Uffz*. Latzig is WIA,lt. during air combat over Rosières in a Hannover Cl.III.
14Sep18	*Uffz*. Heinrich Lins, G, is KIA over Maubeuge.
23Oct18	*Gefr*. Franz Müller is severely WIA over Preux aux Bois. He DOW on 26Oct18 at Maurieux.
12Nov18	*Flg*. August Lüders dies at Namur. Unknown if he was a flight member or ground staff.
Nov18	*Schlachtstaffel 10* is demobilized at *Flieger Bomben Lehr Abteilung*, Frankfurt an der Oder.

The crews of *Schutzstaffel 10* at Escaufourt on 10 December 1917. The aircraft is a Haberstadt Cl.II. Note the captured Lewis machine gun installed on the upper wing. Photo credit: Tobias Weber.

Royal Prussian *Schutzstaffel 11*

Pilot/Gunner	Type	From		To	
		Unit	Date	Date	Unit
Ltn.d.R. Hermann Becker	P	KG 5/29	1Jan17	18May17	Js 12
Uffz. Becker	P	AFP 4	10Nov17	(Sep18)	
Vzfw. Fritz Beckhardt	P	AFP 4	14Nov17	2Feb18	JSch II
Uffz. Behrendt	G			11Mar18	Idflieg
Uffz. Berberich	P		(Aug18)		
Uffz. Büttrich	G			(Sep18)	
Uffz. Johann Brosius	P			21Apr17	POW
Uffz. Cossmann	G		(Aug17)	15Sep17	AFP 4
Vzfw. Cziesla	G		(Jun17)	(Aug18)	
Uffz. Paul Dahms	P	AFP 4	28Sep17	14Oct17	KIC
Uffz. Paul Dorn	P	FA 263A	(Aug17)	29Aug17	AFP 4
Uffz. Paul Dorn	P	JsSch I		12May18	KIA
Vzfw. Wilhelm Elschenbroich	G		(Aug17)	12Apr18	KIA
Sgt. Hans Engel	G			23Apr18	KIA
Flg. Hermann Fischer	G	AFP 4	2Dec17	(Feb18)	
Uffz. Paul Frank	G	Ss 25b	11Sep17		
Uffz. Garnitz	P		(Aug18)		
Uffz. Georg Gruber	P		4Apr17	25May17	WIA,lt.
Uffz. Georg Gruber	P		25May17	13Nov17	KG 2/7
Gefr. Hegger	G		(May17)	5Jun17	WIA,lt.
Vzfw. Johann Heidingsfelder	P	FA 292A	Jan18		FA 292A
Hptm. Heinecke, C.O.	O	AFP 5	19Oct17	28Jan18	FA 45b
Hptm. Heinecke, C.O.	O	FA 45b	2Feb18	4Apr18	
Vzfw. Ernst Henze	P			23Apr18	KIA
Gefr. Walter Herzberg	P	FA 288A		5May17	WIA
Ltn. Martin Heydrich	O	KG 5/29	1Jan17	24Jul17	
Uffz. Emil Holland	G			12May18	KIA
Ltn. Hans-Jürgen Horn	O	KG 5/29	1Jan17	Mar17	FEA 2
Gefr. Jaster	G	AFP 4	21Sep17	21Dec17	BG 1
Gefr. Ernst Jostmeier	G	Ss 23b	9Oct17	21Dec17	BG 1/1
Uffz. Max Wilhelm Kahlhorn	G	Ss 23b	21Sep17	14Oct17	IIC,lt.
Uffz. Max Wilhelm Kahlhorn	G		14Oct17	20Oct17	IIC,lt.
Uffz. Max Wilhelm Kahlhorn	G		20Oct17	7Nov17	KIC
Uffz. Max Kandler	G			10May17	KIA
Flg. Kieckhöfer	G	AFP 4	2Dec17	13Feb18	AFP 4
Uffz. Klebba	G			22Jan18	IIC
Vzfw. Klütz	G	AFP 4	12Aug17	(Dec17)	
Ltn.d.R. Köhler	O			21Apr17	POW
Gefr. Koehling	G	AFP 4	2Dec17	3Jan18	BG 4
Ltn. Caspar Kulenkampff-Post, C.O.	P	FA 261A	4Apr18	1Jun18	Leave
Oblt. Caspar Kulenkampff-Post, C.O.	P	Leave	8Jun18	20Jun18	KIC
Gefr. Leininger	P	AFP 4	25Oct17	30Nov17	FEA 1
Ltn. Eduard Lortz, C.O.	O		(Feb17)	11Feb17	KIA
Offz.Stv. Josef Mai	P	KG 5/29	1Jan17	21Mar17	Jasta 5
Gefr. Mellen	G	AFP 4	23Dec17	8Mar18	AFP 4
Vzfw. Eduard Müller	P		(Aug17)	12Apr18	KIA
Uffz. Hugo Müller	G			14Jun17	Int.
Uffz. Müller	P	AFP 3	17Feb18	27Aug18	WIA,sv.
Vzfw. Nettesheim	G	AFP 4	21Sep17	26Nov17	FEA 12
Vzfw. Ohlf	P	AFP 4	2Dec17	(Jan18)	
Vzfw. Franz-Joseph Ophaus	P	KG 5/29	1Jan17	EOW	
Flg. von Paczynsky	P	AFP 4	29Jan18	15Mar18	FA 221A
Oblt. von Petersdorff					
Flg. Wladsilaus Pockladerki	G			20Jun18	KIC
Gefr. August Raschke	P			14Jun17	Int.
Vzfw. Rebbe	P		(May17)	12Nov17	JsSch I
Uffz. Georg Reichel	P	AFP 4	2Dec17	31Dec17	Intrnd
Ltn. Rompe, OzbV	O	AFP 2	16May18	(Jun18)	
Gefr. Scharfenberg	G	AFP 4	10Jan18	8Mar18	AFP 4

Uffz. Wilhelm Scheffel	P			10May17	KIA
Vzfw. Arnold Scheibchen	G		(Aug18)	EOW	
Ltn.d.R. Julius Schmidt	P	KG 5/29	1Jan17	20Apr17	Js 3
Vzfw. Friedrich August Schönmann	P	Ss 23b	14Oct17	29Mar18	JsSch I
Oblt. Schulte, C.O.		Ss 15	2Oct18	EOW	
Vzfw. Schulz	P	AFP 4	10Sep17	18Sep17	AFP 4
Ltn. Horst-Jörg von Schulz	P	KG 5/29	1Jan17		
Uffz. Fritz Simon	P	Ss 30b	13Oct17	25Oct17	AFP 4
Oblt. Walter Sommé, C.O.	P	Ss 5	Mar17	19Oct17	KG 2/7
Hptm. Erich Sonntag, C.O.	O	SGp 1	21Jun18	1Oct18	KIA
Uffz. Stanischewski	P	AFP 4	2Feb18	17Feb18	AFP 3
Uffz. Stenz	P			2Dec17	AFP 4
Uffz. Stückmann	P	AFP 4	15Oct17	20Oct17	IIC,lt.
Uffz. Stückmann	P		20Oct17	7Nov17	IIC,lt.
Gefr. Guido Thalheim	P	AFP 4	13Jan18	22Jan18	KIC
Vzfw. Gilbert Wagner	P		(Aug17)	19Dec17	JSch II
Gefr. Wilhelm Walter	P	AFP 4	(Aug17)	10Sep17	AFP 4
Gefr. Weiss	P	AFP 4	18Sep17	(Sep18)	
Vzfw. Willy Wenck	P	Ss 4	4Sep17	9Sep17	Ss 4
Vzfw. Adolf Wucherer	G	AFP 4	10Jan18	8Mar18	AFP 4
Vzfw. Adolf Wucherer	G	AFP 4	11Mar18	Apr18	Schwrin
Offz.Stv. Zander	G	AFP 4	31Jan18	(Sep18)	
Ritt. Jürgen *Frhr.* von Zobel zu Giebelstadt, C.O.	O	KG 5/29	1Jan17		
Uffz. Zwick	G			27Aug18	WIA,sv.
Gefr. Zwientak	G		(Mar17)	5Sep17	FEA 12

Schutzstaffel/Schlachtstaffel 11 Airfields

From	To	Location	*Schlachtgruppe* Affiliation	*Armee*
1Jan17	(31Jan17)	Bonne Enfance Ferme	For FA 221(A)	1
(Feb17)	21Mar17	Montauban, Albert	Escort for FA 221(A)	1
21Mar17	(Apr17)	Cantin	Escort for FA 264(A)	6
(27May17)	9Jun17	Corbehem	Escort for FA 264(A)	6
9Jun17	3Aug17	Eeghem	Escort for FA 45b	4
3Aug17	3Sep17	Vlisseghem	Escort for FA 45b	4
3Sep17	(9Sep17)	Engel	Escort for FA 45b	4
(Oct17)	7Oct17	St. Aquaire		7
7Oct17	1Mar18	Eeghem	Escort for FA 45b	4
(7Mar18)	(21Mar18)	Inchy	SGp C (Ss 11,30b) C.O. *Hptm.* Heinecke	2
4Apr18	9Apr18	Haplincourt	SGp B (Ss 4,11,15) C.O. *Ritt.d.R.* Herrmann	2
9Apr18	19Apr18	Herbécourt	SGp B (Ss 4,11,15) C.O. *Ritt.d.R.* Herrmann	2
19Apr18	12May18	Haplincourt	SGp A (Ss 4,11,15,17,22b) C.O. *Hptm.* Zimmermann	2
12May18	9Jun18	Haplincourt	SGp 1 (Ss 4,11,15,17) C.O. *Hptm.* Zimmermann	2
9Jun18	9Jun18	Curchy	SGp 1 (Ss 4,11,15,17) C.O. *Hptm.* Erich Sonntag	18
9Jun18	11Jun18	Haplincourt	SGp 1 (Ss 4,11,15,17) C.O. *Hptm.* Erich Sonntag	2
11Jun18	12Jun18	Curchy	SGp 1 (Ss 4,11,15,17) C.O. *Hptm.* Erich Sonntag	18
12Jun18	10Jul18	Haplincourt	SGp 1 (Ss 4,11,15,17) C.O. *Hptm.* Erich Sonntag	2
10Jul18	8Aug18	Abscon	SGp 2 (Ss 11,27b) C.O. *Hptm.* Erich Sonntag	17
8Aug18	8Aug18	Nurlu	SGp 2 (Ss 11,27b) C.O. *Hptm.* Erich Sonntag	2
8Aug18	9Aug18	Abscon	SGp 2 (Ss 11,27b) C.O. *Hptm.* Erich Sonntag	17

9Aug18	12Aug18	Nurlu	SGp 2 (Ss 11,13,19,27b) C.O. *Hptm.* Erich Sonntag	2
12Aug18	22Aug18	Abscon	SGp 2 (Ss 11,27b) C.O. *Hptm.* Erich Sonntag	17
22Aug18	24Sep18	Abscon	SGp 2 (Ss 9,11,27b) C.O. *Hptm.* Erich Sonntag	17
24Sep18	3Oct18	Abscon	SGp S (Ss 9,11,27b) C.O. *Hptm.* Hugo Weingarth	17
3Oct18	5Oct18	Abscon	SGp S (Ss 4,11,15,27b) C.O. *Hptm.* Hugo Weingarth	17
5Oct18	13Oct18	Marly	SGp S (Ss 4,11,15,27b,35) C.O. *Hptm.* Hugo Weingarth	17
13Oct18	18Oct18	Nouvelles	SGp S (Ss 4,11,15,27b) C.O. *Hptm.* Hugo Weingarth	17
18Oct18	EOW	NW St. Simphorien	SGp S (Ss 4,11,15,27b) C.O. *Hptm.* Hugo Weingarth	17

Royal Prussian *Schutzstaffel 11*

1Jan17 *Schutzstaffel 11* is created from KG 5/Ks 29 by KM Nr.1425.16.g.A.7.L. of 1Jan17.

11Feb17 *Ltn.* Eduard Lortz, O and C.O., is KIA over Montauben, Albert.

6Mar17 *Gefr.* Ophaus-1, *Gefr.* Zweintak-1, B.E. 2e, by Morval
#5823, 52 Sqn. RFC, Lt. J.W. Lockhart,WIA & 2/Lt. G.K. Walker,OK

21Apr17 *Uffz.* Johann Brosius, P, and *Ltn.d.R.* Köhler, O, are shot down and taken POW while on a bombing mission.

5May17 *Gefr.* Walter Herzberg, P, is WIA.

10May17 *Uffz.* Wilhelm Scheffel, P, and *Uffz.* Max Kandler, G, are KIA over Sailly en Ostrevent during air combat in Albatros C.VII 1360/16.

25May17 *Uffz.* Georg Gruber, P, is WIA,lt. during air combat.

27May17 *Vzfw.* Rebbe-1, *Flg.* Hegger-1, Engl. 1, 7.20, by Corbehem
SE 5 #A.4868, 56 Sqn. RFC, 2/Lt. A.P.F. Rhy Davids, FTL, OK

5Jun17 *Uffz.* Ophaus-n/c, *Uffz.* Cziesla-n/c, Sopwith 1, Tilloy

5Jun17 *Gefr.* Hegger, G, is lightly WIA during air combat.

14Jun17 *Gefr.* August Raschke, P, and *Uffz.* Hugo Müller, G, in DFW C.V (Av) 5928/16 become disoriented and make a good landing near Axel, Holland at about 14.15 hours. They are interned.

12Aug17 *Gefr.* Walter-1, *Vzfw.* Klütz-1, Nieup. 1, 8.50, Houthoulster Wood
Spad S.7 #B.1660, 19 Sqn. RFC, 2/Lt. A.A.N.D. Pentland,shotup,OK

17Aug17 *Uffz.* Dorn-1, *Uffz.* Cossmann-1, Sopwith, Houthoulster Wood
Pup #B.1732, 66 Sqn. RFC, 2/Lt. P.A. O'Brien, POW

18Aug17 *Gefr.* Müller-1, *Uffz.* Elschenbroich-1, Sopwith, Hazebrock
S.E. 5a #B.517, 56 Sqn RFC, Capt. H.M. Rushworth, WIA, POW

14Oct17 *Uffz.* Paul Dahms, P, is KIC and *Uffz.* Max Kahlhorn, G, is IIC,lt. during a landing at Eeghem airfield.

20Oct17 *Uffz.* Stückmann, P, and *Uffz.* Max Kahlhorn, G, are IIC,lt. during a landing at Eeghem.

7Nov17 *Uffz.* Stückmann, P, is IIC,lt. and *Uffz.* Max Kahlhorn, G, is KIC at Westroosebeke making a forced landing.

11Nov17 *Uffz.* Müller-2, *Uffz.* Elschenbroich-2, RE 8, 8.30, E. St. Julien
52 Sqn. RFC, Lt. B. Head, WIA

31Dec17 *Uffz.* Georg Reichel, P, is forced to land in Halberstadt Cl.II 6315/17 at Sas van Gent, Holland and is interned.

22Jan18 *Gefr.* Guido Thalheim, P, is KIC and *Uffz.* Klebba, G, is IIC on take-off from Eeghem airfeld.

27Mar18 *Schutzstaffel 11* is renamed *Schlachtstaffel 11* by KM Nr. 5126.18.A.7.L.IV.C. of 27Mar18.

12Apr18 *Vzfw.* Eduard Müller, P, and *Vzfw.* Wilhelm Elschenbroich, G, are KIA over Aveluy-Wald due to ground fire.

23Apr18 *Vzfw.* Ernst Henze, P, and *Sgt.* Hans Engel, G, are KIA by ground fire between Millencourt and Albert.

12May18 *Uffz.* Paul Dorn, P, and *Uffz.* Emil Holland, G, are KIA over Bouillancourt Wald.

20Jun18 *Oblt.* Caspar Kulenkampff-Post, P and C.O., and *Flg.* Wladsilaus Pockladerki, G, are KIC at Ecly during landing, because of propeller damage to their Halberstadt Cl.II which was inflicted by ground fire.

8Aug18 *Uffz.* Becker-1, *Vzfw.* Scheibchen-1, S.E. 5, Herleville

21Aug18 *Uffz.* Garnitz-zLgzw, *Hptm.* Sonntag-zLgzw, 2 Seater, S. St. Léger

27Aug18 *Uffz.* Berberich-1, *Vzfw.* Cziesla-1, Sopwith 1, Sailly-en-Ostrevent

27Aug18 *Uffz.* Müller, P, and *Uffz.* Zwick, G, are WIA,sv. during air combat.

1Oct18 *Hptm.* Erich Sonntag, O and C.O., is KIA over Sancourt, Fressies.

Nov18 *Schlachtstaffel 11* is demobilized at FEA 12, Kottbus.

Above: The men of *Schlachtstaffel 11* at Abscon in the *17. Armee* in July 1918. The C.O., *Hptm.* Erich Sonntag, is seated sixth from the left. Credit: UTD/HAC.

Below: *Vzfw.* Friedrich August Schönmann beside his Halberstadt Cl.II marked "Marianne." He was a pilot with *Schusta 23b* from August 26, 1917, to October 14, 1917, when he was transferred to *Schusta 11*. He later was transferred to *Jasta 77b*, where he served during the middle of 1918. Credit: UTD/HAC.

Royal Prussian *Schutzstaffel 12*

Pilot/Gunner	Type	From		To	
		Unit	Date	Date	Unit
Vzfw. Ernst Bochmann	P		(Dec17)		
Vzfw. Hermann Johann Böttcher	G			12Jul17	POW
Vzfw. Kurt Boje	P			14Aug17	WIA,lt.
Vzfw. Kurt Boje	P	AFP 4	27Oct17	23Dec17	POW,DOW
Uffz. Georg Brix	P	AFP 1	22Jun17	30Aug17	AFP 4
Gefr. Buch	P			8Jun18	JsSch I
Ltn.d.R. Adolf Bundies	O	FA 224A	21Jul17	25Oct17	AFP 6
Charnowsky			(Oct17)		
Ltn.d.R. Heinrich Deilmann	P	KG 5/30	1Jan17	3Jan17	Js 6
Uffz. Dietz	P		(Sep17)	(Mar18)	
Gefr. Drast	G			28Aug18	AFP 4
Oblt. Dreibholz	O	AFP 2	4Jun18	23Jul18	Ss 16
Vzfw. Gustav Droste	G			3Jun18	KIA
Ltn.d.R. Georg van der Emde, C.O.	O	AFP 4	29Jun18	7Aug18	Leave
Flg. Enax			(Apr17)		
Uffz. Feyerherd	G	AFP 4	21Sep17	(Mar18)	
Uffz. Feyerherd	G	FEA 9	20Jul18	12Aug18	AFP 4
Uffz. Feyerherd	G	AFP 4	28Aug18		
Flg. Findeisen	P	AFP 4	8Jun18		
Uffz. Franzen	P			12Sep17	FEA 10
Flg. Robert Gödecke	P			27Jun17	KIC
Flg. Gruhn	P	AFP 4	14Jun18		
Gefr. Max Gutowski	G			8Feb17	KIA
Vzfw. Friedrich Heitsch	G	AFP 4	6Oct17	12Aug18	FA 213A
Gefr. Hermersdörfer	P	AFP 4	31Aug17	(Jan18)	
Ritt.d.R. Herrmann, C.O.		Ss 4	23Apr18	Jul18	
Offz.Stv. Konrad Hesse	P	Js 1	('17)	8Feb17	KIA
Flg. Hinz	P		(Sep17)	13Oct17	JsSch I
Flg. Hinz	P	AFP 4	(Jan18)		
Hptm. Erwin *Frhr.* von Hofmann, C.O.	O	KG 5/30	1Jan17	(May17)	
Uffz. Hermann Hornberger	G			14Aug17	KIA
Uffz. Fritz Jacobs	G			23Jan17	POW
Gefr. Theodor Kaleta	P	Ss 28b	1Sep17	1Feb18	JSch II
Flg. Kommel	P	AFP 4	13Jul18	12Aug18	AFP 4
Uffz. Alfred Kruse	P	AFP 4	23Aug17	23Dec17	FA 8
Gefr. Paul Kühne	G		(May18)		
Uffz. Jakob Lang	G	AFP 18	15Oct18	23Oct18	Ss 30b
Gefr. Lange	P			17Mar18	IIC,lt.
Ltn.d.R. Luesebrink, Stv. C.O.		SGp D	7Aug18		
Mayer			(Oct17)		
Flg. Willy Mees			(Mar18)		
Ltn.d.R. Milbach, OzbV	O		Jul18	Oct18	AFS Ost
Oblt. Johannes Missfelder, Stv. C.O.	O	FA 224A	7Jun17	1Jul17	Ss 12
Oblt. Johannes Missfelder, C.O.	O	Ss 12	1Jul17	5Aug17	Leave
Oblt. Johannes Missfelder, C.O.	O	Leave	23Aug17	24Apr18	SGrp D
Uffz. Möller	G		(Sep17)	7Oct17	AFP 4
Flg. Möller	P	FEA 1	(Jan18)		AFP 4
Oblt. Paul Moosmayer, stv. C.O.	O			7Jun17	FA 224A
Uffz. Müller	G		(Oct17)	17Mar18	IIC,lt.
Flg. Münster	G		(Sep17)	(Jan18)	
Vzfw. Friedrich Niemann	G	AFP 4	24Oct17	23Dec17	KIA
Uffz. Obernier	P			19Jun18	FEA 3
Vzfw. Plantholtz	P	AFP 4	13Oct17	19Jul18	IIC
Vzfw. Reubelt	P			12Jul17	POW
Uffz. Riester	P	AFP 4	22Aug17	31Aug17	FA 8
Flg. Karl Romann	P		(Sep17)	May18	JsSch I
Flg. Friedrich Rügge	G	AFP 4	27Apr18		
Gefr. Rudolf Schadt	G	AFP 4	1Sep17	Oct18	Ss 15
Uffz. Ernst Schaetzle	P			21Jul17	Js 19

Flg. Scharnowsky	G	AFP 4	(Jun18)		
Gefr. Otto Schiebel (DOW 19Feb18)	G	AFP 4	22Aug17	28Sep17	WIA,sv.
Flg. Hans Schlink	G		(Sep17)	19Jun18	FA 250A
Ltn.d.R. Paul Schröder	P	KG 5/30	1Jan17	11Oct17	AFP 4
Gefr. Siemer	G	AFP 4	14Jul18		
Vzfw. Erich Tänzer	P		(Sep17)	3Jun18	KIA
Uffz. Trollmann	G	AFP 4	21Sep17		
Gefr. Uckert	P	AFP 4	21Jul18	3Aug18	Ss 9
Vzfw. Voigt	G		(Sep17)	29Sep18	IIC,sv.
Vzfw. Wagner	P			29Sep18	IIC,sv.
Ltn. Ulrich Wandel, Stv. C.O.	O	FA 224A	5Aug17	23Aug17	Idflieg
Ltn. Wilhelm Weidner	P	KG 5/30	1Jan17	31Mar17	AFP 3
Vzfw. Georg Winkler	G	AFP 4	8Aug17	(Jan18)	

Schutzstaffel/Schlachtstaffel 12 Airfields

From	To	Location	*Schlachtgruppe* Affiliation	*Armee*
1Jan17		Hargicourt	Escort for FA 259(A)	1
(31Jan17)	1Mar17	Mörchingen	Escort for FA 257(A)	AAA
1Mar17	16Apr17	Juniville	Escort for FA 17	3
16Apr17	27Jun17	Juniville	Escort for FA 203(A)	1
27Jun17	18Jul17	Faumont	Escort for FA 211(A)	6
18Jul17	18Sep17	Bisseghem	Escort for FA 224(A)w	4
18Sep17	26Sep17	Wynghene	Escort for FA 40, FA 224(A)w	4
26Sep17	27Oct17	Wynghene	Escort for FA 238(A)	4
27Oct17	15Nov17	Maria Aalter	Escort for FA 40	4
15Nov17				6
(22Nov17)	(29Jan18)		Escort for FA 40	2
(31Jan18)		Wynghene		4
(Feb18)	17Mar18	Caudry		2
17Mar18	(21Mar18)	Quiévy	SGp D (Ss 12,23b) C.O. *Oblt.* Johannes Missfelder	2
(9Apr18)	12Apr18	Römer Ferme	SGp D (Ss 12,23b,26b) C.O. *Oblt.* Johannes Missfelder	2
12Apr18	18Apr18	Linselles	SGp D (Ss 9,12,16,24b) C.O. *Oblt.* Johannes Missfelder	4
18Apr18	30Apr18	Linselles	SGp D (Ss 9,12,16,24b,25b) C.O. *Oblt.* Johannes Missfelder	4
30Apr18	(Jun18)	Linselles	SGp D (Ss 9,12,16,24b) C.O. *Oblt.* Johannes Missfelder	4
(Jun18)		Mariakerke	SGp D (Ss 9,12,16,24b) C.O. *Oblt.* Johannes Missfelder	4
(9Jun18)		Linselles	SGp D (Ss 9,12,16,24b) C.O. *Oblt.* Johannes Missfelder	4
(15Jul18)				6
(29Jul18)		Linselles	SGp D (Ss 9,12,16) C.O. *Oblt.d.R.* Hermann Schulz	4
(7Aug18)	16Aug18	Villeselve		18
16Aug18	30Aug18	Villeselve	SGp 3 (Ss 6,12,18,26b,34,38s) C.O. *Oblt.* Friedrich-Carl Hanesse	18
30Aug18	7Sep18	Ronchin		6
7Sep18	9Sep18	Moved		
9Sep18	18Oct18	Landrecies		18
18Oct18	EOW	Feuchères	SGp 3 (Ss 6,12,23b,38s) C.O. *Oblt.* Friedrich-Carl Hanesse	7

Royal Prussan *Schutzstaffel 12*

1Jan17 — *Schutzstaffel 12* is created from KG 5/Ks 30 by KM Nr.1425.16.g.A.7.L. of 1Jan17.

23Jan17 — *Uffz.* Fritz Jacobs, G, is taken POW at Vauq, near Nancy. He and his pilot, an unknown *Ltn.d.R.*, ran out of fuel and were forced to land.

8Feb17	*Offz.Stv.* Konrad Hesse, P, and *Gefr*. Max Gutowski, G, are KIAover Golancourt.
27Jun17	*Flg*. Robert Goedecke, P, and *Ltn*. Siegfried Lischke, O of Fl.Abt.211(A), are KIC at Faumont airfield.
12Jul17	*Vzfw*. Reubelt, P, and *Vzfw*. Hermann Johann Böttcher, G, are taken POW at Lens in a DFW C.V.
14Aug17	*Vzfw*. Kurt Boje, P, is WIA,lt. and *Uffz*. Hermann Hornberger, G, is KIA over Langemarck during air combat.
28Sep17	*Gefr*. Otto Schiebel, G, is WIA,sv. over Le Cateau. He DOW on 19Feb18 at Caudry.
30Oct17	*Uffz*. Kruse, P, and *Uffz*. Voigt, G, crash land LVG C.V 3342/17. Both men are unhurt.
30Nov17	*Uffz*. Kruse-zLg, *Uffz*. Voigt-zLg, Sopwith 1, Trescault S.E. 5a #B.4871, 56 Sqn. RFC, 2/Lt. G.A. Cawson, KIA
23Dec17	*Vzfw*. Kurt Boje, P, and *Vzfw*. Friedrich Niemann, G, are KIA over Metz en Couture during air combat in LVG C.V 9446/17.
29Jan18	*Flg*. Romann-1, *Vzfw*. Winckler-1, D.H. 4, 12.45, SW Cambrai
17Mar18	*Gefr*. Lange, P, and *Uffz*. Müller, G, are IIC,lt. at Caudry.
27Mar18	*Schutzstaffel 12* is renamed *Schlachtstaffel 12* by KM Nr. 5126.18.A.7.L.IV.C. of 27Mar18.
3Jun18	*Vzfw*. Erich Tänzer, P, and *Vzfw*. Gustav Droste, G, are KIA at Mariakerke.
19Jul18	*Vzfw*. Plantholtz, P, is IIC in a crash landing.
29Sep18	*Vzfw*. Wagner, P, and *Vzfw*. Voigt, G, are IIC,sv.
Nov18	*Schlachtstaffel 12* is demobilized at FEA 14, Halle a.d. Salle.

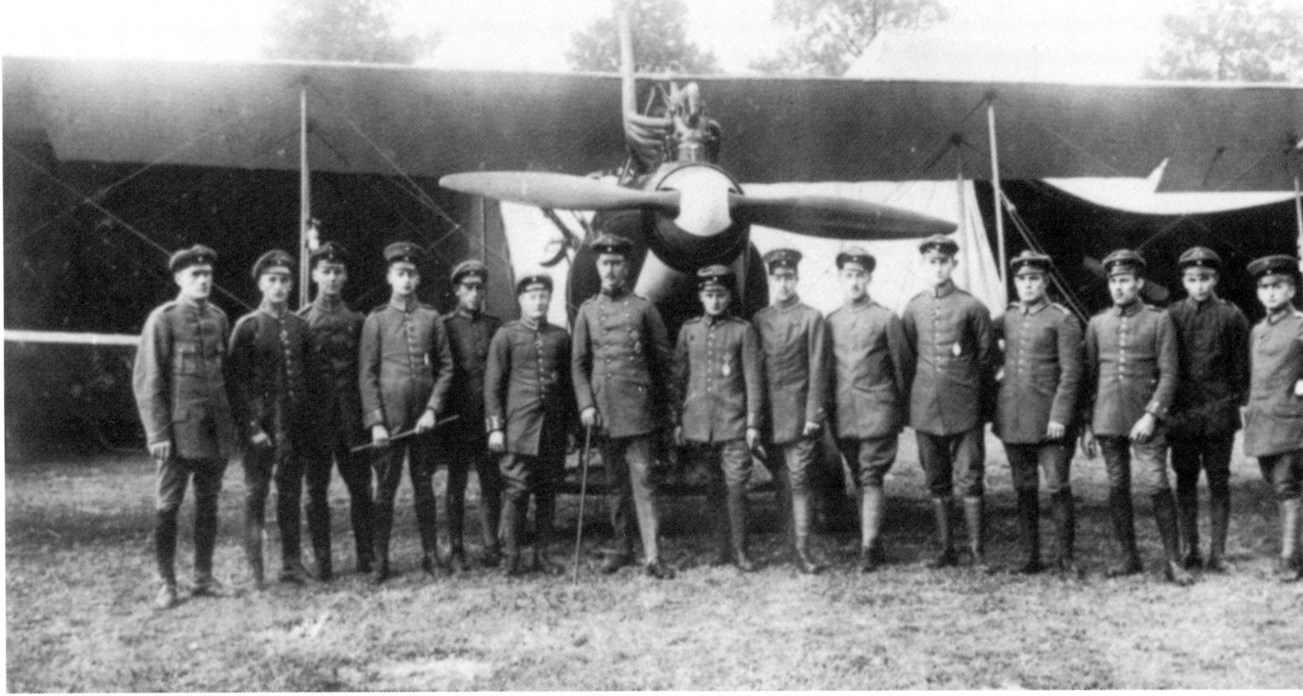

Above: The men of *Schutzstaffel 12* at Wynghene in September 1917. Left to right: *Flg.* Karl Romann, *Flg.* Möller, *Flg.* Hans Schlink, *Uffz.* Dietz, *Gefr.* Hemersdörfer, *Flg.* Münster, the C.O. *Oblt.* Johannes Missfelder, *Flg.* Hinz, *Gefr.* Rudolf Schadt, *Vzfw.* Georg Winkler, *Vzfw.* Erich Tänzer, *Vzfw.* Voigt, *Uffz.* Kruse, *Gefr.* Theodor Kaleta, and *Gefr.* Otto Schiebel. The aircraft is an early DFW C.V with the curved side radiators.

Right: Hannover Cl.II C.9301/17 marked '01' of *Schusta 12*. The pilot is *Flg.* Karl Romann.

Above: Halberstadt Cl.II 6313/17 with *Gefr.* Hermersdörfer, pilot, and *Flg.* Münster, gunner, of *Schusta 12*.

Right: LVG C.V 3349/17 of *Schusta 12* after a severe combat. *Flg.* Münster, the gunner, is on the right. Again note that the aircraft number (49) is based on the serial number (3349).

Below: *Schusta 12* in September 1917. The crew of *Gefr.* Theodor Kaleta and *Gefr.* Otto Schiebel. The aircraft is a DFW C.V.

Bottm right: *Flg.* Hans Schlink and *Uffz.* Dietz of *Schusta 12* in September 1917 posing in front of the same DFW C.V.

The *Schusta 12* crew of *Flg.* Hinz and *Gefr.* Rudolf Schadt.

Gefr. Rudolf Schadt, *Schusta 12*. The aircraft is a LVG B.II and is unarmed. The Hazet side radiators were eliminated in 1916 on operational aircraft which would indicate that this machine was probably used as the squadron 'hack.'

Left: *Schusta 12* at Wynghene in September 1917.

The *Schusta 12* crew of *Flg.* Karl Romann and *Vzfw.* Georg Winkler in their Hannover Cl.II 9301/17 marked '01'.

The *Schusta 12* crew of *Flg.* Karl Romann and *Vzfw.* Georg Winkler beside their Hannover Cl.II 9301/17.

Schusta 12 at Wynghene.

Gefr. Theodor Kaleta posing with LVG C.V marked '13'.

Royal Prussian *Schutzstaffel 13*

Pilot/Gunner	Type	From		To	
		Unit	Date	Date	Unit
Ltn. Otto Abernetty	O	AFP 4	5May18	4Jul18	Kofl 9
Ltn. Otto Abernetty, C.O.	O	Kofl 9	14Sep18	EOW	
Uffz. Kurt Ackenhausen	P	AFP 4	(May18)	23Aug18	POW
Flg. Amzehnhoff	G			23Aug18	POW
Flg. Adam Bätz	G	AFP 4	12Jan18	16Feb18	AFP 4
Vzfw. Bendig	P			30Sep17	AFP 4
Offz.Stv. Bertelsmeier	P	AFP 4	23Dec17	1Mar18	POW
Flg. Bischoff	G	AFP 4	2Dec17	30Dec17	FEA 5
Flg. Boltz	G	AFP 4	2Dec17	21Dec17	BG 1
Gefr. Brunner	P	FA 19	20May18	30May18	AFP 4
Gefr. Franz Budny	P			24Jan17	KIA
Oblt. Helmut Bühling	O	Grufl 3	15Mar18	27May18	WIA,lt.
Oblt. Helmut Bühling, C.O.	O	Ss 13	24Mar18	27May18	WIA,lt.
Oblt. Helmut Bühling, C.O.	O		27May18	9Aug18	WIA
Oblt. Helmut Bühling, C.O.	O	Hosp.	Aug18	7Sep18	SGp 2
Vzfw. Josef Degen	P	AFP 4	29Jul17	25Mar18	AFP 17
Ltn. Karl Drum	O	KG 7/37	1Jan17	10Feb17	FA 23
Sgt. Heinrich Dung	G	Ss 30b	4Jan18	16Feb18	AFP 4
Uffz. Feicke	G	AFP 4	29Aug17		AFP 4
Uffz. Feicke	G	AFP 4	14Nov17	4Dec17	WIA
Ltn.d.R. Julius Fichter	P	KG 7/37	1Jan17	11Jan17	AFP 7
Uffz. Franz Gieler	G	AFP B	18Apr17	26Apr17	Ss 23b
Uffz. Gerschel	P	AFP 4	15Nov17		
Flg. Goralewski	G	AFP 4	2Dec17	21Dec17	BG 1
Uffz. Hartje	G	AFP 4	21Dec17	3Jan18	BG 4
Uffz. Hans Herbert	G			15Jul18	KIA
Vzfw. Hermann Hoos	P			24Sep18	KIA
Gefr. Ernst Jacksch	P	Ss 23b	2May18	15Jul18	KIA
Ltn.d.R. Dieter Jacobi	P	FA 7	(Jan17)		KG 2/7
Vzfw. Mathias Hubert Jorissen	G	AFP 4	23Aug17	26Aug17	AFP 4
Sgt. Karl Jurzitza	P	Ss 23b	19Jul17	23Dec17	AFP 4
Vzfw. Kohlweyer	P			22Jan18	JSch II
Uffz. Kurt Koch			(Aug18)		
Sgt. Gottfried Kort	G			24Jan17	KIA
Gefr. Krüger	P	AFP 4	20Jan18		
Uffz. Karl Kubitza	G	KG 7/37	1Jan17	20Nov17	AFP 8
Uffz. Peter Küchen	P	AFP 4	13Sep17	21Sep17	Ss 17
Gefr. Paul Kühne	G			28Jul17	KIA
Gefr. Kuesler	P			9Jun18	POW
Vzfw. Kunze	G			31May18	AFP 4
Vzfw. Wilhelm Littig	P	KG 7/37	1Jan17	8May18	FEA 10
Vzfw. Erhard Lorenz	G		(Nov17)	13Nov17	AFP 4
Vzfw. Albert Lux	P	AFP 2	10Feb17	4Apr17	FA 293A
Vzfw. Müllenbach	G			9Jun18	POW
Oblt. Müller, C.O.	O		(Nov17)	24Mar18	Ss 13
Oblt. Müller, OzbV	O	Ss 13	24Mar18	29Apr18	WIA,sv.
Vzfw. Josef Nolte	G			1Mar18	KIA
Vzfw. Oppermann	G		(Aug17)	10Dec17	FEA 5
Flg. Pawlack	G			31Jul18	IIC,F/L
Gefr. Radtke	P	AFP 4	20Jan18	(Feb18)	
Flg. Friedrich Rügge	G	AFP 4	10Jan18	16Feb18	AFP 4
Flg. Samol	P			31Jul18	WIA
Gefr. Scharfenberg	G	AFP 4	(May18)	16Aug18	WIA,sv.
Vzfw. Wilhelm Georg Scheerer	P	AFP 2	27Jan17	28Mar17	AFP 2
Vzfw. Wilhelm Georg Scheerer	P	AFP 2	5Apr17	13Sep17	AFP 4
Flg. Ludwig Schmelter	G	AFP 4	10Jan18	15Feb18	AFP 4
Vzfw. Wilhelm Schröder	P	KG 7/37	1Jan17		KG 4/24
Gefr. Karl Schott	G	Ss 5	13Nov17	25May18	FEA 9
Flg. Schuttenhauer	G	AFP 4	(May18)		
Uffz. Simmat	G	AFP 4	23Dec17	16Feb18	AFP 4

Uffz. Ferdinand Vieth	P	AFP 4	20Jan18	16Feb18	AFP 4
Flg. Hans Vollmeyer	P			29Apr18	KIA
Vzfw. Richard Wagner	G			24Sep18	KIA
Vzfw. Rudolf Warschun	P		(Aug17)	22Jan18	JSch II
Ltn.d.R. Ernst Emil Weil	O	FA 287A	27Mar17	10May17	FA 213A
Uffz. Paul Weyher	G	AFP 4	21Sep17	29Apr18	KIA
Vzfw. Reiner Wirtz	P	Ss 28b	14Oct17	4Jan18	IIC,lt.
Vzfw. Reiner Wirtz	P		4Jan18	22Jan18	JSch II
Flg. Zink	G	AFP 4	21Sep17	4Jan18	IIC

Schutzstaffel/Schlachtstaffel 13 Airfields

From	To	Location	*Schlachtgruppe* Affiliation	*Armee*
1Jan17	(31Jan17)	Ham, Süd	For FA 234(A),266(A),287(A)b	2
(24Feb17)	21Mar17	Grand Priel by St. Verquier, NW St. Quentin		2
22Mar17	(Apr17)	Pont à Marcq	Escort for FA 8, 240(A)	6
(May17)	3Jun17	Corbehem	Escort for FA 256(A)	6
3Jun17	26Jun17	Beveren	Escort for FA 213(A)	4
26Jun17	10Dec17	Beveren-Roulers	Escort for FA 213(A)	4
10Dec17	(16Feb18)	Eeghem		4
(1Mar18)	19Mar18	Roeulx	Escort for FA 231(A)	17
19Mar18	21Mar18	Bancourt Ost	SGp A (Ss 13,27b) C.O. *Oblt.* Müller	17
21Mar18	24Apr18	Neuville	SGp A (Ss 13,27b) C.O. *Oblt.* Müller	17
24Apr18	17May18	Ingelmunster	SGp C (Ss 3,13,19,29b) C.O. *Hptm.* Wilhelm Aschenborn	4
17May18	3Jun18	Ingelmunster	SGp 2 (Ss 3,13,19,29b) C.O. *Hptm.* Wilhelm Aschenborn	4
4Jun18	9Jul18	Bonneuil-Ferme	SGp 3 (Ss 3,13,19,29b) C.O. *Oblt.* Helmut Bühling	18
10Jul18	29Jul18	Mont Notre Dame	SGp B (Ss 3,13,19,29b) C.O. *Oblt.* Helmut Bühling	7
29Jul18	10Aug18	Liéramont	SGp 2 (Ss 3,13,19,29b) C.O. *Oblt.* Helmut Bühling	6
10Aug18	12Aug18	Nurlu	SGp 2 (Ss 11,13,19,27b) C.O. *Hptm.* Erich Sonntag	2
12Aug18	26Aug18	Longavesnes	SGp 2 (Ss 3,13,19) C.O. *Oblt.d.R.* Jaspers	2
26Aug18	26Sep18	St. Vaast	SGp 2 (Ss 3,13,19,29b) C.O. *Oblt.d.R.* Jaspers	2
26Sep18	6Oct18	Preutin	SGp 2 (Ss 3,13,19,29b) C.O. *Oblt.* Helmut Bühling	5
6Oct18	21Oct18	Preutin	SGp 2 (Ss 3,13,19,26b,29b) C.O. *Oblt.* Helmut Bühling	5
21Oct18	31Oct18	Mercy le Haut	SGp 2 (Ss 3,13,19,26b,29b) C.O. *Oblt.* Helmut Bühling	5
1Nov18	EOW	Stenay	SGp 2 (Ss 3,13,19,26b,29b) C.O. *Oblt.* Helmut Bühling	5

Royal Prussian *Schutzstaffel 13*

1Jan17	*Schutzstaffel 13* is created from KG 7/Ks 37 by KM Nr.1425.16.g.A.7.L. of 1Jan17.
5Jan17	*Ltn.d.R.* Jacobi-1, Feindl. D.D. type nicht festzustellen, Roye D.H. 2 #A.2581, 24 Sqn. RFC, Lt. W.F.T. James, WIA
24Jan17	*Gefr.* Franz Budny, P, and *Sgt.* Gottfried Kort, G, are KIA over Le Quesnoy at 15.25 hours.
21Jul17	A *Schusta 13* aircraft is forced to land and both unidentified crew men are slightly WIA.
29Jul17	*Vzfw.* Paul Kühne, G, is WIA during air combat and DOW after landing at Beveren.
16Aug17	*Vzfw.* Oppermann-1, *Flg.* Warschun-1, R.E. 8, Houthoulster Wald
6Nov17	*Vzfw.* Wirtz-1, *Flg.* Zink-1, Sopwith Camel, 8.20, W. Poelkapelle S.E. 5a #B.512, 60 Sqn. RFC, Lt W. Duncan, shot up, OK
4Dec17	*Uffz.* Feicke, G, is WIA during air combat.

4Jan18	*Vzfw.* Reiner Wirtz, P, and *Gefr.* Zink, G, are forced to land and are lightly IIC.
16Feb18	*Gefr.* Radtke-1, *Uffz.* Weyher-1, D.H., 11.00, NW Paschendaele
1Mar18	*Offz.Stv.* Bertelsmeier, P, is taken POW and *Vzfw.* Josef Nolte, G, is KIA at Marcoing.
27Mar18	*Schutzstaffel 13* is renamed *Schlachtstaffel 13* by KM Nr. 5126.18.A.7.L.IV.C. of 27Mar18.
29Apr18	*Oblt.* Müller, O and OzbV, is WIA,sv.
29Apr18	*Flg.* Hans Vollmeyer, P, and *Uffz.* Paul Weyher, G, are KIA over Bailleul.
27May18	*Oblt.* Helmut Bühling, O and C.O., is WIA,lt. by ground fire, shot in the upper left arm, and briefly to Field Hospital 109 but returns to the unit.
9Jun18	*Gefr.* Kuesler, P, and *Vzfw.* Müllenbach, G, are taken POW at Villers Bocage in Halberstadt Cl.II 15342/17.
15Jul18	*Gefr.* Ernst Jacksch, P, and *Uffz.* Hans Herbert, G, are KIA over Suippes.
31Jul18	*Flg.* Samol, P, is WIA during air combat and *Flg.* Pawlack, G, is IIC in the ensuing forced landing.
9Aug18	*Oblt.* Helmut Bühling, O and C.O., is WIA by Flak, grazing shot to the lower right arm and the upper lip and to Field Hospital 85. He shortly returns to the unit.
16Aug18	*Gefr.* Scharfenberg, G, is WIA,sv.
23Aug18	*Uffz.* Kurt Ackenhausen, P, and *Flg.* Amzehnhoff, G, are taken POW at Chipilly at 11.30 hours in Halberstadt Cl.IV 4675/18 when they shoot off their own propeller.
24Sep18	*Vzfw.* Hermann Hoos, P, and *Vzfw.* Richard Wagner, G, are KIA over St. Emilie-Roussay by Flak fire in LVG C.VI 7631/18.
Nov18	*Schlachtstaffel 13* is demobilized at FEA 5, Hannover.

Halberstadt Cl.III marked II with white stripes on the upper wing. The Roman numeral clearly identifies that this is a *Schlasta 13* aircraft.

Royal Prussian *Schutzstaffel 14*

Pilot/Gunner	Type	From		To	
		Unit	Date	Date	Unit
Gefr. Karl Beck			(Jul18)		
Gefr. Behrendt	P	FA 256A	20Apr18		
Vzfw. Bremer	G			26Apr18	POW
Flg. Karl Brömel			(Feb18)		
Vzfw. Otto Bruns	G	AFP 17	18Mar18	21Jun18	AFP 7
Ltn.d.R. Cohs	O			3Aug18	WIA,lt.
Uffz. Kurt Erbe			(Jul18)		
Vzfw. Georg Fuchs	P			30Aug18	KIA
Ltn.d.R. Gerlt	P	FA 9		24Jan17	Js 19
Flg. Otto Göbel	M			19Jul18	Died
Uffz. Bruno Grabs				4Sep17	KIA
Uffz. Hans Gross	P			15Feb17	KIA
Flg. Richard Hannig	G			16Jul18	KIA
Uffz. Isphording	P		(Jul18)		
Uffz. H. Kamrath	P			26Apr18	POW
Vzfw. Wilhelm Karcher	G			13May17	KIA
Gefr. Max Kintof	P		(Apr17)	13May17	KIA
Gefr. Wilhelm Knerr	P			26Jul17	KIA
Uffz. Kurt Knoll	G			17Jun17	KIA
Uffz. Koennecke	G		(May17)	(Aug17)	

Vzfw. Krimm	P		(Mar18)		
Flg. Albert Kuhn (+ 4Jun18)				3Jun18	WIA,sv.
Gefr. Paul Max	G		(Jul18)		
Sgt. Max Meinhardt	P			16Jul18	KIA
Uffz. Willy Meyer	G			26Jul17	KIA
Ltn. Modler, C.O.	O		Sep18	EOW	
Gefr. Wilhelm Neumann				15Jul17	KIC
Vzfw. Alfred Nössler			(Mar18)	(Jul18)	
Uffz. Wilhelm Piepenkötter	G		(Aug17)		BG 6/8
Vzfw. Pohler	P			27Feb17	Js 21
Ltn.d.R. Reiner, Schlagru A Stab		AFP 4	6Jun18		
von Renner			(Nov17)		
Uffz. Riebe	G		(Mar18)		
Gefr. Ernst Schild	G	AFP 4	18Apr18		Ss 5
Hptm. Theodor Schubert, C.O.	O	KG 7/38	1Jan17	20Feb17	AFP A
Vzfw. Josef Schwendemann	P		Feb17	27Aug17	JsSch I
Vzfw. Hugo Schwinning				4Sep17	KIA
Uffz. Hans Ernst Seidel	P		(Feb17)	17Jun17	KIA
Uffz. Heinrich Sieber				15Jul17	KIC
Ltn.d.R. Hugo Sillus, C.O.	O		(Jul18)	30Aug18	KIA
Vzfw. Spittel			(May17)		
Hptm. Ernst Josef Stabl, Stv. C.O.	O	FA 296A	5Sep17	18Sep17	FA 296A
Flg. Josef Staeves	G	Ss 22b	22Jun17		
Vzfw. Emil Stiller	G			15Feb17	KIA
Vzfw. Werner Wagener	P	KG 7/38	1Jan17	27Feb17	Js 21
Ltn.d.R. Werner Wagener, OzbV	P	KEST 5	('18)	EOW	
Vzfw. Otto Weimar	P	KG 7/38	1Jan17	(Apr17)	
Vzfw. Wimmer	P		(May17)	(Aug18)	
Uffz. Wittenfeld	P		(Aug17)	('18)	Js
Oblt. Emil Ziegler gen Stege, C.O.	O		(Mar17)	5Sep17	Leave
Oblt. Emil Ziegler gen Stege, C.O.	O	Leave	18Sep17	(May18)	SGp A

Schutzstaffel/Schlachtstaffel 14 Airfields

From	To	Location	*Schlachtgruppe* Affiliation	*Armee*
1Jan17	(31Jan17)	Vrizy	Escort for FA 271(A)	3
(Feb17)				AAA
(1Mar17)		Perthes	Escort for FA 203(A)	3
(Mar17)	(Apr17)	Cuirieux	Escort for FA 10	7
(Apr17)				6
(16Apr17)	(Jul17)			3
(15Jul17)	19Aug17	La Neuville		7
19Aug17		Boulain Ferme	Escort for FA 296(A)b	5
(Sep17)	(Oct17)			7
(Nov17)	(Feb18)	Cuirieux	Escort for FA 10	7
21Mar18		Villers-au-Tertre	SGp B (Ss 14,19,24b,25b,29b) C.O. *Hptm.* Wilhelm Aschenborn	17
3Apr18	(9Apr18)	Framerville	SGp C (Ss 14,28b,30b) C.O. *Oblt.d.R.* August Ertl	2
(12Apr18)	26May18	Heule	SGp A (Ss 1,14,21,28b) C.O. *Oblt.* Emil Ziegler gen Stege	4
26May18		Eppes	SGp A (Ss 1,8,10,14,21) C.O. *Oblt.* Emil Ziegler gen Stege	7
(6Jun18)	(Jul18)	La Pavillon Ferme	SGp Staabs (Ss 1,8,10,14,21) C.O. *Oblt.* Emil Ziegler gen Stege	7
(15Jul18)	3Aug18	Eppes	SGp A (Ss 1,8,10,14,21) C.O. *Oblt.* Emil Ziegler gen Stege	7
3Aug18		Aubry	SGp A (Ss 1,8,10,14,21) C.O. *Oblt.* Emil Ziegler gen Stege	7
8Aug18	9Aug18	Curchy	SGp A (Ss 1,8,10,14,21) C.O. *Oblt.* Emil Ziegler gen Stege	2
9Aug18	11Aug18	Guizancourt	SGp A (Ss 1,8,10,14,21) C.O. *Oblt.* Emil Ziegler gen Stege	18

11Aug18	22Aug18	Eppes	SGp A (Ss 1,8,10,14,21) C.O. *Oblt.* Emil Ziegler gen Stege	7
22Aug18	31Aug18	Eswars	SGp A (Ss 1,8,10,14) C.O. *Oblt.* Emil Ziegler gen Stege	17
31Aug18	25Sep18	Bouchain	SGp A (Ss 1,8,10,14) C.O. *Oblt.* Emil Ziegler gen Stege	17
25Sep18	7Oct18	Bühl	SGp A (Ss 1,8,10,14) C.O. *Oblt.* Emil Ziegler gen Stege	AAA
7Oct18	21Oct18	Croix-les-Rouveroy	SGp A (Ss 1,8,10,14,17) C.O. *Oblt.* Emil Ziegler gen Stege	2
21Oct18	31Oct18	Croix-les-Rouveroy	SGp A (Ss 1,14,17) C.O. *Hptm.* Hermann Krüger	2
31Oct18	EOW	Trazegnies	SGp A (Ss 1,14,17) C.O. *Hptm.* Hermann Krüger	2

Royal Prussian *Schutzstaffel 14*

1Jan17	*Schutzstaffel 14* is created from KG 7/Ks 38 by KM Nr.1425.16.g.A.7.L. of 1Jan17.
15Feb17	*Uffz.* Hans Gross, P, and *Vzfw.* Emil Stiller, G, are KIA over Ripont.
13May17	*Gefr.* Max Kintof, P, and *Vzfw.* Wilhelm Karcher, G, are KIA over St. Souplet.
20May17	*Uffz.* Wimmer-1, *Uffz.* Könnecke-1, Spad, Auberive
17Jun17	*Uffz.* Hans Seidel, P, and *Uffz.* Kurt Knoll, G, are KIA over Laon at 10.35 hours.
15Jul17	*Gefr.* Wilhelm Neumann and *Uffz.* Heinrich Sieber are KIC at La Neuville.
26Jul17	*Gefr.* Wilhelm Knerr, P, and *Uffz.* Willy Meyer, G, are KIA over Laffaux.
20Aug17	*Uffz.* Wittenfeld-1, *Uffz.* Piepenkötter-1, Spad, zw. Wald von Cheppy and Wald von Avocourt Esc. N.80, Cpl. C. Coatsworth, WIA
21Aug17	*Uffz.* Wimmer-2, *Uffz.* Könnecke-2, Spad, zw. Höhe 304 & Toter Mann
4Sep17	*Uffz.* Bruno Grabs and *Vzfw.* Hugo Schwinning are KIA over Epinonville.
23Mar18	*Vzfw.* Krimm-1, *Uffz.* Riebe-1, Sopwith 1
27Mar18	*Schutzstaffel 14* is renamed *Schlachtstaffel 14* by KM Nr. 5126.18.A.7.L.IV.C. of 27Mar18.
26Apr18	*Uffz.* H. Kamrath, P, and *Vzfw.* Bremer, G, are downed by Flak fire and taken POW near Wieltje, NE Ypres in a Halberstadt Cl.II.
3Jun18	*Flg.* Albert Kuhn is WIA,sv. at La Grange by ground fire. He DOW 4Jun18.
16Jul18	*Uffz.* Isphording-1, *Gefr.* Max-1, Spad, SW Dormans
16Jul18	*Sgt.* Max Meinhardt, P, and *Flg.* Richard Hannig, G, are KIA over Treloup, Marne, during an air combat.
19Jul18	*Flg.* Otto Göbel dies in the hospital at Carlandon. It is assumed that he is a member of the ground crew of the unit.
3Aug18	*Ltn.d.R.* Cohs, O, is WIA,lt. by ground fire.
8Aug18	*Vzfw.* Wimmer-3, *Ltn.d.R.* Sillus-1, Sopwith
30Aug18	*Vzfw.* Georg Fuchs, P, and *Ltn.d.R.* Hugo Sillus, O and C.O., are KIA between Beugny and Vaulx-Vraucourt by Flak fire.
Nov18	*Schlachtstaffel 14* is demobilized at FEA 14, Halle a.d. Salle.

Left: *Uffz.* Kurt Knoll was a gunner with *Schusta 14* until being killed in action on 17 June 1917 near Laon.

Right: The obituary of *Gefr.* Wilhelm Meyer and *Uffz.* Willy Knerr of *Schusta 14* and signed by their C.O. *Oblt.* Emil Ziegler gen Stege. Photo credit: Immo Frese.

Im Felde, den 29. Juli 1917.

Am 26. Juli 1917 fielen im Luftkampf gegen Uebermacht unsere lieben Kameraden. 14/24828

Fliegerschütze Unteroffizier

Willy Meyer

Inhaber der Hessischen Tapferkeitsmedaille,

Flugzeugführer Gefreiter

Wilhelm Knerr

Inhaber des Eisernen Kreuzes II. Klasse.

Wir werden ihnen ein treues Andenken bewahren.

Ziegler gen. Stege,

Oberleutnant u. Führer einer Schutzstaffel.

Royal Prussian *Schutzstaffel 15*

Pilot/Gunner	Type	From Unit	From Date	To Date	To Unit
Uffz. von Bartdorff	P		(Jun18)		
Uffz. Arthur Bartsch	P			28Apr18	KIA
Ltn. Gerhard Bassenge	P	KG 7/39	1Jan17	17Jan17	AFP 2
Sgt. Otto Becker	G	Ss 23b	14Jul18	13Oct18	POW
Gefr. Beese	P	KG 7/39	1Jan17		
Uffz. Berling	P			12Apr17	WIA
Uffz. Berling	P		(Sep17)		
Vzfw. Brenner	P				
Vzfw. Gottfried Ehmann	G		(Oct17)	(Aug18)	
Uffz. Walter Enders	G	AFP 5	27Nov17	19Apr18	FA 207A
Ltn.d.R. Erich Fehser	P	FA 44		27Aug18	KIA
Sgt. Michael Fischer	G	AFP 2	2May18	17May18	AFP 2
Flg. Albert Fickus	G		5Jun18	(Jul18)	
Ltn.d.R. Gerhard Wilhelm Flecken	P	Js 20		6Mar17	Js 20
Vzfw. Ernst Flöel	G	KG 7/39	1Jan17	(Apr18)	
Oblt. Florig	O	KG 7/39	1Jan17	(Mar17)	
Vzfw. Willi Gabriel	P	Js 19	21Jul17	17May18	Js 11
Oblt. Gerhardt	O				
Gefr. Herbert Goldberg	P	FA 219A		7Jul18	KIC
Uffz. Max Graf				23Aug17	KIC
Gefr. Hanke	G		(Apr18)	22Aug18	WIA,lt.
Oblt. Hauff, C.O.			2Oct18	EOW	
Uffz. Hilsebein	G	FA 207A	Jul17	5Jun18	WIA,lt.
Uffz. Johannes Hohmann	G		(May18)	5May18	IIC,lt.
Uffz. Johannes Hohmann	G		5May18	5Jun18	IIC,lt.
Uffz. Johannes Hohmann	G		5Jun18	(Jul18)	
Vzfw. Friedrich Huffzky	P		(Dec17)	(Aug18)	
Flg. Wilhelm Kemper	M			9Mar18	KIA
Uffz. Hermann Klein	P			31May18	KIA
Ltn. Gustav Koch	P	KG 7/39	1Jan17	9Feb17	Js 6
Uffz. Josef Köck	G	AFP 5	9Sep17	1Dec17	AFP 5
Gefr. Otto Krüger	M			9Mar18	KIA
Uffz. Krumm	P		5Jun18	(Jul18)	
Sgt. Kuchenbacher	P		6Sep18	13Oct18	POW
Ltn.d.R. Julius Kuse, Stv. C.O.	O	Ss 22b	24Mar18	29Mar18	Rümania
Flg. Ernst Lipka	G			28Apr18	KIA
Flg. Philipp Maltry	M			9Mar18	KIA
Ltn. Werner Meiss	P	KG 7/39	1Jan17	25Jan17	Js 20
Flg. Meister			(Apr17)		
Gefr. Mellen	G	AFP 4	5Jun18	(Jul18)	
Uffz. Müller	P		(Apr18)	29Aug18	IIC
Sgt. Paul Nowotny	G			31May18	KIA
Vzfw. Otte			(Sep17)		
Ltn.d.R. Hans Peters	P	KG 7/39	1Jan17	10Mar17	AFP 2
Oblt. Heinz Pflugk-Harttung, C.O.	O	KG 7/39	1Jan17	(Mar17)	
Vzfw. Pohland	G		(Apr18)	7Aug18	WIA
Uffz. Kurt Rebischke	G			27Aug18	KIA
Uffz. Reck	P		5Jun18	5Jun18	WIA,lt.
Uffz. Reck	P	Hosp.	(Jul18)		Js 8
Vzfw. Hermann Reinecke	G			7Jul18	KIC
Vzfw. Ridder	P		(Dec17)	(Apr18)	
Ltn. Gotthardt Rossteuscher	O	KG 7/39	1Jan17		
Gefr. Rudolf Schadt	G	Ss 12	Oct18	EOW	
Uffz. Ewald Schröder				23Aug17	KIC
Oblt. Schröter, Stv. C.O.			11Mar18	(Apr18)	
Oblt. Schulte, C.O.			Sep18	2Oct18	Ss 11
Gefr. Josef Schulte-Schmale	G			24Mar18	KIA
Ltn.d.R. Julius Schwörer, C.O.	O	FA 207A	28May18	7Sep18	Infntry
Uffz. Täubner	P			24Apr18	WIA

Oblt. Wilhelm Uhlig	O	KG 7/38	1Jan17	30Jun17	Ss 15
Hptm. Wilhelm Uhlig, C.O.	O	Ss 15	30Jun17	May18	
Uffz. Warda	P		(Oct17)	25Apr18	WIA
Ltn. Georg Weiner	P	KG 7/38	1Jan17	25Jan17	Js 20
Vzfw. Woetzold	G			24Apr18	WIA

Schutzstaffel/Schlachtstaffel 15 Airfields

From	To	Location	*Schlachtgruppe* Affiliation	*Armee*
1Jan17	(31Jan17)	Artemps, SW St. Quentin	For FA 206(A)	2
(Feb17)				2
(1Mar17)		Bergnicourt	Escort for FA 290(A)b	3
(Mar17)	31Mar17	Cappy		2
31Mar17				6
(Apr17)	16Apr17	Annelles	Escort for FA 296(A)b	3
16Apr17	30Jun17	Annelles	Escort for FA 296(A)b	1
30Jun17	15Aug17	Alincourt		1
15Aug17	(Feb18)	Marville, Dun sur Meuse	For FA 228(A)	5
(7Mar18)	11Mar18	Escaufourt	Escort for FA 207(A)	2
11Mar18	21Mar18	Aizecourt le Haut	SGp B (Ss 4,15,26b,28b) C.O. *Ritt.d.R.* Herrmann	2
21Mar18		Reumont	SGp B (Ss 4,15,26b,28b) C.O. *Ritt.d.R.* Herrmann	2
(Mar18)		Cappy	SGp B (Ss 4,15,26b,28b) C.O. *Ritt.d.R.* Herrmann	2
(4Apr18)	19Apr18	Herbécourt	SGp B (Ss 4,11,15) C.O. *Ritt.d.R.* Herrmann	2
19Apr18	12May18	Cappy	SGp A (Ss 4,11,15,17,22b) C.O. *Hptm.* Zimmermann	2
12May18	9Jun18	Cappy	SGp 1 (Ss 4,11,15,17) C.O. *Hptm.* Zimmermann	2
9Jun18	9Jun18	Curchy	SGp 1 (Ss 4,11,15,17) C.O. *Hptm.* Erich Sonntag	18
9Jun18	11Jun18	Cappy	SGp 1 (Ss 4,11,15,17) C.O. *Hptm.* Erich Sonntag	2
11Jun18	12Jun18	Curchy	SGp 1 (Ss 4,11,15,17) C.O. *Hptm.* Erich Sonntag	18
12Jun18	6Jul18	Cappy	SGp 1 (Ss 4,11,15,17) C.O. *Hptm.* Erich Sonntag	2
7Jul18	10Jul18	Assevillers	SGp J (Ss 4,15,24b,25b) C.O. *Oblt.d.R.* Franz Albertshauser	2
11Jul18	11Aug18	St. Loup	SGp J (Ss 4,15,24b,25b) C.O. *Oblt.* Erhardt Egerer	1
11Aug18	12Aug18	NW Athies	SGp J (Ss 4,15,24b,25b,35) C.O. *Oblt.* Erhardt Egerer	2
13Aug18	20Aug18	St. Loup	SGp J (Ss 4,15,24b,25b,35) C.O. *Oblt.* Erhardt Egerer	1
21Aug18	1Sep18	Beuvry	SGp J (Ss 4,15,24b,25b) C.O. *Oblt.* Erhardt Egerer	17
2Sep18	8Sep18	Abscon	SGp J (Ss 4,15,24b,25b,35) C.O. *Oblt.* Erhardt Egerer	17
9Sep18	3Oct18	Abscon	SGp J (Ss 4,15,24b,25b,35) C.O. *Oblt.* Friedrich von Krausser	17
4Oct18	13Oct18	Marly	SGp S (Ss 4,11,15,27b,35) C.O. *Hptm.* Hugo Weingarth	17
13Oct18	18Oct18	Nouvelles	SGp S (Ss 4,11,15,27b) C.O. *Hptm.* Hugo Weingarth	17
18Oct18	EOW	NW St. Simphorien	SGp S (Ss 4,11,15,27b) C.O. *Hptm.* Hugo Weingarth	17

Royal Prussian *Schutzstaffel 15*

1Jan17	*Schutzstaffel 15* is created from KG 7/Ks 39 by KM Nr.1425.16.g.A.7.L. of 1Jan17.
12Apr17	*Uffz.* Berling, P, is WIA during air combat.
23Aug17	*Uffz.* Max Graf and *Uffz.* Ewald Schröder are KIC at Marville, Dun sur Meuse.
18Sep17	*Uffz.* Berling-1, *Vzfw.* Otte-1, Spad, Douaumont
30Oct17	*Flg.* Warda-1, *Flg.* Ehmann-1, Spad, by Fort Douaumont
9Mar18	Mechanics *Flg.* Wilhelm Kemper, *Gefr.* Otto Krüger and *Flg.* Philipp Maltry are KIA at Escaufourt during a British bombing attack.
21Mar18	*Gefr.* Warda-2, *Gefr.* Ehmann-2, Sopwith
22Mar18	*Uffz.* Gabriel-1, *Gefr.* Hilsebein-1, Spad
24Mar18	*Gefr.* Josef Schulte-Schmale, G, is KIA over the Somme River.
27Mar18	*Schutzstaffel 15* is renamed *Schlachtstaffel 15* by KM Nr. 5126.18.A.7.L.IV.C. of 27Mar18.
24Apr18	*Uffz.* Warda-3, *Uffz.* Ehmann-3, AWFK 8, N. Cachy
24Apr18	*Uffz.* Täubner, P, and *Vzfw.* Woetzold, G, are WIA.
25Apr18	*Uffz.* Warda, P, is WIA over Herbécourt while *Uffz.* Gottfried Ehmann, G, is OK.
28Apr18	*Uffz.* Arthur Bartsch, P, and *Flg.* Ernst Lipka, G, are KIA over Valenciennes.
5May18	*Uffz.* Johannes Hohmann, G, is IIC,lt. at Cappy in a Halb. Cl.II.
31May18	*Uffz.* Hermann Klein, P, and *Sgt.* Paul Nowotny, G, are KIA over Lamotte-Warfusée during air combat in a Halb. Cl.II.
4Jun18	*Sgt.* Huffzky-1, *Vzfw.* Ehmann-4, A.R. 2, NE Villers-Bretonneux
5Jun18	*Uffz.* Reck, P, is lightly WIA and *Uffz.* Johannes Hohmann, G, is lightly IIC at Cappy in the crash landing of their Halb. Cl.II.
5Jun18	*Uffz.* Hilsebein, G, is lightly WIA in a Halb. Cl.II.
6Jun18	*Uffz.* von Bartdorff-1, *Ltn.d.R.* Schwörer-1, Camel, Aubigny
25Jun18	*Vzfw.* Huffzky-2, *Vzfw.* Ehmann-5, R.E. 8, NE Villers-Bretonneux
5Jul18	*Vzfw.* Huffzky-n/c, *Vzfw.* Ehmann-n/c, Spad 2
5Jul18	*Vzfw.* Huffzky-3, *Vzfw.* Ehmann-6, Sopwith Dolphin, S. Memel
•	23 Sqn. RAF, Lt. R.D. McPherson, WIA
5Jul18	*Uffz.* Krumm-1, *Gefr.* Mellen-1, Sopwith Camel, Villers-Bretonneux
5Jul18	*Vzfw.* Friedrich Huffzky, P, and *Vzfw.* Gottfried Ehmann, G, are forced to land with shots in the engine of their Halberstadt Cl.II. They are OK.
5Jul18	*Uffz.* Krumm, P, and *Gefr.* Mellen, G, are forced to land in their Halb. Cl.II following the above combat. They are OK.
6Jul18	*Uffz.* Reck-1, *Gefr.* Hohmann-1, Sopwith Camel, Hamel-Bouyencourt
7Jul18	*Gefr.* Herbert Goldberg, P, and *Vzfw.* Hermann Reinecke, G, are KIC on the airfield at Assevillers during take-off of their Halb. Cl.II.
18Jul18	*Vzfw.* Huffzky-4, *Vzfw.* Ehmann-7, Spad 1, Prosnes
18Jul18	*Uffz.* Huffzky-5, *Vzfw.* Ehmann-8, Spad 1, 20.20, Beaumont s/Vesle
21Jul18	*Vzfw.* Huffzky-6, *Vzfw.* Ehmann-9, Spad S.11, 20.50, Minaucourt
21Jul18	*Vzfw.* Huffzky-7, *Vzfw.* Ehmann-10, Spad, 20.50, Malmy
21Jul18	*Vzfw.* Huffzky-n/c, *Vzfw.* Ehmann-n/c, Spad, 20.50, Malmy
25Jul18	*Vzfw.* Huffzky-8, *Vzfw.* Ehmann-11, French 2, 21.00, Prosnes

Schutzstaffel 15 celebrating Christmas Eve 1917. Second from the left is *Offz.Stv.* Warda. The two-seater gunner ace *Vzfw.* Gottfried Ehmann is seated dead center while *Vzfw.* Friedrich Huffzky is seated directly in front of Ehmann.

Schlachtstaffel 15 taken 20Apr18 at their airfield at Cappy, left to right: 1st row: *Uffz.* Hilsebein, *Uffz.* Arthur Bartsch, *Uffz.* Täubner, *Vzfw.* Pohland. 2nd row: *Uffz.* Warda, *Uffz.* Walter Enders, *Vzfw.* Friedrich Huffzky, *Vzfw.* Gottfried Ehmann. 3rd row: Standing: *Gefr.* Müller, *Gefr.* Hanke, *Vzfw.* Ridder, *Vzfw.* Ernst Flöel, *Vzfw.* Willy Gabriel, *Vzfw.* Woetzold. Photo Credit: Jan Vancoillie.

29Jul18	*Vzfw.* Huffzky-9, *Vzfw.* Ehmann-12, Sopwith 1, 20.35, Sept-Saulx
7Aug18	*Vzfw.* Pohland, G, is WIA by ground fire.
22Aug18	*Vzfw.* Hanke, G, is WIA,lt. by ground fire.
27Aug18	*Ltn.d.R.* Erich Fehser, P, and *Uffz.* Kurt Rebischke, G, are KIA over Arras.
29Aug18	*Uffz.* Müller, P, is IIC in a landing accident.
13Oct18	*Sgt.* Kuchenbacher, P, and *Sgt.* Otto Becker, G, are taken POW at Solesmes in a Halberstadt Cl.II.
Nov18	*Schlachtstaffel 15* is demobilized at FEA 5, Hannover.

Royal Prussian *Schutzstaffel 16*

Pilot/Gunner	Type	From		To	
		Unit	Date	Date	Unit
Uffz. Alfred Baumann	P			5Jul18	KIA
Gefr. Wilhelm Becker	P	AFP 4	21Jul18	3Sep18	KIA
Gefr. Bischoff	G		(Jul18)	31Jul18	IIC,lt.
Vzfw. Robert Blechmann	G			8Mar18	KIA
Ltn.d.R. Friedrich Boetheld, C.O.	O			17Jul18	KIA
Gefr. Borchert	P		(Aug17)		
Gefr. Brömmer	P	AFP 4	5Sep17		
Uffz. Buch	P	AFP 4	(Sep18)	14Oct18	POW
Uffz. Kurt Busch	G	AFP 4	21Sep17	21Oct17	KIA
Oblt. Dreibholz, C.O.	O	Ss 12	23Jul18	26Aug18	Kofl 7
Gefr. Franz Dutkowski	G	Ss 16	12Jun18	13Jul18	FEA 14
Gefr. Ernst Ebner	G	AFP 4	10Aug17	23Aug17	AFP 4
Flg. Ermisch	G		4Aug18		
Ltn. Günther von Fichte	P			Sep18	Js 54s
Ltn. Hans von Fichte, OzbV	O	AFP 4	6Jun18	14Oct18	POW
Ltn. Hans von Fichte, stv. C.O.	O	Ss 16	18Jul18	23Jul18	Ss 16
Uffz. Flohr	P	AFP 4	16Oct18	EOW	
Gefr. Paul Gebhardt	P	AFP 4	3Oct18		
Vzfw. Gruhl	G	AFP 4	11Jun18		
Vzfw. Gruhl	G	AFP 4	3Oct18		
Flg. Haase	P		(Aug18)		
Vzfw. Max Häser	P	AFP 1	21Jun17	21Oct17	KIA
Uffz. Heberlin	G	AFP 4	4Aug18		
Uffz. Heger	P			4Jul18	JsSch I
Uffz. Hermann	P	AFP 4	8Jun18	16Sep18	JsSch I
Feldw. Friedrich Hilbert			(Apr17)		
Uffz. Hugo Holtmeier	G	Ss 26b	8Oct17	3Sep18	KIA
Gefr. Jaffé				25Nov17	AFP 6
Uffz. Franz Kälker	G			3Jan18	KIC
Flg. Wilhelm Kraatz	G	AFP 4	6Aug17	(Jun18)	
Uffz. Landrock	G		(Feb17)	27Sep17	AFP 4
Ltn. Ludewig, OzbV	O	AFP 4	16Oct18	EOW	
Uffz. Curt Lustig	G		(Jun18)		
Uffz. Hans Lustig	P		13Jul18	11Aug18	Rea
Vzfw. Martin Meister	P	AFP 4	23Aug17	3Jan18	KIC
Uffz. Mertens	P			8Jun18	JsSch I
Sgt. Meyer	G	AFP 4	7Aug18		
Gefr. Misiak	G		(May17)	31Jul17	WIA,sv.
Gefr. Franz Müller	G	AFP 4	23Aug17	27Sep17	AFP 4
Gefr. Müller	G	AFP 4	13Jul18		
Vzfw. Muschen	P	AFP 4	11Jun18	(Jun18)	
Uffz. Niemeyer	P	AFP 4	9Jul18		
Uffz. Wilhelm Osterwald (+ 9Jul18)	G	AFP 4	29Aug17	5Jul18	IIC,sv.
Vzfw. Plachta	G	Ss 19	27Sep17		
Oblt. Hermann Ramdohr, C.O.	O		(Mar18)	9Apr18	KIA
Uffz. Walter Reichenbach	P		(May17)	21Jun17	Js 5
Uffz. Fritz Rittershofer	P	FA 268A	(Jun17)	(Feb18)	
Gefr. Wilhelm Ritzhaupt	P	AFP 4	16Sep18	1Oct18	+ i.Kr.
Ltn.d.R. Werner Roloff, Stv. C.O.	O	FA 211A	16Apr18	6Jun18	Ss 4
Flg. Friedrich Rügge	G	AFP 4		13Jul18	KIC

Sgt. Schaub	G	AFP 4	5Sep18		
Flg. Hunibald Saupp					
Vzfw. Alfred Schmidt	P	Ss 10	24Oct17	17Jul18	KIA
Vzfw. Georg Schneider	P		(Feb17)	9Apr18	KIA
Uffz. Scholz	P	FA 48b	22Oct17	24Oct17	FA 48b
Uffz. Edwin Schuster	G		(Aug18)		
Oblt. Paul Seiffart, C.O.	O		(Jul17)	(Dec17)	
Uffz. Otto Stadter	P	AFP 1	26Apr17	22Aug17	AFP 1
Ltn.d.R. Stephan, stv. C.O.	O	Ss 9	26Aug18	29Sep18	Kofl 4
Ltn.d.R. Strunk	G		(Jul18)	4Aug18	AFP 4
Ltn. Karl Töpfer	P	KG 7/40	1Jan17		FA 253A
Vzfw. Oswald Tränker	G		(May17)	(Jan18)	
Vzfw. Heinrich Traub	P	FA 7	21Feb18	8Mar18	KIA
Sgt. Walter Wachtel	P		(Jun18)	1Oct18	KIA
Ltn.d.R. Warstadt, OzbV	O			6Jun18	FA 8
Pion. Gottfried Weber	P	AFP 7	17May18	25May18	Ss 23b
Ltn.d.R. Richard Wundt	O	KG 7/40	1Jan17	19Apr17	FA 286A

Schutzstaffel/Schlachtstaffel 16 Airfields

From	To	Location	*Schlachtgruppe* Affiliation	*Armee*
1Jan17	(31Jan17)	Matigny, NW Ham	Escort for FA 225(A)	2
(Feb17)		Lihons, Chaulnes area		1,2
(Mar17)	17Mar17			2
18Mar17	(26Apr17)		Escort for FA 228(A)	1
(May17)				7
(Jun17)	22Jun17			1
23Jun17	15Nov17	Engel, Ichteghem	Escort for FA 231(A)	4
15Nov17	1Feb18	Dorignies	Escort for FA 268(A)	6
1Feb18	21Mar18	Dorignies	Escort for FA 268(A)	17
21Mar18	25Mar18	Dorignies	SGp C (Ss 3,9,16) C.O. *Oblt.* Hermann Ramdohr	17
25Mar18	28Mar18	Epinoy	SGp C (Ss 3,9,16) C.O. *Oblt.* Hermann Ramdohr	17
28Mar18	9Apr18	Pont de la Deule	SGp C (Ss 3,9,16) C.O. *Oblt.* Hermann Ramdohr	17
9Apr18	12Apr18	Tourmignies	SGp B (Ss 16,29b) C.O. *Ritt.* Jürgen *Frhr.* von Zobel	6
12Apr18	18Apr18	Linselles	SGp D (Ss 9,12,16,24b) C.O. *Oblt.* Johannes Missfelder	4
18Apr18	30Apr18	Linselles	SGp D (Ss 9,12,16,24b,25b) C.O. *Oblt.* Johannes Missfelder	4
30Apr18	(9Jun18)	Linselles	SGp D (Ss 9,12,16,24b) C.O. *Oblt.* Johannes Missfelder	4
(Jun18)	15Jul18	Stalhille	SGp D (Ss 9,12,16,24b) C.O. *Oblt.* Johannes Missfelder	4
15Jul18		Varsenaere	SGp D (Ss 9,16) C.O. *Oblt.d.R.* Hermann Schulz	4
(29Jul18)		Varsenaere	SGp D (Ss 9,12,16) C.O. *Oblt.d.R.* Hermann Schulz	4
(7Aug18)	22Aug18	Varsenaere	SGp D (Ss 9,16) C.O. *Oblt.d.R.* Hermann Schulz	4
22Aug18	7Oct18	Varsenaere		4
7Oct18	13Oct18	Oudenaarde	SGp J (Ss 9,16,24b,25b) C.O. *Oblt.* Friedrich von Krausser	4
13Oct18	21Oct18			17
21Oct18	EOW		SGp A (Ss 8,10,16,35) C.O. *Oblt.* Emil Ziegler gen Stege	17

Royal Prussian *Schutzstaffel 16*

1Jan17 — *Schutzstaffel 16* is created from KG 7/Ks 40 by KM Nr.1425.16.g.A.7.L. of 1Jan17.
2Feb17 — *Uffz.* Schneider-1, *Uffz.* Landrock-1, Nieuport, Trapezwald by Lihons, W. Chaulnes
5May17 — *Uffz.* Reichenbach-1, *Uffz.* Tränker-1, Nieuport, Gegend Pontavert
5May17 — *Uffz.* Reichenbach-2, *Uffz.* Tränker-2, Caudron, La Ville aux Bois
10May17 — *Uffz.* Reichenbach-3, *Flg.* Misiak-1, Spad 1, Berry au Bac
7Jul17 — *Sgt.* Häser-1, *Vzfw.* Tränker-3, Sopwith, 19.05, Mannekensveere-Nieuport Pup #N.6460, Naval 3, F/S/Lt. L.L. Lindsay, FTL, OK
31Jul17 — *Gefr.* Misiak, G, is WIA,sv. over Bixschoote. His pilot, *Uffz.* Fritz Rittershofer, is OK.
9Aug17 — *Gefr.* Borchert-zLgzw, *Flg.* Kraatz-zLgzw, Ponnier, by Dixmuiden
3Sep17 — *Sgt.* Häser-2, *Vzfw.* Tränker-4, Sopwith Pup, 10.20, Oostkerke
11Sep17 — The Ichteghem airfield of *Schusta 16* is bombed and 4 aircraft are damaged.
21Oct17 — *Vzfw.* Max Häser, P, and *Uffz.* Kurt Busch, G, are shot down in flames during air combat over Dixmuiden and are KIA.
3Jan18 — *Vzfw.* Martin Meister, P, and *Uffz.* Franz Kälker, G, are KIC at Dorignies.
24Jan18 — *Vzfw.* Schneider-2, *Vzfw.* Tränker-5, Bristol F.2b, Méricourt D.H. 4, 57 Sqn. RFC,
8Mar18 — *Vzfw.* Heinrich Traub, P, and *Vzfw.* Robert Blechmann, G, are KIA over Beaumont, S. Drocourt.
21Mar18 — The *Schusta 16* Airfield at Dorignies is bombed. There would appear to be no losses.
27Mar18 — *Schutzstaffel 16* is renamed *Schlachtstaffel 16* by KM Nr. 5126.18.A.7.L.IV.C. of 27Mar18.
9Apr18 — *Vzfw.* Georg Schneider, P, and *Oblt.* Hermann Ramdohr, O, are KIA by ground fire over Bailleul, Reims in Hannover Cl.II 13135/17.
29Jun18 — *Vzfw.* Muschen-1, *Flg.* Kraatz-2, Handley Page, 23.40, Veurne SE Wulpen #C.9648, 214 Sqn RAF, Lt. J.D. Vance, 2/Lt. S.B. Potter, Sgt. R.G. Kimberley, interned in Holland.
5Jul18 — *Uffz.* Alfred Baumann, P, is KIA over Dostnickes and *Uffz.* Wilhelm Osterwald, G, is WIA over Stalhille. He DOW 9Jul18 at Brügge.
13Jul18 — *Flg.* Friedrich Rügge, G, is KIC at Mopertingen.
17Jul18 — *Vzfw.* Alfred Schmidt, P, and *Ltn.d.R.* Friedrich Boetheld, O, and C.O. are KIA E. Dünkirchen in LVG C.V 3882/16 during air combat.
31Jul18 — *Gefr.* Bischoff, G, is lightly IIC during a night landing.
21Aug18 — *Flg.* Haase-1, *Flg.* Schuster-1, Spad, Veurne
24Aug18 — The unit conducts a night bombing raid on the British airfield at Bertangles and destroys 10 Bristol F.2bs of 48 Sqn. RAF and one S.E. 5a of 84 Sqn. RAF. In addition many men are killed and wounded.
3Sep18 — *Gefr.* Wilhelm Becker, P, and *Uffz.* Hugo Holtmeier, G, are KIAover Jonkershove.
1Oct18 — *Sgt.* Walter Wachtel, P, is KIA at Jabbeke.
1Oct18 — *Gefr.* Wilhelm Ritzhaupt, P, dies at an unknown location. He is buried in Langemarck Cemetery, Belgium.
14Oct18 — *Uffz.* Buch, P, and *Ltn.* Hans von Fichte, O and OzbV, are taken POW at Moorslede in Halberstadt Cl.IV 1566/18.
Nov18 — *Schlachtstaffel 16* is demobilized at *Militär Fliegerschule* Lübeck.

Royal Prussian *Schutzstaffel 17*

Pilot/Gunner	Type	From		To	
		Unit	Date	Date	Unit
Flg. Bartels	G			4Jul18	WIA
Ltn.d.R. Fritz Baucus, OzbV	O	FA 207A	30Sep18	EOW	
Uffz. Bauer	P		(Oct18)		
Oblt. Wolf Frhr. von Biedermann, C.O.	P	Idflieg	30Aug18	EOW	
Gefr. Bilitza	G	AFP 4	21Sep17	1Mar18	IIC,sv.
Oblt. Johann Brosius, C.O.		KG 7/41	1Jan17	(May17)	
Ltn. Bühle	P			13Aug17	WIA
Ltn.d.R. Gustav Bürck	P		(Sep17)	13Sep17	FA 233A
Flg. Robert Busch	G			11Jun18	KIA
Uffz. Christiani	P		(Feb18)		
Uffz. Bernhard Conze	P			20Jan18	WIA,lt.
Uffz. Bernhard Conze	P			16Feb18	WIA
Uffz. Bernhard Conze	P			11Jun18	KIA
Ltn.d.R. Friedrich Döring	O	KG 7/41	1Jan17	20Feb17	Js 34
Vzfw. Ernst Ebner	G	AFP 4	23Aug17	26Apr18	WIA,lt.
Vzfw. Rudolf Francke	P	KG 7/41	1Jan17	9Apr17	WIA,lt.
Vzfw. Rudolf Francke	P		9Apr17	24Apr17	AFP 6

Above: The crews of *Schlachtstaffel 16* in front of a Halberstadt Cl.II. *Uffz.* Fritz Rittershofer is on the extreme right.

Right: *Uffz.* Fritz Rittershofer a pilot with *Schusta 16*.

Ltn.d.R. Friedrich Geiger	O	FA 207A	3Apr18	22Aug18	KIA
Ltn.d.R. Friedrich Geiger, C.O.	O	Ss 17	21Jul18	22Aug18	KIA
Uffz. Gerhard Greulich	G			8Oct18	KIA
Uffz. Otto Haack	P	Ss 26b	19Sep17		
Vzfw. Häckel	P		(Feb18)		
Uffz. Heinz	G		(Oct18)		
Vzfw. Richard Hertel	G		(Jan18)		
Gefr. Hetjens	G				
Flg. Paul Huse				8May18	KIA
Flg. Richard Jaekel	P			1Mar18	KIC
Uffz. Jahn	P	AFP 4	13Sep17	20Sep17	AFP 4
Oblt. Walther Karjus, C.O.	P	AFP 2	9Jun18	21Jul18	AFP B
Uffz. Kath	P			6Jun18	WIA
Flg. Kielgas	G	AFP 4	21Sep17	(Oct17)	
Flg. Klatte	P	AFP 4	23Aug17	13Sep17	AFP 4
Uffz. Kotzybick	G			6Jun18	WIA
Vzfw. Krämer	P	AFP 4	13Sep17	(Jan18)	
Flg. Krebs	P		('17)		
Uffz. Kruetzfeld	G	AFP 4	21Sep17	13Jan18	WIA
Uffz. Peter Küchen	P	Ss 13	21Sep17	12Dec17	KIC
Vzfw. Kühn	P	KG 7/41	1Jan17	(Jun17)	
Vzfz. G. Lange	G	AFP 4	15Sep17	26May18	
Ltn.d.R. G. Lange	O	Ss 17	26May18	EOW	
Ltn.d.R. P. Lingens	O			20Jan18	WIA,lt.
Ltn.d.R. P. Lingens	O		20Jan18	31Jan18	FA 224A
Gefr. Adolf Märtens			(Apr18)		
Ltn. Miller	P		(Oct17)		
Vzfw. Müller	G		(Feb18)		
Hptm. Werner Mundt, C.O.	O	AFP 4	17Oct17	27Jan18	BS Jtbg
Gefr. Ludwig Neeb	G	Ss 25b	18Oct17	28Jan18	KIA
Vzfw. Adolf Niess	P	AFP 4	10Jun17	13Sep17	AFP 4
Sgt. Ostermann	P		('17)	16Sep17	Hosp.
Uffz. Kurt Perlhoefter	P			7Jul17	KIA
Flg. Peters	P	AFP 4	1Sep17		
Ltn. Johann Raddatz	O				FA 7
Flg. Adolf Richter	G	Ss 29b	6Oct17		
Uffz. Paul Richter	G		(Jun17)	13Aug17	WIA
Uffz. Paul Richter	G	AFP 4	8Nov17	12Dec17	KIC
Uffz. Georg Rösen (+ 25Apr18)	G	Ss 21		15Mar18	WIA,sv.
Uffz. Kurt Perlhoefter	P			7Jul17	KIA
Flg. Schadt	G			3May18	WIA
Gefr. Schilling	G				
Vzfw. Schrey	G		('17)	16Sep17	AFP 4
Vzfw. Seeger	P			15Jun17	WIA
Uffz. Siering	P			21Sep17	AFP 4
Offz.Stv. Fritz Stephan	P			8Oct18	POW
Hptm. Paul Wilhelm Stoewer, C.O.	P			17Oct17	FA 272A
Ltn. Ernst Umlauff	O			2May18	WIA,sv.
Gefr. Wilhelm Walter	P	Ss 27b	27Sep17	28Jan18	KIA
Uffz. Albert Wildermuth	G	Ss 21	1Scp17	26Sep17	KIA
Vzfw. Wüllner	G			21Sep17	AFP 4
Uffz. Wulff	P			13Aug17	IIC
Hptm. Zimmermann, C.O.	O		27Jan18	10Feb18	FA 224A
Hptm. Zimmermann, C.O.	O	FA 224A	17Feb18	9Jun18	

Schutzstaffel/Schlachtstaffel 17
Mitgemachte Schlachten und Gefechte
(Battles and combat actions in which Ss 17 participated)
(From 26Apr17 - 2Jul18)

26Apr17	9Jun17	*Frühjahrsschlacht bei Arras* (Spring battle of Arras)

10Jun17	24Nov17	*Schlacht in Flandern* (Battle in Flanders)
25Nov17	29Nov17	*Tankschlacht bei Cambrai* (Tank battle of Cambrai)
30Nov17	7Dec17	*Angriffschlacht bei Cambrai* (Offensive battle of Cambrai)
8Dec17	15Dec17	*Stellungskämpfe bei Cambrai* (Trench fighting by Cambrai)
16Dec17	18Feb18	*Stellungskämpfe im Artois und französisch Flandern* (Trench fighting in Artois and French Flanders)
19Feb18	20Mar18	*Kämpfe in der Siegfriedstellung. Vorbereitungzseit für die Grosse Schlacht in Frankreich* (Fighting in the Siegfried Line. Preparation for the Great Battle in France)
21Mar18	6Apr18	*Grosse Schlacht in Frankfreich, darunter* (The Great Battle in France, specifically)
21Mar18	22Mar18	*Druchbruch zwischen Gouzeaucourt und Vermand* (Penetration between Gouzeaucourt and Vermand)
23Mar18	26Mar18	*Verfolgungskämpfe im Sommegebeit* (Pursuit fighting in the Somme area)
23Mar18	25Mar18	*Sommeübergang* (Crossing the Somme)
27Mar18	23Apr18	*Kämpfe an der Ancre, Somme und Avre* (Fighting on the Ancre, the Somme and the Avre)
24Apr18	26Apr18	*Schlacht bei Villers-Brettoneux an Luce und Avre* (Battle at Villers-Brettoneux on the Luce and on the Avre)
27Apr18	2Jul18	*Kämpfe an der Ancre, Somme und Avre* (Fighting on the Ancre, the Somme and the Avre)

Schutzstaffel/Schlachtstaffel 17 Airfields

From	To	Location	*Schlachtgruppe* Affiliation	*Armee*
1Jan17	1Feb17	Le Verquier, NW St. Quentin	For FA 231(A)	2
2Feb17	15Mar17	Pontruet, NW St. Quentin	For FA 235(A), 211(A)	2
15Mar17	23Mar17	Escaufort		2
23Mar17	9Jun17	Faumont Nord	Escort for FA 235(A)	6
10Jun17	17Oct17	Heule		4
17Oct17	24Nov17	Heule	Escort for FA 250(A)	4
25Nov17	15Dec17		Escort for FA 259(A)	2
16Dec17	(13Jan18)	Faumont Nord	Escort for FA 6, FA 292(A)b	6
(27Jan18)	18Feb18	Tourmignies	Escort for FA 224(A)w	6
19Feb18	(1Mar18)	Bertry		2
(11Mar18)	(21Mar18)	Busigny	SGp A (Ss 10,17,22b) C.O. *Hptm*. Zimmermann	2
(4Apr18)		Cappy	SGp A (Ss 10,17,22b) C.O. *Hptm*. Zimmermann	2
(9Apr18)	19Apr18	Caix	SGp A (Ss 10,17,22b) C.O. *Hptm*. Zimmermann	2
19Apr18	12May18	Cappy	SGp A (Ss 4,11,15,17,22b) C.O. *Hptm*. Zimmermann	2
12May18	9Jun18	Cappy	SGp 1 (Ss 4,11,15,17) C.O. *Hptm*. Zimmermann	2
9Jun18	9Jun18	Curchy	SGp 1 (Ss 4,11,15,17) C.O. *Hptm*. Erich Sonntag	18
9Jun18	11Jun18	Cappy	SGp 1 (Ss 4,11,15,17) C.O. *Hptm*. Erich Sonntag	2
11Jun18	12Jun18	Curchy	SGp 1 (Ss 4,11,15,17) C.O. *Hptm*. Erich Sonntag	18
12Jun18		Cappy	SGp 1 (Ss 4,11,15,17) C.O. *Hptm*. Erich Sonntag	2
(15Jul18)	(11Aug18)	Bouvincourt		2
(1Sep18)	7Oct18	Avelu		2
7Oct18	21Oct18	Croix-les-Rouveroy	SGp A (Ss 1,8,10,14,17) C.O. *Oblt*. Emil Ziegler gen Stege	2

21Oct18	31Oct18	Croix-les-Rouveroy	SGp A (Ss 1,14,17) C.O. *Hptm.* Hermann Krüger	2
31Oct18	EOW	Trazegnies	SGp A (Ss 1,14,17) C.O. *Hptm.* Hermann Krüger	2

Royal Prussian *Schutzstaffel 17*

1Jan17	*Schutzstaffel 17* is created from KG 7/Ks 41 by KM Nr.1425.16.g.A.7.L. of 1Jan17.
9Apr17	*Vzfw.* Rudolf Franke, P, is WIA,lt. by ground fire.
1Jun17	*Vzfw.* Kühn-1, *Uffz.* Richter-1, Sopwith 2, Avion by Méricourt Sopwith 1 1/2 #A.2392, 45 Sqn. RFC, Lt. J. Potter,OK & 2/Lt. W.B. Giles,OK, forced to land.
15Jun17	*Vzfw.* Seeger, P, is WIA during air combat.
7Jul17	*Uffz.* Kurt Perlhoefter, P, is KIA at Kortryk during a bombing raid.
13Aug17	*Ltn.* Bühle, P, and *Uffz.* Paul Richter, G, are WIA during air combat.
13Aug17	*Uffz.* Wulff, P, is IIC during a forced landing.
21Sep17	*Flg.* Klatte-1, *Gefr.* Ebner-1, Spad 1, Comines
26Sep17	*Uffz.* Albert Wildermuth, G, is KIA at Heule.
12Dec17	*Uffz.* Peter Küchen, P, and *Uffz.* Paul Richter, G, are KIC at Villers Outreaux.
13Jan18	*Vzfw.* Johann Heidingsfelder, P, Fl.Abt. 292(A)b and *Uffz.* Kruetzfeld, G, are WIA in air combat.
20Jan18	*Uffz.* Bernhard Conze, P, and *Ltn.d.R.* P. Lingens, O, are WIA,lt.
28Jan18	*Gefr.* Wilhelm Walter, P, and *Gefr.* Ludwig Neeb, G, are KIA over Salome by La Bassée at 12.05 hours during air combat in a Hannover Cl.II.
29Jan18	*Vzfw.* Krämer-1, *Vzfw.* Lange-1, Sopwith Camel, Richebourg #B.5427, 3 Sqn. RFC, 2/Lt. C.L. Van der Hoff, KIA
16Feb18	*Uffz.* Christiani-1, *Vzfw.* Ebner-2, D.H. 4, Violains
16Feb18	*Uffz.* Bernhard Conze, P, is WIA,lt. during air combat.
21Feb18	*Vzfw.* Häckel-1, *Vzfw.* Müller-1, Camel, 10.50, NW Bellenglise
1Mar18	*Flg.* Richard Jaekel, P, is KIC and *Gefr.* Bilitza, G, is IIC,sv. during a crash at Bertry.
15Mar18	*Uffz.* Georg Rösen, G, is WIA,sv. over Bellincourt during air combat. He DOW 25Apr18 in Berlin.
27Mar18	*Schutzstaffel 17* is renamed *Schlachtstaffel 17* by KM Nr. 5126.18.A.7.L.IV.C. of 27Mar18.
26Apr18	*Vzfw.* Ernst Ebner, G, is lightly WIA during air combat and to hospital.
2May18	*Ltn.* Ernst Umlauff, O, is WIA,sv. in Albatros J.I 734/17.
3May18	*Flg.* Schadt, G, is WIA by a grenade splinter and the crew is forced to land.
8May18	*Flg.* Paul Huse is KIA at Rosières. Uncertain if he was a flying member of the unit or a mechanic.
6Jun18	*Uffz.* Kath, P, and *Uffz.* Kotzybick, G, are WIA during air combat.
11Jun18	*Uffz.* Bernhard Conze, P, and *Flg.* Robert Busch, G, are KIA over Le Ployron by Flak fire.
4Jul18	*Flg.* Bartels, G, is WIA,sv.
22Aug18	*Ltn.d.R.* Friedrich Geiger, O and CO, is severely WIA by ground fire over Bray sur Somme and DOW at Albert.
8Oct18	*Uffz.* Bauer-1, *Uffz.* Heinz-1, Inf. a/c, E. Prémont R.E. 8 #F.6013, 6 Sqn. RAF, Capt. W. Walker,DFC,KIA & Lt. M.A. Webster,WIA,DOW
8Oct18	*Offz.Stv.* Fritz Stephan, P, is taken POW and *Uffz.* Gerhard Greulich, G, is KIA at Avelu.
Nov18	*Schlachtstaffel 17* is demobilized at *Militär Fliegerschule* Lübeck.

Opposite: The "oily brethren", aircraft and engine mechanics of *Schutzstaffel 17* photographed at Bertry in February 1918. The aircraft is an LVG C.V with an odd upper cowl which is non-specification. Photo credit: Thorsten Pietsch.

Right: *Ltn.d.R.* Friedrich Geiger in the observer's cockpit while serving with *FA 207(A)* during 1916-1917. He became the *Schlasta 17* C.O. on 3 April 1918.

Royal Prussian *Schutzstaffel 18*

Pilot/Gunner	Type	From		To	
		Unit	Date	Date	Unit
Uffz. Beermann	G		(Mar17)	17Mar17	WIA,sv.
Vzfw. Wilhelm Befort	G			15Dec17	KIA
Vzfw. Karl Bickelmann	P	FA 266A	29Jan17	1Jul17	AFP 1
Oblt. Ernst Bonatz, C.O.	P	Kofl 9	18Jun18	EOW	
Vzfw. Brüne	P		(Mar18)	24Apr18	POW
Ltn.d.R. Wilhelm Finhold	P	KG 7/42	1Jan17	5Jan17	FEA 7
Sgt. Hermann Fröhner	P			3Feb18	KIA
Vzfw. Grimm	G		(Sep18)	(Oct18)	
Vzfw. Erich Haase	G	KG 1/2	(Mar17)	Aug18	GS Fkf
Vzfw. Haikert					
Oblt. Georg Henke, C.O.	O		Nov17	4Apr18	WIA,sv.
Vzfw. Rudolf Kausmann	P			15Dec17	KIA
Uffz. Klomp	G			13Apr18	WIA,lt.
Gefr. Josef Kremp	G			1Nov17	KIA
Feldw. Kulke	G		(Aug17)		
Hptm. Richard Lauer, C.O.	P		(Mar17)	Nov17	
Vzfw. Josef Leppich	P		(Mar17)	1Nov17	KIA
Gefr. Georg Post	G	Ss 2		3Feb18	KIA
Vzfw. Max Rossbach		Ss 2	('18)		
Ltn.d.R. Werner Roloff	O	KG 7/42	1Jan17	4Feb17	FA 211A
Oblt. Ulrich von Schimony-Schimonsky	O	FA 270A	26Mar17	25Apr17	Ss 5
Vzfw. Anton Schnabel			(Nov17)		
Ltn. Willi Schunke	P	KG 7/42	1Jan17	13Feb17	Js 20
Flg. Hans Silberstorff	G			4Aug18	KIA
Vzfw. Erwin Thomas	P		(Jun18)	EOW	
Vzfw. Hermann Vehmeier			(Jul18)		
Vzfw. Vetterlein			(Jul18)		
Vzfw. Kurt-Georg Wagner	G		(Mar18)	24Apr18	POW

Schutzstaffel/Schlachtstaffel 18 Airfields

From	To	Location	*Schlachtgruppe* Affiliation	*Armee*
1Jan17	(31Jan17)	Etreillers, W. St. Quentin	For FA 214(A)	2
(Feb17)	1Mar17			2
1Mar17	20Apr17	l'Ecaille	Escort for FA 206(A)	3
22Apr17	19Aug17	Alincourt	For FA 252(A)w, FA 272(A)	1
19Aug17	8Oct17		Escort for FA 44	5
8Oct17	(17Oct17)		Escort for FA 7, FA 202(A)	4
(31Oct17)	(Feb18)	Grandlup-et-Fay	Escort for FA 265(A)	7

(21Mar18)	(24Mar18)	Lesquielles-St. Germain	SGp 2 (Ss 7,18,37) C.O. *Oblt.* Walter Lackner	18
(4Apr18)	Dury		SGp 3 (Ss 6,8,18) C.O. *Oblt.* Kurt Messow	18
(9Apr18)	14Apr18	Dury	SGp 3 (Ss 6,8,18,32) C.O. *Oblt.* Kurt Messow	18
14Apr18	(25Apr18)	Dury	SGp 3 (Ss 6,18,34)	18
(27May18)		Dury	SGp 3 (Ss 6,18,34,35,38s) C.O. *Ritt.* Herrmann	18
(6Jun18)	(24Jun18)	Dury	SGp 2 (Ss 6,18,34,35,38s) C.O. *Ritt.* Herrmann	18
(1Jul18)		Dricourt	SGp 3 (Ss 6,7,18,34,38s) C.O. *Oblt.* Friedrich-Carl Hanesse	3
(15Jul18)		Dury	SGp 3 (Ss 6,18,34,38s) C.O. *Oblt.* Friedrich-Carl Hanesse	9
(29Jul18)	3Aug18	Toulis	SGp 3 (Ss 6,18,34,38s) C.O. *Oblt.* Friedrich-Carl Hanesse	9
4Aug18	9Aug18	Toulis	SGp 3 (Ss 6,18,26b,34,38s) C.O. *Oblt.* Friedrich-Carl Hanesse	9
9Aug18	12Aug18	Bouvincourt	SGp 3 (Ss 6,18,34,38s) C.O. *Oblt.* Friedrich-Carl Hanesse	2
13Aug18	16Aug18	Toulis	SGp 3 (Ss 6,7,18,26b,34,38s) C.O. *Oblt.* Friedrich-Carl Hanesse	9
16Aug18	28Aug18	Villeselve	SGp 3 (Ss 6,12,18,26b,34,38s) C.O. *Oblt.* Friedrich-Carl Hanesse	18
28Aug18	18Sep18	Toulis	SGp 3 (Ss 6,18,26b,34,38s) C.O. *Oblt.* Friedrich-Carl Hanesse	9
18Sep18	6Oct18		SGp B (Ss 6,18,34,38s) C.O. *Oblt.* Friedrich-Carl Hanesse	3
6Oct18	13Oct18	Toulis	SGp B (Ss 6,7,18,34,38s) C.O. *Oblt.* Friedrich-Carl Hanesse	7
13Oct18	18Oct18	Toulis	SGp B (Ss 7,18,34,38s) C.O. *Oblt.* Friedrich-Carl Hanesse	7
18Oct18	29Oct18		SGp B (Ss 7,18,34) C.O. *Oblt.* Ernst Bonatz	7
29Oct18	EOW		SGp B (Ss 7,18,32,34) C.O. *Oblt.* Ernst Bonatz	3

Royal Prussian *Schutzstaffel 18*

1Jan17	*Schutzstaffel 18* is created from KG 7/Ks 42 by KM Nr.1425.16.g.A.7.L. of 1Jan17.
17Mar17	*Uffz.* Beermann, G, is severely WIA, shot twice in the leg during air combat. His pilot, *Uffz.* Josef Leppich, makes a good landing at Lavannes.
20Aug17	*Vzfw.* Leppich-1, *Feldw.* Kulke-1, Nieuport, Mermont Ferme
20Aug17	*Vzfw.* Leppich-2, *Feldw.* Kulke-2, Nieuport, Mermont Ferme
1Nov17	*Vzfw.* Josef Leppich, P, and *Gefr.* Josef Kremp, G, are KIA over Laon at 13.45 hours.
15Dec17	*Vzfw.* Rudolf Kausmann, P, and *Vzfw.* Wilhelm Befort, G, are KIA over Braye at 12.25 hours.
3Feb18	*Sgt.* Hermann Fröhner, P, and *Gefr.* Georg Post, G, are KIA at Grandlup-et-Fay.
24Mar18	*Vzfw.* Brüne-1, *Vzfw.* Wagner-1, Breguet 14B2 Esc. Br.126, M.d.L. Cheudet,MIA & Asp. E. Roux,MIA
27Mar18	*Schutzstaffel 18* is renamed *Schlachtstaffel 18* by KM Nr. 5126.18.A.7.L.IV.C. of 27Mar18.
4Apr18	*Oblt.* Georg Henke, O and C.O., is severely WIA by ground fure, shot in the chest over Sourdon, NW Montdidier and to hospital.
13Apr18	*Uffz.* Klomp, G, is WIA,lt.
24Apr18	*Vzfw.* Brüne, P, and *Vzfw.* Kurt-Georg Wagner, G, are taken POW.
4Aug18	*Flg.* Hans Silberstroff, G, is KIA over Toulis. He parachutes but it fails to hold.
Sep18	*Vzfw.* Thomas-1, *Vzfw.* Grimm-1, a/c
Nov18	*Schlachtstaffel 18* is demobilized at FEA 1, Altenburg.

Royal Prussian *Schutzstaffel 19*

Pilot/Gunner	Type	From Unit	From Date	To Date	To Unit
Sgt. Kurt Andres	P	Ss 8		22May18	KIA
Hptm. Wilhelm Aschenborn, C.O.	O	FA 255A	10Oct17	2Nov17	Leave
Hptm. Wilhelm Aschenborn, C.O.	P	Leave	6Nov17	24Apr18	SGp C
Gefr. Gerhard Baehnisch	M			22Jul18	KIC
Uffz. Barkmann	G	FA 266A	26May18		
Uffz. Johannes Binsfeld	P			17Oct17	KIA
Vzfw. Gustav Böhl	P	AFP 4	13Oct17	5Nov18	WIA
Ltn. Oskar Frhr. von Boenigk	O	Ks S.II	1Jan17	6Apr17	FEA 7
Gefr. Philipp Born (DOW 22Aug18)	G			21Aug18	POW
Gefr. Paul Casto				17May18	KIA
Uffz. Diefenthaler	P			30May18	AFP 4
Vzfw. Dietz	P		(May17)	13Oct17	JsSch I
Sgt. Wilhelm Dülger	P			22Jul18	KIC
Uffz. Dynhausen	P	FA 211A	30Apr17		
Gefr. Eckerle	G	AFP 4	29Aug17	30Nov17	POW
Vzfw. Emrich	G			19May18	BS
Ltn.d.R. Ewald Erdmann	P	KG 4/19	1Jan17	25Jan17	KIA
Vzfw. Eugen Fleischer	G	AFP 4	14May18	24May18	Ss 24b
Vzfw. Wilhelm Florig	P			6Nov17	IIC,lt.
Vzfw. Wilhelm Florig	P		6Nov17	30Nov17	POW
Vzfw. Ernst Friedberg	P	KG 4/19	1Jan17	26Sep17	KIA
Ltn.d.R. Werner Gaasch	O	KG 4/19	1Jan17	11Aug17	KIC
Pion. Georg Gilg	G	Ss 25b	20Nov17		
Gefr. Robert Godlewski	G	AFP 2	17Feb17	21Mar17	AFP 2
Uffz. Gruhl	G	AFP 4	28Oct17	27May18	FA 266A
Oblt. Karl von Gynz-Rekowsky, stv. C.O.	O	FA 202A	2Nov17	6Nov17	FA 202A
Uffz. Otto Haase	G	AFP 4	21Sep17	6Nov17	IIC,lt.
Uffz. Otto Haase	G		6Nov17	25Jan18	KIA
Uffz. Hardel	P			24Sep17	AFP 4
Uffz. Hassler	G	AFP 4	27May18		
Vzfw. Henkenhaf	G			30May18	AFP 4
Ltn.d.R. Herrmann, C.O.	O		21Oct18	5Nov18	WIA
Uffz. Heuer	G		(May17)	7Jun17	WIA,lt.
Vzfw. Heuer	G		7Jun17	11Apr18	WIA,sv.
Uffz. Huber	P		(Jul17)		
Flg. Jäger	G	AFP 4	21Sep17	6Oct17	AFP 4
Gefr. Bernhard Kahlke	P	AFP 4	29May18	2Jun18	AFP 4
Vzfw. Karl Kieling	P	Ss 24b	27Sep17	15Oct17	FEA 7
Uffz. Kontert	G	AFP 4	(May18)		
Sgt. Hans Kracht	G	Ss 24b	23May18	31Jul18	KIA
Vzfw. Krömmelbein	G			2Oct17	FEA 7
Vzfw. Kummetz	G		(Apr17)		
Oblt.d.R. Lantzius, C.O.	O	KG 4/19	1Jan17	10Oct17	FS Nmur
Vzfw. Ludwig	G			31Oct17	IIC,lt.
Vzfw. Ludwig	G		(Apr18)		
Ltn.d.R. Mehne	P		(Oct17)	(Dec17)	
Uffz. Rudolf Mittag	P	KG 4/19	1Jan17	11Aug17	KIC
Uffz. Mittwich	G		(Mar17)		
Uffz. Gustav Mückenhaupt	G	KG 4/19	1Jan17	26Sep17	KIA
Vzfw. Paul Ostrop	P	Ks S.II	1Jan17	8Jan17	Js 2
Vzfw. Plachta	G	AFP 4	21Sep17	27Sep17	Ss 16
Uffz. Reichmann	G	AFP 4	21Sep17	29Nov17	AFP 4
Flg. Ernst Reuter	G	Ss 28b	8Oct17		
Flg. Willi Roeder				13May17	KIA
Uffz. Rogge	G	AFP 4	(May18)	(Sep18)	
Gefr. Max Heinrich Sames	G	Ss 25b	5Oct17	29Jan18	IIC
Vzfw. Reinhard Schmiedel	P			23Aug18	WIA,sv.
Vzfw. Reinhard Schmiedel	P	Hosp.	(Oct18)	EOW	

Gefr. Wilhelm Schreiber	P	AFP 4	13Oct17	25Jan18	KIA
Vzfw. Hans Schuldt	P	AFP 4	10Nov17	31Jul18	KIA
Vzfw. Seemann	G		(Jan18)		
Gefr. Erwin Sommer	G			17Oct17	KIA
Uffz. Sonnenborn	P		(May17)	7Jun17	WIA
Gefr. Clemens Strauf	P	AFP 4	24May18	31Jul18	F/L IIC
Gefr. Clemens Strauf	P			21Aug18	KIA
Uffz. Teske	P			31Aug18	WIA
Flg. Tolle	P	AFP 4	(May18)		
Vzfw. Ulber	G	Ss 4	22Aug17	23Aug17	AFP 4
Vzfw. Karl Voigt	P		(Mar17)	29Jan18	IIC
Gefr. Weissenborn	P	AFP 4	2Jun18		
Uffz. Hans Wenner	G			22May18	KIA
Gefr. Wielpütz	P	AFP 4	15Oct17	31Oct17	IIC,lt.
Uffz. Wielpütz	P		(Sep18)		
Uffz. Woidt	G		(Apr17)	26Oct17	Idflieg

Schutzstaffel/Schlachtstaffel 19 Airfields

From	To	Location	*Schlachtgruppe* Affiliation	*Armee*
1Jan17	(9Jan17)	Villeveque		2
(31Jan17)		Grand Priel, NW St. Quentin	For FA 216(A)w	2
(Feb17)	21Mar17			2
21Mar17	29May17	Faumont Nord	Escort for FA 211(A)	6
29May17	Aug17	St. Denis-Westrem	Escort for FA 204(A)	4
Aug17		Ingelmunster		4
(19Sep17)	(Oct17)	Eeghem	Escort for FA 255(A)	4
(27Oct17)	20Nov17	Oostkamp	Escort for FA 202(A)	4
20Nov17	12Dec17	Boussières	For FA 210(A), 294(A)b	2
12Dec17	20Feb18	Tourmignies	Escort for FA 294(A)b	6
20Feb18	21Mar18	Tourmignies	Escort for FA 224(A)w	6
21Mar18		Cantin	SGp B (Ss 14,19,24b,25b,29b) C.O. *Hptm.* Wilhelm Aschenborn	17
(9Apr18)	24Apr18	Faumont Nord	SGp A (Ss 3,19) C.O. *Hptm.* Wilhelm Aschenborn	6
24Apr18	17May18	Ingelmunster	SGp C (Ss 3,13,19,29b) C.O. *Hptm.* Wilhelm Aschenborn	4
17May18	3Jun18	Ingelmunster	SGp 2 (Ss 3,13,19,29b) C.O. *Hptm.* Wilhelm Aschenborn	4
4Jun18	9Jul18	Bonneuil-Ferme	SGp 3 (Ss 3,13,19,29b) C.O. *Oblt.* Helmut Bühling	18
10Jul18	29Jul18	Mont Notre Dame	SGp B (Ss 3,13,19,29b) C.O. *Oblt.* Helmut Bühling	7
29Jul18	9Aug18	Liéramont	SGp 2 (Ss 3,13,19,29b) C.O. *Oblt.* Helmut Bühling	6
9Aug18	9Aug18	Nurlu	SGp 2 (Ss 3,13,19,29b) C.O. *Oblt.* Helmut Bühling	2
9Aug18	10Aug18	Liéramont	SGp 2 (Ss 3,13,19,29b) C.O. *Hptm.* Erich Sonntag	6
10Aug18	12Aug18	Nurlu	SGp 2 (Ss 11,13,19,27b) C.O. *Hptm.* Erich Sonntag	2
12Aug18	23Aug18	Longvesnes	SGp 2 (Ss 3,13,19) C.O. *Oblt.d.R.* Jaspers	2
24Aug18	26Sep18	St. Aubert	SGp 2 (Ss 3,13,19,29b) C.O. *Oblt.d.R.* Jaspers	2
26Sep18	6Oct18	Preutin	SGp 2 (Ss 3,13,19,29b) C.O. *Oblt.* Helmut Bühling	5
6Oct18	21Oct18	Preutin	SGp 2 (Ss 3,13,19,26b,29b) C.O. *Oblt.* Helmut Bühling	5
21Oct18	31Oct18	Preutin	SGp 2 (Ss 3,13,19,26b,29b) C.O. *Oblt.* Helmut Bühling	5
1Nov18	EOW	Stenay	SGp 2 (Ss 3,13,19,26b,29b) C.O. *Oblt.* Helmut Bühling	5

Royal Prussian *Schutzstaffel 19*

1Jan17	*Schutzstaffel 19* is created from Ks S.2 by KM Nr.1425.16.g.A.7.L. of 1Jan17.
25Jan17	*Ltn.d.R.* Ewald Erdmann, P, and *Ltn.d.R.* Günther Kallenbach, O, FA 216(A)w, are KIA over Clery sur Somme.
18Mar17	*Vzfw.* Voigt-1, *Uffz.* Mittwich-1, Caudron, Verpillieres, E. Roye
30Apr17	*Vzfw.* Voigt-2, *Vzfw.* Woidt-1, Spad 1, Sallaumines Spad S.7, Esc. N.15, Sgt. H. Baudson, WIA
13May17	*Flg.* Willi Roeder is KIA at Douai. Uncertain if he was a flying member or a mechanic of the unit.
26May17	*Vzfw.* Dietz-1, *Vzfw.* Woidt-2, a/c, 12.45, Lens-Avion S.E. 5 #A.8902, 56 Sqn. RFC, Lt. J. Toogood, WIA, POW
7Jun17	*Uffz.* Sonnenborn, P, and *Uffz.* Heuer (Hever), G, are WIA during air combat.
11Aug17	*Uffz.* Rudolf Mittag, P, and *Ltn.d.R.* Werner Gaasch, O, are KIC during takeoff from St. Denis-Westrem airfield.
26Sep17	*Vzfw.* Ernst Friedberg, P, and *Uffz.* Gustav Mückenhaupt, G, are KIA over Zonnebeke in an LVG C.V by ground fire.
17Oct17	*Uffz.* Johannes Binsfeld, P, and *Gefr.* Erwin Sommer, G, are KIA over Westroosebeke.
31Oct17	*Gefr.* Wielpütz, P, and *Vzfw.* Ludwig, G, are IIC,lt. during takeoff and to hospital.
6Nov17	*Vzfw.* Wilhelm Florig, P, and *Uffz.* Otto Haase, G, are IIC,lt. during landing.
30Nov17	*Vzfw.* Wilhelm Florig, P, and *Gefr.* Eckerle, G, are taken POW near Havrincourt in LVG C.V 9458/17 following air combat.
9Jan18	*Vzfw.* Voigt-3, *Vzfw.* Seemann-1, Nieuport, W. Warneton, Messines Nieuport 24 #B.3607, 1 Sqn. RFC, Lt. E.K. Skelton, KIA
25Jan18	*Gefr.* Wilhelm Schreiber, P, and *Uffz.* Otto Haase, G, are KIA over Warneton by Flak fire.
29Jan18	*Vzfw.* Karl Voigt, P, and *Gefr.* Max Heinrich Sames, G, are IIC.
27Mar18	*Schutzstaffel 19* is renamed *Schlachtstaffel 19* by KM Nr. 5126.18.A.7.L.IV.C. of 27Mar18.
11Apr18	*Vzfw.* Heuer (Hever), G, is WIA,sv.
12Apr18	*Vzfw.* Schuldt-1, *Vzfw.* Ludwig-1, Camel, Pont du Hem
17May18	*Gefr.* Paul Casto is KIA over Lendelede.
22May18	*Sgt.* Kurt Andres, P, and *Uffz.* Hans Wenner, G, are KIA over Abeele, Thelus by Flak fire in Halberstadt Cl.II 1209/18.
22Jul18	*Sgt.* Wilhelm Dülger, P, and *Gefr.* Gerhard Baehnisch, M, are KIC at Mont Notre Dame.
31Jul18	*Vzfw.* Hans Schuldt, P, and *Sgt.* Hans Kracht, G, are KIA over Le Marais Ferme, SE of Lestrem. They are mistakenly shot down by a German fighter.
31Jul18	*Gefr.* Clemens Strauf, P, is forced to land and is IIC.
21Aug18	*Gefr.* Clemens Strauf, P, is KIA, and *Gefr.* Philipp Born, G, is taken POW at Quéant while on a Schlacht flight for the *17. Armee*. Born DOW the next day.
23Aug18	*Vzfw.* Reinhard Schmiedel, P, is WIA,sv.
31Aug18	*Uffz.* Teske, P, is WIA by Flak.
25Sep18	*Uffz.* Wielpütz-1, *Uffz.* Rogge-1, S.E. 5a, Nurlu
5Nov18	*Vzfw.* Gustav Böhl, P, and *Ltn.d.R.* Herrmann, O and C.O., are WIA.
Nov18	*Schlachtstaffel 19* is demobilized at FEA 5, Hannover.

A Halberstadt Cl.II of *Schusta 19*, individually marked '1.' The black and white wheel covers were the unit marking of the former unit, *Ks S.II.*

Royal Prussian *Schutzstaffel 20*

Pilot/Gunner	Type	From		To	
		Unit	Date	Date	Unit
Bahlau					
Ltn. Barber	P			18Jul18	POW
Flg. Hugo Barthel			(May18)		
Gefr. Bartikowski	P	Ks S.I	1Jan17		
Vzfw. Bauschke	P	AFP 13			
Uffz. Behrendt					
Uffz. Heinrich Beneking	G			4Oct18	KIA
Uffz. Blanck					
Vzfw. Bürger					
Uffz. Otto Busch	P			Sep17	AFP 6
Clausnitzer					
Uffz. Deterre					
Uffz. Otto Eisele	P			4Oct18	KIA
Uffz. Ellert	G			18Jul18	POW
Uffz. Ferber					
Vzfw. Frank					
Vzfw. Friedrich					
Flg. Albert Gamradt				29Sep18	Died
Gast					
Ltn. Hilmar Glöcklen	O	Ks S.I	1Jan17		
Ltn. Gottberg					
Gefr. Alwin Grothe	P		(Sep18)	18Oct18	KIA
Grüsse					
Ltn. Günther					
Vzfw. Friedrich auf der Haar	P				
Uffz. Rudolf Hager	P			4Oct18	KIA
Flg. Eduard Haring				4Nov18	Died
Uffz. Heilmann					
Ltn. Heinrichshofen, OzbV	O	Ks S.I	1Jan17		KG 1
Vzfw. Hertsch					
Uffz. Hesse	P	Ks S.I	1Jan17		
Offz.Stv. Hettling	P	Ks S.I	1Jan17		
Ltn.d.R. Friedrich Hochstetter	P	Ks S.I	1Jan17	28Mar17	AFP 1
Flg. Paul Hundt				18Oct18	Died
Uffz. Reinhold Joerke	P	Ks S.I	1Jan17	27Feb17	Js 12
Uffz. Emil Karnapke	P			11Jun18	KIA
Uffz. Kirchhoff	G	Ks S.I	1Jan17		
Flg. Hasso Klein			(Jan18)		
Vzfw. Knauf	P				
Koch					
Vzfw. Kremling					
Vzfw. Arnold Küster	G		(Sep18)	4Oct18	POW
Oblt. Walter Lackner, Stv. C.O.	O	Kofl 7	4Dec17	30Jan18	Ss 7
Oblt. Werner Lange, C.O.	O	Ss 34	14Apr18	15May18	SGp B
Uffz. Laubschat					
Ltn. Lüttig					
Vzfw. Eduard Marcard	P			27May17	Js 9
Oblt. Mersmann, C.O.		Ks S.I	1Jan17		FA 237A
Vzfw. Metzner	P				
Vzfw. Josef Müller					
Gefr. Max Müller	P				MIA/POW
Ltn.d.R. Müller-Friedel	O	Ks S.I	1Jan17	Jan17	FA 256A
Ltn. Siegfried von Natzmer	P			Mar18	JSch II
Flg. Ludwig Neeb	G	AFP 1	7Feb17	14Feb17	Hosp.
Ltn. Neumüller	O	Ks S.I	1Jan17		
Vzfw. Nitsche					
Nolte					
Vzfw. Petersen					
Vzfw. Piechowiak	P		(Nov18)	EOW	
Uffz. Emil Piffczyk	G			29Aug18	POW

Vzfw. Plewa	G				Ss 33
Vzfw. Poffpaft					
Ltn.d.R. Wilhelm Prien, Stv. C.O.	P	AFP 6	31Mar18	12Apr18	AFP 6
Hptm. Waldemar Reinicke, C.O.	O		(Apr17)	(Mar18)	FA 210A
Vzfw. Edgar Rosenbaum	P				
Uffz. Robert Rosenkranz	G		(Sep18)	18Oct18	POW
Ltn. Wilhelm Roth					
Oblt.d.R. Rupke, OzbV	O	AFP 7	Jul18		
Gefr. Sammet	G			18Jul18	WIA,sv.
Ltn. Schaarschmidt	O	Ks S.I	1Jan17		
Uffz. Wilhelm Scharg	G		(Sep17)	6Sep18	POW
Gefr. Max Schlüssler	G			11Jun18	KIA
Flg. Ludwig Schmelter	G				
Vzfw. Schulz					
Ltn.d.R. Karl Semmler	O	Ks S.I	1Jan17		FA 245A
Vzfw. Stahl					
Ltn. Stapelberg					
Vzfw. Stenzel					
Uffz. Hugo Strangmeyer	P		(Sep17)		FA 206A
Ernst Szameitat					
Oskar Szameitat					
Ltn. Tauchnitz					
Oblt. Herbert Theurich	P	Ks S.I	1Jan17		Js 1
Gefr. Ullmer	P	Ks S.I	1Jan17	(Aug18)	
Uffz. Wagner					
Uffz. Otto Weber	G		(Sep18)	4Oct18	POW
Uffz. Paul Weisser	P			29May18	IIC,lt.
Uffz. Paul Weisser	P		29May18	6Sep18	POW
Offz.Stv. Willy Westphal	G	Ks S.I	1Jan17	(Aug18)	
Ltn.d.R. Willy Westphal	G		(Aug18)	EOW	
Ltn. Wetzchewald			(Mar17)		
Uffz. Hermann Zimmer	P		(Sep18)	4Oct18	POW
Oblt. Bruno Zipplies, C.O.	O	Ss 5	15May18	EOW	

Schusta 20 had a very colorful formation. Originally formed as *Kasta Köln* on 8Jul15, it was renamed *Kasta Trier* on 17Aug15. This unit was renamed *Kasta 31* on 19Jan16 (not to be confused with the Bavarian KG 6/Ks 31). *Kasta 31* was renamed Ks S.1 or *Sonderstaffel 1* on 29Jun16. Ks S.1 finally became *Schusta 20* on 1Jan17. The point being that some of the personnal given in the above roster may have been members of one or another of these former units without actually having been a member of *Schusta 20*. The existing records just are not sufficiently clear.

Schutzstaffel/Schlachtstaffel 20 Airfields

From	To	Location	*Schlachtgruppe* Affiliation	*Armee*
1Jan17		Ecourt St. Quentin	For FA 288(A)b	1
	(31Jan17)	Rumaucourt	Escort for FA 288(A)b	1
(Feb17)	(Mar17)	Froidmont	Escort for FA 209(A), 212(A)	7
(Mar17)	(Apr17)	Goudelancourt	Escort for FA 234(A)	7
(May17)	19Aug17			7
19Aug17	(Sep17)	Remonville	Escort for FA 278(A)	5
(30Sep17)	10Dec17	Froidmont	Escort for FA 212(A)	7
10Dec17		Erkeghem		4
(Dec17)		Cohartille	Escort for FA 212(A)	7
(Jan18)	(Feb18)	Froidmont		7
(21Mar18)	(24Mar18)	Marchavenne	SGp 4 (Ss 2,5,20,33) C.O. *Oblt.* Werner Lange	18
(9Apr18)	(14Apr18)	Omiécourt	SGp 4 (Ss 2,5,20,33) C.O. *Oblt.* Werner Lange	18
(25Apr18)	15May18	Omiécourt	SGp 4 (Ss 5,20,32,33) C.O. *Oblt.* Werner Lange	18
15May18	(6Jun18)	St. Erme	SGp C (Ss 5,20,32,33,37) C.O. *Oblt.* Werner Lange	7
(9Jun18)	(25Jun18)	Raperie Ferme	SGp Wichura (Ss 5,20,32,33,37) C.O. *Oblt.* Werner Lange	7

(15Jul18)	18Jul18	Anoux	SGp 1 (Ss 5,20,33,37) C.O. *Oblt.* Werner Lange	3
18Jul18	28Jul18	Seringes	SGp B (Ss 5,20,33,37) C.O. *Oblt.* Werner Lange	7
29Jul18	7Aug18	St. Loup	SGp B (Ss 5,20,33,35,37) C.O. *Oblt.* Werner Lange	1
7Aug18	1Sep18	Chivres-en-Laonnois	SGp C (Ss 5,20,33,35,37) C.O. *Oblt.* Werner Lange	7
2Sep18	6Sep18	Briey	SGp B (Ss 5,20,32,37) C.O. *Oblt.* Werner Lange	5
6Sep18	15Sep18	Anoux-le-Grange	SGp B (Ss 5,20,32,37) C.O. *Oblt.* Werner Lange	AAC
16Sep18	26Sep18	Thonne-les-Prés	SGp B (Ss 5,20,21,26b,33) C.O. *Oblt.* Bruno Zipplies	5
27Sep18	13Oct18	Thonne-les-Prés	SGp B (Ss 5,20,21,33) C.O. *Oblt.* Bruno Zipplies	5
13Oct18	23Oct18	St. Mard Vitron	SGp B (Ss 5,20,21,33) C.O. *Oblt.* Bruno Zipplies	5
23Oct18	29Oct18	Louppy-sur-Loison	SGp B (Ss 5,20,21,32,33) C.O. *Oblt.* Hans Ebel	5
29Oct18	6Nov18	St. Mard Vitron	SGp B (Ss 5,20,21,33) C.O. *Oblt.* Hans Ebel	5
6Nov18	EOW	Habay-la-Vieille	SGp B (Ss 5,20,21,33) C.O. *Oblt.* Hans Ebel	5

Royal Prussian *Schutzstaffel 20*

1Jan17	*Schutzstaffel 20* is created from Ks S.1 by KM Nr.1425.16.g.A.7.L. of 1Jan17.
17Mar17	*Gefr.* Ullmer-1, *Offz.Stv.* Westphal-1, Caudron, by Veuilly-Boucy
4Sep17	*Uffz.* Strangmeyer-1, *Gefr.* Scharg-1, Spad 1, Hessenwald
27Mar18	*Schutzstaffel 20* is renamed *Schlachtstaffel 20* by KM Nr. 5126.18.A.7.L.IV.C. of 27Mar18.
29May18	*Uffz.* Paul Weisser, P, is IIC,lt.
11Jun18	*Uffz.* Emil Karnapke, P, and *Gefr.* Max Schlüssler, G, are KIA over Soissons.
18Jul18	*Ltn.* Barber, P, and *Uffz.* Ellert, G, are taken POW.
18Jul18	*Ltn.d.R.* Hermann Wolf, P, *Schlasta 37*, and *Gefr.* Sammet, G, are WIA,sv. by ground fire and to hospital.
29Aug18	*Uffz.* Emil Piffczyk, G, and his pilot, whose name is completely illegible in the Zinn papers but whose rank and first names are *Flg.* Paul Peter Berthold, are taken POW at St. Paul-aux-Bois. They were shot down by French ground fire in Hannover Cl.IIIa 2747/18 at 12.15 hours.
6Sep18	*Uffz.* Paul Weisser, P, and *Uffz.* Wilhelm Scharg, G, are shot down in air combat, FTL, and taken POW at 13.15 hours at Romain, W of Bayon while on an orientation flight, Hannover Cl.IIIa 13369/17.
29Sep18	*Flg.* Albert Gamradt dies at Köslin.
4Oct18	*Uffz.* Otto Eisele, P, and *Uffz.* Heinrich Beneking, G, are KIA over Malancourt.
4Oct18	*Uffz.* Rudolf Hager, P, is KIA and *Uffz.* Otto Weber, G, is taken POW at Epinonville in Hannover Cl.IIIa 3892/18 after being shot down by American ground fire.
4Oct18	*Uffz.* Hermann Zimmer, P, and *Vzfw.* Arnold Küster, G, are taken POW.
18Oct18	*Gefr.* Alwin Grothe, P, is KIA and *Uffz.* Robert Rosenkranz, G, is taken POW at Sommerance at about 16.35 hours in a Halberstadt Cl.II.
18Oct18	*Flg.* Paul Hundt dies in Berlin.
4Nov18	*Vzfw.* Piechowiak-1, *Feldw.Ltn.* Westphal-2, Spad 1, German Lines
4Nov18	*Flg.* Eduard Haring dies in Stuttgart.
	Gefr. Max Müller, P, is reported MIA and presumed taken POW. Details, including even the date, are not known.
Nov18	*Schlachtstaffel 20* is demobilized at *Flieger Bomben Lehr Abteilung*, Frankfurt an der Oder.

Offz.Stv. Willy Westphal, a gunner with *Schlasta 20* from its formation until the end of the war. In August 1918 he was promoted to *Ltn.d.R.* Credit: UTD/HAC.

Royal Prussian *Schutzstaffel 21*

Pilot/Gunner	Type	From		To	
		Unit	Date	Date	Unit
Ltn.d.R. Armbrecht	P	Ks S.3	1Jan17	10Feb17	Js 1
Sgt. Friedrich Bachert (+16Oct)	P		(May18)	30Jul18	WIA,sv.
Gefr. Adam Bätz	G	Ss 26b	26Apr18		
Sgt. Bartsch	G		(May18)		
Offz.Stv. Beckmann	P	AFP 4	15Oct17		
Uffz. Walter Binder	P	AFP 1	27Jan17	13Apr17	WIA,sv.
Vzfw. Hans Birmolin	G	AFP 6	Apr18	8Aug18	KIA
Vzfw. Block	G		(Feb17)	(Jul17)	
Flg. Heinrich Bock	P			8Aug18	KIA
Uffz. Herbert Boy	P	AFP 4	24Sep17	13Oct17	AFP 4
Vzfw. Brabant	G		(Mar18)	2Oct18	WIA,lt.
Uffz. Josef Butzbach	P	AFP 4	25Mar17	5Jan18	AFP 6
Oblt. Hans Ebel, C.O.	O		(Jun18)	EOW	
Ltn. Paul Erbguth	P		(Feb17)	10Mar17	Js 30
Gefr. Fickel	G		(Feb17)	(May17)	
Flg. Max Gebhardt				13May18	KIA
Uffz. Gerschel	P		(Feb17)	23Aug17	FEA 1
Feldw. Gönkler	P		(Feb17)		
Feldw. Götze	P	KG 1/5	1Jan17	(Feb17)	FA 238A
Ltn. Haertel	O		(Feb17)		
Vzfw. Oskar Hassler	P		(Feb17)	12Sep17	IIC,lt.
Vzfw. Oskar Hassler	P		12Sep17	23May18	KIC
Uffz. Georg Hett	P	FA 7		EOW	
Uffz. Hencke	G	AFP 4	21Sep17		
Uffz. Oswald Hornig	P		(Jul18)	8Aug18	POW
Vzfw. Richard Hort	P		(Aug17)	(Mar18)	
Uffz. Hummel	P		(Oct18)		
Uffz. Kasper	P		(Feb17)		
Uffz. Klappstein	G		(Feb17)		

Gefr. Klein	G		(Oct18)		
Vzfw. Rudolf Kolodzicj	G		(Sep18)	2Oct18	POW
Uffz. Kurt Krause	P	FA 238A	15Sep17	21Sep17	KIA
Vzfw. Krüger	P		(Feb17)	(May17)	
Uffz. Krull	G			10Apr18	POW
Uffz. Lasslau	P		(Feb17)		
Oblt. Eberhard Leu, C.O.			(Mar18)	(Apr18)	
Uffz. Llotz	G		(Feb17)		
Flg. Fritz Löper			(Aug17)		
Flg. Luft	G			9Aug17	IIC,lt.
Vzfw. Ernst Mass	G	Ss 25b	9Sep17	10Apr18	POW
Uffz. Mau	P	Ss 10	14Sep17	15Sep17	Ss 10
Uffz. Herbert Mauss	G		(Jul18)	8Aug18	KIA
Gefr. Erich Mix	P	AFP 6	22Apr18	15May18	Js 54s
Ltn.d.R. Model	O		(Feb17)		
Uffz. Munz	P		(Aug17)	15Oct17	Idflieg
Uffz. Mutsch	P	AFP 4	13Oct17		
Uffz. Max Niemann	P	Ss 28b	26Apr18	2Oct18	POW
Uffz. Oberhülsmann	P		(Oct18)		
Ltn. Paetzold	O		(May17)		
Vzfw. Petersen	P			24May17	WIA,lt.
Vzfw. Petersen	P		(Dec17)		
Ltn.d.R. Wilhelm Prien, Stv. C.O.	P	AFP 6	12Apr18	24Apr18	AFP 4
Uffz. Richter	P			9Aug17	IIC
Oblt. Robrade, C.O.	O		21May18	23May18	IIC,sv.
Uffz. Georg Rösen	G	AFP 4	21Sep17		Ss 17
Uffz. Wilhelm Schieber	G	AFP 4	1Sep17	21Sep17	KIA
Sgt. Richard Schmidt	P			6Aug17	FA 258A
Vzfw. Seeger	P	AFP 4	13Sep17	14Sep17	AFP 4
Vzfw. Albert Steinberg	G	Ss 30b	27Sep17	23Jul18	KIA
Vzfw. Stork	G		(Feb17)		
Uffz. Stratmann	P	AFP 6	29Nov17		
Flg. Tiedke	G			7Jul17	IIC,sv.
Vzfw. Unger	G		(Aug17)	26Apr18	AFP 4
Ritt. Voss, C.O.		Ks S.3	1Jan17		
Flg. Voss	G			24May17	WIA,lt.
Gefr. Voss	G	AFP 4	1Sep17	7Sep17	AFP 4
Vzfw. Wenter	G			26Apr17	AFP 4
Uffz. Albert Wildermuth	G	AFP 4	22Aug17	1Sep17	Ss 17
Ltn.d.R. Wolf	O		(Feb17)		

Schutzstaffel/Schlachtstaffel 21 Airfields

From	To	Location	*Schlachtgruppe* Affiliation	*Armee*
1Jan17	26Feb17	Baralle	Escort for FA 226(A)s	1
26Feb17	(14Apr17)	Corbehem	Escort for FA 202(A)	6
(21May17)	4Jun17		Escort for FA 202(A)	6
4Jun17	22Nov17	Oostkamp	Escort for FA 227(A)	4
22Nov17	19Jan18	Dorignies	Escort for FA 288(A)b	6
19Jan18	Feb18	Halluin		4
Feb18	21Mar18	Dorignies		6
21Mar18	9Apr18	Ingelmunster		4
9Apr18	24Apr18	Houplin	SGp C (Ss 9,21) C.O. *Oblt.* Friedrich Carl Hanesse	6
24Apr18	17May18	Heule	SGp A (Ss 1,14,21,28b) C.O. *Oblt.* Emil Ziegler gen Stege	4
17May18	(27May18)	Eppes	SGp A (Ss 1,8,10,14,21) C.O. *Oblt.* Emil Ziegler gen Stege	7
(9Jun18)	(25Jun18)	La Pavillon Ferme	SGp Staabs (Ss 1,8,10,14,21) C.O. *Oblt.* Emil Ziegler gen Stege	7
(Jul18)		Seringes	SGp A (Ss 1,8,10,14,21) C.O. *Oblt.* Emil Ziegler gen Stege	7

(15Jul18)	(29Jul18)	Eppes	SGp A (Ss 1,8,10,14,21) C.O. *Oblt.* Emil Ziegler gen Stege	7
(3Aug18)			SGp A (Ss 1,8,10,14,21) C.O. *Oblt.* Emil Ziegler gen Stege	17
	8Aug18	Eppes	SGp A (Ss 1,8,10,14,21) C.O. *Oblt.* Emil Ziegler gen Stege	7
8Aug18	9Aug18	Curchy	SGp A (Ss 1,8,10,14,21) C.O. *Oblt.* Emil Ziegler gen Stege	2
9Aug18	10Aug18	Guizancourt	SGp A (Ss 1,8,10,14,21) C.O. *Oblt.* Emil Ziegler gen Stege	18
11Aug18	22Aug18	Eppes	SGp A (Ss 1,8,10,14,21) C.O. *Oblt.* Emil Ziegler gen Stege	7
22Aug18	16Sep18	Eppes		7
16Sep18	26Sep18	Thonne-les-Prés	SGp B (Ss 5,20,21,26b,33) C.O. *Oblt.* Bruno Zipplies	5
27Sep18	13Oct18	Thonne-les-Prés	SGp B (Ss 5,20,21,33) C.O. *Oblt.* Bruno Zipplies	5
13Oct18	23Oct18	St. Mard, Vitron	SGp B (Ss 5,20,21,33) C.O. *Oblt.* Bruno Zipplies	5
23Oct18	29Oct18	Louppy-sur-Loison	SGp B (Ss 5,20,21,32,33) C.O. *Oblt.* Hans Ebel	5
29Oct18	6Nov18	St. Mard, Vitron	SGp B (Ss 5,20,21,33) C.O. *Oblt.* Hans Ebel	5
6Nov18	EOW	Habay-la-Vieille	SGp B (Ss 5,20,21,33) C.O. *Oblt.* Hans Ebel	5

Royal Prussian *Schutzstaffel 21*

1Jan17	*Schutzstaffel 21* is created from Ks S.3 by KM Nr.1425.16.g.A.7.L. of 1Jan17.
13Apr17	*Uffz.* Walter Binder, P, is WIA,sv. in Albatros C.VII 3008/16 and is forced to land at Heule.
13May17	*Ltn.* Paetzold-1, *Vzfw.* Hassler-1, e/a, Monchy
24May17	*Vzfw.* Petersen, P, and *Flg.* Voss, G, are lightly WIA during air combat over Goeulzin in DFW C.V (Av) 5945/16.
25May17	*Vzfw.* Krüger-1, *Gefr.* Fickel-1, Spad, 11.40, Feuchy
7Jul17	*Vzfw.* Hassler-2, *Vzfw.* Block-1, Sopwith, 12.05, Quesnoy Sopwith 1 1/2 #A.8281, 45 Sqn. RFC, Lt. J.V.A. Gleed,KIA & Lt. J.B. Fotheringham,KIA
7Jul17	*Flg.* Tiedke, G, is IIC,sv. during a forced landing.
9Aug17	*Uffz.* Richter, P, and *Flg.* Luft, G, are IIC,lt. during a forced landing between Lille and Roubaix.
21Aug17	*Uffz.* Unger-1, *Uffz.* Munz-1, Sopw. Tripe, 11.25, S. Ploegsteert Wald, #N.6308, Naval 1, F/S/Lt. F.C. Lewis, KIA
12Sep17	*Vzfw.* Oskar Hassler, P, is IIC,lt. during a forced landing.
21Sep17	*Uffz.* Kurt Krause, P, and *Uffz.* Wilhelm Schieber, G, are KIA over Verlinghem during air combat.
15Dec17	*Vzfw.* Petersen-1, *Uffz.* Steinberg-1, Sopwith 1, Bailleul, SW Oppy
8Mar18	*Vzfw.* Hort-n/c, *Sgt.* Brabant-n/c, a/c, Laventie
27Mar18	*Schutzstaffel 21* is renamed *Schlachtstaffel 21* by KM Nr. 5126.18.A.7.L.IV.C. of 27Mar18.
10Apr18	*Uffz.* Krull, P, and *Vzfw.* Ernst Mass, G, are taken POW, left from Dorignies airfield.
13May18	*Flg.* Max Gebhardt is KIA at Anor. Unknown if he is a flying member or ground crew member of the unit.
23May18	*Vzfw.* Oskar Hassler, P, is KIC and *Oblt.* Robrade, O and C.O., is IIC,sv. when they strike a high tension line while landing at Charleville.
28May18	*Uffz.* Bachert-1, *Sgt.* Bartsch-1, Spad 1 Spad S.7, Esc. Spa.62, Adj. L. Blanc, MIA
16Jul18	*Gefr.* Hornig-1, *Uffz.* Mauss-1, Spad S.11 Esc. Spa.212, Adj. J. Bohan,WIA & Lt. E. Cassé,WIA
23Jul18	*Vzfw.* Albert Steinberg, G, is KIA over Fronley.
30Jul18	*Sgt.* Friedrich Bachert, P, is WIA,sv. He DOW 16Oct18 at Graudenz.
8Aug18	*Uffz.* Oswald Hornig, P, is taken POW and *Uffz.* Herbert Mauss, G, is KIA at Harbonnières.
8Aug18	*Flg.* Heinrich Bock, P, and *Vzfw.* Hans Birmolin, G, are KIA over Marcelcave.
2Oct18	*Uffz.* Oberhülsmann-1, *Vzfw.* Brabant-1, Spad
2Oct18	*Vzfw.* Brabant, G, is WIA,lt. in the above combat.
2Oct18	*Uffz.* Max Niemann, P, and *Vzfw.* Rudolf Kolodzicj, G, are taken POW at Nixéville Bois. They are shot down in air combat at 18.15 hours in Halberstadt Cl.II 5720/17.
8Oct18	*Uffz.* Hummel-1, *Gefr.* Klein-1, Balloon 26e Cie. Aerostieres
Nov18	*Schlachtstaffel 21* is demobilized at FEA 12, Kottbus.

Right: A Halberstadt Cl.II of *Schusta 21*. The gunner is not identified. Photo credit: UTD/HAC.

Below: The yellow/red Halberstadt Cl.II marked 'Martha/Elsa' of *Schlasta 21*.

Royal Bavarian *Schutzstaffel 22*

Pilot/Gunner	Type	From		To	
		Unit	Date	Date	Unit
Uffz. Peter Paul Bäumler	P	AFP 5	21Dec17	19Apr18	WIA,POW
Vzfw. Karl Behringer	P	AFP 7	4Jun17	11Mar18	JsSch I
Pion. Otto Behringer	G	AFP 2	18Mar18	27Apr18	KIA
Gefr. Otto Biedermann	G	AFP 2	18Mar18	10May18	AFP 2
Vzfw. Ludwig Bott	P	AFP 7	6Apr17	31May18	WIA,sv.
Vzfw. Fritz Karl Brandstädter	G	FA 286A	29May18	EOW	
Vzfw. Franz Braukmann	G	AFP 5	17Feb17	13Aug17	AFP 7
Vzfw. Franz Braukmann	G	AFP 19	30Oct18	EOW	
Gefr. Friedrich Bromberger	G	AFP 1	12Jun18	EOW	
Vzfw. Heinrich Christl	G	AFP 7	30Jun17	9Mar18	FS Asch
Oblt. Hanns Adolf *Frhr.* von Crailsheim, C.O.	P	FA 294A	4Aug17	4Mar18	BG 8/25
Vzfw. Philipp Däuwel	P	AFP 7	8Jul17	23Sep18	FEA 1b
Flg. Ernst Deutschmann	G	AFP 7	9Apr17	29Apr17	KIA
Ltn.d.R. Karl Döring	O	KG 6/31	1Jan17	1Apr17	FEA 1b
Vzfw. Heinrich Eder	G	AFP 7	6Jun17	12Feb18	AFP 5
Uffz. Heinrich Elend	P	AFP 7	6Apr17	15Apr17	Hosp.
Uffz. Bernhard Endres	G	AFP 7	23Jun17	12Mar18	WIA,sv.
Vzfw. Bernhard Endres	G	FEA 1b	24Aug18	EOW	
Gefr. Michael Engert (+ 18Feb19)	G	AFP 2	2Apr18	19Apr18	WIA,POW
Flg. Otto Erdmann	P	KG 6/31	1Jan17	13Feb17	FEA 1b
Pion. Engelbert Esser	G	AFP 7	6Jun17	12Jun17	POW
Gefr. Josef Fink	G	AFP 2	12Apr18	12Jun18	WIA,sv.
Vzfw. Eugen Fleischer	G	AFP 19	13Oct18	29Oct18	Hosp.
Uffz. Alfred Fliegel	P	AFP 7	26Apr17	20Jul17	AFP 7
Vzwachtmstr. Franz Freytag	G	FA 272A	16Jun18	16Jul18	IIC
Vzwachtmstr. Franz Freytag	G	FEA 1	5Sep18	23Oct18	FEA 3
Vzfw. Josef Gerl	G	Ss 26b	13Jul18	21Jul18	AFP 1
Vzfw. Friedrich Gömann	G	AFP 7	9Apr17	28May18	WIA,DOW
Ltn.d.R. Max Gossner	O	KG 6/31	1Jan17	24Apr17	FEA 1b
Vzfw. Josef Groiss	G	AFP 2	29Apr18	EOW	
Oblt. Carl von Grossmann, Stv. C.O.	O	FA 212A	20Jul17	4Aug17	FA 212A
Pion. Ludwig Grünwald	P	FA 296A	17Nov17	2Dec17	AFP 5
Oblt.d.R. Karl *Ritter* von Gruny, CO	O	FEA 1b	7Oct18	EOW	
Uffz. Robert Günther (DOW 10May)	G	AFP 2	22Mar18	3May18	WIA
Vzfw. Wilhelm Harz	P	AFP 2	24Apr18	EOW	
Uffz. Karl Herold	P	AFP 18	15Aug18	EOW	
Uffz. Christoph Hertel	P	FA 265A	6Apr17	20Apr17	JsSch I
Uffz. Martin Höntsch	P	AFP 2	2May18	15Jun18	KIA
Uffz. Franz Kienass	G	AFP 1	2Jun18	EOW	
Gefr. Rudolf Kott	P	AFP 1	17Jul18	EOW	
Uffz. Josef Krebs	P	AFP 19	26Sep18	EOW	
Ltn.d.R. Julius Kuse, Stv. C.O.	O	Kofl 2	4Mar18	23Mar18	Ss 15
Gefr. Alfred Richard Lämmel	P	AFP 5	3Jan18	27Apr18	WIA
Gefr. Alfred Richard Lämmel	P			28Apr18	DOW
Offz.Stv. Anton Leupold	G	AFP 7	30Jun17	3Aug18	AFP 1
Ltn.d.R. Hermann Mader	P	KG 6/31	1Jan17	1Apr17	FA 265A
Oblt.d.R. Ludwig Männer	O	FA 288A	23Mar18	15Oct18	FEA 1b
Gefr. Erich Martens	P	AFP 2	22Mar18	10May18	AFP 2
Gefr. Bonifaz Metz	G	AFP 7	21Apr17	25May17	WIA
Vzfw. Ludwig Müller	G	AFP 7	21Apr17	22Mar18	WIA
Gefr. Wilhelm Naroska	G	AFP 1	2Jun18	15Jun18	KIA
Vzfw. Anton Neuber	P	KG 6/31	1Jan17	4May17	Leave
Vzfw. Anton Neuber	P	Leave	9May17	2Mar18	GS Pdbn
Vzfw. Luitpold Offenbacher	P	KG 6/31	1Jan17	6Aug17	AFP 7
Uffz. Frank Oppenheimer	G	AFP 7	26May17	7Jun17	AFP 7
Gefr. Franz Osiander	G	AFP 1	17Jul18	5Sep18	AFP 1
Uffz. Hermann Pauli	G	FEA 1b	10Jan17	13Feb17	FEA 1b
Gefr. Georg Post	G	AFP 7	4Jun17	17Jun17	AFP 7

Vzfw. Otto Rosenkranz	P	AFP 7	6Apr17	15Apr18	AFP 2
Vzfw. Gustav Lazarus Samuel	G	AFP 7	21Apr17	7Jun17	AFP 7
Vzfw. Josef Schäfer	P	AFP 7	29Jul17	4Jan18	JsSch I
Vzfw. Max Schiffler	P	AFP 2	24Apr18	EOW	
Ltn.d.R. Alfred Schillinger	P	KG 6/31	1Jan17	15Apr17	KSch Pd
Flg. Max Schlender	G	AFP 7	17Jun17	30Jun17	AFP 7
Vzfw. Paul Schrader	P	AFP 7	4Jun17	12Jun17	POW
Uffz. Wilhelm Schreiber	P	AFP 1	4Jun18	EOW	
Flg. Richard Senst	G	AFP 18	15Aug18	EOW	
Uffz. Walter Siedschlag	P	AFP 1	20Jun18	EOW	
Flg. Josef Staeves	G	AFP 7	17Jun17	22Jun17	Ss 14
Uffz. Karl Maria Stauber	G	AFP 5	21Feb18	22Mar18	IIC,lt.
Vzfw. Karl Maria Stauber	G		22Mar18	24Aug18	FEA 1b
Vzfw. Ernst Tautz	G	AFP 7	21May17	22Mar18	IIC
Vzfw. Rudolf Töninges	P	AFP 5	2Jan18	14Feb18	FEA 2b
Oblt. Theodor Triendl, C.O.	O	KG 6/31	1Jan17	20Jul17	FEA 1b
Vzfw. Paul Wagner	P	KG 6/31	1Jan17	1Apr17	AFP 4
Uffz. Augustin Waibel	P	AFP 2	10Mar18	13Aug18	WIA
Vzfw. Siegfried Walther	P	AFP 7	18May17	13Oct17	JSch II
Uffz. Gotthold Walz	P	FA 286A	21May18	16Jul18	KIC
Pion. Eugen Weber	G	AFP 2	9May18	2Jun18	AFP 1
Vzfw. Max Wimmer	P	KG 6/31	1Jan17	1Apr17	AFP 4
Ltn.d.R. Adam Wolff	O	KG 6/31	1Jan17	1Apr17	FEA 1b
Gefr. Josef Zach	G	AFP 2	7May18	12Jun18	AFP 1
Ltn.d.R. Kurt Ziegler	O	KG 6/31	1Jan17	1Apr17	FEA 1b

Royal Bavarian *Schutzstaffel 22*

Mechanics and Ground Personnel

Name	From		To	
	Unit	Date	Date	Unit
Pion. Heinrich Alber	KG 6/31	1Jan17	4Nov17	KWP 5
Kraftf. Friedrich Albinius	AFP 1	17Jul18	1Aug18	AFP 1
Pion. Hans Alt	KG 6/31	1Jan17	17Jul17	FEA 1b
Pion. Max Appel	FEA 1b	10Aug17	17Apr18	Hosp.
Pion. Josef Bauer	FEA 1b	20Jun18	EOW	
Gefr. Ludwig Becker	KG 6/31	1Jan17	3Feb17	FEA 1b
Pion. Alois Beger	KG 6/31	1Jan17	19Jan17	AFP 5
Gefr. Hubert Belasini	KG 6/31	1Jan17	EOW	
Gefr. Peter Bergmeier	FEA 1b	19Jul17	23Oct18	Hosp.
Uffz. Fritz Bickel	KG 6/31	1Jan17	27Mar18	BG 8/25
Pion. Theodor Bolz	KG 6/31	1Jan17	17Oct17	Hosp.
Vzfw. August Bosch	FEA 1b	22Jan18	EOW	
Gefr. Josef Bott	KG 6/31	1Jan17	14Dec17	AFP 5
Pion. Alois Braun	FEA 1b	19Nov17	EOW	
Pion. Ludwig Braun	FEA 1b	10Aug17	EOW	
Pion. Ludwig Breitsameter	AFP 5	9Sep17	14Oct17	AFP 5
Gefr. Eugen Brög	FEA 1b	5Aug17	EOW	
Pion. Richard Brucher	KG 6/31	1Jan17	25Apr17	FEA 1b
Gefr. Josef Brückl	KG 6/31	1Jan17	20Jul17	FEA 1b
Pion. Johann Buberger	FEA 1b	14Jul17	19Jun18	Artllry
Pion. Friedrich Burger	BG 8/25	26Mar18	EOW	
Pion. Walter Dietrich	FEA 1b	10Aug17	EOW	
Pion. Johann Dietz	FEA 1b	3Jan17	27Jan17	FEA 1b
Gefr. Wolfgang Dietz	AFP 5	1Nov17	26May18	FA 286A
Gefr. Franz Diller	KG 6/31	1Jan17	EOW	
Pion. Gottlieb Dilling	AFP 5	2Jan18	20Mar18	FEA 1b
Gefr. Emeran Dosch	Hosp.	24Feb17	24Sep17	Hosp.
Pion. Karl Drechsel	FEA 2b	4Dec17	EOW	
Pion. Georg Dümmler	FEA 1b	10Aug17	15Sep17	Artllry
Pion. Georg Dümmler	Artllry	8Mar18	20Jun18	Hosp.

Pion. Georg Dümmler	Hosp.	2Jul18	EOW	
Pion. Georg Dürsch	KG 6/31	1Jan17	19Jan17	AFP 5
Pion. Karl Ecker	KG 6/31	1Jan17	19Jan17	AFP 5
Pion. Albert Eireiner	Js 16b	20Dec17	EOW	
Pion. Josef Eisner	KG 6/31	1Jan17	26Feb17	Dschrgd
Vzfw. Johann Enzensperger	FEA 1b	21Sep17	EOW	
Sgt. Otto Ernst	KG 6/31	1Jan17	23Sep18	Hosp.
Pion. Rudolf Exel	FEA 1b	2Nov18	10Nov18	AFP 19
Pion. Edmund Fischer	KG 6/31	1Jan17	2Apr17	FA 265A
Uffz. Josef Freisinger	KG 6/31	1Jan17	17Jul17	FEA 1b
Pion. Jacob Fusseder	FEA 1b	10Dec17	EOW	
Pion. Georg Gehring	KG 6/31	1Jan17	19Mar17	FEA 1b
Pion. Alois Geier	KG 6/31	1Jan17	20Jul17	FEA 1b
Pion. Franz Geist	KG 6/31	1Jan17	15Jan17	AFP 5
Pion. Ferdinand Gerauer	FEA 1b	3Aug18	EOW	
Gefr. Wolfgang Gisl	KG 6/31	1Jan17	19Jan17	AFP 5
Uffz. Georg Gmeiner	KG 6/31	1Jan17	1Feb18	FEA 1b
Uffz. Heinrich Goldfuss	KG 6/31	1Jan17	28Oct17	Kn Btln
Pion. Max Gossmann	FEA 1b	20Sep18	EOW	
Pion. Xaver Grotz	KG 6/31	1Jan17	EOW	
Kraftf. August Grünholz	AFP 19	13Oct18	EOW	
Kraftf. Rudolf Hallanzy	KEA 1	23Jul18	EOW	
Pion. Wilhelm Hangenstein	KG 6/31	1Jan17	20Jun17	FEA 1b
Gefr. Karl Hartkorn	KG 6/31	1Jan17	EOW	
Pion. Adam Hauswurz	FEA 1b	8Sep17	7Nov17	FEA 1b
Gefr. Heinrich Heinlein	KG 6/31	1Jan17	10Sep17	FEA 1b
Gefr. Alois Herrschaft	FEA 1b	22Sep17	3Oct17	FEA 1b
Pion. Georg Hirschmann	KG 6/31	1Jan17	19Jan17	AFP 5
Pion. Josef Hirschmüller	FEA 1b	10Aug17	7Nov17	FEA 1b
Gefr. Xaver Hofbauer	KG 6/31	1Jan17	EOW	
Pion. Michael Holzfurtner	KG 6/31	1Jan17	27Jan17	FEA 1b
Pion. Ernst Holzschuher	KG 6/31	1Jan17	20Jul17	FEA 1b
Pion. Anton Huber	KG 6/31	1Jan17	2Sep18	FEA 1b
Pion. Karl Huber	KG 6/31	1Jan17	19Jul18	Infntry
Pion. Peter Huber	FA 22	10Oct18	EOW	
Vzfw. Karl Hummel	KG 6/31	1Jan17	27Feb17	FEA 1b
Pion. Ludwig Jordan	FA 292A	20Sep18	EOW	
Pion. Reinhard Jung	BG 8/25	26Mar18	7Jun18	Hosp.
Pion. Mathäus Kammerer	FEA 1b	10Aug18	EOW	
Pion. Georg Kellner	KG 6/31	1Jan17	27Jan17	FEA 1b
Uffz. Jakob Keyl	KG 6/31	1Jan17	EOW	
Pion. Christoph Kibinger	KG 6/31	1Jan17	26Jun17	AFP 7
Pion. Michael Kleinschrod	FEA 2b	4Dec17	25Feb18	FA 291A
Pion. August Kolb	FEA 2b	7Dec17	EOW	
Uffz. Johann Kramer	KG 6/31	1Jan17	EOW	
Unterzahlmstr. Georg Kraus	FEA 1b	2Nov18	EOW	
Pion. Albert Kübel	FEA 1b	15Sep17	7Nov17	FEA 1b
Pion. Gustav Kuhn	KG 6/31	1Jan17	22Jun17	AFP 7
Gefr. Martin Kurth	FA 291A	27Nov17	EOW	
Pion. Heinrich Lang	KG 6/31	1Jan17	11Apr17	FA 257A
Pion. Franz Lauber	FEA 2b	4Dec17	7Sep18	Hosp.
Pion. Josef Lehnerer	FEA 1b	10Dec17	2Apr18	Hosp.
Sgt. Wilhelm Leiner	KG 6/31	1Jan17	15Sep17	FEA 1b
Pion. Josef Liebenthal	KG 6/31	1Jan17	9Nov17	FEA 1b
Pion. Karl Limmer	KG 6/31	1Jan17	EOW	
Pion. Johann Linner	FEA 1b	20Jun18	19Jul18	Infntry
Pion. Georg Lindner	FEA 1b	4Mar18	26Mar18	Hosp.
Pion. Friedrich Listek	FEA 1b	13Mar18	31Mar18	Hosp.
Pion. Simon Löll	KG 6/31	1Jan17	EOW	
Gefr. Josef Maier	BG 8/25	26Mar18	EOW	
Uffz. Simon Maier	FEA 1b	19Jul17	EOW	
Gefr. Johann Mauer	KG 6/31	1Jan17	EOW	
Gefr. Heinrich Mayer	FS II	22May18	4Jun18	AFP 1
Pion. Friedrich Meisner	KEA 1b	5Nov17	EOW	
Pion. Michael Mendl	KG 6/31	1Jan17	3Feb17	FEA 1b

Pion. Georg Meyer	KG 6/31	1Jan17	3Feb17	FEA 1b
Pion. Christian Mittring	FEA 1b	19Jul17	6May18	Hosp.
Pion. Christian Mittring	Hosp.	28Jun18	EOW	
Pion. Karl Müller	KG 6/31	1Jan17	2May17	FEA 1b
Kraftf. Otto Müller	AFP 1	14Jun18	1Aug18	AKP 1
Gefr. August Münzer	KG 6/31	1Jan17	4May17	Hosp.
Gefr. August Münzer	Hosp.	29May17	30Dec17	Daimler
Uffz. August Münzer	Daimler	8Mar18	EOW	
Pion. Johann Baptist Näger	FEA 1b	19Jul17	7Nov17	FEA 1b
Uffz. Karl Nervegno	KG 6/31	1Jan17	11Jun17	FEA 1b
Pion. Karl Neumayer	BG 8/25	26Mar18	EOW	
Pion. Johann Niederwinkler	KG 6/31	1Jan17	15Aug17	FEA 1b
Werkmstr.Stv. Georg Oberreuther	FEA 1b	5Mar17	11Oct17	FEA 1b
Gefr. Albert Ortloff	AFP 4	19Jul17	EOW	
Pion. Bruno Ostermeier	FBS I	17Jan18	19Jun18	Infntry
Feldw. Philipp Pallmer	KG 6/31	1Jan17	9Oct17	FEA 1b
Gefr. Ernst Paschke	KG 6/31	1Jan17	19Dec17	Js 16
Pion. Max Penn	FEA 1b	11Jul17	3Oct17	FEA 1b
Pion. Johann Petri	KG 6/31	1Jan17	27Jan17	FEA 1b
Pion. Georg Petz	FEA 1b	5Sep17	22Oct17	Hosp.
Gefr. Georg Petz	Hosp.	12Nov17	EOW	
Pion. Sebastian Pölzl	KG 6/31	1Jan17	3Feb17	FEA 1b
Gefr. Georg Rauh	AFP 5	7Sep17	27Jun18	FEA 1b
Kraftf. Bartholomäus Rechthaler	KEA 1b	23Jul18	EOW	
Vzfw. Georg Regler	KG 6/31	1Jan17	1Oct17	FEA 1b
Pion. Georg Rehm	FEA 1b	19Jul17	2Nov17	FEA 1b
Uffz. Anton Reitberger	KG 6/31	1Jan17	23Oct18	Hosp.
Gefr. Christian Renftle	KG 6/31	1Jan17	23Oct17	Hosp.
Uffz. Michael Rentemann	KG 6/31	1Jan17	27Mar18	BG 8/25
Gefr. Friedrich Rentz	AFP 5	13Dec17	27Mar18	BG 8/25
Pion. Andreas Rieder	KG 6/31	1Jan17	19Jan17	AFP 5
Pion. Adam Ring	FEA 1b	18Jun18	EOW	
Pion. Johann Rogner	KG 6/31	1Jan17	22Aug17	FEA 2b
Pion. Erich Rother	FEA 1b	10Aug17	22Apr18	Hosp.
Pion. Johann Rottner	KG 6/31	1Jan17	EOW	
Pion. Ludwig Sappler	KEA 1b	5Nov17	26Nov17	FA 291A
Gefr. Alfred Schäfer	FEA 1b	10Aug17	21Jul18	Hosp.
Uffz. Franz Scheidmeyer	KG 6/31	1Jan17	20Jul17	FEA 1b
Pion. Franz Schmid	AFP 1	10Aug18	EOW	
Pion. Johann Schmid	BG 8/25	26Mar18	19Jun18	Infntry
Uffz. Johann Schmierlein	KG 6/31	1Jan17	EOW	
Gefr. Markus Schömig	KG 6/31	1Jan17	24Sep18	FEA 1b
Uffz. Karl Scholz	KG 6/31	1Jan17	19Jan17	AFP 5
Kraftf. Hans Schretzmeier	KEA 1b	24Oct18	EOW	
Pion. Ludwig Schwarz	KG 6/31	1Jan17	20Jul17	FEA 1b
Uffz. Karl Seeberger	KG 6/31	1Jan17	11Jan17	Hosp.
Uffz. Karl Seeberger	Hosp.	20Jan17	EOW	
Uffz. Heinrich Seehofer	KG 6/31	1Jan17	16Sep17	FA 291A
Gefr. Leonhard Seierlein	KG 6/31	1Jan17	8Jul17	Hosp.
Pion. Hans Sehlmacher	FEA 1b	19Jul17	28Jun18	FEA 2b
Uffz. Wilhelm Sontheimer	KG 6/31	1Jan17	14Dec17	Js 16
Uffz. Fritz Specht	KG 6/31	1Jan17	EOW	
Vzfw. Konrad Spegele	FEA 1b	9Aug18	21Oct18	Hosp.
Vzfw. Konrad Spegele	Hosp.	27Oct18	1Nov18	FEA 1b
Pion. Wilhelm Spötle	KG 6/31	1Jan17	EOW	
Gefr. Peter Stadler	FEA 1b	26Jul18	EOW	
Pion. Josef Standl	KG 6/31	1Jan17	5May17	AFP 5
Pion. Josef Standl	AFP 5	22May17	20Jul17	FEA 1b
Uffz. Karl Staub	KG 6/31	1Jan17	27Mar18	BG 8/25
Gefr. Ludwig Steger	FA 293A	4Aug17	6Mar18	BG 8/25
Pion. Theodor Steger	FEA 1b	20Jun18	EOW	
Gefr. Jakob Steibel	KG 6/31	1Jan17	19Jan17	AFP 5
Sgt. Jakob Steibel	AFP 5	11Aug17	EOW	
Pion. Johann Steinbauer	FEA 1b	19Sep18	EOW	
Pion. August Steiner	Hosp.	23Mar17	4Apr17	Hosp.

Pion. August Steiner	Hosp.	3May17	1Apr18	Hosp.
Gefr. Georg Steinmetz	KG 6/31	1Jan17	14Dec17	FBLA
Gefr. Georg Steinmetz	FBLA	14Jan18	1Feb18	FEA 1b
Gefr. Michael Stellwag	FA 288A	22Mar18	10Oct18	FEA 1b
Pion. Johann Stössl	FEA 1b	19Sep18	EOW	
Pion. Friedrich Strauss	KG 6/31	1Jan17	3Feb17	FEA 1b
Pion. Johann Streibel	KG 6	1Jan17	3Feb17	FEA 1b
Pion. Josef Ströhlein	KG 6/31	1Jan17	EOW	
Pion. Johann Synderhauf	KG 6/31	1Jan17	27Jan17	FEA 1b
Gefr. Josef Tobias	KG 6/31	1Jan17	20Jul17	FEA 1b
Pion. Philipp Träser	KG 6/31	1Jan17	19Jan17	AFP 5
Sgt. Karl Triller	KG 6/31	1Jan17	EOW	
Pion. Heinrich Trunk	FEA 1b	19Jul17	EOW	
Pion. Albert Ulrich	FEA 1b	20Jun18	19Jul18	Infntry
Pion. Johann Unfricht	BG 8/25	26Mar18	22Oct18	Hosp.
Pion. Max Vogler	FEA 1b	19Nov17	EOW	
Pion. Johann Waschhauser	KG 6/31	1Jan17	EOW	
Pion. Karl Weber	KG 6/31	1Jan17	7Nov17	FEA 1b
Pion. Josef Weidinger	KG 6/31	1Jan17	EOW	
Uffz. Fritz Weig	KG 6/31	1Jan17	EOW	
Offz.Stv. Georg Weinzierl	FEA 1b	22Sep17	22May18	FEA 2b
Uffz. Karl Weiss	KG 6/31	1Jan17	27Mar18	BG 8/25
Sgt. Josef Welte	KG 6/31	1Jan17	20Jul17	FEA 1b
Gefr. Josef Wendl	KG 6/31	1Jan17	26Mar18	BG 8/25
Pion. Johann Werner	Fnk Sch	3Aug18	EOW	
Uffz. Karl Wieland	KG 6/31	1Jan17	21Mar17	Hosp.
Pion. Ottmar Wieser	KG 6/31	1Jan17	1May17	Daimler
Uffz. Ottmar Wieser	Daimler	30Jun17	EOW	
Pion. Josef Wittmann	KG 6/31	1Jan17	EOW	
Pion. August Witzgall	FEA 1b	9Aug18	EOW	
Pion. Franz Wolf	FEA 1b	23Sep17	EOW	
Sgt. Max Zeitler	KG 6/31	1Jan17	23Jun18	Hosp.
Uffz. Josef Zenzelhuber	KG 6/31	1Jan17	EOW	
Pion. Otto Zimmermann	KG 6/31	1Jan17	19Jan17	AFP 5

Schutzstaffel/Schlachtstaffel 22b
Mitgemachte Schlachten und Gefechte

(Battles and combat actions in which Ss 22b participated)

10Sep16	3Mar17	*Stellungskämpfe vor Verdun* (Trench fighting at Verdun)
4Mar17	5Apr17	*Kämpfe an der Aisne* (Fighting on the Aisne)
6Apr17	27May17	*Doppelschlacht Aisne-Champagne* (The double battle of Aisne-Champagne)
25May17	13Aug17	*Stellungskämpfe am Chemin-des-Dames* (Trench fighting for the Chemin-des-Dames)
14Aug17	9Oct17	*Abwehrschlacht vor Verdun* (Defensive battle at Verdun)
10Oct17	4Mar18	*Stellungskämpfe vor Verdun* (Trench fighting at Verdun)
5Mar18	12May18	*Kämpfe vor der Siegfried Front und an der Ancre* (Fighting on the Siegfried front and on the Ancre)
13May18	13Sep18	*Stellungskämpfe vor Reims* (Trench fighting at Reims)
14Sep18	11Nov18	*Stellungskämpfe in Lothringen* (Trench fighting in Lorraine)

Schutzstaffel/Schlachtstaffel 22b Airfields

From	To	Location	*Schlachtgruppe* Affiliation	*Armee*
1Jan17	10Jan17	Mont		5
10Jan17	3Mar17	Jametz	Escort for FA 203(A)	5
4Mar17	24Apr17	Cohartille		7
24Apr17	13Aug17	Froidmont	Escort for FA 212(A)	7
14Aug17	4Mar18	Mercy le Bas	Escort for FA 291(A)b	5
5Mar18	21Mar18	Busigny	Escort for FA 269(A)	2
21Mar18	28Mar18	Busigny	SGp A (Ss 10,17,22b) C.O. *Hptm.* Zimmermann	2
28Mar18	19Apr18	Caix	SGp A (Ss 10,17,22b) C.O. *Hptm.* Zimmermann	2
19Apr18	12May18	Cappy	SGp A (Ss 4,11,15,17,22b) C.O. *Hptm.* Zimmermann	2
12May18	28May18	Tagnon	SGp 1 (Ss 2,7,22b,31b) C.O. *Oblt.* Walter Lackner	1
28May18	(6Jun18)	Magneux	SGp 1 (Ss 2,7,22b,31b) C.O. *Oblt.* Walter Lackner	1
(9Jun18)	(Jul18)	Magneux		1
	15Jul18	St. Loup	SGp 2 (Ss 22b,28b,30b,31b,32) C.O. *Oblt.d.R.* August Ertl	1
15Jul18	18Jul18	Autrecourt		1
18Jul18	3Aug18	Le Chesne	SGp 2 (Ss 7,22b,23b,26b,36) C.O. *Oblt.* Walter Lackner	3
4Aug18	9Aug18	Neuflize	SGp B (Ss 2,22b,23b,36) C.O. *Oblt.d.R.* Ludwig Männer	1
9Aug18	9Aug18	Villeselve	SGp B (Ss 2,22b) C.O. *Oblt.d.R.* Ludwig Männer	18
10Aug18	10Aug18	St. Loup	SGp B (Ss 2,22b,23b,36) C.O. *Oblt.d.R.* Ludwig Männer	1
10Aug18	12Aug18	Villeselve	SGp B (Ss 2,22b) C.O. *Oblt.d.R.* Ludwig Männer	18
13Aug18	9Sep18	St. Loup	SGp B (Ss 2,22b,23b,36) C.O. *Oblt.d.R.* Ludwig Männer	1
9Sep18	13Sep18	St. Loup	SGp B (Ss 2,22b,23b,36) C.O. *Oblt.d.R.* Sigmund Kreitmair	1
14Sep18	28Sep18	Autrecourt	SGp 3 (Ss 2,22b,23b) C.O. *Oblt.d.R.* Sigmund Kreitmair	3
28Sep18	19Oct18	Autrecourt	SGp 3 (Ss 2,22b,23b) C.O. *Oblt.* Karl *Ritter* von Gruny	3
19Oct18	EOW	Diffenbach-lès-Puttelange	SGp 2 (Ss 2,22b,28b,36) C.O. *Oblt.* Karl *Ritter* von Gruny	19

Royal Bavarian *Schutzstaffel 22b*

1Jan17	*Schutzstaffel 22b* is created from KG 6/Ks 31 by BKM Nr. 148032 of 31Dec16.
29Apr17	*Flg.* Ernst Deutschmann, G, is KIA over Braye-en-Laonnois during air combat.
25May17	*Gefr.* Bonifaz Metz, G, is WIA during air combat.
12Jun17	*Vzfw.* Paul Schrader, P, and *Pion.* Engelbert Esser, G, are taken POW by the French W. Jouy at 11.15 hours.
18Sep17	*Vzfw.* Behringer-1, *Vzfw.* Eder-1, Spad, Fort Vaux
17Oct17	*Vzfw.* Bott-1, *Vzfw.* Leupold-1, Spad, 11.40, Verdun
12Mar18	*Uffz.* Bernhard Endres, G, is WIA,sv. during air combat, shot in the arm and thigh, and to hospital at Maurois.
22Mar18	*Vzfw.* Ludwig Müller, G, is WIA, shot in the lower right arm, and to hospital at Maurois.
22Mar18	*Vzfw.* Ernst Tautz, G, is IIC, injures left ankle, and to hospital at Maurois.
22Mar18	*Uffz.* Karl Maria Stauber, G, is IIC,lt., contusion of left thigh and light head trauma, remains with the unit.
27Mar18	*Schutzstaffel 22b* is renamed *Schlachtstaffel 22b* by KM Nr. 5126.18.A.7.L.IV.C. of 27Mar18.
31Mar18	*Pion.* Waibel-1, *Flg.* Biedermann-1, D.H. 4 #A.7674, 57 Sqn. RFC, Capt. P.D. Robinson,MC,KIA & 2/Lt. J.F.Q. Walker,KIA
19Apr18	*Uffz.* Peter Paul Bäumler, P, and *Gefr.* Michael Engert, G, are WIA and taken POW S. Rouvrel. Their Halberstadt Cl.II was hit by Flak fire while on an escort mission for Fl.Abt. 239(A). Engert DOW on 8Feb19 as a POW at Lunèville.

22Apr18 *Pion.* Erich Rother, M, is hit in the left knee by a propeller and to hospital.
27Apr18 *Gefr.* Alfred Richard Lämmel, P, is WIA,sv., lung shot, and *Pion.* Otto Behringer, G, is KIA over Morisel-Rouvrel during air combat. Lämmel DOW on 28Apr18 in the hospital at Rosières.
3May18 *Gefr.* Robert Günther, G, is severely WIA during air combat. He DOW on 10May18 at Demuin.
28May18 *Vzfw.* Friedrich Gömann, G, is WIA,sv., during air combat, shot in the head and DOW in the hospital at Tagnon.
31May18 *Vzfw.* Ludwig Bott, P, is WIA,sv. by ground fire, shot in the left thigh, and to hospital at Tagnon.
12Jun18 *Gefr.* Josef Fink, G, is WIA,sv. by ground fire, shot in the lower leg, and to hospital.
15Jun18 *Uffz.* Martin Höntsch, P, and *Gefr.* Wilhelm Naroska, G, are KIA at St. Thierry during air combat.
16Jul18 *Uffz.* Gotthold Walz, P, is KIC and *Vzwachtmstr.* Franz Freytag, G, is IIC, head injuries, at St. Loup-en-Champ and to hospital at Tagnon.
13Aug18 *Uffz.* Augustin Waibel, P, is WIA.
26Nov18 *Schlachtstaffel 22b* is demobilized at FEA 1b, Schleissheim.

Royal Bavarian *Schutzstaffel 23*

Pilot/Gunner	Type	From		To	
		Unit	Date	Date	Unit
Sgt. Karl Auerbach	P	AFP 7	19May18	EOW	
Sgt. Anton Bachlehner	G	FA 13	23Apr18	29May18	KIA
Uffz. Peter Baer	G	BS II	18Apr17	11May17	KIA
Uffz. Alois Bagh	G	AFP 1	8Jul18	EOW	
Oblt. Joseph Bauch, C.O.	O	BS I	28Mar17	22Jun17	FA 291A
Uffz. Otto Becker	G	AFP 7	24May18	14Jul18	Ss 15
Offz.Stv. Konrad Bischoff	P	SGp 1	12Jul18	21Jul18	Ss 31b
Uffz. Robert Bitzer	G	AFP 4	27Aug17	20Sep17	KIA
Uffz. Franz Breitsameter	G	FA 13	23Apr18	EOW	
Uffz. Max Franz Brückner	G	AFP 9	30Aug18	EOW	
Vzfw. Willy Brückner	G	AFP B	18Apr17	21Aug17	FEA 1b
Uffz. Johann Bucher	G	AFP 9	5Sep18	10Sep18	Ss 6
Uffz. Ludwig Büttner	P	KG 6/32	1Jan17	17Mar17	Hosp.
Uffz. Ludwig Büttner	P	FEA 1b	3May17	11May17	KIA
Uffz. Adam Deutsch	P	AFP 4	3Mar18	29Apr18	IIC
Uffz. Heinrich Dippach	G	AFP B	18Apr17	5Dec17	WIA,lt.
Uffz. Heinrich Dippach	G		5Dec17	28Dec17	Hosp.
Uffz. Heinrich Dippach	G	Hosp.	29Dec17	18Jan18	Leave
Uffz. Heinrich Dippach	G	Leave	24Jan18	24Jan18	Hosp.
Uffz. Heinrich Dippach	G	Hosp.	9Feb18	2Mar18	AFP 4
Ltn.d.R. Georg van der Emde, stv. C.O.	O	FA 19	4Nov17	8Dec17	FA 19
Pion. Fritz Emmert	G	AFP 1	13Jul18	10Sep18	AFP 9
Vzfw. Bernhard Ennenga	P	Ss 30b	26Aug18	EOW	
Uffz. Philipp Feiner	P	FS II	1Oct17	12Oct17	AFP 4
Pion. Georg Fink	P	AFP 4	19Apr18	20Apr18	Ss 28b
Ltn.d.R. Hermann Fränkel	O		(Aug17)		
Uffz. Fritz Friedel	G	AFP 4	12Jul17	25Jul17	AFP 4
Uffz. Fritz Friedel	G	AFP 4	19Sep17	20Oct17	FEA 1b
Uffz. Helmut Gotthilf Gelsz	P	AFP B	23Apr17	14Sep17	AFP 4
Uffz. Franz Geritau	P	Ss 24b	21Jul17	9Aug17	FA 7
Vzfw. Friedrich Geys	P	AFP 4	28Dec17	5May18	AFP 4
Vzfw. Friedrich Geys	P	JsSch I	10May18	EOW	
Uffz. Franz Gieler	G	Ss 13	26Apr17	2Jul17	WIA
Ltn.d.R. Josef Gramp	O	KG 6/32	1Jan17	3Apr17	BSch I
Gefr. Wilhelm Günzel	P	AFP 2	11Apr18	14Apr18	Ss 28b
Uffz. Anton Haberl	G	AFP 7	20May18	24May18	Ss 37
Uffz. Anton Haberl	G	AFP 9	24Aug18	5Sep18	AFP 6
Vzfw. Ernst Haegely	G	AFP B	29Mar17	23May17	WIA
Gefr. Michael Hennrich	G	AFP 18	22Oct18	EOW	
Ltn.d.R. Josef Herz	O	KG 6/32	1Jan17	28Apr17	AFP 1
Uffz. Leonhard Höhn	G	AFP 4	21Aug17	22Aug17	WIA
Ltn. Karl Hoffmann	P	KG 6/32	1Jan17	15Feb17	KIC
Oblt.d.R. Konrad Hoffmann	O	KG 6/32	1Jan17	30Apr17	FA 286A
Uffz. Heinrich Hülle	P	AFP 4	20Apr18	EOW	

Pion. Karl Hundertmark	G	AFP 7	23Jun18	30Jun18	AFP 7
Pion. Ernst Jacksch	P	FEA 6	1May18	2May18	Ss 13
Gefr. Karl Jeckstat	G	AFP 7	4Aug18	30Aug18	AFP 9
Uffz. Bernhard Jokisch	P	AFP 1	20May17	20Sep17	WIA,sv.
Gefr. Ernst Jostmeier	G	AFP 4	25Sep17	9Oct17	Ss 11
Sgt. Karl Jurzitza	P	AFP 4	20Aug17	13Sep17	Ss 13
Uffz. Max Wilhelm Kahlhorn	G	AFP 1	25May17	21Sep17	Ss 11
Pion. Wilhelm Adam Keiz	P	AFP 4	8Jul17	11Jul17	KIC
Ltn.d.R. Walter Kirchbach	P	KG 6/32	1Jan17	23Feb17	FA 296A
Ltn.d.R. Hanns Koch, OzbV	O	Ss 28b	21May18		
Vzfw. Alois Köhler	G	FS IV	4Sep17	21Jul18	Hosp.
Vzfw. Alois Köhler	G	Hosp.	30Jul18	EOW	
Uffz. Franz Kornder	P	AFP 1	23May17	2Jul17	WIA
Oblt. Friedrich Lorenz *Ritter* von Krausser, C.O.	O	BSch I	15Jun17	4Nov17	WIA
Oblt. Friedrich Lorenz *Ritter* von Krausser, C.O.	O	Leave	8Dec17	1Feb18	FA 45b
Vzfw. Josef Lautenschlager	P	KG 6/32	1Jan17	19May17	AFP 6
Gefr. Heinrich Lechleitner	G	AFP 4	29Aug17	10Sep17	AFP 4
Gefr. Franz Lorenz	G	AFP B	23Mar17	10Apr17	AFP B
Gefr. Otto Lorenz	P	AFP B	23Feb17	18Mar17	KIA
Pion. Ludwig Maar	G	AFP 4	8Feb18	22Jun18	AFP 4
Vzfw. Johann Wilhelm Märklin	P	AFP B	23Apr17	8May17	FA 280A
Ltn.d.R. Wilhelm Ernst Maser	O	KG 6/34	1Jan17	1May17	FS V
Oblt.d.R. Wilhelm Ernst Maser, C.O.	P	FA 293A	7Jun18	EOW	
Pion. Friedrich Mayr	P	AFP 4	13Oct17	13Oct17	AFP 4
Pion. Rudolf Meutzner	P	AFP 4	17Aug17	25Aug17	AFP 4
Vzfw. Johann Meyer	G	AFP 4	6Feb18	22Jun18	AFP 7
Vzfw. Robert Mitterer	G	KG 6/32	1Jan17	18Feb17	FEA 1b
Vzfw. Gerhard Möhlenbeck	P	AFP 4	26Aug17	20Sep17	KIA
Ltn.d.R. Johann Mohr	O	KG 6/32	1Jan17	18Mar17	KIA
Uffz. Franz Müller (+ 19Aug17)	G	AFP 4	10Jul17	11Aug17	IIC,sv.
Vzfw. Rudolf Nebel	P	KG 6/32	1Jan17	6Mar17	Js 35
Feldw. Josef Niedermayer	G	AFP 4	29Oct17	22Apr18	Hosp.
Feldw. Josef Niedermayer	G	Hosp.	28Apr18	EOW	
Gefr. Michael Oestheimer	G	AFP 7	20May18	28May18	Ss 30b
Pion. Hans Peters	P	Ss 26b	7May18	11May18	AFP 4
Vzfw. Walter Pieck	P	AFP 4	8Aug17	11Aug17	IIC,sv.
Pion. Martin Polzmacher	G	FEA 1b	2Aug18	EOW	
Uffz. Heinrich Postel	G	Ss 26b	12Sep17	3Jan18	WIA,sv.
Vzfw. Karl Rauch	G	FEA 2b	2Feb18	14Sep18	Hosp.
Vzfw. Karl Rauch	G	Hosp.	22Oct18	EOW	
Vzfw. Johann Rodel	G	AFP 4	21Aug17	7Feb18	FEA 1b
Gefr. Waldemar Roeder	P	Ss 27b	23Sep17	7Jan18	AFP 4
Vzfw. Karl Ruppel	P	AFP 4	6Oct17	EOW	
Uffz. Wilhelm Erich Rupprecht	G	AFP 4	18Oct17	17May18	Hosp.
Uffz. Wilhelm Erich Rupprecht	G	Hosp.	30May18	12Jul18	AFP 7
Vzfw. Hans Saupert	P	AFP 4	9May18	EOW	
Vzfw. Wilhelm Friedrich Schäffer	G	AFP 1	1Jun17	4Jul17	WIA
Vzfw. Wilhelm Friedrich Schäffer	G	AFP 4	23Jul17	29Sep17	Ss 27b
Oblt. Karl Willibald Scherer, C.O.	O	FA 47b	10Feb18	7Jun18	
Offz.Stv. Johann Schmid	P	AFP 9	27Aug18	10Sep18	Ss 6
Pion. Josef Schmidt	G	KG 6/32	1Jan17	23Feb17	FA 296A
Uffz. Heinrich Schmitt	G	AFP 4	6Oct17	8Oct18	WIA,lt.
Uffz. Heinrich Schmitt	G		8Oct18	EOW	
Vzfw. Friedrich August Schönmann	P	AFP B	26Aug17	14Oct17	Ss 11
Vzfw. Anton Schreml	G	AFP 4	9Feb18	29Apr18	IIC,lt.
Vzfw. Anton Schreml	G		29Apr18	EOW	
Oblt. Bartholomäus Schröder, C.O.	P	KG 6/32	1Jan17	26Mar17	GS Frbg
Gefr. Karl Schwab	G	AFP 18	23Oct18	EOW	
Vzfw. Joseph Schwarz	G	AFP B	18Apr17	21May18	AFP 7
Ltn. Theodor Seibert	O	KG 6/32	1Jan17	(Mar17)	
Vzfw. Fritz Strunz	P	AFP B	19Feb17	EOW	
Pion. Hubert Stürmer	G	AFP 4	6Oct17	28Dec17	KIA
Vzfw. Ludwig Thaufelder	P	AFP 4	7Oct17	1Aug18	IIC,sv.

Pion. Gottfried Weber	P	Ss 16	25May18	13Jul18	AFP 7
Gefr. Peter Weber	P	FA 293A	16Jun18	16Aug18	Hosp.
Gefr. Peter Weber	P	Hosp.	26Aug18	EOW	
Vzfw. Karl Weckerle	P	AFP 9	27Aug18	10Sep18	Ss 6
Uffz. Alfons Wegmann	P	FA 293A	22Sep17	5Apr18	IIC,lt.
Gefr. Michael Wehr	P	AFP 7	3Jun18	30Jun18	FA 296A
Vzfw. Theodor Weidner	P	AFP B	27Feb17	26Feb18	AFP 4
Pion. Georg Weigert	G	AFP 4	1Jan18	5Jan18	AFP 4
Uffz. Karl Wernsdörfer	G	AFP 4	8Oct17	9Oct17	Ss 26b
Vzfw. Adolf Julius Witt	P	FA 296A	22May18	EOW	
Ltn. Ferdinand Zilcher	P	KG 6/32	1Jan17	14Feb17	FEA 1b
Vzfw. Karl Zimmermann	P	AFP 4	8May18	29May18	KIA

Royal Bavarian *Schutzstaffel 23*

Mechanics and Ground Personnel

Name	From		To	
	Unit	Date	Date	Unit
Gefr. Johann Baptist Aberle	KG 6/32	1Jan17	9Jun17	FEA 1b
Pion. Jakob Acker	KG 6/32	1Jan17	30Apr17	AFP 2
Pion. Josef Ackermann	Ss 28b	6May18	10May18	AFP 4
Pion. Jakob Adrian	FEA 1b	7Jul17	3Nov17	FEA 1b
Gefr. August Albert	KG 6/32	1Jan17	14Feb17	Kea Mch
Pion. Franz Xaver Altmann	KG 6/32	1Jan17	18Jan17	AFP 5
Pion. Karl Altweh	FEA 1b	2Sep17	EOW	
Pion. Otto Amann	KG 6/32	1Jan17	EOW	
Pion. Ferdinand Angart	FEA 1b	5Nov17	1Aug18	IIC
Pion. Josef Anzengruber	KG 6/32	1Jan17	3Feb17	AFP 5
Pion. Johann Bauer	KG 6/32	1Jan17	EOW	
Kraftf. Heinrich Baum	Inftry	17Apr18	7May18	Hosp.
Pion. Andreas Baumann	FA 291A	8Jul17	EOW	
Pion. Paul Bernhard	FEA 1b	28Sep18	18Oct18	Hosp.
Gefr. Johann Binder	KG 6/32	1Jan17	EOW	
Pion. Ernst Bleisteiner	KG 6/32	1Jan17	EOW	
Uffz. August Blomeier	KG 6/32	1Jan17	8Feb17	FEA 2b
Gefr. Karl Braun	FEA 1b	12Mar17	15Mar17	FEA 1b
Pion. Fritz Breitenfeld	KG 6/32	1Jan17	7Mar17	FEA 1b
Pion. Fritz Breitling	KG 6/32	1Jan17	EOW	
Pion. Franz Brummer	FEA 1b	17Jan18	19Jul18	Pioneer
Uffz. Karl Buckler	KG 6/32	1Jan17	9Jan18	Hosp.
Pion. Wilhelm Büchl	FEA 1b	17Aug17	3Sep17	Hosp.
Pion. Wilhelm Büchl	FEA 1b	24Sep18	EOW	
Pion. Friedrich Busch	KG 6/32	1Jan17	18Jan17	AFP 5
Pion. Konrad Buttmann	KG 6/32	1Jan17	6Jul17	FA 291A
Pion. Joseph Dachwald	KG 6/32	1Jan17	20Mar17	Js 35b
Sgt. Josef Dauer	KG 6/32	1Jan17	17Jun18	FEA 1b
Gefr. Georg Dennerlein	FA 47b	17Feb18	15Jun18	FEA 1b
Pion. Georg Dennhöfer	FEA 1b	17Aug17	EOW	
Pion. Karl Dinkel	FEA 1b	19Aug17	3Oct17	FEA 1b
Pion. Leonhard Dobmann	KG 6/32	1Jan17	21Jan18	AFP 4
Pion. Georg Doppel	FEA 1b	18Jan18	1Feb18	AFP 4
Feldw. Alois Eichingen	KG 6/32	1Jan17	18Aug17	Hosp.
Pion. Ludwig Emberger	KG 6/32	1Jan17	18Jan17	AFP 5
Pion. Wilhelm Endres	KG 6/32	1Jan17	20May17	AFP 3
Pion. Josef Engelhardt	KG 6/32	1Jan17	25Apr17	Zeiss
Pion. Johann Eschenbacher	KG 6	1Jan17	17Jan17	AFP 5
Pion. Johann Eschenbacher	AFP B	3Mar17	5May17	FEA 1b
Pion. Otto Färber	FEA 1b	20Apr17	EOW	
Pion. Hans Fischer	KG 6/32	1Jan17	18Jan17	AFP 5
Pion. Karl Förtsch	FEA 2b	19Feb18	EOW	
Pion. Georg Franz	FEA 1b	26Nov17	30Jan18	Hosp.

Pion. Jakob Freiberger	KG 6/32	1Jan17	18Jun18	Inftry
Pion. Alois Frölich	AFP 4	20Apr18	21May18	Ss 30b
Pion. Johann Fuchs	KG 6/32	1Jan17		Js 35b
Pion. Theodor Fuchs	KG 6/32	1Jan17	3Feb17	AFP 5
Pion. Simon Gabler	KG 6/32	1Jan17	18Aug17	Hosp.
Pion. Martin Gebhardt	FEA 1b	7Jul17	19Jul18	Pioneer
Pion. Michael Gleidner	FEA 1b	8Sep17	3Nov17	FEA 1b
Pion. Martin Gleissner	AFP 4	17Aug17	25Aug17	AFP 4
Pion. Josef Gmeiner	KG 6/32	1Jan17	25Jan17	FEA 1b
Uffz. Karl Göss	KG 6/32	1Jan17	20Mar18	Hosp.
Uffz. Karl Göss	Hosp.	22Mar18	14Jun18	FEA 1b
Pion. Wilhelm Gramp	FEA 1b	23Oct18	EOW	
Uffz. Christian Grass	FEA 1b	3Mar17	11Aug18	Hosp.
Pion. Josef Grassl	KG 6/32	1Jan17	16Jul17	FEA 1b
Pion. Hans Haase	KG 6/32	1Jan17	17Feb17	FEA 2b
Gefr. Jakob Hannemann	KG 6/32	1Jan17	26Apr17	AFP B
Pion. Otto Hanutko	KG 6/32	1Jan17	8Jun17	FEA 1b
Vzfw. Paul Hanutko	KG 6/32	1Jan17	15Feb17	KIC
Uffz. Friedrich Hartmann	KG 6/32	1Jan17	9Jun17	FEA 1b
Pion. Jakob Heid	FEA 1b	17Aug18	3Sep17	FEA 1b
Pion. Johann Heil	FEA 1b	12Mar17	7Apr17	Hosp.
Pion. Josef Heil	Hosp.	9May17	23May17	FEA 1b
San.Uffz. Leonhard Heim	KG 6/32	1Jan17	EOW	
Gefr. Karl Heimann	KG 6/32	1Jan17	EOW	
Pion. Karl Hiermann	FEA 1b	Oct18	EOW	
Pion. Hans Helfrich	FEA 1b	7Jul17	16Aug17	FEA 1b
Pion. Albert Herramhof	FEA 1b	21Apr17	19Jul17	FEA 1b
Pion. Michael Herrler	FEA 1b	3Jul17	EOW	
Pion. Anton Herzog	KG 6/32	1Jan17	30Apr17	FA 286A
Pion. Stefan Herzog	FEA 1b	7Jul17	3Nov17	FEA 1b
Uffz. Josef Hochhuber	KG 6/32	1Jan17	EOW	
Unterzahlmstr. Josef Höringer	27Oct18	EOW		
Pion. Max von Hofen	KG 6/32	1Jan17	19Jul17	FEA 1b
Pion. Arthur Holstein	KG 6/32	1Jan17	6Jun17	Hosp.
Pion. Arthur Holstein	Hosp.	11Sep17	EOW	
Gefr. Georg Hopf	KG 6/32	1Jan17	29Jan17	Minden
Pion. Alois Hornung	KG 6/32	1Jan17	25Apr17	FEA 1b
Pion. August Hornung	KG 6/32	1Jan17	EOW	
Pion. Franz Hotz	KG 6/32	1Jan17	EOW	
Uffz. August Huber	FA 227A	20Jan18	EOW	
Pion. Jakob Hütter	KG 6/32	1Jan17	11Jun17	FA 280A
Pion. Johann Huppert	FEA 1b	7Jan18	15Sep18	Injured
Pion. Eugen Huttenberger	FEA 1b	24Mar17	5Oct17	FEA 1b
Pion. Max Hutter	ÜFP Snt	5Nov17	19Jul18	Inftry
Pion. Karl Huttig	KG 6/32	1Jan17	23Apr17	AFP 5
Gefr. Christian Illing	FEA 1b	26May17	EOW	
Pion. Franz Illing	FEA 1b	28Sep18	EOW	
Pion. Franz Xaver Irregen	Inftry	4May18	EOW	
Pion. Martin Jugenheimer	Ss 30b	6Mar17	EOW	
Pion. Karl Kamberger	FEA 1b	Oct18	EOW	
Uffz. Friedriich Kern	KG 6/32	1Jan17	26Jan18	FEA 1b
Pion. Heinrich Keller	KG 6/32	1Jan17	3Feb17	AFP 5
Pion. Johann Kislinger	FEA 1b	6Nov17	EOW	
Gefr. Edwin Kleiner	FEA 1b	9Mar17	19Jul17	FEA 1b
Pion. Josef Klinger	Js 2	25Jan18	EOW	
Pion. Emil Klumb	FEA 1b	Oct18	EOW	
Pion. Georg Kolb	FEA 1b	5Nov17	EOW	
Gefr. Konrad Krauss	FEA 1b	1Feb17	31Dec17	AFP 5
Pion. Otto Kreitmaier	KG 6/32	1Jan17	EOW	
Uffz. Philipp Kronseder	KG 6/32	1Jan17	EOW	
Pion. Georg Lang	KG 6/32	1Jan17	14Feb17	AFP B
Uffz. Ludwig Lanke	KG 6/32	1Jan17	29Sep17	FEA 1b
Pion. Adalbert Lehner	KG 6/32	1Jan17	18Jan17	AFP 5
Offz.Stv. Johann Lehner	FEA 1b	3Mar17	EOW	
Pion. Friedrich Lied	FEA 1b	22Jul18	14Aug18	Posted

Pion. Friedrch Löscher	KG 6/32	1Jan17	EOW	
Gefr. Jakob Magerer	KG 6/32	1Jan17	EOW	
Pion. Karl Mandl	FEA 1b	29Mar17	19Jun17	FEA 1b
Pion. Josef Marte	KG 6/32	1Jan17	27Oct18	Hosp.
Pion. Franz Xaver Maier	FEA 1b	7Jul17	EOW	
Pion. Hermann Meister	FEA 1b	1Apr17	19Feb18	FEA 2b
Uffz. Konrad Meyer	KG 6/32	1Jan17	12Nov17	FEA 1b
Kraftf. Gefr. August Meyer	KG 6/32	1Jan17	EOW	
Uffz. Georg Minderlein	KG 6/32	1Jan17	EOW	
Pion. Friedrich Mohr	KG 6/32	1Jan17	10Jun17	Hosp.
Gefr. Josef Mohr	FEA 3	23May17	1Jun17	AFP 1
Pion. Johann Müller	KG 6/32	1Jan17	18Jan17	AFP 5
Pion. Johann Müller	FEA 1b	17Aug17	EOW	
Pion. Hyronimus Munker	KG 6/32	1Jan17	EOW	
Gefr. Anton Niklas	KG 6/32	1Jan17	3Feb17	AFP 5
Pion. Adolf Orschiedt	KG 6/32	1Jan17	18Jan17	AFP 5
Pion. Johann Partheymüller	Js 7	20Jan18	EOW	
Pion. Wilhelm Pfost	KG 6/32	1Jan17	18Jun18	AFP 7
Pion. Georg Pfrenzinger	KG 6/32	1Jan17	EOW	
Pion. Josef Philipp	KG 6/32	1Jan17	EOW	
Vzfw. Gustav Raebiger	AFP B	23Mar17	29Mar17	AFP B
Pion. Hans Raithel	KG 6/32	1Jan17	11Feb17	
Pion. Alois Rankl	KG 6/32	1Jan17	3Feb17	AFP 5
Vzfw. Friedriich Raux	FEA 1b	22Mar18	EOW	
Uffz. Martn Rebhan	FEA 1b	12Mar17	22Aug17	FEA 1b
Uffz. Richard Rebhuhn	KG 6/32	1Jan17	20Oct17	FEA 1b
Kraftf. Karl Rieber	Kft Prk	24Apr17	26Apr17	Kft Prk
Gefr. Wlhelm Ries	KG 6/32	1Jan17	18Feb17	FEA 1b
Pion. Max Rill	FEA 1b	21Apr17	11Nov17	FEA 1b
Uffz. Karl Rottler	KG 6/32	1Jan17	EOW	
Uffz. Wilhelm Rupprecht	KG 6/32	1Jan17	12Mar17	FEA 1b
Gefr. Walter Sartorius	KG 6/32	1Jan17	27Mar17	FEA 1b
Pion. Friedrich Schäfer	FEA 1b	25Sep17	EOW	
Pion. Henrich Scharrer	FEA 1b	30Nov17	EOW	
Pion. Johann Scheurer	KG 6/32	1Jan17	18Jan17	AFP 5
Pion. Johann Schmidt	AFP 5	18Jan17	22Aug17	FEA 2b
Uffz. Hans Schmitt	KG 6/32	1Jan17	18May18	Hosp.
Uffz. Hans Schmitt	FEA 1b	6Aug18	EOW	
Sgt. Friedrich Schneider	KG 6/32	1Jan17	1Jul17	Daimler
Sgt. Friedrich Schneider	Daimler	31Aug17	EOW	
Pion. Karl Schnurr	FA 280A	11Jun17	2Oct17	FEA 1b
Kraftf. Eduard Schobloch	AFP B	26Apr17	10Aug18	Injured
Gefr. Josef Schönberger	FEA 1b	1Sep17	15May18	Hosp.
Gefr. Josef Schönberger	Hosp.	20May18	EOW	
Pion. Karl Schönung	KG 6/32	1Jan17	EOW	
Uffz. Albert Schulz	AFP 7	24May18	30Jun18	Ss 37
Pion. Adam Schwab	KG 6/32	1Jan17	3Nov17	FEA 1b
Pion. Ludwig Schwenold	FEA 1b	11Jun17	17May18	Hosp.
Pion. Ludwig Schwenold	Hosp.	20May18	EOW	
Gefr. Julius Sebald	KG 6/32	1Jan17	9Jun17	FEA 1b
Pion. Franz Seibold	FEA 1b	5Nov17	EOW	
Vzfw. Georg Anton Selig	KG 6/32	1Jan17	23Mar18	FEA 1b
Pion. Franz Sellmaier	FEA 1b	28Apr18	EOW	
Pion. Joseph Sendlbeck	FEA 1b	8Apr17	3Nov17	FEA 1b
Pion. Karl Sixt	FS Funk	12Dec17	EOW	
Pion. Josef Sohler	KG 6/32	1Jan17	6Feb17	Hosp.
Pion. Michael Sorg	KG 6/32	1Jan17	29Oct17	Hosp.
Uffz. Ludwig Spanlang	KG 6/32	1Jan17	EOW	
Pion. Karl Spegele	FEA 1b	5Apr17	EOW	
Kraftf. Martin Spindler	Kft Prk	15Mar17	EOW	
Gefr. August Stein	KG 6/32	1Jan17	EOW	
Pion. Wilhelm Steinbrecher	FEA 1b	Oct18	EOW	
Uffz. Franz Steinle	KG 6/32	1Jan17	14Feb17	FEA 1b
Pion. Johann Stempfle	KG 6/32	1Jan17	EOW	
Pion. Josef Straub	FEA 1b	17Aug18	EOW	

Pion. Alfred Stich	AFP B	3Mar17	22Mar17	FEA 1b
Uffz. Georg Stohf	KG 6/32	1Jan17	9Sep17	FEA 1b
Pion. Walter Stopfer	KG 6/32	1Jan17	9Aug17	FEA 1b
Uffz. Andreas Strauss	FEA 1b	4Mar17	EOW	
Pion. Johann Strauss	FEA 1b	24Mar17	6Jun17	Dschgd
Pion. Johann Then	KG 6/32	1Jan17	30Apr17	AFP 2
Sgt. Josef Trautner	KG 6/32	1Jan17	EOW	
Gefr. Karl Vogel	Inftry	7Jul18	(Sep18)	
Pion. Karl Vogler	KG 6/32	1Jan17	EOW	
Pion. Udo Voigt	Ss 28b	12Apr18	17Jun18	Ss 8
Gefr. Josef Vonach	FEA 1b	24Mar17	25Jun18	Hosp.
Pion. Georg Wächtler	KG 6/32	1Jan17	3Feb17	AFP 5
Gefr. Klemens Josef Weber	FEA 1b	28Sep18	EOW	
Pion. Josef Wecker	FEA 1b	17Jun17	9Feb18	FA 45b
Uffz. Johann Wedel	KG 6/32	1Jan17	EOW	
Pion. Leopold Weig	KG 6/32	1Jan17	18Jan17	AFP 5
Uffz. Eduard Weiss	KG 6/32	1Jan17	25Sep18	Hosp.
Offz.Stv. Hans Werle	Sonthfn	3Nov17	EOW	
Pion. August Wieser	FEA 1b	7Jul17	11Jul18	Hosp.
Gefr. August Wildgaus	KG 6/32	1Jan17	27Mar17	AOK A
Sgt. Peter Wittmann	KG 6/32	1Jan17	14Jun18	FEA 1b
Gefr. Otto Wittpenig	KG 6/32	1Jan17	EOW	
Pion. Hans Wunderer	FEA 1b	7Jul17	18Jun18	Posted
Uffz. Ludwig Wurdach	KG 6/32	1Jan17	9Apr17	Hosp.
Uffz. Ludwig Wurdach	Hosp.	17May17	EOW	
Kraftf. Lorenz Zeiler	Kft Abt	5May18	EOW	
Pion. Johann Zettl	FEA 1b	27Sep18	EOW	
Pion. Johann Zink	KG 6/32	1Jan17	EOW	
Pion. Heinrich Zins	FEA 1b	Oct18	EOW	

Schutzstaffel/Schlachtstaffel 23b
Mitgemachte Schlachten und Gefechte
(Battles and combat actions in which Ss 23b participated)

10Sep16	11Feb17	*Stellungskämpfe vor Verdun* (Trench fighting at Verdun)
12Feb17	26Apr17	*Stellungskämpfe in Oberelsass* (Trench fighting in Alsace)
28Apr17	27May17	*Doppelschlacht Aisne-Champagne* (The double battle of Aisne-Champagne)
28May17	11Jun17	*Stellungskämpfe vor Reims* (Trench fighting at Reims)
12Jun17	3Dec17	*Schlacht in Flandern* (Battle in Flanders)
4Dec17	10Mar18	*Stellungskämpfe in Flandern* (Trench fighting in Flanders)
11Mar18	20Mar18	*Aufmarsch zur Grossen Schlacht in Frankreich* (Assembly for the Great Battle in France)
21Mar18	12Apr18	*Grosse Schlacht in Frankreich* (Great Battle in France)
13Apr18	29Apr18	*Schlacht um den Kemmel* (Battle for the Kemmel)
30Apr18	13May18	*Stellungskämpfe in Flandern* (Trench fighting in Flanders)
14May18	20May18	*Stellungskämpfe nördlich der Ailette* (Trench fighting north of the Ailette)
27May18	13Jun18	*Schlacht bei Soissons und Reims* (Battle at Soissons and Reims)
27May18		*Erstürmung der Höhen des Chemin des Dames* (Storming the top of the Chemin des Dames)
28May18	1Jun18	*Verfolgungskämpfe zwischen Oise und Aisne und über die Vesle bis zur Marne* (Pursuit fighting between the Oise and the Aisne and across the Vesle to the Marne)

14Jun18	27Jun18	*Stellungskämpfe zwischen Oise und Marne* (Trench fighting between the Oise and the Marne)
28Jun18	14Jul18	*Stellungskämpfe bei Reims* (Trench fighting at Reims)
15Jul18	17Jul18	*Angriffsschlacht an der Marne und in der Champagne* (Offensive battle on the Marne and in the Champagne)
18Jul18	3Aug18	*Abwehrschlacht zwischen Soissons und Reims* (Defensive battle between Soissons and Reims)
4Aug18	16Aug18	*Stellungskämpfe zwischen Oise und Aisne* (Trench fighting between the Oise and the Aisne)
17Aug18	4Sep18	*Abwehrschlacht zwischen Oise und Aisne* (Defensive battle between the Oise and the Aisne)
5Sep18	8Sep18	*Kämpfe vor der Siegfriedstellung* (Battle at the Siegfried Line)
9Sep18	14Sep18	*Kämpfe in der Siegfriedstellung* (Battle in the Siegfried Line)

weitere Eintragungen fehlen (the remainder is not available)

Schutzstaffel/Schlachtstaffel 23b Airfields

From	To	Location	*Schlachtgruppe* Affiliation	*Armee*
1Jan17	10Jan17	Mont		5
10Jan17	11Feb17	Mercy le Bas	Escort for FA 209(A)	5
12Feb17	17Feb17	Hügelheim by Müllheim	For FA 282(A)	AAB
17Feb17		Sierenz	Escort for FA 282(A)	AAB
(Mar17)	26Apr17	Habsheim	Escort for FA 278(A)	AAB
28Apr17	11Jun17	St. Fergeux	Escort for FA 278(A)	1
12Jun17	10Mar18	Ingelmunster	Escort for FA 19	4
11Mar18		Bertry		2
(15Mar18)	(21Mar18)	Quiévy	SGp D (Ss 12,23b) C.O. *Oblt.* Johannes Missfelder	2
(9Apr18)	12Apr18	Römer Ferme	SGp D (Ss 12,23b,26b) C.O. *Oblt.* Johannes Missfelder	2
13Apr18	13May18	Bisseghem	SGp B (Ss 10,23b,26b,30b) C.O. *Oblt.d.R.* August Ertl	4
14May18	13Jun18	Ebouleau, N. Montaigu	SGp B (Ss 23b,26b,28b,30b) C.O. *Oblt.d.R.* August Ertl	7
14Jun18	23Jun18	Cuiry-Housse	SGp Winckler (Ss 23b,26b,28b,30b) C.O. *Oblt.d.R.* August Ertl	7
23Jun18	14Jul18	Neuflize		1
15Jul18	18Jul18	Le Chesne	SGp 2 (Ss 7,23b,26b,35,36) C.O. *Oblt.* Walter Lackner	3
18Jul18	3Aug18	Le Chesne	SGp 2 (Ss 7,22b,23b,26b,36) C.O. *Oblt.* Walter Lackner	3
4Aug18	9Aug18	Neuflize	SGp B (Ss 2,22b,23b,36) C.O. *Oblt.d.R.* Ludwig Männer	1
10Aug18	11Aug18	St. Loup	SGp B (Ss 23b,36) C.O. *Oblt.d.R.* Ludwig Männer	1
11Aug18	6Sep18	Neuflize	SGp B (Ss 2,22b,23b,36) C.O. *Oblt.d.R.* Ludwig Männer	1
6Sep18	12Sep18	Neuflize	SGp B (Ss 2,22b,23b,36) C.O. *Oblt.d.R.* Sigmund Kreitmair	1
12Sep18	17Sep18	St. Loup	SGp B (Ss 2,22b,23b,36) C.O. *Oblt.d.R.* Sigmund Kreitmair	1
17Sep18	28Sep18	Autrecourt	SGp 3 (Ss 2,22b,23b) C.O. *Oblt.d.R.* Sigmund Kreitmair	3
28Sep18	18Oct18	Autrecourt	SGp 3 (Ss 2,22,23b) C.O. *Oblt.* Karl *Ritter* von Gruny	3
18Oct18	EOW	Feuchères	SGp 3 (Ss 6,12,23b,38s) C.O. *Oblt.* Friedrich-Carl Hanesse	7

Royal Bavarian *Schutzstaffel 23b*

1Jan17	*Schutzstaffel 23b* is created from KG 6/Ks 32 by BKM Nr. 148032 of 31Dec16.
15Feb17	*Ltn.* Karl Hoffmann, P, and *Vzfw.* Paul Hanutko, M, are KIC at Hügelheim by Müllheim.
18Mar17	*Gefr.* Otto Lorenz, P, and *Ltn.d.R.* Johann Mohr, O, are KIA over Aspach at 11.00 hours.
11May17	*Uffz.* Ludwig Büttner, P, and *Uffz.* Peter Baer, G, are KIA over Merlet, S. St. Fergeux.
23May17	*Vzfw.* Ernst Haegely, G, is WIA in the hand and arm by Flak fragments at 15.10 hours and to hospital at Althal.
21Jun17	*Gefr.* Gelsz-1, *Uffz.* Schäffer-1, Spad, 8.05, Brielen Nieuport 23 #2783, Esc. N.68, Sgt. P. Castan, KIA
2Jul17	*Uffz.* Franz Kornder, P, and *Uffz.* Franz Gieler, G, are WIA near Ypres, both shot in their right thighs during air combat, while in a DFW C.V.
4Jul17	*Vzfw.* Wilhelm Friedrich Schäffer, G, is WIA, shot in the knee, while in a DFW C.V. and to hospital at Iseghem.
11Jul17	*Pion.* Wilhelm Adam Keiz, P, is KIC at Iseghem.
11Aug17	*Vzfw.* Walter Pieck, P, and *Uffz.* Franz Müller, G, are IIC,sv. during a crash at Iseghem airfield. Müller DOW 19Aug17.
22Aug17	*Uffz.* Leonhard Höhn, G, is WIA during air combat, shot in the foot and lower leg and to hospital at Iseghem.
20Sep17	*Uffz.* Bernhard Jokisch, P, is WIA,sv. by ground fire at 8.45 hours, shot in the chest, and to hospital at St. Eloi. His gunner, *Uffz.* Joseph Schwarz is OK. Jokisch manages to safely land the aircraft between Moorslede and Dadizeele.
20Sep17	*Vzfw.* Gerhard Möhlenbeck, P, and *Uffz.* Robert Bitzer, G, are KIA over Paschendaele by ground fire. They departed at 5.45 hours.
30Oct17	*Uffz.* Ludwig Thaufelder, P, and *Uffz.* Alois Köhler, are shot down near Roulers in aerial combat. Their aircraft is severly damaged but they are OK.
4Nov17	*Oblt.* Friedrich Lorenz *Ritter* von Krausser, O and C.O., is WIA,lt. by ground fire and to hospital.
5Dec17	*Uffz.* Heinrich Dippach, G, is lightly WIA during air combat, remains with the unit.
28Dec17	*Pion.* Hubert Stürmer, G, is KIA at 12.05 hours over Zillebeker See during air combat.
3Jan18	*Uffz.* Heinrich Postel, G, is WIA at 14.50 hours during air combat, shot in the right leg and pelvis, and to hospital at Ingelmünster.
19Jan18	*Pion.* Georg Franz, M, suffers a hernia while closing a hangar door and to hospital at Iseghem on 30Jan18.
25Mar18	*Uffz.* Thaufelder-1, *Uffz.* Köhler-1, Bristol F.2b
27Mar18	*Schutzstaffel 23b* is renamed *Schlachtstaffel 23b* by KM Nr. 5126.18.A.7.L.IV.C. of 27Mar18.
5Apr18	*Uffz.* Alfons Wegmann, P, is lightly IIC and to hospital.
29Apr18	*Uffz.* Adam Deutsch, P, and *Vzfw.* Anton Schreml, G, are IIC during an emergency landing after being shot down. Deutsch incurs a skull fracture and spinal contusion and to Field Hospital 408. Schreml remains with the unit.
29May18	*Vzfw.* Karl Zimmermann, P, and *Sgt.* Anton Bachlehner, G, are KIA over Iuvigny-Crecy-au-Mont.
1Aug18	*Vzfw.* Ludwig Thaufelder, P, and *Pion.* Ferdinand Angart, M, are IIC while on a test flight of a Halberstadt Cl. II and to hospital at St. Martinskirche in Laon. Thaufelder suffers skull and leg fractures, Angart has head injuries.
10Aug18	*Kraftf.* Eduard Schoblock, M, is injured in a motorcycle accident and to hospital at Marle.
15Sep18	*Pion.* Johann Huppert, M, is injured in an auto accident and to hospital.
8Oct18	*Uffz.* Heinrich Schmitt, G, is WIA,lt. by ground fire, grazing shot to the hand, but remains with the unit.
12Nov18	*Gefr.* Karl Heimann, M, dies in the hospital at Deniel.
20Nov18	*Schlachtstaffel 23b* is demobilized at FEA 1b, Schleissheim.

A Halberstadt Cl.II of *Schusta 23b* marked 4 in a blue diamond.

Above: Halberstadt Cl.II aircraft of *Schlasta 23b* lined up on the left. On the right is a line up of Hannover Cl.II aircraft of a sister *Schlasta*. Credit: UTD/HAC.

Right: *Vzfw.* Fritz Strunz and his Halberstadt Cl.II of *Schlasta 23b*. The flowers and placard denote his 200th front flight. Credit: UTD/HAC.

Opposite
The men of *Schusta 23b*. The C.O., *Oblt.* Friedrich *Ritter* von Krausser, is 8th from the left, *Vzfw.* Friedrich Schönmann is 4th from the left, and *Vzfw.* Fritz Strunz is 9th from the left. Credit: UTD/HAC.

Royal Bavarian *Schutzstaffel 24*

Pilot/Gunner	Type	From		To	
		Unit	Date	Date	Unit
Oblt.d.R. Franz Albertshauser,C.O.	O	FA 292A	18Apr18	20Jul18	WIA
Ltn. Oskar Anschütz, OzbV	O	AFP 4	4Jun18	20Jun18	Krgamt
Uffz. Michael Johann Arnold	P	AFP 4	10Jun18	EOW	
Uffz. Heinrich Auer	G	AFP 1	22Jul18	17Oct18	IIC
Oblt. Gustav Bauer, C.O.	O	FA 293A	13Aug18	22Oct18	WIA
Uffz. Josef Bauer	P	AFP 17	4Mar18	18Mar18	FA 293A
Vzfw. Franz Baumeister	P	AFP 4	21Sep17	29Sep17	WIA
Vzfw. Franz Baumeister	P		29Sep17	18Oct17	Hosp.
Flg. August Beckedorf	G	AFP 4	23Sep17	9Oct17	Ss 10
Oblt. Friedrich *Frhr.* von Berchem, C.O.	O	FEA 1b	5Jan18	20Apr18	AFP 6
Uffz. Ludwig Beyer	P	AFP 2	11Jan18	19Jan18	KIA
Uffz. Eduard Binge	P	Ss 29b	31Jan18	6May18	JsSch I
Uffz. Franz Xaver Böck	G	AFP 4	13Jun18	25Sep18	Hosp.
Uffz. Franz Xaver Böck	G	Hosp.	30Sep18	EOW	
Uffz. Franz Xaver Brandl	G	AFP 6	30Apr17	31May17	IIC,lt.
Vzfw. Franz Xaver Brandl	G	Hosp.	4Jun17	22Apr18	Hosp.
Vzfw. Johann Burghauser	P	AFP 4	1Oct17	2Mar18	Hosp.
Vzfw. Johann Burghauser	P	Hosp.	6Mar18	11Apr18	KIA
Ltn.d.R. Erich vom Dorp	O	KG 6/33	1Jan17	24Jan17	FA 249A
Uffz. Willy Richard Ehrlich	P	AFP 2	26Nov17	16Dec17	FA 240A
Pion. Josef Eisenbach	P	AFP 4	18May18	31May18	IIC
Vzfw. Friedrich Emmerich	P	AFP 6	23Apr17	4Jun18	FEA 2b
Uffz. Friedrich Feichtmayr	P	AFP 6	23Apr17	4May18	FA 240A
Oblt. Karl Fillisch, C.O.	O	KG 6/33	1Jan17	16Jul17	BSch
Sgt. Anton Fleck	P	AFP 4	14Jun17	27Jun17	KIC
Vzfw. Eugen Fleischer	G	Ss 19	24May18	12Jun18	AFP 4
Uffz. Wilhelm Flormann (+7Feb18)	G	AFP 2	6Nov17	3Feb18	WIA,sv.
Uffz. Max Forstner	P	AFP 4	3May18	16Jul18	WIA
Uffz. Wilhelm Fried	G	AFP 4	12Jul17	28Sep17	Hosp.
Uffz. Wilhelm Fried	G	Hosp.	10Oct17	28Dec17	Hosp.
Vzfw. Wilhelm Fried	G	Hosp.	31Dec17	1May18	Hosp.
Uffz. Georg Fuchs	G	AFP 6	18Apr17	13Jun18	AFP 6
Vzfw. Johann Baptist Fuchs	P	AFP 4	11Nov17	8Oct18	JsSch I
Uffz. Friedrich Wilhelm Gack	P	AFP 4	8May18	EOW	
Ltn.d.R. Fritz Geiger	P	KG 6/33	1Jan17	25Jan17	AFP 6
Ltn. Aloys Geistbeck	O	KG 6/33	1Jan17	24Jan17	FA 274A
Gefr. Franz Geritau	P	AFP 4	8Jun17	21Jul17	Ss 23b
Gefr. Jakob Grass	G	AFP 4	16Jun17	27Jun17	KIC
Gefr. Wilhelm Günzel	P	AFP 4	4May18	17May18	FA 240A
Pion. Karl Gütz	G	AFP 6	4Jun17	3Jul17	AFP 4
Uffz. Johann Gutneder	G	AFP 6	16Mar18	31May18	IIC
Uffz. Johann Gutneder (+ 9Jul18)	G	Hosp.	7Jun18	28Jun18	Hosp.
Ltn.d.R. Hugo Häusner	O	KG 6/33	1Jan17	20Apr17	AFP 6
Uffz. Thomas Hartig	P	AFP 4	8Oct17	8Dec17	AFP 4
Uffz. Otto Hartung	P	AFP 6	21Mar18	EOW	
Gefr. Karl Heintz	P	AFP 1	16Jul18	EOW	
Pion. Paul Heinze	G	AFP 4	25Sep17	28Oct17	Ss 5
Gefr. Friedrich Heitsch	G	AFP 6	11May17	3Jul17	AFP 4
Vzfw. Albert Hermann	P	AFP 4	28Sep17	14Oct17	JSch II
Ltn.d.R. Albert Hermann	P	AFP 4	23Oct17	10Jul18	Inj,sv.
Uffz. Hans Heuberger	G	AFP 4	13Jun18	16Jul18	WIA
Uffz. Hans Heuberger	G	Hosp.	27Jul18	EOW	
Uffz. Josef Hörmann	G	AFP 6	12Feb18	13Jun18	AFP 6
Uffz. Ernst Julius Hopf	G	AFP 4	13Jun18	25Sep18	KIC
Vzfw. Johann Hübner	P	AFP 4	17May18	1Jun18	AFP 4
Gefr. Josef Anton Humbs	P	AFP 6	13Apr18	29Apr18	WIA,sv.
Uffz. Johannes Ihde	P	AFP 4	9Jun18	25Sep18	KIC
Vzfw. Karl Kallmünzer	P	AFP 4	27Jun17	29Jan18	Js 78b

Vzfw. Karl Kieling	P	KG 6/33	1Jan17	14Sep17	Hosp.
Vzfw. Karl Kieling	P	Hosp.	20Sep17	27Sep17	Ss 19
Vzfw. Friedrich Ludwig Knitl	G	AFP 4	31May18	15Jun18	AFP 6
Uffz. Josef Köck	G	AFP 17	8Apr18	4Jun18	WIA,lt.
Uffz. Josef Köck	G	Hosp.	4Jun18	EOW	
Uffz. Hans Kracht	G	AFP 4	17May18	23May18	Ss 19
Uffz. Max Hermann Lehmann	P	AFP 4	23Aug17	25Sep17	AFP 4
Gefr. Albert Listl	P	AFP 1	17Jul18	EOW	
Gefr. Karl Albin Luthardt	P	AFP 1	17Jul18	18Aug18	AFP 6
Gefr. Karl Albin Luthardt	P	AFP 6	27Sep18	EOW	
Vzfw. Konrad Mann	P	KG 6/33	1Jan17	31May17	KIC
Ltn. Wolf-Magnus von Manteuffel-Szöge	O	KG 6/33	1Jan17	25Jan17	AFP 6
Vzfw. Bruno Marquardt	P	KG 6/33	1Jan17	24Jan17	FA 274A
Vzfw. Bruno Marquardt	P	FA 274A	12Apr17	19Apr17	KSch
Ltn. Theodor Mayer, OzbV	P	AFP 17	6Sep18	19Oct18	Hosp.
Pion. Friedrich Wilhelm Mayr	P	AFP 4	14Oct17	20Oct17	Ss 29b
Vzfw. Andreas Mersch	G	AFP 4	28Jun17	24Nov17	KIC
Uffz. Wilhelm Miltner	P	KG 6/33	1Jan17	25May17	KIA
Uffz. Anton Monz	P	AFP 6	18Apr17	5May17	KIA
Vzfw. Georg Motschiedler	P	KG 6/33	1Jan17	30Dec17	FEA 2b
Vzfw. Johann Müller	G	AFP 6	18Apr17	22Mar18	KIA
Ltn.d.R. Georg Niezoldi	O	KG 6/33	1Jan17	19Apr17	FEA 1b
Vzfw. Friedrich Noder	G	AFP 6	9Jul18	1Sep18	AFP 17
Vzfw. Friedrich Noder	G	AFP 6	27Sep18	EOW	
Uffz. Christian Pabst	G	AFP 4	4May18	EOW	
Vzfw. Franz Pfeffer	P	AFP 2	2Jan18	1May18	AFP 4
Uffz. Anton Raab	G	AFP 4	27Jun17	EOW	
Sgt. Josef Rampp	P	AFP 4	9Oct18	EOW	
Vzfw. Alfred Regensburger	G	FEA 1b	10Jan17	10Aug17	WIA,lt.
Vzfw. Alfred Regensburger	G		10Aug17	21Sep17	WIA,sv.
Gefr. Hugo Reichert	G	AFP 4	26Oct17	19Jan18	WIA,sv.
Uffz. Johann Martin Ritthammer	P	AFP 4	7Nov18	EOW	
Pion. Ludwig Rosenbeck	P	FEA 1b	3Feb17	21Feb17	FEA 1b
Uffz. Ferdinand Schellerer	G	AFP 6	17Apr17	5May17	KIA
Fähnr. Oskar Schlecht	G	AFP 4	7Oct17	11Apr18	KIA
Uffz. Leo Schönhöfer	P	AFP 4	16Jul17	16Sep17	AFP 4
Gefr. Johann Baptist Schreiber	P	AFP 4	9May18	15May18	KIA
Oblt. Karl Schröder, C.O.	O	FBSch I	12Aug17	2Jan18	FA 286A
Ltn.d.R. Edwin Schümichen	O	AFP 5	5Feb17	5Feb17	FA 249A
Ltn. Heinrich Seywald	O	KG 6/33	1Jan17	2May17	AFP 6
Pion. Joachim von Stein zu Lausnitz	P	AFP 4	27Jun17	17Jul17	FA 48b
Pion. Erich Stork	P	AFP 4	4May18	8May18	AFP 4
Gefr. Georg Strauss	G	AFP 17	16Mar18	15May18	KIA
Oblt. Fritz Stumpf, Stv. C.O.	P	FA 48b	25Oct18	1Nov18	FA 48b
Ltn.d.R. Heinrich Tammann	P	KG 6/33	1Jan17	7Jan17	AFP vS
Vzfw. Ludwig Thaufelder	P	KG 6/33	1Jan17	27Mar17	Hosp.
Vzfw. Ludwig Thaufelder	P	Hosp.	2Apr17	19Apr17	FEA 1b
Pion. Peter Weber	G	AFP 4	8May18	30May18	AFP 4
Vzfw. Ferdinand Gisbert Wens	G	AFP 5	26Feb17	25May17	KIA
Uffz. Leo Weth	G	AFP 4	3Oct17	9Mar18	FStzSch
Uffz. Karl Will	P	AFP 6	14May17	24Nov17	KIC
Gefr. Josef Wimmer	G	AFP 17	2Apr18	29Apr18	WIA
Pion. Kaspar Wind	G	FA 13	13Oct18	EOW	
Oblt.d.R. Kurt Ziegler, C.O.	O	FS Asch	1Nov18	EOW	
Sgt. Adolf Zitzelsberger	P	AFP 2	25Jan18	22Mar18	KIA

Royal Bavarian *Schutzstaffel 24*

Mechanics and Ground Personnel

Name	From		To	
	Unit	Date	Date	Unit
Pion. Jean Allgeyer	FEA 1b	29Mar18	19Jul18	Infntry
Pion. Xaver Allmanshofer	KG 6/33	1Jan17	29May17	FEA 1b
Pion. Ernst Altfudisch	AFP 2	18Jan18	3Sep18	Injured
Pion. Wilhelm Ammon	KG 6/33	1Jan17	16Oct18	AFP 4
Pion. Rudolf Otto Baumgärtner	FEA 1b	24Nov17	7Mar18	AFP 17
Pion. Kaspar Theodor Balling	AFP 5	20Feb17	23Apr17	AFP 6
SanSgt. Michael Bayer		16Mar18	2Jul18	Hosp.
SanSgt. Michael Bayer	Hosp.	4Jul18	19Jul18	Hosp.
SanSgt. Michael Bayer	Hosp.	21Jul18	EOW	
Gefr. Josef Berchtold	KG 6/33	1Jan17	25Jan17	FEA 1b
Pion. Otto Berger	FEA 1b	28Nov17	26Mar18	Hosp.
Pion. Otto Berger	Hosp.	28Mar18	1May18	Hosp.
Pion. Otto Berger	Hosp.	5May18	21Jul18	Hosp.
Pion. Otto Berger	Hosp.	12Aug18	EOW	
Pion. Konrad Bieder	KG 6/33	1Jan17	27Oct17	Js 32b
Pion. Paul Beinadseder	AFP 4	6Nov17	5Jul18	Hosp.
Pion. Paul Beinadseder	Hosp.	9Jul18	18Jul18	Hosp.
Gefr. Johann Bierlein	KG 6/33	1Jan17	15Feb17	Hosp.
Gefr. Johann Bierlein	Hosp.	20Feb17	6Mar17	Hosp.
Gefr. Johann Bierlein	Hosp.	11Mar17	16Apr17	Hosp.
Gefr. Johann Bierlein	Hosp.	21Apr17	13Jul18	Hosp.
Gefr. Johann Bierlein	Hosp.	17Jul18	20Sep18	Hosp.
Gefr. Franz Robert Bischof	KG 6/33	1Jan17	EOW	
Pion. Konrad Bosch	KG 6/33	1Jan17	29Sep17	Injured
Pion. Konrad Bosch	FEA 2b	27Aug18	EOW	
Pion. Wilhelm Brandner	FEA 1b	16Jul18	19Aug18	Hosp.
Pion. Johann Brandl	FEA 1b	4Mar17	6Mar17	AFP 5
Pion. Johann Brandl	AFP 5	11Mar17	31Mar18	FEA 1b
Gefr. Anton Braun	KG 6/33	1Jan17	EOW	
Pion. Paul Bretting	FEA 1b	20Aug18	EOW	
Pion. Johann Friedrich Brückner	KG 6/33	1Jan17	4Jan17	Hosp.
Pion. Johann Friedrich Brückner	Hosp.	7Jan17	25Jan17	FEA 1b
Uffz. Ludwig Brunner	KG 6/33	1Jan17	28Feb17	FEA 1b
Uffz. Adolf Bürckle	KG 6/33	1Jan17	EOW	
Pion. Friedrich Bügler	KG 6/33	1Jan17	4Feb17	AFP 5
Gefr. Ludwig Christoph	KG 6/33	1Jan17	10Mar17	Hosp.
Gefr. Ludwig Christoph	Hosp.	17Mar17	13Jun17	FEA 3
Gefr. Ludwig Christoph	FEA 3	31Jul17	EOW	
Pion. Otto Degen	KG 6/33	1Jan17	2Nov17	FEA 1b
Pion. Franz Josef Detzner	FEA 1b	21Dec17	12Jun18	AFP 4
Pion. Friedrich Dill	BS I	2Dec17	10Jan18	Hosp.
Pion. Friedrich Dill	Hosp.	22Jan18	12Jun18	AFP 4
Pion. Hermann Döhler	KG 6/33	1Jan17	10Apr17	Hosp.
Pion. Hermann Döhler	Hosp.	12Apr17	6Jun17	FEA 1b
Pion. Johann Eckl	AFP 4	27Mar18	6Jun18	AFP 4
Gefr. Karl Einloft	KG 6/33	1Jan17	17Sep18	Hosp.
Gefr. Karl Einloft	Hosp.	22Sep18	EOW	
Pion. Leonhard Engelhardt	KG 6/33	1Jan17	2Oct17	AFP 4
Pion. Heinrich Erbe	KG 6/33	1Jan17	25Jul17	FEA 1b
Uffz. Lorenz Eyerkaufer	KG 6/33	1Jan17	12Jun18	FEA 1b
Pion. Ludwig Fertl	FEA 1b	21Mar18	19Jul18	ÜBP Mbg
Kraftf. Benno Fischer	KG 6/33	1Jan17	3May17	Hosp.
Kraftf. Benno Fischer	Hosp.	10May17	15Jun17	Hosp.
Kraftf. Benno Fischer	Hosp.	21Jun17	EOW	
Sgt. Otto Fischer	FEA 1b	1Feb18	11Apr18	FEA 1b
Pion. Georg Fleischberger	FEA 1b	16Mar17	7Apr17	Hosp.
Pion. Georg Fleischberger	Hosp.	9Apr17	2Oct18	Hosp.

Pion. Georg Fleischberger	Hosp.	8Oct18	EOW	
Pion. Erich Frank	FEA 1b	6Sep17	24Sep17	Hosp.
Pion. Erich Frank	Hosp.	29Sep17	16Nov17	FA 288A
Gefr. Georg Franz	KG 6/33	1Jan17	13Aug17	Injured
Gefr. Georg Franz	Hosp.	25Aug17	EOW	
Uffz. Hermann Franken	KG 6/33	1Jan17	EOW	
Gefr. Johann Rudolf Forster	KG 6/33	1Jan17	15Aug18	FEA 1b
Pion. Josef Gadhammer	FEA 1b	28Nov17	2Jul18	Hosp.
Pion. Josef Gadhammer	Hosp.	5Jul18	EOW	
Sgt. Johann Gastl	KG 6/33	1Jan17	EOW	
Pion. Georg Gerneth	FA 286A	19Jul18	EOW	
Pion. Christof Gietl	FEA 1b	16Jul18	EOW	
Pion. Rupert Grill	KG 6/33	1Jan17	4Feb17	AFP 5
Feldw. Josef Gierl	KG 6/33	1Jan17	EOW	
Pion. Josef Götz	KG 6/33	1Jan17	4Feb17	AFP 5
Gefr. Jakob Grass	KG 6/33	1Jan17	16Feb17	FEA 1b
Kraftf. Pion. Max Greineder	KG 6/33	1Jan17	22Feb17	AFP 5
Pion. August Haass	KG 6/33	1Jan17	14Feb17	Hosp.
Pion. August Haass	Hosp.	18Feb17	EOW	
Gefr. Ludwig Hahn	FEA 1b	13Aug17	1Jan18	FA 286A
Pion. Otto Hammerer	AFP 5	20Feb17	6Mar17	AFP 5
Gefr. Georg Hartmann	KG 6/33	1Jan17	EOW	
Gefr. Georg Konrad Hein	KG 6/33	1Jan17	30Mar18	Hosp.
Gefr. Georg Konrad Hein	Hosp.	5Apr18	EOW	
Pion. Karl Franz Heller	KG 6/33	1Jan17	17Sep17	Hosp.
Pion. Karl Franz Heller	Hosp.	26Sep17	12Feb18	Hosp.
Pion. Karl Franz Heller	Hosp.	20Feb18	7Mar18	AFP 17
Gefr. Josef Helminger	KG 6/33	1Jan17	29Jun17	Hosp.
Gefr. Josef Helminger	Hosp.	16Jul17	16Aug18	Hosp.
Gefr. Friedrich Ludwig Hensler	KG 6/33	1Jan17	4Feb17	AFP 5
Uffz. Jakob Hepp	KG 6/33	1Jan17	EOW	
Feldw. Michael Herrmann	FEA 1b	2Nov17	15Dec17	FEA 1b
Pion. Johann Hertreiter	FEA 1b	16Jul18	19Aug18	Hosp.
Pion. Ludwig Hess	KG 6/33	1Jan17	2May17	AFP 4
Pion. Alois Hirnsberger		14Jan18	21Apr18	Hosp.
Pion. Alois Hirnsberger	Hosp.	25Apr17	7Jul18	Hosp.
Pion. Alois Hirnsberger	Hosp.	9Jul18	EOW	
Pion. Gottfried Hölzl	FEA 1b	27Jun18	EOW	
Uffz. Johannes Hörig	KG 6/33	1Jan17	EOW	
Uffz. Andreas Markus Hofmann	KG 6/33	1Jan17	2Oct17	AFP 4
Uffz. Stefan Hofmann	KG 6/33	1Jan17	28Feb17	FEA 1b
Pion. Georg Huber	KG 6/33	1Jan17	19Apr17	FEA 1b
Pion. Heinrich Hübner	KG 6/33	1Jan17	19Jul17	FEA 1b
Uffz. Edmund Igel	KG 6/33	1Jan17	8Apr18	IIC
Uffz. Edmund Igel	Hosp.	23Apr18	26May18	Hosp.
Uffz. Edmund Igel	Hosp.	28May18	EOW	
Kraftf. Erich Junggebauer	Js 26	22Jul17	6Jan18	Hosp.
Kraftf. Erich Junggebauer	Hosp.	10Jan18	19Apr18	Hosp.
Kraftf. Erich Junggebauer	Hosp.	22Apr18	4May18	Hosp.
Kraftf. Erich Junggebauer	Hosp.	6May18	EOW	
Pion. Leopold Keller	KG 6/33	1Jan17	2Nov17	FEA 1b
Pion. Xaver Kermer	KG 6/33	1Jan17	EOW	
Pion. Paul Kick	FEA 1b	5Jan17	6Jan17	FEA 1b
Uffz. Robert Kirch	KG 6/33	1Jan17	6May17	Hosp.
Pion. Richard Klein	FEA 1b	4Jan17	24May17	Hosp.
Pion. Richard Klein	Hosp.	29May17	17Jun17	AFP 4
Pion. Richard Klein	AFP 4	17Oct17	2Nov17	FEA 1b
Gefr. Theodor Klüpfel	KG 6/33	1Jan17	18Sep18	Injured
Vzfw. Karl Knöfel	KG 6/33	1Jan17	30Sep17	FEA 1b
Vzfw. Georg Kölbl	KG 6/33	1Jan17	EOW	
Pion. Friedrich Körner	FEA 1b	9Sep17	27Sep17	Hosp.
Pion. Friedrich Körner	Hosp.	21Oct17	19Mar18	Hosp.
Pion. Friedrich Körner	Hosp.	22Mar18	EOW	
Uffz. Emil Koester	KG 6/33	1Jan17	10Oct17	FEA 1b
Pion. Josef Anton Kohlhaupt	FEA 1b	24Jun17	16Aug17	Hosp.

Pion. Josef Anton Kohlhaupt	Hosp.	18Aug17	EOW	
Pion. Georg Kohlmann	KG 6/33	1Jan17	4Feb17	AFP 5
Gefr. Karl Koller	KG 6/33	1Jan17	EOW	
Gefr. Johann Kornberger	KG 6/33	1Jan17	16Jul17	FEA 3
Gefr. Johann Kornberger	FEA 3	30Jul17	4Jul18	Hosp.
Pion. Stefan Kratzer	FEA 1b	22Aug18	EOW	
Pion. Josef Krieger	FEA 1b	16Jul18	4Aug18	Hosp.
Pion. Josef Krieger	Hosp.	11Aug18	EOW	
Gefr. Johann Peter Küspert	KG 6	1Jan17	28Jan17	FEA 1b
Pion. Otto Kullmann	AFP 4	5Nov17	7Mar18	AFP 17
Pion. Josef Längst	FEA 1b	5Nov17	EOW	
Pion. Christoph Lang	KG 6/33	1Jan17	4Feb17	AFP 5
Pion. Rudolf Lankes	AFP 4	5Nov17	10May18	Hosp.
Pion. Rudolf Lankes	Hosp.	13May18	EOW	
Uffz. Jakob Lenz	KG 6/33	1Jan17	EOW	
Pion. Christian Linder	FA 293A	12Sep18	EOW	
Gefr. Johann Lohneis	KG 6/33	1Jan17	4Feb17	AFP 5
Pion. Karl Luft	FEA 1b	2Jan17	2Jan17	FEA 1b
Pion. Friedrich Lutz	FEA 1b	16Jul18	EOW	
Pion. Pius Lutz	KG 6/33	1Jan17	6Mar17	Hosp.
Pion. Pius Lutz	Hosp.	8Mar17	16Apr17	Hosp.
Pion. Pius Lutz	Hosp.	30Apr17	2Oct17	AFP 4
Pion. Georg Maas	KG 6/33	1Jan17	EOW	
Pion. Karl Friedrich Mathes	AFP 4	30Sep18	28Oct18	Hosp.
Pion. Richard Mauzmann	KfPk 6	4Mar18	27Mar18	KfPk 23
Pion. Simon Mayr	KG 6/33	1Jan17	14Nov17	FEA 1b
Pion. Josef Meder	FEA 1b	13Aug17	16Sep17	Hosp.
Pion. Josef Meder	Hosp.	22Sep17	1Jan18	FA 286A
Uffz. Ludwig Meindl	KG 6/33	1Jan17	12Apr17	FEA 1b
Gefr. Lorenz Meister	FEA 1b	9Aug17	29May18	Benz Wk
Gefr. Lorenz Meister	Benz Wk	14Jul18	EOW	
Pion. Johann Merkle	FEA 1b	23Jun18	8Jul18	FEA 1b
Pion. Ludwig Meyer	FEA 1b	9Oct18	EOW	
Gefr. Wolfgang Meyer	KG 6/33	1Jan17	30May18	Hosp.
Pion. Albert Mooswang	FEA 1b	24Jun17	9Aug17	Injured
Uffz. Philipp Müller	KG 6/33	1Jan17	EOW	
Gefr. Konrad Muth	KG 6/33	1Jan17	14Feb18	FEA 1b
Pion. Karl Oberländer	FEA 1b	2Oct18	EOW	
Pion. Julius Pangerl	AFP 2	16Jan18	17Jan18	FA 293A
Pion. Georg Paringer	KG 6/33	1Jan17	20Dec17	AFP 2
Feldw. Josef Parzefall	KG 6/33	1Jan17	2Mar17	Hosp.
Feldw. Josef Parzefall	Hosp.	22Mar17	12Jul17	Hosp.
Feldw. Josef Parzefall	Hosp.	3Aug17	6Oct17	FEA 1b
Uffz. Franz Pauli	FEA 1b	16Jul18	EOW	
Pion. Hermann Pauli	AFP 18	16Jul18	EOW	
Pion. Johann Pittner	AFP 2	14Jan18	2Apr18	Hosp.
Pion. Johann Evangelist Piendl	AFP 4	5Nov17	EOW	
Pion. Johann Ponath	KG 6/33	1Jan17	19Apr17	Hosp.
Pion. Johann Ponath	Hosp.	23Apr17	14Aug17	Hosp.
Pion. Johann Ponath	Hosp.	2Sep17	12Nov17	Hosp.
Pion. Johann Ponath	Hosp.	6Dec17	15Dec17	Hosp.
Pion. Johann Ponath	Hosp.	3Jan18	EOW	
Uffz. Ludwig Preisser	FEA 1b	17Oct17	14Mar18	Hosp.
Pion. Michael Pschörer	AFP 4	30May18	EOW	
Pion. Rupert Rathspieler	KG 6/33	1Jan17	5Jul18	Hosp.
Pion. Rupert Rathspieler	Hosp.	18Jul18	EOW	
Gefr. Josef Reiser	FEA 1b	5Jan18	20Apr18	AFP 6
Uffz. Emil Rettich	KG 6/33	1Jan17	19Aug17	FEA 1b
Gefr. Leonhard Richter	KG 6/33	1Jan17	7Mar17	FEA 1b
Uffz. Albert Römer	KG 6/33	1Jan17	19Feb17	Hosp.
Uffz. Albert Römer	Hosp.	25Feb17	30Jul17	FEA 1b
Pion. Karl Roth	FEA 1b	21Dec17	12Jun18	AFP 4
Pion. Leonhard Scheck	KG 6/33	1Jan17	19Jan17	FEA 1b
Pion. Lorenz Scheibeck	Infntry	3Nov18	EOW	
Pion. Franz Scheidweiler	KG 6/33	1Jan17	11Aug17	Hosp.

Pion. Franz Scheidweiler	Hosp.	24Aug17	14Jul18	Hosp.
Pion. Franz Scheidweiler	Hosp.	23Jul18	EOW	
Pion. Johann Schemer	KG 6/33	1Jan17	17Feb17	Hosp.
Pion. Johann Schemer	Hosp.	21Feb17	26Apr17	Hosp.
Pion. Johann Schemer	Hosp.	29Apr17	19Jul17	FEA 1b
Uffz. Maximilian Schlickling	FEA 1b	28Feb17	18Sep17	FEA 1b
Uffz. Eugen Schmieg	KG 6/33	1Jan17	10Aug18	Hosp.
Uffz. Eugen Schmieg	Hosp.	13Aug18	EOW	
Gefr. Bernhard Schmitt	KG 6/33	1Jan17	13Apr17	Hosp.
Gefr. Bernhard Schmitt	Hosp.	25Apr17	EOW	
Pion. Georg Schmitzer	KG 6/33	1Jan17	7Jan17	Js 23
Gefr. Josef Schneider	KG 6/33	1Jan17	25Mar17	Hosp.
Gefr. Josef Schneider	Hosp.	30Mar17	EOW	
Pion. Franz Schöndorfer	KG 6/33	1Jan17	7Jan17	Js 23
Pion. Nikolaus Schops	KG 6/33	1Jan17	7Jan17	Js 23
Pion. Konrad Schrimpf	KG 6/33	1Jan17	22Mar17	Hosp.
Pion. Konrad Schrimpf	Hosp.	5May17	2Nov17	FEA 1b
Pion. Johann Schroth	KG 6/33	1Jan17	EOW	
Pion. Georg Schuster	FA 292A	18Apr18	19Aug18	FEA 1b
Uffz. Jakob Schwarz	KG 6/33	1Jan17	27Sep17	AFP 4
Uffz. Wilhelm Seidenspinner	KG 6/33	1Jan17	4Feb17	AFP 5
Gefr. Karl Seidl	KG 6/33	1Jan17	EOW	
Uffz. Maximilian Seifried	KG 6/33	1Jan17	EOW	
Kraftf. Sebastian Seisenberger	KG 6/33	1Jan17	13Jul17	FEA 1b
Gefr. Vitus Sellmaier	FA 293A	13Aug18	17Sep18	Hosp.
Gefr. Vitus Sellmaier	Hosp.	25Sep18	EOW	
Sgt. Josef Sinzinger	KG 6/33	1Jan17	EOW	
Pion. Josef Sollfrank	AFP 4	5Nov17	17Jan18	Hosp.
Pion. Josef Sollfrank	Hosp.	22Jan18	30Jan18	Hosp.
Pion. Michael Sprenger	FEA 1b	10Sep17	4Jul18	Hosp.
Pion. Michael Sprenger	Hosp.	10Aug18	EOW	
Pion. Emil Steiner	KG 6/33	1Jan17	10Aug17	KIA
Pion. Fritz Stephan	KG 6/33	1Jan17	15Dec17	AFP 2
Pion. Jakob Stiegel	KG 6/33	1Jan17	4Feb17	AFP 5
Pion. Hubert Stürmer	KG 6/33	1Jan17	4Feb17	AFP 5
Pion. August Thaler	FEA 1b	17Sep17	10Aug18	Hosp.
Pion. August Thaler	Hosp.	18Aug18	EOW	
Gefr. Walter Tausch	KG 6/33	1Jan17	1Oct17	Hosp.
Gefr. Walter Tausch	Hosp.	21Oct17	22Oct17	FA 45b
Gefr. Gottlieb Thumm	KG 6/33	1Jan17	7Jan17	Js 23
Pion. Josef Vogler	KG 6/33	1Jan17	3Mar17	Hosp.
Pion. Josef Vogler	Hosp.	10Mar17	29May17	Hosp.
Pion. Josef Vogler	Hosp.	30May17	2Nov17	FEA 1b
Pion. Martin Vornberger	KG 6/33	1Jan17	EOW	
Vzfw. Johann Baptist Wachter	KG 6/33	1Jan17	13Jun17	Hosp.
Vzfw. Johann Baptist Wachter	Hosp.	28Jun17	10Jul17	Hosp.
Vzfw. Johann Baptist Wachter	Hosp.	24Jul17	EOW	
Gefr. Heinrich Wartenfelser	KG 6/33	1Jan17	9Mar17	Hosp.
Gefr. Heinrich Wartenfelser	Hosp.	12Mar17	14May18	Hosp.
Gefr. Heinrich Wartenfelser	Hosp.	8Jun18	EOW	
Kraftf. Josef Wendl	KG 6/33	1Jan17	16Feb17	Hosp.
Kraftf. Josef Wendl	Hosp.	20Feb17	16Apr17	Hosp.
Kraftf. Josef Wendl	Hosp.	21Apr17	19Jul17	FEA 1b
Unterzalmstr. Peter Westiner	FEA 1b	7Nov18	EOW	
Pion. Karl Widmer	KG 6/33	1Jan17	6Jul18	Hosp.
Pion. Karl Widmer	Hosp.	9Jul18	5Aug18	Hosp.
Pion. Karl Widmer	Hosp.	8Aug18	EOW	
Pion. Xaver Winter	FEA 1b	25Sep17	EOW	
Pion. Johann Wisgückl	AFP 2	18Jan18	25Jun18	Hosp.
Pion. Johann Wisgückl	Hosp.	2Jul18	18Jul18	Hosp.
Pion. Johann Wisgückl	Hosp.	22Jul18	EOW	
Pion. Paul Wolf	KfPk 6	7Mar18	20Mar18	KfPk 23
Vzfw. Georg Zahn	KG 6/33	1Jan17	EOW	
Gefr. Johannes Zimmermann	Js 27	15Jan17	3Mar17	Hosp.
Gefr. Johannes Zimmermann	Hosp.	8Mar17	25Mar17	Hosp.

Gefr. Johannes Zimmermann	Hosp.	2Apr17	24Jun17	Hosp.
Gefr. Johannes Zimmermann	Hosp.	9Jul17	16Jan18	Hosp.
Gefr. Johannes Zimmermann	Hosp.	28Jan18	EOW	

Schutzstaffel/Schlachtstaffel 24b
Mitgemachte Schlachten und Gefechte
(Battles and combat actions in which Ss 24b participated)

10Sep16	3Apr17	*Stellungskämpfe vor Verdun* (Trench fighting at Verdun)
5Apr17	31May17	*Frühjahrsschlacht bei Arras* (Spring battle of Arras)
1Jun17	20Nov17	*Schlacht in Flandern* (Battle in Flanders)
21Nov17	31Jan18	*Kämpfe in der Siegfriedstellung* (Fighting in the Siegfried Line)
1Feb18	20Mar18	*Stellungskämpfe im Artois und Aufmarsch zur Grossen Schlacht in Frankreich* (Trench fighting in Artois and assembly for the Great Battle in France)
21Mar18	6Apr18	*Grosse Schlacht in Frankreich und zwar im Besonderen:* (Great Battle in France and especially:)
21Mar18	23Mar18	*Durchbruchsschlacht Monchy-Cambrai* (Penetration battle Monchy-Cambrai)
24Mar18	25Mar18	*Schlacht bei Bapaume* (Battle at Bapaume)
7Apr18	12Apr18	*Kämpfe zwischen Arras und Albert* (Fighting between Arras and Albert)
13Apr18	18Apr18	*Schlacht bei Armentières* (Battle at Armentières)
19Apr18	23Apr18	*Stellungskämpfe in französisch Flandern* (Trench fighting in French Flanders)
24Apr18	29Apr18	*Schlacht um den Kemmel* (Battle for the Kemmel)
30Apr18	8Jul18	*Stellungskrieg in Flandern* (Trench war in Flanders)
9Jul18	14Jul18	*Stellungskämpfe bei Reims* (Trench fighting at Reims)
15Jul18	17Jul18	*Angriffsschlacht an der Marne und in der Champagne* (Offensive battle on the Marne and in the Champagne)
18Jul18	25Jul18	*Abwehrschlacht zwischen Soissons und Reims* (Defensive battle between Soissons and Reims)
26Jul18	3Aug18	*Die Bewegliche Schlacht zwischen Marne und Vesle* (The mobile battle between the Marne and the Vesle)
4Aug18	19Aug18	*Stellungskämpfe bei Reims* (Trench fighting at Reims)
20Aug18	29Aug18	*Stellungskämpfe in französisch Flandern* (Trench fighting in French Flanders)
30Aug18	27Sep18	*Stellungskämpfe in Flandern* (Trench fighting in Flanders)
28Sep18	11Nov18	*Abwehrschlacht in Flandern* (Defensive battle in Flanders)

Schutzstaffel/Schlachtstaffel 24b Airfields

From	To	Location	*Schlachtgruppe* Affiliation	*Armee*
1Jan17	10Jan17	Mont		5
10Jan17	31Jan17	Briey (Temporary)	Escort For FA 245(A)	5
31Jan17	(11Mar17)	Charmois	Schusta 24b Headquarters	5
31Jan17		2 a/c at Mont	Escort for FA 245(A)	5
31Jan17		2 a/c at Stenay	Escort for FA 274(A)	5
31Jan17		2 a/c at Cunel	Escort for FA 249(A)	5
3Apr17		Pont-de-la-Deule		1

5Apr17	31May17	Auby by Douai	Escort for FA 268(A)	6
1Jun17	(7Jun17)	Heule	Escort for FA 6	4
(Jul17)	1Sep17	Geluveld	Escort for FA 6	4
1Sep17	8Nov17	Wevelghem	Escort for FA 6	4
8Nov17	20Nov17	Maria Aalter	Escort for KG 1 (Day Bombing)	4
20Nov17	31Jan18	Abscon	Escort for FA 240(A)	6
1Feb18	21Mar18	Erchin	Escort for FA 240(A)	17
21Mar18	8Apr18	Erchin	SGp B (Ss 14,19,24b,25b,29b) C.O. *Hptm.* Wilhelm Aschenborn	17
8Apr18	18Apr18	Wasquehal	SGp D (Ss 24b,25b) C.O. *Oblt.* Hugo Miller	6
18Apr18	24Apr18	Heule	SGp D (Ss 9,12,16,24b,25b) C.O. *Oblt.* Johannes Missfelder	4
25Apr18	8Jul18	Linselles	SGp D (Ss 9,12,16,24b) C.O. *Oblt.* Johannes Missfelder	4
9Jul18	10Jul18	Assevillers	SGp J (Ss 4,15,24b,25b) C.O. *Oblt.d.R.* Franz Albertshauser	2
11Jul18	11Aug18	St. Loup	SGp J (Ss 4,15,24b,25b) C.O. *Oblt.* Erhardt Egerer	1
11Aug18	12Aug18	NW Athies	SGp J (Ss 4,15,24b,25b,35) C.O. *Oblt.* Erhardt Egerer	2
13Aug18	19Aug18	St. Loup	SGp J (Ss 4,15,24b,25b,35) C.O. *Oblt.* Erhardt Egerer	1
20Aug18	31Aug18	Beuvry Ost	SGp J (Ss 4,15,24b,25b) C.O. *Oblt.* Erhardt Egerer	17
1Sep18	8Sep18	Abscon	SGp J (Ss 4,15,24b,25b,35) C.O. *Oblt.* Erhardt Egerer	17
9Sep18	7Oct18	Abscon	SGp J (Ss 4,15,24b,25b,35) C.O. *Oblt.* Friedrich von Kraußer	17
7Oct18	13Oct18	Oudenaarde	SGp J (Ss 9,16,24b,25b) C.O. *Oblt.* Friedrich von Kraußer	4
13Oct18	23Oct18	Oudenaarde	SGp J (Ss 9,24b,25b) C.O. *Oblt.* Friedrich von Kraußer	4
23Oct18	EOW	Deinze	SGp J (Ss 9,24b,25b) C.O. *Oblt.* Friedrich von Kraußer	4

Royal Bavarian *Schutzstaffel 24b*

1Jan17	*Schutzstaffel 24b* is created from KG 6/Ks 33 by BKM Nr. 148032 of 31Dec16.
5May17	*Uffz.* Anton Monz, P, and *Uffz.* Ferdinand Schellerer, G, are KIA 1 km. N. of Quiery-la-Motte between 10.00 - 11.00 hours due to air combat. They are downed in flames in DFW C.V (LVG) 5231/16.
25May17	*Uffz.* Wilhelm Miltner, P, and *Vzfw.* Ferdinand Wens, G, are KIA over Flers, NW Douai in Albatros C.VII C.1237/16, during an air combat at 7.50 hours. They are downed in flames.
31May17	*Vzfw.* Konrad Mann, P, is KIC and *Uffz.* Franz Xaver Brandl, G, is IIC,lt. at Auby, Flers NW of Douai, at 16.30 hours on a practice flight over Rimbeaucourt in DFW C.V (Av) 9018/16. They collided with *Uffz.* Christoph Hertel of *Jasta* 10 who was also IIC,sev.
27Jun17	*Sgt.* Anton Fleck, P, and *Gefr.* Jakob Grass, G, are KIC at Bousbecque at 9.35 hours.
9Aug17	*Pion.* Albert Mooswang, M, is injured by a propeller and to hospital at Kortryk.
10Aug17	*Flg.* Emil Steiner, M, and *Vzfw.* Alfred Regensburger, G, are WIA at Watermolen by Kortryk at 16.50 hours during a bombing raid. Steiner DOW 11Aug17 while Regensburger remains with the unit.
13Aug17	*Gefr.* Georg Franz, M, is injured when he walks into a propeller and to hospital.
16Aug17	*Uffz.* Emmerich-1, *Uffz.* Brandl-1, Spad 1, 11.30, E. Bellewarde-Teich, Spad S.7 #B.3471, 19 Sqn. RFC, Lt. C.D. Thompson, POW
21Sep17	*Vzfw.* Alfred Regensburger, G, is WIA over Zillebeker due to air combat and to hospital.
29Sep17	*Vzfw.* Franz Baumeister, P, is WIA at 8.20 hours over Bisseghem by Kortryk by ground fire. He is shot in the foot and sent to hospital on 18Oct17 when an infection developes.
29Sep17	*Pion.* Konrad Bosch, M, is injured when a detonator accidently explodes and to hospital at Bisseghem.
5Oct17	*Vzfw.* Albert Hermann, P, and *Vzfw.* Franz Xaver Brandl, G, are forced to land E. Wevelghem, after DFW C.V (Av) 145/17 catches fire in the air. They are OK.
24Nov17	*Uffz.* Karl Will, P, and *Vzfw.* Andreas Mersch, G, are KIC at Abscon airfield during take-off at 8.20 hours.
15Dec17	*Vzfw.* Kallmünzer-zLg, *Uffz.* Raab-zLg, Sopwith Camel, 11.30, Boiry
19Jan18	*Uffz.* Ludwig Beyer, P, is KIA and *Gefr.* Hugo Reichert, G, is WIA,sv. N. Biache at 13.00 hours during air combat.
3Feb18	*Uffz.* Wilhelm Flormann, G, is WIA,sv. E. Monchy during air combat. His pilot, *Vzfw.* Franz Pfeffer, lands the aircraft OK. Flormann DOW 7Feb18 at Erchin.

17Feb18 *Vzfw.* Albert Hermann, P, and *Vzfw.* Franz Xaver Brandl, G, are forced to land at 11.20 hours at Abscon, after Halberstadt Cl.II 6348/17 receives a flak splinter in its engine. They are OK.

8Mar18 *Vzfw.* Hermann-n/c, *Vzfw.* Brandl-n/c, S.E. 5, 11.40, Bourlon Wood
(Credited to *Ltn.* Wolf Baron von Manteuffel-Szöge, *Jasta 35b*)

22Mar18 *Sgt.* Adolf Zitzelsberger, P, and *Vzfw.* Johann Karl Heinrich Müller, G, are KIA at 18.30 hours between Beaumetz-les-Cambrai and Mory-St. Leger by ground fire in Hannover Cl.II 9398/17.

27Mar18 *Schutzstaffel 24b* is renamed *Schlachtstaffel 24b* by KM Nr.
5126.18.A.7.L.IV.C. of 27Mar18.

8Apr18 *Uffz.* Edmund Igel, M, is IIC when the aircraft he is in crashes during a check flight.

11Apr18 *Vzfw.* Hermann-1, *Vzfw.* Brandl-2, Sopwith Camel, 15.50, Erquinghem, Steenwerk. #B.5750, 210 Sqn. RAF, F/S/Lt. M.T. McKelvey, WIA, POW.

11Apr18 *Vzfw.* Johann Burghauser, P, and *Fähnr.* Oskar Schlecht, G, are KIA over Lys-Bogen, Erquinghem in an Albatros C.VII during air combat at 15.48 hours.

29Apr18 *Gefr.* Josef Anton Humbs, P, and *Gefr.* Josef Wimmer, G, are WIA,sv. at 8.00 hours over Westoutre by ground fire.

15May18 *Gefr.* Johann Schreiber, P, and *Gefr.* Georg Strauss, G, are KIA over Dranoutre at 18.15 hours by ground fire while on an orientation flight. Strauss fell out of the aircraft.

31May18 *Pion.* Josef Eisenbach, P, and *Uffz.* Johann Gutneder, G, are IIC at Linselles and to hospital.

4Jun18 *Uffz.* Josef Köck, G, is WIA at 11.45 hours over Hooglede by ground fire.

28Jun18 *Uffz.* Johann Gutneder, G, catches pneumonia and is taken to the hospital at Mouvaux. He DOW 9Jul18 at Tourcoing.

10Jul18 *Ltn.d.R.* Albert Hermann, P, is severely injured at Assevillers at 5.45 hours during a horse back riding accident and to hospital.

16Jul18 *Uffz.* Max Forstner, P, and *Uffz.* Hans Heuberger, G, are WIA at 12.15 hours at Mourmelon by ground fire and to hospital.

20Jul18 *Oblt.d.R.* Franz Albertshauser, O and C.O., is WIA by ground fire at 7.45 hours W. Vierzy, S. Soissons and to hospital.

3Sep18 *Pion.* Ernst Altfudisch, M, squashes his hand and to hospital.

18Sep18 *Gefr.* Theodor Klüpfel, M, breaks his left arm when he is struck by a propeller and to hospital.

25Sep18 *Uffz.* Johannes Helmuth Richard Ihde, P, and *Uffz.* Ernst Julius Hopf, G, are KIC at Blaudain during a night take-off at 21.45 hours in LVG C.VI 3937/18.

17Oct18 *Uffz.* Heinrich Auer, G, is IIC in a landing accident at Oudenaarde when a hand grenade accidently detonates.

22Oct18 *Oblt.* Gustav Bauer, O, and C.O., is WIA by ground fire at 16.40 hours over Deerlijk, NE of Kortryk and to hospital.

16Nov18 *Schlachtstaffel 24b* is demobilized at FEA 2b, Fürth.

The men of *Schustzstaffel 24b* in December 1917 at Abscon. From left to right: *Vzfw.* Karl Kallmünzer, *Uffz.* Wilhelm Flormann, *Vzfw.* Albert Hermann, *Vzfw.* Friedrich Emmerich, *Vzfw.* Johann Fuchs, *Vzfw.* Georg Motschiedler, *Vzfw.* Johann Müller, *Fähnr.* Oskar Schlecht, *Uffz.* Willy Ehrlich, *Uffz.* Wilhelm Fried, *Uffz.* Anton Raab, *Vzfw.* Georg Fuchs, *Vzfw.* Franz Xaver Brandl, *Vzfw.* Johann Burghauser, *Uffz.* Leo Weth and *Gefr.* Hugo Reichert. The photo had to have been taken before December 16th, as that is the date Ehrlich left the unit. Photo credit: Werner Walter.

Hannover Cl.IIIa 7005/18 of *Schlachtstaffel 24b* photographed at Coblenz post-war. The cockade is in the U.S. colors.

Another photo of the *Schlasta 24b* Hannover Cl.IIIa 7005/18 post-war at Coblenz. The men are Bartlett Beaman and Phil Henderson of the 12th Aero Sqn. USAS.

Royal Bavarian *Schutzstaffel 25*

Pilot/Gunner	Type	From		To	
		Unit	Date	Date	Unit
Vzfw. Leopold Ballin	G	FEA 1b	20Oct17	13Jun18	AFP 6
Gefr. Franz Bauer	P	AFP 4	30Sep18	EOW	
Uffz. Wilhelm Friedrich Berkowsky	P	KG 6/34	1Jan17	12Feb17	FEA 1b
Oblt. Friedrich Berthold, C.O.	O	Grfl 12	12Jul17	17Jul17	FEA 1b
Vzfw. Konrad Bischoff	P	AFP 5	6Mar17	24Apr18	AFP 6
Pion. Paul Breitling	G	AFP 7	21Apr17	6May17	AFP 7
Gefr. Adolf Brüstle	G	FEA 1b	6Feb17	13Feb17	FEA 1b
Vzfw. Wilhelm Büssing	P	FA 48b	22Sep17	29Sep17	Ss 27b
Oblt. Alfred Colomb, Stv. C.O.	O	Kofl 6	1Jul17	10Jul17	Kofl 6
Oblt. Alfred Colomb, Stv. C.O.	O	Kofl 6	18Jul17	30Jul17	Kofl 6
Sgt. Andreas Dachwald	P	AFP 6	14May18	18Jun18	IIC,lt.
Uffz. Max Dantonello	G	AFP 1	13Jul18	19Jul18	IIC,sv.
Uffz. Doell (Kofl 6 Report)	G			6May18	IIC,sv.
Uffz. Wilhelm Dörfler	P	AFP 6	7Jan18	9Jan18	IIC,lt.
Vzfw. Wilhelm Dörfler	P	Hosp.	10Jan18	26May18	WIA
Vzfw. Konrad Dumpert	P	AFP 5	6Mar17	16Feb18	KIA
Vzfw. Ludwig Dutz	G	AFP 17	28Mar18	17Jul18	IIC
Vzfw. Ludwig Dutz	G	AFP 1	23Jul18	EOW	
Uffz. Mathias Endl	P			19Jul18	IIC,sv.
Vzfw. Ernst Fettinger (KIC 19Nov)	P	AFP 1	10Jul18	EOW	
Oblt. Hermann von Fichte	O		19Apr18	26May18	BG 5/4
Vzfw. Hans Fischer	G	KG 6/34	1Jan17	23Jan17	Hosp.
Vzfw. Hans Fischer	G	Hosp.	12Feb17	29Mar17	FEA 1b
Vzfw. Karl Fischer	G	AFP 17	19Apr18	13Jun18	AFP 6
Uffz. Paul Frank	G	AFP 7	17May17	11Sep17	Ss 11
Gefr. Emil Frey	G	AFP 17	27Oct18	EOW	
Uffz. Fritz Fromme	P	FA 208A	4Mar17	6Mar17	AFP 5
Oblt. Ernst Galle, C.O.	P	KG 6/34	1Jan17	30Jun17	Ss 2
Vzfw. Arnulf Gegerle	P	AFP 6	20Feb18	3May18	FEA 1b
Pion. Georg Gilg	G	AFP 4	10Nov17	20Nov17	Ss 19
Gefr. Friedrich Gross	G	AFP 4	18Oct18	EOW	
Vzfw. Friedrich Hartl (+ 10Mar18)	G	BS II	20Jul17	9Mar18	WIA,sv.
Pion. Maximilian Hartmann	G	AFP 7	30May17	22Jun17	AFP 7
Vzfw. Paul Heim	G	AFP 7	8May17	25Apr18	AFP 6
Ltn. Friedrich Hermann	O	KG 6/34	1Jan17	27Mar17	FEA 1b
Gefr. Hirschel	G	AFP 7	30Apr17	8May17	AFP 7
Vzfw. Leonhard Hitzler	P	AFP 4	20Jun18	EOW	
Vzfw. Joseph Hochholzer	G	AFP 4	15Aug17	8Jun18	FEA 1b
Pion. Heinrich Janz	G	AFP 7	5Apr17	1May17	AFP 7
Vzfw. Mathias Hubert Jorissen	G	AFP 7	7May17	23Aug17	AFP 4
Vzfw. Mathias Hubert Jorissen	G	AFP 4	26Aug17	20Sep17	Ss 2
Vzfw. Leonhard Käppner	P	AFP 6	22Feb18	21Oct18	AFP 4
Vzfw. Ludwig Kapfhammer	P	FA 295A	25May17	7Jun17	AFP 7
Oblt. Alwin Kinkelin, C.O.	O	FA 298A	10Jun18	16Oct18	FEA 1b
Gefr. Bruno Knöfel	G	AFP 4	11Jun18	18Jun18	IIC,lt.
Uffz. Bruno Knöfel	G		18Jun18	17Sep18	IIC
Uffz. Bruno Knöfel	G	Hosp.	25Sep18	EOW	
Vzfw. Alfons Konradt	P	KG 6/34	1Jan17	14May17	WIA
Vzfw. Ludwig Kraus	G	AFP 4	6Aug17	25Mar18	Hosp.
Vzfw. Ludwig Kraus	G	FS IV	22Jun18	22Jul18	Hosp.
Uffz. Michael Krauss	P	AFP 17	5Oct18	EOW	
Vzfw. Jakob Krüger	G	FS I	8Jan18	9Aug18	AFP 1
Uffz. Christian Kurth	G	FEA 1b	9Aug18	EOW	
Vzfw. Walter Lagershausen	P	KG 6/34	1Jan17	4May17	KIA
Pion. Heinrich Lauer	G	AFP 4	6Aug17	26Sep17	KIA
Vzfw. Johann Lottes	P	KG 6/34	1Jan17	18Jul17	FEA 1b
Pion. Heinrich Lübbecke	G	AFP 7	5Apr17	1May17	AFP 7
Uffz. Gerhard Masolyn	G	AFP 7	19May17	31May17	Hosp.
Vzfw. Ernst Mass	G	FEA 1	6May17	9Sep17	Ss 21

Vzfw. Edwin Matthes	P	AFP 1	21Jul18	EOW	
Oblt. Hugo Miller, C.O.	O	FEA 1b	19Dec17	10Jun18	SGp Wnk
Pion. Nikolaus Mosbach	G	AFP 4	5Oct18	EOW	
Vzfw. Franz Müller	G	AFP 4	27Sep17	EOW	
Gefr. Konrad Müller	G	AFP 6	20Feb18	9Apr18	KIA
Gefr. Ludwig Neeb	G	FEA 5	26Sep17	18Oct17	Ss 17
Vzfw. Wilhelm Obernöder	G	AFP 4	5Sep17	8May18	FEA 1b
Gefr. Michael Oestheimer	G	AFP 4	21Jul17	8Aug17	Hosp.
Ltn.d.R. Ernst Poetsch	O	KG 6/34	1Jan17	20Apr17	KG 2
Vzfw. Emil Prime	P	AFP 7	6May17	8Jan18	AFP 6
Pion. Max Ramet	P	AFP 4	18Jun18	21Jun18	KIC
Pion. Michael Ringler	P	AFP 6	30Apr18	6May18	KIC
Oblt. Josef Rittmann, C.O.	O	Ss 29b	30Jul17	10Dec17	FEA 1b
Pion. Max Heinrich Sames	G	AFP 4	23Sep17	5Oct17	Ss 19
Vzfw. Anton Schädle	P	AFP 4	6Oct17	12Jul18	SGp 1
Uffz. Paul Schmidt	G	AFP 1	9Aug18	31Oct18	WIA
Pion. Otto Heinrich Schmitt	G	AFP 4	3Nov18	EOW	
Vzfw. Oskar Schmeckenbecher	P	AFP 6	18Feb18	28Aug18	AFP 6
Vzfw. Josef Schneider	P	FA 238A	17Jul17	EOW	
Uffz. Josef Schreiner	G	AFP 6	15May18	2Oct18	KIA
Uffz. Theodor Schrimpf	P	AFP 17	3Sep18	EOW	
Vzfw. Max Sefferin	G	AFP 6	10Apr18	EOW	
Offz.Stv. Joseph Siegl	P	KG 6/34	1Jan17	24Jan17	WIA
Vzfw. Hugo Sillus	G	AFP 5	27Feb17	30Apr17	AFP 7
Pion. Sebastian Simson	G	AFP 4	11Jun18	21Jun18	KIC
Vzfw. Adalbert Solleder	P	FEA 1b	7Jun17	8Jan18	AFP 6
Uffz. Martin Staber	G	AFP 6	28Mar18	11May18	KIC
Uffz. Robert Staiger	G	KG 6/34	1Jan17	17May17	FEA 1b
Vzfw. Max Stattenberger	P	FA 294A	14Apr18	21Aug18	AFP 4
Oblt.d.R. Ferdinand Wilhelm Frhr. von Stein-Liebenstein zu Barchfeld, C.O.	P	BLA Fnk	29Oct18	EOW	
Ltn.d.R. Stephan, Stv. C.O.	O	Kofl 4	16Oct18	29Oct18	Kofl 4
Gefr. Ernst Tautz	G	AFP 7	5Apr17	1May17	AFP 7
Vzfw. Friedrich Ulber	G	AFP 7	6May17	22Aug17	WIA
Uffz. Franz Völkle	P	AFP 6	5Mar18	10Mar18	AFP 6
Uffz. Franz Völkle	P	AFP 6	3Apr18	9Apr18	KIA
Sgt. Thomas Wagner	P	AFP 6	7May18	11May18	KIC
Pion. Johann Weidmann	G	AFP 7	21Apr17	4May17	KIA
Vzfw. August Wisslicen	P	KG 6/34	1Jan17	18Jun17	Hosp.
Vzfw. August Wisslicen	P	Hosp.	6Jul17	13Feb18	FEA 2b
Vzfw. Franz Wittig	G	KG 6/34	1Jan17	26Aug17	WIA,lt.
Ltn.d.R. Franz Wittig	G		26Aug17	10Jan18	FEA 1b
Vzfw. Benedikt Wölfle	G	AFP 4	5Oct17	16Feb18	KIA
Ltn. Heinrich Zahler	O	KG 6/34	1Jan17	5Jan17	FEA 1b

Royal Bavarian *Schutzstaffel 25*

Mechanics and Ground Personnel

Name	From		To	
	Unit	Date	Date	Unit
Pion. Georg Ackermann	KG 6/45	1Jan17	7Jan17	AFP 5
Gefr. Georg Adolph	KG 6/34	1Jan17	18Feb18	Hosp.
Gefr. Georg Adolph	Hosp.	26Mar18	22Jul18	FEA 1b
Pion. Alfred Aumüller	FEA 1b	4Jan18	20Jun18	FEA 1b
Vzfw. Lorenz Baiermann	KG 6/34	1Jan17	10Dec17	FEA 1b
Pion. Anton Bauer	Ss 27b	10Sep18	EOW	
Pion. Heinrich Baur	KG 6/34	1Jan17	EOW	
Uffz. Johann Peter Baumeister	FEA 1b	15Aug17	12Oct17	FEA 1b
Gefr. Johann Beck	KG 6/34	1Jan17	EOW	
Sgt. Michael Beyer	KG 6/34	1Jan17	26Oct18	FEA 1b
Pion. Emil Bieber	RHBZ 20	16Jun17	11Feb18	Js 29

Pion. Heinrich Bieber	FEA 1b	3Jul18	14Jul18	FEA 1b
Pion. Hermann Billowie	KG 6/34	1Jan17	EOW	
Pion. Paul Bischoff (+ 16Oct18)	Js 23	17Jan17	29Sep18	Hosp.
Pion. Ottmar Blaschke	FEA 1b	2Jul18	EOW	
Pion. Karl Bleistein	KG 6/34	1Jan17	EOW	
Pion. Heinrich Borst	FEA 1b	30Dec17	12Jun18	AFP 4
Gefr. Otto Breitneicher	EAbt 2	29Dec17	14Jul18	Hosp.
Gefr. August Brenner (+ 23Sep18)	Ss 27b	10Sep18	20Sep18	Hosp.
Pion. Otto Brückner	FEA 1b	18Nov17	EOW	
Gefr. Josef Brunner	KG 6/34	1Jan17	EOW	
Sgt. Reinhold Buhrmann	FEA 1b	2May18	EOW	
Gefr. Bernhard Bunk	Ss 29b	30Jul17	22Nov17	FEA 1b
Uffz. Georg Damm	KG 6/34	1Jan17	EOW	
Gefr. Georg Daser	KG 6/34	1Jan17	6Jan18	FEA 1b
Uffz. Wilhelm Diehl	KG 6/34	1Jan17	7Jan17	AFP 5
Uffz. Viktor Döhlemann	KG 6/34	1Jan17	6Oct17	FEA 1b
Vzfw. Leonhard Dorn	KG 6/34	1Jan17	EOW	
Pion. Adolf Ebert	FA 290A	4Sep17	EOW	
Uffz. Christian Eckert	KG 6/34	1Jan17	1Sep17	Dschrgd
Pion. Albert Ehrenbauer	FEA 1b	28Dec17	29Jan18	Hosp.
Pion. Albert Ehrenbauer	Hosp.	21Mar18	13May18	Hosp.
Pion. Albert Ehrenbauer	Hosp.	19Jun18	EOW	
Uffz. Johann Anton Eichhorn		23Aug18	EOW	
Pion. Karl Eichschmidt	KG 6/34	1Jan17	26Aug17	Hosp.
Pion. Josef Johann Enders	KG 6/34	1Jan17	7Jan17	FEA 1b
Pion. Josef Erber	KG 6/34	1Jan17	17Jul17	FEA 1b
Pion. Josef Erdner	FEA 1b	28Dec17	8Oct18	FEA 1b
Uffz. Magnus Ettenreich	KG 6/34	1Jan17	17Jan17	Js 23
Gefr. Matthäus Eurich	KG 6/34	1Jan17	EOW	
Pion. Franz Faber	FEA 1b	30Dec17	EOW	
Vzfw. Max Faber	FEA 1b	30Dec17	21Jun18	Infntry
Pion. Richard Fehlner	KG 6/34	1Jan17	2Nov17	FEA 1b
Pion. Johann Finkenzeller	Hosp.	2Jan17	26Feb17	FEA 1b
Uffz. Ludwig Floss	KG 6/34	1Jan17	17Jan17	Js 23
Pion. Martin Frech	FEA 1b	18Nov17	EOW	
Gefr. Johann Ganzelmeier	KG 6/34	1Jan17	EOW	
Pion. Joseph Gareis	FEA 1b	13Jan18	19Jul18	Kofl 1
Pion. Michael Geier	FEA 1b	4Sep17	2Oct17	FEA 1b
Gefr. Josef Gewolf	FEA 1b	9Aug18	EOW	
Uffz. Hans Gierstorfer	KG 6/34	1Jan17	EOW	
Pion. Karl Gleissner	FEA 1b	13Jan18	EOW	
Gefr. Albert Gmyreck	FEA 1b	3Apr17	2Nov17	FEA 1b
Uffz. Alfred Gräfe	FEA 1b	5Feb17	EOW	
Pion. Heinrich Grümm	AFP 6	24Apr18	25May18	BG 5
Pion. Karl Greinwald	FEA 1b	20Jul18	EOW	
Gefr. Johann Griesberger	KG 6/34	1Jan17	EOW	
Pion. Hans Grünwald	FEA 2b	2Nov17	1May18	Hosp.
Pion. Georg Guckenberger	FEA 1b	18Nov17	9Sep18	Hosp.
Pion. Otto Guggenmos	KG 6/34	1Jan17	28Feb17	FEA 1b
Pion. Konrad Hartel	FEA 1b	3May18	EOW	
Gefr. Johann Hein	FEA 1b	2Feb18	EOW	
Gefr. Heinrich Held	KG 6/34	1Jan17	7Jan17	AFP 5
Uffz. Jakob Hilgert	FEA 1b	30Dec17	19Jul18	Kofl 1
Gefr. Heinrich Höhn	FEA 1b	2Jul18	EOW	
Uffz. Paul Hofmann	KG 6/34	1Jan17	16Nov17	FEA 1b
Pion. Philipp Hofmann	KG 6/34	1Jan17	20Apr18	Hosp.
Pion. Gregor Holzer	FA 298A	17Jun18	EOW	
Pion. Roman Hoschar	KG 6/34	1Jan17	15Feb17	Hosp.
Pion. Josef Huber	AFP 4	8Jun18	EOW	
Gefr. Josef Hufnagel	AKP 6	15Jan18	20Apr18	AKP 6
Vzfw. Johann Jäger	KG 6/34	1Jan17	17Jan17	FEA 1b
Uffz. Ewald Jörn	KG 6/34	1Jan17	EOW	
Pion. Wilhelm Käppel	KG 6/34	1Jan17	20Apr17	KG 2
Pion. Wilhelm Käppel	KG 2	21May17	Sep17	FA 290A
Pion. Hermann Kapp	FEA 1b	28Dec17	EOW	

Uffz. Joseph Wolff Kapfhammer	KG 6/34	1Jan17	EOW	
Pion. Georg Kast	FEA 1b	13Jan18	11Feb18	FSSch
Pion. Karl Kern	KG 6/34	1Jan17	8Jan17	Lnz Kdo
Pion. Fritz Knöchel	KG 6/34	1Jan17	3Jul17	FEA 1b
Uffz. Martin Körner	KG 6/34	1Jan17	1Jul18	Hosp.
Uffz. Martin Körner	Hosp.	20Jul18	1Nov18	AFP 4
Uffz. Max Kotzan		30Oct18	EOW	
Pion. Karl Krämer	FEA 1b	14Jan18	EOW	
Pion. Ludwig Kraus	FEA 1b	11Mar17	28Mar17	FEA 1b
Gefr. Johann Georg Kreuzer	KG 6/34	1Jan17	2Feb17	FEA 1b
Pion. Ludwig Krüninger	FEA 1b	18Feb18	22Mar18	Hosp.
Gefr. Karl Kürth	KG 6/34	1Jan17	21Jun17	Hosp.
Gefr. Karl Kürth	Hosp.	3Jul17	23Jan18	AFP 6
Gefr. Jakob Kugler	KG 6/34	1Jan17	4Jan17	FEA 1b
Pion. Alois Kunkel	KG 6/34	1Jan17	20Feb17	Hllnbau
Pion. Alois Kunkel	Hllnbau	7Mar17	12Jun18	Ss 30b
Uffz. Wilhelm Kunze	FEA 1b	13Jan18	3Nov18	Hosp.
Uffz. Andreas Lehr	KG 6/34	1Jan17	28Jul17	Hosp.
Pion. Max Leithe	FEA 1b	25May18	5Oct18	Hosp.
Pion. Jakob Lenhard	KG 6/34	1Jan17	7Jan17	AFP 5
Werkmstr.Stv. Georg Leonhardt	FEA 1b	11Oct17	EOW	
Pion. Andreas Liegel	KG 6/34	1Jan17	8Jun18	FEA 1b
Pion. Lorenz Lindau	KG 6/34	1Jan17	12Mar17	Hosp.
Uffz. Wilhelm Louis	KG 6/34	1Jan17	7Jul18	KIAcc
Pion. Mathias Ludwig	FEA 1b	2Jul18	EOW	
Gefr. Andreas Linder	FEA 1b	17Nov17	EOW	
Pion. Friedrich Lutz	FEA 1b	5Feb17	3Jul17	FEA 1b
Pion. Karl Maier	FEA 1b	5Feb17	2Oct17	FEA 1b
Uffz. Rupert Maier	KG 6/34	1Jan17	EOW	
Vzfw. Willi Maier	AFP 6	23Apr18	26Sep18	Hosp.
Vzfw. Willi Maier	Hosp.	8Oct18	EOW	
Pion. Paul Mallunat	KG 6/34	1Jan17	18Sep18	Ss 27b
Pion. Anton Mayer	KG 6/34	1Jan17	7Jan17	AFP 5
Pion. Ludwig Merk	FEA 1b	30Dec17	6Oct18	Sick Lv
Pion. Josef Messmann	FEA 1b	3Apr17	29Nov17	FEA 1b
Uffz. Johann Mittring	KG 6/34	1Jan17	8Jun17	FEA 1b
Offz.Stv. Johann Motschiedler	KG 6/34	1Jan17	EOW	
Pion. Franz Müller	FEA 1b	27Nov17	EOW	
Uffz. Hans Müller	AFP 1	10Jul18	EOW	
Uffz. Wilhelm Muth	KG 6/34	1Jan17	19Feb17	Hosp.
Sgt. Wilhelm Muth	FEA 1b	30Jul17	23Mar18	Hosp.
Gefr. Hans Obser	KG 6/34	1Jan17	15Nov17	FEA 1b
Gefr. Karl Ott	AKP 6	20Apr18	EOW	
Pion. Alois Pech	KG 6/34	1Jan17	EOW	
Pion. Josef Philipp	KG 6/34	1Jan17	7Jan17	FEA 1b
Pion. Hans Pinzer	AFP 4	8Oct18	EOW	
Pion. Max Pongratz	FEA 1b	Jun17	16Jul17	FEA 1b
Pion. Otto Preiss	KG 6/34	1Jan17	2Nov17	FEA 1b
Vzfw. Georg Puchner	KG 6/34	1Jan17	9Aug18	FEA 1b
Pion. Karl Simon Ranft	KG 6/34	1Jan17	1May17	FEA 1b
Pion. Ernst Rehm	FEA 1b	31Dec17	11Jun18	AFP 4
Pion. Ernst Rehm	AFP 4	21Jul18	EOW	
Pion. Blasius Reiser	FEA 1b	2Jul18	EOW	
Gefr. Josef Reuter	KG 6/34	1Jan17	EOW	
Pion. Franz Rixner	FEA 1b	28Dec17	25Jan18	Hosp.
Pion. Franz Rixner	Hosp.	2Mar18	24Jun18	Hosp.
Pion. Franz Rixner	Hosp.	20Jul18	23Aug18	Hosp.
Pion. Isidor Roll	FEA 1b	24Nov17	16May18	Hosp.
Pion. Isidor Roll	Hosp.	11Jun18	7Jul18	Hosp.
Pion. Isidor Roll	Hosp.	15Sep18	EOW	
Gefr. Hans Christian Rügemer	KG 6/34	1Jan17	EOW	
Uffz. Georg Ruhland	KG 6/34	1Jan17	EOW	
Uffz. Gottlieb Rupp	KG 6/34	1Jan17	3Jan18	Hosp.
Pion. Johann Schabert	KG 6/34	1Jan17	17Jul17	AFP 6
Pion. Heinrich Schaffhauser	KG 6/34	1Jan17	2Dec17	Hosp.

Pion. Gottfried Schaumann	KG 6/34	1Jan17	17Jan17	FA 47
Uffz. Karl Schleicher	KG 6/34	1Jan17	8Aug17	Hosp.
Pion. Adolf Schmid	FEA 1b	2May18	19Jul18	Kofl 7
Pion. Josef Schmid	KG 6/34	1Jan17	3Jan17	FEA 1b
Pion. Josef Schmid	FEA 1b	2Apr17	14Apr18	FEA 1b
Pion. Albert Schmidt	FEA 1b	4Sep17	16Sep17	AFP 4
Pion. Wolfgang Schmitt	FEA 1b	2Aug18	EOW	
Pion. Clemens Schramm	KG 6/34	1Jan17	20Nov17	Hosp.
Pion. Philipp Schrenker	KG 6/34	1Jan17	29Jan17	FEA 1b
Pion. Franz Schwägerl	KG 6/34	1Jan17	30Jun17	Ss 2
Pion. Georg Sehner	KG 6/34	1Jan17	15May18	Hosp.
Pion. Georg Sehner	FEA 1b	2Jul18	EOW	
Uffz. Ludwig Speckner	KG 6/34	1Jan17	EOW	
Pion. Karl Söllner	BG 8/26	28Apr18	EOW	
Pion. Erwin Sommerfeld	FEA 1b	30Dec17	EOW	
Pion. Erhardt Sondheimer	KG 6/34	1Jan17	21Nov17	FEA 1b
Pion. Karl Stölting	Js 23	17Jan17	14Feb17	Hosp.
Pion. Karl Stölting	Hosp.	17May17	18May17	AFP 7
Pion. Mathias Stölzl	KG 6/34	1Jan17	8Sep17	FEA 1b
Uffz. Florian Stoll	KG 6/34	1Jan17	7May18	Hosp.
Uffz. Florian Stoll	Hosp.	17May18	1Jun18	FEA 1b
Gefr. Johann Karl Strecker	KG 6/34	1Jan17	6Jan17	AFP 5
Pion. Ignatz Thäter	FEA 1b	11Dec17	11Jun18	AFP 4
Gefr. Franz Trier	KG 6/34	1Jan17	EOW	
Gefr. Georg Friedrich Unterberger	KG 6/34	1Jan17	7Jan17	AFP 5
Pion. Anton Urban	KG 6/34	1Jan17	7Jan17	AFP 5
Uffz. Heinrich Vogelmann	KG 6/34	1Jan17	EOW	
Gefr. Georg Vogelmeier	KG 6/34	1Jan17	EOW	
Pion. Oskar Wahl	KG 6/34	1Jan17	EOW	
Uffz. Ludwig Wallner	KG 6/34	1Jan17	EOW	
Pion. Georg Vinzenz Walz	FEA 1b	13Jan18	11Jun18	AFP 4
Pion. Peter Weber	Hosp.	20Feb17	27Apr17	FEA 1b
Uffz. Georg Weidner	KG 6/34	1Jan17	EOW	
Uffz. Max Weidner	KG 6/34	1Jan17	4Jan17	FEA 1b
Gefr. Ernst Weigand	FEA 1b	20Apr17	EOW	
Pion. Josef Weinzierl	FEA 1b	3Apr17	EOW	
Pion. Max Weiss	FEA 1b	30Dec17		
Pion. Josef Weninger	FEA 1b	12Jan18	EOW	
Pion. Nikolaus Werner	FEA 1b	20Aug18	EOW	
Werkmstr.Stv. Anton Wiedemann	KG 6/34	1Jan17	25Jul17	FEA 1b
Pion. Georg Wieland	FEA 1b	3May18	EOW	
Uffz. Josef Winterholler	KG 6/34	1Jan17	12Mar17	Hosp.
Sgt. Josef Winterholler	Hosp.	24Mar17	EOW	
Pion. Georg Wirth	Hosp.	9Jan17	26Feb17	Hosp.
Pion. Georg Wirth	Hosp.	5Mar17	24Apr18	BG 6/26
Pion. August Wohlmacher	KG 6/34	1Jan17	7Jan17	AFP 5
Gefr. Otto Wüst	KG 6/34	1Jan17	EOW	

Schutzstaffel/Schlachtstaffel 25b
Mitgemachte Schlachten und Gefechte

(Battles and combat actions in which Ss 25b participated)

10Sep16	4Mar17	*Stellungskämpfe vor Verdun* (Trench fighting at Verdun)
5Mar17	23Jun17	*Doppelschlacht Aisne-Champagne* (The double battle of Aisne-Champagne)
24Jun17	18Jul17	*Stellungskämpfe im Artois* (Trench fighting in Artois)
19Jul17	24Nov17	*Schlacht im Flandern* (Battle in Flanders)
25Nov17	29Nov17	*Tankschlacht bei Cambrai* (Tank battle of Cambrai)
30Nov17	7Dec17	*Angriffsschlacht bei Cambrai* (Offensive battle of Cambrai)

8Dec17	10Mar18	*Stellungskämpfe in französisch Flandern* (Trench fighting in French Flanders)
11Mar18	20Mar18	*Stellungskämpfe im Artois und Aufmarsch zur Grossen Schlacht in Frankreich* (Trench fighting in Artois and assembly for the Great Battle in France)
ab 21Mar18		*Grosse Schlacht in Frankreich* (Great Battle in France)
21Mar18	23Mar18	*Durchbruchsschlacht Monchy-Cambrai* (Penetration battle Monchy-Cambrai)
24Mar18	25Mar18	*Schlacht bei Bapaume* (Battle at Bapaume)
28Mar18		*Angriff an der Scarpe* (Offensive on the Scarpe)
29Mar18	8Apr18	*Stellungskämpfe in Flandern* (Trench fighting in Flanders)
9Apr18	18Apr18	*Schlacht bei Armentières* (Battle at Armentières)
19Apr18	12May18	*Stellungskämpfe in französisch Flandern* (Trench fighting in French Flanders)
13May18	7Jul18	*Stellungskrieg in Flandern* (Trench war in Flanders)
8Jul18	14Jul18	*Stellungskämpfe bei Reims* (Trench fighting at Reims)
15Jul18	17Jul18	*Angriffsschlacht an der Marne und in der Champagne* (Offensive battle on the Marne and in the Champagne)
18Jul18	25Jul18	*Abwehrschlacht zwischen Soissons und Reims* (Defensive battle between Soissons and Reims)
26Jul18	3Aug18	*Bewegliche Abwehrschlacht zwischen Marne und Vesle* (The mobile battle between the Marne and the Vesle)
4Aug18	21Aug18	*Stellungskämpfe bei Reims* (Trench fighting at Reims)
22Aug18	27Sep18	*Kämpfe bei Cambrai* (Fighting at Cambrai)
28Sep18	11Nov18	*Abwehrschlacht in Flandern* (Defensive battle in Flanders)

Schutzstaffel/Schlachtstaffel 25b Airfields

From	To	Location	*Schlachtgruppe* Affiliation	*Armee*
1Jan17	10Jan17	Mont		5
10Jan17	4Mar17	Briey	Escort for FA 208(A)	5
5Mar17	28Jun17	Notre Dame de Liesse	For FA 216(A)w	7
29Jun17	18Jul17	Abscon	Escort for FA 238(A), 263(A)	6
19Jul17	30Oct17	Bavikhove	Escort for FA 13	4
30Oct17	24Nov17	Desselghem	Escort for FA 13	4
25Nov17	7Dec17	Briastre	Escort for FA 202(A)	2
8Dec17	19Mar18	Villers-au-Tertre	Escort for FA 48b	6
20Mar18	9Apr18	Wasnes-au-Bac	SGp B (Ss 14,19,24b,25b,29b) C.O. *Hptm.* Wilhelm Aschenborn	17
9Apr18	18Apr18	Ronchin	SGp D (Ss 24b,25b) C.O. *Oblt.* Hugo Miller	6
18Apr18	30Apr18	Linselles	SGp D (Ss 9,12,16,24b,25b) C.O. *Oblt.* Johannes Missfelder	4
30Apr18	9Jun18	Ronchin		6
9Jun18	7Jul18	Lambersart	SGp Miller (Ss 25b,36) C.O. *Oblt.* Hugo Miller	6
7Jul18	10Jul18	Assevillers	SGp J (Ss 4,15,24b,25b) C.O. *Oblt.d.R.* Franz Albertshauser	2
11Jul18	11Aug18	St. Loup	SGp J (Ss 4,15,24b,25b) C.O. *Oblt.* Erhardt Egerer	1
11Aug18	12Aug18	NW Athies	SGp J (Ss 4,15,24b,25b,35) C.O. *Oblt.* Erhardt Egerer	2
13Aug18	21Aug18	St. Loup	SGp J (Ss 4,15,24b,25b,35) C.O. *Oblt.* Erhardt Egerer	1

22Aug18	31Aug18	Beuvry Ost	SGp J (Ss 4,15,24b,25b) C.O. *Oblt.* Erhardt Egerer	17
1Sep18	8Sep18	Abscon	SGp J (Ss 4,15,24b,25b,35) C.O. *Oblt.* Erhardt Egerer	17
9Sep18	7Oct18	Abscon	SGp J (Ss 4,15,24b,25b,35) C.O. *Oblt.* Friedrich von Kraussser	17
7Oct18	13Oct18	Oudenaarde	SGp J (Ss 9,16,24b,25b) C.O. *Oblt.* Friedrich von Kraussser	4
13Oct18	23Oct18	Oudenaarde	SGp J (Ss 9,24b,25b) C.O. *Oblt.* Friedrich von Kraussser	4
23Oct18	EOW	Deinze	SGp J (Ss 9,24b,25b) C.O. *Oblt.* Friedrich von Kraussser	4

Royal Bavarian *Schutzstaffel 25b*

1Jan17	*Schutzstaffel 25b* is created from KG 6/Ks 34 by BKM Nr. 148032 of 31Dec16.
23Jan17	*Vzfw.* Hans Fischer, G, is sent to the hospital with a frozen hand.
24Jan17	*Offz.Stv.* Joseph Siegl, P, is WIA by shrapnel, broken right leg and to hospital at Briey.
4May17	*Vzfw.* Walter Lagershausen, P, and *Pion.* Johann Weidmann, G, are KIA over Courtecon at 16.08 hours in Albatros C.VII 3519/16 during an air combat.
14May17	*Vzfw.* Alfons Konradt, P, is WIA by ground fire, shot in the right leg and to hospital.
14Jun17	*Uffz.* Dumpert-1, *Uffz.* Jorissen-1, Spad, Cerny-Vendresse Spad S.7, Esc. N.69, Lt. H. de Bonald, WIA
22Aug17	*Vzfw.* Friedrich Ulber, G, is WIA,sv., shot in the left thigh during air combat and to hospital in Kortryk.
26Aug17	*Vzfw.* Franz Wittig, G, is WIA,lt. by ground fire over Zillebeker See, shot in the shoulder.
26Sep17	*Pion.* Heinrich Lauer, G, is KIA over Becelaere.
15Nov17	*Vzfw.* Schneider-1, *Vzfw.* Obernöder-1, a/c, 13.45, Tenbrielen, Houthem.
9Jan18	*Vzfw.* Wilhelm Dörfler, P, is IIC,lt. during a forced landing and to hospital at Tournai. He suffers contusions of the forehead.
16Feb18	*Vzfw.* Konrad Dumpert, P, and *Vzfw.* Benedikt Wölfle, G, are KIA over Lagnicourt by ground fire in Halberstadt Cl.II 5751/17.
9Mar18	*Vzfw.* Friedrich Hartl, G, is WIA,sv. over Armentières, DOW 10Mar18 at Roubaix.
27Mar18	*Schutzstaffel 25b* is renamed *Schlachtstaffel 25b* by KM Nr. 5126.18.A.7.L.IV.C. of 27Mar18.
9Apr18	*Uffz.* Franz Völkle, P, and *Gefr.* Konrad Müller, G, are KIA over Armentières at 15.30 hours by ground fire.
6May18	*Pion.* Michael Ringler, P, is KIC and *Uffz.* Doell, G, is IIC,sv. at Ronchin.
11May18	*Sgt.* Thomas Wagner, P, and *Uffz.* Martin Staber, G, are KIC at Lompert, NW of Lille while on a practice flight.
26May18	*Vzfw.* Wilhelm Dörfler, P, is WIA during air combat, a grazing shot to the head, and to hospital.
18Jun18	*Sgt.* Andreas Dachwald, P, and *Pion.* Bruno Knöfel, G, are IIC,lt. at Lambersart during a landing accident.
21Jun18	*Pion.* Max Ramet, P, and *Pion.* Sebastian Simson, G, are KIC at Lambersart at 17.00 hours during a practice flight.
7Jul18	*Uffz.* Wilhelm Louis, M, dies at Lambersart of injuries suffered in an automobile accident.
17Jul18	*Vzfw.* Ludwig Dutz, G, is IIC, head injury, and to hospital at Rethel.
19Jul18	*Uffz.* Mathias Endl, P, and *Uffz.* Max Dantonello, G, are IIC,sv.
30Aug18	*Vzfw.* Käppner-n/c, *Vzfw.* Müller-n/c, English Infantry a/c.
17Sep18	*Uffz.* Bruno Knöfel, G, is IIC,lt. in a landing accident, and to hospital.
20Sep18	*Gefr.* August Brenner, M, is sent to the hospital at St. Amand because of the flu. He dies there on 23Sep18.
2Oct18	*Uffz.* Josef Schreiner, G, is KIA over Moorslede at 15.30 hours.
16Oct18	*Flg.* Paul Bischoff, M, dies at Aachen due to the Spainish influenza.
31Oct18	*Uffz.* Paul Schmidt, G, is WIA by shrapnel in the lower left leg and to hospital at Deinze.
19Nov18	*Vzfw.* Ernst Fettinger, P, and *Werkmstr.Stv.* Georg Leonhardt, M, are KIC at Rothenburg a.d. Tauber on the flight home from Krefeld.
23Nov18	*Schlachtstaffel 25b* is demobilized at FEA 2b, Fürth.

Royal Bavarian *Schutzstaffel 26*

Pilot/Gunner	Type	From		To	
		Unit	Date	Date	Unit
Gefr. Peter Adams	P	AFP B	5May17	8Jul17	Hosp.
Pion. Bruno Allert	G	AFP 2	4Apr18	27Apr18	Ss 9
Pion. Bruno Allert	G	Ss 9	10May18	EOW	
Uffz. Albert Arnold	P	AFP 4	3May18	13May18	AFP 4
Uffz. Georg Auer	P	AFP 5	25Oct18	EOW	
Sgt. Ludwig Bachmaier	P	AFP 1	7Sep18	EOW	

Pion. Adam Bätz	G	AFP 4	11Apr18	26Apr18	Ss 21
Uffz. Ludwig Bauer	G	AFP 4	2Dec17	1Apr18	WIA
Uffz. Karl Beck	P	FEA 1b	4Jun17	16Jul17	KIA
Vzfw. Friedrich Beisecker	P	AFP B	15May17	3Jun17	KIA
Pion. Karl Bentz	G	FEA 1b	13Jul17	EOW	
Uffz. Martin Bergmann	P	AFP 4	30Apr18	EOW	
Sgt. Joseph Biermeier	G	AFP 4	27Apr18	EOW	
Ltn.d.R. Julius Brecht	P	KG 6/35	1Jan17	8Jan17	AFP B
Vzfw. Franz Bucher	P	KG 6/35	1Jan17	16Feb17	FEA 1b
Pion. Pirmin Bücklein	G	AFP B	15May17	3Jun17	KIA
Vzfw. Wilhelm Büssing	P	AFP 4	24Jul17	14Aug17	AFP 4
Ltn.d.R. Xaver Dannhuber	P	KG 6/35	1Jan17	8May17	JsSch I
Pion. Georg Danzer	P	FA 45b	25Feb18	EOW	
Uffz. Edmund Darozalski	G	AFP B	19Feb17	27Feb17	AFP B
Vzfw. Ludwig Demmel	P	KG 6/35	1Jan17	14Apr17	KIC
Uffz. Alois Donaubauer	P	AFP 4	7Nov17	2Oct18	Idflieg
Uffz. August Dorner	P	AFP B	19Mar17	12Apr17	FA 296A
Vzfw. Josef Duna	P	FA 287A	24May18	EOW	
Gefr. Wilhelm Eilemann	P	AFP 7	28May18	23Jun18	POW
Vzfw. Heinrich Eissner	P	Ss 28b	24Sep17	3Jun18	AFP 7
Pion. Ernst Fritzsche	P	AFP B	23Apr17	2May17	AFP B
Uffz. Franz Gallenmüller	P	AFP 4	9Aug17	26Feb18	AFP 4
Uffz. Friedrich Galonske	P	AFP B	28Apr17	27Jun17	WIA
Gefr. Rudolf Gassenhuber	G	BS II	13Feb17	11May17	POW
Ltn. Wilhelm Gebhardt	O	KG 6/35	1Jan17	3May17	FEA 1b
Uffz. Josef Gerl	G	AFP 4	24Jul17	13Jul18	Ss 22b
Gefr. Robert Godlewski	G	AFP 7	13Jun17	30Jun17	WIA
Uffz. Kurt Gross	G	AFP 4	24Sep17	11Nov17	Ss 5
Uffz. Otto Haack	P	AFP B	5May17	19Sep17	Ss 17
Pion. Wilhelm Herbert	P	AFP 2	7Apr18	8May18	FTL IIC
Pion. Ludwig Herrndobler	P	Ss 4	13Jul17	18Aug17	FEA 1b
Uffz. Georg Hess	G	AFP B	27Feb17	2Apr17	IIC
Uffz. Georg Hess	G	Hosp.	13Apr17	16Jul17	KIA
Ltn.d.R. Ludwig Hörmann	P	KG 6/35	1Jan17		
Oblt.d.R. Konrad Hoffmann, C.O.	O	FEA 1b	23Feb18	3Oct18	FTL
Oblt.d.R. Konrad Hoffmann, C.O.	O		5Oct18	EOW	
Vzfw. Ewald Hofmann	G	AFP B	15Apr17	10Aug17	FEA 1b
Pion. Hugo Holtmeier	G	AFP 4	23Sep17	8Oct17	Ss 16
Uffz. Karl Hopf	P	AFP 4	17Jul17	12Nov17	AFP 4
Vzfw. Anton Kammermeier	G	AFP 4	21Apr18	EOW	
Vzfw. Ludwig Kapfhammer	P	AFP 7	27Jun17	18Jul17	FEA 1b
Uffz. Georg Kern	G	AFP 4	27Jul17	15Oct17	WIA,sv.
Uffz. Alois Köchel	G	AFP B	17Apr17	25May17	WIA,sv.
Sgt. Wilhelm Kolm	P	AFP C	7Oct18	EOW	
Vzfw. Camille Kopp	P	KG 6/35	1Jan17	4Jun17	JsSch I
Gefr. Jakob Kopp	P	AFP 4	17Oct17	25Mar18	WIA,sv.
Vzfw. Jakob Kopp	P	FEA 2b	21May18	EOW	
*Oblt.*d.R. Sigmund Kreitmair	O	KG 6/35	1Jan17	12Feb17	AFP 5
Oblt. Reinhard Kriegelsteiner, CO	O	KG 6/35	1Jan17	24Aug17	FA 293A
Uffz. Fritz Kuhlmann	P	AFP 4	7Jul17	19Dec17	WIA,lt.
Vzfw. Fritz Kuhlmann	P		19Dec17	30Mar18	WIA,sv.
Ltn.d.R. Alfred Kuhn, OzbV	P	AFP 1	16May18	8Sep18	Ss 28b
Ltn.d.R. Alfred Kuhn, OzbV	P	Ss 28b	27Sep18	EOW	
Vzfw. Erwin Lauster	G	AFP 4	8Nov17	EOW	
Uffz. Johann Loritz	G	AFP 4	21Jan18	9Mar18	AFP 4
Vzfw. Hermann Lübking	P	AFP 7	19May18	7Oct18	Hosp.
Vzfw. Hermann Lübking	P	Hosp.	22Oct18	EOW	
Vzfw. Heinrich Mann	G	AFP 7	9Jun17	20Jun18	AFP 7
Uffz. Johann Mehltretter	G	AFP 4	8Nov17	13Dec17	Hosp.
Uffz. Karl Meissner	G	BS II	6Feb17	15Feb17	FEA 1b
Uffz. Adam Hermann Müller	G	AFP 4	1Nov17	5Dec17	WIA,lt.
Vzfw. Adam Hermann Müller	G	AFP 4	6Jan18	5Apr18	WIA,sv.
Vzfw. Ludwig Müller	P	AFP 4	16Jul17	3Oct18	FTL
Vzfw. Ludwig Müller	P		5Oct18	21Oct18	Hosp.
Gefr. Franz Osiander	G	AFP 1	7Sep18	EOW	

Vzfw. Georg Passan	G	KG 6/35	1Jan17	10Nov17	AFP 4
Pion. Hans Peters	P	AFP 2	5Apr18	7May18	Ss 23b
Uffz. Ludwig Pflüger	P	AFP 18	29May18	3Oct18	KIA
Uffz. Lorenz Pichler	P	Ss 1	11Jul17	18Oct17	AFP 4
Pion. Karl Pollinger	G	AFP 4	12Feb18	Feb18	BG 8/25
Uffz. Heinrich Postel	G	AFP 4	27Jul17	12Sep17	Ss 23b
Uffz. Valentin Racke	G	AFP B	17Apr17	26Sep17	FEA 1b
Ltn.d.R. Adolf Reinlein	O	KG 6/35	1Jan17	Jan17	FA 292A
Vzfw. Otto Richter	G	AFP 7	26May18	23Jun18	POW
Uffz. Sebastian Ritzinger	G	Ss 1	11Jul17	19Dec17	WIA,sv.
Pion. Josef Scherl	G	AFP 7	20May18	20Jul18	AFP 1
Vzfw. Georg Scheuchl	P	AFP 4	15Aug17	22Mar18	WIA
Oblt. Benedikt Schmalschläger, CO	O	Kofl C	19Sep17	27Jan18	Leave
Oblt. Benedikt Schmalschläger, CO	O	Leave	10Feb18	23Feb18	FA 294A
Oblt.d.R. Schmidt, stv. C.O.	O	FA 227A	27Jan18	10Feb18	FA 227A
Uffz. Gottfried Schober	P	AFP 5	13Oct18	EOW	
Vzfw. Johann Schroth	P	KG 6/35	1Jan17	16Mar17	Js 35
Uffz. Franz Schumm	G	AFP 4	26Sep17	2May18	KIC
Pion. Paul Schwarze	P	AFP 2	24Mar18	2May18	IIC,sv.
Uffz. Alois Semar	G	AFP 7	9Jun17	28Dec17	WIA,sv.
Vzfw. Alois Semar	G	AFP 4	9Jan18	EOW	
Uffz. Simon Stebel	G	AFP 5	24Feb17	14Apr17	KIC
Uffz. Heinrich Stümpert	P	AFP 4	10Aug17	14Sep17	AFP 4
Gefr. August Thäder	G	AFP 7	23Jun18	3Oct18	KIA
Oblt. Theodor Triendl, C.O.	O	FEA 1b	25Aug17	23Sep17	FA 287A
Uffz. Alois Weingärtner	P	KG 6/35	1Jan17	11May17	POW
Vzfw. Karl Wernsdörfer	G	Ss 23b	9Oct17	EOW	
Vzfw. Bruno Wiedemann	P	AFP 4	3Aug17	14Aug17	AFP 4
Gefr. August Wiesler	G	AFP 4	27Dec17	12Jan18	AFP 4
Gefr. Theodor Wilbrandt	P	AFP 4	8May18	29May18	AFP 7
Hptm. Karl Wild	O			15Oct18	FEA 1b
Uffz. Johann Wilhelm	P	AFP B	19Feb17	18Jun17	Hosp.
Uffz. Wilhelm Winterling	P	AFP 7	2Jun17	27Jun17	Hosp.

Royal Bavarian *Schutzstaffel 26*

Mechanics and Ground Personnel

Name	From		To	
	Unit	Date	Date	Unit
Uffz. Karl Aufschneider	KG 6/35	1Jan17	27Feb17	FEA 1b
Pion. Hans Bär	FEA 1b	27Jun17	3Oct17	FEA 1b
Vzfw. Josef Baer	KG 6/35	1Jan17	EOW	
Pion. Georg Barthmann	KG 6/35	1Jan17	7Jun17	Dschrgd
Pion. August Bauer	AFP 4	22Jun17	18Jun18	Infntry
Pion. Jakob Bauer	FEA 1b	1Dec17	22Jul18	Lft Trp
Gefr. Karl Alois Beck	KG 6/35	1Jan17	EOW	
Uffz. Karl Beck	KG 6/35	1Jan17	5Jan17	FEA 1b
Gefr. Konrad Beck	FEA 1b	20Nov17	EOW	
Pion. Georg Beil	KG 6/35	1Jan17	19Oct17	AFP 4
Pion. Johann Berthel	FEA 1b	20Nov17	EOW	
Pion. Benedikt Bestler	KG 6/35	1Jan17	4Mar17	FEA 1b
Pion. Georg Betz	FEA 1b	23Nov17	29Sep18	Hosp.
Pion. Georg Betz	Hosp.	22Oct18	EOW	
Pion. Kaspar Bieringer	FEA 1b	21Sep17	1Nov17	FEA 1b
Pion. Johann Bögl	Kft Ers	11Jun18	EOW	
Pion. Leonhard Bohlig	FEA 2b	5Apr18	EOW	
Pion. Franz Bohnenkamp	KG 6/35	1Jan17	18Jun17	Hosp.
Pion. Peter Boll	KG 6/35	1Jan17	2Feb17	AFP 5
Pion. Josef Brand	FEA 2b	7Aug18	EOW	
Pion. Emil Braun	FEA 2b	11Aug18	EOW	
Feldw. Fritz Braun	KG 6/35	1Jan17	23Feb17	FEA 1b

Pion. Johann Breu	FEA 1b	31May17	18Jun18	Artllry
Gefr. Simon Breunig	KG 6/35	1Jan17	1Feb17	AFP 5
Uffz. Friedrich Brunner	KG 6/35	1Jan17	EOW	
Gefr. Johann Bubel	KG 6/35	1Jan17	10Nov18	Dschrgd
Uffz. Johann Bucher	KG 6/35	1Jan17	30Sep17	FEA 1b
Pion. Ludwig Burkhardt	FEA 2b	26Mar18	29Sep18	Hosp.
Pion. Ludwig Burkhardt	Hosp.	22Oct18	EOW	
Pion. Xaver Dafelmaier	KG 6/35	1Jan17	EOW	
Gefr. Karl Diemer	KG 6/35	1Jan17	22Apr18	FEA 2b
Gefr. Wolfgang Dietz	KG 6/35	1Jan17	1Feb17	AFP 5
Offz.Stv. Hermann Dilg	FEA 2b	2Sep18	EOW	
Pion. Hans Dörr	FEA 1b	20Mar18	EOW	
Uffz. Peter Dorsch	KG 6/35	1Jan17	18Jun18	FEA 1b
Pion. Martin Drechsel	FEA 1b	12Jan18	4Feb18	AFP 4
Gefr. Helmut Drude	KG 6/35	1Jan17	5Nov17	FEA 1b
Uffz. Georg Durchdenwald	KG 6/35	1Jan17	EOW	
Uffz. Friedrich Ebert	KG 6/35	1Jan17	7Jun17	Hosp.
Feldw. Adolf Ehemann	FEA 1b	27Mar17	14Aug17	FEA 1b
Pion. August Eiffert	FA 227A	8Dec17	EOW	
Pion. Johannes Enk	KG 6/35	1Jan17	19Jan17	AFP 5
Uffz. Franz Ernst	FEA 1b	24May17	3Nov18	FEA 2b
Uffz. Xaver Faderl	KG 6/35	1Jan17	14Nov17	FEA 1b
Sgt. Johann Färber	KG 6/35	1Jan17	10Jun18	FEA 2b
Pion. Ernst Farnbacher	KG 6/35	1Jan17	23Apr17	Hosp.
Uffz. Emil Feist	KG 6/35	1Jan17	EOW	
Pion. Ernst Feldhäusser	FEA 2b	7Jun18	14Oct18	FEA 2b
Pion. Ludwig Fischer	FEA 1b	7Dec17	EOW	
Pion. Max Fischer	FEA 1b	7Dec17	EOW	
Pion. Xaver Fischer	KG 6/35	1Jan17	16May17	AFP B
Pion. Josef Fleischmann	FEA 2b	5Oct18	EOW	
Pion. Karl Friedrich Flori	KG 6/35	1Jan17	30Aug17	Hosp.
Gefr. Johann Franz	AFP C	25Oct18	EOW	
Pion. Josef Füller	Ss 30b	28Jun18	4Aug18	Ss 30b
Pion. Josef Füssl	FEA 1b	12Jul17	EOW	
Gefr. Johann Gammel	KG 6/35	1Jan17	19Oct17	AFP 4
Gefr. Alfred Gass	KG 6/35	1Jan17	EOW	
Pion. Martin Gattel		27Mar18	EOW	
Pion. Alois Geier	FEA 1b	27Aug17	26Sep17	FA 287A
Pion. Mathias Geldner	KG 6/35	1Jan17	19Jan17	AFP 5
Pion. Andreas Giessregen	FEA 2b	4Jun18	13Jul18	Hosp.
Pion. Georg Gilg	KG 6/35	1Jan17	29Mar17	AFP B
Pion. Georg Göss	KG 6/35	1Jan17	16May17	AFP B
Pion. Heinrich Götz	FEA 1b	12Jan18	4Feb18	AFP 4
Pion. Michael Graf	FEA 1b	7Dec17	30Jun18	Hosp.
Pion. Walter Grasmück	KG 6/35	1Jan17	10Jan17	Hosp.
Uffz. Johann Gross	FEA 1b	24May17	EOW	
Uffz. Maximilian Gruber	KG 6/35	1Jan17	19Jan17	AFP 5
Gefr. Johann Haberger	FEA 1b	17Jan17	25Oct17	Hosp.
Pion. Karl Hämecke	AFP 4	4May18	10May18	AFP 4
Pion. Johann Hässler	KG 6/35	1Jan17	13Apr17	Hosp.
Pion. Andreas Hagn	KG 6/35	1Jan17	19Jan17	AFP 5
Pion. Eugen Hannes	FEA 2b	26Mar18	9Jul18	Hosp.
Vzfw. Georg Hartlöhner	FEA 2b	4Jun18	EOW	
Pion. Stephan Hauser	FEA 2b	23Aug18	7Oct18	Hosp.
Pion. Otto Heckel	FEA 1b	2Nov17	20Apr18	FEA 2b
Pion. Johann Heckmann	FEA 2b	11Aug18	24Aug18	FEA 2b
Pion. Georg Hees	FEA 1b	31May17	28Feb18	Hosp.
Pion. Ernst Heinemann	FEA 1b	21Nov17	18Mar18	FEA 2b
Werkmstr.Stv. Albin Heinzmann	FEA 1b	24Sep17	EOW	
Gefr. Johann Heiss	FEA 1b	24Sep17	EOW	
Uffz. Ludwig Hehl	KG 6/35	1Jan17	EOW	
Pion. Andreas Hermann	FEA 2b	17Aug18	EOW	
Pion. Friedrich Herrmann	KG 6/35	1Jan17	30May17	FEA 1b
Pion. Anton Herzog	FEA 1b	7Mar18	EOW	
Pion. Hugo Hessler	KG 6	1Jan17	30Jul17	Benz Wk

Pion. Hugo Hessler	Benz Wk	3Oct17	EOW	
Pion. Mathäus Hirl	FEA 1b	31May17	EOW	
Gefr. Friedrich Höltl	KG 6/35	1Jan17	19Oct17	AFP 4
Pion. Adolf Hollreiser	FEA 1b	16Mar18	27Jul17	Infntry
Pion. Johann Holzinger	FEA 1b	20Nov17	25Jun18	FEA 2b
Pion. Andreas Horn	KG 6/35	1Jan17	1Feb17	FEA 1b
Gefr. Alfons Huber	KEA	13Apr18	15Sep18	Desertd
Pion. Johann Huber	FEA 1b	6Aug17	EOW	
Pion. Georg Hufnagel	KG 6/35	1Jan17	21Jan17	FEA 1b
Pion. Josef Hugo	FEA 1b	27Jun17	25Jul17	Hosp.
Pion. Hans Jungkunz	FEA 1b	21Sep17	29Sep17	Hosp.
Pion. Alois Kaiser	KG 6/35	1Jan17	30May17	FEA 1b
Pion. Karl Kaiser	FEA 2b	17Jun18	EOW	
Pion. Otto Kammerer	KG 6/35	1Jan17	17Jan17	AFP 5
Pion. Heinrich Kandler	FEA 2b	17Jun18	EOW	
Feldw. Tedo Kirchhoff	Fnker S	8Aug17	4Jul18	FEA 2b
Pion. Rudolf Klebl	KG 6/35	1Jan17	19Jan17	AFP 5
Gefr. Otto Kohler	FEA 1b	20Nov17	EOW	
Gefr. Gotthilf Kopp	KG 6/35	1Jan17	EOW	
Pion. Michael Kotschenreuther	FEA 2b	10May18	EOW	
Pion. Hans Krämer	KG 6/35	1Jan17	30May17	FEA 1b
Gefr. Josef Kratz	KG 6/35	1Jan17	EOW	
Pion. Helmut Krefft	AFP 1	21Jul18	14Sep18	Ss 28b
Pion. Helmut Krefft	Ss 28b	27Sep18	EOW	
Pion. Georg Kreipl	KG 6/35	1Jan17	1Feb17	AFP 5
Pion. Jakob Kreuzer	KG 6/35	1Jan17	EOW	
Pion. Christoph Krüger	KG 6/35	1Jan17	18Jul18	FEA 1b
Pion. Philipp Kütt	KG 6/35	1Jan17	19Jan17	AFP 5
Uffz. Fritz Kuhlmann	KG 6/35	1Jan17	21Jan17	FEA 1b
Pion. Wilhelm Kuhn	FEA 1b	14Aug18	EOW	
Pion. Karl Lang	KG 6/35	1Jan17	1Feb17	AFP 5
Uffz. Korbinian Lerchenmüller	KG 6/35	1Jan17	2Feb17	KEA
Pion. Georg Lichtenegger	KG 6/35	1Jan17	19Jan17	AFP 5
Pion. Johann Loitfelder	FEA 1b	22Jun17	18Jul17	FEA 1b
Pion. Franz Lorenz	Ss 30b	27Jun18	4Aug18	Ss 30b
Pion. Richard Martin	KG 6/35	1Jan17	19Nov17	FEA 1b
Pion. Richard Martin	FEA 1b	8Dec17	18Dec17	Hosp.
Gefr. Josef Meier	KG 6/35	1Jan17	8Jan17	AFP B
Pion. Alois Metz	KG 6/35	1Jan17	17Jan17	AFP 5
Pion. August Michaeli	KG 6/35	1Jan17	19Jan17	AFP 5
Pion. Mathias Miras	KG 6/35	1Jan17	19Jan17	Hosp.
Pion. Alfred Mockert	FS III	26Mar18	EOW	
Gefr. Robert Mosbacher	KG 6/35	1Jan17	24Aug17	FEA 1b
Vzfw. Georg Moser	KG 6/35	1Jan17	17Feb18	FEA 1b
Pion. Eusebius Müller	KG 6/35	1Jan17	24Aug17	FA 293A
Pion. Rudolf Müller	KG 6/35	1Jan17	6Jan17	AFP 5
Gefr. Michael Naegele	KG 6/35	1Jan17	EOW	
Feldw. Paul Neuner	FEA 2b	3Jul18	5Sep18	FEA 2b
Uffz. August Niedermaier	KG 6/35	1Jan17	25Sep17	FA 48b
Pion. Karl Nirschl	KG 6/35	1Jan17	17Jul17	Hosp.
Pion. Theodor Ortner	Ss 7	26Nov17	EOW	
Pion. Chr. Petri	KG 6/35	1Jan17	20Jun17	Hosp.
Pion. Johann Pfeiffer	KG 6/35	1Jan17	2Jul17	Hosp.
Pion. Johann Pfeiffer	Hosp.	19Jul17	4Mar18	FEA 2b
Pion. Otto Pfluger	KG 6/35	1Jan17	17Jan17	AFP 5
Pion. Johann Rabl	FEA 2b	20Sep18	EOW	
Vzfw. Jakob Redl	KG 6/35	1Jan17	25Jun17	AFP 7
Uffz. Johann Reischl	KG 6/35	1Jan17	EOW	
Pion. Konrad Rieder	KG 6/35	1Jan17	17Jul17	FEA 1b
Pion. Karl Ruckdeschel	FEA 1b	24Sep17	EOW	
Pion. Felix Rüther	FA 264A	8Dec17		Gfl Dix
Pion. Sebastian Sämmer	KG 6/35	1Jan17	19Jan17	AFP 5
Pion. Josef Sager	KG 6/35	1Jan17	8Jan17	AFP B
Pion. Josef Sattler	KG 6/35	1Jan17	EOW	
Pion. August Sauer	KG 6/35	1Jan17	21Jan17	KEA

Uffz. Karl Scharnböck	KG 6/35	1Jan17	EOW	
Gefr. Jakob Scherf	FEA 2b	20Nov17	24Apr18	Hosp.
Gefr. Jakob Scherf	FEA 2b	27Jul18	EOW	
Pion. Josef Scherl	Hosp.	24Jan17	25Jan17	FEA 1b
Uffz. Ferdinand Schittig	KG 6/35	1Jan17	1Jul17	FEA 1b
Uffz. Ferdinand Schittig	FEA 1b	11Sep17	EOW	
Gefr. Otto Schmid	KG 6/35	1Jan17	9Jan17	AFP B
Pion. Georg Scholl	KG 6/35	1Jan17	30May17	FEA 1b
Pion. Josef Schratt	KG 6/35	1Jan17	28Jul17	FEA 1b
Uffz. Karl Schricker	KG 6/35	1Jan17	EOW	
Pion. Heinrich Schumann	FEA 1b	31May17	EOW	
Pion. Josef Schurr	FEA 1b	12Jul17	25Apr18	FEA 2b
Gefr. Franz Schweiger	FEA 1b	22Dec17	24May18	Hosp.
Gefr. Franz Schweiger	FEA 2b	20Sep18	EOW	
Pion. Max Sedlmaier	FEA 1b	7Dec17	22Apr18	FEA 2b
Gefr. Ernst Sehlmacher	KG 6/35	1Jan17	16May17	Hosp.
Uffz. Ernst Sehlmacher	Hosp.	1Aug17	1Oct18	FEA 2b
Pion. Ludwig Silberer	KG 6/35	1Jan17	18Jul17	FEA 1b
Sgt. Gottlieb Sommerer	KG 6/35	1Jan17	6Aug18	FEA 2b
Sgt. Gottlieb Sommerer	FEA 2b	7Oct18	EOW	
Pion. Fritz Steinbauer	KG 6/35	1Jan17	23Mar17	AFP B
Pion. Sebastian Stoib	Kofl C	24Sep17	1Mar18	FA 294A
Pion. Josef Strassinger	KG 6/35	1Jan17	17Feb17	AFP 5
Pion. Heinrich Sturm	FEA 1b	20Nov17	18Jun18	Artllry
Uffz. Joseph Thaler	KG 6/35	1Jan17	EOW	
Gefr. Michael Tiefel	KG 6/35	1Jan17	22Feb18	Hosp.
Gefr. Johann Trisl	KG 6/35	1Jan17	19Nov17	FEA 1b
Uffz. Johann Trisl	FEA 1b	8Dec17	EOW	
Pion. Otto Unkelbach		18Aug18	EOW	
Pion. Johann Unterholzer	KG 6/35	1Jan17	29Aug17	Benz Wk
Pion. Johann Unterholzer	Benz Wk	29Sep17	5Nov17	FEA 1b
Pion. Andreas Voglmeier	FEA 1b	24Sep17	22Jul18	Artllry
Gefr. Jakob Wagner	FEA 1b	31May17	EOW	
Pion. Georg Wahl	KG 6/35	1Jan17	19Jan17	AFP 5
Uffz. Georg Walter	KG 6/35	1Jan17	10Aug17	FEA 1b
Gefr. Johann Weber	KEA 4	11Nov17	19Jun18	KEA 2
Pion. Josef Weber	K Abt 3	29May17	25Aug17	Grfl 11
Pion. Josef Weber	Grfl 11	17Sep17	17Dec17	KEA 9
Pion. Eduard Weggl	FEA 1b	7Dec17	26Apr18	Hosp.
Pion. Karl Wenzl	KG 6/35	1Jan17	5Nov17	FEA 1b
Pion. Wolfgang Westermaier	FEA 1b	2Nov17	9Apr18	Hosp.
Pion. Georg Wimmer	KG 6/35	1Jan17	31May17	KHP 7
Pion. Andreas Winter	FEA 1b	7Dec17	EOW	
Gefr. Johann Winzelmeier	KG 6/35	1Jan17	12Feb17	AFP 5
Werkmstr.Stv. Josef Zerle	KG 6/35	1Jan17	1Oct17	FEA 1b
Uffz. Leonhard Zimmermann	KG 6/35	1Jan17	EOW	
Pion. Christian Zink	FEA 1b	6Aug17	12Oct17	Hosp.
Gefr. Josef Zink	KG 6/35	1Jan17	27Jun17	Hosp.
Uffz. Josef Zink	FEA 1b	20Jul17	EOW	
Pion. Wilhelm Zinkel	FEA 1b	31May17	EOW	

Schutzstaffel/Schlachtstaffel 26b
Mitgemachte Schlachten und Gefechte
(Battles and combat actions in which Ss 26b participated)

10Sep16	11Feb17	*Stellungskämpfe vor Verdun* (Trench fighting at Verdun)
12Feb17	18May17	*Stellungskämpfe in Oberelsass* (Trench fighting in Alsace)
20May17	3Jul17	*Doppelschlacht Aisne-Champagne* (The double battle of Aisne-Champagne)
4Jul17	3Dec17	*Schlacht in Flandern* (Battle in Flanders)

4Dec17	9Mar18	*Stellungskämpfe in Flandern im Winter 17/18* (Trench fighting in Flanders in Winter 17/18)
10Mar18	14Apr18	*Grosse Schlacht in Frankreich* (Great Battle in France)
16Apr18	14May18	*Schlacht am Kemmelberg* (Battle for the Kemmel)
16May18	26May18	*Stellungskämpfe nördlich der Ailette* (Trench fighting north of the Ailette)
27May18	13Jun18	*Schlacht bei Soissons und Reims* (Battle at Soissons and Reims)
14Jun18	28Jun18	*Stellungskämpfe zwischen Oise und Marne* (Trench fighting between the Oise and the Marne)
29Jun18	14Jul18	*Stellungskämpfe bei Reims* (Trench fighting at Reims)
15Jul18	17Jul18	*Angriffsschlacht an der Marne und in der Champagne* (Offensive battle on the Marne and in the Champagne)
18Jul18	24Jul18	*Abwehrschlacht zwischen Soissons und Reims* (Defensive battle between Soissons and Reims)
25Jul18	3Aug18	*Bewegliche Abwehrschlacht zwischen Marne und Vesle* (The mobile battle between the Marne and the Vesle)
4Aug18	16Aug18	*Stellungskämpfe zwischen Oise und Aisne* (Trench fighting between the Oise and the Aisne)
17Aug18	28Aug18	*Abwehrschlacht zwischen Oise und Aisne* (Defensive battle between the Oise and the Aisne)
29Aug18	15Sep18	*Stellungskämpfe bei Reims* (Trench fighting at Reims)
16Sep18	25Sep18	*Stellungskämpfe vor Verdun* (Trench fighting at Verdun)
26Sep18	6Oct18	*Stellungskämpfe in der Wavre Ebene* (Trench fighting on the Wavre Plain)
7Oct18	10Nov18	*Abwehrschlacht in der Champagne und an der Maas* (Defensive battle in the Champagne and on the Maas)

Schutzstaffel/Schlachtstaffel 26b Airfields

From	To	Location	*Schlachtgruppe* Affiliation	*Armee*
1Jan17	11Feb17	Mont	Escort for FA 207(A)	5
11Feb17	18May17	Rüstenhart	Escort for FA 284(A), 289(A)b	AAB
20May17	3Jul17	Marle		7
3Jul17	4Jul17	Aizecourt	For FA 207(A), FA 238(A)	2
4Jul17	26Sep17	Oostkamp	Escort for FA 233(A)	4
26Sep17	6Dec17	Thourout	Escort for FA 48b, FA 211(A)	4
6Dec17	23Feb18	Erkeghem	Escort for FA 211(A), 227(A)	4
23Feb18	9Mar18	Oostkamp	Escort for FA 211(A)	4
10Mar18	21Mar18	Reumont	SGp B (Ss 4,15,26b,28b) C.O. *Ritt.d.R.* Herrmann	2
21Mar18		Römer Ferme	SGp D (Ss 12,23b,26b) C.O. *Oblt.* Johannes Missfelder	2
(9Apr18)	14Apr18	Römer Ferme	SGp D (Ss 12,23b,26b) C.O. *Oblt.* Johannes Missfelder	2
16Apr18	14May18	Bisseghem	SGp B (Ss 10,23b,26b,30b) C.O. *Oblt.d.R.* August Ertl	4
16May18	13Jun18	Ebouleau	SGp B (Ss 23b,26b,28b,30b) C.O. *Oblt.d.R.* August Ertl	7
13Jun18	(23Jun18)	Cuiry-Housse	SGp Winckler (Ss 23b,26b,28b,30b) C.O. *Oblt.d.R.* August Ertl	7
15Jul18	18Jul18	Le Chesne	SGp 2 (Ss 7,23b,26b,35,36) C.O. *Oblt.* Walter Lackner	3
18Jul18	3Aug18	Le Chesne	SGp 2 (Ss 7,22b,23b,26b,36) C.O. *Oblt.* Walter Lackner	3
4Aug18	9Aug18	Toulis	SGp 3 (Ss 6,18,26b,34,38s) C.O. *Oblt.* Friedrich-Carl Hanesse	9

9Aug18	13Aug18	Toulis		9
13Aug18	16Aug18	Toulis	SGp 3 (Ss 6,7,18,26b,34,38s) C.O. *Oblt.* Friedrich-Carl Hanesse	9
16Aug18	28Aug18	Villeselve	SGp 3 (Ss 6,12,18,26b,34,38s) C.O. *Oblt.* Friedrich-Carl Hanesse	18
28Aug18	16Sep18	Toulis	SGp 3 (Ss 6,18,26b,34,38s) C.O. *Oblt.* Friedrich-Carl Hanesse	9
16Sep18	25Sep18	Thonne-les-Prés	SGp B (Ss 5,20,21,26b,33) C.O. *Oblt.* Bruno Zipplies	5
26Sep18	6Oct18	Anoux-le-Grange	SGp 1 (26b,37) C.O. *Oblt.d.R.* Konrad Hoffmann	AAC
6Oct18	31Oct18	La Ferté-sur-Chiers	SGp 2 (Ss 3,13,19,26b,29b) C.O. *Oblt.* Helmut Bühling	5
31Oct18	10Nov18	Habay la Vielle	SGp 2 (Ss 3,13,19,26b,29b) C.O. *Oblt.* Helmut Bühling	5
10Nov18	EOW	Stenay	SGp 2 (Ss 3,13,19,26b,29b) C.O. *Oblt.* Helmut Bühling	5

Royal Bavarian *Schutzstaffel 26b*

1Jan17	*Schutzstaffel 26b* is created from KG 6/Ks 35 by BKM Nr. 148032 of 31Dec16.
2Apr17	*Uffz.* Georg Hess, G, is IIC. He suffers light internal injuries and to hospital.
14Apr17	*Vzfw.* Ludwig Demmel, P, and *Uffz.* Simon Stebel G, are KIC at AFP B at Neu-Breisach, Oberelsass.
11May17	*Uffz.* Alois Weingärtner, P, and *Gefr.* Rudolf Gassenhuber, G, are taken POW.
25May17	*Pion.* Galonske-1, *Uffz.* Köchel-1, Spad 1, by Craonelle
25May17	*Uffz.* Alois Köchel, G, is WIA,sv. in the above combat, shot in lung and right shoulder and to hospital.
3Jun17	*Vzfw.* Friedrich Beisecker, P, and *Flg.* Pirmin Bücklein, G, are KIA over Craonelle at 11.30 hours.
27Jun17	*Uffz.* Friedrich Galonske, P, is WIA in the right hand during air combat and to hospital.
30Jun17	*Gefr.* Robert Godlewski, G, is WIA in air combat and to hospital at Marle.
16Jul17	*Uffz.* Beck-1, *Uffz.* Hess-1, Balloon, 18.30, by Elverdingen British Balloon 38-7-2
16Jul17	*Uffz.* Karl Beck, P, and *Uffz.* Georg Hess, G, are KIA over Westroosebeke at 18.30 hours during an air combat.
9Oct17	*Uffz.* Müller-1, *Uffz.* Semar-1, Spad, 10.40, Veldhoek
15Oct17	*Uffz.* Georg Kern, G, is WIA,sv. during air combat and to hospital.
1Nov17	*Uffz.* Gallenmüller-1, *Uffz.* Gerl-1, S.E. 5, 16.15, Houthoulster Wald
12Nov17	*Uffz.* Kuhlmann-1, *Uffz.* Ritzinger-1, Sopwith, 15.55, NW Houthoulster Wald Camel #B.3641, Naval 10, F/S/Lt. G.L. Trapp, KIA
18Nov17	*Uffz.* Scheuchl-1, *Gefr.* Schumm-1, Sopwith, 15.45, NW Boesinghe
5Dec17	*Pion.* Donaubauer-1, *Uffz.* Mann-1, Spad, 12.00, Langemarck
5Dec17	*Uffz.* Scheuchl-2, *Uffz.* Schumm-2, Sopwith Pup, 14.40, Merkem Camel #B.2470, 70 Sqn. RFC, 2/Lt. C.V.G. Runnels-Moss, KIA
5Dec17	*Uffz.* Adam Müller, G, is WIA,lt. during air combat, a shrapnel wound in the back, and crash lands at Thourout. He remains with the unit.
18Dec17	*Uffz.* Müller-n/c, *Uffz.* Semar-n/c, Sopwith 1
19Dec17	*Uffz.* Kuhlmann-2, *Uffz.* Ritzinger-2, Balloon, 12.10, Boesinghe
19Dec17	*Uffz.* Fritz Kuhlmann, P, is WIA,lt. graze in the lower left leg, and *Uffz.* Sebastian Ritzinger, G, is WIA,sv. during an air combat. Ritzinger suffers a shattered femur and tibia, receives an explosive bullet wound in the hand and two creasing shots, to hospital. Kuhlmann remains with the unit.
22Dec17	*Uffz.* Eissner-1, *Uffz.* Wernsdörfer-1, Sopwith, 15.30, Reningen
28Dec17	*Uffz.* Müller-2, *Uffz.* Semar-2, Sopwith Camel, 11.45, E. Merckem
28Dec17	*Uffz.* Otto Semar, G, is WIA,sv. with two shots in the knee during the above combat and to hospital.
19Jan18	*Uffz.* Gallenmüller-n/c, *Vzfw.* Gerl-n/c, Bristol F.2b
4Feb18	*Uffz.* Eissner-n/c, *Uffz.* Wernsdörfer-n/c, Sopwith 1
21Feb18	*Uffz.* Müller-n/c, *Uffz.* Semar-n/c, Sopwith
23Feb18	*Uffz.* Donaubauer-2, *Vzfw.* Mann-2, Spad, 13.07, Woumen, SE Dixmuide, Belg. Esc. 5me, S/Lt. E. Thieffry, WIA,POW
1Mar18	*Flg.* Schwarze-n/c, *Uffz.* Bauer-n/c, S.E. 5, Morlancourt.
22Mar18	*Vzfw.* Georg Scheuchl, P, is WIA in the left upper arm by ground fire and to hospital at Le Cateau.
25Mar18	*Uffz.* Jakob Kopp, P, is WIA,sv. in the left thigh during air combat and to hospital at Le Cateau.
27Mar18	*Schutzstaffel 26b* is renamed *Schlachtstaffel 26b* by KM Nr. 5126.A.7.L.IV.C. of 27Mar18.
29Mar18	*Vzfw.* Kuhlmann-3, *Oblt.d.R.* Hoffmann-1, S.E. 5a, N. Amiens #C.9625, 32 Sqn. RFC, 2/Lt. W.A. Tyrell, FTL, OK

30Mar18	*Vzfw*. Fritz Kuhlmann, P, is WIA,sv. in the lower left leg and right foot by ground fire and to hospital at Cambrai.
1Apr18	*Uffz*. Ludwig Bauer, G, is WIA in air combat and to hospital at Cambrai.
5Apr18	*Vzfw*. Adam Hermann Müller, G, is WIA,sv. by ground fire over Villers-Bretonneux and to hospital at Cambrai.
2May18	*Pion*. Paul Schwarze, P, is IIC,sv. and *Uffz*. Franz Schumm, G, is KIC at Bisseghem while on a practice flight. They crash from 30 meters altitude in Halberstadt Cl.II 14277/17. Schwarze to hospital in Kortryk.
8May18	*Pion*. Wilhelm Herbert, P, is forced to land, is lightly IIC and to hospital at St. Hendrik.
23Jun18	*Gefr*. Wilhelm Eilemann, P, and *Vzfw*. Otto Richter, G, are taken POW at Lesges, SW Braisne, W. La Ferté Gaucher in a Halberstadt Cl.II.
14Sep18	*Uffz*. Bergmann-1, *Vzfw*. Kammermeier-1, 1 Seater
3Oct18	*Uffz*. Ludwig Pflüger, P, and *Gefr*. August Thäder, G, are KIA over Cierges.
3Oct18	*Vzfw*. Ludwig Müller, P, and *Oblt.d.R.* Konrad Hoffmann, O and C.O., are shot down by ground fire and forced to land between Nantillois and Septsarges Wood. They return to the unit on October 5.
25Nov18	*Schlachtstaffel 26b* is demobilized at FEA 2b, Fürth.

Schutzstaffel 26b, Uffz. Fritz Kuhlmann and *Oblt.* Benedickt Schmalschläger in Flanders in 1918. The unit marking consisted of flames enveloping the forward fuselage. Photo credit: UTD/HAC.

Vzfw. Fritz Kuhlmann and his splendidly marked Halberstadt Cl.II number 6 of *Schusta 26b.* The white mark on his collar is a tear in the original photograph. Photo credit: UTD/HAC.

Right: *Uffz.* Fritz Kuhlmann served as a pilot with *Schusta 26b* from 7 July 1917 to 30 March 1918, when he was severely wounded in action.

A *Schusta 26b* Halberstadt Cl.II.

Royal Bavarian *Schutzstaffel 27*

Pilot/Gunner	Type	From		To	
		Unit	Date	Date	Unit
Ltn. Adolf Bauer	P	KG 6/36	1Jan17		FEA 1b
Uffz. Ludwig Bauer	G	AFP 17	15Oct18	EOW	
Ltn. Konrad Blaufuss	O	KG 6/36	1Jan17	1Feb17	AFP 1
Ltn.d.R. Hans Norbert Boës	O	KG 6/36	1Jan17	1Feb17	AFP 1
Gefr. Hermann Brauer	P	KG 6/36	1Jan17	12Feb17	FEA 1b
Vzfw. Hermann Bronner	P	AFP 4	14Oct17	23Jul18	FEA 1b
Uffz. Robert Bühler	G	AFP 4	26Jul17	EOW	
Vzfw. Wilhelm Büssing	P	Ss 25b	29Sep17	8Nov17	IIC
Vzfw. Reinhard Dick	G	AFP 2	13Dec17	EOW	
Ltn.d.R. Paul Dörr	O	KG 6/36	1Jan17		FA 45b
Vzfw. Philipp Feiner	P	Ss 23b	13Oct17	10Sep18	FEA 2b
Ltn.d.R. Eugen Ludwig Frank	P		(Aug18)	23Oct18	WIA,sv.
Offz.Stv. Friedrich Frank	P	AFP 4	3Oct17	11May18	FEA 1b
Ltn.d.R. Friedrich Frank	P	AFP 17	24Jul18	12Oct18	JSch II
Uffz. Fritz Friedrich	G	BS II	1Feb17	2May17	IIC,lt
Vzfw. Fritz Friedrich	G		2May17	9Nov18	Hosp.
Ltn.d.R. Heinrich Georg Geigl	P	KG 6/36	1Jan17	26Feb17	Js 34
Uffz. Hans Gossler	G			26Sep17	KIA
Vzfw. Bruno Gutensohn	G	AFP 4	12Aug17	4Sep17	IIC,lt.
Vzfw. Bruno Gutensohn	G		4Sep17	5Jun18	AFP 17
Pion. Maximilian Hartmann	G	FA 293A	20Jul18	24Jul18	Hosp.
Gefr. Maximilian Hartmann	G	Hosp.	26Aug18	EOW	
Uffz. Hans Kefer	G	AFP 4	11Oct17	23Feb18	Hosp.
Uffz. Richard Klügl	G	AFP 17	4Jun18	26Aug18	WIA,sv.
Vzfw. Eduard Kolb	P	AFP 2	7Jan18	1Jul18	AFP 17
Gefr. Gottfried Kraus	G	AFP 17	8Apr18	9Aug18	WIA,sv.
Oblt.d.R. Sigmund Kreitmair, C.O.	O	AFP 5	20Feb17	6Sep18	SGp B
Vzfw. Adam Lattrell	P	AFP 17	25Mar18	EOW	
Pion. Josef Lenterer	P	AFP 17	16Jul18	8Aug18	AFP 17
Vzfw. Nikolaus Maier	G	BS II	26Jan17	9Aug17	IIC,lt.

Ltn.d.R. Nikolaus Maier	G	AFP 2	4Jan18	9Aug18	ILuft
Vzfw. Ludwig Marx	G	AFP 6	22Apr17	26Mar18	IIC,lt
Ltn.d.R. Konrad Matt	P		(Aug17)	13Sep17	FA 45b
Uffz. Johann Christian Meeder	P	AFP 17	22Aug18	EOW	
Vzfw. Ludwig Meindl	P	AFP 4	22Oct17	EOW	
Uffz. Jakob Merl	G	AFP 4	6Oct17	25Jan18	WIA,lt.
Vzfw. Jakob Merl	G	Hosp.	5Mar18	22Jun18	Hosp.
Vzfw. Jakob Merl	G	Hosp.	25Aug18	EOW	
Vzfw. Egon Patzer	P			21Jul17	Js 36
Oblt. Curt Pflugbeil, stv. C.O.	P	BG 4/23	23Apr18	28Apr18	IIC,sv
Gefr. Karl Prim	P	AFP 17	2Sep18	EOW	
Uffz. Alfred Puder	G	AFP 17	15Oct18	EOW	
Offz.Stv. Fridolin Redenbach	P	AFP 4	29Jul17	22Aug17	WIA,lt.
Offz.Stv. Fridolin Redenbach	P		22Aug17	1Mar18	FEA 2b
Ltn.d.R. Theodor Rein	O	KG 6/36	1Jan17	10Apr17	FA 46b
Uffz. Andreas Riedl	P	AFP 17	1Sep18	EOW	
Gefr. Waldemar Roeder	P	AFP 4	19Sep17	23Sep17	Ss 23b
Vzfw. Oswald Roithmeier	P	AFP 4	7Oct17	7Oct17	FA 45b
Ltn.d.R. Emil Roth	O	KG 6/36	1Jan17	10Jan17	FA 46b
Vzfw. Franz Rothstein	P	AFP 17	30Jun18	18Jul18	AFP 4
Vzfw. Franz Rothstein	P	AFP 4	14Sep18	EOW	
Vzfw. Wilhelm Friedrich Schäffer	G	Ss 23b	29Sep17	16Oct17	AFP 4
Vzfw. Alfons Scheicher	G	AFP vS	1Feb17	18Dec17	FEA 2b
Uffz. Rudolf Schiessl	G	AFP 4	9Oct17	3Nov17	Ss 30b
Vzfw. Rudolf Schiessl	G	Ss 30b	2Jan18	31Jul18	LSO Grp
Vzfw. Rudolf Schiessl	G	LSO Grp	13Sep18	EOW	
Vzfw. Helmuth Schnabel	P	AFP 4	13Nov17	8May18	FEA 2b
Vzfw. Helmuth Schnabel	P	FEA 1b	3Jul18	EOW	
Uffz. Alois Schönberger	P	AFP 4	6Aug17	21Oct17	AFP 4
Gefr. Friedrich Schülke	G	AFP 17	8Feb18	7May18	BLA Frk
Vzfw. Friedrich Schülke	G	BLA Frk	13May18	EOW	
Oblt. Heinrich Schwandner, C.O.	P	KG 6/36	1Jan17	22Feb17	Js 32
Oblt. Karl Albert Selb		FA 26	23Sep17	13Nov17	Ss 30b
Uffz. Friedel Stegmann	P		(Apr17)	6May17	KIA
Vzfw. Georg Sumser	G	AFP 17	1Apr18	EOW	
Vzfw. Johann Tiefenbacher	P	AFP 17	5Mar18	14Aug18	Hosp.
Uffz. Oskar Traulsen	G	AFP 4	24Sep17	2Nov17	AFP 4
Uffz. Paul Tubbesing	P	KG 6/36	1Jan17	10Sep17	AFP 4
Vzfw. Georg Walcher	P	AFP 6	13May17	17Sep17	JsSch
Vzfw. Georg Walcher	P	JsSch I	22Sep17	31Dec17	KIC
Gefr. Wilhelm Walter	P	AFP 4	10Sep17	27Sep17	Ss 17
Vzfw. Weiss	P			6Sep17	IIC,lt.
Vzfw. Weiss	P		6Sep17	14Oct17	AFP 4
Vzfw. Josef Wenzl	G		(Apr17)	6May17	KIA
Uffz. Bruno Wiedemann	P	AFP 4	13Sep17	26Sep17	KIA
Vzfw. Wiese	P	FA 25		9Mar17	IIC,sv.
Ltn. Heinrich Zahler, Stv. C.O.	P	Js 78b	7Sep18	16Oct18	
Ltn. Heinrich Zahler, C.O.	P		16Oct18	EOW	
Vzfw. Max Zitzelsberger	G	BS II	26Jan17	30Nov17	KIA

Royal Bavarian *Schutzstaffel 27*

Mechanics and Ground Personnel

Name	From		To	
	Unit	Date	Date	Unit
Uffz. Ignatz Amrhein	KG 6/36	1Jan17	EOW	
Pion. Josef Angermeier	KG 6/36	1Jan17	10Nov17	Hosp.
Pion. Josef Angermeier	Hosp.	12Dec17	EOW	
Pion. Anton Bauer	FEA 1b	13Jan18	13May18	Hosp.
Pion. Anton Bauer	Hosp.	23Jul18	10Sep18	Ss 25b
Gefr. Martin Bernhard	KG 6/36	1Jan17	EOW	

Gefr. Hans Bollwein	AFP 5	3Mar17	EOW	
Pion. Josef Borst	FEA 2b	18Jun18	EOW	
Gefr. August Brenner	AFP 17	1Jun18	10Sep18	Ss 25b
Pion. Leonhardt Buchner	Ss 30b	24Aug17	8Dec17	Hosp.
Pion. Leonhardt Buchner	Hosp.	27Dec17	16Jun18	Infntry
Kraftf. Theodor Compensis	Infntry	26Feb18	25Mar18	FS III
Sgt. Eduard Cremer	FEA 1b	24Apr17	14Aug18	FEA 2b
Pion. Wilhelm Cron	KG 6/36	1Jan17	26Sep18	FEA 2b
Pion. Josef Däumling	FEA 1b	13Jan18	EOW	
Pion. Ludwig Deubner	FEA 1b	13Jan18	23Sep18	Hosp.
Pion. Michael Dendorfer	KG 6/36	1Jan17	EOW	
Uffz. Mathias Deutsch	FEA 1b	15Oct18	EOW	
Pion. Benedikt Dillinger	FEA 1b	13Jan18	16Jun18	Infntry
Uffz. Franz Dornhörfer	AFP 17	26Aug18	15Sep18	Hosp.
Pion. Georg Ebert	KG 6/36	1Jan17	3Aug17	FEA 1b
Pion. Lorenz Eckstein	FEA 2b	21Jul18	EOW	
Werkmstr.Stv. Karl Eger	KG 6/36	1Jan17	14Jun18	FEA 2b
Pion. Johann Eichner	KG 6/36	1Jan17	EOW	
Uffz. Johann Eisenbauer	KG 6/36	1Jan17	EOW	
Pion. Alfons Epp	KEA 6a	17May17	4Jun18	AWOL
Pion. Wilhelm Ermark	KG 6/36	1Jan17	20Jan17	Hosp.
Gefr. Wilhelm Ermark (+ 25Oct18)	Hosp.	1Mar17	17Oct18	Hosp.
Pion. Johann Eschenbacher	FEA 2b	6Jul18	EOW	
Pion. Josef Ettl	FEA 2b	4Feb18	EOW	
Vzfw. Otto Feyh	KG 6/36	1Jan17	EOW	
Pion. Ludwig Fischer	FEA 1b	30Dec17	10Jun18	Hosp.
Vzfw. Georg Fischer-Dick	KG 6/36	1Jan17	28Dec17	Hosp.
Sgt. Konrad Freytag	KWP 4	20Aug17	27Apr18	KWP 4
Pion. Karl Fürst	FEA 2b	27Jun18	EOW	
Gefr. Josef Gainhos	FEA 1b	21Feb17	EOW	
Pion. Josef Gebhard	KG 6/36	1Jan17	18Jan17	AFP 5
Pion. Josef Gebhard	AFP 5	17Jun17	23Aug17	AFP 4
Pion. Josef Gebhard	AFP 4	18Sep17	25Mar18	Inj.lt.
Pion. Josef Gebhard	25Mar18	31Mar18	Inj.sv.	
Pion. Hermann Geitz	FEA 2b	20Jan18	EOW	
Gefr. Josef Gehring	KG 6/36	1Jan17	8Dec17	Hosp.
Uffz. Josef Gehring	Hosp.	7Jan18	EOW	
Uffz. Johann Geissler	KG 6/36	1Jan17	EOW	
Pion. Johann Gilg	KG 6/36	1Jan17	EOW	
Pion. Konrad Glenk	FEA 1b	13Jan18	18Jan18	FEA 1b
Pion. Paul Goppert	AFP 4	1Aug17	EOW	
Sgt. Emil Grimm	KEA 23	5Jun18	21Jun18	KWP 23
Uffz. Philipp Gschwend	AFP 4	13Jul17	EOW	
Gefr. Otto Günther	AFP C	3Mar17	19May18	WIA
Gefr. Otto Günther	Hosp.	24Jun18	EOW	
Pion. Sebastian Güthlein	KG 6/36	1Jan17	12Mar18	Hosp.
Pion. Johann Haas	FEA 1b	1Aug17	EOW	
Gefr. Johann Hammhammer	KG 6/36	1Jan17	18Jan17	AFP 5
Pion. Luitpold Hans	FEA 1b	2Nov17	17Jul18	Infntry
Gefr. Johann Hartmann	KG 6/36	1Jan17	EOW	
Uffz. Josef Hau	KG 6/36	1Jan17	31Dec17	KIC
Gefr. Eugen Heck	KG 6/36	1Jan17	4May17	FEA 1b
Pion. Max Hefele	Ss 30b	6Sep17	18Nov17	FEA 1b
Pion. Max Hefele	FEA 1b	8Dec17	13Apr18	AWOL
Pion. Karl Heimisch	FEA 1b	30Jul17	3Nov17	FEA 1b
Pion. Friedrich Heitmann	KG 6/36	1Jan17	EOW	
Pion. Nikolaus Heller	FEA 2b	20Jan18	EOW	
Pion. Georg Hirsch	FEA 1b	15Oct18	EOW	
Pion. Konrad Hirschberger	FEA 1b	14Jan18	21Apr18	WIA
Pion. Konrad Hirschberger	Hosp.	3May18	EOW	
Gefr. Ludwig Holzheid	FEA 1b	26Oct17	27Sep18	Hosp.
Uffz. Andreas Holzmann	AFP C	15Aug17	3Nov17	FEA 1b
Gefr. Andreas Horn	FA 289A	7Sep18	EOW	
Pion. Johann Horndasch	FEA 1b	28Dec17	19Mar18	FA 235A
Pion. Johann Horndasch	AFP 17	17Apr18	EOW	

Pion. Johann Ibler	FEA 2b	20Jan18	EOW	
Pion. Johann Iffland	FEA 1b	12Jan18	18Mar18	Hosp.
Pion. Adam Jäckel	FEA 1b	2Nov17	17Jul18	Infntry
Gefr. Emil Junghänel	KG 6/36	1Jan17	EOW	
Pion. Fritz Kirsten	FEA 1b	2Nov17	EOW	
Pion. Georg Kolbeck	FEA 1b	30Nov17	11Apr18	Hosp.
Pion. Georg Kolbeck	FEA 2b	25Jun18	EOW	
Offz.Stv. Josef Kutzmann	FEA 1b	6Jan18	EOW	
Uffz. Christian Kraus	KG 6/36	1Jan17	EOW	
Gefr. Heinrich Kruse	Infntry	26Mar18	12May18	Infntry
Pion. Thomas Laub	FEA 1b	21Jun17	16Jun18	Infntry
Pion. Georg Laucks	FEA 2b	27Jun18	19Aug18	Hosp.
Pion. Wilhelm Lehnerer	FEA 1b	11Sep17	EOW	
Pion. Josef Lobmeier	Ss 29b	7Aug17	25Aug17	Ss 30b
Pion. Paul Mallunat	Ss 25b	18Sep18	EOW	
Pion. Philipp May	FEA 1b	15Oct18	EOW	
Gefr. Albert Miller	FEA 1b	12Apr17	EOW	
Pion. Otto Moser	KG 6/36	1Jan17	EOW	
Sgt. Josef Mühlbauer	KG 6/36	1Jan17	5Jun18	FEA 2b
Pion. Josef Müller	FEA 1b	13Jan18	19May18	KIA
Uffz. Karl Müller	KG 6/36	1Jan17	EOW	
Uffz. Karl Müller II	KG 6/36	1Jan17	8Jul18	FEA 2b
Uffz. Friedrich Nachtmann	KG 6/36	1Jan17	30Dec17	Hosp.
Uffz. Friedrich Nachtmann	Hosp.	9Jan18	18Jan18	Hosp.
Pion. Rudolf Nell	KWP 23	10Apr18	26Apr18	KWP 23
Sgt. Guido Nitz	KG 6/36	1Jan17	EOW	
Unterzahlmstr. August Obermeier	FEA 2b	16Oct18	EOW	
Gefr. Josef Obermeier	KG 6/36	1Jan17	3Sep17	Hosp.
Gefr. Josef Obermeier	Hosp.	30Nov17	EOW	
Gefr. Wilhelm Ohl	AFP C	2Mar17	21Oct18	Hosp.
Pion. Karl Ostheimer	FEA 1b	30Jul17	EOW	
Werkmstr. Alois Paulus	FEA 2b	6Jul18	EOW	
Kraftf. Josef Rahner	AKP 6	6Jun17	EOW	
Gefr. Wilhelm Reis	KG 6/36	1Jan17	EOW	
Pion. Johann Reitmayer	KG 6/36	1Jan17	EOW	
Gefr. Andreas Röder	KG 6/36	1Jan17	EOW	
Pion. Paulus Rösch	FS III	26Jun18	2Jul18	Hosp.
Gefr. Alois Roth	KG 6/36	1Jan17	EOW	
Pion. Georg Rubenbauer	FEA 1b	22Sep17	EOW	
Uffz. Karl Rubner	KG 6/36	1Jan17	5Aug18	Hosp.
Uffz. Karl Rubner	Hosp.	15Aug18	7Oct18	Hosp.
Pion. Josef Ruelins	KG 6/36	1Jan17	18Jan17	AFP 5
Pion. Josef Ruelins	AFP 5	31Jan17	18Jan18	Hosp.
Gefr. Josef Schad	FEA 1b	15Jan17	24Jun18	Hosp.
Gefr. Josef Schad	Hosp.	9Jul18	10Oct18	Hosp.
Gefr. Josef Schad	Hosp.	15Oct18	EOW	
Uffz. Kasimir Saur	AFP 17	17Oct18	EOW	
Uffz. Richard Schäder	KG 6/36	1Jan17	EOW	
Pion. Valentin Schäfer	AFP 4	27Jun17	EOW	
Pion. Johann Schaffelhuber	FEA 1b	28Dec17	26Apr18	Hosp.
Pion. Artur Schall	FEA 2b	26Jun18	EOW	
Uffz. Anton Schardt	KG 6/36	1Jan17	EOW	
Pion. Fritz Scheffler	FEA 2b	27Jun18	EOW	
Offz. Stv. Ernst Schmidt	KG 6/36	1Jan17	23Dec17	FEA 1b
Pion. Jakob Schmidt	KG 6/36	1Jan17	15Oct18	Hosp.
Gefr. Johann Schneider	KG 6/36	1Jan17	18Jan17	AFP 5
Pion. Simon Schneider	FEA 1b	13Jan18	EOW	*
Pion. Hermann Scholz	AFP 17	7Apr18	12Sep18	Ss 14
Gefr. Johann Schott	AFP C	3Mar17	8Oct18	Hosp.
Pion. Johann Schramm	KG 6/36	1Jan17	16Sep17	AFP 4
Pion. Johann Schramm	AFP 17	8Mar18	11Oct18	Inj.
Pion. Johann Schramm	Hosp.	15Oct18	EOW	
Gefr. Michael Schütz	FEA 1b	7Jul18	EOW	
Pion. Gregor Schuhbauer	KG 6/36	1Jan17	1Jan17	Mrds Wk
Uffz. Gregor Schuhbauer	Mrds Wk	28Feb17	20Sep18	FEA 1b

Pion. Anton Schwager	FEA 1b	2Nov17	12Dec17	Grufl 2
Pion. Anton Schwager	Grufl 2	3Apr18	EOW	
Sgt. Jakob Schwartz	KG 6/36	1Jan17	28Jun18	FEA 2b
Pion. Heinrich Schwegler	KG 6/36	1Jan17	EOW	
Pion. Alois Spreng	FEA 2b	20Jan18	17Jul18	Infntry
Uffz. Kaspar Stockmann	KG 6/36	1Jan17	EOW	
Pion. Christof Stöckel	KG 6/36	1Jan17	EOW	
Uffz. Karl Strössenreuther	KG 6/36	1Jan17	6Feb17	Hosp.
Uffz. Karl Strössenreuther	FEA 1b	12Jan18	EOW	
Pion. Georg Vogel	FEA 1b	28Dec17	EOW	
Pion. Christian Wachter	FEA 1b	14Jan18	11Oct18	JSch II
Kraftf. Karl Weinzierl	KEA I	8May18	EOW	
San.Uffz. Franz Weiss	Infntry	1Apr17	EOW	
Gefr. Fritz Weiss	FEA 1b	23Jan18	EOW	
Pion. Johann Wetzler			25Oct18	Died
Pion. Georg Wieland	KG 6/36	1Jan17	18Jan17	AFP 5
Pion. Karl Wiesnet	FEA 1b	13Jan18	EOW	*
Gefr. Johann Winzelmeier	AFP 5	21Feb17	18Jul18	FEA 2b
Pion. Johann Wirsing	AFP 4	9Jun17	EOW	

* Both Schenider and Wiesnet joined the *Schusta 27b Parkzug* at AFP 17 on 13Jan18 and may never have actually served in *Schusta 27b*. The *Parkzug* was the Support Detachment for *Schusta 27b*.

Schutzstaffel/Schlachtstaffel 27b
Mitgemachte Schlachten und Gefechte
(Battles and combat actions in which Ss 27b participated)

10Sep16	21Jan17	*Stellungskämpfe vor Verdun* (Trench fighting at Verdun)
22Jan17	5Apr17	*Kämpfe zwischen Maas und Mosel* (Fighting between the Maas and the Mosel)
6Apr17	10Jun17	*Frühjahrsschlacht bei Arras* (Spring battle of Arras)
11Jun17	22Nov17	*Schlacht in Flandern* (Battle in Flanders)
23Nov17	29Nov17	*Tankschlacht bei Cambrai* (Tank battle of Cambrai)
30Nov17	7Dec17	*Angriffsschlacht bei Cambrai* (Offensive battle of Cambrai)
8Dec17	1Feb18	*Kämpfe in der Siegfriedstellung* (Fighting in the Siegfried Line)
1Feb18	20Mar18	*Stellungskämpfe im Artois und Aufmarsch zur Grossen Schlacht in Frankreich* (Trench fighting in Artois and assembly for the Great Battle in France)
21Mar18	23Mar18	*Grossen Schlacht in Frankreich* (Great Battle in France)
21Mar18	6Apr18	*Durchbruchsschlacht Monchy-Cambrai* (Penetration battle Moncy-Cambrai)
7Apr18	1Nov18	*Kämpfe zwischen Arras und Albert* (Fighting between Arras and Albert)

weitere Gefechtseinträge fehlen (the remainder is not available)

Schutzstaffel/Schlachtstaffel 27b Airfields

From	To	Location	*Schlachtgruppe* Affiliation	*Armee*
1Jan17	10Jan17	Mont		5
10Jan17	21Jan17	Higny-Preutin	Escort for FA 252(A)w	5
22Jan17	5Apr17	Puxieux	Escort for FA 252(A)w	AAC
6Apr17	10Jun17	Bellincamps	Escort for FA 224(A)w	6
11Jun17	17Oct17			4
17Oct17		Oostkamp	Escort for FA 233(A)	4
(Oct17)	5Nov17	Herseaux	Escort for FA 294(A)b	4
5Nov17	22Nov17	Oostkamp	Escort for FA 258(A)	4

23Nov17	8Dec17	Bertry	Escort for FA 233(A)	2
8Dec17	1Feb18	Villers-au-Tertre	Escort for FA 233(A)	6
1Feb18	19Mar18	Villers-au-Tertre		17
19Mar18	24Apr18	Boucheneuil	SGp A (Ss 13,27b) C.O. *Oblt.* Müller	17
24Apr18	(19May18)	Bancourt Ost		17
(9Jun18)		Boucheneuil		17
15Jul18	8Aug18	Masny Süd	SGp 2 (Ss 11,27b) C.O. *Hptm.* Erich Sonntag	17
8Aug18	12Aug18	Nurlu	SGp 2 (Ss 11,13,19,27b) C.O. *Hptm.* Erich Sonntag	2
12Aug18	22Aug18	Masny Süd	SGp 2 (Ss 11,27b) C.O. *Hptm.* Erich Sonntag	17
22Aug18	24Sep18	Masny Süd	SGp 2 (Ss 9,11,27b) C.O. *Hptm.* Erich Sonntag	17
24Sep18	4Oct18	Masny Süd	SGp S (Ss 9,11,27b) C.O. *Hptm.* Hugo Weingarth	17
9Oct18	13Oct18	Marly	SGp S (Ss 4,11,15,27b,35) C.O. *Hptm.* Hugo Weingarth	17
13Oct18	18Oct18	Nouvelles	SGp S (Ss 4,11,15,27b) C.O. *Hptm.* Hugo Weingarth	17
18Oct18	EOW	NW St. Simphorien	SGp S (Ss 4,11,15,27b) C.O. *Hptm.* Hugo Weingarth	17

Royal Bavarian *Schutzstaffel 27b*

1Jan17	*Schutzstaffel 27b* is created from KG 6/Ks 36 by BKM Nr. 148032 of 31Dec16.
9Mar17	*Vzfw.* Wiese, P, is IIC,sv. during take-off.
24Apr17	*Uffz.* Stegmann-1, *Vzfw.* Wenzl-1, Sopwith Pup, 8.50, Lens either #A.6152, 66 Sqn. RFC, 2/Lt. Morley, shot up, OK or #A.7305, 66 Sqn. RFC, Capt. R. Oxspring, shot up, OK
2May17	*Vzfw.* Fritz Friedrichs, G, is IIC,lt., remains with the unit.
6May17	*Uffz.* Friedel Stegmann, P, and *Vzfw.* Josef Wenzl, G, are KIA over Annay during air combat in Albatros C.VII 3560/16.
9Aug17	*Vzfw.* Nikolaus Maier, G, is IIC,lt. He crashes from 3000 meters, injures his back and head and to hospital.
19Aug17	*Vzfw.* Redenbach-n/c, *Vzfw.* Scheicher-n/c, Sopwith 1 1/2, Zandvoorde #A.8298, 45 Sqn. RFC, Lt. C.M. Ross,KIA & 2/Lt. J.O. Fowler,KIA (Credited to *Ltn.* Bohner of *Flakzug 99*)
22Aug17	*Offz.Stv.* Fridolin Redenbach, P, is slightly WIA during air combat. He remains with the unit.
4Sep17	*Vzfw.* Bruno Gutensohn, G, is IIC,lt. in a landing accident. He remains with the unit.
6Sep17	*Vzfw.* Weiss, P, is lightly IIC, remains with the unit.
26Sep17	*Uffz.* Bruno Wiedemann, P, and *Uffz.* Hans Gossler, G, are KIA over Langemarck in a Rumpler C.V.
8Nov17	*Vzfw.* Wilhelm Büsing, P, is IIC during a crash landing and to hospital at Brügge.
30Nov17	*Vzfw.* Max Zitzelsberger, G, is KIA in a Hannover Cl.II over Bourlon Wald at 15.46 hours during air combat.
31Dec17	*Vzfw.* Georg Walcher, P, and *Uffz.* Josef Hau, M, are KIC at 11.50 hours at the airfield of Villers-au-Tertre during a practice flight.
25Jan18	*Uffz.* Jakob Merl, G, is lightly WIA during air combat over Cambrai and to hospital.
25Mar18	*Pion.* Josef Gebhard, M, is struck by a propeller and is lightly injured in the arm but remains with the unit.
26Mar18	*Vzfw.* Ludwig Marx, G, is IIC,lt., injures his left eye and to hospital at Valenciennes
27Mar18	*Schutzstaffel 27b* is renamed *Schlachtstaffel 27b* by KM Nr. 5126.18.A.7.L.IV.C. of 27Mar18.
31Mar18	*Pion.* Josef Gebhard, M, again is struck by a propeller, severely injures his arm and to hospital.
28Apr18	*Oblt.* Curt Pflugbeil, P and Stv. C.O., is IIC,sv. in a landing accident and to hospital.
21Apr18	*Pion.* Konrad Hirschberger, M, is WIA in the left thigh by a bomb splinter at Bancourt airfield and to hospital.
19May18	*Pion.* Josef Müller, M, is KIA at Bancourt Ost during an English bombing raid on the airfield. *Gefr.* Otto Günther, M, is WIA by a bomb fragment and to hospital.
8Aug18	*Vzfw.* Meindl-1, *Gefr.* Schülke-1, S.E. 5, Vermandovillers
9Aug18	*Ltn.d.R.* Frank-1, *Oblt.* Kreitmair-1, D.H. 9, Proyart
9Aug18	*Gefr.* Gottfried Kraus, G, is accidently WIA,sv. by a Fokker D.VII, and to hospital at Valenciennes.
26Aug18	*Uffz.* Richard Klügl, G, is WIA,sv. by a non-penetrating grenade splinter to the right temple and to hospital at Auberchicourt.
11Oct18	*Pion.* Johann Schramm, M, is injured by a propeller hit and to hospital at Mons.
15Oct18	*Pion.* Jakob Schmidt, M, falls off his motorcycle, breaks his right collar bone, and to hospital.
17Oct18	*Gefr.* Wilhelm Ermark, M, is sent to the hospital at Mons because of the flu. He dies there on 25Oct18.
23Oct18	*Ltn.d.R.* Eugen Ludwig Frank, P, is WIA,sv. at Villers la Chevre. He DOW on 25Dec18 in München.
25Oct18	*Pion.* Johann Wetzler, M, dies at Mons.
23Nov18	*Schlachtstaffel 27b* is demobilized at *Flieger Schule III*, FEA 2b, at Fürth.

The men of *Schusta 27b* in 1917. The C.O., *Oblt.d.R.* Sigmund Kreitmair, is in the center holding the cane. Credit: Michael Stacey.

Above: An Albatros C.III of *KG 6/Ks 36*. This unit later was renamed *Schusta 27b*.

Above right: Albatros C.VII (OAW) of *Schusta 27b* on its nose. Note the white outlines to the crosses on the pale blue undersides of the bottom wing. At this time the unit marking was a black chevron with black individual aircraft numbers, in this case '4.'

Right: A Roland C.II *Walfisch* of *Schusta 27b*. The crew is not identified.

Albatros C.VII (OAW) 3540/16 showing the unit marking of *Schusta 27b*. The photo is dated 22 May 1917.

A Hannover Cl.II of *Schlasta 27b*. Note that the unit marking has now changed to a white chevron and white individual aircraft numerals.

Left: *Uffz.* Fridolin Redenbach served as a pilot with *Schusta 27b* from 29 July 1917 to 1 March 1918. Credit: Michael Stacey. Above: The Halberstadt Cl.II of *Uffz.* Fridolin Redenbach in September 1917 while serving with *Schusta 27b*. Note the unit marking of a white chevron. Credit: Michael Stacey.

Below
Left top: *Schlasta 27b* Halberstadt Cl.II 'Brünhilde.' 'Thea' is in the background. The unit marking is a white chevron. Left bottom: *Schlasta 27b* Halberstadt Cl.II 'Brünhilde.' The stick grenades are being loaded. Right: As above. The mechanic is handing the gunner Priest mortar grenades.

Royal Bavarian *Schutzstaffel 28*

Pilot/Gunner	Type	From		To	
		Unit	Date	Date	Unit
Ltn.d.R. Andreas Aman, C.O.	O	FEA 1b	13Nov18	30Nov18	Demob.
Oblt. Eduard Amann, C.O.	O	FA 294A	14Sep17	24Mar18	KIA
Uffz. Adolf André	G	AFP 1	8May17	20Oct17	FEA 1b
Pion. Albert Asam	G	AFP 4	12Dec17	7Apr18	WIA,POW
Vzfw. Max Bäumler	G	AFP 4	6Aug17	25Mar18	IIC
Vzfw. Max Bäumler	G		25Mar18	28Mar18	Hosp.
Oblt. Oskar Baumann, C.O.	O	FA 287A	4Apr18	11Apr18	IIC,lt.
Oblt. Oskar Baumann, C.O.	O	Hosp.	12Apr18	25Apr18	WIA,lt.
Oblt. Oskar Baumann, C.O.	O	Hosp.	26Apr18	8Sep18	Leave
Oblt. Oskar Baumann, C.O.	O	Leave	27Sep18	EOW	
Pion. Karl Baumgärtler	P	AFP 1	20Jul18	8Sep18	FA 295A
Uffz. Paul Bayer	P	FEA 1b	15Feb17	15Apr17	AFP 6
Uffz. Johann Becker	G	AFP 1	23Apr17	28May17	WIA,DOW
Uffz. Ludwig Bergmann	P	AFP 4	4Aug17	12Apr18	AFP 2
Uffz. Wilhelm Berkowsky	P	FEA 1b	15Feb17	8Aug17	FA 26
Uffz. Michael Boxhammer	P	FA 26	8Aug17	13Dec17	AFP 4
Uffz. Hermann Brauer	P	FEA 1b	15Feb17	27Jul17	KIA
Uffz. Hugo Braun	P	AFP 1	11Jul18	EOW	
Gefr. Georg Brix	P	AFP 4	30Aug17	11Sep17	Ss 30b
Ltn.d.R. Otto Brockert	O	FA 199b	24Nov18	30Nov18	Demob.
Uffz. Adolf Brüstle	G	FEA 1b	15Feb17	29May17	Inj.
Vzfw. Adolf Brüstle	G	FEA 1b	11Aug17	23May18	Hosp.
Vzfw. Adolf Brüstle	G	Hosp.	8Jul18	28Sep18	Hosp.
Vzfw. Adolf Brüstle	G	Hosp.	12Oct18	EOW	
Vzfw. Franz Bucher	P	FEA 1b	15Feb17	18Apr17	AFP 1
Vzfw. Heinrich Carstens	P	AFP 1	20Jun17	24Mar18	KIA
Pion. Wilhelm Chemnitz	P	AFP 1	22May17	21Jun17	FA 17
Uffz. Karl Dennhof	G	FA 26	19Apr18	EOW	
Uffz. Eduard Dietrich	P	FS IV		EOW	
Gefr. Ernst Ebner	G	AFP 1	5May17	10Aug17	AFP 4
Uffz. Heinrich Eissner	P	Ss 30b	16Sep17	24Sep17	Ss 26b
Uffz. Otto Erdmann	P	FEA 1b	15Feb17	20Jul17	Intrnd
Sgt. Ernst Fettinger	P	AFP 4	25Apr18	27Jun18	AFP 7
Uffz. Georg Fink	P	Ss 23b	20Apr18	28Jul18	WIA
Sgt. Michael Fischer	G	AFP 7	4Jun18	10Jul18	Ss 32
Gefr. Emil Frey	G	AFP 4	28Apr18	27May18	WIA,sv.
Uffz. Bruno Fuchs	P	FS IV	6Apr17	20Jun17	AFP 7
Pion. Joseph Fuchs	P	JsSch I	20Jul18	20Aug18	POW
Gefr. Wilhelm Günzel	P	Ss 23b	14Apr18	22Apr18	AFP 4
Pion. Emil Hellwig	P	AFP 4	16Apr18	23Apr18	Ss 3
Offz.Stv. Hermann Herwig	G	FEA 1b	15Feb17	23Mar17	Inj.
Offz.Stv. Hermann Herwig	G	Hosp.	27Mar17	EOW	
Uffz. Karl Hönig	G	AFP 1	14Apr17	27Jul17	KIA
Vzfw. Franz Hutter	G	AFP 4	2Aug17	30Jul18	Hosp.
Uffz. Willy Jutsch	G	AFP 7	24May18	EOW	
Gefr. Theodor Kaleta	P	AFP 4	23Aug17	31Aug17	Ss 12
Pion. Friedrich Karcher	G	AFP 19	13Sep18	EOW	
Gefr. Kastner (KSR papers missing)	G	AFP 1	29May17	(Apr18)	
Offz.Stv. Karl Klein	P	AFP 4	23Apr18	30Oct18	Hosp.
Uffz. Stefan Klosseck	P	AFP 1	8May17	18May17	AFP 13
Ltn.d.R. Hanns Koch, OzbV	O		('17)	21May18	Ss 23b
Flg. Wilhelm Kraatz	G	AFP 1	18Jun17	6Aug17	AFP 4
Uffz. Karl Krämer	G	AFP 4	8Oct17	9Mar18	FS Asch
Vzfw. Heinrich Kratz	P	AFP 7	14May18	EOW	
Ltn.d.R. Alfred Kuhn, Stv. C.O.	P	Ss 26b	8Sep18	27Sep18	Ss 26b
Gefr. Heinrich Lechleitner	G	AFP 7	20Jun17	5Jul17	AFP 6
Sgt. Hermann Lenn	G	AFP 7	23May18	30May18	Ss 31b
Uffz. Adolf Marr	G	AFP 9	27Aug18	EOW	
Uffz. Karl Meissner	G	FEA 1b	15Feb17	14Jun17	Hosp.
Uffz. Karl Meissner	G	Hosp.	1Jul17	5Oct17	AFP 4

Uffz. Wilhelm Menz	P	AFP 4	23Aug17	28Aug17	AFP 4
Vzfw. Robert Mitterer	G	FEA 1b	18Feb17	8May17	Hosp.
Pion. Emil Morlock	P	AFP 4	16Apr18	23Apr18	Ss 3
Uffz. Karl Müller	P	AFP 4	27Dec17	6Apr18	WIA,lt.
Gefr. Otto Müller	G	AFP 4	31Jul17	16Aug17	Ss 29b
Gefr. Max Niemann	P			26Apr18	Ss 21
Uffz. Hermann Pauli	G	FEA 1b	15Feb17	20Jul17	Intrnd
Uffz. Bernhard Peterkord	G	AFP 7	28May18	EOW	
Oblt. Karl Prager, C.O.	O	FA 293A	5May17	25Sep17	FEA 1b
Pion. Ernst Reuter	G	AFP 4	23Sep17	8Oct17	Ss 19
Uffz. Georg Rohde	G	AFP 4	23Sep17	18Oct17	Ss 9
Gefr. Ludwig Rosenbeck	P	FEA 1b	22Feb17	28May17	WIA,lt.
Vzfw. Ludwig Rosenbeck	P	Hosp.	6Jun17	26Dec17	Inj.
Ltn.d.R. Rupke, OzbV	O			1Jul18	AFP 7
Uffz. Bernhard Rupprecht	P	AFP 4	3May18	EOW	
Uffz. Johann Schatt	P	AFP 4	17Jul17	14Sep17	JsSch I
Uffz. Johann Schatt	P	JsSch I	22Sep17	17Feb18	WIA,lt.
Vzfw. Johann Schatt	P		17Feb18	12Jul18	AFP 2
Vzfw. Anton Scherber	G	AFP 4	2Aug17	19Aug18	AFP 9
Oblt.d.R. Eduard Schleich, C.O.	P	FS I	12Feb17	4May17	AFP 1
Uffz. Johann Schlenk	P	AFP 4	5Oct17	6Apr18	AFP 2
Vzfw. Wilhelm Schlör	G	AFP 4	20Oct17	24Mar18	KIA
Vzfw. Max Schmeer (+ 24Nov19)	P	AFP 4	1Oct17	EOW	
Ltn.d.R. Max Schmeer, OzbV	P		20Oct18	EOW	
Uffz. Hans Friedrich Schmidt	P	AFP 4	13Dec17	3Feb18	IIC,lt.
Uffz. Hans Friedrich Schmidt	P		3Feb18	7Apr18	KIA
Uffz. Friedrich Schneider	G	FEA 1b	15Feb17	19Apr17	KIA
Uffz. Julius Scholler	G	AFP 4	5Oct17	26Dec17	WIA,lt.
Uffz. Julius Scholler	G		26Dec17	8Jan18	Sick Lv
Pion. Georg Schott	P	AFP 1	29May17	20Jun17	AFP 1
Gefr. Emil Soetebier	G	AFP 7	29May18	20Aug18	POW
Uffz. Otto Sommerroch	G	AFP 4	18Oct17	8Mar18	FS Asch
Uffz. Hans Täschner	P	AFP 4	20Jun17	17Jul17	FEA 1b
Uffz. Johann Treutlein	G	AFP 4	8May18	EOW	
Gefr. Michael Wehr	P	AFP 2	28Apr18	26May18	AFP 7
Uffz. Heinrich Wingen	P	AFP 4	20May18	EOW	
Vzfw. Georg Winkler	G	AFP A	28May17	6Aug17	AFP 4
Gefr. Johann Winkler	P	AFP 2	12Apr18	25Apr18	AFP 4
Vzfw. Reiner Wirtz	P	AFP 1	5May17	14Oct17	Ss 13
Sgt. Alexander Wittke	P	AFP 7	28May18	15Jun18	JSch II
Flg. Anton Zimmermann (+ 1May18)	G	AFP 4	12Apr18	30Apr18	WIA,POW
Pion. Theobald Zimmermann	P			EOW	
Flg. Ludwig Zippelius	G	FA 26	3May18	27Jun18	AFP 7

Royal Bavarian *Schutzstaffel 28*

Mechanics and Ground Personnel

Name	From		To	
	Unit	Date	Date	Unit
Gefr. Johann Adler	FEA 1b	24Jun17	EOW	
Pion. Karl Artmeier	FEA 1b	15Feb17	EOW	
Pion. Josef Baldauf	FEA 1b	11Jan18	EOW	
Pion. Felix Bartsch	FEA 12	8Jan18	15Jan18	AFP 4
Pion. Karl Bast	FEA 1b	20Jun17	EOW	
Uffz. Oskar Bauer	FEA 1b	15Feb17	1Aug18	SGp B
Uffz. Eugen Bentz	FEA 1b	15Feb17	EOW	
Uffz. Paul Bergold	FEA 1b	15Feb17	EOW	
Gefr. Peter Berwig	AFP 1	7May17	EOW	
Pion. Sebastian Bichlmaier	FEA 1b	13Nov17	EOW	
Pion. Max Bichlmeier	FEA 1b	24Jun17		
Pion. Friedrich Bösinger	FEA 1b	14Aug17	EOW	

Pion. Fritz Bräu	FEA 1b	11Jun17	10Feb18	FEA 1b
Pion. Franz Brandl	FEA 1b	15Feb17	8Mar18	KEA 1b
Pion. Johann Brandl	FS II	25Sep18	EOW	
Pion. Karl Braun	FEA 2b	25Sep18	EOW	
Pion. Johann Breitsameder	FEA 1b	15Feb17	3Nov17	FEA 1b
Uffz. Josef Brem	FEA 1b	11Jan17	17Jul17	FEA 1b
Pion. Otto Brentzel	FEA 1b	5Apr17	5May18	Hosp.
Pion. Otto Brentzel	Hosp.	12Aug18	21Aug18	FEA 1b
Pion. Adolf Buchner	FEA 2b	25Sep18	EOW	
Pion. Johann Christgau	FEA 1b	15Feb17	EOW	
Gefr. Emil Daniel	FEA 2b	13Jun18	31Jul18	Hosp.
Gefr. Emil Daniel	Hosp.	27Aug18	EOW	
Pion. Karl Datschegg	FEA 1b	15Feb17	10Apr17	FEA 1b
Pion. Johann Dengler	FEA 1b	15Feb17	17Jul17	FEA 1b
Pion. Arnold Deufel	FEA 1b	14Aug17	21Nov17	FEA 1b
Gefr. Ernst Dickel	FEA 1b	14May17	EOW	
Uffz. Oskar Dörr	FEA 1b	15Feb17	8May17	AFP 1
Uffz. Philipp Dorn	FEA 1b	15Feb17	EOW	
Pion. Simon Eben	FEA 1b	15Feb17	8Jul17	Inj.
Gefr. Simon Eben	Hosp.	16Jul17	9Jul18	FEA 2b
Gefr. Oswald Eberhardt	FEA 2b	27Jun18	EOW	
Sgt. Georg Ebert	FEA 1b	17Sep17	EOW	
Pion. Michael Eder	FEA 1b	15Feb17	6Apr18	Hosp.
Pion. Rudolf Eggmeier	FEA 2b	9Aug18	EOW	
Pion. Wilhelm Ferstl	FEA 1b	14Aug17	3Nov17	FEA 1b
Pion. Franz Ficker	FEA 1b	15Feb17	31May17	Js 32b
Pion. Friedrich Fink	FEA 2b	25Sep18	EOW	
Pion. Wilhelm Flockerzi	FEA 1b	26May17	5Jun17	Hosp.
Pion. Wilhelm Flockerzi	Hosp.	1Jul17	2Jul17	AFP 6
Pion. Lorenz Forler	FEA 1b	14Jan18	18Oct18	Pioners
Pion. Friedrich Frank	FEA 1b	15Feb17	24Jul17	FEA 1b
Gefr. Josef Freymadl	FEA 1b	23May17	19Aug17	FEA 1b
Pion. Andreas Frosch	FEA 1b	26Nov17	14Feb18	FEA 1
Uffz. August Fürmann	FEA 1b	15Feb17	19Jun18	FEA 1b
Pion. Johann Gauster	FEA 2b	25Sep18	EOW	
Pion. Johann Gebhardt	FEA 2b	9Aug18	30Aug18	Hosp.
Pion. Johann Geutner	FEA 1b	14Jan18	21Oct18	Hosp.
Pion. Johann Geutner	Hosp.	7Nov18	EOW	
Vzfw. Ferdinand Gmach	FEA 1b	15Feb17	8Oct18	+ i.Kr.
Pion. Heinrich Graf	FA 253A	21Jun17	29Dec17	FEA 1
Pion. Karl Grimm	FEA 1b	13Nov17	EOW	
Pion. Thadäus Grönninger	FEA 1b	15Feb17	28Apr17	FEA 1b
Gefr. Heinrich Grosklos	FEA 2b	6Jun18	15Jun18	Hosp.
Pion. Georg Gutting	FEA 1b	3Apr17	3Nov17	FEA 1b
Pion. Friedrich Hacker	AFP 4	16Apr18	EOW	
Pion. Johann Haslbeck	FEA 1b	15Feb17	5May17	AFP 1
Gefr. Johann Heider	FA 293A	1May17	24Sep17	FEA 1b
Pion. Johann Heil	AFP 4	11Apr18	22Jun18	Hosp.
Pion. Johann Heil	Hosp.	3Jul18	21Oct18	Hosp.
Pion. Johann Heil	Hosp.	28Oct18	EOW	
Pion. Leonhardt Heitler	FEA 1b	15Feb17	17Jul17	FEA 1b
Pion. Georg Heberling	FEA 2b	9Aug18	6Sep18	Hosp.
Uffz. Johann Herbst	FEA 1b	15Feb17	EOW	
Uffz. Jakob Hilgert	FEA 1b	15Feb17	7May17	FEA 1b
Pion. Adolf Hoffmann	FEA 1b	15Feb17	EOW	
Uffz. Karl Hoffmann	FEA 1b	15Feb17	EOW	
Pion. Ferdinand Hofstetter	AFP 4	10Apr18	26Jul18	Hosp.
Pion. Balthasar Hopf	FEA 1b	21Sep17	3Nov17	FEA 1b
Pion. Georg Horn	FEA 1b	15Feb17	9Mar17	Hosp.
Pion. Georg Horn	Hosp.	3Apr17	EOW	
Pion. Wilhelm Horn	FEA 1b	15Feb17	18Oct17	Lbr Co.
Gefr. Wilhelm Horn	Lbr Co.	8Mar18	EOW	
Uffz. Otto Jung	FEA 1b	15Feb17	29Jan18	FEA 1b
Uffz. Wilhelm Kiesel	FEA 1b	15Feb17	5May18	IIC,sv.
Pion. Anton Kieser	FEA 2b	9Aug18	10Sep18	Hosp.

Pion. Anton Kieser	Hosp.	4Oct18	EOW	
Pion. Georg Klov	FEA 1b	15Feb17	10Mar17	Hosp.
Pion. Georg Klov	Hosp.	17Mar17	EOW	
Uffz. Karl Knapp	FEA 1b	15Feb17	EOW	
Uffz. Alois Knopf	FEA 1b	25Aug17	EOW	
Pion. Georg Köck	FEA 1b	1Jun17	14Nov17	FEA 1b
Pion. August Krätzer	FEA 1b	Dec17		
Gefr. Michael Krampfl	FA 294A	14Sep17	EOW	
Gefr. Georg Kreiser	FEA 1b	15Feb17	20Dec17	Hosp.
Gefr. Franz Kroiss	AKP 4	10Oct17	23Jan18	AKP 4
Gefr. Johann Küspert	FEA 1b	15Feb17	3Nov17	FEA 1b
Sgt. Max Kurz	FEA 1b	15Feb17	EOW	
Uffz. Philipp Langenstein	FEA 1b	15Feb17	13Apr18	Hosp.
Sgt. Philipp Langenstein	Hosp.	30Apr18	EOW	
Pion. Josef Lasser	FEA 2b	4Oct18	4Oct18	Hosp.
Pion. Felix Latterner	FEA 1b	15Feb17	5May17	AFP 1
Pion. Max Lehner	FEA 1b	30Jul17	EOW	
Pion. Karl Leichte	FEA 1b	13Nov17	EOW	
Pion. Karl Leis	FEA 1b	7Sep17	2Oct18	Hosp.
Pion. Max Liebl	FEA 2b	4Oct18	EOW	
Pion. Josef Listl	AFP 3	16Mar17	EOW	
Uffz. Roman Löchler	FEA 1b	12Jan18	15Jan18	AFP 4
Pion. Friedrich Lux	FEA 1b	15Feb17		
Pion. Ludwig Maar	FEA 1b	15Feb17	1Aug17	FEA 1b
Gefr. Michael Magg	FEA 1b	15Feb17	22Jun17	Hosp.
Gefr. Karl Maier	FEA 2b	10Aug18	EOW	
Gefr. Ludwig Mainz	FEA 2b	10Aug18	EOW	
Uffz. Friedrich Marci	FEA 1b	15Feb17	4Nov17	FEA 1b
Pion. Emil Matheis	FEA 1b	15Feb17	20Apr17	Hosp.
Feldw. Francis Mayer	FEA 1b	15Feb17	EOW	
Pion. Hermann Meier	FEA 1b	13Nov17	EOW	
Pion. Josef Meinhardt	FEA 2b	10Aug18	EOW	
Pion. Franz Melchardt	FEA 1b	30Mar17	7Feb18	FEA 1b
Pion. Michael Metz	FEA 2b	27Jun18	EOW	
Pion. Karl Metzger	AFP 4	14Jan18	19Jul18	Infntry
Pion. Karl Müller	FEA 1b	12Jan18	19Jul18	Infntry
Gefr. Franz Muich	AKP 4	14Sep17	8Oct17	AKP 4
Pion. Josef Murr	FEA 1b	24Jun17	18Jun18	Infntry
Pion. Wilhelm Nennzert	FEA 1b	16Feb17	15Mar17	Hosp.
Pion. Wilhelm Nennzert	Hosp.	17Mar17	29Apr17	KEA
Pion. Richard Opp	FEA 2b	9Aug18	EOW	
Uffz. Michael Ottowitz	AFP 3	29May17	EOW	
Gefr. Herbert Peschke	Js 28w	19Jan18	30Jun18	FEA 1b
Pion. Johann Pimperl	FEA 1b	13Nov17	16Jun18	Hosp.
Pion. Johann Popp	FEA 1b	15Feb17	31Jul18	Inj.
Gefr. Georg Reichel	FEA 2b	8Jun18	EOW	
Wermstr.Stv. Josef Robauer	FEA 1b	15Feb17	EOW	
Pion. Georg Rössler	FEA 2b	9Aug18	EOW	
Gefr. Josef Rosskopf	FEA 1b	15Feb17	25Feb18	Hosp.
Gefr. Josef Rosskopf	FEA 2b	18Jun18	EOW	
Pion. Ferdinand Rüth	FEA 1b	13Nov17	EOW	
Gefr. Marinus Schaber	FEA 1b	15Feb17	4Jul18	FEA 2b
Pion. Paul Schell	FEA 2b	26Jun18	EOW	
Pion. Franz Schellenberger	FEA 1b	15Feb17	25Feb17	AFP 1
Pion. Christoph Schelter	AFP 4	16Apr18	EOW	
Pion. Josef Scherl	FEA 1b	25Feb17	18Aug17	FEA 1b
Gefr. Johann Schimmel	FEA 1b	15Feb17	22May18	Hosp.
Pion. Clemens Schlamp	FEA 1b	24Sep17	EOW	
Pion. Karl Schmitt	FEA 2b	28Jun18	EOW	
Uffz. Albert Schrem	FEA 1b	15Feb17	20Jan18	Js 28w
Pion. Konrad Schumm	FEA 2b	26Sep18	EOW	
Pion. Johann Schwab	FEA 1b	15Feb17	30May17	Hosp.
Pion. Johann Schwab	Hosp.	11Oct17	EOW	
Pion. Heinrich Seidl	FEA 2b	31Aug18	11Sep18	Hosp.
Pion. Heinrich Seidl	Hosp.	5Oct18	EOW	

Gefr. Johann Seidl I	FEA 1b	15Feb17	3Nov17	FEA 1b
Pion. Johann Seidl II	FEA 1b	15Feb17	2Apr17	Hosp.
Pion. Johann Seidl II	Hosp.	15Apr17	3Nov17	FEA 1b
Pion. Heinrich Seidler			4Jun18	+ i.Kr.
Gefr. Wolfgang Seyferth	FEA 1b	15Feb17	18Aug17	FEA 1b
Pion. Karl Siegfarth	FEA 1b	3Aug17	18Oct18	Hosp.
Gefr. Konrad Söllner	FEA 1b	15Feb17	5Oct18	Hosp.
Gefr. Konrad Söllner	Hosp.	16Oct18	2Nov18	Hosp.
Uffz. Wilhelm Solleder	FEA 1b	15Feb17	30Oct18	Hosp.
Pion. Alfred Spier	FEA 1b	15Feb17	7May17	AFP 1
Pion. Karl Steffen	FEA 1b	2Aug17	19Nov17	FEA 1b
Pion. Karl Steffen	FEA 1b	8Dec17	EOW	
Sgt. Jakob Steiger	FEA 1b	15Feb17	EOW	
Gefr. Robert Steiner	FEA 1b	15Feb17	EOW	
Sgt. Heinrich Stephan	FEA 2b	12Jul18	25Aug18	FEA 2b
Gefr. Adolf Sterzer	FEA 1b	15Feb17	18Oct17	FEA 1b
Pion. Alfred Stoffel	FEA 1b	15Feb17	26Oct17	FEA 1b
Pion. Striegel (KST papers missing)	FEA 1b	15Feb17		
Pion. Ludwig Studtrucker	FEA 1b	15Feb17	21Oct18	Hosp.
Pion. Ludwig Studtrucker	Hosp.	29Oct18	EOW	
Uffz. Johann Tischler	FEA 1b	15Feb17	EOW	
Gefr. Josef Veidl	FEA 1b	2Jun17	24Jul17	Hosp.
Uffz. Josef Veidl	Hosp.	1Aug17	17Apr18	Hosp.
Uffz. Josef Veidl	Hosp.	5May18	19Jul18	Infntry
Pion. Karl Weigand	FEA 1b	24Nov17	5Jan18	AFP 4
Vzfw. August Weissenseel	FEA 1b	15Feb17	21Nov17	FEA 1b
Gefr. Wilhelm Wellstein	FEA 1b	15Feb17	EOW	
Pion. Sebastian Wiendl	FEA 1b	10Jan18	26Jul18	Hosp.
Pion. Max Wild	FEA 1b	13Oct17	8Mar18	FEA 1b
Gefr. Hermann Wilke			20Jun18	+ i.Kr.
Unterzahlmstr. Michael Winkler	FEA 2b	9Oct18	EOW	
Gefr. Ludwig Winter	FEA 1b	15Feb17	10Oct17	FEA 1b
Pion. Johann Zech	FEA 1b	24Sep17	EOW	
Gefr. Leodegard Zedelmayr	FEA 1b	12Sep17	18Jun18	Infntry
Pion. Michael Zellerer	FEA 1b	30Mar17	20Jul17	FEA 1b
Pion. August Zirngibl	AFP 3	8May17	24Jan18	Adlrshf
Pion. August Zirngibl	Adlrshf	25Feb18	EOW	

Schutzstaffel/Schlachtstaffel 28b
Mitgemachte Schlachten und Gefechte
(Battles and combat actions in which Ss 28b participated)

25Feb17	15Apr17	*Stellungskämpfe in der Champagne* (Trench fighting in the Champagne)
16Apr17	27May17	*Doppelschlacht Aisne-Champagne* (The double battle Aisne-Champagne)
28May17	21Jun17	*Stellungskämpfe bie Reims* (Trench fighting at Reims)
22Jun17	17Jul17	*Kämpfe in französisch Flandern und im Artois* (Fighting in French Flanders and in Artois)
18Jul17	3Dec17	*Schlacht in Flandern* (Battle in Flanders)
4Dec17	10Mar18	*Stellungskämpfe in Flandern Winter 17/18* (Trench fighting in Flanders Winter 17/18)
11Mar18	20Mar18	*Aufmarsch für die Grosse Schlacht in Frankreich* (Assembly for the Great Battle in France)
21Mar18	27Mar18	*Grosse Schlacht in Frankreich* (Great Battle in France)
28Mar18	15Apr18	*Kämpfe an Ancre, Somme und Avre* (Fighting on the Ancre, the Somme and the Avre)
16Apr18	19Apr18	*Stellungskrieg in Flandern* (Trench war in Flanders)

20Apr18	29Apr18	*Schlacht um den Kemmelberg* (Battle for the Kemmel)
30Apr18	12May18	*Stellungskrieg in Flandern* (Trench war in Flanders)
13May18	26May18	*Stellungskämpfe nördlich der Ailette* (Trench fighting north of the Ailette)
27May18		*Erstürmung der Höhen des Chemin des Dames* (Storming the top of the Chemin des Dames)
28May18	1Jun18	*Verfolgungskämpfe zwischen Oise und Aisne und über die Vesle bis zur Marne* (Pursuit fighting between the Oise and the Aisne and across the Vesle to the Marne)
2Jun18	13Jun18	*Schlacht zwischen Soissons und Reims* (Battle between Soissons and Reims)
14Jun18	27Jun18	*Stellungskämpfe zwischen Oise und Marne* (Trench fighting between the Oise and the Marne)
28Jun18	14Jul18	*Stellungskämpfe bei Reims* (Trench fighting at Reims)
15Jul18	17Jul18	*Angriffsschlacht an der Marne und in der Champagne* (Offensive battle on the Marne and in the Champagne)
18Jul18	25Jul18	*Abwehrschlacht zwischen Soissons und Reims* (Defensive battle between Soissons and Reims)
26Jul18	3Aug18	*Bewegliche Abwehrschlacht zwischen Marne und Vesle* (The mobile battle between the Marne and the Vesle)
4Aug18	16Aug18	*Stellungskämpfe zwischen Oise und Aisne* (Trench fighting between the Oise and the Aisne)
17Aug18	28Aug18	*Abwehrschlacht zwischen Oise und Aisne* (Defensive battle between the Oise and the Aisne)
29Aug18	14Sep18	*Stellungskämpfe vor Reims* (Trench fighting at Reims)
15Sep18	24Sep18	*Stellungskämpfe in Lothringen* (Trench fighting in Lorraine)
25Sep18	28Sep18	*Vorfeldkämpfe um den Kalten Berg (La Cote) im Süden von Metz* (Forefield fighting for the Kalten Berg (La Cote) south of Metz)
29Sep18	11Nov18	*Stellungskämpfe in Lothringen* (Trench fighting in Lorraine)

Schutzstaffel/Schlachtstaffel 28b Airfields

From	To	Location	*Schlachtgruppe* Affiliation	*Armee*
25Feb17	16Apr17	Alincourt	Escort for FA 53, FA 272(A)	3
16Apr17	3May17	Alincourt	For FA 53, 252(A)w, 272(A)	1
3May17	21Jun17	Ancoisne	Escort for FA 252(A)w	1
22Jun17	17Jul17	Ennetières	Escort for FA 292(A)b	6
18Jul17	28Aug17	Snelleghem	Escort for FA 26	4
28Aug17	6Sep17	Ingelmunster	Escort for FA 26	4
6Sep17	10Mar18	Rumbeke	Escort for FA 26	4
11Mar18	21Mar18	Reumont	SGp B (Ss 4,15,26b,28b) C.O. *Ritt.d.R.* Herrmann	2
21Mar18	3Apr18	Longavesnes	SGp B (Ss 4,15,26b,28b) C.O. *Ritt.d.R.* Herrmann	2
3Apr18	19Apr18	Framerville	SGp A (Ss 14,28b,30b) C.O. *Oblt.d.R.* August Ertl	2
20Apr18	12May18	Heule-Bisseghem	SGp A (Ss 1,14,21,28b) C.O. *Oblt.* Emil Ziegler gen Stege	4
13May18	27May18	Montigny le Franc	SGp B (Ss 23b,26b,28b,30b) C.O. *Oblt.d.R.* August Ertl	7
27May18	28May18	Forsthaus Eppes	SGp B (Ss 23b,26b,28b,30b) C.O. *Oblt.d.R.* August Ertl	7
28May18	16Jun18	Monthussart Fe.	SGp B (Ss 23b,26b,28b,30b) C.O. *Oblt.d.R.* August Ertl	7
16Jun18	17Jul18	Cuiry-Housse	SGp Winckler (Ss 28b,30b,31b,32) C.O. *Oblt.d.R.* August Ertl	7

18Jul18	25Jul18	l'Ecaille	SGp B (Ss 28b,30b,31b,32) C.O. *Oblt.d.R.* Josef Gramp	1
26Jul18	14Sep18	Grandlup-et-Fay	SGp B (Ss 28b,30b,31b,32) C.O. *Oblt.d.R.* Josef Gramp	7
15Sep18	24Sep18	Perthes	SGp B (Ss 28b,30b,31b,32) C.O. *Oblt.d.R.* Josef Gramp	1
25Sep18	19Oct18	Antullen by Metz	SGp 2 (Ss 28b,36) C.O. *Oblt.* Oskar Baumann	19
19Oct18	EOW	Diffenbach-lès-Puttelange	SGp 2 (Ss 2,22b,28b,36) C.O. *Oblt.* Karl *Ritter* von Gruny	19

Royal Bavarian *Schutzstaffel 28b*

15Feb17	*Schutzstaffel 28b* is created at FEA 1b by BKM Nr. 21943A. of 15Mar17.
23Mar17	*Vzfw.* Bucher-1, *Offz.Stv.* Herwig-1, Spad, Prosnes
23Mar17	*Offz.Stv.* Hermann Herwig, G, suffers frost bitten hands and to hospital at Juniville.
19Apr17	*Uffz.* Friedrich Schneider, G, is KIA over Prosnes during an air combat with two Spads. *Gefr.* Hermann Brauer, P, is OK and lands safely at Warmeriville.
28May17	*Gefr.* Ludwig Rosenbeck, P, is WIA,lt. during an air combat over Prosnes and to hospital at Juniville. *Uffz.* Johann Becker, G, is severely WIA, shot in the stomach during the same combat, and DOW in the hospital at Juniville.
29May17	*Gefr.* Adolf Brüstle, G, breaks his left arm doing gymnastics and to hospital at Juniville.
14Jun17	*Uffz.* Karl Meissner, G, burns his left hand and to hospital.
8Jul17	*Pion.* Simon Eben, M, is injured in an accident and to hospital.
20Jul17	*Uffz.* Otto Erdmann, P, and *Uffz.* Hermann Pauli, G, while on a flight from Ennetières airfield in the *6. Armee* to Snelleghem air field in the *4. Armee* suffer motor problems, are forced to land in Holland, and are interned with DFW C.V 4982/16.
27Jul17	*Uffz.* Hermann Brauer, P, and *Uffz.* Karl Hönig, G, are KIA over Zonnebeke during air combat.
10Sep17	*Uffz.* Carstens-1, *Uffz.* Meissner-1, Sopwith 1, 18.20, Paschendaele
17Dec17	*Uffz.* Schmidt-1, *Uffz.* Bäumler-1, Sopw. Camel, 15.25, NW Zonnebeke
26Dec17	*Vzfw.* Ludwig Rosenbeck, P, is injured when he walks into a propeller on the Rumbeke airfield, breaks his left arm and to hospital.
26Dec17	*Uffz.* Julius Scholler, G, is WIA,lt. during air combat, a bullet graze to the lower left leg, remains with the unit.
28Dec17	*Uffz.* Carstens-2, *Vzfw.* Schlör-1, Sopw. Camel, 13.30, NW Tenbrielen
28Jan18	*Uffz.* Schatt-1, *Gefr.* Hutter-1, Sopw. Camel, 16.40, Langemarck
29Jan18	*Vzfw.* Carstens-3, *Vzfw.* Schlör-2, Sopw. Camel, 16.27, Frezenberg
3Feb18	*Uffz.* Hans Friedrich Schmidt, P, is IIC,lt. on a practice flight, remains with the unit.
17Feb18	*Uffz.* Johann Schatt, P, is WIA,lt. during an air combat. He suffers a slight injury to his left hand, remains with the unit.
24Mar18	*Uffz.* Bergmann-1, *Vzfw.* Brüstle-1, Spad 1
24Mar18	*Vzfw.* Heinrich Carstens, P, and *Oblt.* Eduard Amann, O and C.O., are KIA over Guillemont in a Halberstadt during air combat.
24Mar18	*Vzfw.* Wilhelm Schlör, G, is KIA over Combles. His pilot, *Uffz.* Johann Schlenk makes a safe return.
25Mar18	*Vzfw.* Max Bäumler, G, is lightly IIC. A glass splinter from his goggles injuries his right eye. He remains with the unit until 28Mar18 when he is transported to hospital at Le Cateau due to infection.
27Mar18	*Schutzstaffel 28b* is renamed *Schlachtstaffel 28b* by KM Nr. 5126.18.A.7.L.IV.C. of 27Mar18.
6Apr18	*Vzfw.* Schmeer-1, *Uffz.* Scherber-1, Spad 1
6Apr18	*Uffz.* Müller-1, *Vzfw.* Brüstle-2, Sopwith 1, Amiens
6Apr18	*Uffz.* Karl Müller, P, is WIA,lt. in the above combat, shot in the upper left arm, and to hospital at Péronne.
7Apr18	*Uffz.* Hans Schmidt, P, is KIA and *Pion.* Albert Asam, G, is WIA and taken POW over Flandern. Shot down by ground fire.
11Apr18	*Oblt.* Oskar Baumann, O and C.O., is lightly IIC and to hospital. The aircraft steering controls are shot up during air combat causing the aircraft to somersault on landing, spraining his right wrist and causing a slight hand injury.
25Apr18	*Oblt.* Oskar Baumann, O and C.O., is lightly WIA in the upper left arm by ground fire and to hospital at Kortryk.
30Apr18	*Vzfw.* Speer, P, *Schlasta 10*, is taken POW and *Flg.* Anton Zimmermann, G, is WIA and taken POW at Dickebusch following air combat in a Halberstadt Cl.II. Zimmermann DOW 1May18 in N. Frankreich.
5May18	*Uffz.* Wilhelm Kiesel, M, is IIC,sv. in an aircraft crash, sustains internal injuries and to hospital at Kortryk.
27May18	*Gefr.* Emil Frey, G, is WIA,sv. over Fismes in air combat, shot in the buttock, and to hospital at Tagnon.
4Jun18	*Pion.* Heinrich Seidler, M, dies at Braisne.
20Jun18	*Gefr.* Hermann Wilke, M, dies at Eichsfeld.
28Jul18	*Uffz.* Georg Fink, P, is WIA, shot in the left thigh by ground fire, and to hospital at Glennes.
31Jul18	*Pion.* Johann Popp, M, is injured in an accident and to hospital at Chambry.
20Aug18	*Pion.* Joseph Fuchs, P, and *Gefr.* Emil Soetebier, G, are taken POW at Osly-Coushl. They give their unit as *Schlasta 57* to the French interrogators.
8Oct18	*Vzfw.* Ferdinand Gmach, M, dies at München.
29Nov18	*Schlachtstaffel 28b* is demobilized at the Kitzingen airfield of FEA 2b, Fürth.
24Nov19	*Ltn.d.R.* Max Schmeer, P and OzbV, dies at Güdingen.

The men of *Schutzstaffel 28b* at Snelleghem airfield in the *4.Armee* in late August 1917. The aircraft is a DFW C.V.

The men of *Schusta 28b.* Credit: UTD/HAC.

A group of *Schusta 28b* crewmen posing beside a DFW C.V (Av) marked 'Betty,' August 1917. Left to right: Unknown, *Uffz.* Ludwig Bergmann, *Vzfw.* Reiner Wirtz, *Gefr.* Theodor Kaleta and *Uffz.* Johann Schatt.

Royal Bavarian *Schutzstaffel 29*

Pilot/Gunner	Type	From		To	
		Unit	Date	Date	Unit
Vzfw. Sebastian Ahr	G	FEA 1b	1Mar17	29Apr17	WIA
Ltn.d.R. Sebastian Ahr	G	Hosp.	10May17	10Nov17	AFP 4
Gefr. Heinrich Auer	G	AFP 4	6Oct17	22Feb18	AFP 6
Gefr. Carl Bäsecke	G	FEA 1b	1Mar17	24Mar17	POW
Pion. Willy Bechert	P	FEA 1b	1Mar17	10Mar17	AFP A
Uffz. Eduard Binge	P	AFP 2	26Jan18	31Jan18	Ss 24b
Uffz. Herbert Boy	P	AFP 4	7Sep17	24Sep17	AFP 4
Uffz. Xaver Brandl	G	BS II	26Feb17	13Dec17	AFP 2
Uffz. Richard Degel	G	FEA 1b	1Mar17	19Apr17	IIC
Uffz. Richard Degel	G	Hosp.	20Apr17	1Jun17	FA 245A
Vzfw. Richard Degel	G	FA 245A	15Jun17	EOW	
Vzfw. Hans Drossel	G	AFP 4	20Nov17	14Jan18	FEA 2b
Oblt.d.R. Hans von Euler-Chelpin,CO	O	FBSch	14Dec17	12Jan18	FEA 1b
Uffz. August Fischer	P	AFP 4	19Jul17	24Dec17	JsSch I
Vzfw. August Fischer	P	JsSch I	31Dec17	EOW	
Uffz. Michael Fischer (+ 24Oct18)	P	FEA 1b	1Mar17	24Mar17	WIA,POW
Uffz. Anton Gänsler	G	AFP 4	23Nov17	15Dec17	Hosp.
Sgt. Anton Gänsler	G	Hosp.	10Jan18	EOW	
Oblt. Wilhelm Gebhardt, C.O.	O	FA 298A	12Jan18	23Aug18	WIA
Oblt. Wilhelm Gebhardt, C.O.	O	Hosp.	21Oct18	EOW	
Sgt. Hans Gömmel	G	AFP 17	13Mar18	EOW	
Vzfw. Friedrich Gütermann	P	FEA 1b	1Mar17	16Sep17	JsSch I
Vzfw. Friedrich Gütermann	P	JsSch I	23Sep17	16Feb18	Hosp.
Ltn.d.R. Friedrich Gütermann	P	Hosp.	24Feb18	13Jul18	Hosp.
Gefr. Friedrich Heitsch	G	FEA 12	26Sep17	6Oct17	AFP 4
Ltn.d.R. Walter Hill	P	FEA 1b	1Mar17	20Oct17	AFP 4
Gefr. Michael Höhne	G	AFP 4	8Nov17	6Dec17	KIC
Uffz. Ulrich Hopfengärtner	P	FA 294A	10Sep17	6Dec17	KIC

Uffz. Josef Huber	P	BS II	1Mar17	1Jun17	FA 245A
Vzfw. Josef Huber	P	FA 245A	15Jun17	1Apr18	AFP 17
Uffz. Otto Huber	G	AFP 17	2Feb18	6Mar18	FS Asch
Pion. Georg Janetzky	P	AFP 2	11Sep18	EOW	
Uffz. Otto Jung	G	FEA 1b	1Mar17	13Jun17	FA 245A
Uffz. Otto Jung	G	FA 245A	15Jun17	21Nov17	AFP 4
Uffz. Hermann Kappel	G	FEA 2b	30Aug18	5Nov18	FTL,IIC
Pion. Friedrich Keller	G	AFP 4	1May18	31Jul18	BG 8/26
Uffz. Bernhard Knorr	G	AFP 2	16Jan18	2Feb18	AFP 2
Uffz. Bernhard Knorr	G	AFP 17	15Mar18	3Apr18	AFP 17
Gefr. Emil Kraft	G	AFP 17	8Feb18	25Jun18	AFP 6
Pion. Adalbert Krieger	G	AFP 18	17Jun18	EOW	
Gefr. Wilhelm Krieger	P	AFP 17	19Mar18	EOW	
Gefr. Heinrich Lechleiter	G	AFP 4	10Sep17	16Feb18	WIA,POW
Gefr. Heinrich Lechleiter	G			17Feb18	DOW
Gefr. Peter Martin	G	AFP 6	1May18	30May18	AFP 4
Pion. Friedrich Wilhelm Mayr	P	Ss 24b	20Oct17	22Feb18	AFP 6
Uffz. Eugen Moser	P	AFP 17	1Mar18	EOW	
Uffz. Otto Müller	G	Ss 28b	16Aug17	1Apr18	AFP 17
Vzfw. Georg Neumaier	P	AFP 17	22Feb18	5Nov18	FTL,IIC
Ltn.d.R. Franz Ortner, OzbV	O	FA 291A	9Jun18	EOW	
Uffz. Karl Pinnow	P	AFP 3	13Jul18	5Nov18	IIC,sv.
Flg. Adolf Richter	G	AFP 4	22Sep17	6Oct17	Ss 17
Oblt. Josef Rittmann	O	FkGp 10	17Jul17	30Jul17	Ss 25b
Sgt. Albert Römer	G	AFP 17	17Mar18	EOW	
Uffz. Thomas Schaller	G	BS II	27Feb17	6Sep17	WIA,sv.
Uffz. Thomas Schaller	G	AFP 4	19Oct17	23Feb18	AFP 4
Uffz. Andreas Schnitzler (+13May18)	G	AFP 2	30Jan18	24Mar18	WIA,sv.
Offz.Stv. Leopold Schönberger	P	AFP 18	14Jun18	29Jun18	AFP 18
Gefr. Erwin Schwarz	G	AFP 17	28Mar18	16May18	FEA 2b
Gefr. Jakob Stiegel	P	AFP 17	24Feb18	13Jun18	AFP 18
Uffz. Bernhard Ultsch	P	FEA 1b	1Mar17	1Jun17	FA 245A
Uffz. Bernhard Ultsch	P	FA 245A	15Jun17	6Sep17	AFP 4
Oblt. Cornelius Vogeley, C.O.	O	FEA 1b	1Mar17	15Dec17	FA 296A
Uffz. Friedrich Wassermann	P	AFP A	26Mar17	17Jul17	AFP 4
Pion. Georg Weigert	G	AFP 4	6Oct17	22Nov17	AFP 4
Vzfw. Josef Wenz	G	FEA 1b	1Mar17	17Jun18	AFP 18
Uffz. Bruno Wichert	P	AFP 2	10Dec17	15Jan18	JsSch I
Uffz. Bruno Wichert	P	JsSch I	21Jan18	6Feb18	AFP 6
Ltn.d.R. Siegfried Wittkowsky	P	AFP 17	1Mar18	EOW	
Uffz. Josef Zahn	P	FEA 1b	1Mar17	22Feb18	Hosp.
Vzfw. Lorenz Zeuch (DOW 17Feb18)	P	AFP 4	1Oct17	16Feb18	WIA,POW
Ritt. Jürgen *Frhr.* von Zobel zu Griebelstadt, OzbV	O		(Mar18)	9Apr18	SGp B

Royal Bavarian *Schutzstaffel 29*

Mechanics and Ground Personnel

Name	From		To	
	Unit	Date	Date	Unit
Pion. Jakob Albrecht	FEA 2b	4Oct18	EOW	
Pion. Johann Ardner	FEA 1b	1Mar17	1Oct17	FEA 1b
Pion. Johann Bachmann	AFP 4	8Jun18	20Jul18	Hosp.
Pion. Ludwig Bäsel	FEA 2b	15Jul18	EOW	
Uffz. Alois Bagh	FEA 1b	1Mar17	8Jul17	Hosp.
Pion. Ludwig Baldauss	FEA 1b	1Mar17	1Jun17	FA 245A
Pion. Ludwig Baldauss	FA 245A	15Jun17	30Jun17	AFP 4
Pion. Ludwig Baldauss	AFP 4	30Jul17	1Oct17	FEA 1b
Uffz. Johann Bals	FEA 1b	1Mar17	EOW	
Pion. Oscar Bauer	FEA 1b	1Mar17	19Jul17	AFP 4
Pion. Ludwig Baumann	FEA 1b	24Nov17	EOW	

Gefr. Ludwig Becker	FEA 1b	1Mar17	3Sep17	Hosp.
Uffz. Ludwig Becker	Hosp.	15Dec17	EOW	
Pion. Carl Bock	FEA 1b	1Mar17	15Jul18	Infntry
Pion. Josef Böck	FEA 1b	12Aug17	2Jun18	Hosp.
Pion. Josef Böck	Hosp.	10Jun18	EOW	
Pion. Ludwig Bögler	AFP 1	17May17	17Jun18	Infntry
Kraftf. Michael Börmann	AKP 3	13Jul18	9Aug18	AKP 6
Pion. Karl Bottner	FEA 2b	27Aug18	EOW	
Gefr. Josef Brand	FEA 1b	1Mar17	EOW	
Pion. Eduard Brandl	FEA 2b	22Jul18	EOW	
Gefr. Friedrich Braun		16Oct18	EOW	
Uffz. Friedrich Breindl	FEA 1b	1Mar17	12May18	Hosp.
Pion. Ludwig Breitsameter	FEA 1b	15May17	9Jun17	FEA 1b
Pion. Alois Brinz	FEA 2b	4Jan18	EOW	
Gefr. Johann Brückert	FA 296A	17Dec17	EOW	
Pion. Georg Brückner	FEA 1b	1Mar17	23Mar17	AFP A
Gefr. Sylvester Bühler	FEA 1b	1Mar17	14Dec17	FA 296A
Pion. Bernhard Bunk	FA 290A	21Jul17	30Jul17	Ss 25b
Pion. Michael Brunner	FEA 2b	26Aug18	9Sep18	Hosp.
Pion. Georg Demas	FEA 2b	8Aug18	9Sep18	Hosp.
Pion. Georh Demas	Hosp.	18Sep18	EOW	
Pion. Friedrich Denk	Grfl 19	6Apr18	7May18	Grfl 19
Gefr. Josef Diepold	FEA 1b	1Mar17	3Nov17	FEA 1b
Gefr. Hans Dimpfl	FEA 2b	26Aug18	EOW	
Pion. Wilhelm Divivier	FEA 1b	19Jul17	EOW	
Gefr. Heinrich Drechsler	FEA 1b	1Mar17	19Jul17	AMT 56
Pion. Jacob Eisenschenk	FEA 1b	1Mar17	11Apr17	Hosp.
Pion. Jacob Eisenschenk	Hosp.	11Jun17	17May18	Hosp.
Gefr. Jacob Eisenschenk	Hosp.	17Jun18	EOW	
Pion. Eduard Eisenmann	FEA 1b	1Mar17	18Mar17	FEA 1b
Pion. Erwin Erich	FEA 1b	25Oct17	30May18	AFP 4
Uffz. Johann Ender	KEA 1	3Oct17	EOW	
Pion. Georg Faatz	FEA 2b	2Sep18	EOW	
Pion. Leonhardt Fessler	FEA 1b	1Mar17	22Aug17	AFP 4
Pion. Gregor Fick	FEA 2b	13May18	4Jul18	Hosp.
Gefr. Ludwig Forster	FEA 1b	1Mar17	EOW	
San.Soldt. Karl Freund	FA 289A	15Jan18	24Jul18	Hosp.
San.Gefr. Karl Freund	Hosp.	27Sep18	EOW	
Pion. Christian Freyermuth	FEA 1b	1Mar17	8Apr17	FEA 1b
Gefr. Wolfgang Fröhlich	FEA 1b	1Mar17	EOW	
Pion. Heinrich Fruth	AFP 4	28Jun17	12Aug18	Hosp.
Pion. Heinrich Fruth	Hosp.	24Sep18	EOW	
Pion. Otto Fuchs	FEA 2b	23Sep18	EOW	
Gefr. Ludwig Gall	AFP 2	8Sep18	EOW	
Pion. Ernst Gardow	FEA 1b	14Jan18	EOW	
Pion. Alois Gessl	FEA 1b	1Mar17	23Mar17	AFP A
Kraftf. Richard Gluth	KFA 2	9Sep18	15Sep18	KFA 2
Pion. Erich Gropp	KFA 3	20Jul18	8Sep18	Heimat
Gefr. Andreas Gruber	FEA 1b	1Mar17	10Aug18	FEA 2b
Gefr. Heinrich Haber	KAbt. 2	16Sep18	EOW	
Uffz. Johann Hammhammer	FEA 1b	1Mar17	13Aug17	AFP 4
Pion. Leonhard Haumann	FEA 2b	13May18	30May18	AFP 4
Pion. Gebhardt Hämmerle	FEA 1b	1Mar17	1Mar17	AFP A
Pion. Gebhardt Hämmerle	AFP A	30Jun17	13Aug17	AFP 4
Uffz. Johann Heider	FEA 1b	1Mar17	25Sep17	FEA 1b
Uffz. Friedrich Heil	FEA 1b	1Mar17	EOW	
Pion. Georg Heinimann	FS III	31Jul18	EOW	
Pion. Johann Henn	FEA 1b	1Mar17	15Aug17	Hosp.
Gefr. Max Hertel	FEA 1b	1Mar17	17Jun17	Hosp.
Uffz. Max Hertel	Hosp.	12Jul17	EOW	
Pion. Hermann Hess	FEA 1b	12Aug17	15Sep17	Wrk Abt
Pion. Hermann Hess	Wrk Abt	8Mar18	EOW	
Pion. Heinrich Hill	FEA 2b	4Jan18	3Jul18	Hosp.
Gefr. Heinrich Höhn	FEA 1b	1Mar17	1May18	Inj.
Pion. Gaudenz Hörmann	FEA 1b	24May17	19Jul17	AFP 4

Gefr. Ernst Hoffmann	FEA 1b	1Mar17	14Sep17	Hosp.
Krftrdf. Heinrich Hoge	KRA 51	21Jun18	13Jul18	KRA 51
Pion. Anton Holleber	FEA 1b	1Mar17	4Jun17	FEA 1b
Gefr. Georg Hopf	AKP 3	5Aug18	EOW	
Pion. Max Hüttner	FEA 2b	18Jul18	EOW	
Pion. Georg Hufnagel I	FEA 1b	1Mar17	23Mar17	AFP A
Pion. Georg Hufnagel I	AFP A	1Jul17	18Jul17	FEA 1b
Pion. Georg Hufnagel II	FEA 1b	1May17	23Jun17	FEA 1b
Pion. Franz Iglhaut	FEA 1b	1Mar17	13Apr17	FEA 1b
Pion. Fritz Joos	FEA 1b	13May17	19Jul17	AFP 4
Pion. Michael Kärtner	FEA 2b	13May18	EOW	
Pion. Alfred Kaiser	FEA 2b	9Oct18	EOW	
Pion. Bartholomäus Kaiser	FEA 2b	4Jan18	17Jun18	Infntry
Uffz. August Kauper	FEA 1b	1Mar17	2Feb18	Hosp.
Sgt. August Kauper	Hosp.	14Feb18	9Jun18	FEA 1b
Sgt. August Kauper	FEA 1b	24Jun18	EOW	
Sgt. Alois Kauschinger	FEA 2b	26Aug18	EOW	
Pion. Georg Kett	FEA 1b	1May17	21Jun17	Hosp.
Pion. Richard Klein	FEA 1b	1Mar17	27Apr17	FEA 1b
Pion. Hermann Klose	FEA 2b	26Aug18	14Sep18	Hosp.
Pion. Anton Knäbl	FEA 1b	19Jul17	EOW	
Pion. Johann Knapp	FEA 2b	22Jul18	EOW	
Gefr. Josef Kubala	FA 293A	17Jan18	EOW	
Uffz. Josef Köberle	FEA 1b	1Mar17	13May17	AFP 1
Pion. Ludwig König	FEA 1b	1Mar17	23Mar17	AFP A
Pion. Ludwig König	AFP A	30Jun17	8Jul17	FEA 1b
Pion. Peter Kolb	FEA 1b	23Sep18	22Oct18	AFP 5
Pion. Rudolf Kraus	FEA 2b	27Aug18	22Oct18	AFP 5
Pion. Wilhelm Kuhlmann	Kofl 4	22May18	30May18	AFP 4
Pion. Rudolf Kuther	FEA 2b	4Oct18	EOW	
Uffz. Otto Lallinger	FEA 1b	1Mar17	EOW	
Pion. Johann Lang	FEA 1b	19Jul17	EOW	
Pion. Julius Lang	FEA 2b	4Jan18	EOW	
Gefr. Ernst Lehmann	AFP 2	27Aug18	15Sep18	Ss 13
Gefr. Martin Leisentritt	AFP 4	28Jun17	18Jul17	AFP 4
Werkmstr.Stv. Eugen Leonhardt	FEA 1b	1Mar17	EOW	
Pion. Wilhelm Liebel	FEA 1b	21Sep17	3Nov17	FEA 1b
Pion. Georg Lingl	FEA 2b	4Jan18	21Feb18	Hosp.
Pion. Georg Lingl	Hosp.	9Mar18	22Jun18	FEA 2b
Pion. Josef Lobmeier	FEA 1b	31Jul17	7Aug17	Ss 27b
Uffz. Heinrich Mayer	FEA 1b	1Mar17	EOW	
Pion. Otto Mayerhofer	AKP 6	12Sep18	EOW	
Pion. Siegfried Meindl	FEA 1b	1Mar17	8Feb18	Hosp.
Uffz. Hans Müller	FEA 1b	1Mar17	30Jun18	Hosp.
Uffz. Hans Müller	Hosp.	20Jul18	22Jul18	FEA 2b
Uffz. Hans Müller II	FEA 1b	1Mar17	EOW	
Pion. Georg Müller	FEA 2b	13May18	30May18	AFP 4
Gefr. Karl Müller	FEA 2b	13May18	EOW	
Feldw. Martin Müller	FEA 1b	1Mar17	22Jun18	Hosp.
Gefr. Karl Neidig	AKP 51	18Jun18	22Sep18	AWOL
Pion. Michael Neubauer	FEA 1b	21Sep17	EOW	
Pion. Josef Neumaier	FEA 1b	1Mar17	12Apr17	FEA 1b
Pion. Ludwig Nürnberger	FEA 1b	1Mar17	5May17	FEA 1b
Uffz. Carl Oswald	FEA 1b	1Mar17	14Dec17	FA 296A
Gefr. Ludwig Overbeck	FEA 1b	1Mar17	EOW	
Gefr. Alfred Paech	FEA 1b	1Mar17	30May18	AFP 4
Uffz. Alois Piemml	FEA 2b	2Jul18	20Oct18	FEA 2b
Pion. Nikolaus Plebst	FEA 2b	16Sep18	EOW	
Pion. Erhard Pöllmann	FEA 1b	2Nov17	17Jun18	Infntry
Pion. Franz Preis	FEA 1b	1Mar17	23Mar17	AFP A
Pion. Georg Rabus	FEA 1b	1May17	10Jun17	Inj.
Pion. Georg Rabus	Hosp.	9Jul17	2Aug17	FEA 1b
Pion. Johann Radlmann	FEA 1b	1Mar17	14Jul17	Hosp.
Pion. Anton Rank	FEA 2b	13May18	30May18	AFP 4
San.Uffz. Alexander Rauber	FEA 1b	1Mar17	17Dec17	Hosp.

Uffz. Kilian Rauch	FEA 1b	1Mar17	5Sep18	Hosp.
Pion. Johann Reichenberger	FEA 1b	14Jan18	3Oct18	FEA 2b
Pion. Franz Reindl	FEA 1b	15Jan18	EOW	
Pion. Hans Reingruber	FEA 1b	15Jan18	EOW	
Uffz. Josef Reisacher	FEA 1b	1Mar17	EOW	
Pion. Jean Reiss		16Oct18	EOW	
Pion. Josef Reithmeier	FEA 1b	1Mar17	EOW	
Uffz. Leo Resch	FEA 1b	1Mar17	EOW	
Pion. Friedrich Richter	FEA 1b	1Mar17	23Mar17	AFP A
Pion. Andreas Rieder	AFP 1	17Jun17	15Jul18	Infntry
Pion. Jakob Ruth	FEA 1b	2Nov17	23Dec17	Inj.
Uffz. Carl Schaaf	FEA 1b	1Mar17	4Aug17	FEA 1b
Pion. Fritz Schäfer	FEA 1b	12Aug17	3Nov17	FEA 1b
Pion. Sigmund Schäfer	FEA 1b	27Jun17	EOW	
Pion. Roman Schedel	FEA 2b	27Jul18	EOW	
Gefr. August Schiedlofsky	FEA 2b	13May18	11Oct18	Hosp.
Pion. Friedrich Schilk	FEA 1b	2Nov17	2Oct18	FEA 2b
Pion. Hans Schiller	FEA 2b	31Jul18	22Oct18	AFP 5
Pion. Carl Schmid	FEA 1b	12Aug17	26May18	Inj.
Uffz. Alois Schmidt	FEA 1b	1Mar17	17Nov17	Hosp.
Uffz. Ludwig Schmidt	FEA 1b	1Mar17	24Jun18	Hosp.
Pion. Carl Schmolke	FEA 1b	1Mar17	29Jun18	FEA 2b
Uffz. Johann Schneider	FEA 1b	1Mar17	7May18	Hosp.
Uffz. Johann Schneider	Hosp.	26May18	9Jun18	Hosp.
Gefr. Josef Schneider	FEA 1b	1Mar17	EOW	
Uffz. Friedrich Scholler	FEA 1b	1Mar17	17Jan18	FA 293A
Gefr. Josef Schratt	FA 298A	24Jan18	EOW	
Pion. Walter Schröter	FEA 1b	1Mar17	19Feb18	Hosp.
Pion. Walter Schröter	Hosp.	26Feb18	EOW	
Pion. Max Seidel	FEA 2b	26Aug18	EOW	
Pion. Karl Setzwein	FEA 1b	14Jan18	20Apr18	Inj.
Pion. Karl Setzwein	Hosp.	10Jun18	EOW	
Pion. Otto Seufert	FEA 1b	1Mar17	23Mar17	AFP A
Pion. Otto Seufert	AFP A	30Jun17	13Aug17	AFP 4
Gefr. Johannes Seybold	FEA 1b	1Mar17	14Nov17	FEA 1b
Pion. Andreas Siebenlist	FEA 2b	13May18	29May18	FEA 2b
Vzfw. Georg Speigl	FEA 2b	9Oct18	EOW	
Sgt. Johann Spiegel	AFP 4	13May18	22Jun18	Hosp.
Pion. Josef Stangl	FEA 1b	1Mar17	7Aug17	Hosp.
Pion. Alfred Stein	FEA 2b	19Jul18	EOW	
Gefr. Heinrich Stephan	BS II	11Jun17	13Aug17	FEA 1b
Gefr. Heinrich Stephan	FEA 1b	23Aug17	25Sep17	FEA 1b
Uffz. Sebastian Stiglauer	FEA 1b	1Mar17	17Jun18	Infntry
Pion. Adam Streit	FEA 2b	13May18	EOW	
Pion. Jacob Strixner	FEA 1b	1Mar17	4Jul18	Hosp.
Pion. Anton Sulzer	FEA 1b	1May17	23Jun17	AFP 4
Pion. Anton Sulzer	AFP 4	30Jun17	3Aug17	Hosp.
Pion. Albin Thomas	FEA 1b	1Mar17	23Mar17	AFP A
Pion. Albin Thomas	AFP A	2Jul17	13Aug17	AFP 4
Feldw. Alois Tremmel	FEA 2b	3Jul18	EOW	
Pion. Gustav Trumpf	FEA 1b	8Oct18	EOW	
Gefr. Wilhelm Vielberth	FEA 1b	1Mar17	EOW	
Pion. Anton Wagner	FEA 2b	23Sep18	EOW	
Pion. Bernhard Wagner	FEA 1b	1Mar17	5Oct17	Hosp.
Gefr. Bernhard Wagner	Hosp.	20Oct17	EOW	
Pion. Ludwig Wagner	FEA 2b	2Sep18	EOW	
Pion. Ludwig Wald	FEA 1b	1Mar17	EOW	
Pion. Franz Waldherr	FEA 1b	1Mar17	23Mar17	AFP A
Vzfw. Georg Waldherr	FEA 1b	1Mar17	EOW	
Unterzahlmstr. Josef Waninger	FEA 2b	28Oct18	EOW	
Sgt. Albert Weber	AFP 1	30Apr17	1Jun17	FA 245A
Sgt. Albert Weber	FA 245A	10Jun17	11Jun17	AFP 1
Pion. Josef Wecker	AFP 2	8Sep18	EOW	
Pion. Alfred Wehner	FEA 1b	15Aug17	22Jan18	Hosp.
Pion. Alfred Wehner	Hosp.	6Mar18		

Pion. Johann Weidling	FEA 1b	1Mar17	14Jul17	Hosp.
Pion. Karl Weidauer	AFP 6	12Aug18	25Aug18	WIA,sv.
Pion. Franz Weinschütz	FEA 1b	2Nov17	EOW	
Gefr. Georg Weissenmayer	FEA 1b	1Mar17	23Mar17	AFP A
Pion. Jacob Weltmaier	FEA 1b	1Mar17	EOW	
Pion. Hermann Wilquet	FEA 1b	23Sep18	22Oct18	AFP 5
Pion. Friedrich Winkelmann	FEA 1b	9May17	EOW	
Pion. Arthur Wulf	AFP 3	13Jul18	EOW	
Uffz. Johann Zieghaus	FEA 1b	1Mar17	15Jul17	FEA 1b
Pion. Karl Zimmermann	FEA 1b	13Jan18	16Jul18	Hosp.
Pion. Max Zimmermann	FEA 1b	15Aug17	EOW	
Pion. Jakob Zink	FEA 2b	13May18	2Jul18	Hosp.

Schutzstaffel/Schlachtstaffel 29b
Mitgemachte Schlachten und Gefechte
(Battles and combat actions in which Ss 29b participated)

10Mar17	14Apr17	*Stellungskämpfe in Lothringen* (Trench fighting in Lorraine)
15Apr17	16Jun17	*Doppelschlacht Aisne-Champagne* (The double battle Aisne-Champagne)
17Jun17	30Nov17	*Schlacht in Flandern* (Battle in Flanders)
1Dec17	31Jan18	*Kämpfe bei Cambrai* (Fighting at Cambrai)
1Feb18	20Mar18	*Stellungskämpfe im Artois and Aufmarsch zur Grossen Schlacht in Frankreich* (Trench fighting in Artois and assembly for the Great Battle in France)
21Mar18	1Apr18	*Grosse Schlacht in Frankreich* (Great Battle in France)
21Mar18	23Mar18	*Druchbruchsschlacht Monchy-Cambrai* (Penetration battle Monchy-Cambrai)
24Mar18	25Mar18	*Schlacht bei Bapaume* (Battle at Bapaume)
1Apr18	8Apr18	*Stellungskämpfe in französisch Flandern und in Artois* (Trench fighting in French Flanders and in Artois)
9Apr18	18Apr18	*Schlacht bei Armentières* (Battle at Armentières)
19Apr18	23Apr18	*Stellungskämpfe in französisch Flandern und in Artois* (Trench fighting in French Flanders and in Artois)
24Apr18	3Jun18	*Schlacht bei Ypern* (Battle at Ypres)
4Jun18	9Jun18	*Kämpfe an der Avre, bei Montdidier und Noyon* (Fighting on the Avre, at Montdidier and Noyon)
9Jun18	13Jun18	*Schlacht bei Noyon* (Battle at Noyon)
14Jun18	9Jul18	*Kämpfe an der Avre und an der Matz* (Fighting on the Avre and on the Matz)
10Jul18	14Jul18	*Stellungskämpfe von der Champagne* (Trench fighting of the Champagne)
15Jul18	17Jul18	*Angriffsschlacht an der Marne und in der Champagne* (Offensive battle on the Marne and in the Champagne)
18Jul18	7Aug18	*Stellungskämpfe in der Champagne und in den Argonnen* (Trench fighting in the Champagne and in the Argonne)
8Aug18	11Aug18	*Stellungskämpfe in Flandern und in Artois* (Trench fighting in Flanders and in Artrois)
12Aug18	20Aug18	*Abwehrschlacht zwischen Scarpe und Somme* (Defensive battle between the Scarpe and the Somme)
21Aug18	2Sep18	*Schlacht Albert-Peronne* (Battle of Albert and Peronne)
3Sep18	26Sep18	*Kämpfe vor der Siegfriedfront* (Battle in front of the Siegfried Front)
26Sep18	11Nov18	*Abwehrschlacht in der Champagne und an der Maas* (Defensive battle in the Champagne and on the Maas)

Schutzstaffel/Schlachtstaffel 29b Airfields

From	To	Location	*Schlachtgruppe* Affiliation	*Armee*
10Mar17	14Apr17	Mörchingen		AAA
15Apr17	16Jun17	Seraincourt by Rethel	For FA 248(A)	1
17Jun17	27Aug17	Ghistel	Escort for FA 293(A)b	4
27Aug17	Sep17	Varsenaere	Escort for FA 269(A)	4
Sep17	22Nov17	Stalhille	Escort for FA 293(A)b	4
22Nov17	30Nov17	Masny Süd	Escort for FA 293(A)b	6
1Dec17	31Jan18	Caudry	Escort for FA 296(A)b	2
1Feb18	20Mar18	Masny Süd	Escort for FA 293(A)b	17
21Mar18	8Apr18	Masny Süd	SGp B (Ss 14,19,24b,25b,29b) C.O. *Oblt.* Hermann Ramdohr	17
9Apr18	18Apr18	Tourmignies	SGp B (Ss 16,29b) C.O. *Ritt.* Jürgen *Frhr.* von Zobel	6
19Apr18	24Apr18	Golancourt		18
24Apr18	17May18	Ingelmunster	SGp C (Ss 3,13,19,29b) C.O. *Hptm.* Wilhelm Aschenborn	4
17May18	3Jun18	Ingelmunster	SGp 2 (Ss 3,13,19,29b) C.O. *Hptm.* Wilhelm Aschenborn	4
4Jun18	9Jul18	Bonneuil-Ferme	SGp 3 (Ss 3,13,19,29b) C.O. *Oblt.* Helmut Bühling	18
10Jul18	29Jul18	Mont Notre Dame	SGp B (Ss 3,13,19,29b) C.O. *Oblt.* Helmut Bühling	7
29Jul18	9Aug18	Liéramont	SGp 2 (Ss 3,13,19,29b) C.O. *Oblt.* Helmut Bühling	6
9Aug18	10Aug18	Nurlu	SGp 2 (Ss 3,13,19,29b)	2
10Aug18	20Aug18	Liéramont		6
21Aug18	26Sep18	St. Aubert	SGp 2 (Ss 3,13,19,29b) C.O. *Oblt.d.R.* Jaspers	2
26Sep18	6Oct18	Preutin	SGp 2 (Ss 3,13,19,29b) C.O. *Oblt.* Helmut Bühling	5
6Oct18	21Oct18	Preutin	SGp 2 (Ss 3,13,19,26b,29b) C.O. *Oblt.* Helmut Bühling	5
1Nov18	EOW	Stenay	SGp 2 (Ss 3,13,19,26b,29b) C.O. *Oblt.* Helmut Bühling	5

Royal Bavarian *Schutzstaffel 29b*

22Feb17	*Schutzstaffel 29b* is created at FEA 1b by BKM Nr. 21943.A. of 15Mar17.
1Mar17	*Schutzstaffel 29b* is mobilized at FEA 1b, Schleissheim.
24Mar17	*Uffz.* Michael Fischer, P, is WIA,sv. and taken POW along with *Gefr.* Carl Bäsecke, G, at Mörching. Fischer DOW on 24Oct18 as a POW in French Hospital 41 at Avignon.
19Apr17	*Uffz.* Richard Degel, G, is IIC during landing, dislocates his tibia and to hospital at Rethel.
29Apr17	*Vzfw.* Sebastian Ahr, G, is WIA, shot in the left thigh during air combat and to hospital at Sevigny.
1Jun17	*Vzfw.* Hill-1, Vzfw. *Ahr*-1, Spad, W. La Neuvillette
10Jun17	*Pion.* Georg Rabus, M, is struck by a propeller in the right forearm and to hospital.
24Jul17	*Uffz.* Ultsch-1, *Uffz.* Wenz-1, Sopwith, 7.40, by Nieuport R.E. 8 #A.4197, 6 Sqn. RFC, Lt. O.L. Burt,KIA & Lt. M.W. Briscoe,KIA
29Jul17	*Uffz.* Huber-1, *Uffz.* Degel-1, Sopwith, 6.40, Lombartzyde
29Jul17	*Uffz.* Ultsch-2, *Uffz.* Wenz-2, B.E. 2, 21.00, Nieuport
15Aug17	*Uffz.* Zahn-1, *Uffz.* Jung-1, Sopwith 1, Oostdynkerke
4Sep17	*Uffz.* Ultsch-3, *Uffz.* Wenz-3, Sopwith 1, 12.15, Nieuport Hanriot #8, Belm. Esc. 1ère, Lt. J. Olieslagers, FTL
6Sep17	*Uffz.* Thomas Schaller, G, is WIA,sv. during air combat, hit in the right hand and left shoulder, and to hospital at Marine Feldlaz. 3.
17Nov17	*Uffz.* Alois Schmidt, M, is struck by a propeller, fractures his left femur and left hand and to hospital at Marine Feldlaz. 3.
6Dec17	*Uffz.* Ulrich Hopfengärtner, P, and *Gefr.* Michael Höhne, G, are KIC at Rumaucourt.
23Dec17	*Pion.* Jakob Ruth, M, is accidently shot in the right forearm and to hospital.
16Feb18	*Vzfw.* Lorenz Zeuch, P, and *Gefr.* Heinrich Lechleiter, G, are WIA W. Quéant in a DFW C.V (LVG), shot down in flames at 11.25 hours during an air combat and taken POW. Both men died the next day at Cagnicourt according to a British report.
26Feb18	*Vzfw.* Neumaier-1, *Uffz.* Müller-1, D.H. 5, Chérisy

24Mar18	*Gefr.* Andreas Schnitzler, G, is severely WIA, shot in the left groin at 13.15 hours during an air combat over St. Leger. He DOW on 13May18 at Montigy as an *Uffz.*
27Mar18	*Schutzstaffel 29b* is renamed *Schlachtstaffel 29b* by KM Nr. 5126.18.A.7.L.IV.C. of 27Mar18.
20Apr18	*Pion.* Karl Setzwein, M, is struck by a propeller, injures his arm and thigh and to hospital.
1May18	*Gefr.* Heinrich Höhn, M, is injured and to hospital.
26May18	*Pion.* Carl Schmid, M, is injured when a flare pistol explodes in his right hand and to hospital at Lille.
23Aug18	*Oblt.* Wilhelm Gebhardt, O and C.O, is WIA over Liéramont and to hospital.
25Aug18	*Pion.* Karl Weidauer, M, is WIA,sv. during aerial bombing of Cambrai, struck in the head at 01.45 hours, and to hospital.
6Sep18	*Vzfw.* Neumaier-2, *Uffz.* Kappel-1, Sopwith Camel, 10.33, S. Brie
21Sep18	*Vzfw.* Neumaier-3, *Uffz.* Kappel-2, D.H. 4, 9.45, NW Epehy
7Oct18	*Uffz.* Moser-1, *Pion.* Krieger-1
5Nov18	*Uffz.* Karl Pinnow, P, is IIC at Preutin by Landres. He is shot down in aerial combat and crash lands from 900 meters altitude. He suffers contusions of the liver and lung and to hospital.
5Nov18	*Vzfw.* Georg Neumaier, P, and *Uffz.* Hermann Kappel, G, are driven down during aerial combat and are forced to land by Sivry (Verdun). Neumaier is IIC sustaining internal injuries and to hospital.
19Nov18	*Schlachtstaffel 29b* is demobilized at FEA 2b, Fürth.

Royal Bavarian *Schutzstaffel 30*

Pilot/Gunner	Type	From		To	
		Unit	Date	Date	Unit
Uffz. Jacob Alkofer	P	AFP 6	16Jun17	24Jul17	FA 292A
Gefr. Artur Arnold	P	AFP 2	16Mar18	17Apr18	AFP 4
Ltn.d.R. Leopold Ballin	G	(Demob. Offizier)		EOW	
Vzfw. Rudolf Besel	P	FEA 1b	17Mar17	27Mar18	AFP 2
Vzfw. Johann Birmolin	G	AFP 2	16Mar18	17Apr18	AFP 2
Ritt.d.R. Julius Bossert, C.O.	O	Ss 35	17Jul18	EOW	
Uffz. Georg Brix	P	Ss 28b	11Sep17	6Jan18	AFP 4
Vzfw. Otto Bruns	G	AFP 7	2Aug18	20Aug18	KIA
Uffz. August Brunthaler	G	AFP 4	5Dec17	1Jan18	WIA,DOW
Pion. Alois Debernitz	P	AFP 7	14Jun18	29Jun18	AFP 7
Uffz. Adam Deutsch	P	AFP 9	29Aug18	EOW	
Vzfw. Eugen Dietz	P	AFP 4	14Dec17	EOW	
Sgt. Anton Dirr	G	AFP 9	7Sep18	EOW	
Offz.Stv. Georg Dörfler	P	AFP 1	14Jul18	20Aug18	KIA
Vzfw. Walter Drechsler	P	FA 45b	25Jan18	10Jul18	Hosp.
Vzfw. Walter Drechsler	P	Hosp.	13Jul18	EOW	
Sgt. Heinrich Dung	G	AFP 4	2Jan18	4Jan18	Ss 13
Vzfw. Michael Duschner	G	BS II	15Mar17	23Jan18	FEA 1b
Uffz. Michael Eberth	G	AFP 4	28Aug17	24Jan18	IIC,lt.
Vzfw. Michael Eberth	G	Hosp.	25Jan18	EOW	
Gefr. Friedrich Ehmann	P	AFP 4	18Jun17	23Jun17	IIC
Uffz. Friedrich Ehmann	P	Hosp.	7Jul17	13Sep17	AFP 4
Uffz. Heinrich Eissner	P	AFP 4	13Sep17	15Sep17	Ss 28b
Gefr. Georg Endres	G	AFP 9	1Oct18	EOW	
Vzfw. Bernhard Ennenga	P	AFP 9	24Aug18	26Aug18	Ss 23b
Uffz. Arthur Erndl	P	AFP 4	20Sep17	2Jan18	AFP 4
Oblt.d.R. August Ertl, C.O.	P	AFP C	23Feb18	3Mar18	Leave
Oblt.d.R. August Ertl, C.O.	P	Leave	13Mar18	19Jul18	FEA 1b
Ltn.d.R. Eusterbrock, stv. C.O.	O	FA 221A	3Mar18	7Mar18	FA 221A
Ltn.d.R. Eusterbrock, stv. C.O.	O	FA 221A	10Mar18	13Mar18	FA 221A
Uffz. Bruno Felten	G	AFP 2	3Apr18	EOW	
Pion. Adam Föller	G	AFP 6	1Apr17	1May17	KIA
Pion. Josef Frank	G	AFP 2	3Apr18	7May18	KIC
Uffz. Georg Graue	G	AFP 7	26May18	9Sep18	AFP 18
Gefr. Heinrich Graebner	G	AFP 4	29Apr18	28May18	POW
Vzfw. Andreas Graf	P	AFP 4	9Sep17	27Mar18	AFP 2
Gefr. Johann Graf	P	AFP 9	30Aug18	EOW	
Uffz. Georg Graue	G	AFP 7	26May18	9Sep18	AFP 18
Uffz. Josef Griebl	P	AFP 4	9May18	28May18	KIA
Pion. Alois Gruber	G	AFP 2	1Apr18	3Apr18	AFP 2

Uffz. Anton Haberl	G	Ss 37	2Aug18	6Aug18	AFP 9
Uffz. Johann Hanauer	P	AFP 4	15Jan18	23Mar18	IIC,lt.
Uffz. Johann Hanauer	P		23Mar18	7May18	KIC
Uffz. Thomas Hartig	P	AFP 4	14Dec17	23Dec17	KIA
Uffz. Josef Hefele	G	AFP 4	12Nov17	22Mar18	WIA,lt.
Uffz. Josef Hefele	G		22Mar18	EOW	
Flg. Max Heilmeier	G	AFP 4	21Sep17	31Oct17	WIA,lt.
Vzfw. Max Heilmeier	G		31Oct17	EOW	
Uffz. Hans Herrmann	P	AFP 2	24Mar18	17Apr18	AFP 2
Uffz. Johann Herrmann	G	FEA 1b	15Mar17	13Jul17	WIA
Ltn.d.R. Wolfgang Hohenadl	P	AFP 4	3Jul17	21Sep17	FA 294A
Uffz. Severin Hornung	G	FEA 1b	15Mar17	17Jun17	KIA
Uffz. Georg Imgrund	P	AFP 4	19Sep17	12Nov17	KIC
Uffz. Wendolin Immler	P	FS IV	27Mar17	2Oct17	Hosp.
Sgt. Valentin Jackl (+ 3Aug18 POW)	P	AFP 2	11Apr18	31Jul18	WIA,POW
Uffz. Justus Kaiser	P	FEA 1b	15Mar17	19Sep17	AFP 4
Uffz. Josef Köck	G	AFP 2	24Mar18	28Mar18	AFP 17
Uffz. Johann Königsreuther	P	FA 287A	26May18	EOW	
Pion. Emil Kratzer	G	AFP 4	23Sep17	8Oct17	Ss 7
Uffz. Jakob Lang	G	AFP 4	9Oct17	6Jan18	AFP 4
Uffz. Jakob Lang	G	Ss 12	23Oct18	EOW	
Pion. Oskar Lantsch	P	AFP 18	22Oct18	2Nov18	IIC
Sgt. Richard Letsch	P	AFP 7	27May18	5Jul18	AFP 9
Uffz. Franz Maier	P	AFP 4	9May18	EOW	
Uffz. Franz Xaver Mall	P	AFP 4	14Oct17	6Mar18	IIC,lt.
Uffz. Franz Xaver Mall	P	Hosp.	7Mar18	22Mar18	WIA,POW
Oblt. Maske, stv. C.O.	O	FA 221A	9Feb18	15Feb18	FA 221A
Gefr. Anton Maurer	G	FEA 1b	15Mar17	17Jun17	AFP 4
Gefr. Anton Maurer	G	AFP 4	25Jun17	13Nov17	FEA 1b
Uffz. Albert Mayer	G	AFP 4	24Jan18	27Mar18	AFP 2
Gefr. Heinrich Metz	G	AFP 4	9Nov17	23Mar18	IIC,lt.
Gefr. Heinrich Metz	G		23Mar18	28May18	KIA
Gefr. Wilhelm Meyer	P	AFP 2	16Mar18	4May18	JsSch I
Gefr. Michael Mois	G	AFP 4	12Nov17	23Dec17	KIA
Vzfw. Franz Mülberger	G	AFP 4	27Sep17	22Mar18	WIA,lt.
Vzfw. Franz Mülberger	G	Hosp.	24Mar18	21May18	KIC
Oblt. Hermann Muggenthaler, C.O.	P	AFP FP A	16Aug17	9Feb18	Leave
Oblt. Hermann Muggenthaler, C.O.	P	Leave	15Feb18	23Feb18	FA 46b
Uffz. Anton Nar	G	AFP 9	30Aug18	EOW	
Vzfw. Robert Neidhart	P	FEA 1b	15Mar17	17Jun17	KIA
Sgt. Alwin Neitsch	G	Kofl 7	7Jun18	31Jun18	FA 265A
Uffz. Peter Neumüller	P	AFP 4	16Oct17	10Jan18	WIA,sv.
Vzfw. Adalbert Niedermeyer	G	FA 288A	8May18	8Jun18	AFP 7
Sgt. Michael Oestheimer	G	Ss 23b	24May18	EOW	
Pion. Gerhard Petersen	P	AFP 7	19May18	28May18	POW
Uffz. Johann Pfann	P	AFP 4	13Sep17	19Sep17	KIC
Gefr. Emil Piffczyk	G	AFP 7	13Jun18	29Jun18	AFP 7
Pion. Johann Pöllmann	P	AFP 4	9May18	21May18	KIC
Vzfw. Heinrich Raab (+ 13Nov17)	G	AFP 4	3Jul17	12Nov17	IIC,sv.
Pion. Paul Raisig	P	AFP 4	15Nov17	1Jan18	WIA,lt.
Vzfw. Paul Raisig	P		1Jan18	EOW	
Pion. Fritz Reiner	G	AFP 4	25Sep17	8Nov17	AFP 4
Ltn.d.R. Reiter, SGp B OzbV	O	FA 204A	20Apr18		
Gefr. Alfred Rösler	G	LSO Cpy	11Jun18	1Aug18	Ss 37
Pion. Karl Sandner	P	FEA 1b	15Mar17	1May17	WIA,lt.
Uffz. Karl Sandner	P		1May17	11Sep17	AFP 4
Uffz. Wilhelm Schäfer	G	AFP 4	29Aug17	27Mar18	AFP 2
Gefr. Karl Scheerer	G	AFP 4	18Jun17	19Sep17	IIC,sv.
Gefr. Wilhelm Schieber	G	AFP 6	8May17	23May17	AFP 6
Uffz. Rudolf Schiessl	G	Ss 27b	4Nov17	2Jan18	Ss 27b
Uffz. Richard Schliermann	G	AFP 6	5May17	31Oct17	AFP 4
Ltn. Hubertus Graf von Schmettow, Stv. C.O.	P	FA 256A	7Mar18	10Mar18	FA 256A
Pion. Emil Schwebius	G	AFP 4	26Apr18	7May18	KIC
Oblt. Karl Albert Selb	Ss 27b		13Nov17		

Gefr. Karl Siegenthaler	G	AFP 1	14Jul18	31Jul18	WIA,POW
Uffz. Fritz Simon	P	AFP 4	21Sep17	13Oct17	Ss 11
Gefr. Friedrich Spindler	P	AFP 4	7Jan18	24Jan18	IIC,sv.
Uffz. Alfred Steinberg	G	AFP 4	21Jun17	27Sep17	Ss 21
Uffz. Erwin Stiefel	G	FEA 1b	15Mar17	23Jun17	IIC,sv.
Vzfw. Gottfried Stumpf	P	FEA 1b	15Mar17	6Jul17	FA 238A
Vzfw. Gottfried Stumpf	P	FA 18	22Jul17	25Jul17	AFP 4
Uffz. Otto Volkelt	G	Kofl 7	7Jun18	11Jun18	FA 265A
Pion. Hermann Weber	P	AFP 2	5Apr18	7May18	KIC
Hptm. Karl Wild, C.O.	O	FEA 1b	15Mar17	21Aug17	AFP C
Vzfw. Hans Zeitler	G	AFP 4	21Jan18	EOW	
Uffz. Karl Zimmermann	G	FEA 1b	15Mar17	26Aug17	FTL,KIC

Royal Bavarian *Schutzstaffel 30*

Mechanics and Ground Personnel

Name	From		To	
	Unit	Date	Date	Unit
Pion. Gustav Achilles	FA 222A	23May18	15Jun18	FA 222A
Pion. Jakob Angermaier	FEA 1b	15Mar17	10Aug17	Hosp.
Gefr. Jakob Angermaier	Hosp.	17Aug17	EOW	
Gefr. Georg Bär	FEA 1b	15Mar17	EOW	
Pion. Rudolf Balthasar	FEA 1b	15Mar17	29Mar17	Hosp.
Uffz. Max Barmann	FEA 1b	15Mar17	16Aug17	Hosp.
Uffz. Max Barmann	Hosp.	22Aug17	5Aug18	FEA 1b
Pion. Heinrich Baumgärtner	FEA 1b	15Mar17	6Jul17	FEA 1b
Pion. Anton Baus	FA 221A	26Sep17	EOW	
Pion. Wilhelm Becher	FEA 1b	17Jan18	18Jun18	Infntry
Pion. Josef Beringer	FEA 1b	14Jan18	24Sep18	FEA 2b
Pion. Friedrich Bernthold	FEA 1b	15Mar17	13Aug17	Hosp.
Pion. Friedrich Bernthold	Hosp.	21Aug17	EOW	
Pion. Alois Binder	FEA 1b	14Jan18	19Jul18	Infntry
Uffz. Max Bissinger	FEA 1b	15Mar17	11Dec17	FEA 1b
Gefr. Nikolaus Bründl	FEA 1b	15Mar17	2Oct17	Hosp.
Gefr. Nikolaus Bründl	Hosp.	11Oct17	3Nov17	FEA 1b
Pion. Leonhardt Buchner	FEA 1b	15Mar17	24Aug17	Ss 27b
Pion. Josef Damböck	FEA 1b	5Nov17	22Dec17	FEA 1b
Gefr. Johann Deller	FEA 1b	15Mar17	EOW	
Gefr. Theodor Dietl	FEA 2b	18Aug18	EOW	
Gefr. Engelbert Dolp	AFP 4	5May18	11May18	AFP 4
Gefr. Georg Dotterweich	FEA 1b	15Mar17	EOW	
Pion. Karl Ecker	Js 7	21Jan18	EOW	
Gefr. Wilhelm Eckert	FEA 1b	15Mar17	16May17	Hosp.
Gefr. Ludwig Eder	FEA 1b	15Mar17	8Jan18	Hosp.
Gefr. Ludwig Eder	Hosp.	18Feb18	6Jun18	Hosp.
Arm.Soldt. Edmund Eskeles	Arm Btl	20Apr18	7May18	Arm Btl
Pion. Leonhard Fessler	AFP 4	6May18	11May18	AFP 4
Pion. Urban Fichter	FEA 1b	19Dec17	22Dec17	FEA 1b
Pion. Georg Fick	FEA 1b	15Mar17	6Jan18	Hosp.
Pion. Friedrich Flessa	FEA 1b	15Mar17	25Jun17	Hosp.
Offz.Stv. Josef Flunk	FEA 1b	15Mar17	21May18	FEA 2b
Pion. Johann Franz	FEA 1b	15Mar17	21Aug17	AFP C
Pion. Hugo Frimberger	FEA 1b	26Sep17	31Nov17	FEA 1b
Pion. Heinrich Fröhlich	FEA 1b	8Sep18	EOW	
Pion. Alois Frölich	Ss 23b	21May18	EOW	
Pion. Adalbert Fuchs	FEA 1b	15Mar17	EOW	
Pion. Josef Füller	AFP 7	26May18	28Jun18	Ss 26b
Pion. Josef Füller	Ss 26b	4Aug18	EOW	
Pion. Thomas Gries	FEA 1b	15Mar17	23Aug17	Hosp.
Pion. Wilhelm Gross	FEA 1b	15Mar17	11Jul17	FEA 1b
Pion. Franz Gumpp	FEA 1b	13Mar17	30May17	KEA Pk

Pion. Franz Gumpp	KEA Pk	19Jun17	EOW	
Pion. Paul Häberle	FEA 1b	15Mar17	EOW	
Fahrer Franz Hallmann	FPK 612	10Aug18	6Sep18	FPK 612
Pion. Johann Heckner	FEA 1b	8Jul17	EOW	
Pion. Max Hefele	FEA 1b	15Aug17	6Sep17	Ss 27b
Pion. Michael Heid	AFP 4	4May18	EOW	
Pion. Paul Heitmann	FA 216A	27May18	27Jun18	SGp B
Pion. Johann Helmbrecht	FEA 1b	12Jan18	18Jun18	Infntry
Pion. Konstantin Hengge	AFP 7	26May18	27Jun18	Ss 26b
Uffz. Emeran Hillinger	FEA 1b	15Mar17	27Jan18	FEA 2b
Uffz. Johann Hinterleitner	FEA 1b	15Mar17	EOW	
Pion. Max Höcherl	FEA 1b	5Nov17	EOW	
Gefr. Johann Hölzl	FEA 1b	15Mar17	25Sep18	Hosp.
Gefr. Johann Holz	FEA 1b	15Mar17	EOW	
Pion. Leonhard Hornfischer	AKP 4	8May18	11May18	AFP 4
Pion. Richard Igl	FEA 1b	14Jan18	EOW	
Pion. Jakob Ihle	FEA 1b	15Mar17	EOW	
Pion. Georg Janson	FEA 1b	14Jan18	EOW	
Pion. Albert Johann	FEA 1b	9Dec17	EOW	
Gefr. Michael Juraszka	FPK 612	10Aug18	6Sep18	FPK 612
Pion. Josef Kaiser (+ i.Kr. 17Jul18)	FEA 1b	15Mar17	13Jul18	Hosp.
Pion. Emil Keil	FEA 1b	15Mar17	EOW	
Pion. Albert Kessler	FEA 1b	10Sep18	EOW	
Pion. Georg Kestler	FEA 2b	24Jul18	EOW	
Gefr. Johann Kistler	Artllry	28Feb18	25Aug18	Hosp.
Gefr. Johann Kistler	Hosp.	3Sep18	EOW	
Pion. Xaver Klein	FEA 2b	13Sep18	25Sep18	Hosp.
Pion. Xaver Klein	Hosp.	27Sep18	5Nov18	FEA 2b
Arm.Soldt. Wilhelm Klempt	Arm Btn	20Apr18	7May18	Arm Btn
Gefr. Johann Kogler	FEA 1b	15Mar17	23Sep17	Hosp.
Pion. Ferdinand Kohl	FEA 1b	17Jan18	18Jun18	Infntry
Pion. Valentin Kormann	AFP 1	21Jul18	EOW	
Gefr. Anton Kraus	FEA 1b	15Mar17	26Mar17	Hosp.
Sgt. Anton Kraus	Hosp.	2Apr17	EOW	
Gefr. Wilhelm Krell	FEA 1b	15Mar17	26Aug17	Js 36
Gefr. Wilhelm Krell	Js 36	31Aug17	1Nov18	Dschrgd
Pion. Johann Kulessa	Grfl 18	26May18	27Jun18	SGp B
Pion. Alois Kunkel	Ss 25b	14Jun18	27Jun18	SGp B
Sgt. Ludwig Ladenberger	FEA 2b	23Jan18	5Jul18	FEA 2b
UnterZahlmstr. Max Landenberger	FEA 2b	17Oct18	EOW	
Pion. Franz Lang	FEA 2b	19Dec17	27May18	Hosp.
Pion. Franz Lang	Hosp.	4Jun18	7Jul18	FEA 1b
Uffz. Georg Leonhardt	FEA 1b	15Mar17	12Jun17	FEA 1b
Gefr. Karl Lindner	FA 276A	21Aug17	28Feb18	FA 46b
Pion. Josef Lobmeier	Ss 27b	25Aug17	EOW	
Sgt. Friedrich Löbcke	FPK 612	10Aug18	6Sep18	FPK 612
Uffz. Roman Löchler	AFP 4	5May18	11May18	AFP 4
Pion. Franz Lorenz	AFP 7	26May18	27Jun18	Ss 26b
Pion. Franz Lorenz	Ss 26b	4Aug18	EOW	
Uffz. Albert Mall	FEA 1b	15Mar17	EOW	
Pion. Thomas Mall	FEA 1b	15Mar17	23Jul17	Hosp.
Uffz. Augustin Mangold	FEA 1b	15Mar17	6Feb18	AFP 4
Pion. Friedrich Marx	FEA 1b	15Jan18	EOW	
Pion. Heinrich Mayer	FEA 1b	15Mar17	12May17	IIC
Gefr. Heinrich Mayer	Hosp.	18May17	20Aug17	FEA 1b
Gefr. Josef Mayer	FEA 1b	15Mar17	26Aug17	AFP 4
Pion. Max Mayr	FEA 1b	26Sep17	3Nov17	FEA 1b
Pion. Johann Meier	KEA I	18Aug18	EOW	
Pion. Johann Meister	AFP 6	5May17	5Jul18	Hosp.
Sgt. Max Michl	FEA 1b	15Mar17	22Aug18	FEA 1b
Feldw. August Moser	FEA 1b	15Mar17	EOW	
Funker Hermann Müller	AFkPk 4	20Apr18	11May18	AFkPk 4
Gefr. Otto Müller	FA 254A	26May18	27Jun18	SGp B
Ltn.d.R. Wilhelm Nebel (*Werkmeister*)	FEA 1b	20Jan18	EOW	

Uffz. Fritz Negle	FA 221A	26Sep17	7Jan18	AFP 4
Pion. Jakob Nicola	AFP 6	24Sep17	11May18	KPA 4
Pion. Friedrich Öed	FEA 1b	15Mar17	20May17	FEA 1b
Pion. Anton Pfenninger	FEA 1b	15Mar17	EOW	
Pion. Josef Pohl	FEA 1b	15Mar17	9Sep17	AFP 4
Sgt. Johann Pröbstl	FEA 1b	15Mar17	19Sep18	Inftry
Pion. Friedrich Rang	FEA 1b	1Nov17	EOW	
Arm.Soldt. Karl Rekitke	Arm Btn	20Apr18	7May18	Arm Btn
Fahrer Eduard Reichert	FPK 612	10Aug18	6Sep18	FPK 612
Pion. Franz Xaver Reischl	FEA 1b	23Jul18	EOW	
Fahrer Karl Rickhoff	FPK 612	10Aug18	6Sep18	FPK 612
Gefr. Otto Richter	KAbt 4	10May18	EOW	
Gefr. Wilhelm Rieckhoff	Kofl 4	21Apr18	11May18	BG 3
Sgt. Josef Rieder	FEA 1b	15Mar17	26Oct18	FEA 2b
Gefr. Georg Rommel	FEA 1b	15Mar17	5Oct17	FEA 1b
Funker Alfred Rothenstein	AFkPk 4	20Apr18	11May18	AFkPk 4
Pion. Otto Ruland	FEA 1b	15Mar17	27Jul17	AFP 4
Gefr. Otto Ruland	AFP 4	4Aug17	14Jan18	Hosp.
Gefr. Otto Ruland	Hosp.	29Jan18	EOW	
Sgt. Johann Rupp	FEA 1b	15Mar17	EOW	
Vzfw. Adam Schildknecht	FEA 1b	15Mar17	11Dec17	FEA 1b
Pion. Max Josef Schindler	FEA 1b	15Mar17	10May17	FEA 1b
Pion. Georg Schlegel	FEA 1b	5Nov17	EOW	
Uffz. Heinrich Schlicht	FEA 1b	15Mar17	EOW	
Pion. Philipp Schlosser	AFP 4	5May18	11May18	AFP 4
Pion. Alois Schmidt	FEA 1b	17Dec17	19Jul18	Artllry
Pion. Ludwig Schneider	FEA 1b	15Mar17	EOW	
Pion. Jakob Schorr	FS II	10Sep18	EOW	
Uffz. Gustav Schulz	FEA 1b	15Mar17	EOW	
Pion. Rudolf Schwarz	FEA 1b	15Mar17	10Apr17	Hosp.
Pion. Rudolf Schwarz	Hosp.	14May17	18May17	FEA 1b
Gefr. Wilhelm Schwarz	FEA 1b	15Mar17	20Aug18	FEA 1b
Pion. Josef Sedelmaier	FEA 1b	10Sep18	EOW	
Uffz. Johann Seidl	FEA 1b	15Mar17	EOW	
Uffz. Rudolf Seiler	FEA 1b	15Mar17	30Jan18	FEA 1b
Pion. Kaspar Seitz	Artllry	15Mar18	EOW	
Pion. Johann Seitzl	FEA 1b	15Mar17	14Aug17	Hosp.
Gefr. Johann Seitzl	Hosp.	15Aug17	12Feb18	FEA 1b
Pion. Max Seubert	AFP 4	20Jan18	12Oct18	Hosp.
Pion. Karl Simon	FEA 2b	10Aug18	EOW	
Uffz. Heinrich Singer	FEA 1b	15Mar17	EOW	
Pion. Heinrich Sonntag	FEA 1b	23May17	EOW	
Gefr. Franz Stein	FEA 1b	9Dec17	EOW	
Pion. Max Stocker	FEA 1b	15Mar17	EOW	
Uffz. Richard Strobl	FEA 1b	15Mar17	19Jul18	Infntry
Pion. Michael Treutterer	Infntry	4Aug18	EOW	
Funker Benedikt Vogel	AFkPk 4	20Apr18	11May18	AFkPk 4
Pion. Valentin Wägele	FEA 1b	15Mar17	3Nov17	FEA 1b
Pion. Richard Wagner	FEA 1b	15Mar17	19Nov17	FEA 1b
Gefr. Richard Wagner	FEA 1b	8Dec17	EOW	
Vzfw. Alois Weber	FEA 1b	15Mar17	EOW	
Uffz. Josef Weinberger	FEA 1b	15Mar17	2Oct17	WIA
Pion. Georg Wieland	AFP 6	16May17	5Oct17	FEA 1b
Uffz. Johann Winter	Infntry	19Dec17	3Feb18	FEA 2b
Pion. Josef Wittmann	FEA 1b	15Mar17	23Jan18	AFP 4
Pion. Konrad Woiczyk	FEA 2b	18Aug18	EOW	
Pion. Strefan Zahn	Infntry	8Sep18	EOW	
Pion. Johann Zeilein	FEA 1b	15Mar17	21Feb18	AFP 2
Pion. Johann Zeilein	AFP 2	15Apr18	EOW	
Sgt. Otto Zipf	FA 45b	28May17	EOW	
Pion. Heinrich Zorn	FEA 1b	15Mar17	7Jun17	Hosp.

Schutzstaffel/Schlachtstaffel 30b
Mitgemachte Schlachten und Gefechte
(Battles and combat actions in which Ss 30b participated)

22Mar17	14Apr17	*Stellungskämpfe in Lothringen* (Trench fighting in Lorraine)
15Apr17	9Jun17	*Frühjahrsschlacht bei Arras* (Spring battle of Arras)
9Jun17	21Jul17	*Kämpfe am Wytschaetebogen und Vorbereitungen* (Fighting on the Wytschaete bend and prepartion for the summer battle of Flanders)
22Jul17	17Sep17	*Sommerschlacht in Flandern* (Summer battle in Flanders)
18Sep17	3Dec17	*Herbstschlacht in Flandern* (Fall battle in Flanders)
4Dec17	10Mar18	*Stellungskämpfe in Flandern Winter 17/18* (Trench fighting in Flanders Winter 17/18)
11Mar18	20Mar18	*Aufmarsch zur Grossen Schlacht in Frankreich* (Assembly for the Great Battle in France)
21Mar18	9Apr18	*Grosse Schlacht in Frankreich* (Great Battle in France)
10Apr18	12Apr18	*Kämpfe an der Ancre, Somme und Avre* (Fighting on the Ancre, the Somme and the Avre)
13Apr18	15May18	*Stellungskrieg in Flandern* (Trench war in Flanders)
16May18	26May18	*Stellungskämpfe nördlich der Ailette* (Trench fighting north of the Ailette)
27May18	13Jun18	*Schlacht bei Soissons und Reims* (Battle at Soissons and Reims)
27May18		*Erstürmung der Höhen des Chemin des Dames* (Storming the top of the Chemin des Dames)
28May18	1Jun18	*Verfolgungskämpfe zwischen Oise und Aisne über die Vesle bis zur Marne* (Pursuit fighting between the Oise and the Aisne and across the Vesle to the Marne)
30May18	13Jun18	*Angriffsschlacht westlich und südwestlich von Soissons* (Offensive battle west and southwest of Soissons)
14Jun18	27Jun18	*Stellungskämpfe zwischen Oise und Aisne* (Trench fighting between the Oise and the Aisne)
28Jun18	14Jul18	*Stellungskämpfe bei Reims* (Trench fighting at Reims)
15Jul18	17Jul18	*Angriffsschlacht an der Marne und in der Champagne* (Offensive battle on the Marne and in the Champagne)
18Jul18	25Jul18	*Abwehrschlacht zwischen Soissons und Reims* (Defensive battle between Soissons and Reims)
26Jul18	3Aug18	*Bewegliche Abwehrschlacht zwischen Marne und Vesle* (The mobile battle between the Marne and the Vesle)
4Aug18	16Aug18	*Stellungskämpfe zwischen Oise und Aisne* (Trench fighting between the Oise and the Aisne)
17Aug18	4Sep18	*Abwehrschlacht zwischen Oise und Aisne* (Defensive battle between the Oise and the Aisne)
5Sep18	8Sep18	*Kämpfe vor der Siegfriedstellung 1918* (Fighting at the Siegfried Line 1918)
9Sep18	12Sep18	*Kämpfe in der Siegfriedstellung 1918* (Fighting in the Siegfried Line 1918)
13Sep18	18Sep18	*Kämpfe vor der Siegfriedstellung 1918* (Fighting at the Siegfried Line 1918)

weitere Gefechtseinträge fehlen (the remainder is not available)

***Schutzstaffel/Schlachtstaffel 30b* Airfields**

From	To	Location	*Schlachtgruppe* Affiliation	*Armee*
22Mar17	14Apr17	Mörchingen		AAA
15Apr17	9Jun17	Abscon	Escort for FA 238(A)	6
9Jun17	10Mar18	Bisseghem	Escort for FA 221(A)	4

11Mar18	21Mar18	Inchy	For FA 221(A), FA 224(A)w	2
21Mar18		Inchy	SGp C (Ss 11,30b) C.O. *Hptm.* Heinecke	2
(24Mar18)	3Apr18	Longavesnes	SGp C (Ss 11,30b) C.O. *Hptm.* Heinecke	2
3Apr18	12Apr18	Framerville	SGp C (Ss 14,28b,30b) C.O. *Oblt.d.R.* August Ertl	2
13Apr18	15May18	Bisseghem	SGp B (Ss 10,23b,26b,30b) C.O. *Oblt.d.R.* August Ertl	4
16May18	13Jun18	Montigny-le-Franc	SGp B (Ss 23b,26b,28b,30b) C.O. *Oblt.d.R.* August Ertl	7
13Jun18	18Jul18	Cuiry-Housse	SGp Winckler (Ss 23b,26b,28b,30b) C.O. *Oblt.d.R.* August Ertl	7
18Jul18	26Jul18	l'Ecaille	SGp 2 (Ss 22b,28b,30b,31b,32) C.O. *Oblt.d.R.* August Ertl	1
26Jul18	10Aug18	Montaigu	SGp B (Ss 28b,30b,31b,32) C.O. *Oblt.d.R.* Josef Gramp	7
10Aug18	10Aug18	Athies	SGp B (Ss 28b,30b,31b,32) C.O. *Oblt.d.R.* Josef Gramp	2
11Aug18	(1Sep18)	Grandlup-et-Fay	SGp B (Ss 28b,30b,31b,32) C.O. *Oblt.d.R.* Josef Gramp	7
(12Sep18)	15Sep18	Grandlup-et-Fay	SGp B (Ss 7,28b,30b,31b,33) C.O. *Oblt.d.R.* Josef Gramp	7
15Sep18	25Sep18	Perthes	SGp B (Ss 28b,30b,31b,32) C.O. *Oblt.d.R.* Josef Gramp	1
25Sep18	13Oct18	Perthes	SGp B (Ss 30b,31b,32) C.O. *Ritt.d.R.* Julius Bossert	1
13Oct18	23Oct18	Ecly	SGp B (Ss 30b,31b,32) C.O. *Ritt.d.R.* Julius Bossert	1
23Oct18	EOW	Ecly	SGp B (Ss 30b,31b) C.O. *Ritt.d.R.* Julius Bossert	1

Royal Bavarian *Schutzstaffel 30b*

15Mar17	*Schutzstaffel 30b* is created at FEA 1b by BKM Nr. 21943.A. of 15Mar17.
23Apr17	*Uffz.* Justus Kaiser, P, and *Pion.* Adam Föller, G, crash land but are unhurt.
1May17	*Pion.* Karl Sandner, P, is WIA,lt. and *Pion.* Adam Föller, G, is WIA,sv. over Gavrelle, 15 km. W. Douai during air combat at 10.00 hours in DFW C.V (LVG) 5073/16. Föller DOW at 13.00 hours at Lambres.
12May17	*Pion.* Heinrich Mayer, M, is IIC during a test flight and to hospital at Guise.
17Jun17	*Vzfw.* Robert Neidhart, P, and *Uffz.* Severin Hornung, G, are KIA at 8.10 hours over Zonnebeke during air combat. They fall in flames in DFW C.V (LVG) 5075/16.
23Jun17	*Gefr.* Friedrich Ehmann, P, and *Uffz.* Erwin Stiefel, G, are IIC during a forced landing. Stiefel suffers a broken leg and to hospital at Gulleghem, Ehmann also to the hospital at Gulleghem.
13Jul17	*Uffz.* Johann Herrmann, P, is WIA during air combat, shot in the left heel and to hospital at Kortryk.
28Jul17	*Uffz.* Sandner-1, *Gefr.* Scheerer-1, Nieuport 1, 9.05, NW Polygon Wald, Nieuport 17 #A.6680, 1 Sqn. RFC, 2/Lt. G.B. Buxton, KIA
18Aug17	*Ltn.d.R.* Zichäus (FA 221A)-1, *Uffz.* Besel-1, Nieuport 1, 8.40, Paschendaele Nieuport 17 #A.6701, 29 Sqn. RFC, 2/Lt. W.B. Styles, WIA,POW
21Aug17	*Uffz.* Besel-2, *Uffz.* Duschner-1, R.E. 8, 19.30, W. Ypern 6 Sqn. RFC, 2/Lt. G.A.S. Nicholson,DOW & Pte. F. Lankshear,KIA
22Aug17	*Uffz.* Besel-3, *Uffz.* Duschner-2, Sopwth Camel, 11.30, Frezenberg Pup #B.1767, 66 Sqn. RFC, 2/Lt. E.H. Garland, POW
26Aug17	*Uffz.* Karl Zimmermann, G, is forced to land at Moorslede by ground fire at 7.10 hours and is KIC. He jumps from the aircraft.
19Sep17	*Uffz.* Johann Pfann, P, is KIC and *Gefr.* Karl Scheerer, G, is IIC,sv. at Marke-Bisseghem at 11.00 hours and to hospital at Gullegehem.
2Oct17	*Uffz.* Josef Weinberger, M, is accidently injured and to hospital. He receives a shot to the right lung and fragments to the back of his head and his right foot.
7Oct17	*Uffz.* Besel-4, *Uffz.* Duschner-3, Engl. Spad, 8.00, W. Geluvelt D.H. 4 #A.7401, 55 Sqn. RFC, Sgt. M. Coomer-Weare,WIA & Gnr. W.G. Osbourne,WIA
31Oct17	*Flg.* Max Heilmeier, G, is WIA,lt. by a bruising shot to the right thigh, remains.
12Nov17	*Uffz.* Georg Imgrund, P, is KIC and *Vzfw.* Heinrich Raab, G, is IIC,sv. at Heule-Bisseghem at 16.15 hours during a practice flight. Raab DOI 13Nov17 in the hospital at Kortryk.
4Dec17	*Vzfw.* Besel-5, *Vzfw.* Duschner-4, Bristol F.2b, 13.20, Bellewarde Lake #B.1153, 22 Sqn. RFC, 2/Lt. A.F. Goodchap,POW & 2/Lt. A.H. Middleton,POW

23Dec17	*Uffz.* Thomas Hartig, P, and *Gefr.* Michael Mois, G, are KIA at 16.25 hours over Kasteelhoek E. Hollebeke during air combat. They fall in flames.
1Jan18	*Vzfw.* Paul Raisig, P, is WIA,lt. and *Uffz.* August Brunthaler, G, is WIA,sv. over Gheluvelt-Zandvoorde during air combat at 11.00 hours. Brunthaler DOW at 11.25 hours during the landing at Bisseghem. Raising receives a bruising shot to his back and remains with the unit.
10Jan18	*Uffz.* Peter Neumüller, P, is WIA,sv. during air combat, shrapnel shot to the right thigh and to hospital at Kortryk.
24Jan18	*Gefr.* Friedrich Spindler, P, and *Uffz.* Michael Eberth, G, crash land 500 meters SW of Lendelede following air combat, are IIC, and to hospital at Winkel St. Eloi. Spindler suffers a broken arm and lower left leg. Eberth merely has a head laceration.
6Mar18	*Uffz.* Franz Xaver Mall, P, is slightly injured in a crash and to hospital for a one day stay.
22Mar18	*Uffz.* Franz Xaver Mall, P, is WIA and taken POW and *Vzfw.* Franz Mülberger, G, is WIA,lt. in the foot near Bernes by artillery fire. Mülberger is briefly taken POW but escapes and returns to the unit the next day.
22Mar18	*Uffz.* Josef Hefele, G, is WIA over Nurlu by ground fire, a bruising shot to the right thigh. He remains with the unit.
23Mar18	*Uffz.* Johann Hanauer, P, and *Gefr.* Heinrich Metz, G, are IIC,lt. when they hit the telephone cable at Longavesnes, both remain with the unit.
27Mar18	*Schutzstaffel 30b* is renamed *Schlachtstaffel 30b* by KM Nr. 5126.18.A.7.L.IV.C. of 27Mar18.
7May18	*Uffz.* Johann Hanauer, P, and *Pion.* Josef Frank, G, are KIC at Lendelede during a practice flight. They collide with Weber and Schwebius.
7May18	*Pion.* Hermann Weber, P, and *Pion.* Emil Schwebius, G, are KIC at Lendelede during a practice flight. They collide with Hanauer and Frank.
21May18	*Pion.* Johann Pöllmann, P, and *Vzfw.* Franz Mülberger, G, are KIC E. Montigny-le-Franc at 19.40 hours during a practice flight.
27May18	*Pion.* Franz Lang, M, suffers a bruised thigh and to hospital at Regensburg.
28May18	*Uffz.* Josef Griebl, P, and *Gefr.* Heinrich Metz, G, are KIA over Mont St. Martin near Fismes.
28May18	*Pion.* Gerhard Petersen, P, and *Gefr.* Heinrich Graebner, G, are taken POW by the French.
18Jul18	*Pion.* Josef Kaiser, M, dies of the flu at Tagnon.
31Jul18	*Sgt.* Valentin Jackl, P, and *Gefr.* Karl Siegenthaler are WIA and taken POW by the French. Jackl dies at Meaux, Seine-et-Marne as a POW on 3Aug18.
20Aug18	*Offz.Stv.* Georg Dörfler, P, and *Vzfw.* Otto Bruns, G, are KIA over Oisne-Aisne.
2Nov18	*Pion.* Oskar Lantsch, P, is IIC and to hospital.
21Nov18	*Schlachtstaffel 30b* is demobilized at FEA 2b, Fürth.

Schusta 30b in March 1918 while serving with the *2.Armee*. The first aircraft is Hannover Cl.II 9390/17.

Royal Bavarian *Schutzstaffel 31*

Pilot/Gunner	Type	From		To	
		Unit	Date	Date	Unit
Ltn.d.R. Guido Barth	O	FA 47b	18Feb18	28Feb18	AFP 3
Ltn. Konrad Bischoff, OzbV	P	Ss 23b	21Jul18	EOW	
Vzfw. August Bonauer	P	AFP 18	20Apr18	EOW	
Gefr. Max Brandl	P	AFP 3	4Mar18	28May18	FLT,POW
Vzfw. Rudolf Dittrich	G	AFP 18	9Apr18	EOW	
Uffz. Johann Dütsch	G	AFP 18	9Apr18	19Jul18	KIA
Vzfw. Theodor Eickhoff	G	FA 252A	29May18	EOW	
Pion. Josef Erhart	P	AFP 3	27Feb18	30Mar18	WIA
Vzfw. Josef Erhart	P	Hosp.	22Apr18	EOW	
Vzfz. Ludwig Fauss	G	AFP 3	26Feb18	EOW	
Vzfw. Martin Fellner	P	AFP 18	14Apr18	EOW	
Gefr. Peter Grotz	G	AFP 18	7Apr18	28May18	FTL,POW
Gefr. Eugen Heck	P	FA 47b	18Feb18	3Mar18	FA 297A

Gefr. Kastulus Huber	P	ArtFlKo	20Sep18	EOW	
Vzfw. Hermann Karwaschewski	P	AFP 18	11Apr18	22Oct18	IIC,sv.
				26Oct18	DOI
Uffz. Georg Kelsch	P	JSch II	30Oct18	EOW	
Vzfw. Friedrich Klein	P	AFP 18	20Apr18	19Sep18	AFP 1
Pion. Josef Koch	G	AFP 3	27Feb18	6Apr18	KIA
Pion. Wilhelm Köppen	G	AFP 3	28Feb18	16May18	AFP 18
Vzfw. Karl Koller	P	FA 273A	28Feb18	17Mar18	JSch II
Gefr. Michael Lang	G	AFP 3	26Feb18	3May18	KIA
Vzfw. Hermann Lenn	G	Ss 28b	30May18	EOW	
Oblt. Friedrich Wilhelm *Ritter und Edler* von Tiechler von Mann, C.O.	O	FA 47b	18Feb18	23Feb18	FEA 1b
Vzfw. Karl Memmel	G	AFP 18	11May18	EOW	
Ltn. Maximilian Müller	O	FA 47b	18Feb18	23Feb18	FEA 2b
Oblt. Heinrich Nopitsch, OzbV	P	FA 47b	18Feb18	6Aug18	Iluft
Oblt. Heinrich Nopitsch, Stv. C.O.	P	Ss 31b	23Feb18	3Mar18	Ss 31b
Vzfw. Karl Peez (+ 9May18)	P	FA 47b	18Feb18	3May18	WIA,POW
Ltn.d.R. Wilhelm Pletsch	P	FA 47b	18Feb18	28Feb18	AFP 3
Uffz. Ludwig Röder	P	AFP 18	10Apr18	16Jun18	FEA 1b
Uffz. Erich Oskar Roland	P			19Jul18	KIA
Gefr. Josef Sauer	G	AFP 1	10Aug18	27Oct18	KIA
Uffz. Friedrich Sattes	P	AFP 1	22Jul18	EOW	
Ltn.d.R. Johann Schaller	O	FA 47b	18Feb18	20Mar18	FEA 1b
Uffz. Ludwig Schwem	G	AFP B	27Mar18	28May18	WIA,sv.
Vzfw. Ludwig Schwem	G	Hosp.	1Oct18	15Oct18	Hosp.
Gefr. Simon Seifried	G	FEA 1b	10May18	1Jun18	WIA,sv.
Uffz. Fritz Seitzinger	P	AFP 3	26Feb18	6Apr18	KIA
Pion. Johann Sichermann (+ 25Mar)	P	AFP 18	13Mar18	23Mar18	WIA,POW
Pion. Michael Sutor	P	AFP 1	Oct18	27Oct18	KIA
Oblt. Max Ungewitter, C.O.	O	ILuft	3Mar18	EOW	
Uffz. Josef Unterberger	P	FA 47b	18Feb18	6Apr18	KIA
Gefr. Eugen Weber	G	AFP 1	14Jun18	12Aug18	AFP 1
Pion. Johannes Weissler	G	AFP 3	26Feb18	6Apr18	KIA
Gefr. Johann Zink	G	AFP 3	26Feb18	23Mar18	POW

Royal Bavarian *Schutzstaffel 31*

Mechanics and Ground Personnel

Name	From		To	
	Unit	Date	Date	Unit
Gefr. Karl Alexander	FA 47b	18Feb18	EOW	
Pion. Wilhelm Amann	FA 47b	18Feb18	16Jun18	IIC,DOW
Gefr. Alois Aschenbrenner	FEA 1b	19Sep18	EOW	
Pion. Benedikt Barnsteiner	FA 47b	18Feb18	EOW	
Kraftf. Heinrich Bäumler	FA 47b	18Feb18	EOW	
Kraftf. Pion. Konrad Baumann	FA 47b	18Feb18	EOW	
Pion. Johann Baur	FA 47b	18Feb18	EOW	
Kraftf. Friedrich Bernard	FA 47b	18Feb18	5Mar18	AFP 3
Gefr. Konrad Bernrieder	FA 47b	18Feb18	EOW	
Uffz. Georg Biebelmann	FA 47b	18Feb18	25Jun18	Hosp.
Gefr. Josef Bindl	FA 47b	18Feb18	9Mar18	FEA 1b
Pion. Karl Birkle	FEA 1b	3May18	EOW	
Pion. Heinrich Brandl	FEA 1b	3May18	EOW	
Pion. Wilhelm Büchl	FA 47b	18Feb18	29Aug18	FEA 1b
Uffz. Ernst Bülow	FA 47b	18Feb18	EOW	
Pion. Johann Bürckmann	FA 47b	18Feb18	2Apr18	WIA
Gefr. Johann Bürckmann	Hosp.	8Apr18	EOW	
Pion. Johann Burkhard	FEA 1b	7Aug18	EOW	
Pion. Johann Busch	FA 47b	18Feb18	EOW	
Pion. Xaver Daigle	FA 47b	18Feb18	26Feb18	AFP 3
Gefr. Heinrich Drebinger	FA 47b	18Feb18	EOW	
Uffz. Theodor Eberle	FA 47b	18Feb18	EOW	

Sgt. Adolf Eckhardt	FA 47b	18Feb18	EOW	
Sgt. Friedrich Egenhofer	FA 47b	18Feb18	EOW	
Sgt. Josef Eiglmeier	FA 47b	18Feb18	EOW	
Pion. Martin Ellenrieder	FA 47b	18Feb18	24Feb18	FEA 1b
Pion. Philipp Emrich	FA 47b	18Feb18	EOW	
Pion. Ludwig Fischer	FA 47b	18Feb18	22Oct18	IIC
Pion. Franz Glaissner	FA 47b	18Feb18	28Feb18	AFP 3
Uffz. Julius Godlewsky	FA 47b	18Feb18	17Mar18	München
Gefr. Franz Grillhösl	FA 47b	18Feb18	EOW	
Sgt. Otto Häufglöckmer	FA 47b	18Feb18	18Jun18	Kofl 1
Vzfw. Georg Hartnagel	FA 47b	18Feb18	5Oct18	FS VII
Pion. Fritz Hegemann	FEA 1b	3May18	18Jun18	Kofl 1
Gefr. Emil Hentzen	FEA 1b	3May18	EOW	
Pion. Franz Herbrand	AFP 3	6Mar18	EOW	
Gefr. Erich Höhne	FA 47b	18Feb18	EOW	
Sgt. Franz Hösl	FA 47b	18Feb18	EOW	
Pion. Hermann Kampmann	FEA 1b	3May18	3Jun18	Injured
Pion. Otto König	FEA 1b	2Mar18	22Mar18	FEA 1b
Gefr. Philipp Kraft	FA 47b	18Feb18	14May18	WIA
Pion. Martin Kriegbaur	FA 47b	18Feb18	EOW	
Gefr. Valentin Küttenbaum	FA 47b	18Feb18	EOW	
Gefr. Leonhard Lehrer	FA 47b	18Feb18	EOW	
Pion. Karl Liebhart	AFP 3	7Mar18	May18	Injured
Pion. Johann Liegsalz	FA 47b	18Feb18	28Feb18	AFP 3
Uffz. Adam Lodes	FA 47b	18Feb18	EOW	
Sgt. Armin Löwenberg	FA 47b	18Feb18	EOW	
Uffz.Werkmstr. Christian Malkomes	FA 47b	18Feb18	EOW	
Gefr. Adam Marg	FA 47b	18Feb18	24Mar18	AFP 18
Pion. Lorenz Mayer	FEA 1b	3May18	19Jul18	Kofl 1
Gefr. Martin Mayer	FA 47b	18Feb18	EOW	
Kraftf. Pion. Joseph Mehler	FA 47b	18Feb18	27Mar17	Kofl 18
Gefr. Adam Merz	FA 47b	18Feb18	24Mar18	AFP 18
Gefr. Michael Mettelsiefen	FA 47b	18Feb18	10Jul18	Artllry
Pion. Xaver Muth	FEA 1b	20May18	18Jul18	FEA 1b
Pion. Georg Nagel	FEA 1b	3May18	18Jun18	Kofl 1
Pion. Xaver Nein	AFP 3	7Mar18	19Mar18	Hosp.
Uffz. Andreas Öttl	FA 47b	18Feb18	30May18	Hosp.
Uffz. Andreas Öttl	Hosp.	11Aug18	EOW	
Sgt. Johann Perzlmayr	FA 47b	18Feb18	EOW	
Sgt. Philipp Pfaff	FA 47b	18Feb18	19Mar18	Hosp.
Gefr. Leopold Pferrer	FA 47b	18Feb18	16May18	FEA 1b
Pion. Johann Baptist Probst	FA 47b	18Feb18	May18	FEA 1b
Pion. Franz Xaver Prutscher	FEA 1b	7Aug18	EOW	
Pion. Louis Rauh	AFP 3	8Mar18	EOW	
Pion. Georg Rieder	FA 47b	18Feb18	EOW	
Pion. Josef Riescher	FEA 1b	3May18	19Jul18	Kofl 1
Sgt. Johann Rink	FA 47b	18Feb18	EOW	
San.Uffz. Josef Rogenhofer	FA 47b	18Feb18	EOW	
Gefr. Rupert Särve	FA 47b	18Feb18	EOW	
Pion. Franz Schäffler	FA 297A	25May18	EOW	
Sgt. Ernst Scheidt	FA 47b	18Feb18	EOW	
Pion. Konrad Schirmer	FA 47b	18Feb18	EOW	
Uffz. Karl Schwind	FA 47b	18Feb18	EOW	
Pion. Xaver Sedelmayr	FA 47b	18Feb18	EOW	
Pion. Hermann Senger	FA 47b	18Feb18	EOW	
Pion. Karl Stephan	FA 47b	18Feb18	EOW	
UnterZahlmstr. Ludwig Stettmeyer	FA 47b	18Feb18	24Mar18	München
Sgt. Adam Stenglein	FA 47b	18Feb18	EOW	
Pion. Edmund Stier	FA 47b	18Feb18	EOW	
Pion. Johann Strasser	FEA 1b	3May18	EOW	
Uffz. Georg Streit	FA 47b	18Feb18	EOW	
Pion. Otto Sutter	FEA 1b	20Sep18	EOW	
Gefr. Alwin Thäter	FA 47b	18Feb18	EOW	
Vzfw. Adam Unold	FA 47b	18Feb18	EOW	
Pion. Johann Wagner	AFP 3	7Mar18	31Aug18	FEA 1b
Sgt. Heinrich Walter	AFP 1	7Jun18	EOW	

Pion. Friedrich Walter	AFP 1	7Jun18	EOW	
Pion. Clemens Weber	FA 47b	18Feb18	22Mar18	FEA 1b
Gefr. Peter Weinberger	FA 47b	18Feb18	EOW	
Pion. Waldemer Weise	FA 47b	18Feb18	EOW	
Pion. Josef Weizenwieser	FA 47b	18Feb18	EOW	
Gefr. Johann Wiesand	FA 47b	18Feb18	15May18	FEA 1b
Uffz. Georg Will	FA 47b	18Feb18	EOW	
Feldw. Jakob Wittlinger	FA 47b	18Feb18	EOW	
Sgt. Johann Zillig	FA 47b	18Feb18	EOW	

Schutzstaffel/Schlachtstaffel 31b
Mitgemachte Schlachten und Gefechte
(Battles and combat actions in which Ss 31b participated)

13Feb18	7Mar18	*Stellungskämpfe zwischen Tahure und der Butte Mesnil* (Trench fighting between Tahure and the Butte Mesnil)
8Mar18	20Mar18	*Stellungskämpfe bei St. Quentin und an der Oise* (Trench fighting at St. Quentin and on the Oise)
ab 21Mar18		*Grosse Schlacht in Frankreich* (Great Battle in France)
21Mar18	22Mar18	*Durchbruchsschlacht bei St. Quentin und La Fère* (Penetration battle of St. Quentin and La Fère)
23Mar18	24Mar18	*Kämpfe beim Übergang über die Somme und den Crozatkanal zwischen St. Christ und Tergnier* (Fighting during the crossing of the Somme and the Crozat Canal between St. Christ and Tergnier)
25Mar18	31Mar18	*Verfolgungskämpfe bis Montdidier und Noyon* (Pursuit fighting at Montdidier and Noyon)
1Apr18	14May18	*Stellungskämpfe an der Avre und bei Montdidier* (Trench fighting on the Avre and at Montdidier)
15May18	26Jun18	*Schlacht bei Soissons und Reims* (Battle at Soissons and Reims)
27Jun18	14Jul18	*Stellungskämpfe bei Reims* (Trench fighting at Reims)
15Jul18	17Jul18	*Angriffsschlacht an der Marne und in der Champagne* (Offensive battle on the Marne and in the Champagne)
18Jul18	25Jul18	*Abwehrschlacht zwischen Soissons und Reims* (Defensive battle between Soissons and Reims)
26Jul18	3Aug18	*Bewegliche Abwehrschlacht zwischen Soissons und Vesle* (The mobile battle between Soissons and the Vesle)
4Aug18	7Nov18	*Stellungskämpfe bei Reims* (Trench fighting at Reims)

Schutzstaffel/Schlachtstaffel 31b Airfields

From	To	Location	*Schlachtgruppe* Affiliation	*Armee*
18Feb18	8Mar18	Mars sous Bourcq		3
8Mar18	(21Mar18)	Faucouzy	SGp 1 (Ss 8,31b,36,38s) C.O. *Oblt.* Walter Lackner	18
(4Apr18)	(14Apr18)	Villeselve	SGp 2 (Ss 7,31b,34,37) C.O. *Oblt.* Walter Lackner	18
(25Apr18)		Bonneuil	SGp 1 (Ss 2,7,31b) C.O. *Oblt.* Walter Lackner	18
(8May18)	(14May18)	Hangest	SGp B (Ss 28b,30b,31b,32) C.O. *Oblt.d.R.* August Ertl	7
(23May18)	7Jun18	Tagnon	SGp 1 (Ss 2,7,22b,31b) C.O. *Oblt.* Walter Lackner	1
7Jun18	(9Jun18)	Villeselve	SGp 1 (Ss 2,7,31b) C.O. *Oblt.* Walter Lackner	18
(14Jun18)	25Jul18	Tagnon	SGp 2 (Ss 22b,28b,30b,31b,32) C.O. *Oblt.d.R.* August Ertl	1
26Jul18	10Aug18	Montaigu	SGp B (Ss 28b,30b,31b,32) C.O. *Oblt.d.R.* Josef Gramp	7

10Aug18	11Aug18	Athies	SGp B (Ss 28b,30b,31b,32) C.O. *Oblt.d.R.* Josef Gramp	2
11Aug18	(1Sep18)	Grandlup-et-Fay	SGp B (Ss 28b,30b,31b,32) C.O. *Oblt.d.R.* Josef Gramp	7
(12Sep18)	25Sep18	Perthes	SGp B (Ss 28b,30b,31b,32) C.O. *Oblt.d.R.* Josef Gramp	1
25Sep18	13Oct18	Perthes	SGp B (Ss 30b,31b,32) C.O. *Ritt.d.R.* Julius Bossert	1
13Oct18	23Oct18	Ecly	SGp B (Ss 30b,31b,32) C.O. *Ritt.d.R.* Julius Bossert	1
23Oct18	EOW	Ecly	SGp B Ss (30b,31b) C.O. *Ritt.d.R.* Julius Bossert	1

Royal Bavarian *Schutzstaffel 31b*

18Feb18	*Schutzstaffel 31b* is created from Fl.Abt. 47b by BKM Nr. 16029 of 18Feb18.
6Mar18	*Uffz.* Unterberger-1, *Pion.* Koch-1, Spad, Blaise
23Mar18	*Pion.* Johann Sichermann, P, is WIA and taken POW and *Gefr.* Johann Zink, G, is taken POW S. Nesle. Sichermann DOW on 25Mar18 as a British POW.
27Mar18	*Schutzstaffel 31b* is renamed *Schlachtstaffel 31b* by KM Nr. 5126.18.A.7.L.IV.C. of 27Mar18.
30Mar18	*Pion.* Josef Erhart, P, is WIA during air combat, shot in the lower left leg and to hospital.
2Apr18	*Pion.* Johann Brückmann, M, is WIA by an aerial bomb fragment and to hospital.
6Apr18	*Uffz.* Fritz Seitzinger, P, and *Pion.* Josef Koch, G, are KIA over Moreuil during air combat.
6Apr18	*Uffz.* Josef Unterberger, P, and *Pion.* Johannes Weissler, G, are KIA over Moreuil during air combat.
2May18	*Uffz.* Karwaschewski-1, *Uffz.* Schwem-1, Spad S.13, 17.50, Thory
3May18	*Vzfw.* Karl Peez, P, is WIA and taken POW and *Gefr.* Michael Lang, G, is KIA over Moreuil in Hannover Cl.II 13282/17. Peez DOW 9May18 on the Somme.
14May18	*Gefr.* Philipp Kraft, M, is WIA by a shell splinter to the head during an artillery attack of the airfield at Hangest and to hospital.
28May18	*Gefr.* Max Brandl, P, and *Gefr.* Peter Grotz, G, are forced to land and are taken POW at Faverolles in a Halberstadt Cl.II.
28May18	*Uffz.* Ludwig Schwem, G, is severely WIA, shot in the upper leg, and to hospital at Tagnon.
May18	*Pion.* Konrad Liebhardt, M, is hit in the left arm by a propeller and to hopsital at Hangest.
1Jun18	*Gefr.* Simon Seifried, G, is WIA,sv. by ground fire and to hospital at Tagnon.
3Jun18	*Pion.* Hermann Kampmann, M, is struck by a propeller and to hospital at Hangest.
16Jun18	*Pion.* Wilhelm Amann, M, is severely injured in an accident and dies in the hospital at Tagnon.
19Jul18	*Uffz.* Erich Oskar Roland, P, and *Uffz.* Johann Dütsch, G, are KIA over Vierzy, S. Soissons at 13.55 hours during air combat.
22Oct18	*Vzfw.* Hermann Karwascheski, P, is IIC,sv. at Ecly during a crash while on a test flight. He DOI in the hospital at Charleville on 26Oct18. *Pion.* Ludwig Fischer, M, suffers a broken left arm in this crash and to hospital at Charleville.
25Oct18	*Uffz.* Bonauer-z.L.gzw., *Vzfw.* Dittrich-z.L.gzw., A.R. 2
27Oct18	*Pion.* Michael Sutor, P, and *Gefr.* Josef Sauer, G, are KIA over Ecly during air combat
21Nov18	*Schlachtstaffel 31b* is demobilizd at FEA 1b, Schleissheim.

A captured *Schlasta 31b* Halberstadt Cl.II. This was the aircraft of *Gefr.* Max Brandl and *Gefr.* Peter Grotz downed on 28 May 1918 at Faverolles. The aircraft has been pretty well 'souvenired,' yet the unit marking of a blue/white bar directly under the gunner's cockpit still shows clearly.

Royal Prussian *Schutzstaffel 32*

Pilot/Gunner	Type	From		To	
		Unit	Date	Date	Unit
Vzfw. Karl Albrecht	P			31May18	WIA,lt.
Sgt. Michael Fischer	G	Ss 28b	10Jul18	6Aug18	POW
Gefr. Wilhelm Gerstenkorn	P			10Aug18	KIA
Gefr. Barnim Kiesel (+ 19Jul18)	P			17Jul18	WIA,sv.
Vzfw. Alfred Krauss	G			15Jun18	KIA
Vzfw. Heinrich Müller	P			15Jun18	KIA
Uffz. Paul Nickel				17Jun18	KIA
Flg. Rudolf Pfeifer			(Oct18)		
Ltn. Ernst Ross, C.O.	P	Js 44s	7Oct18	EOW	
Gefr. Paul Schmich	G			10Aug18	KIA
Uffz. Karl Schuchardt	P			6Aug18	POW
Vzfw. Theodor Schulte-Herweling	G			31May18	KIA
Oblt.d.R. Johann Stolch, C.O.	O		14Apr18	Sep18	FA 262A
Flg. Karl Wintergerst				4Dec18	+ i.Kr.
Uffz. Friedrich Witschakowski				17Jun18	KIA

Schutzstaffel/Schlachtstaffel 32 Airfields

From	To	Location	*Schlachtgruppe* Affiliation	*Armee*
(Feb18)	21Mar18	Gruny	Escort for FA 237(A)	18
21Mar18	5Apr18	Grougis	SGp 3 (Ss 6,32,34) C.O. *Oblt.* Werner Lange	18
5Apr18	14Apr18	Gruny	SGp 3 (Ss 6,8,18,32) C.O. *Oblt.* Kurt Messow	18
14Apr18	15May18	Gruny	SGp 4 (Ss 5,20,32,33) C.O. *Oblt.* Werner Lange	18
15May18	(6Jun18)	St. Erme	SGp C (Ss 5,20,32,33,37) C.O. *Oblt.* Werner Lange	7
(9Jun18)	15Jul18	Raperie Ferme	SGp Wichura (Ss 5,20,32,33,37) C.O. *Oblt.* Werner Lange	7
15Jul18	26Jul18	Tagnon	SGp 2 (Ss 22b,28b,30b,31b,32) C.O. *Oblt.d.R.* August Ertl	1
26Jul18	10Aug18	Montaigu	SGp B (Ss 28b,30b,31b,32) C.O. *Oblt.d.R.* Josef Gramp	7
10Aug18	11Aug18	Athies	SGp B (Ss 28b,30b,31b,32) C.O. *Oblt.d.R.* Josef Gramp	2
11Aug18	12Aug18	Montaigu	SGp B (Ss 28b,30b,31b,32) C.O. *Oblt.d.R.* Josef Gramp	7
12Aug18	1Sep18	Grandlup-et-Fay	SGp B (Ss 28b,30b,31b,32) C.O. *Oblt.d.R.* Josef Gramp	7
1Sep18	6Sep18	Briey	SGp B (Ss 5,20,32,37) C.O. *Oblt.* Werner Lange	5
6Sep18	15Sep18	Anoux-le-Grange	SGp B (Ss 5,20,32,37) C.O. *Oblt.* Werner Lange	AAC
15Sep18	25Sep18	Perthes	SGp B (Ss 28b,30b,31b,32) C.O. *Oblt.d.R.* Josef Gramp	1
25Sep18	23Oct18	Perthes	SGp B (Ss 30b,31b,32) C.O. *Ritt.d.R.* Julius Bossert	1
23Oct18	29Oct18	Louppy-sur-Loison	SGp B (Ss 5,20,21,32,33) C.O. *Oblt.* Hans Ebel	5
29Oct18	EOW		SGp B (Ss 7,18,32,34) C.O. *Oblt.* Ernst Bonatz	3

Royal Prussian *Schutzstaffel 32*

26Jan18	*Schutzstaffel 32* is created from Fl.Abt. 4 by KM Nr.995.18.A.7.L.4C. of 26Jan18.
27Mar18	*Schutzstaffel 32* is renamed *Schlachtstaffel 32* by KM Nr.5126.18.A.7.L.IV.C of 27Mar18.
31May18	*Vzfw*. Albrecht, P, is WIA,lt. and *Vzfw*. Theodor Schulte-Herweling, G, is KIA over Estrepilly during air combat.
15Jun18	*Vzfw*. Heinrich Müller, P, and *Vzfw*. Alfred Krauss, G, are KIA over Villers-Cotterêts.
17Jun18	*Uffz*. Paul Nickel and *Uffz*. Friedrich Witschakowski are KIA over Ambrief in a Halberstadt Cl.II.
17Jul18	*Uffz*. Barnim Kiesel, P, is WIA,sv. during air comabt. DOW 19Jul18 at Beelitz.
6Aug18	*Uffz*. Karl Schuchardt, P, and *Sgt*. Michael Fischer, G, are taken POW while on a practice flight from Montaigu.
10Aug18	*Gefr*. Wilhelm Gerstenkorn, P, and *Gefr*. Paul Schmich, G, are KIA over Warvillers during air combat.
4Dec18	*Flg*. Karl Wintergerst dies at Heidenheim.
Nov18	*Schlachtstaffel 32* is demobilized at FEA 3, Gotha.

Royal Prussian *Schutzstaffel 33*

Pilot/Gunner	Type	From		To	
		Unit	Date	Date	Unit
Gefr. Karl Balhorn				4May18	KIA
Uffz. Borchert	G			2Nov18	IIC,sv.
Uffz. Distel	P			2Nov18	IIC,sv.
Vzfw. Josef Fritz	P	FA 15	26Jan18	EOW	
F.T. Georg Kiefer	M			28Jul18	KIA
Ltn.d.R. Walter Knobel, Stv. C.O.	O		(Jul18)	28Jul18	KIA
Oblt. Mai, C.O.				26Jan18	EOW
Uffz. Wilhelm Mittelbachert	P			28Jul18	KIA
Sgt. Paul Osswald	P			28Jul18	KIA
Gefr. August Penske	P			21Apr18	KIA
Vzfw. Plewa	G	Ss 20		4Oct18	WIA,sv.
Gefr. Redmann	G		(Apr18)		
Uffz. Georg Schrickel				4May18	KIA
Ltn. Albrecht Spiess	O	FA 15	26Jan18	7Apr18	AFP 18
Gefr. Edwin Stich	P	BG 3		4Oct18	KIA
Gefr. Stoll	P		(Jul18)		
Gefr. Johannes Straub	G			21Apr18	KIA
Uffz. Stückemann	P		(Apr18)		
Gefr. Wilhelm Wilde	G			28Jul18	KIA

Schutzstaffel/Schlachtstaffel 33 Airfields

From	To	Location	*Schlachtgruppe* Affiliation	*Armee*
26Jan18	Mar18	Origny		18
(21Mar18)	9Apr18	Matigny, NW Ham	SGp 4 (Ss 2,5,20,33) C.O. *Oblt*. Werner Lange	18
9Apr18	15May18	Curchy-Manicourt	SGp 4 (Ss 2,5,20,33) C.O. *Oblt*. Werner Lange	18
15May18	(6Jun18)	St. Erme	SGp C (Ss 5,20,32,33,37) C.O. *Oblt*. Werner Lange	7
(9Jun18)	(25Jun18)	Raperie Ferme	SGp Wichura (Ss 5,20,32,33,37) C.O. *Oblt*. Werner Lange	7
15Jul18	18Jul18	Anoux	SGp 1 (Ss 5,20,33,37) C.O. *Oblt*. Werner Lange	3
18Jul18	28Jul18	Seringes	SGp B (Ss 5,20,33,37) C.O. *Oblt*. Werner Lange	7
29Jul18	7Aug18	St. Loup	SGp B (Ss 5,20,33,35,37) C.O. *Oblt*. Werner Lange	1
7Aug18	(1Sep18)	Chivres-en-Laonnois	SGp C (Ss 5,20,33,35,37) C.O. *Oblt*. Werner Lange	7
(12Sep18)	17Sep18	Grandlup-et-Fay	SGp B (Ss 7,28b,30b,31b,33) C.O. *Oblt.d.R.* Josef Gramp	7

17Sep18	26Sep18	Immonville	SGp B (Ss 5,20,21,26b,33) C.O. *Oblt*. Bruno Zipplies	5
26Sep18	13Oct18	Thonne-les-Prés	SGp B (Ss 5,20,21,33) C.O. *Oblt*. Bruno Zipplies	5
13Oct18	23Oct18	St. Mard, Vitron	SGp B (Ss 5,20,21,33) C.O. *Oblt*. Bruno Zipplies	5
23Oct18	29Oct18	Louppy-sur-Loison SGp	B (Ss 5,20,21,32,33) C.O. *Oblt*. Hans Ebel	5
29Oct18	EOW	Habay-la-Vieille	SGp B (Ss 5,20,21,33) C.O. *Oblt*. Hans Ebel	5

Royal Prussian *Schutzstaffel 33*

26Jan18	*Schutzstaffel 33* is created from Fl.Abt. 15 by KM Nr.995.18.A.7.L.4C. of 26Jan18.
27Mar18	*Schutzstaffel 33* is renamed *Schlachtstaffel 33* by KM Nr.5126.18.A.7.L.IV.C of 27Mar18.
20Apr18	*Uffz*. Stückemann-1, *Gefr*. Redmann-1, Spad S.13, 17.15, W. Montdidier
21Apr18	*Gefr*. August Penske, P, and *Gefr*. Johannes Straub, G, are KIA over Montdidier during an air combat.
4May18	*Gefr*. Karl Balhorn and *Uffz*. Georg Schrickel are KIA at Liancourt-Fosse, E. of Nesle.
20Jul18	*Ltn.d.R*. Knobel-1, *Gefr*. Stoll-1, French 1 Seater
28Jul18	*F.T*. Georg Kiefer, M, is KIA at Arcy-Ste. Restitue.
28Jul18	*Uffz*. Wilhelm Mittelbachert, P, and *Ltn.d.R*. Walter Knobel, O, are KIA over Villers sur Fère in a collision with Osswald at 20.00 hours.
28Jul18	*Sgt*. Paul Osswald, P, and *Gefr*. Wilhelm Wilde, G, are KIA over Villers sur Fère in a collision with Mittelbachert at 20.00 hours.
4Oct18	*Gefr*. Edwin Stich, P, is KIA and *Vzfw*. Plewa, G, is WIA,sv. shot in the neck, over Verdun.
2Nov18	*Uffz*. Distel, P, and *Uffz*. Borchert, G, are IIC,sv.
Nov18	*Schlachtstaffel 33* is demobilized at *Militär Fliegerschule* Elbing.

Royal Prussian *Schutzstaffel 34*

Pilot/Gunner	Type	From		To	
		Unit	Date	Date	Unit
Uffz. Robert Clashaus	P			10Aug18	KIA
Vzfw. Alfred Hädrich	G			1Oct18	KIA
Rudolf Hooss	G		Jul18	17Aug18	IIC
Flg. Erich Klein	G			10Aug18	KIA
Vzfw. Knauf	P		(May18)	(Jul18)	
Uffz. Ernst Knorth				15Jul18	KIA
Ltn. Herbert Koch, C.O.					
Vzfw. Körver			(Jul18)		
Ltn. Mark Albrecht von Köster, stv. CO		Ss 7	Aug18	4Sep18	Ss 34
Ltn. Mark Albrecht von Köster, C.O.	O		4Sep18	1Oct18	SD
Ltn. Mark Albrecht von Köster, C.O.	O		1Oct18	EOW	
Ladehoff					
Oblt. Werner Lange, C.O.			Jan18	14Apr18	Ss 20
Uffz. Machemehl		AFP 1	19Feb18		
Gefr. Noack	G		(May18)		
Oblt. Podoll, C.O.			14Apr18	Aug18	
Erich Riehm			('18)	EOW	
Vzfw. Schaber			(Oct18)		
Vzfw. Theodor Schäfer	P			1Oct18	KIA
Uffz. Weilhardt	P			10Aug18	WIA,lt.

Schutzstaffel/Schlachtstaffel 34 Airfields

From	To	Location	*Schlachtgruppe* Affiliation	*Armee*
19Feb18		St. Loup by Alincourt		1
21Mar18		Bohéries	SGp 3 (Ss 6,32,34) C.O. *Oblt*. Werner Lange	18

24Mar18		Bohain	SGp 3 (Ss 6,32,34) C.O. *Oblt.* Werner Lange	18
(9Apr18)		Bonneuil	SGp 2 (Ss 7,31b,34,37) C.O. *Oblt.* Walter Lackner	18
(25Apr18)		Bonneuil	SGp 3 (Ss 6,18,34)	18
(27May18)		Dury	SGp 3 (Ss 6,18,34,35,38s) C.O. *Ritt.* Herrmann	18
(9Jun18)	24Jun18	Dury	SGp 2 (Ss 6,18,34,35,38s) C.O. *Ritt.* Herrmann	18
24Jun18	5Jul18	Mons-en-Chaussée	SGp 2 (Ss 6,18,34,35) C.O. *Oblt.* Friedrich-Carl Hanesse	18
5Jul18	(15Jul18)	Dricourt	SGp 3 (Ss 6,7,18,34,38s) C.O. *Oblt.* Friedrich-Carl Hanesse	3
(23Jul18)	29Jul18	Marle	SGp 3 (Ss 6,18,34,38s) C.O. *Oblt.* Friedrich-Carl Hanesse	9
29Jul18	3Aug18	Toulis	SGp 3 (Ss 6,18,34,38s) C.O. *Oblt.* Friedrich-Carl Hanesse	9
4Aug18	9Aug18	Toulis	SGp 3 (Ss 6,18,26b,34,38s) C.O. *Oblt.* Friedrich-Carl Hanesse	9
9Aug18	12Aug18	Bouvincourt	SGp 3 (Ss 6,18,34,38s) C.O. *Oblt.* Friedrich-Carl Hanesse	2
13Aug18	16Aug18	Marle	SGp 3 (Ss 6,7,18,26b,34,38s) C.O. *Oblt.* Friedrich-Carl Hanesse	9
16Aug18	28Aug18	Villeselve	SGp 3 (Ss 6,12,18,26b,34,38s) C.O. *Oblt.* Friedrich-Carl Hanesse	18
28Aug18	18Sep18	Toulis	SGp 3 (Ss 6,18,26b,34,38s) C.O. *Oblt.* Friedrich-Carl Hanesse	9
18Sep18	6Oct18		SGp B (Ss 6,18,34,38s) C.O. *Oblt.* Friedrich-Carl Hanesse	3
9Oct18	13Oct18	Toulis	SGp B (Ss 6,7,18,34,38s) C.O. *Oblt.* Friedrich-Carl Hanesse	7
13Oct18	18Oct18	Toulis	SGp B (Ss 7,18,34,38s) C.O. *Oblt.* Friedrich-Carl Hanesse	7
18Oct18	29Oct18		SGp B (Ss 7,18,34) C.O. *Oblt.* Ernst Bonatz	7
29Oct18	EOW		SGp B (Ss 7,18,32,34) C.O. *Oblt.* Ernst Bonatz	3

Royal Prussian *Schutzstaffel 34*

26Jan18	*Schutzstaffel 34* is created from Fl.Abt. 21 by KM Nr.995.18.A.7.L.4C. of 26Jan18.
27Mar18	*Schutzstaffel 34* is renamed *Schlachtstaffel 34* by KM Nr.5126.18.A.7.L.IV.C. of 27Mar18.
22May18	*Vzfw.* Knauf-1, *Gefr.* Noack-1, Fr. Kamfeinsitzer.
15Jul18	*Uffz.* Ernst Knorth is KIA over Dricourt.
10Aug18	*Uffz.* Robert Clashaus, P, and *Flg.* Erich Klein, G, are KIA over Warvillers during air combat.
10Aug18	*Uffz.* Weilhardt, P, is WIA over Warvillers during air combat.
17Aug18	Rudolf Hooss, G, is IIC.
1Oct18	*Vzfw.* Theodor Schäfer, P, and *Vzfw.* Alfred Hädrich, G, are KIA over Aure at 18.00 hours.
1Oct18	*Ltn.* Mark Albrecht von Köster, O and C.O., is shot down but is OK and manages to get the aircraft back OK.
Nov18	*Schlachtstaffel 34* is demobilized at FEA 1, Altenburg.

Royal Prussian *Schutzstaffel 35*

Pilot/Gunner	Type	From		To	
		Unit	Date	Date	Unit
Gefr. Beoching	G			6Jul18	WIA,sv.
Ritt.d.R. Julius Bossert, Stv C.O.	O	FA 292A	21Jun18	17Jul18	Ss 30b
Flg. Jakob Diehl	P			28Sep18	KIA
Uffz. Martin Duffy	P	AFP 6	9Apr18	18Apr18	Js 41
Uffz. Adolf Eckhoff (DOW 2Jun18)	P		(May18)	2Jun18	WIA,sv.
Vzfw. Rudolf Gemeinder (+ 22Aug)	P			20Aug18	WIA,sv.

Hannover Cl.IIIa 12678/18 shown here in Canada post-war. Note the black and white diagonal fuselage band aft of the cross and the white aircraft number 2 on the fin, the unit markings of *Schlasta 34*.

Flg. Hermann Goebel	G		(Jun18)	17Aug18	KIA
Gefr. Grunow	P		(Aug18)		
Uffz. Alfred Haucke	P		25Aug18		
Uffz. Hebel	G		(Aug18)	18Aug18	WIA,lt.
Uffz. Kämpf	P			7May18	IIC,lt.
Flg. Alfred Käuflin	G			29Apr18	KIC
Gefr. Kontrzonke	G			23Jun18	WIA
Uffz. Erich Lehmald				17Oct18	+ i.Kr.
Vzfw. August Matthies	P	Ss 5	(Aug18)	(Oct18)	
Uffz. Meyer	G			22May18	IIC,F/L
Ltn.d.R. Müller-Friedel, C.O.	O	Js 33	7Apr18	EOW	
Vzfw. Neuenfeld				19Jul18	IIC,lt.
Vzfw. Alfred Poller (+ 8Jul18)	P			21May18	WIA
Flg. Erich Reinke	G			20Aug18	KIA
Vzfw. Roeder	P		(May18)	(Jun18)	
Gefr. Schöckel				12May18	IIC,lt.
Flg. Schubert	G			16Jun18	WIA
Uffz. Robert Topp	P			29Apr18	KIC
Vzfw. Wollgast	G			7May18	WIA,lt.

Schutzstaffel/Schlachtstaffel 35 Airfields

From	To	Location	*Schlachtgruppe* Affiliation	*Armee*
(21Mar18)	(12May18)	Houplin		6
(27May18)	9Jun18	Dury	SGp 3 (Ss 6,18,34,35,38s) C.O. *Ritt.* Herrmann	18
9Jun18	(24Jun18)	Dury	SGp 2 (Ss 6,18,34,35,38s) C.O. *Ritt.* Herrmann	18
(1Jul18)	15Jul18	Dricourt	SGp 2 (Ss 6,18,34,35,38s) C.O. *Oblt.* Friedrich-Carl Hanesse	3
15Jul18	18Jul18	Le Chesne	SGp 2 (Ss 7,23b,26b,35,36) C.O. *Oblt.* Walter Lackner	3
18Jul18	28Jul18	St. Loup		1
29Jul18	7Aug18	St. Loup	SGp B (Ss 5,20,33,35,37) C.O. *Oblt.* Werner Lange	1
7Aug18	11Aug18	Chivres-en-Laonnois	SGp C (Ss 5,20,33,35,37) C.O. *Oblt.* Werner Lange	7

11Aug18	12Aug18	Athies NW	SGp J (Ss 4,15,24b,25b,35) C.O. *Oblt.* Erhardt Egerer	2
12Aug18	15Aug18	Chivres-en-Laonnois	SGp C (Ss 5,20,33,35,37) C.O. *Oblt.* Werner Lange	7
15Aug18	20Aug18	St. Loup	SGp J (Ss 4,15,24b,25b,35) C.O. *Oblt.* Erhardt Egerer	1
21Aug18	1Sep18	Chivres-en-Laonnois	SGp C (Ss 5,20,33,35,37) C.O. *Oblt.* Werner Lange	7
2Sep18	8Sep18	Abscon	SGp J (Ss 4,15,24b,25b,35) C.O. *Oblt.* Erhardt Egerer	17
9Sep18	3Oct18	Abscon	SGp J (Ss 4,15,24b,25b,35) C.O. *Oblt.* Friedrich von Krausser	17
3Oct18	13Oct18	Marly	SGp S (Ss 4,11,15,27b,35) C.O. *Hptm.* Hugo Weingarth	17
13Oct18	21Oct18			17
21Oct18	EOW		SGp A (Ss 8,10,16,35) C.O. *Oblt.* Emil Ziegler gen Stege	17

Royal Prussian *Schutzstaffel 35*

26Jan18	*Schutzstaffel 35* is created from Fl.Abt. 11 by KM Nr.995.18.A.7.L.4C. of 26Jan18.
27Mar18	*Schutzstaffel 35* is renamed *Schlachtstaffel 35* by KM Nr.5126.18.A.7.L.IV.C of 27Mar18.
29Apr18	*Uffz.* Richard Topp, P, and *Flg.* Alfred Käuflin, G, are KIC at Houplin.
7May18	*Uffz.* Kämpf, P, is IIC,lt. at Houplin.
7May18	*Vzfw.* Wollgast, G, is WIA,lt. by ground fire.
12May18	*Gefr.* Schöckel is IIC,lt. at Houplin.
21May18	*Vzfw.* Alfred Poller, P, is WIA,sv. over Béthune during air combat. He DOW 8Jul18 at Bremerhaven.
22May18	*Uffz.* Meyer, G, is IIC in a forced landing.
2Jun18	*Uffz.* Adolf Eckhoff, P, is WIA,sv. during air combat. He dies that day at Laventé.
16Jun18	*Flg.* Schubert, G, is WIA during air combat.
23Jun18	*Gefr.* Kontrzonke, G, is WIA during air combat.
6Jul18	*Gefr.* Beoching, G, is WIA,sv. during air combat.
19Jul18	*Vzfw.* Neuenfeld is IIC,lt.
17Aug18	*Gefr.* Grunow-1, *Uffz.* Hebel-1, Breguet 14B2, 8.35, Sillery Esc. Br.17, Sol. G. Bordas, KIA
17Aug18	*Flg.* Hermann Göbel, G, is KIA over Lomme.
18Aug18	*Uffz.* Hebel, G, is WIA,lt. by ground fire.
20Aug18	*Flg.* Erich Reinke, G, is KIA over Fismes, and *Vzfw.* Rudolf Gemeinder, P, is WIA,sv. over Fismes. He DOW 22Aug18 at Juvigny.
28Sep18	*Flg.* Jakob Diehl, P, is KIA at an unknown location. He is buried in Hooglede.
17Oct18	*Uffz.* Erich Lehmald dies at Sedan. Unknown if he was a flying member or a mechanic of the unit.
Nov18	*Schlachtstaffel 35* is demobilized at *Militär Fliegerschule* Elbing.

Royal Prussian *Schutzstaffel 36*

Pilot/Gunner	Type	From		To	
		Unit	Date	Date	Unit
Flg. Alfred Blind	P			28Apr18	KIC
Oblt. Ernst Bonatz, C.O.	P	FA 25	26Jan18	22Apr18	Grfl 19
Gefr. Erich Dähne	G			28Apr18	KIC
Uffz. Willy Danzmann	P			15Sep18	KIA
Uffz. Erich Dittmar	G		(May18)	15Sep18	KIA
Flg. Rudolf Dreher	P			31May18	KIA
Vzfw. Bernhard Ennenga	P	FA 25	26Jan18	27Apr18	IIC,lt.
Vzfw. Bernhard Ennenga	P		27Apr18	21Aug18	AFP 9
Vzfw. Grunau	G			28Apr18	WIA
Oblt. Karl von Gynz-Rekowsky, C.O.	O	FA 202A	23Apr18	27Apr18	IIC,lt.
Oblt. Karl von Gynz-Rekowsky, C.O.	O		27Apr18	(Jul18)	
Uffz. Keusen	P		(May18)		
Flg. Werner Klauss	P			28Apr18	WIA
Uffz. Werner Klauss	P		(Jul18)	EOW	
Uffz. Edmund Ruch	G			17Aug18	KIA

Gefr. Wilhelm Schoop	P		(May18)	31May18	WIA,sv.
Gefr. Wilhelm Schoop	P			17Aug18	KIA
Uffz. Sindt	G			31May18	WIA,sv.
Flg. Wener	P		(Jun18)	EOW	

Schutzstaffel/Schlachtstaffel 36 Airfields

From	To	Location	*Schlachtgruppe* Affiliation	*Armee*
(21Mar18)		Faucouzy	SGp 1 (Ss 8,31b,36,38s) C.O. *Oblt.* Walter Lackner	18
11Apr18	(14Apr18)	Faucouzy	SGp 1 (Ss 36,38s) C.O. *Ritt.* Herrmann	18
(25Apr18)	9Jun18	Ronchin		6
9Jun18	15Jul18	Ronchin	SGp Miller (Ss 25b,36) C.O. *Oblt.* Hugo Miller	6
15Jul18	18Jul18	Le Chesne	SGp 2 (Ss 7,23b,26b,35,36) C.O. *Oblt.* Walter Lackner	3
18Jul18	3Aug18	Le Chesne	SGp 2 (Ss 7,22b,23b,26b,36) C.O. *Oblt.* Walter Lackner	3
4Aug18	9Sep18	St. Loup	SGp B (Ss 2,22b,23b,36) C.O. *Oblt.d.R.* Ludwig Männer	1
9Sep18	15Sep18	St. Loup	SGp B (Ss 2,22b,23b,36) C.O. *Oblt.d.R.* Sigmund Kreitmair	1
15Sep18	25Sep18	Antullen by Metz		19
25Sep18	19Oct18	Antullen by Metz	SGp 2 (Ss 28b,36) C.O. *Oblt.* Oskar Baumann	19
19Oct18	EOW	Diffenbach-lès-Puttelange	SGp 2 (Ss 2,22b,28b,36) C.O. *Oblt.* Karl *Ritter* von Gruny	19

Royal Prussian *Schutzstaffel 36*

26Jan18	*Schutzstaffel 36* is created from Fl.Abt. 25 by KM Nr.995.18.A.7.L.4C. of 26Jan18.
27Mar18	*Schutzstaffel 36* is renamed *Schlachtstaffel 36* by KM Nr. 5126.18.A.7.L.IV.C of 27Mar18.
27Apr18	*Vzfw.* Bernhard Ennenga, P, and *Oblt.* Karl von Gynz-Rekowsky O, are IIC,lt. Both men remain with the unit.
28Apr18	*Flg.* Alfred Blind, P, and *Gefr.* Erich Dähne, G, are KIC at Ronchin during take-off.
28Apr18	*Flg.* Werner Klauss, P, and *Vzfw.* Grunau, G, are WIA.
31May18	*Flg.* Rudolf Dreher, P, is KIA by Flak over Ronchin.
31May18	*Gefr.* Wilhelm Schoop, P, and *Uffz.* Sindt, G, are WIA,sv. over Ronchin during air combat.
17Aug18	*Uffz.* Wilhelm Schoop, P, and *Uffz.* Edmund Ruch, G, are KIA over Le Marais Ferme, SE of Lestrem.
15Sep18	*Uffz.* Willy Danzmann, P, and *Uffz.* Erich Dittmar, G, are KIA over Antullen by Metz.
Nov18	*Schlachtstaffel 36* is demobilized at *Militär Fliegerschule* Elbing.

Royal Prussian *Schutzstaffel 37*

Pilot/Gunner	Type	From		To	
		Unit	Date	Date	Unit
Flg. F. Brake	P		(Mar18)	6Sep18	Js 26
Uffz. Otto Diederichs	P		(Jul18)		
Vzfw. Erlhoff	G		(Jul18)		
Gefr. Jacob Flott	G		(Jul18)	10Aug18	KIA
Uffz. Anton Haberl	G	Ss 23b	24May18	8Jun18	Hosp.
Uffz. Anton Haberl	G	Hosp.	24Jul18	2Aug18	Ss 30b
Ltn.d.R. Holbeck, C.O.	O	Kofl 4	9Feb18	24Aug18	
Flg. Maniura	G	AFP 1	(Mar18)		
Ltn.d.R. Perleberg	O		18Feb18	(Jul18)	
Uffz. Oswald Pflaum	P		(Jul18)	10Aug18	KIA
Gefr. Alfred Rösler	G	Ss 30b	1Aug18		
Vzfw. August Rottau	P			18Feb18	EOW

Vzfw. Speer	P			24Mar18	WIA,sv.
Ltn. Umlauff	P			24Apr18	WIA,sv.
Ltn.d.R. Hermann Wolf	P	AFP 7	26May18	18Jul18	WIA,sv.

Schutzstaffel/Schlachtstaffel 37 Airfields

From	To	Location	*Schlachtgruppe* Affiliation	*Armee*
19Feb18	Mar18	St. Loup by Alincourt	Escort for FA 252(A)w	1
(21Mar18)	23Mar18	Lesquielles- St. Germain	SGp 2 (Ss 7,18,37) C.O. *Oblt.* Walter Lackner	18
23Mar18		Mont d'Origny	SGp 2 (Ss 7,18,37) C.O. *Oblt.* Walter Lachner	18
(9Apr18)		Bonneuil	SGp 2 (Ss 7,31b,34,37) C.O. *Oblt.* Walter Lackner	18
(25Apr18)		Bonneuil	SGp 2 (Ss 8,37,38s) C.O. *Ritt.* Herrmann	18
(29Apr18)	(6Jun18)	St. Erme	SGp C (Ss 5,20,32,33,37) C.O. *Oblt.* Werner Lange	7
(9Jun18)	(25Jun18)	Raperie Ferme	SGp Wichura (Ss 5,20,32,33,37) C.O. *Oblt.* Werner Lange	7
(15Jul18)	18Jul18	Anoux	SGp 1 (Ss 5,20,33,37) C.O. *Oblt.* Werner Lange	3
18Jul18	28Jul18	Serignes	SGp B (Ss 5,20,33,37) C.O. *Oblt.* Werner Lange	7
29Jul18	7Aug18	St. Loup	SGp B (Ss 5,20,33,35,37) C.O. *Oblt.* Werner Lange	1
7Aug18	11Aug18	Chivres-en-Laonnois	SGp C (Ss 5,20,33,35,37) C.O. *Oblt.* Werner Lange	7
11Aug18	12Aug18	Chivres-en-Laonnois	SGp C (Ss 5,20,33,37) C.O. *Oblt.* Werner Lange	7
12Aug18	1Sep18	Chivres-en-Laonnois	SGp C (Ss 5,20,33,35,37) C.O. *Oblt.* Werner Lange	7
2Sep18	6Sep18	Briey	SGp B (Ss 5,20,32,37) C.O. *Oblt.* Werner Lange	5
6Sep18	15Sep18	Anoux-le-Grange	SGp C (Ss 5,20,32,37) C.O. *Oblt.* Werner Lange	AAC
15Sep18	25Sep18	Anoux-le-Grange		AAC
26Sep18	6Oct18	Anoux-le-Grange	SGp 1 (Ss 26b,37) C.O. *Oblt.d.R.* Konrad Hoffmann	AAC
6Oct18	(23Oct18)	Anoux-le-Grange		AAC
(27Oct18)	EOW			AAC

Royal Prussian *Schutzstaffel 37*

26Jan18	*Schutzstaffel 37* is created from Fl.Abt. 220(A) by KM Nr. 995.18.A.7.L.4C. of 26Jan18.
24Mar18	*Vzfw.* Speer, P, is WIA,sv.
27Mar18	*Schutzstaffel 37* is renamed *Schlachtstaffel 37* by KM Nr. 5126.18.A.7.L.IV.C. of 27Mar18.
24Apr18	*Ltn.* Umlauff, P, is WIA,sv.
18Jul18	*Uffz.* Pflaum-1, *Gefr.* Flott-1, Spad S.11 Esc. Spa.266, M.d.L. L. Quet,OK & S/Lt. Merot,WIA
18Jul18	*Ltn.d.R.* Hermann Wolf, P, and *Gefr.* Sammet, G, *Schlasta 20* are WIA,sv. by ground fire and to hospital.
24Jul18	*Uffz.* Diederichs-1, *Vzfw.* Erlhoff-1, French Breguet
10Aug18	*Uffz.* Oswald Pflaum, P, and *Gefr.* Jakob Flott, G, are KIA over Rosières during an air combat.
Nov18	*Schlachtstaffel 37* is demobilized at FEA 2, Schneidemühl.

A crew of *Schlasta 37,* on the left the pilot *Vzfw.* August Rottau and his observer, *Ltn.d.R.* Perleberg. Credit: UTD/HAC.

Royal Saxon *Schutzstaffel 38*

Pilot/Gunner	Type	From		To	
		Unit	Date	Date	Unit
Vzfw. Blumenthal			(Jul18)		
Gefr. Willi Döhmland				21Mar18	KIA
Ritt. Herrmann, C.O.		FA 259A	9Apr18	7Jul18	
Gefr. Bruno Karcher (+ 30Mar18)	P			29Mar18	POW
Ltn.d.R. Knerlich	O	FA 8	9Feb18	(Sep18)	
Ltn.d.R. Knerlich, C.O.	O	Ss 38s	7Jul18	(Sep18)	
Uffz. Willi Marth	G			6Jun18	KIA
Gefr. Meder	P			23Mar18	POW
Ltn.d.R. Hans Mezger, OzbV	P	AFP 18	3Jun18	EOW	
Uffz. Müller			(Oct18)		
Uffz. Otto Rühle	P		Apr18	Sep18	FEA 6
Uffz. Leo Rupprecht				EOW	
Flg. Paul Schleuder	G			29Mar18	POW
Gefr. Voss	G			23Mar18	POW
Uffz. Wagner			(Jul18)		
Vzfw. Wespisser			(Oct18)		
Gefr. Julius Withenius	P		(May18)	6Jun18	KIA

Schutzstaffel/Schlachtstaffel 38s
Mitgemachte Schlachten und Gefechte

(Battles and combat actions in which Ss 38s participated)
(From 3Jun18 - EOW)

26Jan18	2Jun18	Not available
3Jun18	8Jun18	*Kämpfe an der Aisne und an der Marne* (Fighting on the Aisne and on the Marne)
9Jun18	13Jun18	*Schlacht bei Noyon* (Battle by Noyon)
19Jun18	6Jul18	*Kämpfe an der Avre und an der Matz* (Fighting on the Avre and on the Matz)
10Jul18	17Jul18	*Angriffsschlacht an der Marne und in der Champagne* (Offensive battle on the Marne and in the Champagne)
18Jul18	25Jul18	*Abwehrschlacht zwischen Soissons und Reims* (Defensive battle between Soissons and Reims)
26Jul18	3Aug18	*Abwehrschlacht zwischen Marne und Vesle* (Defensive battle between the Marne and the Vesle)
3Aug18	16Aug18	*Stellungskämpfe zwischen Oise und Aisne* (Trench fighting between the Oise and the Aisne)
17Aug18	4Sep18	*Abwehrschlacht zwischen Oise und Aisne* (Defensive battle between the Oise and the Aisne)
5Sep18	18Sep18	*Kämpfe um die Siegfriedstellung, 1918* (Fighting on the Siegfried Line, 1918)
27Sep18	21Oct18	*Abwehrschlacht in der Champagne und an der Marne* (Defensive battle in the Champagne and on the Marne)
22Oct18	EOW	*Rückzugskämpfe der 7. Armee* (Fighting during the retreat of the 7th Army)

Schutzstaffel/Schlachtstaffel 38s Airfields

From	To	Location	*Schlachtgruppe* Affiliation	*Armee*
26Jan18		Dricourt		3
(21Mar18)	29Mar18	Faucouzy	SGp 1 (Ss 8,31b,36,38s) C.O. *Oblt.* Walter Lackner	18
29Mar18	Villeselve		SGp 1 (Ss 36,38s) C.O. *Ritt.* Herrmann	18
(25Apr18)	Villeselve		SGp 2 (Ss 8,37,38s) C.O. *Ritt.* Herrmann	18
(27May18)	Dury		SGp 3 (Ss 6,18,34,35,38s) C.O. *Ritt.* Herrmann	18
(9Jun18)	13Jun18	Dury	SGp 2 (Ss 6,18,34,35,38s) C.O. *Ritt.* Herrmann	18
(1Jul18)	Dricourt		SGp 3 (Ss 6,7,18,34,38s) C.O. *Oblt.* Friedrich-Carl Hanesse	3
(15Jul18)	Dury		SGp 3 (Ss 6,18,34,38s) C.O. *Oblt.* Friedrich-Carl Hanesse	9
(29Jul18)	3Aug18	Toulis	SGp 3 (Ss 6,18,34,38s) C.O. *Oblt.* Friedrich-Carl Hanesse	9
4Aug18	9Aug18	Toulis	SGp 3 (Ss 6,18,26b,34,38s) C.O. *Oblt.* Friedrich-Carl Hanesse	9
9Aug18	12Aug18	Bouvincourt	SGp 3 (Ss 6,18,34,38s) C.O. *Oblt.* Friedrich-Carl Hanesse	2
13Aug18	16Aug18	Toulis	SGp 3 (Ss 6,7,18,26b,34,38s) C.O. *Oblt.* Friedrich-Carl Hanesse	9
16Aug18	28Aug18	Toulis		9
28Aug18	18Sep18	Toulis	SGp 3 (Ss 6,18,26b,34,38s) C.O. *Oblt.* Friedrich-Carl Hanesse	9
18Sep18	6Oct18		SGp B (Ss 6,18,34,38s) C.O. *Oblt.* Friedrich-Carl Hanesse	3
6Oct18	13Oct18	Toulis	SGp B (Ss 6,7,18,34,38s) C.O. *Oblt.* Friedrich-Carl Hanesse	7

13Oct18	18Oct18	Toulis	SGp B (Ss 7,18,34,38s) C.O. *Oblt.* Friedrich-Carl Hanesse	7
18Oct18	EOW	Feuchères	SGp 3 (Ss 6,12,23b,38s) C.O. *Oblt.* Friedrich-Carl Hanesse	7

Royal Saxon *Schutzstaffel 38s*

26Jan18	*Schutzstaffel 38s* is created from Fl.Abt. 24s by KM Nr.995.18.A.7.L.4C. of 26Jan18.
21Mar18	*Gefr.* Willi Döhmland is KIA over Essigny-le-Grand during air combat.
23Mar18	*Gefr.* Meder, P, and *Gefr.* Voss, G, are taken POW in Hannover Cl.II 13186/17.
27Mar18	*Schutzstaffel 38s* is renamed *Schlachtstaffel 38s* by KM Nr. 5126.18.A.7.L.IV.C. of 27Mar18.
29Mar18	*Gefr.* Bruno Karcher, P, is WIA, POW and *Flg.* Paul Schleuder, G, is taken POW in Hannover Cl.II 13199/17 at Lestrem. Karcher DOW the next day. They were downed by British anti-aircraft fire.
30May18	*Gefr.* Withenius-1, *Ltn.d.R.* Knerlich-2, Balloon 88e Cie. Aerostieres
6Jun18	*Gefr.* Julius Withenius, P, and *Uffz.* Willi Marth, G, are KIA over Frenchies.
27Dec18	*Schlachtstaffel 38s* is demobilized at *Militär Fliegerschule* Wurzen, part of FEA 6 at Grossenhain.

Hannover Cl.II 13199/17 on the ground at the RAF base at Turnbury. This *Schlasta 38s* aircraft, crewed by *Gefr.* Bruno Karcher (P) and *Flg.* Paul Schleuder (G), was captured by the British and given the "G" number G.156. It was brought to England for flight-testing and evalution.

CONCLUSION

The purpose of this book has been to help fill the void created by the almost total lack of information written about the *Schutzstaffeln/Schlachtstaffeln* and to show how their role evolved from purely escort duties to one of infantry support. At the same time an attempt has been made to document not only the equipment used by these units but to also relate at least some information about the brave young men who crewed these two-seaters.

General der Flieger (ret'd) Walter Sommé succinctly summarized the history of the *Schusta/Schlasta* in a short paper, now located in the Military Archives at Freiburg, written after the end of the Second World War entitled, 'From the Beginnings of Ground Attack Flying':

> "In the course of the First World War, the aerial weapon had developed from purely a means of observation to a means for conducting combat which employed its armament not only in battle from one aircraft to another, but also against ground targets. So it came in the year 1915-1916 to the establishment of so-called *Kampfgeschwader*, which were equipped with single-engine two-seater machines of the types Albatros, Rumpler, Aviatik, and LVG. They had at their disposal fixed machine guns firing through the propeller arc and flexible machine guns manned by the observer. Three *Staffeln* of six aircraft each were assembled into a *Geschwader*, *Kampfgeschwader OHL,* abbreviated as *'Kagohl,'* which was proudly worn by the crews as a badge on their sleeves. The aircraft of these *Geschwader* were also capable of carrying small and medium-sized bombs.
>
> "However, it was soon determined that the deployment of these *Geschwader* did not quite live up to one's expectations. This was due not so much to the spirit of the crews as to the aircraft, which could fend off individual fighter aircraft, but really were not suitable for an actual aerial combat. On the other hand, they lacked the performance to be bombers, both in terms of load capacity and ability to climb. It was revealed here, as it was time and again later on, that so called 'compromise aircraft' are out of place. Unfortunately, one fell for them again and again.
>
> "Thus were the *Kagohl* used for barrage patrols in the various battle sectors, i.e., in order to put a stop to the activities of approaching artillery and reconnaissance aircraft. With the further development of fighter aviation, this task too was dropped. The *Geschwader* were disbanded and the individual *Staffeln* made into so-called *Schutzstaffeln* which received the task of protecting the individually flying machines of the reconnaissance and artillery *Fliegerabteilungen.* Now this was a task which demanded to a high degree a sense of responsibility and readiness for action from the crew to whom the reconnaissance or artillery flyers were entrusted. They presented a welcome target for anti-aircraft fire and fighter pilots and had to put up with a lot of criticism, mostly as scapegoats.
>
> "Obviously, *Staffel* commanders as well as crews of these so-called *Schutzstaffeln* yearned for tasks which promised them greater freedom of action. So it came about that almost at the same time *Schutzstaffel 11* of *Oberleutnant* Sommé and that of *Oberleutnant* Zorer made a point of attacking enemy trench sections, troop concentrations, and battery positions at a low level after finishing their escort duties. The effect on the enemy was so novel and surprising and the relief for our own troops so noticeable that the army communiques took notice of it.

Of course, this provided a great incentive for *Staffel* commanders and crews, especially since our own losses were kept entirely within acceptable limits. We now proceeded to bolster our fire with the dropping of hand grenades. The badly suffering infantry was enthusiastic about this aid and on their own accord secured recognition for it.

"This goaded the development departments into action with surprising speed. We received a little 12.5 kilogram fragmentation bomb with an impact fuse. Furthermore, the *Staffeln* which specialized in ground attacks received a new aircraft, the so-called 'Halberstädter.' It was an aircraft resembling a fighter, a single-bay biplane with a fixed machine gun for the pilot and a flexible machine for the gunner and bomb-dropping gear. It was very maneuverable and had a good rate of climb, but unfortunately was somewhat too slow for our taste. But otherwise it was the ideal aircraft for us.

"The appearance of this new machine at the front brought us however an unexpected surprise. Since the machine closely resembled a fighter plane, all enemy reconnaissance aircraft ran away from us. On the other hand, enemy fighters thinking we were fighter aircraft approached us from the rear and then quite surprisingly got a taste of a machine gun burst from the gunner. So in the *Schlachtstaffeln*, as we were now designated, we were very soon able to chalk up a considerable number of confirmed victories. Our self-confidence now increased greatly and with growing general recognition had an effect on the crew's thirst for action. Soon the *Staffeln* were also assembled into *Schlachtfliegergruppen.*"

The role of infantry support has largely remained unchanged since first developed by the *Luftstreitkräfte* in 1917-1918, namely to help the "grunt" on the ground take and hold enemy positions. Granted, the Halberstadt and Hannover aircraft have been replaced by the Bell Huey 'Cobra' Helicopter gunship and the Fairchild Republic A-10 'Warthog' anti-tank aircraft, and the name has changed to Close Air Support (CAS), but the goal has remained the same.

As an aside, for those of you who like to keep track of these things, *Schusta/Schlasta* crews were credited with at least 184 victories (including five balloons), with an additional eight forced to land (*zLgzw*), and at least a dozen unconfirmed, usually counter-claimed by either Flak units or *Jasta* pilots.

APPENDICES

APPENDIX I

TRAINING

Pilot Training
During 1917-1918 the training of pilots was conducted at either one of the many military flying schools which were situated throughout Germany or entirely at one of the 16 *Flieger Ersatz Abteilungen* (*FEA* – Aviation Replacement Sections). To become a pilot it was necessary for the student to pass three examinations (*Prüfungen*). The first two of these could be accomplished at the flying school. However, the third and final *Prüfung* almost invariably had to be taken at one of the *FEA*.

The length of training given to prospective pilots was a function of the candidate's ability to learn how to fly, the weather, training aircraft availability, and military necessity. In 1916 it was deemed appropriate that the student pilot needed at least six months of instruction before being sent to the front. As the conflict wore on this training period became shorter and shorter, as more and more pilots were needed at the front. By 1918 this training period had been reduced to three to four months.

Training was conducted using the usual two-seater B and C Class aircraft, although a few D Class aircraft were available for the prospective fighter pilot to train on. Pilots slated for a *Schusta* might also be required to take a short course at one of the gunnery schools. Upon the completion of training the pilot was assigned to an *Armee Flugpark* and from there to an operational unit. Unlike the Allies, who presented their pilots wings at the completion of training, a German pilot was required to carry out a certain number of missions over hostile territory before being awarded the *Flugzeugführer Abzeichen* or pilot's badge. New pilots to the front were often paired with an experienced gunner who knew the 'lay of the land.' New pilots were also often shadowed in flight by another aircraft comprised by an older more experienced crew, who could keep an eye on them and critique their performance upon their return to the airfield.

Gunner Training
Aerial gunners were trained at special *Flieger Schützen Schulen* or Gunnery Schools. These included the Flg.Sch.Sch. at Asch and the Bavarian Flg.Sch.Sch. at *Flieger Schule IV* located at Lager-Lechfeld. Training could also be received at gunnery schools attached to the *FEA* at Böblingen (*FEA 10*), Breslau (*FEA 11*), Hannover (*FEA 5*), Gotha (*FEA 3*), Schneidemühl (*FEA 2*), etc. Additional training was often provided at the *Geschwader Schulen* at either Freiburg or Paderborn, as well as the *Flieger Bomben Lehr Abteilung* at Frankfurt an der Oder.

Gunnery training comprised target practice, firing on the ground from behind a revolving propeller, firing at targets from fast motor cars, and finally firing from an aircraft at targets on the ground. In addition, as with the training of officer observers, it was necessary for the prospective gunner to photograph an approaching aircraft in flight, being careful to center the aircraft in the exact middle of the frame. This was designed to test the student's ability to track and shoot at an approaching enemy aircraft.

The usual instruction course lasted from eight to ten weeks. At the completion of his training, as with the new pilots, the gunners were forwarded to an *Armee Flugpark* and from there to an operational unit. Also similar to the pilots, the gunner did not receive his gunner's badge – *Fliegerschützen Abzeichen* – until a required number of front flight missions had been carried out. In fact the Gunner's Badge wasn't even authorized until January 27, 1918, in celebration of the 59th birthday of Kaiser Wilhelm II. As with new pilots, a newly arrived gunner was usually paired with a more experienced pilot for his first few operational missions over enemy lines.

Schlachtstaffelschule
According to information provided in the study entitled, "*Die Organisation des deutschen Heeres im Weltkrieg*" by Hermann Cron, a *Schlachtstaffelschule* was established at Saultain in September 1918. The purpose of this school was to provide instruction in flight and squadron formation flying as well as the technique of attacking ground targets of every kind. Little information has come to light regarding this school. It is known that, according to their service records, none of the Bavarian *Schlasta* crew members are noted as having passed through such a school.

However, there is a brief discussion of the *Schlachtstaffelschule* written by *Ltn.d.R.* Herrmann, the last commanding officer of *Schlasta 19,* and presented in Georg Paul Neumann's *"Die deutschen Luftstreitkräfte im Weltkrieg."* The translation is presented here through the courtesy of Hannes Täger. "While each of the individual branches of the air service had their own special schools, *Schlachtstaffeln* developed so quickly that a *Schlachtstaffelschule* could not be set up with comparable speed. So the skills of low-level flying and attacking ground targets had to be instilled into the young new generation when they arrived at the front. Only in the last months of the war was such a facility available. However, it was established too late for the benefits of this new training to be realized".

This photo shows what an experienced Bavarian *Schlachtstaffel* crew would wear into battle: on the left the pilot's badge, on the right the gunner's. Both are replicas. Photo credit: Mark Berger.

APPENDIX II

SCHLACHTGRUPPEN

The *Schlachtstaffeln* were also grouped into *Schlachtgruppen* (*Schlagru*), similar to the more familiar *Jagdgruppen* (*Gruja*). These were temporary groupings of anywhere from two to six *Schlasta* under an experienced senior officer, to be used as the tactical situation dictated. Contrary to previously published information, no *Schlachtgeschwader*, or permanent formation, was ever established. At first the *Schlagru* were placed under the command of the most senior individual *Schlasta* commander. Later in 1918 senior officers were given command of the *Schlagru* independent of the composition of the *Schlasta* involved. This would be comparable to *Hptm.* Erhard Milch being assigned as C.O. of *Gruja 6* or *Ritt.* Anton von Brederlow being placed in charge of *Gruja 11*. Similarly for example, *Hptm.* Wilhelm Aschenborn, *Oblt.* Johannes Missfelder, and *Oblt.* Emil Ziegler gen Stege were assigned as C.O.'s of various *Schlagru* even though the component units were occasionally changing as the situation with the ground forces required.

A continuing area of confusion to aviation historians has been the numbering of the *Schlagru*. In fact the solution is fairly simple for those *Schlagru* having either a number or letter designation. Within each *Armee* the *Schlagru* were usually, but not always, numbered left to right either 1, 2, 3, etc. or A, B, C, etc. Thus there could easily be two or more *Schlagru 1* and *Schlagru 2* in existence at the same time just in different *Armeen*. For example during the assault on the Chemin des Dames, there was a *Schlagru 1* in the *1. Armee* and also a *Schlagru 1* in the *18. Armee*. Likewise, a *Schlagru A* and a *Schlagru B* could also exist at the same time.

However there are reports of a *Schlagru J* and a *Schlagru S*, which present a most interesting problem in identification. At first these were believed to be the initials of the *Schlachtgruppe Führer,* "J" = Jaspers, "S" = Sonntag, but since neither Jaspers nor Sonntag commanded such designated *Schlagru*, this theory was laid aside. It was then thought that these might be the initials of the *Grufl* or even the commander of the ground troops to which these *Schlagru* were assigned. That theory was dashed when it was established that both *Schlagru J* and *Schlagru S* were transferred to various *Armeen*, yet still retained their respective letter designation. That leaves only the explanation that this information was provided by captured crews and that these letter designations came about during POW interrogations. The veracity of the identification of these *Schlagru* must therefore be questioned. In any event, these were no doubt only temporary identifications before a permanent letter or number designation was assigned.

The *Schlagru* could also be identified by a name, which tends to complicate the situation even a little more. Since the *Schlagru* were such loose and changing groups, names were often used to denote either the *Schlagru* C.O., e.g., *Schlagru Lackner* or *Schlagru Miller*, or the *Armee* group to which they were assigned. For the Battle of Matz beginning on June 9, 1918 and spearheaded by the *7. Armee, Schlagru A, B*, and *C*, were redesignated as *Schlagru Staabs, Winckler*, and *Wichura*. These were the names of the *Armee* Corps commanders under which they served and were: *Generalleutnant* Hermann von Staabs who commanded the *XXXIX Reserve-Korps; General der Infanterie* Arnold von Winckler who commmanded the *XXV Reserve-Korps*; and *General der Infanterie* Georg Wichura who commanded the *VIII Reserve-Korps*, respectively. These *Schlagru* reverted to their original letter designations at the conclusion of the battle on approximately June 12th and certainly by June 25, 1918.

The name identification of *Schlagru* could also refer to the airfield where they were located, much as *Gruja Habsheim* or *Gruja Marville*. Recently discovered *Kofl 17* weekly reports indicate that after August 22, 1918 the *Schlagru* in the *17. Armee* were called *Schlagru Abscon* and *Schlagru Beuvry*. These denote *Schlagru 2* (*Schlasta 9, 11*, and *27b*) stationed at Abscon and *Schlagru J* (*Schlasta 4, 15, 24b*, and *25b*) stationed Beuvry. Thus the proper identification of a *Schlagru* can be just as confusing and diverse as the identification of a *Jagdgruppe.*

The next few pages present the service records, or at least as much as could be compiled, of those men who, at one time or another, served as a *Schlachtgruppe* commander. Again, note that they might also be a *Schlachtstaffel* commander at the same time.

Schlachtgruppen Kommandeur

***Oblt.d.R.* Franz Albertshauser, Observer**

FEA 1b	1Sep16	29Sep16	
Beo.Sch Tergnier	29Sep16	14Nov16	
FEA 1b	14Nov16	1Dec16	
Feld Fl.Abt. 4b	1Dec16	7Dec16	
Fl.Abt. 292(A)b	7Dec16	24Jan17	
Berlin	24Jan17	10Feb17	
Fl.Abt. 292(A)b	10Feb17	1Mar17	
FT Course Neuruppin	1Mar17	31Mar17	
Fl.Abt. 292(A)b	31Mar17	18Apr18	
Schlasta 24b C.O.	18Apr18	20Jul18	WIA,sv.
Schlagru D C.O.	2Jul18	10Jul18	
Schlagru J C.O.	10Jul18	20Jul18	WIA,sv.
Hospital	20Jul18	10Aug18	
Idluft	10Aug18	23Aug18	
FEA 1b	23Aug18	EOW	

***Hptm.* Wilhelm Aschenborn, Observer**

Feld Fl.Abt. 62	25Apr15	Jul15	IIC,sv.
Fl.Abt. 255(A)		10Oct17	
Schusta 19 C.O.	10Oct17	2Nov17	
Leave	2Nov17	6Nov17	
Schlasta 19 C.O.	6Nov17	24Apr18	
Schlagru C C.O.	24Apr18	3Jun18	

***Oblt.* Oskar Baumann, Observer**

FEA 1b BeoSch	8Jan16	18Feb16	
FEA 1b	18Feb16	1Apr16	
AFS Jüterbog	1Apr16	9Jun16	
AFP 4	10Jun16	15Jun16	
Art.Fl.Abt. 102b	16Jun16	1Oct16	WIA,lt.
Art.Fl.Abt. 102b	1Oct16	8Dec16	
Fl.Abt. 287(A)b	8Dec16	30Dec16	
AFP 8	31Dec16	31Dec16	
Feld Fl.Abt. 52	31Dec16	11Jan17	
Fl.Abt. 22	11Jan17	8Mar17	WIA,lt.
Hospital	8Mar17	23Mar17	
Fl.Abt. 22	23Mar17	25Sep17	
SFS Windau	25Sep17	26Oct17	
Leave	26Oct17	3Dec17	
AFP B	3Dec17	10Dec17	
Fl.Abt. 289(A)b	10Dec17	12Jan18	
AFP 2	12Jan18	13Jan18	
AFP 18	13Jan18	15Jan18	
Fl.Abt. 287(A)b	15Jan18	4Apr18	
Schlasta 28b C.O.	4Apr18	11Apr18	IIC,lt.
Schlasta 28b C.O.	11Apr18	25Apr18	WIA,lt.
Schlasta 28b C.O.	25Apr18	8Sep18	
Leave	8Sep18	27Sep18	
Schlasta 28b C.O.	27Sep18	EOW	

***Oblt.* Ernst Bonatz, Pilot**

Feld Fl.Abt. 15	24Mar15	20May15
AFP Süd	21May15	4Jun15
Feld Fl.Abt. 26	5Jun15	23Oct17
Fl.Abt. 25 C.O.	24Oct17	26Jan18
Schusta 36 C.O.	26Jan18	22Apr18
Grufl 19 Staff	22Apr18	17Jun18
Schlasta 18 C.O.	17Jun18	EOW
Schlagru B C.O.	18Oct18	EOW

***Rittm.d.R.* Julius Bossert, Observer**

FEA 1b	20Nov15	25Jan16
AFP Falkenhausen	25Jan16	26Jan16
Feld Fl.Abt. 6b	26Jan16	31Jan16
Feld Fl.Abt. 65	31Jan16	15Mar16
KG 6/Ks 33	15Mar16	15May16
AFP 2	15May16	18May16
FEA 1b	18May16	11Aug16
Feld Fl.Abt. 7b	11Aug16	26Oct16
FEA 1b	26Oct16	9Jun17
FBSchule I	9Jun17	19Oct17
AFP 4	19Oct17	20Oct17
Fl.Abt. 294(A)b	20Oct17	16Dec17
FS I	16Dec17	3Apr18
FBS	3Apr18	14May18
AFP 6	14May18	15May18
Fl.Abt. 292(A)b	15May18	21Jun18
Schlasta 35 C.O.	21Jun18	17Jul18
Schlasta 30b C.O.	17Jul18	EOW

***Oblt.* Helmut Bühling, Observer**

FEA 5	15Apr15	15May15	
AFP 6	15May15	20May15	
Feld Fl.Abt. 18	20May15	18Jul15	
AFP 6	18Jul15	19Aug15	
Feld Fl.Abt. 9	19Aug15	6Jun16	
Feld Fl.Abt. 5b	6Jun16	13Jul16	
Fl.Abt. 235(A) OzbV	13Jul16	19Nov16	
Idflieg	19Nov16	26Nov16	
AFS Ost Gross Auz	26Nov16	19Nov17	
AFP 4	19Nov17	23Nov17	
Grufl 3 OzbV	23Nov17	15Mar18	
Schusta 13	15Mar18	24Mar18	
Schlasta 13 C.O.	24Mar18	27May18	WIA,lt.
Schlasta 13 C.O.	27May18	9Aug18	WIA
Hospital	9Aug18	Aug18	
Schlasta 13 C.O.	Aug18	7Sep18	
Schlagru 2 C.O.	7Sep18	EOW	

***Oblt.* Hans Ebel, Observer**

FEA 1b	1Mar15	6May15
AFP von Strantz	6May15	1Sep15
Feld Fl.Abt. 3b	1Sep15	1Aug16
Stofl von Strantz	1Aug16	
Schlasta 21 C.O.	(Jun18)	EOW
Schlagru B C.O.	23Oct18	EOW

***Oblt.* Erhardt Egerer, Pilot**

Feld Fl.Abt. 3b	19Nov14	2Feb16
FEA 1b Instr.	2Feb16	10May16
AFP von Strantz	10May16	12May16
Feld Fl.Abt. 3b	12May16	19Jul16
KEA 1	19Jul16	17Aug16
Feld Fl.Abt. 3b	17Aug16	2Sep16
KG 6/Ks 32 C.O.	2Sep16	15Oct16
Jasta 13 C.O.	15Oct16	27Sep17
FEA 1b	27Sep17	22Oct17
FA Grafenwöhr C.O.	22Oct17	25Oct17
FEA 2b	25Oct17	30Nov17
FS IV C.O.	30Nov17	1Aug18
Schlagru 2 (J) C.O.	1Aug18	9Sep18
AFP 6	9Sep18	EOW

***Oblt.d.R.* August Peter Jacob Ertl, Observer**

Feld Fl.Abt. 42	16	15Feb16	
FEA 5	15Feb16	1Apr16	
Feld Fl.Abt. 42	1Apr16	26Apr16	
Feld Fl.Abt. 6b	26Apr16	1Aug16	WIA,sv.
Hospital	1Aug16	23Aug16	
FEA 1b	23Aug16	16Jan17	
Flg.Sch. V Stv. C.O.	16Jan17	1Mar17	
Flg.Sch. V OzbV	1Mar17	30Jan18	
Flg.Sch. V C.O.	30Jan18	23Feb18	
AFP C	23Feb18	23Feb18	
Schlasta 30b C.O.	23Feb18	12Apr18	
Schlagru B C.O.	12Apr18	19Jul18	
FEA 1b	19Jul18	25Jul18	
Hospital	25Jul18	EOW	

***Oblt.d.R.* Josef Gramp, Pilot**

FEA 1b	1Sep16	29Oct16
KG 6/Ks 32	29Oct16	1Jan17
Schusta 23b	1Jan17	3Apr17
Beo.Sch. I	3Apr17	30Apr17
Flg.Sch. I	30Apr17	11Oct17
JsSch I	11Oct17	10Nov17
Jasta 34b	10Nov17	4Mar18
FEA 1b	4Mar18	22Jul18
Schlagru B C.O.	22Jul18	25Sep18
FEA 1b	25Sep18	

***Oblt.d.R.* Karl *Ritter* von Gruny, Observer**

FEA 1b	15May17	23Aug17	
Fl.Abt. 22 OzbV	23Aug17	9Sep17	
Fl.Abt. 22	9Sep17	19May18	IIC,sv.
Hospital	19May18	10Sep18	
FEA 1b, BeoSch	10Sep18	6Oct18	
Schlasta 22b C.O.	7Oct18	EOW	
Schlagru 3 C.O.	7Oct18	18Oct18	
Schlagru 2 C.O.	18Oct18	EOW	

***Oblt.d.R.* Otto Hafner, Observer**

Fl.Abt. 225(A)	(Dec16)	(Jan17)
Schlagru 3 Stv. C.O.	May18	

***Oblt.* Friedrich-Carl Hanesse, Pilot**

AFP 2	15Feb17	31May17
Fl.Abt. 225(A)	1Jun17	31Mar18
Schlasta 9 C.O.	1Apr18	31May18
Schlasta 2 C.O.	1Jun18	30Jun18
Schlagru 3 C.O.	1Jul18	EOW

***Hptm.* Heinecke, Observer**

AFP 5		19Oct17
Schusta 11 C.O.	19Oct17	28Jan18
Fl.Abt. 45b Stv. CO	28Jan18	2Feb18
Schlasta 11 C.O.	2Feb18	4Apr18
Schlagru C C.O.	(Mar18)	4Apr18

***Ritt.* Herrmann**

Fl.Abt. 259(A)		9Apr18
Schlasta 38s C.O.	9Apr18	7Jul18
Schlagru 1 C.O.	9Apr18	25Apr18
Schlagru 2 C.O.	25Apr18	25May18
Schlagru 3 C.O.	25May18	9Jun18
Schlagru 2 C.O.	9Jun18	7Jul18

***Ritt.d.R.* Herrmann**

Schlasta 4 C.O.	(Aug17)	23Apr18
Schlagru B C.O.	10Mar18	23Apr18
Schlasta 12 C.O.	23Apr18	Jul18

***Oblt.d.R.* Konrad Albrecht Ludwig Hoffmann, Observer**

FEA 1b	18Jul16	1Sep16	
KG 6/Ks 32	1Sep16	1Jan17	
Schusta 23b	1Jan17	30Apr17	
Fl.Abt. 286(A)b	30Apr17	1Nov17	
FEA 1b Instr.	1Nov17	3Dec17	
FEA 1b Stab	3Dec17	23Feb18	
Schlasta 26b C.O.	23Feb18	3Oct18	SD FTL
Schlasta 26b C.O.	5Oct18	EOW	
Schlagru 1 C.O.	26Sep18	6Oct18	

***Oblt.d.R.* Jaspers, Observer**

Fl.Abt. 238(A)		
Hospital		28Sep17
AFP 4	28Sep17	6Oct17
FEA 5	6Oct17	
Schlasta 3 C.O.	(Jul18)	Oct18
Schlagru 2 C.O.	12Aug18	7Sep18

***Oblt.* Friedrich Lorenz *Ritter* von Krausser, Observer**

FEA 1b	3Feb15	6Mar15	
Feld Fl.Abt. 7b	6Mar15	25Oct16	
FEA 1b	25Oct16	14Nov16	
Feld Fl.Abt. 7b	14Nov16	1Dec16	
Funker Erstatz Abt.	1Dec16	30Jan17	
FT Luft. Neuruppin	30Jan17	17Feb17	
FT Lehr. Warschau	17Feb17	20Mar17	
Kofl 6 Stab.	20Mar17	31May17	
Beo.Sch. I	31May17	15Jun17	
Schusta 23b C.O.	15Jun17	4Nov17	WIA
Hospital	4Nov17	8Dec17	
Schusta 23b C.O.	8Dec17	1Feb18	
Fl.Abt. 45b C.O.	1Feb18	8Sep18	
AFP 2	8Sep18	8Sep18	
Schlagru 2 (J) C.O.	8Sep18	EOW	

***Oblt.d.R.* Sigmund Kreitmair, Observer**

FEA 1b	27May16	18Jul16
KG 6/Ks 31	18Jul16	8Oct16
KG 6/Ks 35	8Oct16	1Jan17
Schusta 26b	1Jan17	12Feb17
AFP 5	12Feb17	20Feb17
Schusta 27b C.O.	20Feb17	6Sep18
Schlagru B C.O.	6Sep18	28Sep18
Flg.Schutz.Sch. C.O.	28Sep18	16Oct18
FEA 1b	16Oct18	EOW

***Hptm.* Hermann Krüger, Pilot**

Feld Fl.Abt. 6		13Apr15
EFP 4	13Apr15	Apr15
Feld Fl.Abt. 47 C.O.	Apr15	
FEA 8	(Nov15)	
Feld Fl.Abt. 41 C.O.	(Dec15)	(Jun16)
KG 5/Ks 27 C.O.	(Aug16)	(Dec16)
Kofl 7, Grufl 9	(Aug17)	(Feb18)
Schlagru A C.O.	21Oct18	EOW

***Oblt.* Walter Lackner, Observer**

Unit	From	To
Beo.Sch. Adlershof	29Mar15	12Apr15
Feld Fl.Abt. 11	13Apr15	24Oct15
Feld Fl.Abt. 26	24Oct15	10Dec15
Feld Fl.Abt. 11	10Dec15	18Jul16
AFP 13	18Jul16	31Jul16
AOK von Mackensen	1Aug16	30Sep16
Idflieg	1Oct16	31Mar17
Kofl 6 Stab	1Apr17	13Aug17
Kofl 7 Stab	14Aug17	3Dec17
Schusta 20 Stv. C.O	4Dec17	30Jan18
Schusta 7 C.O.	31Jan18	20Mar18
Schlagru Lackner C.O.	21Mar18	9Aug18
Kofl 9 Stab	10Aug18	1Sep18
Idflieg	2Sep18	25Sep18
Kofl 7 Heimat Stab	25Sep18	EOW

***Oblt.* Werner Lange, Observer**

Unit	From	To
Schusta 34 C.O.	Jan18	14Apr18
Schlasta 20 C.O.	14Apr18	15May18
Schlagru B C.O.	15May18	15Sep18

***Oblt.* Kurt Messow, Observer**

Unit	From	To
Schusta 6 C.O.	(Apr17)	14Apr18
Schlagru 3 C.O.	4Apr18	14Apr18

***Oblt.d.R.* Ludwig Männer, Observer**

Unit	From	To	Notes
FEA 1b	17Mar17	11Apr17	
VÜP Warschau	11Apr17	9Jun17	
FEA 1b	9Jun17	14Jun17	
AFP 6	14Jun17	7Jul17	
Fl.Abt. 211(A)	7Jul17	12Aug17	IIC,sv.
Hospital	12Aug17	11Sep17	
FEA 1b, BS	11Sep17	13Oct17	
AFP 6	13Oct17	17Oct17	
Fl.Abt. 288(A)b OzbV	17Oct17	23Mar18	
Schusta 22b C.O.	23Mar18	15Oct18	
Schlagru B C.O.	4Aug18	9Sep18	
FEA 1b Instr.	15Oct18	EOW	

***Oblt.* Kurt Messow, Observer**

Unit	From	To
Schusta 6 C.O.	(Apr17)	14Apr18
Schlagru 3 C.O.	4Apr18	14Apr18

***Hptm.* Hugo Miller, Observer**

Unit	From	To
FEA 1b	3Aug14	2Sep14
EFP 6	5Sep14	9Sep14
Feld Fl.Abt. 3b	9Sep14	25Oct14
AFP 6	25Oct14	11May15
Stofl C Adj.	11May15	6Jul16
Infantry	6Jul16	6Apr17
FEA 1b	6Apr17	19Dec17
Schusta 25b C.O.	19Dec17	10Jun18
Schlagru Miller C.O.	10Jun18	14Jul18
FEA 1b	14Jul18	13Aug18
FBS Stab	13Aug18	21Oct18
Pulverfbk. Dachau	21Oct18	3Nov18
Fl.Abt. Miller	3Nov18	EOW

***Oblt.* Johannes Missfelder, Observer**

Unit	From	To
FBS Leipzig-Lind.	2Aug14	24Aug14
Feld Fl.Abt. 35	25Aug14	30May16
Fl.Abt. 224(A) OzbV	30May16	7Jun17
Schusta 12 Stv. C.O.	7Jun17	1Jul17
Schusta 12 C.O.	1Jul17	23Apr18
Schlagru D C.O.	24Apr18	1Jul18
AFS Ost II, Abt A C.O.	2Jul18	EOW

***Oblt.* Müller, Observer**

Unit	From	To	Notes
Schusta 13 C.O.	(Nov17)	24Mar18	
Schlasta 13 OzbV	24Mar18	29Apr18	WIA,sv.
Schlagru A C.O.	(Mar18)	29Apr18	

***Oblt.* Hermann Ramdohr, Observer**

Unit	From	To	Notes
Schlasta 16 C.O.	(Mar18)	9Apr18	KIA Bailleul
Schlagru C C.O.	(Mar18)	9Apr18	KIA

***Oblt.d.R.* Hermann Schulz, Observer**

Unit	From	To
Fl.Abt. 211(A)	20Nov15	30Dec16
AFP 8	30Dec16	
Fl.Abt. 217(A)	('17)	
Gross-Auz	('18)	
Schlasta 9 C.O.	Jun18	EOW
Schlagru D C.O.	1Jul18	22Aug18

***Hptm.* Erich Sonntag, Observer**

Unit	From	To	Notes
KG 1/Ks 1 C.O.	1Sep17	18Dec17	
BG 1/Bs 1 C.O.	18Dec17	Feb18	
Schlasta 11 C.O.	21Jun18	1Oct18	KIA Sancourt, Fressies
Schlagru 1 C.O.	9Jun18	15Jul18	
Schlagru 2 C.O.	15Jul18	24Sep18	

***Hptm.* Hugo Weingarth, Observer**

Unit	From	To
Feld Fl.Abt. 25	2Aug14	16Nov14
Flg. Station Metz	16Nov14	21Jan15
Feld Fl.Abt. 25	21Jan15	10Oct15
Idflieg	10Oct15	20Dec15
BS Königsberg	20Dec15	27Jun16
AFP 10	28Jun16	30Jun16
Feld Fl.Abt. 14	1Jul16	10Jul16
Feld Fl.Abt. 4	11Jul16	11Dec16
FA 215(A) Stv C.O.	11Dec16	3Feb17
Fl.Abt. 4	4Feb17	10Apr17
Fl.Abt. 256(A)	10Apr17	27Sep17
AFP 4	27Sep17	27Sep17
FEA 3 Adj.	27Sep17	28Jun18
Kofl 3 Stab	28Jun18	31Jul18
JG II Adj.	31Jul18	24Sep18
Schlagru S C.O.	24Sep18	EOW

***Oblt.* Emil Ziegler gen Stege, Observer**

Unit	From	To
Schusta 14 C.O.	(Mar17)	(May18)
Schlagru A C.O.	24Apr18	EOW

***Hptm.* Zimmermann, Observer**

Unit	From	To
Schusta 17 C.O.	27Jan18	10Feb18
Fl.Abt. 224A Stv. C.O.	10Feb18	17Feb18
Schlasta 17 C.O.	17Feb18	9Jun18
Schlagru A C.O.	Mar18	Apr18
Schlagru 1 C.O.	May18	9Jun18

***Oblt.* Bruno Zipplies, Observer**

AFP 3		25Oct17	
Fl.Abt. 3	25Oct17	29Oct17	IIC,sv.
Hospital	29Oct17	2Nov17	
AFP 4	2Nov17	26Nov17	
Idflieg	26Nov17		
AFP 4		31Jan18	
Jasta 69 OzbV	31Jan18	14Apr18	
Schlasta 5 C.O.	14Apr18	15May18	
Schlasta 20 C.O.	15May18	EOW	
Schlagru B C.O.	16Sep18	21Oct18	

***Ritt.* Jürgen *Frhr.* von Zobel zu Giebelstadt, Observer**

Feld Fl.Abt. 25		Oct16
KG 5/Ks 29 C.O.	Oct16	1Jan17
Schusta 11 C.O.	1Jan17	
Fl.Abt. 228(A) C.O.	(Sep17)	
Schlasta 29b OzbV	(Mar18)	9Apr18
Schlagru B C.O.	9Apr18	12Apr18

APPENDIX III

AWARDS

The higher medals awarded to various personnel of the *Schutzstaffeln/ Schlachtstaffeln* are presented on the following pages. It should be noted that these are all considered major awards, as defined in Neal O'Connor's excellent series of books covering German awards. These do not include such awards as the EK I and II (*Eisernes Kreuz*) of which over 5 million were awarded during the conflict, nor the various grades of the Bavarian Military Merit Order, which came in six classes, and were doled out 380,976 times to all participants of the Great War. Similarly the Saxon Friedrich August Medal in either Bronze, Silver or Gold, which were very common, are also not included.

There are no recipients of Prussia's highest order, the *Order Pour le Mérite*, as none were awarded to *Schusta/Schlasta* personnel while serving with these units. *Oblt.* Friedrich Lorenz *Ritter* von Krausser came closest to receiving this decoration. His name was seconded for the award in late October 1918. The cessation of hostilities prevented any action occurring on his behalf. The next closest was *Hptm.* Eduard Wolfgang Zorer who was nominated for the award at an unknown date in 1917, but who was subsequently shot down and taken POW on September 1, 1917, while C.O. of *KG 1/Ks 1*. The long established tradition was that the *Pour le Mérite* was not awarded to men who were either taken prisoners or deceased. Therefore, no award for Zorer was forthcoming. One report also has *Oblt.* Emil Ziegler gen Stege's name being put forward for the award in November 1918, although there may be confusion with *Ltn.* Johannes Ziegler, an observer with *Fl.Abt. 270(A)*. In any event the abdication of the Kaiser put an end to the process of granting such awards.

Aviation Awards Received by *Schusta* Personnel while serving with the *Schutzstaffeln* (by date of award). (courtesy of Neal W. O'Connor)

Recipient	*Type*	*Schusta*	*Date of Award*
Knight's Cross with Swords of the Royal Hohenzollern House Order			
Oblt. Wilhelm Gebhardt	O	29b	9Nov18
Ltn.d.R. Friedrich Geiger	O	17	3May18
Oblt. Friedrich *Ritter* von Krausser	O	23b	4Dec17
Oblt. Jürgen Lüdeke	O	6	5Jul18
Oblt. Johannes Missfelder	O	Schlagru D	6Jul18
Ltn. Modler	O	14	26Oct18
Oblt. Curt Pflugbeil	P	27b	17Apr18
Oblt.d.R. Konrad Hoffmann	O	26b	13Jun18
Ltn.d.R. Julius Schwörer	O	15	30Aug18
Oblt. Thesing	P	8	10Sep18
Knight's Cross with Swords of the Royal Hohenzollern House Order			
(Received by men who were probably serving in a *Schusta* at the time but where the exact award date is not known)			
Oblt.d.R. Sigmund Kreitmair	O	27b	Aug18
Oblt. Wilhelm Ernst Maser	P	23b	
Member's Cross with Swords of the Royal Hohenzollern House Order			
Vzfw. Josef Schleiffer	P	7	30May17
Vzfw. Franz-Josef Ophaus	P	11	3Oct18
Prussian Golden Military Merit Cross			
Vzfw. Willy Wenck	P	4	11Apr18
Vzfw. Franz-Josef Ophaus	P	11	2Jun18
Vzfw. Wilhelm Krake	G	2	30Jun18
Vzfw. Wilhelm Littig	P	13	8Jul18
Vzfw. August Rottau	P	37	16Jul18
Offz.Stv. Willy Westphal	G	20	7Aug18
Vzfw. Gottfried Ehmann	G	15	9Aug18
Vzfw. Fritz Hankner	G	5	30Sep18
Knight's Cross of the Military Max-Joseph Order			
Oblt. Friedrich *Ritter* von Krausser	O	23b	20Sep17
Bavarian Bravery Medal in Silver [Date of Action]			
Uffz. Fritz Kuhlmann	P	26b	19Dec17
Uffz. Sebastian Ritzinger	G	26b	19Dec17
Vzfw. Adolf Brüstle	G	28b	24Mar18 & 6Apr18
Vzfw. Adam Müller	G	26b	5Apr18
Vzfw. Fritz Strunz	P	23b	27May18
Knight's Cross 2nd Class with Swords of the Württemberg Friedrich Order			
Hptm. Eduard Wolfgang Zorer	O	7	3May17

Württemberg Gold Military Merit Medal

Ltn. Heinrich Sänger	O	7	18May17
Vzfw. Wilhelm Erlewein	P	9	27Jan18
Ltn.d.R. Otto Gawron	G	2	12May18
Ltn.d.R. Hermann Wolf	P	37	7Sep18
Vzfw. Gottfried Ehmann	G	15	Unknown

Württemberg Silver Military Merit Medal

Vzfw. Gottfried Ehmann	G	15	Unknown
Ltn.d.R. Otto Gawron	G	2	Unknown

Württemberg Wilhelm Cross with Swords

Uffz. Eugen Brodbeck	P	7	30May18

Baden Silver Karl Friedrich Military Merit Medal

Uffz. Fritz Rittershofer	P	16	31Jan18
Uffz. Kurt Andres	P	8	18Jul18

Baden Silver Merit Medal on the Ribbon of the Military Karl Friedrich Merit Medal

Vzfw. Wilhelm Littig	P	13	18Jan18

Knight's Cross of the Saxon Military St. Heinrich Order

Ltn. Martin Heydrich	O	11	24Jul17
Oblt. Kurt Messow	O	8	21Nov17
Oblt. Georg Henke	O	18	10Jun18

Knight's Cross 2nd Class with Swords of the Albert Order

Oblt. Oskar Bechtle	O	2	31Mar18
Ltn.d.R. Knerlich	O	38s	14Sep18

Saxon Silver St. Heinrich Medal

Vzfw. Kurt Liehr	G	5	27Sep17
Vzfw. Erhard Lorenz	G	13	11Nov17
Gefr. Kurt Seidel	P	10	11Nov17
Vzfw. Ernst Bochmann	P	12	2Dec17
Vzfw. Richard Hertel	G	17	7Jan18

Note: Other *Schusta* crew members may have received this award, but the roll virtually ends in early 1918.

Saxon Honor Cross with Swords

Vzfw. Wilhelm Hillner	P	1	23Jun17

Baden Order of the Zähringen Lion Knight's Cross 2nd Class with Swords

Ltn.d.R. Gustav Bürck	P	17	15Sep17

Oldenburg Friedrich August Cross 2nd Class

Flg. Albert Fickus		15	9Jul18
Flg. Hermann Lange		3	23Nov17
Gefr. Adolf Märtens		17	16Apr18

Saxe-Meiningen Medal for Merit in War

Uffz. Max Greiner		5	4Jan18
Uffz. August Matthies	P	5	4Jan18
Uffz. Hermann Vichlein		2	4Jan18
Uffz. Mylius Schneider		6	19Apr18
Gefr. Rudolf Schadt	G	15	8Oct18

Saxe-Weimar-Eisenach Wilhelm Ernst War Cross

Vzfw. Max Rossbach		18	1918

Saxe-Weimar-Eisenach General Honor Decoration in Silver with Sword Clasp

Uffz. Horst Rath	P	10	1917
Vzfw. Ernst Flöel	G	15	1917
Uffz. Max Rossbach		2	1917

Gold Merit Medal of the Ducal Saxe-Ernestine House Order

Vzfw. Spittel		14	18May17
Vzfw. Albin Schnabel	P	18	1Nov17
Vzfw. Alfred Nössler		14	1918

Silver Merit Medal of the Ducal Saxe-Ernestine House Order

Flg. Hasso Klein		20	14Jan18
Uffz. Kurt Erbe		14	2Jul18
Gefr. Karl Beck		14	2Jul18
Uffz. Kurt Koch		13	24Aug18
Flg. Rudolf Pfeifer		32	25Oct18

Schwarzburg Silver Medal for Merit in War

Gefr. Kurt Steinecke		6	26Apr17
Flg. Karl Brömel		14	28Feb18
Flg. Hugo Barthel		20	16May18

Brunswick War Merit Cross 2nd Class

Oblt. Theodor Triendl	O	22b	22Mar17
Ltn.d.R. Karl Döring	O	22b	22Mar17

Hessian Warrior's Honor Decoration in Iron

Vzfw. Fritz Beckhardt	P	11	Unknown
Oblt. Friedrich-Carl Hanesse	P	Schlagru 3	Unknown
Oblt. Cornelius Vogeley	O	29b	5Sep17

Hessian General Honor Decoration 'For Bravery'

Oblt. Friedrich-Carl Hanesse	P	Schlagru 3	Unknown
Vzfw. Richard Hort	P	21	14Aug17
Hptm. Eduard Wolfgang Zorer	O	7	Unknown

Princely Hohenzollern Silver Merit Medal with Swords

Vzfw. Fritz Beckhardt	P	11	Unknown
Flg. Hunibald Saupp		16	Unknown

Princely Lippe War Honor Cross for Heroic Deed

Vzfw. Hermann Vehmeier		18	8Jul18

Bremen Hanseatic Cross

Uffz. Wilhelm Lüning		8	1Mar18
Flg. Wilhelm Walter	P	4	2Mar17
Gefr. Georg Andreae		7	11Jun18
Uffz. Otto Diederichs	P	37	30Jul18
Gefr. Heinrich Lüders		5	20Nov20

Hamburg Hanseatic Cross

Oblt. Friedrich-Carl Hanesse	P	Schlagru 3	Unknown
Flgmstr. Willy Ochs	G	M Ss I	Unknown
Oblt. Friedrich *Frhr.* von Berchem	P	24b	30Apr18
Vzfw. Franz Xaver Brandl	G	24b	30Apr18
Vzfw. Georg Fuchs	G	24b	30Apr18
Vzfw. Karl Kieling	P	24b	30Apr18
Vzfw. Johann Müller	G	24b	30Apr18

Lübeck Hanseatic Cross

Flg. Fritz Löper		21	29Aug17

Note: Where the Type is not given, the man could either be a Pilot, Gunner or Ground Crew. The relevant details are lacking.

APPENDIX IV

THE HIGH SCORING SCHUSTA/SCHLASTA FLYERS

(Those with three or more victories scored while with the Schusta)

Name	*Victories* *Ss*	*Ttl*	*Schusta*	*P/G*	*Notes*
Vzfw. Gottfried Ehmann	12	12	15	Gunner	a.
Vzfw. Friedrich Huffzky	9	9	15	Pilot	
Vzfw. Rudolf Besel	5	5	30b	Pilot	b.
Vzfw. Oswald Tränker	5	5	16	Gunner	
Vzfw. Michael Duschner	4	4	30b	Gunner	
Uffz. Ernst Noerthen	4	4	10	Gunner	
Vzfw. Heinrich Carstens	3	3	28b	Pilot	
Vzfw. Georg Neumaier	3	3	27b	Pilot	
Uffz. Walter Reichenbach	3	3	16	Pilot	c.
Vzfw. Karl Waldemar Ritscherle	3	8	8	Gunner	d.
Uffz. Artur Roesler	3	3	10	Gunner	
Gefr. Kurt Seidel	3	4	10	Pilot	e.
Uffz. Bernhard Ultsch	3	11	29b	Pilot	f.
Vzfw. Karl Voigt	3	3	19	Pilot	
Uffz. Warda	3	3	15	Pilot	
Vzfw. Fritz Weber	3	3	8	Pilot	g.
Uffz. Josef Wenz	3	3	29b	Gunner	
Vzfw. Wimmer	3	3	14	Pilot	

a. For being the top German aerial gunner of World War I, the details of Ehmann's career are sadly lacking. It is known that he was born in 1894 and that he received the Golden Military Merit Cross on August 9, 1918, and also both the Gold and Silver Military Merit Medals on unknown dates.

b. *Vzfw*. Rudolf Besel served in *Schusta 30b* from March 17, 1917 to March 27, 1918. He was posted to *Bavarian Flg.Sch. V* on an unknown date to serve as an instructor. He died in the hospital at Gablingen on 7Sep18 after suffering a crash that day at Gersthofen airfield.

c. Walter Reichenbach was KIA on 25Jul17 at Busigny as a member of *Jasta 5*.

d. Karl Ritscherle's post *Schusta 8* war record is a little more detailed. He went to FEA 1 (Altenburg) on 7Jan18 to begin training as a pilot. On 14Jun18 he went to *JsSch I* for a short fighter pilot course, and then on to *Jasta 60* on 22Jun18 where he saw out the war. Here he was promoted to *Ltn.d.R.* and scored an additional 5 victories.

e. Kurt Seidel attended *JsSch I* from 2Oct17 to 16Oct17 whereupon he reported to *Jasta 3*. Here he was promoted to *Uffz*. and scored his fourth and final victory on 26Sep18.

f. After leaving *Schusta 29b*, Bernhard Ultsch spent 5 days at *JsSch I* and then reported to *Jasta 39* on 10Sep17 shortly before it departed for the Italian front. He scored an additional 5 victories with this unit before transferring to *Jasta 77b* on 9Feb18. He was to gain 3 more victories here, where he finished out the war. He was awarded two classes of the Bavarian Military Merit Cross. The 3rd Class with Crown and Swords was bestowed on June 18, 1917 and the 2nd Class with Swords was awarded in September 1918.

g. Fritz Weber was promoted to *Ltn.d.R.* while serving with *Jasta 44s*. He was forced to leave this unit and report to the hospital on 24Sep18 during the influenza outbreak.

Vzfw. Gottfried Ehmann of *Schlasta 15*, the highest scoring gunner in the *Luftstreitkräfte* with 12 confirmed victories. Credit: UTD/HAC.

APPENDIX V

FIGHTER PILOTS

As noted in Chapter VI a good many *Schusta/Schlasta* pilots became *Jasta* pilots. The following photographs present a few examples of those men who had tiger's blood in their veins.

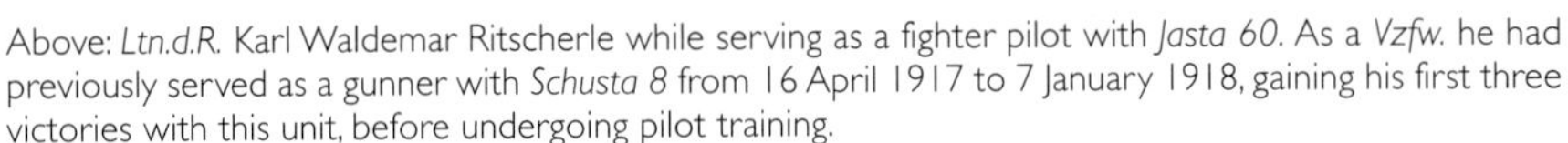

Above: *Ltn.d.R.* Karl Waldemar Ritscherle while serving as a fighter pilot with *Jasta 60*. As a *Vzfw.* he had previously served as a gunner with *Schusta 8* from 16 April 1917 to 7 January 1918, gaining his first three victories with this unit, before undergoing pilot training.

Top right: *Ltn.d.R.* Hans Hinsch was an original member of *Schutzstaffel 7* and served with the unit for three months. He was then transferred to *Jasta 11* where he was KIC on 25May17. Note that the correct spelling of his name is Hinsch, not Hintsch as given in the von Eberhardt necrology. Photo credit: Thorsten Pietsch.

Right: *Vzfw.* Reinhold Joerke, later a 14 victory ace with *Jasta 12, 13* and *39*, was an original member of *Schutzstaffel 20*.

Ltn.d.R. Xaver Dannhuber shown while a pilot with *Jagdstaffel 26.* He was an original member of *Schutzstaffel 26b* serving until May 8, 1917.

Vzfw. Albert Haussmann shown here while a member of *Jagdstaffel 13.* He was an original member of *Schutzstaffel 8* serving until 12 April 1917. He was slated to be killed on 16 October 1918.

Ltn.d.R. Hermann Becker, pictured here while C.O. of *Jasta 12.* He was an original pilot with *Schutzstaffel 11* where he served until May 18, 1917.

Oblt. Eduard Schleich shown here as the C.O. of *Jagdgruppe 8.* He was the first C.O. of *Schutzstaffel 28b*, which he led until 4 May 1917. He received the Bavarian Military Max-Joseph Order on 14 June 1918, which automatically elevated him to nobility and he became *Ritter* von Schleich. Credit: Darren Whiteside.

Oblt. Oskar *Frhr.* von Boenigk was an original member of *Schusta 19* serving until 6 April 1917. He went on to a most succesful fighter pilot career serving in *Jasta 4*, *Jasta 21*, and was the last commander of *JG II.*

Ltn.d.R. Heinrich Bongartz was an original member of *Schusta 9* until 11 March 1917 when he was posted to *Jasta 36*. Here he was able to rack up 33 victories before being severely WIA on 23 April 1918.

Vzfw. Willi Gabriel served with *Schusta/Schlasta 15* from July 1917 to May 1918 before being posted to *Jasta 11*. Here he was to claim 10 of his 11 confirmed victories before earning the wrath of his commander, *Oblt.* Hermann Göring, and being posted out of the unit.

Hptm.d.R. Eberhard von Seel was the initial commander of *Schusta 8*. He is shown here as the C.O. of *Jasta 17*.

Ltn.d.R. Paul Bäumer. As a *Gefr.*, he served very briefly with *Schusta 5* in February 1917. He later had an illustrious fighter pilot career with *Jasta 2*, scoring 43 victories.

Ltn.d.R. Friedrich Hengst was an original member of *Schusta 3* where he served until February 6, 1918 when he was posted to *Jasta 64w*. He is shown here on the right in the car next to Lt. Oskar J. Gude of the 93 Sqn. USAS on the date of Gude's capture – October 22, 1918. Photo credit: The Lafayette Foundation.

Right: *Offz.Stv.* Bernhard Ultsch. He achieved two victories with *Schusta 29b* and then transferred to fighter aircraft and was very successful with both *Jasta 39* and *Jasta 77b*. The photograph is one of the Sanke postcards, in this case No. 663.

Far right: The "obligatory" photograph of Manfred *Freiherr* von Richthofen. Although never a *Schusta* pilot, Manfred is quoted as saying in his book, *Der Rote Kampfflieger*, "Had I not become a fighter pilot I would have selected being an infantry flier. It is a great satisfaction to be able to provide direct assistance to our hardest fighting troops. After many a pursuit flight I have fired my remaining bullets into the enemy trenches. Although I may have done little practical good, it makes an impression on their morale."

Ltn.d.R. August Raben was an original member of *Schusta 7* serving until February 17, 1917 when he was posted to *Jasta Schule I* before being sent onto *Jasta 36*. He is shown here with the later unit. Photo credit: The Lafayette Foundation.

APPENDIX VI

SCHLACHTSTAFFEL CREW MEMBER'S POW OBFUSCATION

Undoubtedly most German airmen when captured and interrogated would attempt to provide false information to the enemy. It would appear, however, that at least certain *Schlasta* crews had an affinity for supplying their interrogators with convincing stories regarding their unit and its prior movements. The first such example concerns the *Schlasta 22b* crew of *Uffz.* Peter Paul Bäumler, pilot, and *Gefr.* Michael Engert, gunner, who were captured on 19 April 1918 along with their Halberstadt Cl.II. Their interrogations have been admirably presented by Peter Kilduff in the *Over the Front Journal* Volume 2, Number 3, Autumn 1987 and will not be repeated here. Suffice to say that they handed out a lot of erroneous information, even contradicting each other at times. What is interesting is that the pilot is reported as having been killed, yet his interrogation report is presented following the gunner's. In reality the gunner, Engert, succumbed to his wounds during captivity, but not until 8 February 1919. Information gleaned from this crew was reported in the RFC/RAF Summary of Air Intelligence bulletins #62, dated 21Apr18, #65, dated the 24th and #69, dated the 28th.

A much more serious matter was reported in Air Intelligence Summary Bulletin #186 (25Aug18) which noted the existence of a new unit, *Schlasta 52*, which was said to be in the Champagne sector, Rethel area. This information came from a non-*Schlasta* prisoner who had been captured on 31 July 1918. If this information were true, it would indicate that the number of *Schlachtstaffeln* had been increased.

Then on 20 August the French captured *Pion.* Josef Fuchs, pilot, and *Gefr.* Emil Soetebier, gunner, who identified themselves as being members of *Schlasta 57*. The captives emphatically claimed that this was a new unit formed from a nucleus of *Schlasta 28b*. The British reported this finding in RFC/RAF Air Intelligence Summary #191 of 30 August, stating further that *Schlasta 57* was based at Foreste, NE of Ham. This report was so convincing that it has contributed to the bafflement of researchers right up to the present day. Only recently has the true identity of their unit, *Schlasta 28b*, been unearthed.

That these two reports were upsetting to both the French and English Intelligence officers was quite understandable. Knowing the Germans numbered their units from one upwards, the existence of *Schlasta 52* and *57* would indicate at least a 50% increase in the number of operational *Schlasta* acting on the Western Front. However, for both intelligence services, further confirmation would be required before they would commit to such a conclusion.

That confirmation was forthcoming in British Air Bulletin #206, dated 14 September 1918, stating that the French had captured a crew from *Schlasta 45* on the 6th, whose unit had been formed from a nucleus of *Schlasta 20*. The crew, *Uffz.* Weisser, pilot, and *Uffz.* Wilhelm Scharg, gunner, even provided the name of their commanding officer, *Oblt.* Zipplies, who is known was the C.O. of *Schlasta 20*, and their airfield location at Chivres. Still more "proof" was reported in RAF Bulletin #212 of 20 September, which noted the existence of an unknown *Schlasta 47* from a non-*Schlasta* crew member who had been taken POW.

At this point British Air Intelligence pretty much had it nailed down. With confirmed reports of the existence of *Schlasta 45, 47, 52* and *57*, clearly the Germans had increased the number of *Schlachtstaffeln* by 50%. WRONG! All of this 'air intelligence' was essentially based on the statements of two POW *Schlasta* crews and some miscellaneous POW reports which, in hindsight, were clearly red herrings. Still, it kept the Allied Intelligence Services jumping right up to the end of the war.

APPENDIX VII

THE MYSTERY SURROUNDING HANNOVER CL.IIIA 3892/18, NUMBER 4

This is probably by far and away the most photographed *Schlachtstaffel* aircraft in Allied hands, yet its *Schlasta* and crew identity have remained a mystery for over 80 years. Hannover Cl.IIIa 3892/18 was shot down on 4 October 1918 between Montfaucon and Cierges as recorded on at least two US Signal Corps photos, numbers 26544 and 26545, which were taken of the downed aircraft. It was the victim of American ground gunners.

Yet, this same aircraft is displayed in numerous photos as being the Hannover shot down by Eddie Rickenbacker and Reed Chambers of the 94th Aero Squadron, USAS, on October 2nd. Furthermore, not only was this aircraft extensively photographed during its stay at the 94th, it was also featured in a movie made for public consumption engaging in a 'dog fight' with members of the 94th Squadron taken during October 1918.

In his book "Fighting the Flying Circus," Rickenbacker goes into some detail as to how this aircraft was shot down. Catching it unawares, he attacked and killed the gunner. Then his guns jammed, but Reed Chambers swooped down, wounded the pilot and the Hannover came down north of Montfaucon within the American lines. In his autobiography "Rickenbacker," Eddie alters his story slightly to state that the pilot was killed and the gunner wounded.

In any event, three days later on October 5th, the 94th Aero Squadron was notified of a downed Hannover Cl.IIIa north of Montfaucon and asked if they would like to have it. Would they!? They hurried over and took possession of 3892/18. The only problem was, this was NOT the aircraft downed by Rickenbacker and Chambers on the 2nd. Their victim had actually gone down south of Montfaucon, near Véry, and the *Schlasta 5* crew, Holtmann and Hankner, both apparently unwounded, had been taken into captivity. In his original combat report, written before the enemy aircraft was recovered, Eddie claimed a Halberstadt, with which *Schlasta 5* was equipped. As Rickenbacker notes, it was extremely unusual for a captured German aircraft to remain long on the ground before it was ravaged by souvenir hunters. This form of destruction no doubt occurred to the Halberstadt of Holtmann and Hankner.

The Hannover given to the 94th had been downed by American ground fire on the 4th and came down near Epinonville. The *Schlasta 20* crew of *Uffz.* Rudolf Hager, the pilot, was killed, while the gunner, *Uffz.* Otto Weber, was taken prisoner. Epinonville is roughly half way between Montfaucon and Cierges to the north, and slightly east of both towns. The US ground authorities, knowing the 94th had downed a two-seater on the 2nd, presented them with the WRONG aircraft! And since it was recovered north of Montfaucon with a dead and buried pilot and a captured gunner, Rickenbacker merely slightly modified the circumstances of its capture to conform to the known facts. Thus the *Schlasta 20* Hannover Cl.IIIa 3892/18 came to the airfield of the 94th Aero Squadron on October 5th, where it was extensively photographed, and has been a source of confusion for WWI aviation researchers ever since.

The question is not *whether* Rickenbacker and Chambers achieved a victory on October 2, 1918. They very definitely *did*, downing the *Schlasta 5* crew of Holtmann and Hankner. However, they did not down Hannover Cl.IIIa 3892/18 from *Schlasta 20*, individually marked as Number 4 and with the large white arrow which was the unit marking. Hopefully, this matter can finally be put to rest.

The following pages show a series of ten photos relating to the capture of Hannover Cl.IIIa 3892/18 marked '4' of *Schlachtstaffel 20* on 4 October 1918 near Epinonville. The crew was *Uffz.* Rudolf Hager, the pilot, who was killed and *Uffz.* Otto Weber, the gunner, who was taken prisoner.

U.S. Signal Corp photo #26544 taken shortly after its capture before the aircraft was moved. It was downed by American ground fire. Photo credit: Charles Woolley.

U.S. Signal Corps photo #26545 taken on October 4, 1918 showing the aircraft in its original, as captured, markings.

The captured aircraft photographed at the Rembercourt airfield of the USAS 94th Aero. Squadron before the 'repainting' had begun. Photo credit: Charles Woolley.

Capt. Reed Chambers of the 94th Aero. Sqn. pointing to the bullet hole that 'he' put into the aircraft.

Tail section showing the serial number photographed at the airfield of the 94th Aero. Sqn.

The captured Hannover at Rembercourt after having been repainted by the 94th Aero. Sqn. The mechanics are not identified.

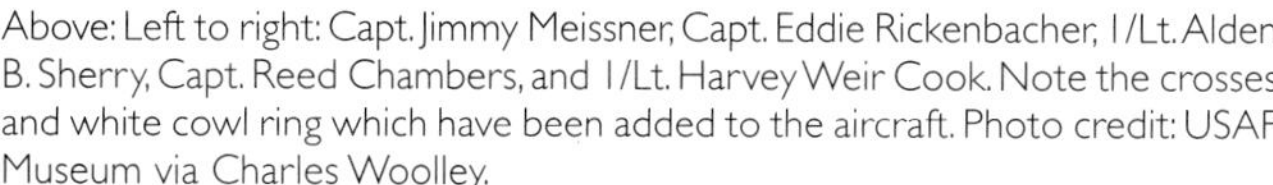

Above: Left to right: Capt. Jimmy Meissner, Capt. Eddie Rickenbacher, 1/Lt. Alden B. Sherry, Capt. Reed Chambers, and 1/Lt. Harvey Weir Cook. Note the crosses and white cowl ring which have been added to the aircraft. Photo credit: USAF Museum via Charles Woolley.

Top right: Capt. Eddie Rickenbacher posing beside 'his kill'. The aircraft has now undergone significant repainting.

Right: A group of the 94th Aero. Sqn. mechanics posing with the considerably retouched aircraft. Photo credit: Charles Woolley.

Below: Hannover Cl.IIIa 3892/18 photographed after being totally redecorated. Photo credit: The Lafayette Foundation.

APPENDIX VIII

MARINE SCHUTZSTAFFELN

Despite the almost total lack of information in the current English language publications regarding the *Marine Schutzstaffeln* of the German Naval Air Service, the *Kaiserliche Marine* did operate two such units in Flanders. These were very similar to their early Army counterparts in that they were used exclusively in the role of escort or protection flights of the Naval artillery spotting aircraft. They were known as Marine *Schusta I* and *II* and were under the operational control of the *Küstenflieger Abteilung (KFA) Flandern* or Coastal Aviation Command, Flanders, also known as the *Grufl Küst.*

Formed on 20 July 1917, *KFA Flandern* was commanded by *Korvettenkapitän* Franz Schröter. Subordinate to *KFA Flandern* were six units, four *Küsten-Artillerie-Staffeln (Küsta)* and the two *Küstenschutzstaffel (Schusta)*. *Küsta I*, stationed at Zeebrügge, was assembled on 28 July 1917 under the command of *Ltn.d.R.* Hans Block. He remained in command until 14 September when he was succeeded by *Ltn.z.S.d.R.* Ernst Thormählen. *Küsta II* was organized at Ostend on 9 September 1917 and was led by *Ltn.z.S.* Ludwig von Frankenberg und Proschlitz until the 24th. Command was then turned over to *Oblt.d.R.* Martin Schatz. *Küsta I* and *II* flew seaplanes, with each unit having a nominal strength of four aircraft and two in reserve.

Küsta III and *IV* were stationed at Uitkerke. *Küsta III* commanded by *Oblt.d.R.* Fritz Schwarzlose was formed on 23 September 1917 and *Küsta IV* led by *Ltn.d.R.* Bruno Majewski, was not established until 5 March 1918. *Küsta III* and *IV* flew landplanes with a nominal unit strength of six aircraft and three in reserve.

Schusta I and *II* also flew landplanes, the unit strength also being six aircraft, but with only two in reserve. The original complement of *Schusta I* was three Albatros C.VII's and three DFW C.V's. In late 1917 and early 1918 the landplane of choice for both the *Küsta* and *Schusta* appears to have been the LVG C.V. In 1918 the *Schusta* were also equipped with the Halberstadt Cl.II.

Among other duties, the *Küsta* ranged the large Naval artillery batteries established along the Flanders coast. These batteries included *Deutschland* at Bredene, *Württemberg* and *Goeben* near Zeebrügge and *Friedrich, Ludendorff*, and *Jacobynessen* near Ostend, as well as *Langer Max* (Long Max) of the *Pommern Batterie* and *Batterie Aachen* at Raversyde, to name a few. The *Küsta* also performed coastal patrol and reconnaissance. The *Schusta* acted as escort and protection to the various *Küsta* artillery spotting flights.

Marine Schusta I was formed on September 23, 1917, at Vlissegem, but the unit first assembled on the 23rd at Neumünster under the command of *Ltn.d.R.* Paul Leffler who had been appointed commander on the 14th. On the 30th of the month they moved to Uitkerke near Blankenberge and settled in with *Küsta III.*

Marine Schusta II was established on 4 March 1918 and became operational on 12 April 1918 under the command of *Ltn.d.R.* Lothar Nagel. It was also stationed at Uitkerke. Both *Schusta* remained at this location almost throughout the war, only being forced to pull back to Eeklo, NNW of Gent, on 16 October 1918 during the German *4. Armee* withdrawal due to the Belgium attack in Flanders commencing on October 14, 1918. On this same date *Küsta III* and *Küsta IV* were combined and renamed *Marine Schlachtstaffel I.* Similarly *Schutzstaffeln I* and *II* were combined and were renamed *Marine Schlachtstaffel II,* as they were no longer protecting the *Küsten-Artillerie-Staffeln*. The commands were given to *Oblt.d.R.* Albert Reusch and *Ltn.d.R.* Bruno Majewski, respectively.

Day-to-day details of their operational duties have yet to be uncovered, but it is known that it was not unusual for three *Schusta* aircraft to escort two *Küsta* aircraft during the artillery spotting missions. As far as can be determined, only one *Schusta* crew was lost in action, that of *Flugmaat* Bernitzky and *Flugobermaat* Sielaff of *Schusta II* who were taken POW over the North Sea on 31 July 1918. *Obmtr*. Adolf Flink, a gunner with *Schusta II*, and *Flugzgobermtr*. Paul Reipschläger, a pilot from *Küstenstaffel IV*, were both WIA on 12 August 1918. Additionally, *Flugzeugobermaat* Richter, a *Schusta I* pilot, was interned at Teinhovenpolder, Cadzand, Holland on 21 August 1918 when his LVG C.VI number 1698/18 was shot down. Finally *Ltn.d.R.* Herbert Plechati, an observer with *Schusta II*, was WIA on 28 August 1918 and *Ltn.z.S.* Hans-Günther Eckhardt was lightly WIA on the 31st.

The following pages present those few snippets of information that have been uncovered on the two *Marine Schutzstaffeln*. The rosters have been most graciously supplemented by data from the personnel archives of Ron Kintner and Gunnar Söderbaum to whom much appreciation is owed.

Marine Schutzstaffel I

Pilot/Gunner	Type	From		To	
		Unit	Date	Date	Unit
Flgobmtr. Erich Aland	P	MFJ I	23Sep17	Mar18	Küst IV
Flgmstr. Martin Bauer	P	Küst III	(Apr18)	Apr18	M Ss II
Flgmt. Birnbaum	G		(Jul18)		
Flgmt. Bulzer	P		(Sep18)		
Ltn.d.R. Hans Conrad, Stv. C.O.	P	M Ss II	19Mar18	21Mar18	M Ss II
Flgobmtr. Wilhelm Cranel	G	SEE III	4Sep18		
Flgmtr. Dietrich	G		(Aug18)		
Flgobmt. Erdmann			(Jan18)	17Jun18	Sndstfl
Ltn.d.R. Arthur Greiser, Stv. C.O.	O	Küst II	8Dec17	Jan18	Lngfhr
Flgobmtr. Gerhard Götze	G	SEE III	4Sep18	EOW	
Flgobmtr. Rudolf Heimel	P		(Mar18)		M Ss II
Flgobmt. Otto Hess	P		23Sep17	Oct17	SEE I
Vzfw. Franz Hofer	G		(Nov17)	17Mar18	SEE II
Flgobmt. Hugo Klimke	P		15Dec17	(Aug18)	
Flgmtr. Kochendörfer	G	MLFA	27Jan18	(Jul18)	
Flgobmtr. Koppel	G	MLFA	17Mar18	(Jul18)	
Ltn.d.R. Friedrich Lange	P	MFLA	30Apr18	16Oct18	MFJ I
Ltn.d.R. Friedrich Lange, C.O.	P	M Ss I	24May18	16Oct18	MFJ I
Flgobmt. Lange	G	MLFA	30Apr18	23Aug18	M-Zug
Ltn.d.R. Paul Leffler, C.O.	O	M Kofl	14Sep17	8Dec17	Leave
Ltn.d.R. Paul Leffler, C.O.	O	Leave	Jan18	19Mar18	Küst III
Flgmtr. Rudolf Löwenstein	G	MLFA	27Jan18	(Mar18)	M Ss II
Flgobmtr. Mader			(Jul18)		
Vzfw. Johannes Mann	G	MFA II	23Sep17		Küst IV
Flgmt. Melbak	P		23Sep17		
Flgmt. Noak	P		23Sep17	2Sep18	M Ss II
Flgmstr. Willy Ochs	G	MFA II	23Sep17	11Oct17	MFA I
Flgmstr. Willy Ochs	G	MFA I	(Feb18)	23Aug18	M-Zug
Ltn.d.R. Erich Piontek	O	Küst III	9Mar18	(Sep18)	
Flgmstr. Udo Plazikowski	P	MFA II	23Sep17	(Jul18)	M Ss II
Flgmt. Gustav Raschke	P	MFA I	23Sep17	(Mar18)	Küst IV
Oblt.d.R. Albert Reusch, C.O.	P	MFJ II	21Mar18	24May18	M Ss II
Oblt.d.R. Albert Reusch, C.O.	P	M Ss II	16Oct18	EOW	
Flgobmt. Richter	P		15Dec17	21Aug18	Intrnd
Flgobmtr. Riess	P		(Apr18)	10Sep18	MFJ I
Vizefeuerwerker Karl Rippen	G		23Sep17		Küst III
Flgmt. Ritter			(Mar18)		
Flgmt. Rössle	P	MFA I	23Sep17		
Ltn.d.R. Ernst Rutenkolk	O	FS Asch	29Aug18		SEE I
Flgobmt. Schmidtke	G	MFA II	23Sep17		MFA II
Flgmt. Franz Schönen	P	MFA II	23Sep17	(Feb18)	Küst III
Vizefeuerwerker Schorr	G		23Sep17		
Vizefeuerwerker Walter Spöring	G	MFA II	23Sep17	23Aug18	M-Zug
Flgobmtr. Stratemann	P		(Apr18)	17Jun18	Sndstfl
Flgmtr. Paul Tschuschke	G	MLFA	27Jan18	(Mar18)	M Ss II
Flgobmtr. Wallbrecht			(Apr18)		
Flgobmt. Weber		MLFA	20Feb18	(May18)	
Flgmstr. Wilhelm Zimpel	P	MFJ II	27Mar18	26Aug18	MLFA

Marine Schutzstaffel II

Pilot/Gunner	Type	From		To	
		Unit	Date	Date	Unit
Flgmech. Otto Bäppler	M			15Sep18	KIA*
Flgobmstr. Martin Bauer	P	M Ss I	Apr18	(Jul18)	
Flgmt. Bernitzky	P		(Jun18)	31Jul18	POW
Flgmtr. Walter Borchert	P		(Apr18)	21May18	MFJ I
Flgobmt. Felix Borske	P	M AFP	17Aug18		

Flgmtr. Richard Bürger	P		(Apr18)	20Apr18	Küst III
Flgobmtr. Richard Bürger	P	Küst III	(May18)	23Jun18	MFJ III
Ltn.d.R. Hans Conrad	P	Küst III	9Mar18	19Mar18	M Ss I
Ltn.d.R. Hans Conrad	P	M Ss I	21Mar18	27Aug18	M FA II
Ltn.z.S. Hans-Günther Eckhardt				31Aug18	WIA,lt.
Flgobmtr. Adolf Flink	G		(Apr18)	12Aug18	WIA
Flgobmtr. Gustav Fuchs	G		(Apr18)	(Sep18)	
Flgobmtr. Rudolf Heimel	P	M Ss I	(Apr18)	21May18	MFJ I
Flgmtr. Friedrich Hintz	G		(Apr18)	(Jun18)	M Sdr
Flgmt. Hüber	P		(May18)		
Flgmt. Fritz Kirsten	P	Küst III	(Apr18)	(Sep18)	
Vzfw. Kühn			(Apr18)		
Ltn.d.R. Georg von Landgraf, OzvB	O	MFJ II	5Jun18	(Sep18)	
Flgobmtr. Rudolf Löwenstein	G	M Ss I	(Apr18)	(Sep18)	
Ltn.d.R. Bruno Majewski, C.O.	P	M Sdr	16Oct18	EOW	
Ltn.d.R. Friedrich Möller	P	MFA II	27Aug18		
Ltn.d.R. Lothar Nagel, C.O.	O	Küst III	7Mar18	24May18	Küst I
Obmtr. Neinaber	G		(Apr18)	(Sep18)	
Flgobmt. Noak	P	M Ss I	2Sep18		
Flgobmtr. Kurt Ortmann	P	Küst III	9Mar18	(Apr18)	
Flgmstr. Udo Plazikowski	P	M Ss I	(Aug18)	12Sep18	Kofl MK
Ltn.d.R. Herbert Plechati	O	M Kofl	Apr18	28Aug18	WIA
Ltn.d.R. Herbert Plechati	O		(Sep18)	Oct18	
Oblt.d.R. Albert Reusch, C.O.	P	M Ss I	24May18	16Oct18	
Flgmech. Waldemar Reinecke	M			15Sep18	KIA*
Vizefeuerwerker Karl Rippen	G	Küst II	(Jul18)		
Flgmt. Schmidt	P		(Sep18)		
Flgmt. Franz Schönen	P	Küst III	(Apr18)	(Aug18)	
Flgobmt. Hugo Schwörer	P	Küst III	20Apr18	(Jun18)	
Flgobmt. Sielaff	G	Soko	5Jun18	31Jul18	POW
Flgmtr. Stegemann			(Jul18)		
Flgobmtr. Paul Tschuschke	G	M Ss I	(Apr18)	(Sep18)	
Flgobmtr. Werler	G		(Aug18)	(Sep18)	
Flgmtr. Wernicke			(May18)		

* Both Bäppler and Reinecke were killed at Uitkerke during a British bombing attack on the airfield.

Marine Schutzstaffeln Airfields

Unit	From	To	Location	*Armee*
M Schusta I	14Sep17		formed at Vlissegem	4
M Schusta I	14Sep17	23Sep17	Vlissegem	4
M Schusta I	23Sep17	30Sep17	operational at Neumünster	4
M Schusta I	30Sep17	16Oct18	Uitkerke near Blankenberge	4
M Schusta I	16Oct18	29Oct18	Eeklo, NW Brügge	4
M Schusta I	29Oct18	EOW	near St. Nicolas	4
M Schusta II	4Mar18		formed at Uitkerke near Blankenberge	4
M Schusta II	12Apr18		operational at Uitkerke	4
M Schusta II	12Apr18	16Oct18	Uitkerke near Blankenberge	4
M Schusta II	16Oct18	29Oct18	Eeklo, NW Brügge	4
M Schusta II	29Oct18	EOW	near St. Nicolas	4

A Marine *Schusta* Halberstadt with a white triangular marking. It is not known if this was a unit or an individual marking. Crew, date, and location are all unknown, but the photo was most likely taken at Uitkerke. Photo credit: Johan Ryheul.

APPENDIX IX

SCHUTZSTAFFELN/SCHLACHTSTAFFELN 'G' NUMBERS

This explanation of numbering of captured German aircraft by the British was previously detailed in "The Jasta Pilots", but will be repeated here for the sake of clarity. Toward the end of 1916 it was decided for Intelligence purposes to allocate a 'G' serial number to those German aircraft which came down on the British side of the lines. Despite the main volume of air action being fought on the German side, there were a surprising number of aircraft which did come down on the British side. Not all were in any condition to be deemed a captured machine, many were no more than smoldering wrecks. But once the system was in place, 'all' such machines, whether wreckage or intact aeroplanes, were generally given a 'G' number.

There is evidence, however, that when aircraft came down in an active battle front, there was not always time to salvage anything from the machines and so a 'G' number was not allocated. There are also some 'G' numbers that were not allocated at all. As the war progressed, allocation of these numbers was broken down into Brigade; thus from early April 1918, numbers will show individual Brigade allocations, e.g. G/5/16 is the 5th Brigade's No.16.

Some captured aircraft became quite famous photographically or were shown at wartime exhibitions, while others were test-flown, etc. Where little more than wreckage resulted, just bits and pieces, parts were sometimes salvaged, such as the guns or the engine. Because there seems to be no definitive 'G' list, the one following has been compiled from several sources, both official and unofficial. Note that despite the fact that during 1918 the *Schusta/Schlasta* operated very close to or over the front-line trenches, very few captured aircraft are reported by the British. Perhaps the rapid fluctuation of the battle lines precluded such identification. Or perhaps these machines were merely lost in the 'fog of war.'

For the sake of completeness, the 'G' list of *Schusta/Schlasta* aircraft presented herein, has been augmented with further details of 'G' numbers, dates, unit crew, and aircraft not presented in previously published lists. It is felt that this additional information will prove to be worthwhile to the serious WWI aviation researcher.

***SCHUTZSTAFFELN* 'G' NUMBERS**

No.	Date	A/C Type S/N	Location	Crew	*Schusta*	Remarks
G 35	6May17	Alb. C	Annay	*Uffz.* Stegmann *Vzfw.* Wenzl	27b	2/Lt. Babbage 2/AM Aldred 20 Sqn. RFC
G 52	12Jul17	DFW C.V	S. Lens	*Vzfw.* Reubelt *Vzfw.* Böttcher	12	2/Lt. Mannock 40 Sqn. RFC
G 73	27Sep17	Rumpler C.V	Langemarck	*Uffz.* Wiedemann *Uffz.* Gossler	27b	Capt. McCudden 56 Sqn. RFC
G 76	26Sep17	LVG C.V	Polygon Wood	*Vzfw.* Friedberg *Uffz.* Mückenhaupt	19	Infantry Fire
G 94	30Nov17	LVG C.V 9458/17	Bourlon Wood	*Vzfw.* Florig *Gefr.* Eckerle	19*	Capt. McCudden 56 Sqn. RFC
G 102	10Dec17	2 Seater	Cambrai	*Uffz.* Uhe *Vzfw.* Wieczorek	1	Infantry Fire
G 104	22Dec17	DFW C.V	St. Quentin	*Uffz.* Biesenbach *Uffz.* Bode	5	Capt. McCudden 56 Sqn. RFC
G 108	23Dec17	LVG C.V 9446/17	near Metz	*Vzfw.* Boje *Vzfw.* Niemann	12	Capt. McCudden 56 Sqn. RFC
G 118	29Dec17	LVG C	Gomelien	*Vzfw.* Gerschel *Uffz.* Lehnert	10	Capt. McCudden 56 Sqn. RFC

G 137	16Feb18	Rumpler C.IV	Lagnicourt	*Vzfw*. Zeuch *Gefr*. Lechleiter	29b	Capt. McCudden 56 Sqn. RFC
G 139	16Feb18	Halb. Cl.II Wk. Nr.549/17	Lagnicourt	*Vzfw*. Dumpert *Vzfw*. Wölfle	25b	Infantry Fire
G 156	29Mar18	Hann. Cl.II 13199/17	Lestrem	*Gefr*. Karcher *Flg*. Schleuder	38s	AA Fire
G 165	9Apr18	Hann. Cl.II 13135/17	Bailleul, Reims	*Vzfw*. Schneider *Oblt*. Ramdohr	16	Infantry Fire
G/2/5	26Apr18	Halb. Cl.II	near Wieltje NE Ypres	*Uffz*. Kammrath *Vzfw*. Bremer	14	AA Fire
G/2/6	30Apr18	Halb. Cl.II	Dickebusch	*Vzfw*. Speer *Flg*. Zimmermann	28b	Lt. Dolan 74 Sqn, RAF
G/2/11	22May18	Halb. Cl.II 1209/18	Poperinghe	*Sgt*. Andres *Uffz*. Wenner	19	Infantry Fire
G/2/30	14Oct18	Halb. Cl.IV 1556/18	Moorslede	*Uffz*. Buch *Ltn*. von Fichta	16	Found during advance
G/3/26	25Sep18	LVG C.VI 3937/18	Blaudain	*Uffz*. Ihde *Uffz*. Hopf	24b	Located 27Sep18 during advance
G/5/6	3May18	Hann. Cl.II 13282/17	Moreuil	*Vzfw*. Peez *Gefr*. Lang	31b	Capt. Whitehead 65 Sqn. RAF
G/5/11	27May18	LVG C.II 3871/16	Crugny	Crew POW	1	Lt. May 209 Sqn. RAF
G/5/16	9Jun18	Halb. Cl.II 15342/17	Villers Bocage	*Gefr*. Kuesler *Vzfw*. Müllenbach	13	Lt. Armstrong Lt. Mart 3 Sqn. AFC
G/5/18	17Jul18	LVG C.V 3882/16	Dunkirk	*Vzfw*. Schmidt *Ltn*. Boethold	16	Capt. Foster Lt. Gracie 209 Sqn. RAF
G/5/22	23Aug18	Halb. Cl.IV 4675/18	Chipilly	*Flg*. Amzehnhoff *Uffz*. Ackenhausen	13	Forced to Land
G/5/29	24Sep18	LVG C.VI 7631/18	St. Quentin	*Vzfw*. Hoos *Vzfw*. Wagner	13	AA Fire

* Although long recorded as a FA 19 aircraft, this is actually a *Schusta 19* aircraft and crew.

The *Schlasta 13* Halberstadt Cl.II 15342/17 captured on 9 June 1918 and given the British capture number G/5/16. The crew was *Gefr.* Kuesler and *Vzfw.* Müllenbach who were both taken POW. Photo Credit: Johan Ryheul.

Halberstadt Cl.II 15342/17 of *Schlasta 13* in British hands, clearly showing the white and black tailplane which was part of the unit marking.

Hannover Cl.II 13199/17 marked '2' at Turnbury during a flight test. It was captured on 29 March 1918 and given the "G" number G.156.

APPENDIX X

SCHUSTA/SCHLASTA MISCELLANEOUS

Personnel known to have served in a *Schutzstaffel/Schlachtstaffel* but whose unit has yet to be identified:

Uffz. Arthur Arnold	P		7Jul18	KIA
Vzfw. Kurt Berger	P	('17)		
Vzfw. Kurt Gaede	G	KG 3/13	5Jul18	KIA
Gelpke				
Vzfw. Wilhelm Güdemann	P	('17)		BG 7/23
Uffz. Kirstein	G	(Jul18)		
Gefr. Klemm	G	(Jul18)		
Gefr. Karl Klinck	G		7Jul18	KIA
Gefr. Kriegel	P	(Jul18)		
Uffz. Meder	P	(Jun18)		
Vzfw. Georg Müller	P		5Jul18	KIA
Vzfw. Pelz	P	(Jul18)		
Uffz. Schonegg	G	(Jun18)		
Vzfw. Hermann Schorling	P	('17)	('18)	

APPENDIX XI

ARMEEN KOMMANDEUREN

As the activities of the *Schusta/Schlasta* were so closely tied to the ground activities, especially the *Schlasta* during 1918, and since these activities entailed such close support with the respective *Armeen*, whose commanders names have been liberally sprinkled throughout the text, it was felt prudent to present a list of these *Armee* commanders during the period of 1917-1918. Note that the following list is not complete with respect to the entire war. It does not present information during 1914-1916, that is, before the initial *Schusta* were formed. It is complete for 1917-1918 when the *Schusta/Schlasta* were active on the Western Front. Likewise, no mention is given to the Eastern or Italian Fronts, as the *Schusta/Schlasta* were not involved in any of these campaigns. Hopefully this appendix may prove useful and serve as a guideline to the general activities of the *Schusta/Schlasta.*

OHL

29Aug16 - 11Nov18 — *Chef des OHL General-Feldmarschall* Paul von Beneckendorff und von Hindenburg
29Aug16 - 27Oct18 — *Generalquartiermeister der OHL General der Infanterie* Erich Ludendorff
28Oct18 - 11Nov18 — *Generalquartiermeister der OHL Generalleutnant* Wilhelm Groener

4. Armee

2Aug14 - 24Feb17 — *General-Feldmarschall* Herzog Albrecht von Württemberg
25Feb17 - 11Nov18 — *General der Infanterie* Friedrich Sixt von Arnim

6. Armee

28Aug16 - 21Apr17 — *Generaloberst* Ludwig *Frhr.* von Falkenhausen
22Apr17 - 9Sep17 — *General der Infanterie* Otto von Below
9Sep17 - 11Nov18 — *General der Infanterie* Ferdinand von Quast

17. Armee

1Feb18 - 12Oct18 — *General der Infanterie* Otto von Below
12Oct18 - 11Nov18 — *General der Infanterie* Bruno von Mudra

2. Armee

17Dec16 - 21Sep18 — *General der Kavallerie* Georg von der Marwitz
22Sep18 - 11Nov18 — *General der Infanterie* Adolph von Carlowitz

18. Armee

27Dec17 - 11Nov18 — *General der Infanterie* Oskar von Hutier

9. Armee

18Jun18 - 6Aug18 — *General der Infanterie* Fritz von Below
7Aug18 - 22Sep18 — *General der Infanterie* Adolph von Carlowitz

7. Armee

28Aug16 - 21Apr17 — *Generaloberst* Richard von Schubert
11Mar17 - 6Aug18 — *General der Infanterie* Max von Boehn
6Aug18 - 31Oct18 — *General der Infanterie* Magnus von Eberhardt
31Oct18 - 11Nov18 — *General der Infanterie* Max von Boehn

1. Armee	
19Jul16 - 18Jun18	*General der Infanterie* Fritz von Below
18Jun18 - 11Oct18	*General der Infanterie* Bruno von Mudra
12Oct18 - 8Nov18	*General der Infanterie* Otto von Below
8Nov18 - 11Nov18	*General der Infanterie* Magnus von Eberhardt
3. Armee	
28Aug16 - 11Nov18	*Generaloberst* Karl von Einem gen. von Rothmaler
5. Armee	
17Dec16 - 22Sep18	*General der Artillerie* Max von Gallwitz
22Sep18 - 11Nov18	*General der Kavallerie* Georg von dcr Marwitz
Armee Abteilung C.	
2Feb17 - 11Mar17	*General der Infanterie* Max von Boehn
11Mar17 - 11Nov18	*General der Infanterie* Georg Fuchs
19. Armee	
5Feb18 - 8Nov18	*Generaloberst* Felix Graf von Bothmer
8Nov18 - 11Nov18	*General der Infanterie* Karl *Ritter* von Fasbender
Armee Abteilung A.	
2Jan17 - 17Jun18	*General der Infanterie* Bruno von Mudra
18Jun18 - 11Nov18	*General der Infanterie* Johannes von Eben
Armee Abteilung B.	
2Sep16 - 11Nov18	*General der Infanterie* Erich von Gündell

REFERENCES

Abbott, Dan-San. *The Colours of the Halberstadt-Built DFW C.V, Part 1*. Wetherby, England: *Cross & Cockade International Journal*, Vol. 30, No. 2, 1999.

—. *The Colours of the Halberstadt-Built DFW C.V, Part 2*. Wetherby, England: *Cross & Cockade International Journal*, Vol. 32, No. 3, 2001

—. *Albatros C.VII. Over the Front*, Vol. 11, No. 3, Fall 1996.

—. *Camouflage and Markings of the AEG C.IV. WWI Aero, No. 178, Journal of Early Aeroplanes*. Poughkeepsie, NY: November 2002.

Air Ministry (A.1.2.), Handbook of German Military and Naval Aviation (War) 1914-1918. London: The Imperial War Museum, Department of Printed Books, October, 1918.

Alter, Junius. *Ein Armeeführer erlebt den Weltkrieg, Persönliche Aufzeichnungen des Generalobersten von Einem*. Leipzig: von Hase & Koehler Verlag, 1938.

Angle, Glenn D. *Aerosphere 1939*. New York, NY: Aircraft Publications, 1940.

Arndt, *Major a.D.* Hans. *Die Fliegerwaffe*. From Sesselberg, Friedrich, ed. *Der Stellungskrieg, 1914 - 1918*. Berlin: Verlag bei E.S. Mittler & Sohn, 1926.

Bailey, Frank W. and Cony, Christophe. *The French Air Service War Chronology, 1914-1918*. London: Grub Street, 2001.

Baker, David. *Manfred von Richthofen: The Man and the Aircraft He Flew*. London: Outline Press, 1990.

Baur de Bétaz, Wilhelm. *Generalmajor*, et.al., *Die Luftstreitkräfte in der Abwehrschlacht zwischen Somme und Oise vom 8. bis 12. August 1918 und Rückblicke auf ihre vorangegangene Entwicklung*. Berlin: Ernst Siegfried Mittler und Sohn, 1942.

Bodenschatz, Karl. *Jagd in Flanderns Himmel- Aus den sechzehn Kampfmonaten des Jagdgeschwaders Freiherr von Richthofen*. München: Verlag Knorr & Hirth, 1938.

Chant, Christopher. *How Weapons Work*. London: Marshall Cavendish Publications Ltd., 1976.

Clark, Chad G. *Trampled Underfoot: The Story of Attack Aviation in the German Spring Offensives of 1918*. Air Power History, Vol. 45, Issue 2, Summer 1998.

Cooper, Bryan. *The Battle of Cambrai*. New York: Stein and Day, Publishers, 1968.

Cron, Hermann. *Die Organisation des deutschen Heeres im Weltkrieg*. Berlin: E.S. Mittler, 1923.

—. *Geschichte des deutschen Heeres im Weltkrieg 1914-1918*. Berlin: *Geschichte der Kgl. Preussischen Armee und des Deutsches Reichsheeres Bd. V*, 1937.

Cross & Cockade Journal. The Society of World War I Aero Historians. Various Issues.

Cuneo, John R. *The Air Weapon 1914-1916, Vol. II of Winged Mars*. Harrisburg, PA: Military Service Publishing Co., 1947.

Deneckere, Bernard. *Luchtoorlog Boven West-Vlaanderen, 1914-1918*. Kortrijk, Belgium: Uitgeverji Groeninghe n.v. Budastraat 56-8500, 2000.

Dooly, William G. Jr. *Great Weapons of World War I*. New York: Walker and Company, 1969.

Von Eberhardt, *Generalleutnant a.D.* Walter. *Unsere Luftstreifkräfte 1914-18*. Berlin: Vaterländischer Verlag C.A. Weller, 1930.

Fitzsimons, Bernard. *Warplanes & Air Battles of World War I*. London: BPC Publishing Ltd., 1973.

Foerster, Wolfgang and Greiner, Helmuth. *Wir Kämpfer im Weltkrieg 1914-1918*. Berlin: F.W. Peters Verlag, G.m.b.h., ca. 1936.

Franks, Norman L.R., Bailey, Frank W., and Guest, Russell. *Bloody April ... Black September*. London: Grub Street, 1995.

—. *Above the Lines*. London: Grub Street, 1997.

Fredette, Major Raymond H. *The Sky on Fire, the First Battle of Britain*. New York: Holt, Rinehart, and Winston, 1966.

Gies, Joseph. *Crisis 1918*. New York: W. W. Norton Co., Inc., 1974.

Gray, Peter and Thetford, Owen. *German Aircraft of the First World War*. London: Putnam & Company Ltd., 1962.

—. *German Aircraft of the First World War, Second Edition*. London: Putnam & Company Ltd., 1970.

Greenwood, Paul. *The Second Battle of the Marne, 1918*. Shrewsbury, England: Airlife Publishing, Ltd., 1998.

Grosz, Peter M. *AEG C.IV*. Windsock Datafile No. 67, Part 1. Berkhamsted, Hertfordshire, England: Albatros Publications, Ltd., 1998.

—. *ALBATROS C.III*. Windsock Datafile No. 13. Berkhamsted, Hertfordshire, England: Albatros Publications, Ltd., 1989.

—. *ALBATROS C.V*. Windsock Datafile No. 81. Berkhamsted, Hertfordshire, England: Albatros Publications, Ltd., 2000.

—. *ALBATROS C.VII*. Windsock Datafile No. 77. Berkhamsted, Hertfordshire, England: Albatros Publications, Ltd., 1999.

—. *DFW C.V*. Windsock Datafile No. 53. Berkhamsted, Hertfordshire, England: Albatros Publications, Ltd., 1995.

—. *HALBERSTADT CL.II*. Windsock Datafile No. 27, Revised 2nd Edition. Herts, England: Albatros Publications, Ltd., 1999.

—. *HALBERSTADT CL.IV*. Windsock Datafile No, 43. Herts, England: Albatros Publications, Ltd., 1994.

—. *HANNOVER CL.III*. Windsock Datafile No. 23, Revised 2nd Edition. Herts, England: Albatros Publications, Ltd., 1990.

—. *JUNKERS J.I.* Windsock Datafile No. 39. Berkhamsted, Hertfordshire, England: Albatros Publications, Ltd., 1993.

—. *LFG ROLAND C.II.* Windsock Datafile No. 49. Berkhamsted, Hertfordshire, England: Albatros Publications, Ltd., 1995.

—. *LVG C.V.* Windsock Datafile No. 71. Berkhamsted, Hertfordshire, England: Albatros Publications, Ltd., 1998.

—. *RUMPLER C.I.* Windsock Datafile No. 79. Berkhamsted, Hertforschire, England: Albatros Publications, Ltd., 1995.

—. *RUMPLER C.IV.* Windsock Datafile No. 35. Berkhamsted, Hertfordshire, England: Albatros Publications, Ltd., 1992.

—. *Hannover Aircraft 1915-1919.* Air Pictorial, July 1971 Part 1, August 1971, Part 2. London: Journal of the Air League, 1971.

—. Archiv: Peter M. Grosz, ed. *Frontbestand Part 1. WWI Aero, No. 107, The Journal of Early Aeroplanes.* Poughkeepsie, New York: December, 1985.

—. Archiv: Peter M. Grosz, ed. *Frontbestand Part 2. WWI Aero, No. 108, The Journal of Early Aeroplanes.* Poughkeepsie, New York: February 1986.

Haddow, G.W. and Grosz, Peter M. *The German Giants, The German R-Planes 1914-1918*, Third Edition. London: Putnam, 1998.

Haehnelt, *Major* Wilhelm, ed. *Ehrentafel der in Flugdienst während des Weltkriegs gefallenen Offiziere der Deutschen Fliegerverbände. Inspektion der Fliegertruppen.* Berlin: Mittler, 1920.

—. *Inspektion der Fliegertruppen Nr. 10/3.19 Abt I b - Verteilungsplan der Auflösungsstellen.* Berlin: Mittler, March 1, 1919. (Courtesy of Jörg Mückler).

Hallion, Dr. Richard P. *Battlefield Air Support, A Retrospective Assessment.* Airpower Journal, Spring 1990.

Hayzlett, Jan. *Hunting with Richthofen.* An English translation of *Jagd in Flanders Himmel.* Bodenschatz, Karl. London: Grub Street, 1996.

Henshaw, Trevor. *The Sky Their Battlefield.* London: Grub Street, 1995.

Herwig, Hermann. *Die Bayerische Schlachtfliegerstaffel 28.* Würzburg: Perschmann, 1933.

Hildebrand, Karl Friedrich. *Die Generale der deutschen Luftwaffe 1935-1945.* Osnabrück: Biblio Verlag, Vol. 1; 1990, Vol. 2; 1991, Vol. 3; 1992.

History of Aviation Collection, University of Texas at Dallas, Richardson, Texas.

von Hoeppner, Ernst Wilhelm. *Deutschlands Krieg in der Luft.* Leipzig: von Hase and Köhler, 1921.

—. *Germany's War in the Air.* Nashville, TN: The Battery Press, 1994.

Hoffschmidt, Edward J. *German Aircraft Guns WWI amd WWII.* Old Greenwich, Conn: WE Inc., 1969.

Idflieg ZAK VII, Geschichte der deutschen Flugzeugindustrie, Band IIa: Bauaufsichten 1 bis 10, Stand von Sommer, 1918. Berlin: Gedruckt in der Reichsdruckerie, 1918.

Idflieg ZAK VII, Geschichte der deutschen Flugzeugindustrie, Band IIb: Bauaufsichten 11 bis 45, Stand von Sommer 1918. Berlin: Gedruckt in der Reichsdruckerie, 1918.

Idflieg ZAK KdoStat., B.-Nr.298/18 Art der Königl. Inspektions des Militär-Luftfahrwesens. Kontingentierung unter Berucksichtigung des Amerika-Programm für Januar-Dezember 1918.

Imrie, Alex. *Pictorial History of the German Army Air Service.* Shepperton, Surrey, England: Ian Allan, Ltd., 1971.

. *German Naval Air Service.* London: Arms and Armour Press, Ltd., 1989.

—. *German Bombers of World War One.* London: Arms and Armour Press, Ltd., 1990.

Jones, H.A. *The War in the Air.* Oxford, England: Oxford at the Clarendon Press, Vol IV, 1934 and Vol. VI, 1937.

Kennett, Lee. *The First Air War 1914-1918.* New York: The Free Press, a Division of Macmillian, Inc., 1991.

Kilduff, Peter. *Germany's First Air Force 1914-1918.* Osceola, WI: Motorbooks International, 1991.

—. *Over the Battlefields, Amazing Air Action of World War One.* London, England: Arms and Armour Press, 1996.

Kogenluft. Nachrichtenblatt der Luftstreitkräfte. Berlin: Vol. 1, 1917 and Vol. 2, 1918.

Kommandeur der Flieger Wochenberichte (*Kofl* Weekly Reports) of the 1, 2, 3, 4, 5, 6, 7, 9, 17, 18, 19 Army's and Army Detachment C. Various Issues.

Kriegsministerium, Teil 10 Abschnitt B, Flieger-Formationen, Berlin, 1918.

Kroschel, Günter and Stützer, Helmut. *Die Deutschen Militärflugzeug 1910-1918.* Wilhelmshaven: Verlag Lohse-Eissing, 1977.

KrStR 17.987. Kriegsstammrolle der Königlich Bavarian Schlachtstaffel Nr. 22. Münich, Germany: Bavarian Military Archives, ca. 1920.

KrStR 17.989. Kriegsstammrolle der Königlich Bavarian Schlachtstaffel Nr. 23. Münich, Germany: Bavarian Military Archives, ca. 1920.

KRL 17.990. Kriegs-Rangliste der Königlich Bavarian Schlachtstaffel Nr. 24. Münich, Germany: Bavarian Military Archives, ca. 1920.

KrStR 17.991. Kriegsstammrolle der Königlich Bavarian Schlachtstaffel Nr. 24. Münich, Germany: Bavarian Military Archives, ca. 1920.

KrStR 17.993. Kriegsstammrolle der Königlich Bavarian Schlachtstaffel Nr. 25. Münich, Germany: Bavarian Military Archives, ca. 1920.

KrStR 17.994. Kriegsstammrolle der Königlich Bavarian Schlachtstaffel Nr. 26. Münich, Germany: Bavarian Military Archives, ca. 1920.

KrStR 17.995. Kriegsstammrolle der Königlich Bavarian Schlachtstaffel Nr. 27. Münich, Germany: Bavarian Military Archives, ca. 1920.

KrStR 17.996. Kriegsstammrolle der Königlich Bavarian Schlachtstaffel Nr. 28. Münich, Germany: Bavarian Military Archives, ca. 1920.

KrStR 17.997. Kriegsstammrolle der Königlich Bavarian Schlachtstaffel Nr. 29. Münich, Germany: Bavarian Military Archives, ca. 1920.

KsStR 18.000. Kriegsstammrolle der Königlich Bavarian Schlachtstaffel Nr. 30. Münich, Germany: Bavarian Military Archives, ca. 1920.

KrStR 18.003. Kriegsstammrolle der Königlich Bavarian Schlachtstaffel Nr. 31. Münich, Germany: Bavarian Military Archives, ca. 1920.

Kulenkampff-Post, Caspar. *Reiter unterm Himmel: Kriegsbriefe eines jungen Ulanen und Fliegers.* Stuttgart: Rowohlt, 1939.

von Lowenstern, Baron Elard. *Eine falsche englische Rechnung, Die Fliegerschlacht von Amiens am 8 August 1918.* Berlin: Verlag Bernard & Graefe, 1938.

Ministry of Munitions, I.C. 652. *Report of the Halberstadt Fighter, Type C.L.IV.* October, 1918.

Ministry of Munitions, H.B. 805. *Report on the 180 H.P. Mercedes Aero Engine.* March, 1918.

Morrow, John H. Jr. *German Air Power in World War I.* Lincoln, Neb.: University of Nebraska Press, 1982.

von Moser, Otto. *Die Württemberger im Weltkriege.* Stuttgart: 1938.

Musgrave, Daniel D. and Oliver, Smith Hempstone. *German Machineguns.* Hyattsville, MD: Creative Printing, Inc., 1971.

Neumann, Georg Paul. *In der Luft Unbesiegt.* München: J.F. Lehmanns Verlag, 1923.

—. *Die deutschen Luftstreitkräfte im Weltkrieg.* Berlin: Ernst Siegfried Mittler & Sohn, 1920.

O'Connor, Neal W. *Aviation Awards of Imperial Germany and the Men Who Earned Them. Volume I. The Aviation Awards of the Kingdom of Bavaria*. Foundation for Aviation for World War One. Stratford, Connecticut: Flying Machines Press, 1998.

—. *Volume II. The Aviation Awards of the Kingdom of Prussia*. 1990.

—. *Volume III. The Aviation Awards of the Kingdom of Saxony*. 1993.

—. *Volume IV. The Aviation Awards of the Kingdom of Württemberg*. 1995.

—. *Volume V. The Aviation Awards of the Eight Thuringian States and the Duchy of Anhalt*. 1998.

—. *Volume VI. The Aviation Awards of the Grand Duchies of Baden and Oldenburg*. 1999.

—. *Volume VII. The Aviation Awards of Eight German States and the Three Free Cities*. Atglen, PA: Schiffer Publishing Ltd., 2002.

Over the Front. Journal of the League of World War I Aviation Historians. Various Issues.

Paschall, Rod. *The Defeat of Imperial Germany, 1917-1918*. Chapel Hill, NC: Algonquin Books of Chapel Hill, 1989.

Pieters, Walter M. *Above Flanders' Fields*. London: Grub Street, 1998.

Pitt, Barrie. *1918, the Last Act*. New York: Ballantine Books, 1963.

Postma, Thijs. *Fokker Aircraft Builders of the World*. London: Janes Publishing Co., Ltd., 1979.

Potempa, Harald. *Die Königlich-Bayerische Fliegertruppe 1914-1918, Europäishe Hochschulschriften, Bd./Vol. 727*. Frankfurt am Main: Peter Lang, 1997.

Revell, Alex. *High in the Empty Blue*. Mountain View, CA: Flying Machines Press, 1995.

von Richthofen, Manfred *Frhr. Der Rote Kampfflieger*. Berlin: Verlag Ullstein, 1933.

RFC Periodical Summary of Aeronautical Information. #1 dated 22 May 1917 through #30, dated 11 February 1918.

RFC/RAF Summaries of Air Intelligence (1918). #1 dated 12 February 1918 through #263, dated 11 November 1918.

Schilling, Friedrich. *Flieger an allen Fronten*. Berlin: Verlag Scherl, 1936.

Sherman, William C. *Air Warfare*. New York: The Ronald Press Company, 1926.

Sloan, James J. Jr. *Wings of Honor*. Atglen, PA: Schiffer Publishing Ltd., 1994

Stallings, Laurence. *The Doughboys*. New York: Popular Library, 1964.

Stutz, *Hptm.a.D.* Dr. Georg. *Band 31, Die Tankschlacht bei Cambrai, 20-29 November 1917* of *Schlachten des Weltkriegs. In Einzeldarstellungen bearbeitet und herausgegeben im Auftrag des Reicharchives*. Berlin: Oldenburg, 1929.

Theilhaber, Felix A. *Jüdische Flieger im Weltkrieg*. Berlin: Verlag der Schild, 1924.

Toland, John. *No Man's Land, 1918 - the Last Year of the Great War*. Garden City, New York: Doubleday & Co., Inc., 1980.

Vanoverbeke, Lothair. *Moorsele, één dorp, twee vliegvelden*. Kortrijk: Groeninghe, 1993.

VanWyngarden, Greg. *An Unpublished Listing of British 'G' Numbers*. Based On Information Contained in PRO Files Air 1: 4/26/24, 4/26/25, 3/4/26/22, 1061/204/5/1578 and 1714/204/123/124.

Wagner, Ray and Nowarra, Heinz. *German Combat Planes*. New York: Doubleday & Co., Inc., 1971.

Weyl, A.R. *FOKKER: The Creative Years*. London: Putnam and Co., Ltd., 1965.

Woodman, Harry. *Early Aircraft Armament, The Aeroplane and the Gun up to 1918*. Washington D.C.: Smithsonian Institution Press, 1989.

Woolley, Charles. *First to the Front, The Aerial Adventures of 1/Lt. Waldo Heinrichs and the 95th Aero Squadron, 1917-1918*. Atglen, PA: Schiffer Publishing Ltd., 1999.

—. *The Hat in the Ring Gang, The Combat History of the 94th Aero Squadron in World War I*. Atglen, PA: Schiffer Publishing Ltd., 2001.

Yeates, Victor M. *Winged Victory*. London: Jonathan Cape, 1934.

Zeidelhack, Max. *Bayerische Flieger im Weltkrieg*. München: 1919.

Zinn, Major Frederick W. *German Aviators Lost over the Lines*. Letter addressed to the Chief of the Air Servce AEF, June 30, 1919, in Zinn Papers, US Air Force Museum, Wright-Patterson AFB, Dayton, Ohio.

INDEX

(Parts I through IV)